LAN Times Guide to SQL

About the Author...

James R. Groff was the cofounder of Network Innovations Corporation, a developer of SQL-based networking software that links personal computers to corporate databases. Founded in 1984, Network Innovations was acquired by Apple Computer in 1988. Prior to founding Network Innovations, Groff held marketing positions at Hewlett-Packard and Plexus Computers, a manufacturer of UNIX-based microcomputer systems. He is a frequent speaker and author of technical articles on SQL and UNIX topics. Groff holds a B.S. degree in mathematics from the Massachusetts Institute of Technology and an M.B.A. degree from Harvard University.

Paul N. Weinberg was the cofounder of Network Innovations Corporation. Prior to founding Network Innovations, he held software development and marketing positions at Bell Laboratories, Hewlett-Packard, and Plexus Computers. Weinberg is the co-author, with Jim Groff, of *Understanding UNIX: A Conceptual Guide*, a best-selling overview of the UNIX operating system for managers and data processing professionals. He holds a B.S. degree from the University of Michigan and an M.S. degree from Stanford University, both in computer science. While at Stanford, Weinberg collaborated on *The Simple Solution to Rubik's Cube*, the best-selling book of 1981, with more than seven million copies in print.

Includes coverage of Oracle, SQL/DS, ODBC, Sybase, Ingres, Informix, SQL Server, SQLBase, and DB2.

LAN Times Guide to SQL

James R. Groff
and
Paul N. Weinberg

Osborne **McGraw-Hill**

Berkeley   New York   St. Louis   San Francisco
Auckland   Bogotá   Hamburg   London   Madrid
Mexico City   Milan   Montreal   New Delhi   Panama City
Paris   São Paulo   Singapore   Sydney
Tokyo   Toronto

Osborne **McGraw-Hill**
2600 Tenth Street
Berkeley, California 94710
U.S.A.

LAN Times Guide to SQL

4567890 DOC 998765

ISBN 0-07-882026-X

Contents at a Glance

Contents

Part II

Retrieving Data

Part III

Updating Data

Part IV

Database Structure

Appendixes

Preface

L AN Times Guide to SQL provides a comprehensive, in-depth treatment of the SQL language for both technical and non-technical users, programmers, data processing professionals and managers who want to understand the impact of SQL in the computer market. This book offers a conceptual framework for understanding and using SQL, describes the history of SQL and SQL standards, and explains the role of SQL in the computer industry today. It will show you, step-by-step, how to use SQL features, with many illustrations and realistic examples to clarify SQL concepts. The book also compares SQL products from leading DBMS vendors, describing their advantages, benefits, and trade-offs, to help you select the right product for your application.

In some of the chapters in this book, the subject matter is explored at two different levels—a fundamental description of the topic, and an advanced discussion intended for computer professionals who need to understand some of the "internals" behind SQL. The more advanced information is covered in sections marked with an asterisk (*). You do not need to read these sections to obtain an understanding of what SQL is and what it does.

How this Book Is Organized

The book is divided into six parts that cover various aspects of the SQL language:

- Part One, "An Overview of SQL," provides an introduction to SQL and a market perspective of its role as a database language. Its four chapters describe the history of SQL, the evolution of SQL standards, and how SQL relates to the relational data model and to earlier database technologies. Part One also contains a quick tour of SQL that briefly illustrates its most important features and provides you with an overview of the entire language early in the book.

- Part Two, "Retrieving Data," describes the features of SQL that allow you to perform database queries. The first chapter in this part describes the basic structure of the SQL language. The next four chapters start with the simplest SQL queries, and progressively build to more complex queries, including multi-table queries, summary queries, and queries that use subqueries.

- Part Three, "Updating Data," shows how you can use SQL to add new data to a database, delete data from a database, and modify existing database data. It also describes the database integrity issues that arise when data is updated, and how SQL addresses these issues. The last of the three chapters in this part discusses the SQL transaction concept and SQL support for multi-user transaction processing.

- Part Four, "Database Structure," deals with creating and administering a SQL-based database. Its four chapters tell you how to create the tables, views, and indexes that form the structure of a relational database. It also describes the SQL security scheme that prevents unauthorized access to data, and the SQL system catalog that describes the structure of a database. This part also discusses the significant differences between the database structures supported by various SQL-based DBMS products.

- Part Five, "Programming with SQL," describes how application programs use SQL for database access. It discusses the embedded SQL specified by the ANSI standard and used by IBM, Oracle, Ingres, Informix, and most other SQL-based DBMS products. It also describes the dynamic SQL interface that is used to build general-purpose database tools, such as report writers and database browsing programs. Finally, this part describes the SQL APIs provided by SQL Server, Oracle, and SQLBase, and contrasts them with the embedded IBM and ANSI interfaces.

- Part Six, "Future Directions," examines the state of SQL-based DBMS products today, the directions that SQL will take during the rest of the decade, and the likely impact of SQL in various segments of the computer market. It describes the intense current activity in distributed databases, the continuing evolution of SQL standards, and the role of SQL-based databases in online transaction processing applications. This part also discusses the rapid growth of SQL in the

PC local area network market, and the impact that object-oriented databases may have on the evolution of SQL in the 1990s.

Conventions Used in this Book

LAN Times Guide to SQL describes the SQL features and functions that are available in the most popular SQL-based DBMS products and those that are described in the ANSI/ISO SQL standards. Whenever possible, the SQL statement syntax described in the book and used in the examples applies to all dialects of SQL. When the dialects differ, the differences are pointed out in the text, and the examples follow the most common practice. In these cases, you may have to modify the SQL statements in the examples slightly to suit your particular brand of DBMS.

Throughout the book, technical terms appear in italics the first time that they are used and defined. SQL language elements, including SQL keywords, table and column names, and sample SQL statements appear in an uppercase monospace font. SQL API function names appear in a lowercase monospace font. Program listings also appear in monospace font, and use the normal case conventions for the particular programming language (uppercase for COBOL and FORTRAN, lowercase for C). Note that these conventions are used solely to improve readability; most SQL implementations will accept either uppercase or lowercase statements. Many of the SQL examples include query results, which appear immediately following the SQL statement as they would in an interactive SQL session. In some cases, long query results are truncated after a few rows; this is indicated by a vertical ellipsis (. . .) following the last row of query results.

Why this Book Is for You

LAN Times Guide to SQL is the right book for anyone who wants to understand and learn SQL, including database users, data processing professionals, programmers, students, and managers. It describes—in simple, understandable language liberally illustrated with figures and examples—what SQL is, why it is important, and how you use it. This book is not specific to one particular brand or dialect of SQL. Rather, it describes the standard, central core of the SQL language and then goes on to describe the differences among the most popular SQL products, including DB2, SQL/DS, Oracle, Ingres, Sybase, Informix, SQL Server, SQLBase, and others. It also explains the importance of new SQL-based standards, such as ODBC and the new SQL2 standard.

If you are a new user of SQL, this book offers a comprehensive, step-by-step treatment of the language, building from simple queries to more advanced concepts. The structure of the book will allow you to quickly start using SQL, but the book will continue to be valuable as you begin to use more complex features of the language.

If you are a data processing professional or a manager, this book will give you a perspective on the impact that SQL is having in every segment of the computer market—from personal computers to mainframes to local area networks to OLTP systems. The early chapters of the book describe the history of SQL, its role in the market, and its evolution from earlier database technologies. The final chapters describe the future of SQL and the development of distributed databases and other database technologies of the 1990s.

If you are a programmer, this book offers a very complete treatment of programming with SQL. Unlike the reference manuals of many DBMS products, it offers a conceptual framework for SQL programming, explaining the *why* as well as the *how* of developing a SQL-based application. It contrasts the SQL programming interfaces offered by all of the leading SQL products (ODBC, embedded SQL, dynamic SQL, SQL Server's dblib, and other SQL APIs), providing a perspective not found in any other book.

If you are selecting a DBMS product, this book offers a detailed comparison of the SQL features, advantages, and benefits offered by the various DBMS vendors. The differences between leading DBMS products are explained, not only in technical terms, but also in terms of their impact on applications and their competitive position in the marketplace.

In short, both technical and non-technical users can benefit from this book. It is the most comprehensive source of information available about the SQL language, SQL features and benefits, popular SQL-based products, the history of SQL, and the impact of SQL on the future direction of the computer market.

PART ONE

An Overview of SQL

The first four chapters of this book provide a perspective and a quick introduction to SQL. Chapter 1 describes what SQL is and explains its major features and benefits. In Chapter 2, a quick tour of SQL shows you many of its capabilities with simple, rapid-fire examples. Chapter 3 offers a market perspective of SQL by tracing its history, describing the SQL standards and the major vendors of SQL-based products, and identifying the reasons for SQL's prominence today. Chapter 4 describes the relational data model upon which SQL is based and compares it to earlier data models.

Chapter One

Introduction

The exploding popularity of SQL is one of the most important trends in the computer industry today. Over the last few years, SQL has become *the* standard computer database language. Over 100 database management products now support SQL, running on computer systems from personal computers to mainframes. An official international SQL standard has been adopted and expanded. SQL plays a central role in every major computer vendor's database architecture, and it is at the core of Microsoft's database strategy. From its obscure beginnings as an IBM research project, SQL has leaped to prominence as both an important computer technology and a powerful market force.

What, exactly, is SQL? Why is it important? What can it do, and how does it work? If SQL is really a standard, why are there so many different versions and dialects? What is Microsoft's ODBC standard, and how does it relate to SQL? How do popular SQL products like SQL Server, Oracle, Ingres, Informix, Sybase, SQLBase, and DB2 compare? Is SQL really important on personal computers and local area networks? Can it meet the demands of high-volume transaction processing? How will SQL impact the way you use computers, and how can you get the most out of this important data management tool?

The SQL Language

SQL is a tool for organizing, managing, and retrieving data stored by a computer database. The name "SQL" is an abbreviation for *Structured Query Language*. For historical reasons, SQL is usually pronounced "sequel," but the alternate pronunciation "S.Q.L." is also used. As the name implies, SQL is a computer *language* that you use to interact with a database. In fact, SQL works with one specific type of database, called a *relational database*.

Figure 1-1 shows how SQL works. The computer system in the figure has a *database* that stores important information. If the computer system is in a business, the database might store inventory, production, sales, or payroll data. On a personal computer, the database might store data about the checks you have written, lists of people and their phone numbers, or data extracted from a larger computer system. The computer program that controls the database is called a *database management system*, or DBMS.

When you need to retrieve data from the database, you use the SQL language to make the request. The DBMS processes the SQL request, retrieves the requested data, and returns it to you. This process of requesting data from the database and receiving back the results is called a database *query*; hence the name Structured *Query* Language.

The name Structured Query Language is actually somewhat of a misnomer. First of all, SQL is far more than a query tool, although that was its original purpose and retrieving data is still one of its most important functions. SQL is used to control all of the functions that a DBMS provides for its users, including:

- *Data definition.*   SQL lets a user define the structure and organization of the stored data and relationships among the stored data items.

- *Data retrieval.*   SQL allows a user or an application program to retrieve stored data from the database and use it.

- *Data manipulation.*   SQL allows a user or an application program to update the database by adding new data, removing old data, and modifying previously stored data.

- *Access control.*   SQL can be used to restrict a user's ability to retrieve, add, and modify data, protecting stored data against unauthorized access.

- *Data sharing.*   SQL is used to coordinate data sharing by concurrent users, ensuring that they do not interfere with one another.

- *Data integrity.*   SQL defines integrity constraints in the database, protecting it from corruption due to inconsistent updates or system failures.

SQL is thus a comprehensive language for controlling and interacting with a database management system.

Secondly, SQL is not really a complete computer language like COBOL, FORTRAN, or C. SQL contains no IF statement for testing conditions, no GOTO statement for branching, and no DO or FOR statements for looping. Instead, SQL is a database *sublanguage,* consisting of about thirty statements specialized for database management tasks. These SQL statements are *embedded* into another language, such as COBOL, FORTRAN, or C, to extend that language for use in database access. Alternatively, they can be explicitly sent to a database management system for processing, via a *call level interface* from a language such as C.

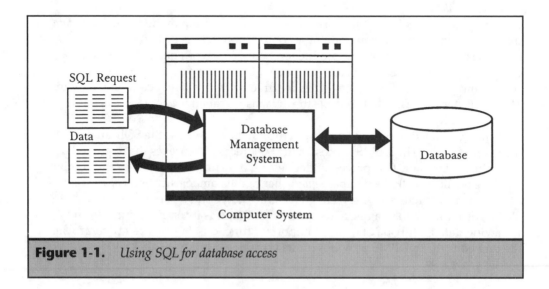

Figure 1-1.   *Using SQL for database access*

Finally, SQL is not a particularly structured language, especially when compared to a highly structured language such as C or Pascal. Instead, SQL statements resemble English sentences, complete with "noise words" that don't add to the meaning of the statement but make it read more naturally. There are quite a few inconsistencies in the SQL language, and there are also some special rules to prevent you from constructing SQL statements that look perfectly legal, but don't make sense.

Despite the inaccuracy of its name, SQL has emerged as *the* standard language for using relational databases. SQL is both a powerful language and one that is relatively easy to learn. The quick tour of SQL in the next chapter will give you a good overview of the language and its capabilities.

The Role of SQL

SQL is not itself a database management system, nor is it a stand-alone product. You cannot go into a computer store and "buy SQL." Instead, SQL is an integral part of a database management system, a language and a tool for communicating with the DBMS. Figure 1-2 shows some of the components of a typical DBMS, and how SQL acts as the "glue" that links them together.

The *database engine* is the heart of the DBMS, responsible for actually structuring, storing, and retrieving the data on the disk. It accepts SQL requests from other DBMS

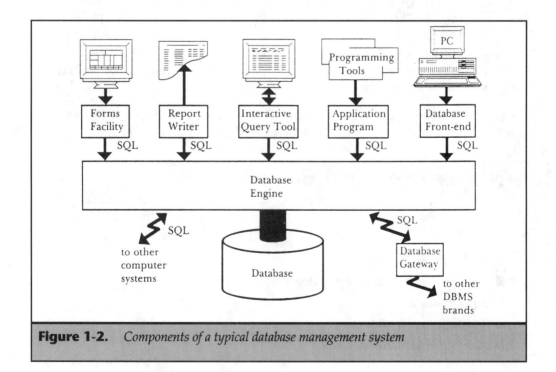

Figure 1-2.   *Components of a typical database management system*

components, such as a forms facility, report writer, or interactive query facility, from user-written application programs, and even from other computer systems. As the figure shows, SQL plays many different roles:

■ SQL is an *interactive query language*.   Users type SQL commands into an interactive SQL program to retrieve data and display it on the screen, providing a convenient, easy-to-use tool for ad hoc database queries.

■ SQL is a *database programming language*.   Programmers embed SQL commands into their application programs to access the data in a database. Both user-written programs and database utility programs (such as report writers and data entry tools) use this technique for database access.

■ SQL is a *database administration language*.   The database administrator responsible for managing a minicomputer or mainframe database uses SQL to define the database structure and control access to the stored data.

■ SQL is a *client/server language*.   Personal computer programs use SQL to communicate over a local area network with database servers that store shared data. Many new applications are using this client/server architecture, which minimizes network traffic and allows both PCs and servers to do what they do best.

■ SQL is a *distributed database language*.   Distributed database management systems use SQL to help distribute data across many connected computer systems. The DBMS software on each system uses SQL to communicate with the other systems, sending requests for data access.

■ SQL is a *database gateway language*.   In a computer network with a mix of different DBMS products, SQL is often used in a *gateway* that allows one brand of DBMS to communicate with another brand.

SQL has thus emerged as a useful, powerful tool for linking people, computer programs, and computer systems to the data stored in a relational database.

SQL Features and Benefits

SQL is both an easy-to-understand language and a comprehensive tool for managing data. Here are some of the major features of SQL and the market forces that have made it successful:

■ Vendor independence
■ Portability across computer systems
■ SQL standards
■ IBM endorsement (DB2)
■ Microsoft commitment (ODBC)

- Relational foundation
- High-level, English-like structure
- Interactive, ad hoc queries
- Programmatic database access
- Multiple views of data
- Complete database language
- Dynamic data definition
- Client/server architecture

These are the reasons why SQL has emerged as the standard tool for managing data on personal computers, minicomputers, and mainframes. They are described in the sections that follow.

Vendor Independence

SQL is offered by all of the leading DBMS vendors, and no new database product can be successful without SQL support. A SQL-based database and the programs that use it can be moved from one DBMS to another vendor's DBMS with minimal conversion effort and little retraining of personnel. PC database tools, such as query tools, report writers, and application generators, work with many different brands of SQL databases. The vendor independence thus provided by SQL is one of the most important reasons for its popularity.

Portability Across Computer Systems

SQL-based DBMS vendors offer their products on computer systems ranging from personal computers and workstations to local area networks, minicomputers, and mainframes. SQL-based applications that begin on single-user systems can be moved to larger minicomputers or mainframe systems as they grow. Data from corporate SQL-based databases can be extracted and downloaded into departmental or personal databases. Finally, economical personal computers can be used to prototype a SQL-based database application before moving it to an expensive multi-user system.

SQL Standards

An official standard for SQL was published by the American National Standards Institute (ANSI), and the International Standards Organization (ISO) in 1986, and was significantly expanded in 1992. SQL is also a U.S. Federal Information Processing Standard (FIPS), making it a key requirement for large government computer contracts. In Europe, X/OPEN, a standard for a portable, UNIX-based application environment, includes SQL as its standard for database access. SQL Access Group, a consortium of database and computer vendors, specified a call-level standard for SQL that is the basis for Microsoft's ODBC and is also an X/OPEN standard. These standards serve as an official stamp of approval for SQL, and have speeded its market acceptance.

IBM Endorsement (DB2)

SQL was originally invented by IBM researchers and has since become a strategic product for IBM based on its flagship DB2 database. SQL support is available on all major IBM product families, including PS/2 personal computers, AS/400 midrange systems, RS/6000 UNIX-based systems, and IBM mainframes running both the MVS and VM operating systems. This broad support by IBM has speeded the market acceptance of SQL, and provided a clear signal of IBM's direction for other database and system vendors to follow early in the growth of the database market.

ODBC and Microsoft

Microsoft considers database access a key part of its Windows personal computer software architecture. Microsoft's standard for providing database access is Open Database Connectivity (ODBC), a SQL-based facility. ODBC is supported by leading Windows software applications (spreadsheets, word processors, databases, etc.) from Microsoft and from other leading Windows applications vendors, and ODBC access is available or announced for all of the leading SQL databases. In addition, ODBC is based on standards adopted by the SQL Access Group, a vendor consortium, giving it status as both a *de facto*, Microsoft-backed standard and a "vendor-independent" standard.

Relational Foundation

SQL is a language for relational databases, and it has become popular along with the relational database model. The tabular, row/column structure of a relational database is intuitive to users, keeping the SQL language simple and easy to understand. The relational model also has a strong theoretical foundation that has guided the evolution and implementation of relational databases. Riding a wave of acceptance brought about by the success of the relational model, SQL has become *the* database language for relational databases.

High-Level, English-Like Structure

SQL statements look like simple English sentences, making SQL easy to learn and understand. This is in part because SQL statements describe the *data* to be retrieved, rather than specifying *how* to find the data. Tables and columns in a SQL database can have long, descriptive names. As a result, most SQL statements "say what they mean," and can be read as clear, natural sentences.

Interactive, Ad Hoc Queries

SQL is an interactive query language that gives users ad hoc access to stored data. Using SQL interactively, a user can get answers even to complex questions in minutes or seconds, in sharp contrast to the days or weeks it would take for a programmer to write a custom report program. Because of SQL's ad hoc query power, data is more accessible, and can be used to help an organization make better, more informed decisions.

Programmatic Database Access

SQL is also a database language used by programmers to write applications that access a database. The same SQL statements are used for both interactive and programmatic access, so the database access parts of a program can be tested first with interactive SQL, and then embedded into the program. In contrast, traditional databases provided one set of tools for programmatic access and a separate query facility for ad hoc requests, without any synergy between the two modes of access.

Multiple Views of Data

Using SQL, the creator of a database can give different users of the database different *views* of its structure and contents. For example, the database can be constructed so that each user sees only data for their own department or sales region. In addition, data from several different parts of the database can be combined and presented to the user as a simple row/column table. SQL views can thus be used to enhance the security of a database, and tailor it to the particular needs of individual users.

Complete Database Language

SQL was first developed as an ad hoc query language, but its powers now go far beyond data retrieval. SQL provides a complete, consistent language for creating a database, managing its security, updating its contents, retrieving data, and sharing data among many concurrent users. SQL concepts that are learned in one part of the language can be applied to other SQL commands, making users more productive.

Dynamic Data Definition

Using SQL, the structure of a database can be changed and expanded dynamically, even while users are accessing database contents. This is a major advance over static data definition languages, which prevented access to the database while its structure was being changed. SQL thus provides maximum flexibility, allowing a database to adapt to changing requirements while on-line applications continue uninterrupted.

Client/Server Architecture

SQL is a natural vehicle for implementing applications using a distributed, client/server architecture. In this role, SQL serves as the link between "front-end" computer systems optimized for user interaction and "back-end" systems specialized for database management, allowing each system to do what it does best. SQL also allows personal computers to function as front-ends to network servers or to larger minicomputer and mainframe databases, providing access to corporate data from personal computer applications.

Chapter Two

A Quick Tour of SQL

12

Before diving into the details of SQL, it's a good idea to develop an overall perspective on the language and how it works. This chapter contains a quick tour of SQL that illustrates its major features and functions. The goal of the quick tour is not to make you proficient in writing SQL statements; that is the goal of Part Two of this book. Rather, by the time you've finished this chapter, you will have a basic familiarity with the SQL language, and an overview of its capabilities.

A Simple Database

The examples in the quick tour are based on a simple relational database for a small distribution company. The database, shown in Figure 2-1, stores the information needed to implement a small order processing application. Specifically, it stores the following information:

- the *customers* who buy the company's products,
- the *orders* placed by those customers,
- the *salespeople* who sell the products to customers, and
- the *sales offices* where those salespeople work.

This database, like most others, is a model of the "real world." The data stored in the database represents real entities—customers, orders, salespeople, and offices. There is a separate table of data for each different kind of entity. The database requests that you make using the SQL language parallel real-world activities, as customers place, cancel, and change orders, you hire and fire salespeople, and so on. Let's see how you can use SQL to manipulate data.

Retrieving Data

First, let's list the sales offices, showing the city where each one is located and its year-to-date sales. The SQL statement that retrieves data from the database is called SELECT. This SQL statement retrieves the data you want:

```
SELECT CITY, OFFICE, SALES
  FROM OFFICES

CITY          OFFICE        SALES
------------  ------  ------------
Denver            22  $186,042.00
New York          11  $692,637.00
Chicago           12  $735,042.00
Atlanta           13  $367,911.00
Los Angeles       21  $835,915.00
```

ORDERS Table

ORDER_NUM	CUST	PRODUCT	QTY	AMOUNT
112961	2117	2A44L	7	$31,500.00
113012	2111	41003	35	$3,745.00
112989	2101	114	6	$1,458.00
113051	2118	XK47	4	$1,420.00
112968	2102	41004	34	$3,978.00
113036	2107	4100Z	9	$22,500.00
113045	2112	2A44R	10	$45,000.00
112963	2103	41004	28	$3,276.00
113013	2118	41003	1	$652.00
113058	2108	112	10	$1,480.00
112997	2124	41003	1	$652.00
112983	2103	41004	6	$702.00
113024	2114	XK47	20	$7,100.00
113062	2124	114	10	$2,430.00
112979	2114	4100Z	6	$15,000.00
113027	2103	41002	54	$4,104.00
113007	2112	773C	3	$2,925.00
113069	2109	775C	22	$31,350.00
113034	2107	2A45C	8	$632.00
112992	2118	41002	10	$760.00
112975	2111	2A44G	6	$2,100.00
113055	2108	4100X	6	$150.00
113048	2120	779C	2	$3,750.00
112993	2106	2A45C	24	$1,896.00
113065	2106	XK47	6	$2,130.00
113003	2108	779C	3	$5,625.00
113049	2118	XK47	2	$776.00
112987	2103	4100Y	11	$27,500.00
113057	2111	4100X	24	$600.00
113042	2113	2A44R	5	$22,500.00

CUSTOMERS Table

CUST_NUM	COMPANY	CUST_REP	CREDIT_LIMIT
2111	JCP Inc.	103	$50,000.00
2102	First Corp.	101	$65,000.00
2103	Acme Mfg.	105	$50,000.00
2123	Carter & Sons	102	$40,000.00
2107	Ace International	110	$35,000.00
2115	Smithson Corp.	101	$20,000.00
2101	Jones Mfg.	106	$65,000.00
2112	Zetacorp	108	$50,000.00
2121	QMA Assoc.	103	$45,000.00
2114	Orion Corp.	102	$20,000.00
2124	Peter Brothers	107	$40,000.00
2108	Holm & Landis	109	$55,000.00
2117	J.P. Sinclair	106	$35,000.00
2122	Three-Way Lines	105	$30,000.00
2120	Rico Enterprises	102	$50,000.00
2106	Fred Lewis Corp.	102	$65,000.00
2119	Solomon Inc.	109	$25,000.00
2118	Midwest Systems	108	$60,000.00
2113	Ian & Schmidt	104	$20,000.00
2109	Chen Associates	107	$25,000.00
2105	AAA Investments	101	$45,000.00

SALESREPS Table

NAME	REP_OFFICE	QUOTA	SALES
Bill Adams	13	$350,000.00	$367,911.00
Mary Jones	11	$300,000.00	$392,725.00
Sue Smith	21	$350,000.00	$474,050.00
Sam Clark	11	$275,000.00	$299,912.00
Bob Smith	12	$200,000.00	$142,594.00
Dan Roberts	12	$300,000.00	$305,673.00
Tom Snyder	NULL	NULL	$75,985.00
Larry Fitch	21	$350,000.00	$361,865.00
Paul Cruz	12	$275,000.00	$286,775.00
Nancy Angelli	22	$300,000.00	$186,042.00

OFFICES Table

OFFICE	CITY	REGION	TARGET	SALES
22	Denver	Western	$300,000.00	$186,042.00
11	New York	Eastern	$575,000.00	$692,637.00
12	Chicago	Eastern	$800,000.00	$735,042.00
13	Atlanta	Eastern	$350,000.00	$367,911.00
21	Los Angeles	Western	$725,000.00	$835,915.00

Figure 2-1. *A simple relational database*

The SELECT statement asks for three pieces of data—the city, the office number, and the sales—for each office. It also specifies that the data comes from the OFFICES table, which stores data about sales offices. The results of the query appear, in tabular form, immediately after the request.

The SELECT statement is used for all SQL queries. For example, here is a query that lists the names and year-to-date sales for each salesperson in the database. It also shows the quota (sales target) and the office number where each person works. In this case, the data comes from SALESREPS table:

```
SELECT NAME, REP_OFFICE, SALES, QUOTA
   FROM SALESREPS
```

NAME	REP_OFFICE	SALES	QUOTA
Bill Adams	13	$367,911.00	$350,000.00
Mary Jones	11	$392,725.00	$300,000.00
Sue Smith	21	$474,050.00	$350,000.00
Sam Clark	11	$299,912.00	$275,000.00
Bob Smith	12	$142,594.00	$200,000.00
Dan Roberts	12	$305,673.00	$300,000.00
Tom Snyder	NULL	$75,985.00	NULL
Larry Fitch	21	$361,865.00	$350,000.00
Paul Cruz	12	$286,775.00	$275,000.00
Nancy Angelli	22	$186,042.00	$300,000.00

SQL also lets you ask for calculated results. For example, you can ask SQL to calculate the amount by which each salesperson is over or under quota:

```
SELECT NAME, SALES, QUOTA, (SALES - QUOTA)
   FROM SALESREPS
```

NAME	SALES	QUOTA	(SALES-QUOTA)
Bill Adams	$367,911.00	$350,000.00	$17,911.00
Mary Jones	$392,725.00	$300,000.00	$92,725.00
Sue Smith	$474,050.00	$350,000.00	$124,050.00
Sam Clark	$299,912.00	$275,000.00	$24,912.00
Bob Smith	$142,594.00	$200,000.00	-$57,406.00
Dan Roberts	$305,673.00	$300,000.00	$5,673.00
Tom Snyder	$75,985.00	NULL	NULL
Larry Fitch	$361,865.00	$350,000.00	$11,865.00
Paul Cruz	$286,775.00	$275,000.00	$11,775.00
Nancy Angelli	$186,042.00	$300,000.00	-$113,958.00

The requested data (including the calculated difference between sales and quota for each salesperson) once again appears in a row/column table. Perhaps you would like to focus on the salespeople whose sales are less than their quotas. SQL lets you retrieve that kind of selective information very easily, by adding a mathematical comparison to the previous request:

```
SELECT NAME, SALES, QUOTA, (SALES - QUOTA)
  FROM SALESREPS
 WHERE SALES < QUOTA

NAME                    SALES          QUOTA (SALES-QUOTA)
---------------    ------------    ------------  -------------
Bob Smith          $142,594.00    $200,000.00    -$57,406.00
Nancy Angelli      $186,042.00    $300,000.00   -$113,958.00
```

The same technique can be used to list large orders in the database, and find out which customer placed the order, what product was ordered, and in what quantity. You can also ask SQL to sort the orders based on the order amount:

```
SELECT ORDER_NUM, CUST, PRODUCT, QTY, AMOUNT
  FROM ORDERS
 WHERE AMOUNT > 25000.00
 ORDER BY AMOUNT

ORDER_NUM  CUST  PRODUCT   QTY     AMOUNT
---------- ----- --------- ----  -----------
   112987  2103  4100Y      11   $27,500.00
   113069  2109  775C       22   $31,350.00
   112961  2117  2A44L       7   $31,500.00
   113045  2112  2A44R      10   $45,000.00
```

Summarizing Data

SQL not only retrieves data from the database, it can be used to summarize the database contents as well. What's the average size of an order in the database? This request asks SQL to look at all the orders and find the average amount:

```
SELECT AVG(AMOUNT)
  FROM ORDERS

AVG(AMOUNT)
-----------
  $8,256.37
```

You could also ask for the average amount of all the orders placed by a particular customer:

```
SELECT AVG(AMOUNT)
  FROM ORDERS
 WHERE CUST = 2103

AVG(AMOUNT)
-----------
  $8,895.50
```

Finally, let's find out the total amount of the orders placed by each customer. To do this, you can ask SQL to group the orders together by customer number, and then total the orders for each customer:

```
SELECT CUST, SUM(AMOUNT)
  FROM ORDERS
 GROUP BY CUST

CUST   SUM(AMOUNT)
-----  -----------
2101     $1,458.00
2102     $3,978.00
2103    $35,582.00
2106     $4,026.00
2107    $23,132.00
2108     $7,255.00
2109    $31,350.00
2111     $6,445.00
2112    $47,925.00
2113    $22,500.00
2114    $22,100.00
2117    $31,500.00
2118     $3,608.00
2120     $3,750.00
2124     $3,082.00
```

Adding Data to the Database

SQL is also used to add new data to the database. For example, suppose you just opened a new Western region sales office in Dallas, with target sales of $275,000.

Here's the INSERT statement that adds the new office to the database, as office number 23:

```
INSERT INTO OFFICES (CITY, REGION, TARGET, SALES, OFFICE)
    VALUES ('Dallas', 'Western', 275000.00, 0.00, 23)

1 row inserted.
```

Similarly, if Mary Jones (employee number 109) signs up a new customer, Acme Industries, this INSERT statement adds the customer to the database as customer number 2125 with a $25,000 credit limit:

```
INSERT INTO CUSTOMERS  (COMPANY, CUST_REP, CUST_NUM, CREDIT_LIMIT)
    VALUES ('Acme Industries', 109, 2125, 25000.00)

1 row inserted.
```

Deleting Data

Just as the SQL INSERT statement adds new data to the database, the SQL DELETE statement removes data from the database. If Acme Industries decides a few days later to switch to a competitor, you can delete them from the database with this statement:

```
DELETE FROM CUSTOMERS
 WHERE COMPANY = 'Acme Industries'

1 row deleted.
```

And if you decide to terminate all salespeople whose sales are less than their quotas, you can remove them from the database with this DELETE statement:

```
DELETE FROM SALESREPS
 WHERE SALES < QUOTA

2 rows deleted.
```

Updating the Database

The SQL language is also used to modify data that is already stored in the database. For example, to increase the credit limit for First Corp. to $75,000, you would use the SQL UPDATE statement:

```
UPDATE CUSTOMERS
   SET CREDIT_LIMIT = 75000.00
 WHERE COMPANY = 'First Corp.'

1 row updated.
```

The UPDATE statement can also make many changes in the database at once. For example, this UPDATE statement raises the quota for all salespeople by $15,000:

```
UPDATE SALESREPS
   SET QUOTA = QUOTA + 15000.00

8 rows updated.
```

Protecting Data

An important role of a database is to protect the stored data from access by unauthorized users. For example, suppose your secretary, named Mary, was not previously authorized to insert data about new customers into the database. This SQL statement grants her that permission:

```
GRANT INSERT
   ON CUSTOMERS
   TO MARY

Privilege granted.
```

Similarly, the following SQL statement gives Mary permission to update data about customers, and to retrieve customer data with the SELECT statement:

```
GRANT UPDATE, SELECT
   ON CUSTOMERS
   TO MARY

Privilege granted.
```

If Mary is no longer allowed to add new customers to the database, this REVOKE statement will disallow it:

```
REVOKE INSERT
    ON CUSTOMERS
  FROM MARY

Privilege revoked.
```

Similarly, this REVOKE statement will revoke all of Mary's privileges to access customer data in any way:

```
REVOKE ALL
    ON CUSTOMERS
  FROM MARY

Privilege revoked.
```

Creating a Database

Before you can store data in a database, you must first define the structure of the data. Suppose you want to expand the sample database by adding a table of data about the products sold by your company. For each product, the data to be stored includes:

- a three-character manufacturer ID code,
- a five-character product ID code,
- a description of up to thirty characters,
- the price of the product, and
- the quantity currently on hand.

This SQL CREATE TABLE statement defines a new table to store the products data:

```
CREATE TABLE PRODUCTS
    (MFR_ID CHAR(3),
  PRODUCT_ID CHAR(5),
  DESCRIPTION VARCHAR(20),
       PRICE MONEY,
  QTY_ON_HAND INTEGER)

Table created.
```

Although more cryptic than the previous SQL statements, the CREATE TABLE statement is still fairly straightforward. It assigns the name "PRODUCTS" to the new table, and specifies the name and type of data stored in each of its five columns.

Once the table has been created, you can fill it with data. Here's an INSERT statement for a new shipment of 250 size 7 widgets (product ACI-41007), which cost $225.00 apiece:

```
INSERT INTO PRODUCTS (MFR_ID, PRODUCT_ID, DESCRIPTION, PRICE, QTY_ON_HAND)
    VALUES ('ACI', '41007', 'Size 7 Widget', 225.00, 250)

1 row inserted.
```

Finally, if you discover later that you no longer need to store the products data in the database, you can erase the table (and all of the data it contains) with the DROP TABLE statement:

```
DROP TABLE PRODUCTS

Table dropped.
```

Summary

This quick tour of SQL showed you what SQL can do and illustrated the style of the SQL language, using eight of the most commonly used SQL statements. To summarize:

- SQL is used to *retrieve* data from the database, using the SELECT statement. You can retrieve all or part of the stored data, sort it, and ask SQL to summarize the data, using totals and averages.

- SQL is used to *update* the database, by adding new data with the INSERT statement, deleting data with the DELETE statement, and modifying existing data with the UPDATE statement.

- SQL is used to *control access* to the database, by granting and revoking specific privileges for specific users.

- SQL is used to *create* the database by defining the structure of new tables and dropping tables when they are no longer needed.

Chapter Three

SQL in Perspective

S QL is both a *de facto* and an official standard language for database management. What does it mean for SQL to be a standard? What role does SQL play as a database language? How did SQL become a standard, and what impact is the SQL standard having on personal computers, local area networks, minicomputers, and mainframes? To answer these questions, this chapter traces the history of SQL and describes its current role in the computer market.

SQL and Database Management

One of the major tasks of a computer system is to store and manage data. To handle this task, specialized computer programs known as database management systems began to appear in the late 1960s and early 1970s. A database management system, or DBMS, helped computer users to organize and structure their data, and allowed the computer system to play a more active role in managing the data. Although database management systems were first developed on large mainframe systems, their popularity has spread to minicomputers, personal computers, and workstations.

Today, database management is big business. Independent software companies and computer vendors ship billions of dollars worth of database management products every year. Computer industry experts say that mainframe and mini-computer database products each account for about 20 percent of the database market, and personal computer database products account for 40 percent or more. Database servers are the most rapidly growing segment of the PC-LAN market, with databases on UNIX, OS/2, Netware, and Windows NT based servers. Database management thus touches every segment of the computer market.

Since the late 1980s a specific type of DBMS, called a *relational* database management system (RDBMS), has exploded in popularity, and has become *the* standard database form. Relational databases organize data in a simple, tabular form, and provide many advantages over earlier types of databases. SQL is specifically a relational database language used to work with relational databases.

A Brief History of SQL

The history of the SQL language is intimately intertwined with the development of relational databases. Table 3-1 shows some of the milestones in its twenty-year history. The relational database concept was originally developed by Dr. E.F. "Ted" Codd, an IBM researcher. In June 1970 Dr. Codd published an article entitled "A Relational Model of Data for Large Shared Data Banks" that outlined a mathematical theory of how data could be stored and manipulated using a tabular structure. Relational databases and SQL trace their origins to this article, which appeared in the *Communications of the Association for Computing Machinery.*

Date	Event
1970	Codd defines relational database model
1974	IBM's System/R project begins
1974	First article describing the SEQUEL language
1978	System/R customer tests
1979	Oracle introduces first commercial RDBMS
1981	Relational Technology introduces Ingres
1981	IBM announces SQL/DS
1982	ANSI forms SQL standards committee
1983	IBM announces DB2
1986	ANSI SQL standard ratified
1986	Sybase introduces RDBMS for transaction processing
1987	ISO SQL standard ratified
1988	Ashton-Tate and Microsoft announce SQL Server for OS/2
1988	IBM announces DB2 Version 2
1989	First shipment of SQL database servers for OS/2
1989	SQL Access Group founded
1991	SQL Access Group specification published
1992	Microsoft publishes ODBC specification
1992	First shipment of SQL database servers for Netware
1992	ANSI SQL2 standard ratified
1993	First shipment of ODBC products

Table 3-1.   *Milestones in the Development of SQL*

The Early Years

Codd's article triggered a flurry of relational database research, including a major research project within IBM. The goal of the project, called System/R, was to prove the workability of the relational concept and to provide some experience in actually implementing a relational DBMS. Work on System/R began in the mid-1970s at IBM's Santa Teresa laboratories in San Jose, California.

In 1974 and 1975 the first phase of the System/R project produced a minimal prototype of a relational DBMS. In addition to the DBMS itself, the System/R project included work on database query languages. One of these languages was called SEQUEL, an acronym for Structured English Query Language. In 1976 and 1977 the System/R research prototype was rewritten from scratch. The new implementation supported multi-table queries, and allowed several users to share access to the data.

The System/R implementation was distributed to a number of IBM customer sites for evaluation in 1978 and 1979. These early customer sites provided some actual user experience with System/R and its database language, which had been renamed SQL, or Structured Query Language, for legal reasons. Despite the name change, the SEQUEL pronunciation remained, and continues to this day. In 1979 the System/R research project came to an end, with IBM concluding that relational databases were not only feasible, but could be the basis for a useful commercial product.

Early Relational Products

The System/R project and its SQL database language were well-chronicled in technical journals during the 1970s. Seminars on database technology featured debates on the merits of the new and "heretical" relational model. By 1976 it was apparent that IBM was becoming enthusiastic about relational database technology, and that it was making a major commitment to the SQL language.

The publicity about System/R attracted the attention of a group of engineers in Menlo Park, California, who decided that IBM's research foreshadowed a commercial market for relational databases. In 1977 they formed a company named Relational Software, Inc., to build a relational DBMS based on SQL. The product, named Oracle, shipped in 1979, and became the first commercially-available relational DBMS. Oracle beat IBM's first product to market by a full two years, and ran on Digital's VAX minicomputers, which were less expensive than IBM mainframes. Today the company, renamed Oracle Corporation, is a leading vendor of relational database management systems, with annual sales well over one billion dollars.

Professors at the University of California's Berkeley computer laboratories were also researching relational databases in the mid-1970s. Like the IBM research team, they built a prototype of a relational DBMS, and called their system Ingres. The Ingres project included a query language named QUEL which, although more "structured" than SQL, was less English-like. Many of today's database experts trace their involvement with relational databases back to the Berkeley Ingres project, including the founders of Sybase, and many of the object-oriented database startup companies.

In 1980 several professors left Berkeley and founded Relational Technology, Inc., to build a commercial version of Ingres, announced in 1981. Relational Technology, renamed Ingres Corporation in 1989, and now part of the ASK Group, remains a leading relational DBMS vendor, with annual sales of several hundred million dollars. The original QUEL query language was effectively replaced by SQL in 1986, a testimony to the market power of the SQL standard.

IBM Products

While Oracle and Ingres raced to become commercial products, IBM's System/R project had also turned into an effort to build a commercial product, named SQL/Data System (SQL/DS). IBM announced SQL/DS in 1981, and began shipping the product in 1982. In 1983 IBM announced a version of SQL/DS for VM/CMS, an operating system that is frequently used on IBM mainframes in corporate "information center" applications.

In 1983 IBM also introduced Database 2 (DB2), another relational DBMS for its mainframe systems. DB2 operated under IBM's MVS operating system, the workhorse operating system used in large mainframe data centers. The first release of DB2 began shipping in 1985, and IBM officials hailed it as a strategic piece of IBM software technology. DB2 has since become IBM's flagship relational DBMS, and with IBM's weight behind it, DB2's SQL language became the de facto standard database language. DB2 technology has now migrated across all IBM product lines, from personal computers to network servers to mainframes.

Commercial Acceptance

During the first half of the 1980s, the relational database vendors struggled for commercial acceptance of their products. The relational products had several disadvantages when compared to the traditional database architectures. The performance of relational databases was inferior to that of traditional databases. Except for the IBM products, the relational databases came from small "upstart" vendors. And, except for the IBM products, the relational databases tended to run on minicomputers rather than on IBM mainframes.

The relational products did have one major advantage, however. Their relational query languages (SQL, QUEL, and others) allowed users to pose ad hoc queries to the database, and get immediate answers, without writing programs. As a result, relational databases began slowly turning up in information center applications as decision-support tools. By May 1985 Oracle proudly claimed to have "over 1000" installations. Ingres was installed in a comparable number of sites. DB2 and SQL/DS were also being slowly accepted, and counted their combined installations at slightly over 1000 sites.

During the last half of the 1980s, SQL and relational databases were rapidly accepted as the database technology of the future. The performance of the relational database products improved dramatically. Ingres and Oracle, in particular, leapfrogged with each new version claiming superiority over the competitor and two or three times the performance of the previous release. Improvements in the processing power of the underlying computer hardware also helped to boost performance.

Market forces also boosted the popularity of SQL in the late 1980s. IBM stepped up its evangelism of SQL, positioning DB2 as the data management solution for the 1990s. Publication of the ANSI/ISO standard for SQL in 1986 gave SQL "official" status as a standard. SQL also emerged as a standard on UNIX-based computer systems, whose popularity accelerated in the 1980s. As personal computers became more powerful and were linked in local area networks, they needed more sophisticated database management. PC database vendors embraced SQL as the solution to these needs, and minicomputer database vendors moved "down market" to compete in the emerging PC local area network market. By the early 1990s, better SQL implementations and faster processors also made SQL a solution for transaction-processing applications. Finally, SQL became a key part of the client/server architecture that links PCs and network servers into low cost information processing systems. Table 3-2 shows some of the most popular SQL-based database management systems on different types of computer systems.

As the computer industry entered the 1990s, SQL installations numbered in the hundreds of thousands. SQL was clearly established as the standard database language. Database vendors who didn't already support SQL were scrambling to provide it, and any new database product required SQL as a "checklist" item to be taken seriously. SQL had become both an official and a de facto standard for relational databases.

SQL Standards

One of the most important developments in the market acceptance of SQL is the emergence of SQL standards. References to "the SQL standard" usually mean the official standard adopted by the American National Standards Institute (ANSI) and the International Standards Organization (ISO). However, there are other important SQL standards including the SQL defined by IBM's DB2 and the X/OPEN standard for SQL under UNIX.

The ANSI/ISO Standards

Work on the official SQL standard began in 1982, when ANSI charged its X3H2 committee with defining a standard relational database language. At first the

DBMS	Computer Systems
DB2	IBM mainframes under MVS; IBM UNIX systems
SQL/DS	IBM mainframes under VM and DOS/VSE
Rdb/VMS	Digital VAX/VMS minicomputers
Oracle	Mainframes, minicomputers, servers, and PCs
Ingres	Minicomputers, servers, and PCs
Sybase	Minicomputers, servers, and PC LANs
Informix-SQL	UNIX-based minicomputers, servers, and PCs
SQL Server	OS/2- and Windows NT-based PC LANs
SQL Base	DOS- and OS/2-based PC LANs

Table 3-2.   *Leading SQL-Based Database Management Systems*

committee debated the merits of various proposed database languages. However, as IBM's commitment to SQL increased and SQL emerged as a de facto standard in the market, the committee selected SQL as their relational database language, and turned their attention to standardizing it.

The resulting ANSI standard for SQL was largely based on DB2 SQL, although it contains some major differences from DB2. After several revisions, the standard was officially adopted as ANSI standard X3.135 in 1986, and as an ISO standard in 1987. The ANSI/ISO standard has since been adopted as a Federal Information Processing Standard (FIPS) by the U.S. Government. This standard, slightly revised and expanded in 1989, is usually called the "SQL-89" or "SQL1" standard. References in this book to the "ANSI/ISO standard" refer to SQL1, which is still the basis for most commercial products.

Many of the ANSI and ISO standards committee members were representatives from database vendors who had existing SQL products, each implementing a slightly different SQL dialect. Like dialects of human languages, the SQL dialects were generally very similar to one another, but were incompatible in their details. In many areas the committee simply sidestepped these differences by omitting some parts of the language from the standard and specifying others as "implementor-defined." These decisions allowed existing SQL implementations to claim broad adherence to the resulting ANSI/ISO standard, but made the standard relatively weak.

To address the holes in the original standard, the ANSI committee continued its work, and drafts for a new more rigorous SQL2 standard were circulated. Unlike the 1989 standard, the SQL2 drafts specified features considerably beyond those found in current commercial SQL products. Even more far-reaching changes were proposed for a follow-on SQL3 standard. As a result, the proposed SQL2 and SQL3 standards were a good deal more controversial than the initial SQL standard. The SQL2 standard weaved its way through the ANSI approval process, and was finally approved in October, 1992. While the original 1986 standard took less than 100 pages, the official SQL2 standard takes nearly six hundred.

Despite the existence of a SQL2 standard, no commercial SQL product available today implements all of its features, and no two commercial SQL products support exactly the same SQL dialect. Moreover, as database vendors introduce new capabilities, they are expanding their SQL dialects, and moving them even further apart. The central core of SQL language has become fairly standardized, however. Where it can be done without hurting existing customers or features, vendors have brought their products into conformance with the SQL-89 standard, and the same will slowly happen with SQL2.

The "real" SQL standard, of course, is the SQL implemented in products that are broadly accepted by the marketplace. Which parts of the standard will come from the official standards committees, from the market power of IBM or Microsoft, or from the entrepreneurial efforts of the independent database vendors remains to be seen.

Other SQL Standards

Although it is the most widely recognized, the ANSI/ISO standard is not the only standard for SQL. X/OPEN, a European vendor group, has also adopted SQL as part of its suite of standards for a "portable application environment" based on UNIX. The X/OPEN standards play a major role in the European computer market, where portability among computer systems from different vendors is a key concern. Unfortunately, the X/OPEN standard differs from the ANSI/ISO standard in several areas.

IBM also included SQL in the specification of its Systems Application Architecture blueprint, promising that all of its SQL products would eventually move to this SAA SQL dialect. Although SAA failed to achieve its promise of unifying the IBM product line, the momentum toward a unified IBM SQL continued. With its mainframe DB2 database as the flagship, IBM has introduced DB2 implementations for OS/2, its personal computer operating system, and for its RS/6000 line of UNIX-based workstations and servers. Thus the DB2 version is a very powerful *de facto* standard.

ODBC and the SQL Access Group

An important area of database technology not addressed by official standards is *database interoperability* — the methods by which data can be exchanged among different databases, usually over a network. In 1989, a group of vendors formed the SQL Access Group to address this problem. The resulting SQL Access Group specification for Remote Database Access (RDA) was published in 1991. Unfortunately, the RDA specification is closely tied to the OSI protocols, which have not been widely accepted, so it has had little impact. Transparent interoperability among different vendors' databases remains an elusive goal.

A second standard from SQL Access Group has had far more market impact. At Microsoft's urging and insistence, SQL Access Group expanded its focus to include a call-level interface for SQL. Based on a draft from Microsoft, the resulting Call-Level Interface (CLI) specification was published in 1992. Microsoft's own Open Database Connectivity (ODBC) specification, based on the CLI standard, was published the same year. With the market power of Microsoft behind it, and the "open standards" blessing of SQL Access Group, ODBC has emerged as the *de facto* standard interface for PC access to SQL databases. Apple and Microsoft announced an agreement to support ODBC on Macintosh and Windows in the Spring of 1993, giving ODBC "standard" status in both popular graphical user interface environments.

The Portability Myth

The existence of published SQL standard has spawned quite a few exaggerated claims about SQL and applications portability. Diagrams such as the one in Figure 3-1 are frequently drawn to show how an application using SQL can work interchangeably with any SQL-based database management system. In fact, the holes in the SQL-89 standard and the current differences between SQL dialects are significant enough that an application must *always* be modified when moved from one SQL database to another. These differences, many of which are eliminated by the SQL2 standard but not yet implemented in commercial products, include:

- *Error codes.* The SQL-89 standard does not specify the error codes to be returned when SQL detects an error, and all of the commercial implementations use their own set of error codes. The SQL2 standard specifies standard error codes.

- *Data types.* The SQL-89 standard defines a minimal set of data types, but it omits some of the most popular and useful types, such as variable-length character strings, dates and times, and money data. The SQL2 standard addresses these, but not "new" data types such as graphics and multimedia objects.

- *System tables.* The SQL-89 standard is silent about the system tables that provide information regarding the structure of the database itself. Each vendor has its own structure for these tables, and even IBM's four SQL implementations differ from one another. The tables are standardized in SQL2.

- *Interactive SQL.* The standard specifies only the *programmatic* SQL used by an application program, not interactive SQL. For example, the SELECT statement used to query the database in interactive SQL is absent from the standard.

- *Programmatic interface.* The original standard specifies an abstract technique for using SQL from within an applications program written in COBOL, C, FORTRAN, and other programming languages. No commercial SQL product uses this technique, and there is considerable variation in the actual programmatic interfaces used. The SQL2 standard specifies an embedded SQL interface for popular programming languages, but not a call-level interface.

- *Dynamic SQL.* The SQL-89 standard does not include the features required to develop general-purpose database front-ends, such as query tools and report writers. These features, known as *dynamic SQL*, are found in virtually all SQL database systems, but they vary significantly from product to product. SQL2 includes a standard for dynamic SQL.

- *Semantic differences.* Because the standards specify certain details as "implementor-defined," it's possible to run the same query against two different conforming SQL implementations, and produce two different sets of query results. These differences occur in the handling of NULL values, column functions, and duplicate row elimination.

- *Collating sequences.* The SQL-89 standard does not address the collating (sorting) sequence of characters stored in the database. The results of a sorted query will be different if the query is run on a personal computer (with ASCII characters) and a mainframe (with EBCDIC characters). The SQL2 standard includes an elaborate specification for how a program or a user can request a specific collating sequence.

■ *Database structure.*   The SQL-89 standard specifies the SQL language to be used once a particular database has been opened and is ready for processing. The details of database naming and how the initial connection to the database is established vary widely, and are not portable. The SQL2 standard creates more uniformity, but cannot completely mask these details.

Despite these differences, commercial database tools boasting portability across several different brands of SQL databases began to emerge in the early 1990s. In every case, however, the tools require a special adapter for each supported DBMS, which generates the appropriate SQL dialect, handles data type conversion, translates error codes, and so on. Transparent portability across different DBMS brands based on standard SQL is the major goal of SQL2 and ODBC, but widespread, transparent, uniform access to SQL databases remains in the future.

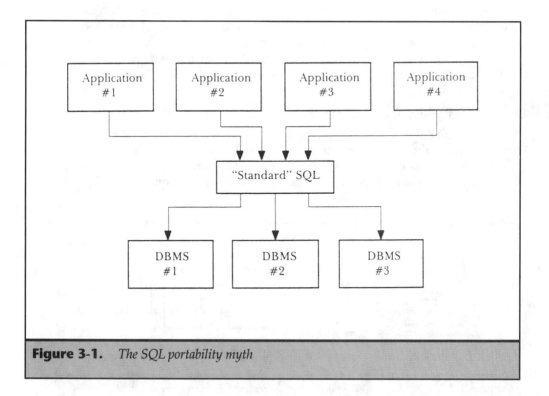

Figure 3-1.   *The SQL portability myth*

SQL and Networking

The growing popularity of computer networking over the last few years has had a major impact on database management and given SQL a new prominence. As networks become more common, applications that have traditionally run on a central minicomputer or mainframe are moving to local area networks of desktop workstations and servers. In these networks SQL plays a crucial role as the link between an application running on a desktop workstation and the DBMS that manages shared data on the server.

Centralized Architecture

The traditional database architecture used by DB2, SQL/DS, and minicomputer databases such as Oracle and Ingres is shown in Figure 3-2. In this architecture the DBMS and the physical data both reside on a central minicomputer or mainframe system, along with the application program that accepts input from the user's terminal and displays data on the user's screen.

Suppose that the user types a query that requires a sequential search of a database, such as a request to find the average amount of merchandise of all orders. The DBMS receives the query, scans through the database fetching each record of data from the disk, calculates the average, and displays the result on the terminal screen. Both the application processing and the database processing occur on the central computer, and since the system is shared by many users, each user experiences degraded performance as the system becomes more heavily loaded.

File Server Architecture

The introduction of personal computers and local area networks led to the development of the *file server* architecture, shown in Figure 3-3. In this architecture, an application running on a personal computer can transparently access data located on a file server, which stores shared files. When a PC application requests data from a

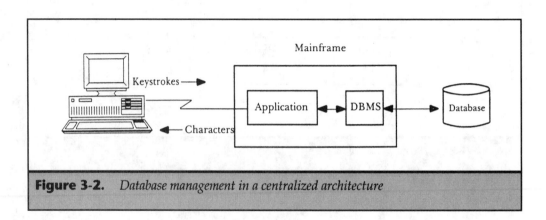

Figure 3-2. *Database management in a centralized architecture*

shared file, the networking software automatically retrieves the requested block of the file from the server. Popular PC databases, including Microsoft Access, Paradox, and dBASE, support this file server approach, with each personal computer running its own copy of the DBMS software.

For typical queries this architecture provides excellent performance, because each user has the full power of a personal computer running its own copy of the DBMS. However, consider the query made in the previous example. Because the query requires a sequential scan of the database, the DBMS repeatedly requests blocks of data from the database, which is physically located across the network on the server. Eventually *every* block of the file will be requested and sent across the network. Obviously this architecture produces very heavy network traffic and slow performance for queries of this type.

Client/Server Architecture

Figure 3-4 shows the emerging *client/server* architecture for database management. In this architecture, personal computers are combined in a local area network with a *database server* that stores shared databases. The functions of the DBMS are split into two parts. Database "front-ends," such as interactive query tools, report writers, and

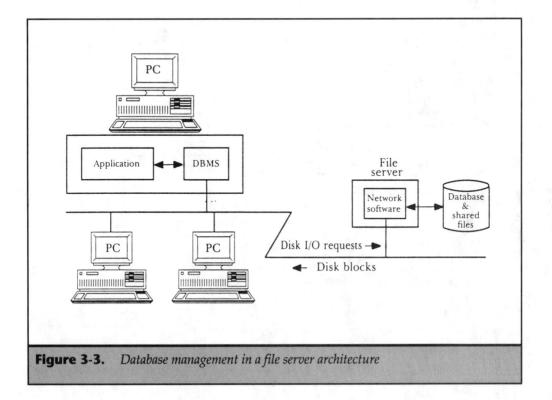

Figure 3-3.   *Database management in a file server architecture*

application programs, run on the personal computer. The back-end database engine that stores and manages the data runs on the server. SQL has become the standard database language for communication between the front-end tools and the back-end engine in this architecture.

Consider once more the query requesting the average order size. In the client/server architecture, the query travels across the network to the database server as a SQL request. The database engine on the server processes the request and scans the database, which also resides on the server. When the result is calculated, the database engine sends it back across the network as a single reply to the initial request, and the front-end application displays it on the PC screen.

The client/server architecture reduces the network traffic and splits the database workload. User-intensive functions, such as handling input and displaying data, are concentrated on the user's PC. Data-intensive functions, such as file I/O and query processing, are concentrated in the database server. Most importantly, the SQL language provides a well-defined interface between the front-end and back-end systems, communicating database access requests in an efficient manner.

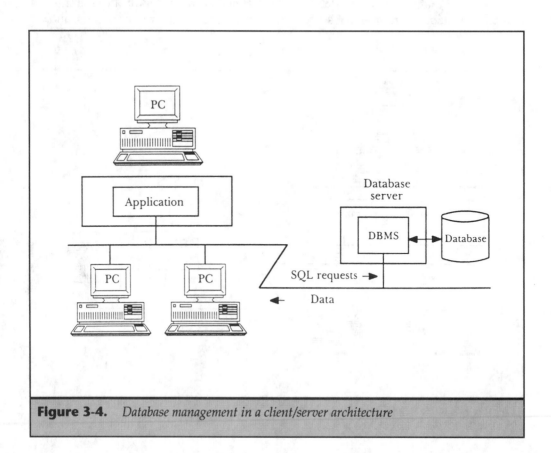

Figure 3-4.   *Database management in a client/server architecture*

The client/server architecture has received a great deal of attention with the proliferation of PC networks based on OS/2, Novell Netware and Windows NT servers. SQL Server, the Oracle, Informix and Ingres implementation for PC LANs, and Gupta Technologies' SQLBase all use this approach.

The Impact of SQL

As the standard for relational database access, SQL has had a major impact on all parts of the computer market. IBM has adopted SQL as a unifying database technology for its product line. All minicomputer vendors offer SQL-based databases, and SQL-based databases dominate the market for UNIX-based computer systems. SQL is also reshaping the personal computer database market as stand-alone personal computers give way to client/server personal computer networks. SQL is even emerging as a technology for on-line transaction processing, thus refuting the conventional wisdom that relational databases would never offer good enough performance for transaction processing applications.

SQL and IBM's SAA

SQL plays a key role as the database access language that unifies IBM's multiple incompatible computer families. Originally, this role was part of IBM's Systems Application Architecture (SAA) strategy, announced in March 1987. Although IBM's grand goals for SAA were not achieved, the unifying role of SQL has grown even more important over time. The strategic products in IBM's SQL database product line are:

- *DB2.* IBM's flagship relational database manager is the SQL standard-bearer for IBM mainframes running MVS.

- *SQL/DS.* SQL/DS is the relational database system for VM, another operating system for IBM mainframes.

- *SQL/400.* This SQL implementation for IBM's mid-range system supports the built-in relational database of the AS/400.

- *DB2/6000.* This implementation of DB2 runs on IBM's RS/6000 family of RISC-based workstations and servers, under a UNIX operating system.

- *DB2/2.* This SQL implementation for IBM personal computers is based on the DB2 mainframe implementation. It replaced OS/2 Extended Edition, which was IBM's initial SQL product for PCs, and provides better compatibility with mainframe DB2.

SQL on Minicomputers

Minicomputers were one of the most fertile early markets for SQL-based database systems. Oracle and Ingres were both originally marketed on Digital's VAX/VMS minicomputer systems. Both products have since been ported to many other platforms. Sybase, a later database system specialized for on-line transaction processing, also targeted the VAX as one of its primary platforms.

The minicomputer vendors have also developed their own proprietary relational databases featuring SQL. Digital considers relational databases so important that it is shipping a run-time version of its Rdb/VMS database with every VAX/VMS system. Hewlett-Packard offers Allbase, a database that supports both its HPSQL dialect and a non-relational interface. Data General's DG/SQL database has replaced its older non-relational databases as DG's strategic data management tool. In addition, many of the minicomputer vendors resell relational databases from the independent database software vendors.

SQL on UNIX Systems

SQL has firmly established itself as the data management solution of choice for UNIX-based computer systems. Originally developed at Bell Laboratories, UNIX became very popular in the 1980s as a vendor-independent, standard operating system. It runs on a wide range of computer systems, from workstations to mainframes, and has become the standard operating system for scientific and engineering applications.

In the early 1980s there were already four major databases available for UNIX systems. Two of them, Ingres and Oracle, were UNIX versions of the products that ran on DEC's proprietary minicomputers. The other two, Informix and Unify, were written specifically for UNIX. Neither of them originally offered SQL support, but by 1985 Unify offered a SQL query language and Informix had been rewritten as Informix-SQL, with full SQL support. Oracle, Ingres and Informix, as well as Sybase, are now available on all of the leading UNIX systems.

SQL and Transaction Processing

SQL and relational databases historically had very little impact in on-line transaction processing (OLTP) applications. With their emphasis on queries, relational databases were confined to decision support and low-volume on-line applications, where their slower performance was not a disadvantage. For OLTP applications, where hundreds of users needed on-line access to data and sub-second response times, IBM's nonrelational Information Management System (IMS) reigned as the dominant DBMS.

In 1986 a new DBMS vendor, Sybase, introduced a new SQL-based database especially designed for OLTP applications. The Sybase DBMS ran on VAX/VMS minicomputers and Sun workstations, and focused on maximum on-line performance. Oracle Corporation and Relational Technology followed shortly with announcements that they, too, would offer OLTP versions of their popular Oracle and Ingres database systems. In the UNIX market, Informix announced an OLTP version of its DBMS, named Informix-Turbo.

In April 1988 IBM jumped on the relational OLTP bandwagon with DB2 Version 2, with benchmarks showing the new version operating at over 250 transactions per second on large mainframes. IBM claimed that DB2 performance was now suitable for all but the most demanding OLTP applications, and encouraged customers to consider it as a serious alternative to IMS. OLTP benchmarks have now become a standard sales tool for relational databases, despite serious questions about how well the benchmarks actually measure performance in real applications.

The suitability of SQL for OLTP continues to improve, with advances in relational technology and more powerful computer hardware both leading to ever-higher transaction rates. Customers are now considering and using DB2 and relational databases for OLTP applications, and transaction rates have risen several fold.

SQL on Personal Computers

Databases have been popular on personal computers since before the introduction of the IBM PC. Ashton-Tate's dBASE product has been installed on over one million MS-DOS-based PCs, and other products such as R:BASE, PFS:File, and Paradox have also achieved significant success. On the Macintosh, databases such as 4th Dimension combined data management and a graphical user interface. Although these PC databases often presented data in tabular form, they lacked the full power of a relational DBMS and a relational database language such as SQL.

SQL had little impact on personal computers until the late 1980s. By then, powerful PCs supporting tens or hundreds of megabytes of disk storage were common. Users also were linking personal computers into local area networks, and wanted to share databases. In short, PCs began to need the features that SQL and relational databases could provide.

The early SQL-based databases for personal computers were versions of popular minicomputer products that barely fit on personal computers. Professional Oracle, announced in 1984, required two megabytes of memory on an IBM PC, and Oracle for Macintosh, announced in 1988, had similar requirements. A PC version of Ingres, announced in 1987, fit (just barely) within the 640KB limitation of MS-DOS. Informix-SQL for MS-DOS was announced in 1986, providing a PC version of the popular UNIX database. Also in 1986, Gupta Technologies, a company founded by an ex-Oracle manager, announced SQLBase, a database for PC local area networks. SQLBase was among the first PC products to offer a client/server architecture, a preview of the PC LAN database announcements to come.

The real impact of SQL on personal computers began with the announcement of OS/2 by IBM and Microsoft in April 1987. In addition to the standard OS/2 product, IBM announced a proprietary OS/2 Extended Edition (OS/2 EE) with a built-in SQL database and communications support. With the introduction, IBM again signalled its strong commitment to SQL, saying in effect that SQL was so important that it belonged in the computer's operating system.

OS/2 Extended Edition presented Microsoft with a problem. As the developer and distributor of standard OS/2 to other personal computer manufacturers, Microsoft needed an alternative to the Extended Edition. Microsoft responded by licensing the Sybase DBMS, which had been developed for the VAX, and began porting it to OS/2.

In January 1988, in a surprise move, Microsoft and Ashton-Tate announced that they would jointly sell the resulting OS/2-based product, renamed SQL Server. Microsoft would sell SQL Server with OS/2 to computer manufacturers; Ashton-Tate would sell the product through retail channels to PC users. In September 1989, Lotus Development added its endorsement of SQL Server by investing in Sybase. Later that year, Ashton-Tate relinquished its exclusive retail distribution rights and sold its investment to Lotus. Although SQL Server for OS/2 met with only limited success, SQL Server continues to play a key role in Microsoft's product plans. It is Microsoft's relational database for Windows NT, Microsoft's flagship operating system for client/server computing, which began shipping in 1993.

SQL on PC Local Area Networks

The introduction of OS/2 Extended Edition and the Ashton-Tate/Microsoft SQL Server focused attention on the potential of SQL in local area networks. Customers began looking seriously at networks of personal computers and the client/server architecture as an alternative to a centralized minicomputer or mainframe for database applications.

Initially, the market for SQL on PC LANs focused on OS/2 as a database server platform. Unlike MS-DOS, OS/2 had no 640KB memory limit, and its multitasking architecture made it an excellent technical foundation for a database server. By the end of 1989, IBM, Microsoft, Oracle, Gupta and others had introduced OS/2 products. But OS/2's sales fell well below initial expectations, while sales of Microsoft Window began to soar with the introduction of Windows 3.0. Despite attempts to paper over their differences in public, the resulting rivalry between OS/2 and Windows produced a deeper and deeper rift between IBM and Microsoft. In the end, Microsoft acknowledged its commitment to Windows and its lack of support for OS/2, leaving OS/2 with an "IBM proprietary" status. OS/2 continues to be an important platform for some large IBM corporate accounts, but its chance to become the dominant "industrial-strength" PC operating system—and hence the preferred platform for SQL on local area networks—is gone.

While the Windows versus OS/2 battle raged on the desktop, SQL database sales on other PC LAN platforms began to grow significantly. UNIX-based computers steadily dropped in price, and a version of UNIX from the Santa Cruz Operation (SCO UNIX) became a favorite platform for Intel-based PCs. In the early 1990s, SCO UNIX added support for multiprocessing, a technique for spreading the workload of a computer over two, three or more microprocessors. With the processing power of four or eight microprocessors working together, UNIX-based versions of Oracle, Informix and Sybase could now deliver minicomputer-level performance on PC servers starting at $20,000. Multiprocessing servers from Compaq, Dell, IBM and other leading PC vendors currently offer the best performance for the price of any computer system available.

Although UNIX became a popular platform for database servers, the vast majority of PC LAN servers were still used for file and printer sharing, and most of those servers used Novell's Netware as a server operating system. Netware lacked the sophistication of UNIX or OS/2, but it had a major advantage—sales volume. The early Netware SQL databases were inferior to those available for UNIX or OS/2, but beginning in 1992 the major database vendors introduced Netware versions. Sales of these products quickly became very strong, and Netware has emerged as a viable PC LAN database platform.

In competition with UNIX, OS/2 and Netware, Microsoft has thrown its weight behind Windows NT as a PC LAN client/server platform. Windows NT has some major technical advantages over the competition; it is a new, modern operating system without the "baggage" of backward compatibility. But the lack of installed base, few applications, and the need to build an entire sales and support infrastructure slowed the acceptance of NT. With Microsoft's weight behind it, however, most analysts believed that NT would eventually assume a prominent role in client/server LANs. As a result, all of the leading database vendors have announced NT versions of their products. The first of these products began shipping in 1993.

The market for client/server databases on PC LANs has developed more slowly than the file server and print server markets, but it reached a turning point by 1993. It is now the fastest growing segment of the PC LAN server market. Most analysts expect that growth to accelerate further and to continue into the late 1990s, eventually making PC LAN servers the largest market for SQL-based databases.

Summary

This chapter described the development of SQL and its role as a standard language for relational database management:

- SQL was originally developed by IBM researchers, and IBM's strong support of SQL is a key reason for its success.

- There are official ANSI/ISO SQL standards and several other SQL standards, each slightly different from the ANSI/ISO standards.

- Despite the existence of standards, there are many small variations among commercial SQL dialects; no two SQLs are exactly the same.

- SQL is having an impact on database management in many different segments of the computer market, including mainframes, OLTP systems, workstations, personal computers, and especially in client/server local area networks.

Chapter Four

Relational Databases

D atabase management systems organize and structure data so that it can be retrieved and manipulated by users and application programs. The data structures and access techniques provided by a particular DBMS are called its *data model*. The data model determines the "personality" of a DBMS, and the applications for which it is particularly well suited.

SQL is a database language for relational databases, and uses the *relational data model*. What exactly is a relational database? How is data stored in a relational database? How do relational databases compare to earlier technologies, such as hierarchical and network databases? What are the advantages and disadvantages of the relational model? This chapter describes the relational data model supported by SQL, and compares it to earlier strategies for database organization.

Early Data Models

As database management became popular during the 1970s and 1980s, a handful of popular data models emerged. Each of these early data models had advantages and disadvantages that played key roles in the development of the relational data model. In many ways the relational data model represented an attempt to streamline and simplify the earlier data models. In order to understand the role and contribution of SQL and the relational model, it would be useful to examine briefly some data models that preceded the development of SQL.

File Management Systems

Before the introduction of database management systems, all data permanently stored on a computer system, such as payroll and accounting records, was stored in individual files. A *file management system*, usually provided by the computer manufacturer as part of the computer's operating system, kept track of the names and locations of the files. The file management system basically had no data model; it knew nothing about the internal contents of files. To the file management system, a file containing a word processing document and a file containing payroll data appeared the same.

Knowledge about the contents of a file—what data it contained and how the data was organized—was embedded in the application programs that used the file, as shown in Figure 4-1. In this payroll application, each of the COBOL programs that processed the employee master file contained a *file description* (FD) that described the layout of the data in the file. If the structure of the data changed—for example, if an additional item of data was to be stored for each employee—every program that accessed the file had to be modified. As the number of files and programs grew over time, more and more of a data processing department's effort went into maintaining existing applications rather than developing new ones.

The problems of maintaining large file-based systems led in the late 1960s to the development of database management systems. The idea behind these systems was

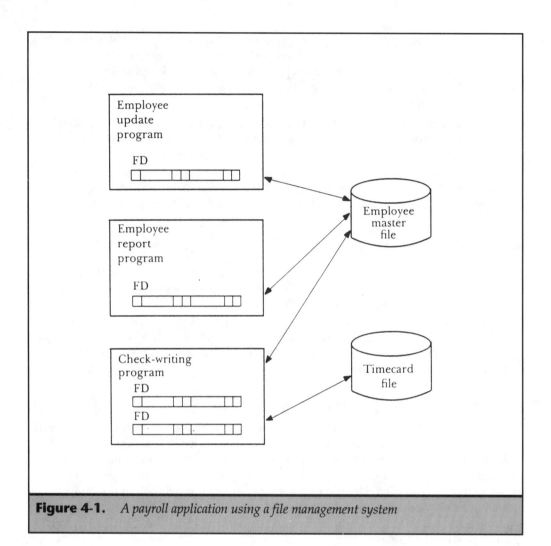

Figure 4-1.   *A payroll application using a file management system*

simple: take the definition of a file's content and structure out of the individual programs, and store it, together with the data, in a database. Using the information in the database, the DBMS that controlled it could take a much more active role in managing the data and changes to the database structure.

Hierarchical Databases

One of the most important applications for the earliest database management systems was production planning for manufacturing companies. If an automobile manufacturer decided to produce 10,000 units of one car model and 5,000 units of another model, it needed to know how many parts to order from its suppliers. To answer the question, the product (a car) had to be decomposed into assemblies (engine, body, chassis), which were decomposed into subassemblies (valves, cylinders, spark plugs), and then into sub-subassemblies, and so on. Handling this list of parts, known as a *bill of materials*, was a job tailor-made for computers.

The bill of materials for a product had a natural hierarchical structure. To store this data, the *hierarchical* data model, illustrated in Figure 4-2, was developed. In this model, each *record* in the database represented a specific part. The records had *parent/child relationships*, linking each part to its subpart, and so on.

To access the data in the database, a program could:

■ find a particular part by number (such as the left door),

■ move "down" to the first child (the door handle),

■ move "up" to its parent (the body), or

■ move "sideways" to the next child (the right door).

Retrieving the data in a hierarchical database thus required *navigating* through the records, moving up, down, and sideways one record at a time.

One of the most popular hierarchical database management systems was IBM's Information Management System (IMS), first introduced in 1968. The advantages of IMS and its hierarchical model follow.

■ *Simple structure.*   The organization of an IMS database was easy to understand. The database hierarchy paralleled that of a company organization chart or a family tree.

■ *Parent/child organization.*   An IMS database was excellent for representing parent/child relationships, such as "A is a part of B" or "A is owned by B."

■ *Performance.*   IMS stored parent/child relationships as physical pointers from one data record to another, so that movement through the database was rapid. Because the structure was simple, IMS could place parent and child records close to one another on the disk, minimizing disk input/output.

IMS is still the most widely installed DBMS on IBM mainframes. It is used on over 25 percent of IBM mainframe installations.

Network Databases

The simple structure of a hierarchical database became a disadvantage when the data had a more complex structure. In an order-processing database, for example, a single order might participate in three *different* parent/child relationships, linking the order to the customer who placed it, the salesperson who took it, and the product ordered,

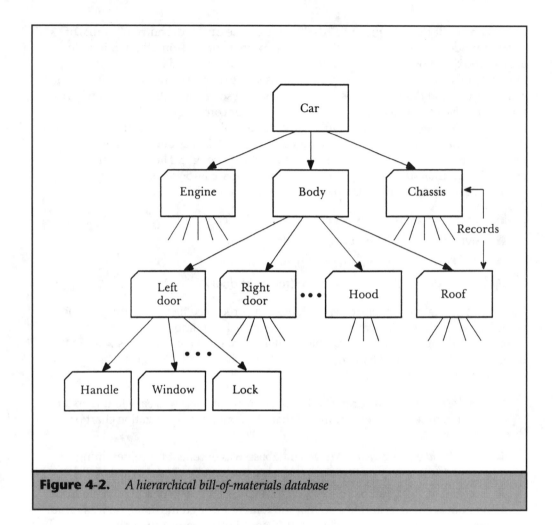

Figure 4-2. *A hierarchical bill-of-materials database*

as shown in Figure 4-3. The structure of this type of data simply didn't fit the strict hierarchy of IMS.

To deal with applications such as order processing, a new *network* data model was developed. The network data model extended the hierarchical model by allowing a record to participate in multiple parent/child relationships, as shown in Figure 4-4. These relationships were known as *sets* in the network model. In 1971 the Conference on Data Systems Languages published an official standard for network databases, which became known as the CODASYL model. IBM never developed a network DBMS of its own, choosing instead to extend IMS over the years. But during the 1970s independent software companies rushed to embrace the network model, creating

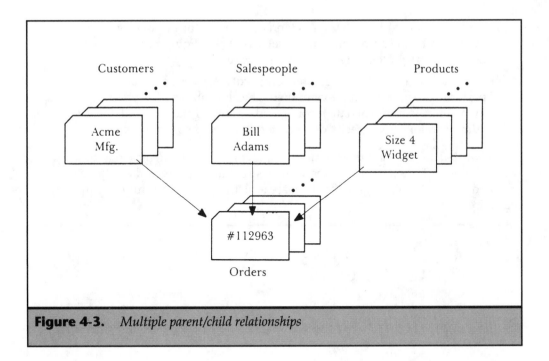

Figure 4-3. *Multiple parent/child relationships*

products such as Cullinet's IDMS, Cincom's Total, and the Adabas DBMS that became very popular.

For a programmer, accessing a network database was very similar to accessing a hierarchical database. An application program could:

- find a specific parent record by key (such as a customer number),
- move down to the first child in a particular set (the first order placed by this customer),
- move sideways from one child to the next in the set (the next order placed by the same customer), or
- move up from a child to its parent in another set (the salesperson who took the order).

Once again the programmer had to navigate the database record-by-record, this time specifying which relationship to navigate as well as the direction.

Network databases had several advantages:

- *Flexibility.* Multiple parent/child relationships allowed a network database to represent data that did not have a simple hierarchical structure.

■ *Standardization.* The CODASYL standard boosted the popularity of the network model, and minicomputer vendors such as Digital Equipment Corporation and Data General implemented network databases.

■ *Performance.* Despite their greater complexity, network databases boasted performance approaching that of hierarchical databases. Sets were represented by pointers to physical data records, and on some systems, the database administrator could specify data clustering based on a set relationship.

Network databases had their disadvantages, too. Like hierarchical databases, they were very rigid. The set relationships and the structure of the records had to be specified in advance. Changing the database structure typically required rebuilding the entire database.

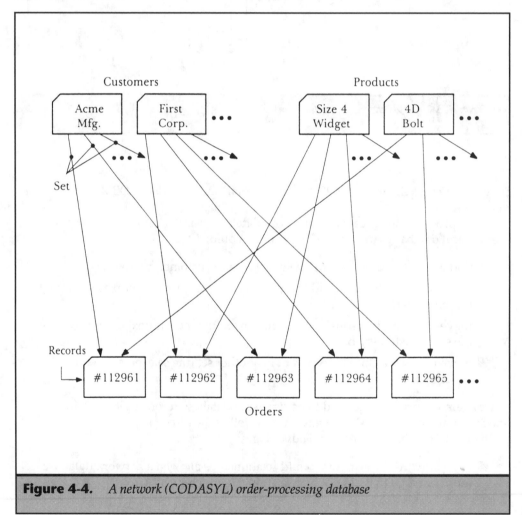

Figure 4-4. *A network (CODASYL) order-processing database*

Both hierarchical and network databases were tools for programmers. To answer a question such as "What is the most popular product ordered by Acme Manufacturing?" a programmer had to write a program that navigated its way through the database. The backlog of requests for custom reports often stretched to weeks or months, and by the time the program was written the information it delivered was often worthless.

The Relational Data Model

The disadvantages of the hierarchical and network models led to intense interest in the new *relational* data model when it was first described by Dr. Codd in 1970. The relational model was an attempt to simplify database structure. It eliminated the explicit parent/child structures from the database, and instead represented all data in the database as simple row/column tables of data values. Figure 4-5 shows a relational version of the network order-processing database in Figure 4-4.

Unfortunately, the practical definition of "What is a relational database?" became much less clear-cut than the precise, mathematical definition in Codd's 1970 paper. Early relational database management systems failed to implement some key parts of Codd's model, which are only now finding their way into commercial products. As

PRODUCTS Table

DESCRIPTION	PRICE	QTY_ON_HAND
Size 3 Widget	$107.00	207
Size 4 Widget	$117.00	139
Hinge Pin	$350.00	14
⋮		

ORDERS Table

ORDER_NUM	COMPANY	PRODUCT	QTY
112963	Acme Mfg.	41004	28
112975	JCP Inc.	2A44G	6
112983	Acme Mfg.	41004	6
113012	JCP Inc.	41003	35
⋮			

CUSTOMERS Table

COMPANY	CUST_REP	CREDIT_LIMIT
Acme Mfg.	105	$50,000.00
JCP Inc.	103	$50,000.00
⋮		

Figure 4-5. *A relational order-processing database*

the relational concept grew in popularity, many databases that were called "relational" in fact were not.

In response to the corruption of the term "relational," Dr. Codd wrote an article in 1985 setting forth twelve rules to be followed by any database that called itself "truly relational." Codd's twelve rules have since been accepted as *the* definition of a truly relational DBMS. However, it's easier to start with a more informal definition:

> A relational database is a database where all data visible to the user is organized strictly as tables of data values, and where all database operations work on these tables.

The definition is intended specifically to rule out structures such as the embedded pointers of a hierarchical or network database. A relational DBMS can represent parent/child relationships, but they are represented strictly by the data values contained in the database tables.

The Sample Database

Figure 4-6 shows a small relational database for an order-processing application. This sample database is used throughout this book, and provides the basis for most of the examples. Appendix A contains a complete description of the database structure and its contents.

The sample database contains five tables. Each table stores information about one particular *kind* of entity:

- The CUSTOMERS table stores data about each customer, such as the company name, credit limit, and the salesperson who calls on the customer.

- The SALESREPS table stores the employee number, name, age, year-to-date sales, and other data about each salesperson.

- The OFFICES table stores data about each of the five sales offices, including the city where the office is located, the sales region to which it belongs, and so on.

- The ORDERS table keeps track of every order placed by a customer, identifying the salesperson who took the order, the product ordered, the quantity and amount of the order, and so on. For simplicity, each order is for only one product.

- The PRODUCTS table stores data about each product available for sale, such as the manufacturer, product number, description and price.

Tables

The organizing principle in a relational database is the *table,* a rectangular, row/column arrangement of data values. Each table in a database has a unique *table name* that identifies its contents. (Actually, each user can choose their own table names without worrying about the names chosen by other users, as explained in Chapter 5.)

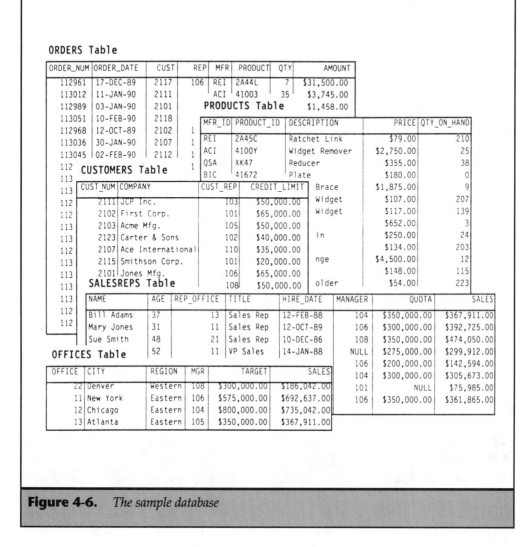

Figure 4-6. *The sample database*

The row/column structure of a table is shown more clearly in Figure 4-7, which is an enlarged view of the OFFICES table. Each horizontal *row* of the OFFICES table represents a single physical entity—a single sales office. Together the five rows of the table represent all five of the company's sales offices. All of the data in a particular row of the table applies to the office represented by that row.

Each vertical *column* of the OFFICES table represents one item of data that is stored in the database for each office. For example, the CITY column holds the location of each

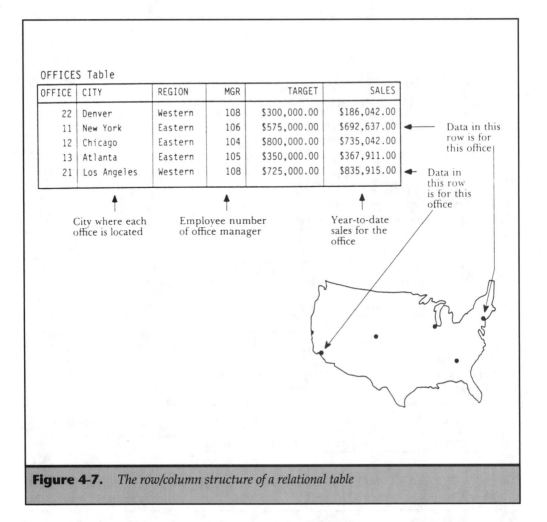

OFFICES Table

OFFICE	CITY	REGION	MGR	TARGET	SALES
22	Denver	Western	108	$300,000.00	$186,042.00
11	New York	Eastern	106	$575,000.00	$692,637.00
12	Chicago	Eastern	104	$800,000.00	$735,042.00
13	Atlanta	Eastern	105	$350,000.00	$367,911.00
21	Los Angeles	Western	108	$725,000.00	$835,915.00

City where each office is located

Employee number of office manager

Year-to-date sales for the office

Data in this row is for this office

Data in this row is for this office

Figure 4-7. *The row/column structure of a relational table*

office. The SALES column contains each office's year-to-date sales total. The MGR column shows the employee number of the person who manages the office.

Each row of a table contains exactly one data value in each column. In the row representing the New York office, for example, the CITY column contains the value "New York." The SALES column contains the value $692,637.00, which is the year-to-date sales total for the New York office.

For each column of a table, all of the data values in that column hold the same type of data. For example, all of the CITY column values are words, all of the SALES values are money amounts, and all of the MGR values are integers (representing employee numbers). The set of data values that a column can contain is called the *domain* of the column. The domain of the CITY column is the set of all names of cities. The domain of the SALES column is any money amount. The domain of the REGION column is just two data values, "Eastern" and "Western," because those are the only two sales regions the company has!

Each column in a table has a *column name,* which is usually written as a heading at the top of the column. The columns of a table must all have different names, but there is no prohibition against two columns in two different tables having identical names. In fact, frequently used column names, such as NAME, ADDRESS, QTY, PRICE, and SALES, are often found in many different tables of a production database.

The columns of a table have a left-to-right order, which is defined when the table is first created. A table always has at least one column. The ANSI/ISO SQL standard does not specify a maximum number of columns in a table, but almost all commercial SQL products do impose a limit. Usually the limit is 255 columns per table or more.

Unlike the columns, the rows in a table do *not* have any particular order. In fact, if you use two consecutive database queries to display the contents of a table, there is no guarantee that the rows will be listed in the same order twice. Of course you can ask SQL to sort the rows before displaying them, but the sorted order has nothing to do with the actual arrangement of the rows within the table.

A table can have any number of rows. A table of zero rows is perfectly legal, and is called an *empty* table (for obvious reasons). An empty table still has a structure, imposed by its columns; it simply contains no data. The ANSI/ISO standard does not limit the number of rows in a table, and many SQL products will allow a table to grow until it exhausts the available disk space on the computer. Other SQL products impose a maximum limit, but it is always a very generous one—two billion rows or more is common.

Primary Keys

Because the rows of a relational table are unordered, you cannot select a specific row by its position in the table. There is no "first row," "last row," or "thirteenth row" of a table. How then can you specify a particular row, such as the row for the Denver sales office?

In a well-designed relational database every table has some column or combination of columns whose values uniquely identify each row in the table. This column (or columns) is called the *primary key* of the table. Look once again at the OFFICES table in Figure 4-7. At first glance, either the OFFICE column or the CITY column could serve as a primary key for the table. But if the company expands and opens two sales offices in the same city, the CITY column could no longer serve as the primary key. In practice, "ID numbers," such as an office number (OFFICE in the OFFICES table), an employee number (EMPL_NUM in the SALESREPS table), and customer numbers (CUST_NUM in the CUSTOMERS table) are often chosen as primary keys. In the case of the ORDERS table there is no choice—the only thing that uniquely identifies an order is its order number (ORDER_NUM).

The PRODUCTS table, part of which is shown in Figure 4-8, is an example of a table where the primary key must be a *combination* of columns. The MFR_ID column identifies the manufacturer of each product in the table, and the PRODUCT_ID column specifies the manufacturer's product number. The PRODUCT_ID column might make a

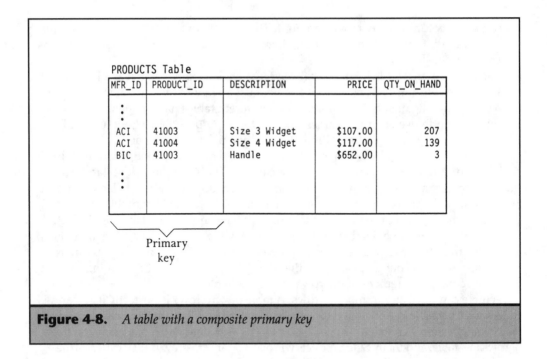

PRODUCTS Table

MFR_ID	PRODUCT_ID	DESCRIPTION	PRICE	QTY_ON_HAND
.				
ACI	41003	Size 3 Widget	$107.00	207
ACI	41004	Size 4 Widget	$117.00	139
BIC	41003	Handle	$652.00	3
.				

Primary
key

Figure 4-8. *A table with a composite primary key*

good primary key, but there's nothing to prevent two different manufacturers from using the same number for their products. Therefore, a combination of the MFR_ID and PRODUCT_ID columns must be used as the primary key of the PRODUCTS table. Every product in the table is guaranteed to have a unique combination of data values in these two columns.

The primary key has a different unique value for each row in a table, so no two rows of a table with a primary key are exact duplicates of one another. A table where every row is different from all other rows is called a *relation* in mathematical terms. The name "relational database" comes from this term, because relations (tables with distinct rows) are at the heart of a relational database.

Although primary keys are an essential part of the relational data model, early relational database management systems (System/R, DB2, Oracle, and others) did not provide explicit support for primary keys. Database designers usually ensured that all of the tables in their databases had a primary key, but the DBMS itself did not provide a way to identify the primary key of a table. DB2 Version 2, introduced in April 1988, finally added primary key support to IBM's commercial SQL products. The ANSI/ISO standard was subsequently expanded to include support for primary keys.

Relationships

One of the major differences between the relational model and earlier data models is that explicit pointers, such as the parent/child relationships of a hierarchical database, are banned from relational databases. Yet obviously these relationships exist in a relational database. For example, in the sample database, each of the salespeople is assigned to a particular sales office, so there is an obvious relationship between the rows of the OFFICES table and the rows of the SALESREPS table. Doesn't the relational model "lose information" by banning these relationships from the database?

As shown in Figure 4-9, the answer to the question is "no." The figure shows a close-up of a few rows of the OFFICES and SALESREPS tables. Note that the REP_OFFICE column of the SALESREPS table contains the office number of the sales

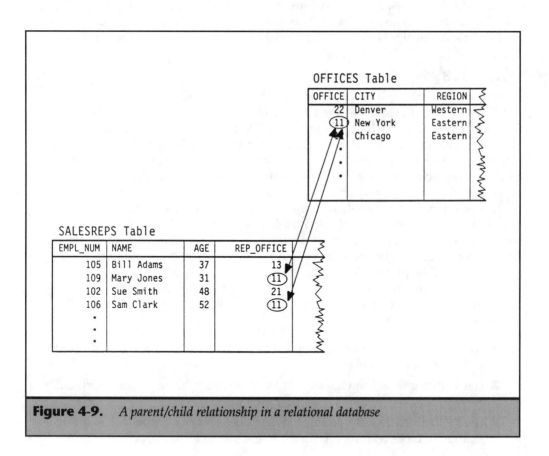

Figure 4-9. *A parent/child relationship in a relational database*

office where each salesperson works. The domain of this column (the set of legal values it may contain) is *precisely* the set of office numbers found in the OFFICE column of the OFFICES table. In fact, you can find the sales office where Mary Jones works by finding the value in Mary's REP_OFFICE column (11), and finding the row of the OFFICES table that has a matching value in the OFFICE column (in the row for the New York office). Similarly, to find all the salespeople who work in New York, you could note the OFFICE value for the New York row (11), and then scan down the REP_OFFICE column of the SALESREPS table looking for matching values (in the rows for Mary Jones and Sam Clark).

The parent/child relationship between a sales office and the people who work there isn't lost by the relational model, it's just not represented by an explicit pointer stored in the database. Instead, the relationship is represented by *common data values* stored in the two tables. All relationships in a relational database are represented this way. One of the main goals of the SQL language is to let you retrieve related data from the database by manipulating these relationships in a simple, straightforward way.

Foreign Keys

A column in one table whose value matches the primary key in some other table is called a *foreign key*. In Figure 4-9 the REP_OFFICE column is a foreign key for the OFFICES table. Although it's a column in the SALESREPS table, the values that this column contains are office numbers. They match values in the OFFICE column, which is the primary key for the OFFICES table. Together, a primary key and a foreign key create a parent/child relationship between the tables that contain them, just like the parent/child relationships in a hierarchical database.

Just as a combination of columns can serve as the primary key of a table, a foreign key can also be a combination of columns. In fact, the foreign key will *always* be a compound (multi-column) key when it references a table with a compound primary key. Obviously the number of columns and the data types of the columns in the foreign key and the primary key must be identical to one another.

A table can contain more than one foreign key if it is related to more than one other table. Figure 4-10 shows the three foreign keys in the ORDERS table of the sample database:

- The CUST column is a foreign key for the CUSTOMERS table, relating each order to the customer who placed it.

- The REP column is a foreign key for the SALESREPS table, relating each order to the salesperson who took it.

- The MFR and PRODUCT columns together are a composite foreign key for the PRODUCTS table, relating each order to the product being ordered.

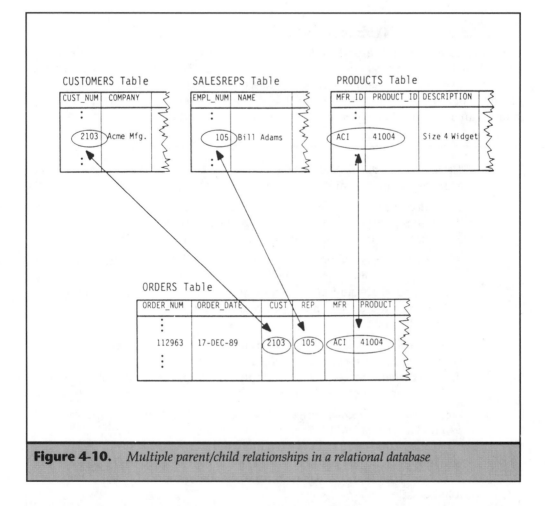

Figure 4-10. *Multiple parent/child relationships in a relational database*

The multiple parent/child relationships created by the three foreign keys in the ORDERS table may seem familiar to you, and they should. They are precisely the same relationships as those in the network database of Figure 4-4. As the example shows, the relational data model has all of the power of the network model to express complex relationships.

Foreign keys are a fundamental part of the relational model because they create relationships among tables in the database. Unfortunately, as with primary keys, foreign key support was missing from early relational database management systems. They were added to DB2 Version 2 and have since been added to the ANSI/ISO standard, and now appear in many commercial products.

Codd's Twelve Rules *

In his 1985 *Computerworld* article, Ted Codd presented twelve rules that a database must obey if it is to be considered truly relational. Codd's twelve rules, shown in Table 4-1, have since become a semi-official definition of a relational database. The rules come out of Codd's theoretical work on the relational model, and actually represent more of an ideal goal than a definition of a relational database.

---

1. *The information rule.* All information in a relational database is represented explicitly at the logical level and in exactly one way—by values in tables.

2. *Guaranteed access rule.* Each and every datum (atomic value) in a relational database is guaranteed to be logically accessible by resorting to a combination of table name, primary key value and column name.

3. *Systematic treatment of null values.* Null values (distinct from the empty character string or a string of blank characters and distinct from zero or any other number) are supported in fully relational DBMS for representing missing information and inapplicable information in a systematic way, independent of data type.

4. *Dynamic on-line catalog based on the relational model.* The database description is represented at the logical level in the same way as ordinary data, so that authorized users can apply the same relational language to its interrogation as they apply to the regular data.

5. *Comprehensive data sublanguage rule.* A relational system may support several languages and various modes of terminal use (for example, the fill-in-the-blanks mode). However, there must be at least one language whose statements are expressible, per some well-defined syntax, as character strings, and which is comprehensive in supporting all of the following items:

   - Data definition

   - View definition

   - Data manipulation (interactive and by program)

   - Integrity constraints

   - Authorization

   - Transaction boundaries (begin, commit and rollback)

Table 4-1.   *Codd's Twelve Rules for Relational DBMS*

6. *View updating rule.* All views that are theoretically updatable are also updatable by the system.

7. *High-level insert, update, and delete.* The capability of handling a base relation or a derived relation as a single operand applies not only to the retrieval of data but also to the insertion, update, and deletion of data.

8. *Physical data independence.* Application programs and terminal activities remain logically unimpaired whenever any changes are made in either storage representations or access methods.

9. *Logical data independence.* Application programs and terminal activities remain logically unimpaired when information preserving changes of any kind that theoretically permit unimpairment are made to the base tables.

10. *Integrity independence.* Integrity constraints specific to a particular relational database must be definable in the relational data sublanguage and storable in the catalog, not in the application programs.

11. *Distribution independence.* A relational DBMS has distribution independence.

12. *Nonsubversion rule.* If a relational system has a low-level (single record at a time) language, that low level cannot be used to subvert or bypass the integrity rules and constraints expressed in the higher-level relational language (multiple records at a time).

Table 4-1.   *Codd's Twelve Rules for Relational DBMS (continued)*

No currently available relational DBMS fully satisfies all twelve of Codd's rules. In fact, it's become a popular practice to compile "scorecards" for commercial DBMS products, showing how well they satisfy each of the rules. Unfortunately, the rules are subjective so the scorecards are usually full of footnotes and qualifications, and don't reveal a great deal about the products.

Rule 1 is basically the informal definition of a relational database presented at the beginning of this section. Rule 2 stresses the importance of primary keys for locating data in the database. The table name locates the correct table, the column name finds the correct column, and the primary key value finds the row containing an individual data item of interest. Rule 3 requires support for missing data through NULL values, which are described in Chapter 5.

Rule 4 requires that a relational database be self-describing. In other words, the database must contain certain *system tables* whose columns describe the structure of the database itself. These tables are described in Chapter 16.

Rule 5 mandates using a relational database language, such as SQL, although SQL is not specifically required. The language must be able to support all the central functions of a DBMS—creating a database, retrieving and entering data, implementing database security, and so on.

Rule 6 deals with views, which are *virtual tables* used to give various users of a database different views of its structure. It is one of the most challenging rules to implement in practice, and no commercial product fully satisfies it today. Views and the problems of updating them are described in Chapter 14.

Rule 7 stresses the set-oriented nature of a relational database. It requires that rows be treated as sets in insert, delete, and update operations. The rule is designed to prohibit implementations that only support row-at-a-time, navigational modification of the database.

Rule 8 and Rule 9 insulate the user or application program from the low-level implementation of the database. They specify that specific access or storage techniques used by the DBMS, and even changes to the structure of the tables in the database, should not affect the user's ability to work with the data.

Rule 10 says that the database language should support integrity constraints that restrict the data that can be entered into the database and the database modifications that can be made. This is another of the rules that is not supported in most commercial DBMS products.

Rule 11 says that the database language must be able to manipulate distributed data located on other computer systems. Distributed data and the challenges of managing it are described in Chapter 20. Finally, Rule 12 prevents "other paths" into the database that might subvert its relational structure and integrity.

Summary

SQL is based on the relational data model that organizes the data in a database as a collection of tables:

- Each table has a table name that uniquely identifies it.
- Each table has one or more named columns, which are arranged in a specific, left-to-right order.
- Each table has zero or more rows, each containing a single data value in each column. The rows are unordered.
- All data values in a given column have the same data type, and are drawn from a set of legal values called the domain of the column.

Tables are related to one another by the data they contain. The relational data model uses primary keys and foreign keys to represent these relationships among tables:

■ A primary key is a column or combination of columns in a table whose value(s) uniquely identify each row of the table. A table has only one primary key.

■ A foreign key is a column or combination of columns in a table whose value(s) are a primary key value for some other table. A table can contain more than one foreign key, linking it to one or more other tables.

■ A primary key/foreign key combination creates a parent/child relationship between the tables that contain them.

PART TWO

Retrieving Data

Queries are the heart of the SQL language, and many people use SQL exclusively as a database query tool. The next five chapters describe SQL queries in depth. Chapter 5 describes the basic SQL language structures that you use to form SQL statements. Chapter 6 discusses simple queries that draw data from a single table of data. Chapter 7 expands the discussion to multi-table queries. Queries that summarize data are described in Chapter 8. Finally, Chapter 9 explains the SQL subquery capability that is used to handle complex queries.

Chapter Five

SQL Basics

This chapter begins a detailed description of the features of SQL. It describes the basic structure of a SQL statement, and the basic elements of the language, such as keywords, data types, and expressions. The way that SQL handles missing data through NULL values is also described. Although these are basic features of SQL, there are some subtle differences in the way they are implemented by various popular SQL products, and in many cases the SQL products provide significant extensions to the capabilities specified in the ANSI/ISO SQL standard. These differences and extensions are also described in this chapter.

Statements

The SQL language consists of about thirty statements, which are summarized in Table 5-1. Each statement requests a specific action from the DBMS, such as creating a new table, retrieving data, or inserting new data into the database. All SQL statements have the same basic form, illustrated in Figure 5-1.

Every SQL statement begins with a *verb*, a keyword that describes what the statement does. CREATE, INSERT, DELETE, and COMMIT are typical verbs. The statement continues with one or more *clauses*. A clause may specify the data to be acted upon by the statement, or provide more detail about what the statement is supposed to do. Every clause also begins with a keyword, such as WHERE, FROM, INTO, and HAVING. Some clauses are optional; others are required. The specific structure and content vary from one clause to another. Many clauses contain table or column names; some may contain additional keywords, constants or expressions.

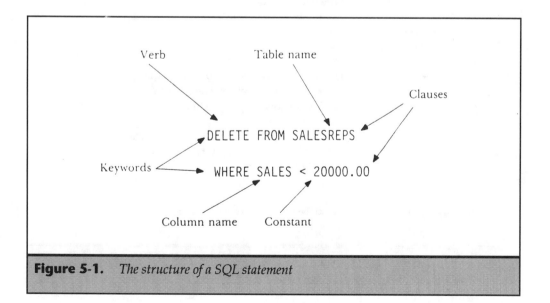

Figure 5-1. *The structure of a SQL statement*

Statement	Description
Data Manipulation	
SELECT	Retrieves data from the database
INSERT	Adds new rows of data to the database
DELETE	Removes rows of data from the database
UPDATE	Modifies existing database data
Data Definition	
CREATE TABLE	Adds a new table to the database
DROP TABLE*	Removes a table from the database
ALTER TABLE*	Changes the structure of an existing table
CREATE VIEW	Adds a new view to the database
DROP VIEW*	Removes a view from the database
CREATE INDEX*	Builds an index for a column
DROP INDEX*	Removes the index for a column
CREATE SYNONYM*	Defines an alias for a table name
DROP SYNONYM*	Removes an alias for a table name
COMMENT*	Defines remarks for a table or column
LABEL*	Defines a title for a table or column
Access Control	
GRANT	Grants user access privileges
REVOKE	Removes user access privileges
Transaction Control	
COMMIT	Ends the current transaction
ROLLBACK	Aborts the current transaction
Programmatic SQL	
DECLARE	Defines a cursor for a query
EXPLAIN*	Describes the data access plan for a query
OPEN	Opens a cursor to retrieve query results
FETCH	Retrieves a row of query results
CLOSE	Closes a cursor
PREPARE*	Prepares a SQL statement for dynamic execution
EXECUTE*	Executes a SQL statement dynamically
DESCRIBE*	Describes a prepared query

*Not part of the ANSI/ISO SQL1 standard, but found in many popular SQL-based products.

Table 5-1.   *Major SQL Statements*

The ANSI/ISO SQL1 standard specifies the SQL keywords that are used as verbs and in statement clauses. According to the standard, these keywords cannot be used to name database objects, such as tables, columns and users. Many SQL implementations relax this restriction, but it's generally a good idea to avoid the keywords when you name your tables and columns. Table 5-2 lists the keywords included in the ANSI/ISO SQL1 standard. The SQL2 standard expanded the list to over 300 keywords.

Throughout this book, the acceptable forms of a SQL statement are illustrated by a syntax diagram, such as the one shown in Figure 5-2. A valid SQL statement or clause is constructed by "following the line" through the syntax diagram to the dot that marks the end of the diagram. Keywords in the syntax diagram and in the examples (such as DELETE and FROM in Figure 5-2) are always shown in UPPERCASE, but almost all SQL implementations accept both uppercase and lowercase keywords, and it's often more convenient to actually type them in lowercase.

ADA	CURRENT	GO	OF	SOME
ALL	CURSOR	GOTO	ON	SQL
AND	DEC	GRANT	OPEN	SQLCODE
ANY	DECIMAL	GROUP	OPTION	SQLERROR
AS	DECLARE	HAVING	OR	SUM
ASC	DEFAULT	IN	ORDER	TABLE
AUTHORIZATION	DELETE	INDICATOR	PASCAL	TO
AVG	DESC	INSERT	PLI	UNION
BEGIN	DISTINCT	INT	PRECISION	UNIQUE
BETWEEN	DOUBLE	INTEGAR	PRIMARY	UPDATE
BY	END	INTO	PRIVILEGES	USER
C	ESCAPE	IS	PROCEDURE	VALUES
CHAR	EXEC	KEY	PUBLIC	VIEW
CHARACTER	EXISTS	LANGUAGE	REAL	WHENEVER
CHECK	FETCH	LIKE	REFERENCES	WHERE
CLOSE	FLOAT	MAX	ROLLBACK	WITH
COBOL	FOR	MIN	SCHEMA	WORK
COMMIT	FOREIGN	MODULE	SECTION	
CONTINUE	FORTRAN	NOT	SELECT	
COUNT	FOUND	NULL	SET	
CREATE	FROM	NUMERIC	SMALLINT	

Table 5-2. *ANSI/ISO SQL1 Keywords*

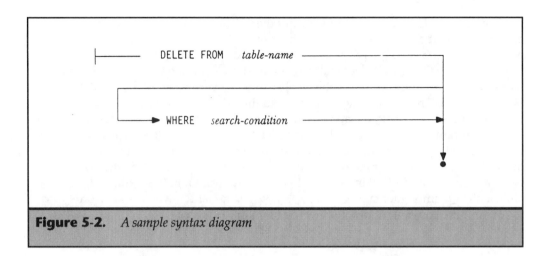

Figure 5-2. *A sample syntax diagram*

Variable items in a SQL statement (such as the table name and search condition in Figure 5-2) are shown in *lowercase italics*. It's up to you to specify the appropriate item each time the statement is used. Optional clauses and keywords, such as the WHERE clause in Figure 5-2, are indicated by alternate paths through the syntax diagram. When a choice of optional keywords is offered, the default choice (that is, the behavior of the statement if no keyword is specified) is <u>UNDERLINED</u>.

Names

The objects in a SQL-based database are identified by assigning them unique names. Names are used in SQL statements to identify the database object on which the statement should act. The ANSI/ISO SQL standard specifies table names (which identify tables), column names (which identify columns) and user names (which identify users of the database). Many SQL implementations support additional named objects, such as stored procedures (Sybase and SQL Server), primary key/foreign key relationships (DB2), and data entry forms (Ingres).

The ANSI/ISO standard specifies that SQL names must contain 1 to 18 characters, begin with a letter, and may not contain any spaces or special punctuation characters. The SQL2 standard increased the maximum to 128 characters. In practice the names supported by SQL-based DBMS products vary significantly. DB2, for example, restricts user names to 8 characters, but allows 18 characters in table and column names. Oracle allows 30-character table and column names, and many other SQL implementations also permit names longer than the ANSI/ISO limits. The various products also differ in the special characters they permit in table names. For portability it's best to keep names relatively short, and to avoid the use of special characters.

Table Names

When you specify a table name in a SQL statement, SQL assumes that you are referring to one of your own tables (that is, a table that you created). With the proper permission, you can also refer to tables owned by other users, by using a *qualified table name*. A qualified table name specifies both the name of the table's owner and the name of the table, separated by a period (.). For example, the table BIRTHDAYS, owned by the user named SAM, has the qualified table name:

```
SAM.BIRTHDAYS
```

A qualified table name generally can be used in a SQL statement wherever a table name can appear.

Column Names

When you specify a column name in a SQL statement, SQL can normally determine from the context which column you intend. However, if the statement involves two columns with the same name from two different tables, you must use a *qualified column name* to unambiguously identify the column you intend. A qualified column name specifies both the name of the table containing the column and the name of the column, separated by a period (.). For example, the column named SALES in the SALESREPS table has the qualified column name:

```
SALESREPS.SALES
```

If the column comes from a table owned by another user, a qualified table name is used in the qualified column name. For example, the BIRTHDATE column in the BIRTHDAYS table owned by the user SAM is specified by the fully qualified column name:

```
SAM.BIRTHDAYS.BIRTH_DATE
```

Qualified column names can generally be used in a SQL statement wherever a simple (unqualified) column name can appear; exceptions are noted in the descriptions of the individual SQL statements.

Data Types

The ANSI/ISO SQL standards specify various types of data that can be stored in a SQL-based database and manipulated by the SQL language. The data types specified by the SQL1 standard are only a minimal set, but almost all commercial SQL products

Data Type	Description
CHAR(*len*) CHARACTER(*len*)	Fixed-length character strings
VARCHAR(*len*) CHAR VARYING(*len*) CHARACTER VARYING(*len*)	Variable-length character strings*
NCHAR(*len*) NATIONAL CHAR(*len*) NATIONAL CHARACTER(*len*)	Fixed-length national character strings*
NCHAR VARYING(*len*) NATIONAL CHAR VARYING(*len*) NATIONAL CHARACTER VARYING(*len*)	Variable-length national character strings*
INTEGER INT	Integer numbers
SMALLINT	Small integer numbers
BIT(*len*)	Fixed-length bit string*
BIT VARYING(*len*)	Variable-length bit string*
NUMERIC(*precision,scale*) DECIMAL(*precision,scale*) DEC(*precision,scale*)	Decimal numbers
FLOAT(*precision*)	Floating point numbers
REAL	Low-precision floating point numbers
DOUBLE PRECISION	High-precision floating point numbers
DATE	Calendar date*
TIME(*precision*)	Clock time*
TIMESTAMP(*precision*)	Date and time*
INTERVAL	Time interval*

*new data type in SQL2

Table 5-3. *ANSI/ISO SQL Data Types*

support them or have data types that are very similar to them. The ANSI/ISO SQL1 and SQL2 data types are listed in Table 5-3. The SQL1 data types consist of:

- *Fixed-length character strings.* Columns holding this type of data typically store names of people and companies, addresses, descriptions, and so on.

- *Integers.* Columns holding this type of data typically store counts, quantities, ages, and so on. Integer columns are also frequently used to contain id numbers, such as customer, employee, and order numbers.

■ *Decimal numbers.* Columns with this data type store numbers that have fractional parts and must be calculated exactly, such as rates and percentages. They are also frequently used to store money amounts.

■ *Floating-point numbers.* Columns with this data type are used to store scientific numbers that can be calculated approximately, such as weights and distances. Floating-point numbers can represent a larger range of values than decimal numbers, but can produce round-off errors in computations.

Extended Data Types

Most commercial SQL products offer a much more extensive set of data types than those specified in the SQL1 standard, and the SQL2 standard has included many of these. Some of the more popular or important extended data types are:

■ *Variable-length character strings.* Almost every SQL product supports VARCHAR data, which allows a column to store character strings that vary in length from row to row, up to some maximum length. The SQL1 standard specifies only fixed-length strings, which are padded on the right with trailing blanks.

■ *Money amounts.* Many SQL products support a MONEY or CURRENCY type, which is usually stored as a decimal or floating-point number. Having a distinct money type allows the DBMS to properly format money amounts when they are displayed.

■ *Dates and times.* Support for date/time values is also common in SQL products, although the details vary dramatically from one product to another. Various combinations of dates, times, timestamps, time intervals, and date/time arithmetic are generally supported. The SQL2 standard includes an elaborate specification for DATE, TIME, TIMESTAMP and INTERVAL data types, including support for time zones and time precision (e.g. tenths or hundredths of seconds).

■ *Boolean data.* Some SQL products (including dBASE IV) support logical (TRUE or FALSE) values as an explicit type.

■ *Long text.* Several SQL-based databases support columns that store long text strings (typically up to 32,000 or 65,000 characters, and in some cases even larger). The DBMS usually restricts the use of these columns in interactive queries and searches.

■ *Unstructured byte streams.* Oracle and several other products allow unstructured, variable-length sequences of bytes to be stored and retrieved. Columns containing this data are used to store compressed video images, executable code, and other types of unstructured data.

■ *Asian characters.* DB2 supports fixed-length and variable-length strings of 16-bit characters used to represent Kanji and other Asian characters. Searching and sorting on these GRAPHIC and VARGRAPHIC types is not permitted, however.

Table 5-4 summarizes the data types supported by several popular SQL-based database products.

Data Type*	DB2 and SQL/DS	Oracle[1]	Ingres	Rdb/VMS[2]
Fixed-Length Character	CHARACTER(*n*)		CHAR(*n*)	CHAR(*n*)
Variable-Length Character	VARCHAR(*n*)	CHAR(*n*)	VARCHAR(*n*)	VARCHAR(*n*) LONG VARCHAR
Long Text	LONG VARCHAR	LONG		
Integer	SMALLINT INTEGER		INTEGER1 INTEGER2 INTEGER4	SMALLINT(*n*) INTEGER(*n*) QUADWORD(*n*)
Decimal	DECIMAL(*p,s*)	NUMBER(*p,s*)		DECIMAL(*p,s*)
Money			MONEY	
Floating Point	FLOAT(*p*) REAL DOUBLE PRECISION		FLOAT4 FLOAT8	FLOAT(*n*) REAL DOUBLE PRECISION
Date/Time	DATE TIME TIMESTAMP	DATE[3]	DATE[4]	DATE
Boolean				
Byte Stream		RAW LONG RAW		
Other	GRAPHIC(*n*) VARGRAPHIC(*n*) LONG VARGRAPHIC			

*Many of the products also support the ANSI/ISO types as synonyms to their own types.

[1]Oracle stores all numbers using its own internal format with 40 digits of precsion.

[2]Rdb/VMS actually supports additional data types that are not available through VAX SQL.

Table 5-4.   *Data Types Supported by Popular SQL Products*

Informix	**Sybase and SQL Server**	**OS/2 EE**	**dBASE IV**	**SQLBase**[5]
CHAR(*n*)	CHAR(*n*)	CHAR(*n*)	CHAR(*n*)	
	VARCHAR(*n*)	VARCHAR(*n*)		VARCHAR(*n*)
	TEXT	LONG VARCHAR		LONG VARCHAR
SMALLINT INTEGER	TINYINT SMALLINT INT	SMALLINT INTEGER	SMALLINT INTEGER	SMALLINT(*n*) INTEGER NUMBER
DECIMAL(*p,s*)		DECIMAL	DECIMAL(*p,s*)	DECIMAL(*p,s*)
MONEY(*p,s*)	MONEY			
SMALLFLOAT FLOAT	FLOAT	FLOAT	FLOAT(*p,s*)	FLOAT(*s*) REAL DOUBLE PRECISION
DATE	DATETIME	DATE DATE TIMESTAMP	DATE	DATE TIME DATETIME
	BIT		LOGICAL	
	BINARY(*n*) VARBINARY(*n*) IMAGE			
SERIAL	SYSNAME USER_TYPE_NAME			

[3] The Oracle DATE data type is really a timestamp. Oracle built-in functions can be used to isolate the date and time parts.

[4] The Ingres DATE data type stores both timestamps and durations. Ingres supports "meaningful" date arithmetic on both.

[5] SQLBase stores all numbers using its own internal format with 22 digits of precision.

Table 5-4. *Data Types Supported by Popular SQL Products* (continued)

Data Type Differences

The differences between the data types offered in various SQL implementations is one of the practical barriers to the portability of SQL-based applications. Date/time data provides an excellent example of these differences. DB2, for example, supports three different date/time data types:

- DATE, which stores a date like June 30, 1991,

- TIME, which stores a time of day like 12:30 P.M., and

- TIMESTAMP, which is a specific instant in history, with a precision down to the nanosecond.

Specific dates and times can be specified as string constants, and date arithmetic is supported. Here is an example of a valid query using DB2 dates, assuming that the HIREDATE column contains DATE data:

```
SELECT NAME, HIRE_DATE
  FROM SALESREPS
 WHERE HIRE_DATE >= '05/30/1989' + 15 DAYS
```

OS/2 Extended Edition supports the same three data types as DB2, but does not support date arithmetic, so the previous query must be rewritten as:

```
SELECT NAME, HIRE_DATE
  FROM SALESREPS
 WHERE HIRE_DATE >= '06/14/1989'
```

SQL Server provides a single date/time data type, called DATETIME, which closely resembles the DB2 TIMESTAMP data type. If HIRE_DATE contained DATETIME data, SQL Server could accept the OS/2 Extended Edition version of the query. Since no specific time on June 14, 1989, is specified in the query, SQL Server defaults to midnight on that date. The SQL Server query thus *really* means:

```
SELECT NAME, HIRE_DATE
  FROM SALESREPS
 WHERE HIRE_DATE >= '06/14/1989 12:00AM'
```

If a salesperson's hire date was stored in the database as midday on June 14, 1989, the salesperson would not be included in the SQL Server query results, but would have been included in the OS/2 Extended Edition or DB2 results (because only the date would be stored). SQL Server also supports date arithmetic through a set of built-in functions. Thus the DB2-style query can also be specified, in this way:

```
SELECT NAME, HIRE_DATE
  FROM SALESREPS
 WHERE HIRE_DATE >= DATEADD(DAY, 15, '05/30/1989')
```

which, of course, is considerably different from the DB2 syntax.

Oracle also supports date/time data, with a single data type called DATE. Like SQL Server's DATETIME type, an Oracle DATE is, in fact, a timestamp. Also like SQL Server, the time part of an Oracle DATE value defaults to midnight if no time is explicitly specified. The default Oracle date format is different from the DB2 and SQL Server formats, so the Oracle version of the query becomes:

```
SELECT NAME, HIRE_DATE
  FROM SALESREPS
 WHERE HIRE_DATE >= '14-JUN-89'
```

Oracle also supports limited date arithmetic, so the DB2-style query can also be specified, but without the DAYS keyword:

```
SELECT NAME, HIRE_DATE
  FROM SALESREPS
 WHERE HIRE_DATE >= '30-MAY-89' + 15
```

As these examples illustrate (in vivid detail!), the subtle differences in data types among various SQL products lead to some significant differences in SQL statement syntax. They can even cause the same SQL query to produce slightly different results on different database management systems. The widely praised portability of SQL is thus true, but only at a general level. An application can be moved from one SQL database to another. However, the subtle variations in SQL implementations mean that data types and SQL statements must almost always be adjusted somewhat in the process. Transparent portability of SQL-based applications remains a goal, but not a reality.

Constants

In some SQL statements a numeric, character, or date data value must be expressed in text form. For example, in this INSERT statement, which adds a salesperson to the database:

```
INSERT INTO SALESREPS (EMPL_NUM, NAME, QUOTA, HIRE_DATE, SALES)
     VALUES (115, 'Dennis Irving', 175000.00, '21-JUN-90', 0.00)
```

the value for each column in the newly inserted row is specified in the VALUES clause. Constant data values are also used in expressions, such as in this SELECT statement:

```
SELECT CITY
  FROM OFFICES
 WHERE TARGET > (1.1 * SALES) + 10000.00
```

The ANSI/ISO SQL standard specifies the format of numeric and string constants, or *literals*, which represent specific data values. These conventions are followed by most SQL implementations.

Numeric Constants

Integer and decimal constants (also called *exact numeric literals*) are written as ordinary decimal numbers in SQL statements, with an optional leading plus or minus sign.

```
21    -375    2000.00    +497500.8778
```

You must not put a comma between the digits of a numeric constant, and not all SQL dialects allow the leading plus sign, so it's best to avoid it. For money data, most SQL implementations simply use integer or decimal constants, although some allow the constant to be specified with a currency symbol:

```
$0.75    $5000.00    $-567.89
```

Floating-point constants (also called *approximate numeric literals*) are specified using the E notation commonly found in programming languages such as C and FORTRAN. Here are some valid SQL floating-point constants:

```
1.5E3    -3.14159E1    2.5E-7    0.783926E21
```

The E is read "times ten to the power of," so the first constant becomes "1.5 times ten to the third power," or 1500.

String Constants

The ANSI/ISO standard specifies that SQL constants for character data be enclosed in single quotes ('. . .'), as in these examples:

```
'Jones, John J.'    'New York'    'Western'
```

If a single quote is to be included in the constant text, it is written within the constant as two consecutive single quote characters. Thus this constant value:

```
'I can''t'
```

becomes the seven-character string "I can't."

Some SQL implementations, such as dBASE IV, SQL Server and Informix, accept string constants enclosed in double quotes ("..."):

```
"Jones, John J."   "New York"   "Western"
```

Unfortunately, the double quotes pose portability problems with other SQL products, including some unique portability problems with SQL/DS. SQL/DS allows column names containing blanks and other special characters (in violation of the ANSI/ISO standard). When these characters appear as names in a SQL statement, they must be enclosed in double quotes. For example, if the NAME column of the SALESREPS table were called "FULL NAME" in a SQL/DS database, this SELECT statement would be valid:

```
SELECT "FULL NAME", SALES, QUOTA
  FROM SALESREPS
 WHERE "FULL NAME" = 'Jones, John J.'
```

The SQL2 standard provides the additional capability to specify string constants from a specific national character set (e.g. French, German) or from a user-defined character set. These capabilities have not yet found their way into mainstream SQL implementations.

Date and Time Constants

In SQL products that support date/time data, constant values for dates, times, and time intervals are specified as string constants. The format of these constants varies from one DBMS to the next. Even more variation is introduced by the differences in the way dates and times are written in different countries.

Both DB2 and OS/2 Extended Edition support several different international formats for date, time, and timestamp constants, as shown in Table 5-5. The choice of format is made when the DBMS is installed. DB2 (but currently not OS/2 Extended Edition) also supports durations specified as "special" constants, as in this example:

```
HIRE_DATE + 30 DAYS
```

Format Name	DATE Format	DATE Example	TIME Format	TIME Example
American	*mm/dd/yyyy*	5/19/1960	*hh:mm am/pm*	2:18 PM
European	*dd.mm.yyyy*	19.5.1960	*hh.mm.ss*	14.18.08
Japanese	*yyyy-mm-dd*	1960-5-19	*hh:mm:ss*	14:18:08
ISO	*yyyy-mm-dd*	1960-5-19	*hh.mm.ss*	14.18.08

TIMESTAMP format: *yyyy-mm-dd-hh.mm.ss.nnnnnn*

TIMESTAMP example: 1960-05-19-14.18.08.048632

Table 5-5. *IBM SQL Date and Time Formats*

Note that a duration can't be stored in the database, however, because DB2 doesn't have an explicit DURATION data type.

SQL Server also supports date/time data, and accepts a variety of different formats for date and time constants. The DBMS automatically accepts all of the alternate formats, and you can intermix them if you like. Here are some examples of legal SQL Server date constants:

```
March 15, 1990    Mar 15 1990    3/15/1990    3-15-90    1990 MAR 15
```

and here are some legal time constants:

```
15:30:25    3:30:25 PM    3:30:25 pm    3 PM
```

Oracle dates and times are also written as string constants, using this format:

```
15-MAR-90
```

You can also use Oracle's built-in TO_DATE() function to convert date constants written in other formats, as in this example:

```
SELECT NAME, AGE
  FROM SALESREPS
  WHERE HIRE_DATE = TO_DATE('JUN 14 1989', 'MON DD YYYY')
```

The SQL2 standard specifies a format for date and time constants, based on the ISO format in Table 5-5, except that time constants are written with colons instead of periods separating the hours, minutes and seconds.

Symbolic Constants

In addition to user-supplied constants, the SQL language includes special symbolic constants that return data values maintained by the DBMS itself. The OS/2 Extended Edition symbolic constant CURRENT DATE yields the value of the current date and can be used in queries such as the following, which lists the salespeople whose hire date is still in the future.

```
SELECT NAME, HIRE_DATE
  FROM SALESREPS
 WHERE HIRE_DATE > CURRENT DATE
```

The SQL1 standard specifies only a single symbolic constant (the USER constant described in Chapter 15), but most SQL products provide many more. Symbolic constants that are commonly found in SQL implementations are listed in Table 5-6. Generally, a symbolic constant can appear in a SQL statement anywhere that an ordinary constant of the same data type could appear. The SQL2 standard adopted the most useful symbolic constants from current SQL implementations, and provides for CURRENT_DATE, CURRENT_TIME and CURRENT_TIMESTAMP (note the underscores!) as well as USER, SESSION_USER and SYSTEM_USER.

Constant	Description
USER	The user name under which you are currently accessing a database (DB2, SQL/DS, Oracle, VAX SQL, SQLBase, and also specified in the ANSI/ISO standard)
CURRENT DATE	The current date (DB2, SQL/DS, SQLBase)
CURRENT TIME	The current time of day (DB2, SQL/DS, SQLBase)
CURRENT TIMESTAMP	The current date and time (DB2, SQL/DS)
CURRENT TIMEZONE	A time duration specifying the difference between this time zone and GMT (DB2, SQL/DS, SQLBase)
SYSDATE	The current date and time (Oracle, SQLBase)
ROWNUM	The internal "row ID number" of a row (Oracle)
ROWID	The internal "row ID number" of a row (SQLBase)

Table 5-6. *SQL Symbolic Constants*

Some SQL products, including SQL Server, provide access to system values through built-in functions rather than symbolic constants. The SQL Server version of the preceding query is:

```
SELECT NAME, HIRE_DATE
  FROM SALESREPS
 WHERE HIRE_DATE > GETDATE()
```

Built-in functions are described later in this chapter.

Expressions

Expressions are used in the SQL language to calculate values that are retrieved from a database and to calculate values used in searching the database. For example, this query calculates the sales of each office as a percentage of its target:

```
SELECT CITY, TARGET, SALES, (SALES/TARGET) * 100
  FROM OFFICES
```

and this query lists the offices whose sales are more than $50,000 over target:

```
SELECT CITY
  FROM OFFICES
 WHERE SALES > TARGET + 50000.00
```

The ANSI/ISO SQL standard specifies four arithmetic operations that can be used in expressions: addition (X + Y), subtraction (X - Y), multiplication (X * Y), and division (X / Y). Parentheses can also be used to form more complicated expressions, like this one:

```
(SALES * 1.05) - (TARGET * .95)
```

Strictly speaking, the parentheses are not required in this query, because the ANSI/ISO standard specifies that multiplication and division have a higher precedence than addition and subtraction. However, you should always use parentheses to make your expressions unambiguous, because different SQL dialects may use different rules. The parentheses also increase the readability of the statement and make programmatic SQL statements easier to maintain.

The ANSI/ISO standard also specifies automatic data type conversion from integers to decimal numbers, and from decimal numbers to floating-point numbers, as required. You can thus mix these data types in a numeric expression. Many SQL implementations support other operators and allow operations on character and date data. DB2, for example, supports a string concatenation operator, written as two consecutive vertical bar characters (||). If two columns named FIRST_NAME and LAST_NAME contain the values "Jim" and "Jackson," then this DB2 expression:

```
('Mr./Mrs. ' || FIRST_NAME || ' ' || LAST_NAME)
```

produces the string "Mr./Mrs. Jim Jackson." As already mentioned, DB2 also supports addition and subtraction of DATE, TIME, and TIMESTAMP data, for occasions when those operations make sense. This capability has been included in the SQL2 standard.

Built-In Functions

Although the SQL1 standard doesn't specify them, most SQL implementations include a number of useful *built-in functions*. These facilities often provide data type conversion facilities. For example, DB2's built-in MONTH() and YEAR() functions take a DATE or TIMESTAMP value as their input and return an integer that is the month or year portion of the value. This query lists the name and month of hire for each salesperson in the sample database:

```
SELECT NAME, MONTH(HIRE_DATE)
  FROM SALESREPS
```

and this one lists all salespeople hired in 1988:

```
SELECT NAME, MONTH(HIRE_DATE)
  FROM SALESREPS
 WHERE YEAR(HIRE_DATE) = 1988
```

Built-in functions also are often used for data reformatting. Oracle's built-in TO_CHAR() function, for example, takes a DATE data type and a format specification as its arguments, and returns a string containing a formatted version of the date. In the results produced by this query:

```
SELECT NAME, TO_CHAR(HIRE_DATE,'DAY MONTH DD, YYYY')
  FROM SALESREPS
```

the hire dates will all have the format "Wednesday June 14, 1989"' because of the built-in function.

In general, a built-in function can be specified in a SQL expression anywhere that a constant of the same data type can be specified. The built-in functions supported by popular SQL dialects are too numerous to list here. The IBM SQL dialects include about two dozen built-in functions, Oracle supports a different set of about two dozen built-in functions, and SQL Server has several dozen. The SQL2 standard incorporated the most useful built-in functions from these implementations, in many cases with slightly different syntax. These functions are summarized in Table 5-7.

Missing Data (NULL Values)

Because a database is usually a model of a real-world situation, certain pieces of data are inevitably missing, unknown, or don't apply. In the sample database, for example,

Function	Returns
BIT_LENGTH(*string*)	number of bits in a bit string
CAST(*value* AS *data_type*)	the value, converted to the specified data type (e.g. a date converted to a character string)
CHAR_LENGTH(*string*)	length of a character string
CONVERT(*string* USING *conv*)	string converted as specified by a named conversion function
CURRENT_DATE	current date
CURRENT_TIME(*precision*)	current time, with the specified precision
CURRENT_TIMESTAMP(*precision*)	current date and time, with the specified precision
EXTRACT(*part* FROM *source*)	specified part (DAY, HOUR, etc.) from a DATETIME value
LOWER(*string*)	string converted to all lowercase letters
OCTET_LENGTH(*string*)	number of 8-bit bytes in a character string
POSITION(*target* IN *source*)	position where the *target* string appears within the *source* string
SUBSTRING(*source* FROM *n* FOR *len*)	a portion of the *source* string, beginning at the *n*-th character, for a length of *len*
TRANSLATE(*string* USING *trans*)	string translated as specified by a named translation function
TRIM(BOTH *char* FROM *string*)	string with both leading and trailing occurrences of *char* trimmed off
TRIM(LEADING *char* FROM *string*)	string with any leading occurrences of *char* trimmed off
TRIM(TRAILING *char* FROM *string*)	string with any trailing occurrences of *char* trimmed off
UPPER(*string*)	string converted to all uppercase letters

Table 5-7. *Built-in SQL2 Functions*

the QUOTA column in the SALESREPS table contains the sales goal for each salesperson. However, the newest salesperson has not yet been assigned a quota; this data is missing for that row of the table. You might be tempted to put a zero in the column for this salesperson, but that would not be an accurate reflection of the situation. The salesperson does not have a zero quota; the quota is just "not yet known."

Similarly, the MANAGER column in the SALESREPS table contains the employee number of each salesperson's manager. But Sam Clark, the Vice President of Sales, has no manager in the sales organization. This column does not apply to Sam. Again, you might think about entering a zero, or a 9999 in the column, but neither of these values would really be the employee number of Sam's boss. No data value is applicable to this row.

SQL supports missing, unknown, or inapplicable data explicitly, through the concept of a *null value*. A null value is an *indicator* that tells SQL (and the user) that the data is missing or not applicable. As a convenience, a missing piece of data is often said to have the value NULL. But the NULL value is not a real data value like 0, 473.83, or "Sam Clark." Instead, it's a signal, or a reminder, that the data value is missing or unknown. Figure 5-3 shows the contents of the SALESREPS table. Note that the QUOTA and REP_OFFICE values for Tom Snyder's row and the MANAGER value for Sam Clark's row of the table all contain NULL values.

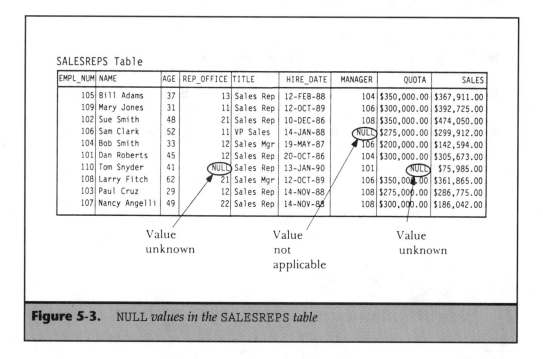

Figure 5-3. NULL *values in the* SALESREPS *table*

In many situations NULL values require special handling by the DBMS. For example, if the user requests the sum of the QUOTA column, how should the DBMS handle the missing data when computing the sum? The answer is given by a set of special rules that govern NULL value handling in various SQL statements and clauses. Because of these rules, some leading database authorities feel strongly that NULL values should not be used. Others, including Dr. Codd, have advocated the use of multiple NULL values, with distinct indicators for "unknown" and "not applicable" data.

Regardless of the academic debates, NULL values are a part of the ANSI/ISO SQL standard, and are supported in virtually all commercial SQL products. They also play an important, practical role in production SQL databases. The special rules that apply to NULL values (and the cases where NULL values are handled inconsistently by various SQL products) are pointed out in the relevant sections of this book.

Summary

This chapter described the basic elements of the SQL language. The basic structure of SQL can be summarized as on the following page.

- The SQL language that is in common use includes about thirty statements, each consisting of a verb and one or more clauses. Each statement performs a single, specific function.

- SQL-based databases can store various types of data, including text, integers, decimal numbers, floating-point numbers, and usually several more vendor-specific data types.

- SQL statements can include expressions that combine column names, constants, and built-in functions, using arithmetic and other vendor-specific operators.

- Variations in data types, constants, and built-in functions make portability of SQL statements more difficult than it may seem at first.

- NULL values provide a systematic way of handling missing or inapplicable data in the SQL language.

Chapter Six

Simple Queries

In many ways, queries are the heart of the SQL language. The SELECT statement, which is used to express SQL queries, is the most powerful and complex of the SQL statements. Despite the many options afforded by the SELECT statement, it's possible to start simply and then work up to more complex queries. This chapter discusses the simplest SQL queries — those that retrieve data from a single table in the database.

The SELECT Statement

The SELECT statement retrieves data from a database and returns it to you in the form of query results. You have already seen many examples of the SELECT statement in the quick tour presented in Chapter 2. Here are several more sample queries that retrieve information about sales offices:

List the sales offices with their targets and actual sales.

```
SELECT CITY, TARGET, SALES
  FROM OFFICES

CITY              TARGET         SALES
- - - - - - - -   - - - - - - -  - - - - - - -
Denver        $300,000.00  $186,042.00
New York      $575,000.00  $692,637.00
Chicago       $800,000.00  $735,042.00
Atlanta       $350,000.00  $367,911.00
Los Angeles   $725,000.00  $835,915.00
```

List the Eastern region sales offices with their targets and sales.

```
SELECT CITY, TARGET, SALES
  FROM OFFICES
 WHERE REGION = 'Eastern'

CITY              TARGET         SALES
- - - - - - - -   - - - - - - -  - - - - - - -
New York      $575,000.00  $692,637.00
Chicago       $800,000.00  $735,042.00
Atlanta       $350,000.00  $367,911.00
```

List Eastern region sales offices whose sales exceed their targets, sorted in alphabetical order by city.

```
SELECT CITY, TARGET, SALES
  FROM OFFICES
 WHERE REGION = 'Eastern'
   AND SALES > TARGET
 ORDER BY CITY

CITY                TARGET         SALES
------------    ------------    ------------
Atlanta         $350,000.00    $367,911.00
New York        $575,000.00    $692,637.00
```

What are the average target and sales for Eastern region offices?

```
SELECT AVG(TARGET), AVG(SALES)
  FROM OFFICES
 WHERE REGION = 'Eastern'

AVG(TARGET)    AVG(SALES)
------------   ------------
$575,000.00    $598,530.00
```

For simple queries, the English language request and the SQL SELECT statement are very similar. When the requests become more complex, more features of the SELECT statement must be used to specify the query precisely.

Figure 6-1 shows the full form of the SELECT statement, which consists of six clauses. The SELECT and FROM clauses of the statement are required. The remaining four clauses are optional. You include them in a SELECT statement only when you want to use the functions they provide. The function of each clause is summarized below:

■ The SELECT clause lists the data items to be retrieved by the SELECT statement. The items may be columns from the database, or columns to be calculated by SQL as it performs the query. The SELECT clause is described in later sections of this chapter.

■ The FROM clause lists the tables that contain the data to be retrieved by the query. Queries that draw their data from a single table are described in this chapter. More complex queries that combine data from two or more tables are discussed in Chapter 7.

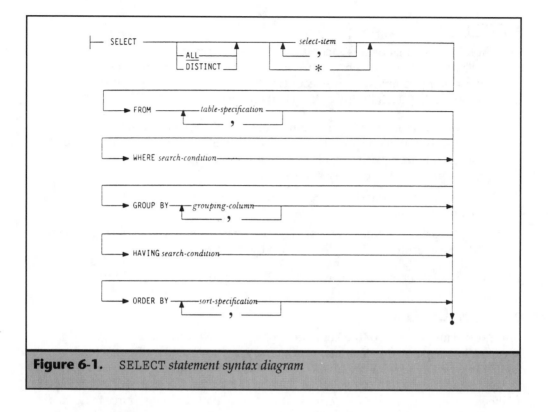

Figure 6-1. SELECT *statement syntax diagram*

- The WHERE clause tells SQL to include only certain rows of data in the query results. A *search condition* is used to specify the desired rows. The basic uses of the WHERE clause are described later in this chapter. Those that involve subqueries are discussed in Chapter 9.

- The GROUP BY clause specifies a summary query. Instead of producing one row of query results for each row of data in the database, a summary query groups together similar rows and then produces one summary row of query results for each group. Summary queries are described in Chapter 8.

- The HAVING clause tells SQL to include only certain groups produced by the GROUP BY clause in the query results. Like the WHERE clause, it uses a search condition to specify the desired groups. The HAVING clause is described in Chapter 8.

- The ORDER BY clause sorts the query results based on the data in one or more columns. If it is omitted, the query results are not sorted. The ORDER BY clause is described later in this chapter.

The `SELECT` **Clause**

The `SELECT` clause that begins each `SELECT` statement specifies the data items to be retrieved by the query. The items are usually specified by a *select list*, a list of *select items* separated by commas. Each select item in the list generates a single column of query results, in left-to-right order. A select item can be:

- a *column name*, identifying a column from the table(s) named in the FROM clause. When a column name appears as a select item, SQL simply takes the value of that column from each row of the database table and places it in the corresponding row of query results.

- a *constant*, specifying that the same constant value is to appear in every row of the query results.

- a *SQL expression*, indicating that SQL must calculate the value to be placed into the query results, in the style specified by the expression.

Each type of select item is described later in this chapter.

The `FROM` **Clause**

The `FROM` clause consists of the keyword `FROM`, followed by a list of table specifications separated by commas. Each table specification identifies a table containing data to be retrieved by the query. These tables are called the *source tables* of the query (and of the `SELECT` statement), because they are the source of all of the data in the query results. All of the queries in this chapter have a single source table, and every `FROM` clause contains a single table name.

Query Results

The result of a SQL query is always a table of data, just like the tables in the database. If you type a `SELECT` statement using interactive SQL, the DBMS displays the query results in tabular form on your computer screen. If a program sends a query to the DBMS using programmatic SQL, the table of query results is returned to the program. In either case, the query results always have the same tabular, row/column format as the actual tables in the database, as shown in Figure 6-2. Usually the query results will be a table with several columns and several rows. For example, this query produces a table of three columns (because it asks for three items of data) and ten rows (because there are ten salespeople):

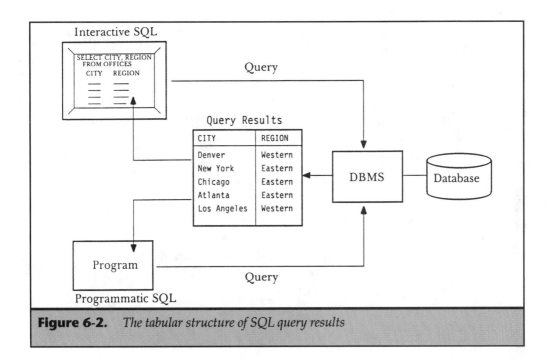

Figure 6-2. *The tabular structure of SQL query results*

List the names, offices, and hire dates of all salespeople.

```
SELECT NAME, REP_OFFICE, HIRE_DATE
  FROM SALESREPS

NAME             REP_OFFICE  HIRE_DATE
-------------    ----------  ----------
Bill Adams               13  12-FEB-88
Mary Jones               11  12-OCT-89
Sue Smith                21  10-DEC-86
Sam Clark                11  14-JUN-88
Bob Smith                12  19-MAY-87
Dan Roberts              12  20-OCT-86
Tom Snyder             NULL  13-JAN-90
Larry Fitch              21  12-OCT-89
Paul Cruz                12  01-MAR-87
Nancy Angelli            22  14-NOV-88
```

In contrast, the following query produces a single row, because there is only one salesperson with the requested employee number. Even though this single row of query results looks less "tabular" than the multi-row results, SQL still considers it to be a table of three columns and one row.

What are the name, quota, and sales of employee number 107?

```
SELECT NAME, QUOTA, SALES
  FROM SALESREPS
 WHERE EMPL_NUM = 107

NAME                    QUOTA          SALES
--------------    -------------    ------------
Nancy Angelli    $300,000.00    $186,042.00
```

In some cases the query results can be a single value, as in the following example:

What are the average sales of our salespeople?

```
SELECT AVG(SALES)
  FROM SALESREPS

  AVG(SALES)
------------
 $289,353.20
```

These query results are still a table, although it's a very small one consisting of one column and one row.

Finally, it's possible for a query to produce *zero* rows of query results, as in this example:

List the name and hire date of anyone with sales over $500,000.

```
SELECT NAME, HIRE_DATE
  FROM SALESREPS
 WHERE SALES > 500000.00

NAME              HIRE_DATE
------------     ---------
```

Even in this situation, the query results are still a table. This one is an empty table with two columns and zero rows.

Note that SQL's support for missing data extends to query results as well. If a data item in the database has a NULL value, the NULL value appears in the query results when the data item is retrieved. For example, the SALESREPS table contains NULL values in its QUOTA and MANAGER columns. The following query returns these NULL values in the second and third columns of query results:

List the salespeople, their quotas, and their managers.

```
SELECT NAME, QUOTA, MANAGER
   FROM SALESREPS

NAME                  QUOTA MANAGER
-------------- ------------- -------
Bill Adams       $350,000.00     104
Mary Jones       $300,000.00     106
Sue Smith        $350,000.00     108
Sam Clark        $275,000.00    NULL
Bob Smith        $200,000.00     106
Dan Roberts      $300,000.00     104
Tom Snyder              NULL     101
Larry Fitch      $350,000.00     106
Paul Cruz        $275,000.00     104
Nancy Angelli    $300,000.00     108
```

The fact that a SQL query always produces a table of data is very important. It means that the query results can be stored back into the database as a table. It means that the results of two similar queries can be combined to form a larger table of query results. Finally, it means that the query results can themselves be the target of further queries. A relational database's tabular structure thus has a very synergistic relationship with the relational query facilities of SQL. Tables can be queried, and queries produce tables.

Simple Queries

The simplest SQL queries request columns of data from a single table in the database. For example, this query requests three columns from the OFFICES table:

List the location, region, and sales of each sales office.

```
SELECT CITY, REGION, SALES
   FROM OFFICES
```

```
CITY            REGION          SALES
------------    --------    ------------
Denver          Western     $186,042.00
New York        Eastern     $692,637.00
Chicago         Eastern     $735,042.00
Atlanta         Eastern     $367,911.00
Los Angeles     Western     $835,915.00
```

The SELECT statement for simple queries like this one includes only the two required clauses. The SELECT clause names the requested columns; the FROM clause names the table that contains them.

Conceptually, SQL processes the query by going through the table named in the FROM clause, one row at a time, as shown in Figure 6-3. For each row, SQL takes the values of the columns requested in the select list and produces a single row of query results. The query results thus contain one row of data for each row in the table.

Calculated Columns

In addition to columns whose values come directly from the database, a SQL query can include *calculated columns* whose values are calculated from the stored data values. To request a calculated column, you specify a SQL expression in the select list. As discussed in Chapter 5, SQL expressions can involve addition, subtraction,

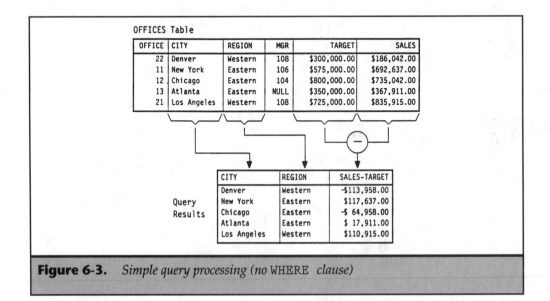

Figure 6-3.   *Simple query processing (no* WHERE *clause)*

multiplication, and division. You can also use parentheses to build more complex expressions. Of course the columns referenced in an arithmetic expression must have a numeric type. If you try to add, subtract, multiply, or divide columns containing text data, SQL will report an error.

This query shows a simple calculated column:

List the city, region and amount over/under target for each office.

```
SELECT CITY, REGION, (SALES - TARGET)
  FROM OFFICES

CITY          REGION    (SALES-TARGET)
------------  --------  --------------
Denver        Western     -$113,958.00
New York      Eastern      $117,637.00
Chicago       Eastern      -$64,958.00
Atlanta       Eastern       $17,911.00
Los Angeles   Western      $110,915.00
```

To process the query, SQL goes through the offices, generating one row of query results for each row of the OFFICES table, as shown in Figure 6-4. The first two columns of query results come directly from the OFFICES table. The third column of query results is calculated, row by row, using the data values from the current row of the OFFICES table.

Here are other examples of queries that use calculated columns:

Show the value of the inventory for each product.

```
SELECT MFR_ID, PRODUCT_ID, DESCRIPTION, (QTY_ON_HAND * PRICE)
  FROM PRODUCTS

MFR_ID PRODUCT_ID DESCRIPTION        (QTY_ON_HAND*PRICE)
------ ---------- -----------------  -------------------
REI    2A45C      Ratchet Link             $16,590.00
ACI    4100Y      Widget Remover           $68,750.00
QSA    XK47       Reducer                  $13,490.00
BIC    41672      Plate                         $0.00
IMM    779C       900-lb Brace             $16,875.00
ACI    41003      Size 3 Widget            $22,149.00
ACI    41004      Size 4 Widget            $16,263.00
BIC    41003      Handle                    $1,956.00
  .
  .
  .
```

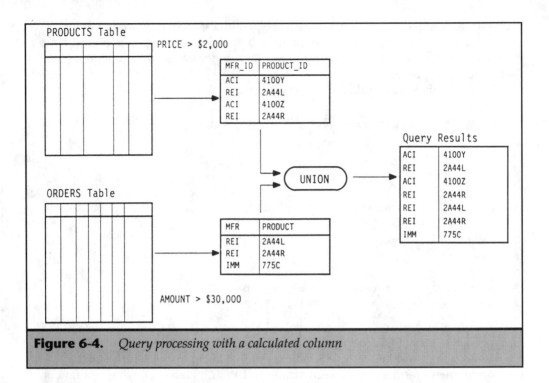

Figure 6-4. *Query processing with a calculated column*

Show me the result if I raised each salesperson's quota by 3% of their year-to-date sales.

```
SELECT NAME, QUOTA, (QUOTA + (.03 * SALES))
  FROM SALESREPS
```

NAME	QUOTA	(QUOTA+(.03*SALES))
Bill Adams	$350,000.00	$361,037.33
Mary Jones	$300,000.00	$311,781.75
Sue Smith	$350,000.00	$364,221.50
Sam Clark	$275,000.00	$283,997.36
Bob Smith	$200,000.00	$204,277.82
Dan Roberts	$300,000.00	$309,170.19
Tom Snyder	NULL	NULL
Larry Fitch	$350,000.00	$360,855.95
Paul Cruz	$275,000.00	$283,603.25
Nancy Angelli	$300,000.00	$305,581.26

As mentioned in Chapter 5, many SQL products provide additional arithmetic operations, character string operations, and built-in functions that can be used in SQL expressions. These can appear in select list expressions, as in this DB2 example:

List the name and month and year of hire for each salesperson.

```
SELECT NAME, MONTH(HIRE_DATE), YEAR(HIRE_DATE)
  FROM SALESREPS
```

SQL constants can also be used by themselves as items in a select list. This can be useful for producing query results that are easier to read and interpret, as in this example:

List the sales for each city.

```
SELECT CITY, 'has sales of', SALES
  FROM OFFICES

CITY          HAS SALES OF        SALES
------------  ------------  ------------
Denver        has sales of  $186,042.00
New York      has sales of  $692,637.00
Chicago       has sales of  $735,042.00
Atlanta       has sales of  $367,911.00
Los Angeles   has sales of  $835,915.00
```

The query results appear to consist of a separate "sentence" for each office, but they're really a table of three columns. The first and third columns contain values from the OFFICES table. The second column always contains the same 12-character text string. This distinction is subtle when the query results are displayed on a screen, but it is crucial in programmatic SQL, when the results are being retrieved into a program and used for calculations.

Selecting All Columns (SELECT *)

Sometimes it's convenient to display the contents of all the columns of a table. This can be particularly useful when you first encounter a new database and want to get a quick understanding of its structure and the data it contains. As a convenience, SQL lets you use an asterisk (*) in place of the select list as an abbreviation for "all columns":

Show me all the data in the OFFICES *table.*

```
SELECT *
  FROM OFFICES
```

OFFICE	CITY	REGION	MGR	TARGET	SALES
22	Denver	Western	108	$300,000.00	$186,042.00
11	New York	Eastern	106	$575,000.00	$692,637.00
12	Chicago	Eastern	104	$800,000.00	$735,042.00
13	Atlanta	Eastern	105	$350,000.00	$367,911.00
21	Los Angeles	Western	108	$725,000.00	$835,915.00

The query results contain all six columns of the OFFICES table, in the same left-to-right order as in the table itself.

The ANSI/ISO SQL standard specifies that a SELECT statement can either have an all-column selection or a select list, but not both, as shown in Figure 6-1. However, many SQL implementations treat the asterisk (*) as just another element of the select list. Thus the query:

```
SELECT *, (SALES - TARGET)
  FROM OFFICES
```

is legal in most commercial SQL dialects (for example in DB2, Oracle, and SQL Server), but it is not permitted by the ANSI/ISO standard.

The all-columns selection is most appropriate when you are using interactive SQL casually. It should be avoided in programmatic SQL, because changes in the database structure can cause a program to fail. For example, suppose the OFFICES table were dropped from the database and then re-created with its columns rearranged and a new seventh column added. SQL automatically takes care of the database-related details of such changes, but it cannot modify your application program for you. If your program expects a SELECT * FROM OFFICES query to return six columns of query results with certain data types, it will almost certainly stop working when the columns are rearranged and a new one is added.

These difficulties can be avoided if you write the program to request the columns it needs by name. For example, the following query produces the same results as SELECT * FROM OFFICES. It is also immune to changes in the database structure, so long as the named columns continue to exist in the OFFICES table:

```
SELECT OFFICE, CITY, REGION, MGR, TARGET, SALES
  FROM OFFICES
```

Duplicate Rows (`DISTINCT`)

If a query includes the primary key of a table in its select list, then every row of query results will be unique (because the primary key has a different value in each row). If the primary key is not included in the query results, duplicate rows can occur. For example, suppose you made this request:

List the employee numbers of all sales office managers.

```
SELECT MGR
  FROM OFFICES

MGR
----
 108
 106
 104
 105
 108
```

The query results have five rows (one for each office), but two of them are exact duplicates of one another. Why? Because Larry Fitch manages both the Los Angeles and Denver offices, and his employee number (108) appears in both rows of the `OFFICES` table. These query results are probably not exactly what you had in mind. If there are four different managers, you might have expected only four employee numbers in the query results.

You can eliminate duplicate rows of query results by inserting the keyword `DISTINCT` in the `SELECT` statement just before the select list. Here is a version of the previous query that produces the results you want:

List the employee numbers of all sales office managers.

```
SELECT DISTINCT MGR
  FROM OFFICES

MGR
----
 104
 105
 106
 108
```

Conceptually, SQL carries out this query by first generating a full set of query results (five rows), and then eliminating rows that are exact duplicates of one another to form the final query results. The DISTINCT keyword can be specified regardless of the contents of the SELECT list (with certain restrictions for summary queries, as described in Chapter 8).

If the DISTINCT keyword is omitted, SQL does not eliminate duplicate rows. You can also specify the keyword ALL to explicitly indicate that duplicate rows are to be retained, but it is unnecessary since this is the default behavior.

Row Selection (WHERE Clause)

SQL queries that retrieve all rows of a table are useful for database browsing and reports, but for little else. Usually you'll want to select only some of the rows in a table, and include only these rows in the query results. The WHERE clause is used to specify the rows you want to retrieve. Here are some examples of simple queries that use the WHERE clause:

Show me the offices where sales exceed target.

```
SELECT CITY, SALES, TARGET
  FROM OFFICES
 WHERE SALES > TARGET

CITY                SALES        TARGET
------------    ------------  ------------
New York        $692,637.00  $575,000.00
Atlanta         $367,911.00  $350,000.00
Los Angeles     $835,915.00  $725,000.00
```

Show me the name, sales, and quota of employee number 105.

```
SELECT NAME, SALES, QUOTA
  FROM SALESREPS
 WHERE EMPL_NUM = 105

NAME                SALES        QUOTA
--------------  ------------  ------------
Bill Adams      $367,911.00  $350,000.00
```

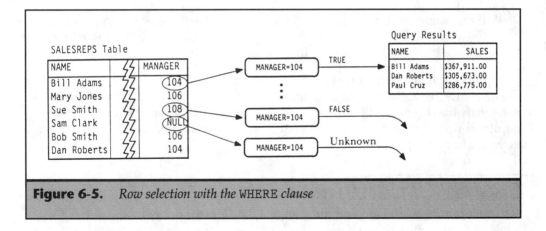

Figure 6-5. *Row selection with the WHERE clause*

Show me the employees managed by Bob Smith (employee 104).

```
SELECT NAME, SALES
  FROM SALESREPS
 WHERE MANAGER = 104

NAME               SALES
------------    ------------
Bill Adams      $367,911.00
Dan Roberts     $305,673.00
Paul Cruz       $286,775.00
```

The WHERE clause consists of the keyword WHERE followed by a search condition that specifies the rows to be retrieved. In the previous query, for example, the search condition is MANAGER = 104. Figure 6-5 shows how the WHERE clause works. Conceptually, SQL goes through each row of the SALESREPS table, one by one, and applies the search condition to the row. When a column name appears in the search condition (such as the MANAGER column in this example), SQL uses the value of the column in the current row. For each row, the search condition can produce one of three results:

■ If the search condition is TRUE, the row is included in the query results. For example, the row for Bill Adams has the correct MANAGER value, and is included.

■ If the search condition is FALSE, the row is excluded from the query results. For example, the row for Sue Smith has the wrong MANAGER value, and is excluded.

■ If the search condition has a NULL (unknown) value, the row is excluded from the query results. For example, the row for Sam Clark has a NULL value for the MANAGER column, and is excluded.

Figure 6-6 shows another way to think about the role of the search condition in the WHERE clause. Basically, the search condition acts as a filter for rows of the table. Rows that satisfy the search condition pass through the filter and become part of the query results. Rows that do not satisfy the search condition are trapped by the filter and are excluded from the query results.

Search Conditions

SQL offers a rich set of search conditions that allow you to specify many different kinds of queries efficiently and naturally. Five basic search conditions (called *predicates* in the ANSI/ISO standard) are summarized here, and are described in the sections that follow:

■ *Comparison test.* Compares the value of one expression to the value of another expression. Use this test to select offices in the Eastern region, or salespeople whose sales are above their quotas.

■ *Range test.* Tests whether the value of an expression falls within a specified range of values. Use this test to find salespeople whose sales are between $100,000 and $500,000.

■ *Set membership test.* Checks whether the value of an expression matches one of a set of values. Use this test to select offices located in New York, Chicago, or Los Angeles.

■ *Pattern matching test.* Checks whether the value of a column containing string data matches a specified pattern. Use this test to select customers whose names start with the letter "E".

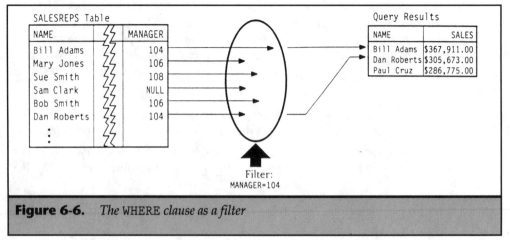

Figure 6-6. *The WHERE clause as a filter*

■ *Null value test.* Checks whether a column has a NULL (unknown) value. Use this test to find the salespeople who have not yet been assigned to a manager.

Comparison Test (=, <>, <, <=, >, >=)

The most common search condition used in a SQL query is a comparison test. In a comparison test, SQL computes and compares the values of two SQL expressions for each row of data. The expressions can be as simple as a column name or a constant, or they can be more complex arithmetic expressions. SQL offers six different ways of comparing the two expressions, as shown in Figure 6-7. Here are some examples of typical comparison tests:

Find salespeople hired before 1988.

```
SELECT NAME
  FROM SALESREPS
 WHERE HIRE_DATE < '01-JAN-88'

NAME
--------------
Sue Smith
Bob Smith
Dan Roberts
Paul Cruz
```

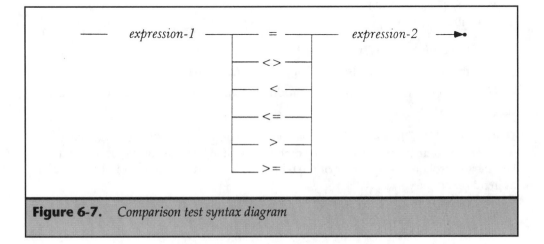

Figure 6-7. *Comparison test syntax diagram*

List the offices whose sales fall below 80 percent of target.

```
SELECT CITY, SALES, TARGET
  FROM OFFICES
 WHERE SALES < (.8 * TARGET)
```

```
CITY              SALES        TARGET
------------  ------------  ------------
Denver        $186,042.00   $300,000.00
```

List the offices not managed by employee number 108.

```
SELECT CITY, MGR
  FROM OFFICES
 WHERE MGR <> 108
```

```
CITY          MGR
------------  ----
New York      106
Chicago       104
Atlanta       105
```

As shown in Figure 6-7, the inequality comparison test is written as "A < > B" according to the ANSI/ISO SQL specification. Several SQL implementations use alternate notations, such as "A != B" (used by SQL Server) and "A¬ =B" (used by DB2 and SQL/DS). In some cases, these are alternative forms; in others, they are the only acceptable form of the inequality test.

When SQL compares the values of the two expressions in the comparison test, three results can occur:

- If the comparison is true, the test yields a TRUE result.
- If the comparison is false, the test yields a FALSE result.
- If either of the two expressions produces a NULL value, the comparison yields a NULL result.

SINGLE-ROW RETRIEVAL The most common comparison test is one that checks whether a column's value is equal to some constant. When the column is a primary key, the test isolates a single row of the table, producing a single row of query results, as in this example:

Retrieve the name and credit limit of customer number 2107.

```
SELECT COMPANY, CREDIT_LIMIT
  FROM CUSTOMERS
 WHERE CUST_NUM = 2107

COMPANY             CREDIT_LIMIT
------------------  ------------
Ace International    $35,000.00
```

This type of query is the foundation of forms-based database retrieval programs. The user enters a customer number into the form, and the program uses the number to construct and execute a query. It then displays the retrieved data in the form.

Note that the SQL statements for retrieving a specific customer by number, as in this example, and retrieving all customers with a certain characteristic (such as those with credit limits over $25,000), both have exactly the same form. These two types of queries (retrieval by primary key and retrieval based on a search of the data) would be very different operations in a nonrelational database. This uniformity of approach makes SQL much simpler to learn and use than earlier query languages.

NULL VALUE CONSIDERATIONS The behavior of NULL values in comparison tests can reveal some "obviously true" notions about SQL queries to be, in fact, not necessarily true. For example, it would seem that the results of these two queries:

List salespeople who are over quota.

```
SELECT NAME
  FROM SALESREPS
 WHERE SALES > QUOTA

NAME
--------------
Bill Adams
Mary Jones
Sue Smith
Sam Clark
Dan Roberts
Larry Fitch
Paul Cruz
```

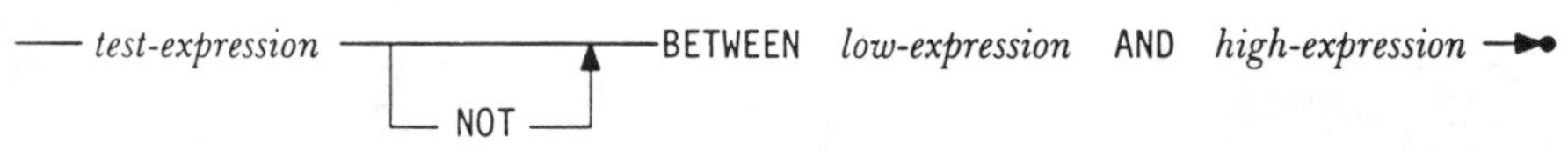

Figure 6-8. *Range test (BETWEEN) syntax diagram*

List salespeople who are under or at quota.

```
SELECT NAME
  FROM SALESREPS

 WHERE SALES < = QUOTA

NAME
- - - - - - - - - - - - - -
Bob Smith
Nancy Angelli
```

would include every row of the SALESREPS table, but the queries produce seven and two rows, respectively, for a total of nine rows, while there are ten rows in the SALESREPS table. Tom Snyder's row has a NULL value in the QUOTA column, because he has not yet been assigned a quota. This row is not listed by either query; it "vanishes" in the comparison test.

As this example shows, you need to think about NULL value handling when you specify a search condition. In SQL's three-valued logic, a search condition can yield a TRUE, FALSE or NULL result. Only rows where the search condition yields a TRUE result are included in the query results.

Range Test (BETWEEN)

SQL provides a different form of search condition with the range test (BETWEEN) shown in Figure 6-8. The range test checks whether a data value lies between two specified values. It involves three SQL expressions. The first expression defines the value to be tested; the second and third expressions define the low and high ends of the range to be checked. The data types of the three expressions must be comparable.

This example shows a typical range test:

Find orders placed in the last quarter of 1989.

```
SELECT ORDER_NUM, ORDER_DATE, MFR, PRODUCT, AMOUNT
  FROM ORDERS
 WHERE ORDER_DATE BETWEEN '01-OCT-89' AND '31-DEC-89'

ORDER_NUM ORDER_DATE MFR  PRODUCT      AMOUNT
--------- ---------- ---- ------- -----------
   112961 17-DEC-89  REI  2A44L    $31,500.00
   112968 12-OCT-89  ACI  41004     $3,978.00
   112963 17-DEC-89  ACI  41004     $3,276.00
   112983 27-DEC-89  ACI  41004       $702.00
   112979 12-OCT-89  ACI  4100Z    $15,000.00
   112992 04-NOV-89  ACI  41002       $760.00
   112975 12-OCT-89  REI  2A44G     $2,100.00
   112987 31-DEC-89  ACI  4100Y    $27,500.00
```

The BETWEEN test includes the endpoints of the range, so orders placed on October 1 or December 31 are included in the query results. Here is another example of a range test:

Find the orders that fall into various amount ranges.

```
SELECT ORDER_NUM, AMOUNT
  FROM ORDERS
 WHERE AMOUNT BETWEEN 20000.00 AND 29999.99

ORDER_NUM      AMOUNT
--------- -----------
   113036  $22,500.00
   112987  $27,500.00
   113042  $22,500.00

SELECT ORDER_NUM, AMOUNT
  FROM ORDERS
 WHERE AMOUNT BETWEEN 30000.00 AND 39999.99

ORDER_NUM      AMOUNT
--------- -----------
   112961  $31,500.00
   113069  $31,350.00
```

```
SELECT ORDER_NUM, AMOUNT
  FROM ORDERS
 WHERE AMOUNT BETWEEN 40000.00 AND 49999.99

ORDER_NUM      AMOUNT
---------- -----------
   113045  $45,000.00
```

The negated version of the range test (NOT BETWEEN) checks for values that fall outside the range, as in this example:

List salespeople whose sales are not between 80 percent and 120 percent of quota.

```
SELECT NAME, SALES, QUOTA
  FROM SALESREPS
 WHERE SALES NOT BETWEEN (.8 * QUOTA) AND (1.2 * QUOTA)

NAME                  SALES        QUOTA
--------------- ------------- ------------
Mary Jones      $392,725.00   $300,000.00
Sue Smith       $474,050.00   $350,000.00
Bob Smith       $142,594.00   $200,000.00
Nancy Angelli   $186,042.00   $300,000.00
```

The test expression specified in the BETWEEN test can be any valid SQL expression, but in practice it's usually just a column name, as in the previous examples.

The ANSI/ISO standard defines relatively complex rules for the handling of NULL values in the BETWEEN test:

- If the test expression produces a NULL value, or if *both* expressions defining the range produce NULL values, then the BETWEEN test returns a NULL result.
- If the expression defining the lower end of the range produces a NULL value, then the BETWEEN test returns FALSE if the test value is greater than the upper bound, and NULL otherwise.
- If the expression defining the upper end of the range produces a NULL value, then the BETWEEN test returns FALSE if the test value is less than the lower bound and NULL otherwise.

Before relying on this behavior, it's a good idea to experiment with your DBMS.

It's worth noting that the BETWEEN test doesn't really add to the expressive power of SQL, because it can be expressed as two comparison tests. The range test:

```
A BETWEEN B AND C
```

is completely equivalent to:

```
(A >= B) AND (A < = C)
```

However, the BETWEEN test is a simpler way to express a search condition when you're thinking of it in terms of a range of values.

Set Membership Test (IN)

✕

Another common search condition is the set membership test (IN), shown in Figure 6-9. It tests whether a data value matches one of a list of target values. Here are several queries that use the set membership test:

List the salespeople who work in New York, Atlanta or Denver.

```
SELECT NAME, QUOTA, SALES
  FROM SALESREPS
 WHERE REP_OFFICE IN (11, 13, 22)

NAME                   QUOTA          SALES
---------------  -------------  -------------
Bill Adams       $350,000.00    $367,911.00
Mary Jones       $300,000.00    $392,725.00
Sam Clark        $275,000.00    $299,912.00
Nancy Angelli    $300,000.00    $186,042.00
```

Find all orders placed on a Thursday in January 1990.

```
SELECT ORDER_NUM, ORDER_DATE, AMOUNT
  FROM ORDERS
 WHERE ORDER_DATE IN ('04-JAN-90', '11-JAN-90', '18-JAN-90', '25-JAN-90')

ORDER_NUM ORDER_DATE     AMOUNT
--------- ---------- -----------
   113012 11-JAN-90    $3,745.00
   113003 25-JAN-90    $5,625.00
```

Find all orders placed with four specific salespeople.

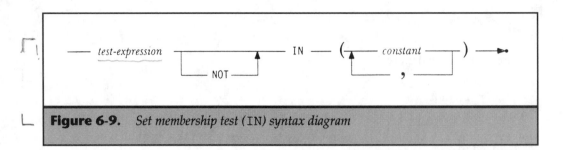

Figure 6-9.   *Set membership test (IN) syntax diagram*

```
SELECT ORDER_NUM, REP, AMOUNT
  FROM ORDERS
 WHERE REP IN (107, 109, 101, 103)

ORDER_NUM  REP      AMOUNT
---------  ----  -----------
   112968  101    $3,978.00
   113058  109    $1,480.00
   112997  107      $652.00
   113062  107    $2,430.00
   113069  107   $31,350.00
   112975  103    $2,100.00
   113055  101      $150.00
   113003  109    $5,625.00
   113057  103      $600.00
   113042  101   $22,500.00
```

You can check if the data value does *not* match any of the target values by using the NOT IN form of the set membership test. The test expression in an IN test can be any SQL expression, but it's usually just a column name, as in the preceding examples. If the test expression produces a NULL value, the IN test returns NULL. All of the items in the list of target values must have the same data type, and that type must be comparable to the data type of the test expression.

Like the BETWEEN test, the IN test doesn't add to the expressive power of SQL, because the search condition:

```
X IN (A, B, C)
```

is completely equivalent to:

```
(X = A) OR (X = B) OR (X = C)
```

However, the IN test offers a much more efficient way of expressing the search condition, especially if the set contains more than a few values. The ANSI/ISO SQL standard doesn't specify a maximum limit to the number of items that can appear in the value list, and most commercial implementations do not state an explicit upper limit either. For portability reasons, it's generally a good idea to avoid lists with only a single item, such as this one:

```
CITY IN ('New York')
```

and replace them with a simple comparison test:

```
CITY = 'New York'
```

Pattern Matching Test (LIKE)

A simple comparison test can be used to retrieve rows where the contents of a text column match some particular text. For example, this query retrieves a row of the CUSTOMERS table by name:

Show the credit limit for Smithson Corp.

```
SELECT COMPANY, CREDIT_LIMIT
  FROM CUSTOMERS
 WHERE COMPANY = 'Smithson Corp'.
```

However, you might easily forget whether the company's name was "Smith," "Smithson," or "Smithsonian." SQL's pattern matching test can be used to retrieve the data based on a partial match of the customer's name.

The pattern matching test (LIKE), shown in Figure 6-10, checks to see whether the data value in a column matches a specified *pattern*. The pattern is a string that may include one or more *wildcard* characters. These characters are interpreted in a special way.

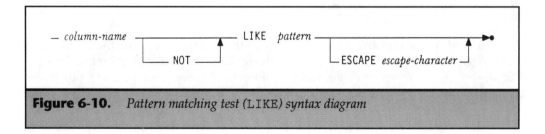

Figure 6-10. *Pattern matching test (LIKE) syntax diagram*

WILDCARD CHARACTERS   The percent sign (%) wildcard character matches any sequence of zero or more characters. Here's a modified version of the previous query that uses the percent sign for pattern matching:

```
SELECT COMPANY, CREDIT_LIMIT
  FROM CUSTOMERS
 WHERE COMPANY LIKE 'Smith% Corp.'
```

The LIKE keyword tells SQL to compare the NAME column to the pattern "Smith% Corp." Any of the following names would match the pattern:

```
Smith Corp.   Smithson Corp.   Smithsen Corp.   Smithsonian Corp.
```

but these names would not:

```
SmithCorp    Smithson Inc.
```

The underscore (_) wildcard character matches any single character. If you are sure that the company's name is either "Smithson" or "Smithsen," for example, you can use this query:

```
SELECT COMPANY, CREDIT_LIMIT
  FROM CUSTOMERS
 WHERE COMPANY LIKE 'Smiths_n Corp.'
```

In this case, any of these names will match the pattern:

```
Smithson Corp.   Smithsen Corp.   Smithsun Corp.
```

but these names will not:

```
Smithsoon Corp.   Smithsn Corp.
```

Wildcard characters can appear anywhere in the pattern string, and there can be several wildcard characters within a single string. This query allows either the "Smithson" or "Smithsen" spelling, and will also accept "Corp.", "Inc.", or any other ending on the company name:

```
SELECT COMPANY, CREDIT_LIMIT
  FROM CUSTOMERS
 WHERE COMPANY LIKE 'Smiths_n %'
```

You can locate strings that do *not* match a pattern by using the NOT LIKE form of the pattern matching test. The LIKE test must be applied to a column with a string data type. If the data value in the column is NULL, the LIKE test returns a NULL result.

If you have used personal computers, you've probably seen string pattern matching before. For example, in the MS-DOS or OS/2 command language, you can type the command:

```
DIR D*
```

to list all files whose names begin with the letter "D". In MS-DOS commands, the asterisk (*) is used instead of SQL's percent sign (%), and the question mark (?) is used instead of SQL's underscore (_), but the pattern matching capabilities themselves are the same.

ESCAPE CHARACTERS * One of the problems with string pattern matching is how to match the wildcard characters themselves as literal characters. To test for the presence of a percent sign character in a column of text data, for example, you can't simply include the percent sign in the pattern, because SQL will treat it as a wildcard. With most commercial SQL products, you cannot literally match the two wildcard characters. This usually doesn't pose serious problems, because the wildcard characters don't frequently appear in names, product numbers, and other text data of the sort that is usually stored in a database.

The ANSI/ISO SQL standard does specify a way to literally match wildcard characters, using a special *escape character*. When the escape character appears in the pattern, the character immediately following it is treated as a literal character rather than a wildcard character. (The latter character is said to be *escaped*.) The escaped character can be either of the two wildcard characters, or the escape character itself, which has now taken on a special meaning within the pattern.

The escape character is specified as a one-character constant string in the ESCAPE clause of the search condition, as shown in Figure 6-10. Here is an example using a dollar sign ($) as the escape character:

Find products whose product id's start with the four letters "A%BC".

```
SELECT ORDER_NUM, PRODUCT
  FROM ORDERS
 WHERE PRODUCT LIKE 'A$%BC%' ESCAPE '$'
```

The first percent sign in the pattern, which follows an escape character, is treated as a literal percent sign; the second functions as a wildcard.

The use of escape characters is very common in pattern matching applications, which is why the ANSI/ISO standard specified it. However, it was not a part of the early SQL implementations, and has not been widely adopted. To insure portability, the ESCAPE clause should be avoided.

Null Value Test (IS NULL)

NULL values create a three-valued logic for SQL search conditions. For any given row, the result of a search condition may be TRUE or FALSE, or it may be NULL because one of the columns used in evaluating the search condition contains a NULL value. Sometimes it's useful to check explicitly for NULL values in a search condition and handle them directly. SQL provides a special null value test (IS NULL), shown in Figure 6-11, to handle this task.

This query uses the null value test to find the salesperson in the sample database who has not yet been assigned to an office:

Find the salesperson not yet assigned to an office.

```
SELECT NAME
  FROM SALESREPS
 WHERE REP_OFFICE IS NULL

NAME
- - - - - - - - - - - - - -
Tom Snyder
```

The negated form of the null value test (IS NOT NULL) finds rows that do not contain a NULL value:

List the salespeople who have been assigned to an office.

```
SELECT NAME
  FROM SALESREPS
 WHERE REP_OFFICE IS NOT NULL

NAME
- - - - - - - - - - - - - -
Bill Adams
Mary Jones
Sue Smith
```

```
Sam Clark
Bob Smith
Dan Roberts
Larry Fitch
Paul Cruz
Nancy Angelli
```

Unlike the previously described search conditions, the null value test cannot yield a NULL result. It is always either TRUE or FALSE.

It may seem strange that you can't just test for a NULL value using a simple comparison search condition, such as this:

```
SELECT NAME
  FROM SALESREPS
 WHERE REP_OFFICE = NULL
```

The NULL keyword can't be used here because it isn't really a value; it's just a signal that the value is unknown. Even if the comparison test:

```
REP_OFFICE = NULL
```

were legal, the rules for handling NULL values in comparisons would cause it to behave differently from what you might expect. When SQL encountered a row where the REP_OFFICE column was NULL, the search condition would test:

```
NULL = NULL
```

Is the result TRUE or FALSE? Because the values on both sides of the equal sign are unknown, SQL can't tell, so the rules of SQL logic say that the search condition itself must yield a NULL result. Because the search condition doesn't produce a true result, the row is excluded from the query results— precisely the opposite of what you

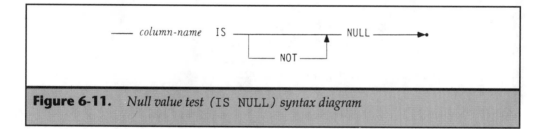

Figure 6-11. *Null value test (IS NULL) syntax diagram*

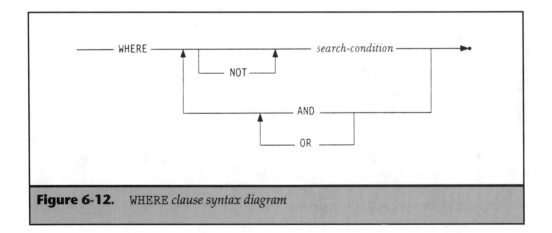

Figure 6-12. WHERE *clause syntax diagram*

wanted to happen! As a result of the way SQL handles NULLs in comparisons, you must explicitly use the null value test to check for NULL values.

Compound Search Conditions (AND, OR, **and** NOT)

The simple search conditions described in the preceding sections return a value of TRUE, FALSE, or NULL when applied to a row of data. Using the rules of logic, you can combine these simple SQL search conditions to form more complex ones, as shown in Figure 6-12. Note that the search conditions combined with AND, OR, and NOT may themselves be compound search conditions.

The keyword OR is used to combine two search conditions when one or the other (or both) must be true:

Find salespeople who are under quota or with sales under $300,000.

```
SELECT NAME, QUOTA, SALES
   FROM SALESREPS
 WHERE SALES < QUOTA
    OR SALES < 300000.00
```

NAME	QUOTA	SALES
Sam Clark	$275,000.00	$299,912.00
Bob Smith	$200,000.00	$142,594.00
Tom Snyder	NULL	$75,985.00
Paul Cruz	$275,000.00	$286,775.00
Nancy Angelli	$300,000.00	$186,042.00

ter4444444444444444

You can also use the keyword AND to combine two search conditions which must both be true:

Find salespeople who are under quota and with sales under $300,000.

```
SELECT NAME, QUOTA, SALES
  FROM SALESREPS
 WHERE SALES < QUOTA
   AND SALES < 300000.00

NAME                 QUOTA        SALES
-------------- ------------ ------------
Bob Smith      $200,000.00 $142,594.00
Nancy Angelli  $300,000.00 $186,042.00
```

Finally, you can use the keyword NOT to select rows where a search condition is false:

Find all salespeople who are under quota, but whose sales are not under $150,000.

```
SELECT NAME, QUOTA, SALES
  FROM SALESREPS
 WHERE SALES < QUOTA
   AND NOT SALES < 150000.00

NAME                 QUOTA        SALES
-------------- ------------ ------------
Nancy Angelli  $300,000.00 $186,042.00
```

Using the logical AND, OR, and NOT keywords and parentheses to group the search criteria, you can build very complex search criteria, such as the one in this query:

Find all salespeople who either: (a) work in Denver, New York, or Chicago; or (b) have no manager and were hired since June 1988; or (c) are over quota, but have sales of $600,000 or less.

```
SELECT NAME
  FROM SALESREPS
 WHERE (REP_OFFICE IN (22, 11, 12))
    OR (MANAGER IS NULL AND HIRE_DATE >= '01-JUN-88')
    OR (SALES > QUOTA AND NOT SALES > 600000.00)
```

Exactly why you might want to see this particular list of names is a mystery, but the example does illustrate a reasonably complex query.

As with simple search conditions, NULL values influence the outcome of compound search conditions, and the results are subtle. In particular, the result of (NULL OR TRUE) is TRUE, not NULL as you might expect. Tables 6-1, 6-2 and 6-3 specify truth tables for AND, OR, and NOT, respectively, and show the impact of NULL values.

When more than two search conditions are combined with AND, OR, and NOT, the ANSI/ISO standard specifies that NOT has the highest precedence, followed by AND and then OR. To ensure portability, it's always a good idea to use parentheses and remove any possible ambiguity.

AND	TRUE	FALSE	NULL
TRUE	TRUE	FALSE	NULL
FALSE	FALSE	FALSE	FALSE
NULL	NULL	FALSE	NULL

Table 6-1. AND *Truth Table*

OR	TRUE	FALSE	NULL
TRUE	TRUE	TRUE	TRUE
FALSE	TRUE	FALSE	NULL
NULL	TRUE	NULL	NULL

Table 6-2. OR *Truth Table*

NOT	TRUE	FALSE	NULL
	FALSE	TRUE	NULL

Table 6-3. NOT *Truth Table*

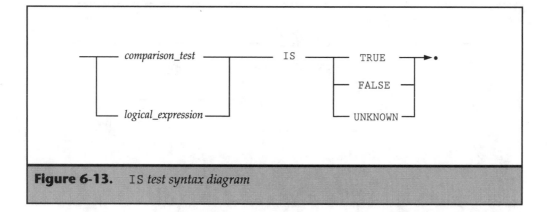

Figure 6-13. IS *test syntax diagram*

The SQL2 standard adds another logical search condition, the IS test, to the logic provided by AND, OR and NOT. Figure 6-13 shows the syntax of the IS test, which checks to see whether the logical value of an expression or comparison test is TRUE, FALSE or UNKNOWN (NULL).

For example, the IS test:

```
((SALES - QUOTA) > 10000.00) IS UNKNOWN
```

can be used to find rows where the comparison cannot be done because either SALES or QUOTA has a NULL value. Similarly, the IS test:

```
((SALES - QUOTA) > 10000.00) IS FALSE
```

will select rows where SALES are not significantly above QUOTA. As this example shows, the IS test doesn't really add to the expressive power of SQL, since the test could just as easily have been written:

```
NOT ((SALES - QUOTA) > 10000.00)
```

For maximum portability, it's a good idea to avoid the tests and write the expressions using only AND, OR and NOT. It's not always possible to avoid the IS UNKNOWN from the test.

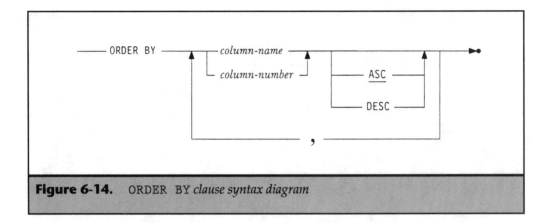

Figure 6-14. ORDER BY *clause syntax diagram*

Sorting Query Results (ORDER BY Clause)

Like the rows of a table in the database, the rows of query results are not arranged in any particular order. You can ask SQL to sort the results of a query by including the ORDER BY clause in the SELECT statement. The ORDER BY clause, shown in Figure 6-14, consists of the keywords ORDER BY, followed by a list of sort specifications separated by commas. For example, the results of this query are sorted on two columns, REGION and CITY:

Show the sales for each office, sorted in alphabetical order by region, and within each region by city.

```
SELECT CITY, REGION, SALES
  FROM OFFICES
 ORDER BY REGION, CITY

CITY            REGION          SALES
------------    --------    ------------
Atlanta         Eastern     $367,911.00
Chicago         Eastern     $735,042.00
New York        Eastern     $692,637.00
Denver          Western     $186,042.00
Los Angeles     Western     $835,915.00
```

The first sort specification (REGION) is the *major* sort key; those that follow (CITY, in this case) are progressively more *minor* sort keys, used as "tie breakers" when two rows of query results have the same values for the more major keys. Using the ORDER

BY clause, you can request sorting in an ascending or descending sequence, and you can sort on any item in the select list of the query.

By default, SQL sorts data in ascending sequence. To request sorting in descending sequence, the keyword DESC is included in the sort specification, as in this example:

List the offices, sorted in descending order by sales, so that the offices with the largest sales appear first.

```
SELECT CITY, REGION, SALES
  FROM OFFICES
 ORDER BY SALES DESC

CITY          REGION         SALES
------------  --------  ------------
Los Angeles   Western   $835,915.00
Chicago       Eastern   $735,042.00
New York      Eastern   $692,637.00
Atlanta       Eastern   $367,911.00
Denver        Western   $186,042.00
```

As indicated in Figure 6-14, you can also use the keyword ASC to specify an ascending sort, but because that's the default sorting sequence, the keyword is usually omitted.

If the column of query results to be used for sorting is a calculated column, it has no column name to be used in a sort specification. In this case, you must specify a column number instead of a column name, as in this example:

List the offices, sorted in descending order by sales performance, so that the offices with the best performance appear first.

```
SELECT CITY, REGION, (SALES - TARGET)
  FROM OFFICES
 ORDER BY 3 DESC

CITY          REGION    (SALES-TARGET)
------------  --------  --------------
New York      Eastern      $117,637.00
Los Angeles   Western      $110,915.00
Atlanta       Eastern       $17,911.00
Chicago       Eastern      -$64,958.00
Denver        Western     -$113,958.00
```

These query results are sorted on the third column, which is the calculated difference between the SALES and TARGET for each office. By combining column numbers, column names, ascending sorts, and descending sorts, you can specify quite complex sorting of the query results, as in the following final example.

List the offices, sorted in alphabetical order by region, and within each region in descending order by sales performance.

```
SELECT CITY, REGION, (SALES - TARGET)
  FROM OFFICES
 ORDER BY REGION ASC, 3 DESC

CITY           REGION    (SALES-TARGET)
------------   --------  --------------
New York       Eastern       $117,637.00
Atlanta        Eastern        $17,911.00
Chicago        Eastern       -$64,958.00
Los Angeles    Western       $110,915.00
Denver         Western      -$113,958.00
```

The SQL2 standard allows you to control the sorting order used by the DBMS for each sort key. This can be important when working with international character sets or to insure portability between ASCII and EBCDIC character set systems. However, this area of the SQL2 specification is quite complex, and most SQL implementations either ignore sorting sequence issues or use their own proprietary scheme for user control of the sorting sequence.

Rules for Single-Table Query Processing

Single-table queries are generally simple, and it's usually easy to understand the meaning of a query just by reading the SELECT statement. As queries become more complex, however, it's important to have a more precise "definition" of the query results that will be produced by a given SELECT statement. Figure 6-15 describes the procedure for generating the results of a SQL query that includes the clauses described in this chapter.

As Figure 6-15 shows, the query results produced by a SELECT statement are specified by applying each of its clauses, one by one. The FROM clause is applied first (selecting the table containing data to be retrieved). The WHERE clause is applied next (selecting specific rows from the table). The SELECT clause is applied next (generating the specific columns of query results and eliminating duplicate rows, if requested). Finally, the ORDER BY clause is applied to sort the query results.

To generate the query results for a SELECT statement:

1. Start with the table named in the FROM clause.

2. If there is a WHERE clause, apply its search condition to each row of the table, retaining those rows for which the search condition is TRUE, and discarding those for which it is FALSE or NULL.

3. For each remaining row, calculate the value of each item in the select list to produce a single row of query results. For each column reference, use the value of the column in the current row.

4. If SELECT DISTINCT is specified, eliminate any duplicate rows of query results that were produced.

5. If there is an ORDER BY clause, sort the query results as specified.

The rows generated by this procedure comprise the query results.

Figure 6-15. *SQL query processing rules (single-table queries)*

The "rules" for SQL query processing in Figure 6-15 will be expanded several times in the next three chapters to include the remaining clauses of the SELECT statement.

Combining Query Results (UNION) *

Occasionally, it's convenient to combine the results of two or more queries into a single table of query results. SQL supports this capability through the UNION feature of the SELECT statement. Figure 6-16 illustrates how the UNION operation can be used to satisfy the following request:

"List all the products where the price of the product exceeds $2,000 or where more than $30,000 of the product has been ordered in a single order."

The first part of the request can be satisfied with the top query in the figure:

List all the products whose price exceeds $2,000.

```
SELECT MFR_ID, PRODUCT_ID
  FROM PRODUCTS
  WHERE PRICE > 2000.00
```

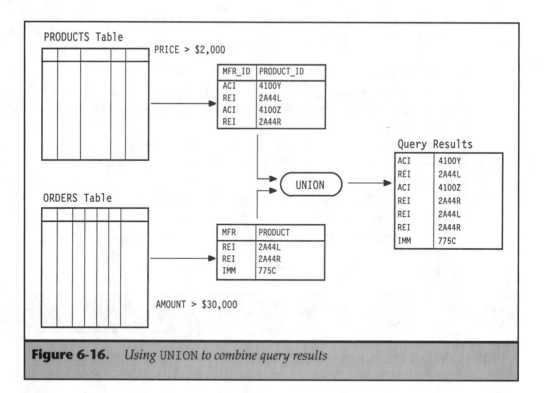

Figure 6-16. *Using UNION to combine query results*

```
MFR_ID PRODUCT_ID
------ ----------
ACI    4100Y
REI    2A44L
ACI    4100Z
REI    2A44R
```

Similarly, the second part of the request can be satisfied with the bottom query in the figure:

List all the products where more than $30,000 of the product has been ordered in a single order.

```
SELECT DISTINCT MFR, PRODUCT
  FROM ORDERS
 WHERE AMOUNT > 30000.00
```

```
MFR   PRODUCT
----  -------
IMM   775C
REI   2A44L
REI   2A44R
```

As shown in the figure, the UNION operation produces a single table of query results that combines the rows of the top query results with the rows of the bottom query results. The SELECT statement that specifies the UNION operation looks like this:

List all the products where the price of the product exceeds $2,000 or where more than $30,000 of the product has been ordered in a single order.

```
SELECT MFR_ID, PRODUCT_ID
  FROM PRODUCTS
 WHERE PRICE > 2000.00
 UNION
SELECT DISTINCT MFR, PRODUCT
  FROM ORDERS
 WHERE AMOUNT > 30000.00

ACI    4100Y
ACI    4100Z
IMM    775C
REI    2A44L
REI    2A44R
```

There are severe restrictions on the tables that can be combined by a UNION operation:

- The two tables must contain the same number of columns.
- The data type of each column in the first table must be the same as the data type of the corresponding column in the second table.
- Neither of the two tables can be sorted with the ORDER BY clause. However, the combined query results can be sorted, as described in the following section.

Note that the column names of the two queries combined by a UNION do not have to be identical. In the preceding example, the first table of query results has columns named MFR_ID and PRODUCT_ID, while the second table of query results has columns named MFR and PRODUCT. Because the columns in the two tables can have different names, the columns of query results produced by the UNION operation are unnamed.

The ANSI/ISO SQL standard specifies a further restriction on a SELECT statement that participates in a UNION. It permits only column names or an "all columns" specification (SELECT *) in the select list, and prohibits expressions in the select list. Most commercial SQL implementations relax this restriction and permit simple expressions in the select list. However, many SQL implementations do not allow the SELECT statements to include the GROUP BY or HAVING clauses, and some do not allow column functions in the select list (prohibiting summary queries as described in Chapter 8). In fact, some SQL implementations (including SQL Server and dBASE IV) do not support the UNION operation at all.

Unions and Duplicate Rows *

Because the UNION operation combines the rows from two sets of query results, it would tend to produce query results containing duplicate rows. For example, in the query of Figure 6-16, product REI-2A44L sells for $4,500.00, so it appears in the top set of query results. There is also an order for $31,500.00 worth of this product in the ORDERS table, so it also appears in the bottom set of query results. By default, the UNION operation *eliminates* duplicate rows as part of its processing. Thus, the combined set of query results contains only *one* row for product REI-2A44L.

If you want to retain duplicate rows in a UNION operation, you can specify the ALL keyword immediately following the word UNION. This form of the query produces two duplicate rows for product REI-2A44L:

List all the products where the price of the product exceeds $2,000 or where more than $30,000 of the product has been ordered in a single order.

```
SELECT MFR_ID, PRODUCT_ID
  FROM PRODUCTS
 WHERE PRICE > 2000.00
 UNION ALL
SELECT DISTINCT MFR, PRODUCT
  FROM ORDERS
 WHERE AMOUNT > 30000.00

  ACI    4100Y
  REI    2A44L
  ACI    4100Z
  REI    2A44R
  IMM    775C
  REI    2A44L
  REI    2A44R
```

Note that the default duplicate row handling for the UNION operation and for the simple SELECT statement are exact opposites. For the SELECT statement, SELECT ALL (duplicates retained) is the default. To eliminate duplicate rows, you must explicitly specify SELECT DISTINCT. For the UNION operation, UNION (duplicates eliminated) is the default. To retain duplicate rows, you must explicitly specify UNION ALL.

Database experts have criticized the handling of duplicate rows in SQL, and point to this inconsistency as an example of the problems. The reason for the inconsistency is that the SQL defaults were chosen to produce the correct behavior most of the time:

- In practice, most simple SELECT statements do not produce duplicate rows, so the default is no duplicate elimination.

- In practice, most UNION operations would produce unwanted duplicate rows, so the default is duplicate elimination.

Eliminating duplicate rows from query results is a very time-consuming process, especially if the query results contain a large number of rows. If you know, based on the individual queries involved, that a UNION operation cannot produce duplicate rows, you should specifically use the UNION ALL operation, because the query will execute much more quickly.

Unions and Sorting *

The ORDER BY clause cannot appear in either of the two SELECT statements combined by a UNION operation. It wouldn't make much sense to sort the two sets of query results anyway, because they are fed directly into the UNION operation and are never visible to the user. However, the *combined* set of query results produced by the UNION operation can be sorted by specifying an ORDER BY clause after the second SELECT statement. Since the columns produced by the UNION operation are not named, the ORDER BY clause must specify the columns by column number.

Here is the same products query as that shown in Figure 6-16, with the query results sorted by manufacturer and product number:

List all the products where the price of the product exceeds $2,000 or where more than $30,000 of the product has been ordered in a single order, sorted by manufacturer and product number.

```
SELECT MFR_ID, PRODUCT_ID
  FROM PRODUCTS
 WHERE PRICE > 2000.00
 UNION
SELECT DISTINCT MFR, PRODUCT
  FROM ORDERS
 WHERE AMOUNT > 30000.00
```

```
    ORDER BY 1, 2

ACI     4100Y
ACI     4100Z
IMM     775C
REI     2A44L
REI     2A44R
```

Multiple Unions *

The UNION operation can be used repeatedly to combine three or more sets of query results, as shown in Figure 6-17. The union of Table B and Table C in the figure produces a single, combined table. This table is then combined with Table A in another UNION operation. The query in the figure is written this way:

```
SELECT *
  FROM A
  UNION (SELECT *
           FROM B
          UNION
         SELECT *
          FROM C)

Bill
Mary
George
Fred
Sue
Julia
Harry
```

The parentheses in the query indicate which UNION should be performed first. In fact, if all of the UNIONs in the statement eliminate duplicate rows, or if all of them retain duplicate rows, the order in which they are performed is unimportant. These three expressions are completely equivalent:

```
A UNION (B UNION C)

(A UNION B) UNION C

(A UNION C) UNION B
```

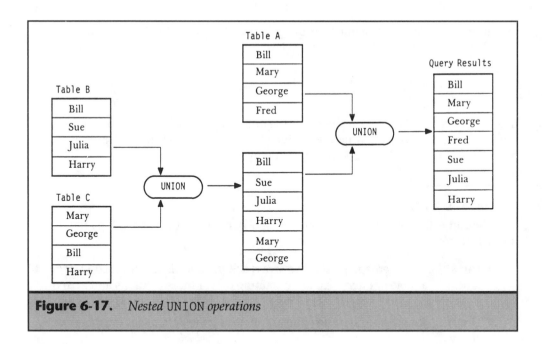

Figure 6-17. *Nested* UNION *operations*

and produce seven rows of query results. Similarly, the following three expressions are completely equivalent and produce twelve rows of query results, because the duplicates are retained:

```
A UNION ALL (B UNION ALL C)

(A UNION ALL B) UNION ALL C

(A UNION ALL C) UNION ALL B
```

However, if the unions involve a mixture of UNION and UNION ALL, the order of evaluation matters. If this expression:

```
A UNION ALL B UNION C
```

is interpreted as:

```
A UNION ALL (B UNION C)
```

then it produces ten rows of query results (six from the inner UNION, plus four rows from Table A). However, if it is interpreted as

```
(A UNION ALL B) UNION C
```

then it produces only four rows, because the outer UNION eliminates all duplicate rows. For this reason, it's always a good idea to use parentheses in UNIONs of three or more tables to specify the order of evaluation intended.

Summary

This chapter is the first of four chapters about SQL queries. It described the following query features:

- The SELECT statement is used to express a SQL query. Every SELECT statement produces a table of query results containing one or more columns and zero or more rows.
- The FROM clause specifies the table(s) containing the data to be retrieved by a query.
- The SELECT clause specifies the column(s) of data to be included in the query results, which can be columns of data from the database, or calculated columns.
- The WHERE clause selects the rows to be included in the query results by applying a search condition to rows of the database.
- A search condition can select rows by comparing values, by checking a value against a range or set of values, by matching a string pattern, and by checking for NULL values.
- Simple search conditions can be combined with AND, OR, and NOT to form more complex search conditions.
- The ORDER BY clause specifies that the query results should be sorted in ascending or descending order, based on the values of one or more columns.
- The UNION operation can be used within a SELECT statement to combine two or more sets of query results into a single set.

Chapter Seven

Multi-Table
Queries (Joins)

M any useful queries request data from two or more tables in the database. For example, these requests for data in the sample database draw data from two, three, or four tables:

■ List the salespeople and the offices where they work (SALESREPS and OFFICES tables).

■ List each order placed last week, showing the order amount, the name of the customer who placed it, and the name of the product ordered (ORDERS, CUSTOMERS, and SALESREPS tables).

■ Show all orders taken by salespeople in the Eastern region, showing the product description and salesperson (ORDERS, SALESREPS, OFFICES, and PRODUCTS tables).

SQL allows you to retrieve data that answers these requests through multi-table queries that *join* data from two or more tables. These queries and the SQL join facility are described in this chapter.

A Two-Table Query Example

The best way to understand the facilities that SQL provides for multi-table queries is to start with a simple request that combines data from two different tables:

"List all orders, showing the order number and amount, and the name and account balance of the customer who placed it."

The four specific data items requested are clearly stored in two different tables, as shown in Figure 7-1:

■ The ORDERS table contains the order number and amount of each order, but doesn't have customer names or credit limits.

■ The CUSTOMERS table contains the customer names and balances, but it lacks any information about orders.

There is a link between these two tables, however. In each row of the ORDERS table, the CUST column contains the customer number of the customer who placed the order, which matches the value in the CUST_NUM column in one of the rows in the CUSTOMERS table. Clearly, the SELECT statement that handles the request must somehow use this link between the tables to generate its query results.

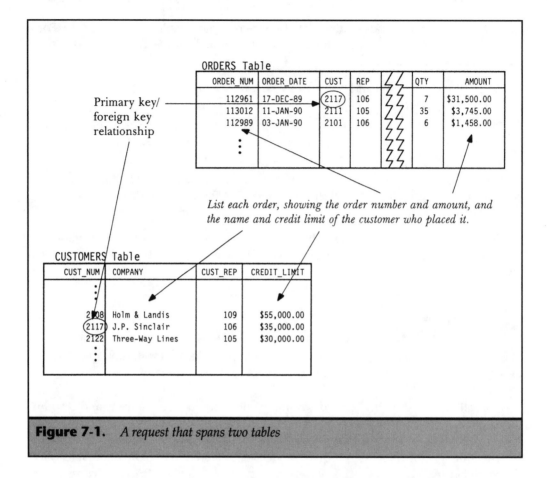

Primary key/
foreign key
relationship

List each order, showing the order number and amount, and
the name and credit limit of the customer who placed it.

Figure 7-1. *A request that spans two tables*

Before examining the SELECT statement for the query, it's instructive to think
about how you would manually handle the request, using paper and pencil. Figure 7-2
shows what you would probably do:

1. Start by writing down the four column names for the query results. Then move
   to the ORDERS table, and start with the first order.

2. Look across the row to find the order number (112961) and the order amount
   ($31,500.00) and copy both values to the first row of query results.

3. Look across the row to find the number of the customer who placed the order
   (2117), and move to the CUSTOMERS table to find customer number 2117 by
   searching the CUST_NUM column.

4. Move across the row of the CUSTOMERS table to find the customer's name ("J.P.
   Sinclair") and credit limit ($35,000.00), and copy them to the query results table.

5. You've generated a row of query results! Move back to the ORDERS table, and go to the next row. Repeat the process, starting with Step 2, until you run out of orders.

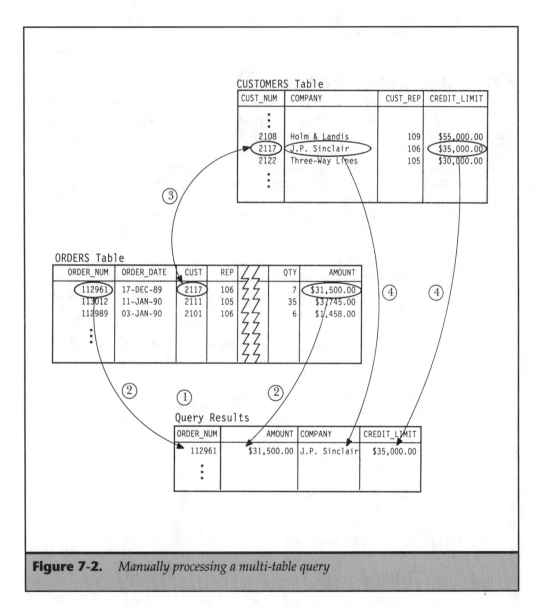

Figure 7-2. *Manually processing a multi-table query*

Of course this isn't the only way to generate the query results, but regardless of how you do it, two things will be true:

■ Each row of query results will draw its data from a specific *pair* of rows, one from the ORDERS table and one from the CUSTOMERS table.

■ The pair of rows will be found by matching the contents of *corresponding columns* from the tables.

Simple Joins (Equi-Joins)

The process of forming pairs of rows by matching the contents of related columns is called *joining* the tables. The resulting table (containing data from both of the original tables) is called a *join* between the two tables. (A join based on an exact match between two columns is more precisely called an *equi-join*. Joins can also be based on other kinds of column comparisons, as described later in this chapter.)

Joins are the foundation of multi-table query processing in SQL. All of the data in a relational database is stored in its columns as explicit data values, so that all possible relationships between tables can be formed by matching the contents of related columns. Joins thus provide a powerful facility for *exercising* the data relationships in a database.

Because SQL handles multi-table queries by matching columns, it should come as no surprise that the SELECT statement for a multi-table query must contain a search condition that specifies the column match. Here is the SELECT statement for the query that was performed manually in Figure 7-2:

List all orders showing order number, amount, customer name, and the customer's credit limit.

```
SELECT ORDER_NUM, AMOUNT, COMPANY, CREDIT_LIMIT
  FROM ORDERS, CUSTOMERS
 WHERE CUST = CUST_NUM

ORDER_NUM      AMOUNT COMPANY              CREDIT_LIMIT
---------  ----------- --------------------  ------------
   112989   $1,458.00 Jones Mfg.             $65,000.00
   112968   $3,978.00 First Corp.            $65,000.00
   112963   $3,276.00 Acme Mfg.              $50,000.00
   112987  $27,500.00 Acme Mfg.              $50,000.00
   112983     $702.00 Acme Mfg.              $50,000.00
   113027   $4,104.00 Acme Mfg.              $50,000.00
   112993   $1,896.00 Fred Lewis Corp.       $65,000.00
   113065   $2,130.00 Fred Lewis Corp.       $65,000.00
```

```
113036    $22,500.00 Ace International   $35,000.00
113034       $632.00 Ace International   $35,000.00
113058     $1,480.00 Holm & Landis       $55,000.00
113055       $150.00 Holm & Landis       $55,000.00
113003     $5,625.00 Holm & Landis       $55,000.00
       .
       .
       .
```

This looks just like the queries from the previous chapter, with two new features. First, the FROM clause lists two tables instead of just one. Second, the search condition:

```
CUST = CUST_NUM
```

compares columns from two different tables. We call these two columns the *matching* columns for the two tables. Like all search conditions, this one restricts the rows that appear in the query results. Because this is a two-table query, the search condition restricts the *pairs* of rows that generate the query results. In fact, the search condition specifies the same matching columns you used in the paper-and-pencil query processing. It actually captures the spirit of the manual column matching very well, saying:

"Generate query results only for pairs of rows where the customer number (CUST) in the ORDERS table matches the customer number (CUST_NUM) in the CUSTOMERS table."

Notice that the SELECT statement doesn't say anything about *how* SQL should execute the query. There is no mention of "starting with orders" or "starting with customers." Instead, the query tells SQL *what* the query results should look like, and leaves it up to SQL to decide how to generate them.

Parent/Child Queries

The most common multi-table queries involve two tables that have a natural parent/child relationship. The query about orders and customers in the preceding section is an example of such a query. Each order (child) has an associated customer (parent), and each customer (parent) can have many associated orders (children). The pairs of rows that generate the query results are parent/child row combinations.

You may recall from Chapter 4 that foreign keys and primary keys create the parent/child relationship in a SQL database. The table containing the foreign key is the child in the relationship; the table with the primary key is the parent. To exercise the parent/child relationship in a query, you must specify a search condition that compares the foreign key and the primary key. Here is another example of a query that exercises a parent/child relationship, shown in Figure 7-3:

List each salesperson and the city and region where they work.

```
SELECT NAME, CITY, REGION
  FROM SALESREPS, OFFICES
 WHERE REP_OFFICE = OFFICE

NAME               CITY           REGION
--------------     ------------   --------
Mary Jones         New York       Eastern
Sam Clark          New York       Eastern
Bob Smith          Chicago        Eastern
Paul Cruz          Chicago        Eastern
Dan Roberts        Chicago        Eastern
Bill Adams         Atlanta        Eastern
Sue Smith          Los Angeles    Western
Larry Fitch        Los Angeles    Western
Nancy Angelli      Denver         Western
```

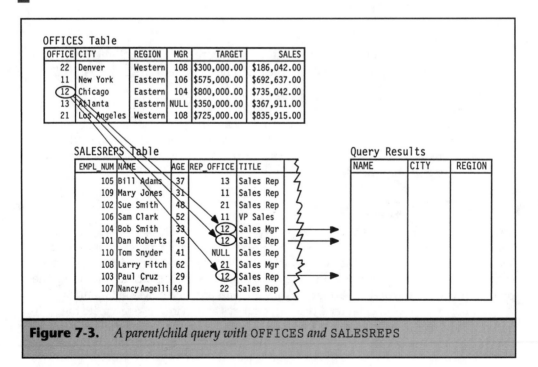

Figure 7-3. *A parent/child query with* OFFICES *and* SALESREPS

The SALESREPS (child) table contains REP_OFFICE, a foreign key for the OFFICES (parent) table. This relationship is used to find the correct OFFICE row for each salesperson, so that the correct city and region can be included in the query results.

Here's another query involving the same two tables, but with the parent and child roles reversed, as shown in Figure 7-4:

List the offices and the names and titles of their managers.

```
SELECT CITY, NAME, TITLE
  FROM OFFICES, SALESREPS
 WHERE MGR = EMPL_NUM
```

```
CITY            NAME            TITLE
------------    -------------   ----------
Chicago         Bob Smith       Sales Mgr
Atlanta         Bill Adams      Sales Rep
New York        Sam Clark       VP Sales
Denver          Larry Fitch     Sales Mgr
Los Angeles     Larry Fitch     Sales Mgr
```

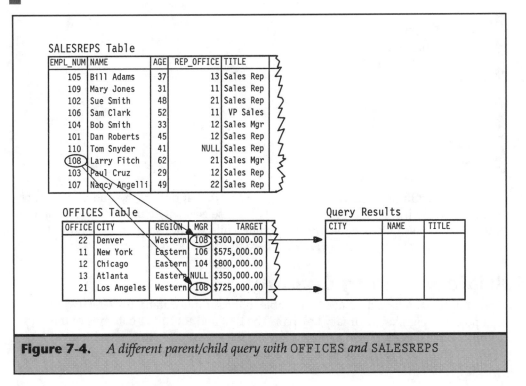

Figure 7-4. *A different parent/child query with* OFFICES *and* SALESREPS

The OFFICES (child) table contains MGR, a foreign key for the SALESREPS (parent) table. This relationship is used to find the correct SALESREPS row for each salesperson, so that the correct name and title of the manager can be included in the query results.

SQL does not require that the matching columns be included in the results of a multi-table query. They will often be omitted in practice, as in the two preceding examples. That's because primary keys and foreign keys are often id numbers (such as the office numbers and employee numbers in the examples), which humans find hard to remember, while the associated names (cities, regions, names, titles) are easier to understand. It's quite common for id numbers to be used in the WHERE clause to join two tables, and for more descriptive names to be specified in the SELECT clause to generate columns of query results.

Joins with Row Selection Criteria

The search condition that specifies the matching columns in a multi-table query can be combined with other search conditions to further restrict the contents of the query results. Suppose you want to rerun the preceding query, showing only offices with large sales targets:

List the offices with a target over $600,000.

```
SELECT CITY, NAME, TITLE
  FROM OFFICES, SALESREPS
 WHERE MGR = EMPL_NUM
   AND TARGET > 600000.00

CITY          NAME              TITLE
------------  ----------------  ----------
Chicago       Bob Smith         Sales Mgr
Los Angeles   Larry Fitch       Sales Mgr
```

With the additional search condition, the rows that appear in the query results are further restricted. The first test (MGR=EMPL_NUM) selects only pairs of OFFICES and SALESREPS rows that have the proper parent/child relationship; the second test further selects only those pairs of rows where the office is above target.

Multiple Matching Columns

The ORDERS table and the PRODUCTS table in the sample database are related by a composite foreign key/primary key pair. The MFR and PRODUCT columns of the ORDERS table together form a foreign key for the PRODUCTS table, matching its MFR_ID and PRODUCT_ID columns, respectively. To join the tables based on this parent/child relationship, you must specify *both* pairs of matching columns, as shown in this example:

List all the orders, showing amounts and product descriptions.

```
SELECT ORDER_NUM, AMOUNT, DESCRIPTION
  FROM ORDERS, PRODUCTS
 WHERE MFR = MFR_ID
   AND PRODUCT = PRODUCT_ID

ORDER_NUM      AMOUNT DESCRIPTION
--------- ----------- ------------------
   113027  $4,104.00 Size 2 Widget
   112992    $760.00 Size 2 Widget
   113012  $3,745.00 Size 3 Widget
   112968  $3,978.00 Size 4 Widget
   112963  $3,276.00 Size 4 Widget
   112983    $702.00 Size 4 Widget
   113055    $150.00 Widget Adjuster
   113057    $600.00 Widget Adjuster
      .
      .
      .
```

The search condition in the query tells SQL that the related pairs of rows from the ORDERS and PRODUCTS tables are those where both pairs of matching columns contain the same values. Multi-column joins are less common than single-column joins, and are usually found in queries involving compound foreign keys such as this one.

Queries with Three or More Tables

SQL can combine data from three or more tables using the same basic techniques used for two-table queries. Here is a simple example of a three-table join:

List orders over $25,000, including the name of the salesperson who took the order and the name of the customer who placed it.

```
SELECT ORDER_NUM, AMOUNT, COMPANY, NAME
  FROM ORDERS, CUSTOMERS, SALESREPS
 WHERE CUST = CUST_NUM
   AND REP = EMPL_NUM
   AND AMOUNT > 25000.00
```

```
ORDER_NUM      AMOUNT COMPANY              NAME
--------- ----------- -------------------- --------------
   112987 $27,500.00 Acme Mfg.            Bill Adams
   113069 $31,350.00 Chen Associates      Nancy Angelli
   113045 $45,000.00 Zetacorp             Larry Fitch
   112961 $31,500.00 J.P. Sinclair        Sam Clark
```

This query uses two foreign keys in the ORDERS table, as shown in Figure 7-5. The CUST column is a foreign key for the CUSTOMERS table, linking each order to the customer who placed it. The REP column is a foreign key for the SALESREPS table, linking each order to the salesperson who took it. Informally speaking, the query links each order to its associated customer and salesperson.

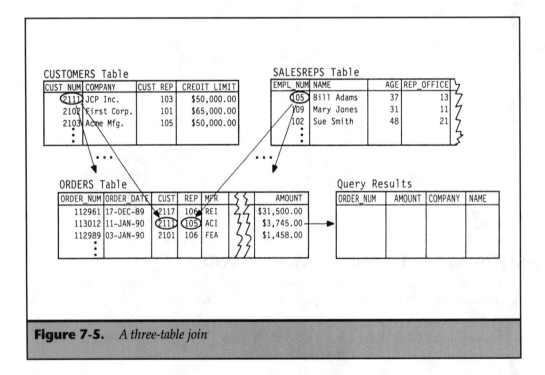

Figure 7-5. *A three-table join*

Here is another three-table query that uses a different arrangement of parent/child relationships:

List the orders over $25,000, showing the name of the customer who placed the order and the name of the salesperson assigned to that customer.

```
SELECT ORDER_NUM, AMOUNT, COMPANY, NAME
  FROM ORDERS, CUSTOMERS, SALESREPS
 WHERE CUST = CUST_NUM
   AND CUST_REP = EMPL_NUM
   AND AMOUNT > 25000.00
```

ORDER_NUM	AMOUNT	COMPANY	NAME
112987	$27,500.00	Acme Mfg.	Bill Adams
113069	$31,350.00	Chen Associates	Paul Cruz
113045	$45,000.00	Zetacorp	Larry Fitch
112961	$31,500.00	J.P. Sinclair	Sam Clark

Figure 7-6 shows the relationships exercised by this query. The first relationship again uses the CUST column from the ORDERS table as a foreign key to the CUSTOMERS table. The second uses the CUST_REP column from the CUSTOMERS table as a foreign key to the SALESREPS table. Informally speaking, this query links each order to its customer, and each customer to their salesperson.

It's not uncommon to find three-table or even four-table queries used in production SQL applications. Even within the confines of the small, five-table sample database, it's not too hard to find a four-table query that makes sense:

List the orders over $25,000, showing the name of the customer who placed the order, the customer's salesperson, and the office where the salesperson works.

```
SELECT ORDER_NUM, AMOUNT, COMPANY, NAME, CITY
  FROM ORDERS, CUSTOMERS, SALESREPS, OFFICES
 WHERE CUST = CUST_NUM
   AND CUST_REP = EMPL_NUM
   AND REP_OFFICE = OFFICE
   AND AMOUNT > 25000.00
```

```
ORDER_NUM       AMOUNT COMPANY              NAME            CITY
---------- ------------ ------------------- --------------- ---------
   112987  $27,500.00 Acme Mfg.            Bill Adams      Atlanta
   113069  $31,350.00 Chen Associates      Paul Cruz       Chicago
   113045  $45,000.00 Zetacorp             Larry Fitch     Los Angeles
   112961  $31,500.00 J.P. Sinclair        Sam Clark       New York
```

Figure 7-7 shows the parent/child relationships in this query. Logically, it extends the *join* sequence of the previous example one more step, linking an order to its customer, the customer to their salesperson, and the salesperson to their office.

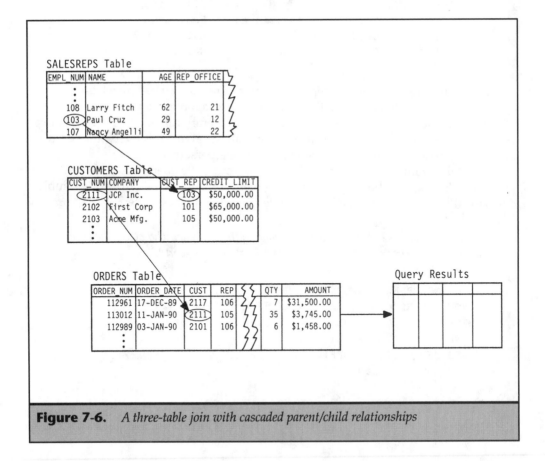

Figure 7-6. *A three-table join with cascaded parent/child relationships*

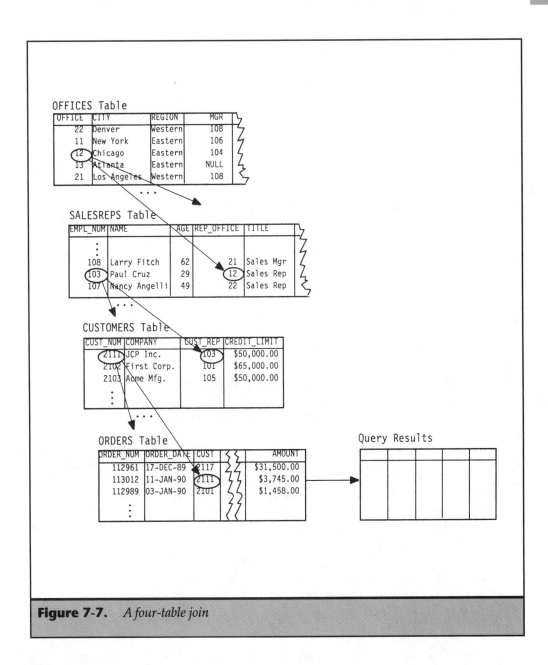

Figure 7-7. *A four-table join*

Other Equi-Joins

The vast majority of multi-table queries are based on parent/child relationships, but SQL does not require that the matching columns be related as a foreign key and primary key. Any pair of columns from two tables can serve as matching columns, provided they have comparable data types. Here is an example of a query that uses a pair of dates as matching columns:

Find all orders received on days when a new salesperson was hired.

```
SELECT ORDER_NUM, AMOUNT, ORDER_DATE, NAME
  FROM ORDERS, SALESREPS
 WHERE ORDER_DATE = HIRE_DATE

ORDER_NUM       AMOUNT ORDER_DATE NAME
--------- ------------ ---------- --------------
   112968    $3,978.00 12-OCT-89  Mary Jones
   112979   $15,000.00 12-OCT-89  Mary Jones
   112975    $2,100.00 12-OCT-89  Mary Jones
   112968    $3,978.00 12-OCT-89  Larry Fitch
   112979   $15,000.00 12-OCT-89  Larry Fitch
   112975    $2,100.00 12-OCT-89  Larry Fitch
```

The results of this query come from pairs of rows in the ORDERS and SALESREPS tables where the ORDER_DATE happens to match the HIRE_DATE for the salesperson, as shown in Figure 7-8. Neither of these columns is a foreign key or a primary key, and the relationship between the pairs of rows is admittedly a strange one—the only thing the matched orders and salespeople have in common is that they happen to have the same dates. However, SQL happily joins the tables anyway.

Matching columns like the ones in this example generate a many-to-many relationship between the two tables. There can be many orders that share a single salesperson's hire date, and more than one salesperson may have been hired on a given order's order date. For example, note that three different orders (112968, 112975, and 112979) were received on October 12, 1989, and two different salespeople (Larry Fitch and Mary Jones) were hired that same day. The three orders and two salespeople produce six rows of query results.

This many-to-many relationship is different from the one-to-many relationship created by primary key/foreign key matching columns. The situation can be summarized as follows:

■ Joins that match primary keys to foreign keys always create one-to-many, parent/child relationships.

■ Other joins may also generate one-to-many relationships, if the matching column in at least one of the tables has unique values for all rows of the table.

■ In general, joins on arbitrary matching columns generate many-to-many relationships.

Note that these three different situations have nothing to do with how you write the SELECT statement that expresses the join. All three types of joins are written the same way—by including a comparison test for the matching column pairs in the WHERE clause. Nonetheless, it's useful to think about joins in this way to understand how to turn an English-language request into the correct SELECT statement.

Non-Equi-Joins

The term "join" applies to any query that combines data from two tables by comparing the values in a pair of columns from the tables. Although joins based on equality

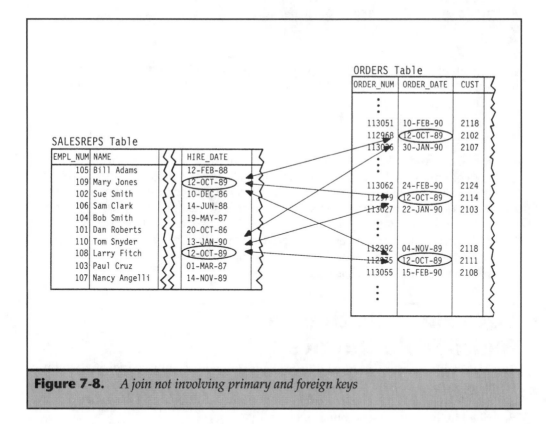

Figure 7-8. *A join not involving primary and foreign keys*

between matching columns (equi-joins) are by far the most common joins, SQL also allows you to join tables based on other comparison operators. Here's an example where a greater than (>) comparison test is used as the basis for a join:

List all combinations of salespeople and offices where the salesperson's quota is more than the office's target.

```
SELECT NAME, QUOTA, CITY, TARGET
  FROM SALESREPS, OFFICES
 WHERE QUOTA > TARGET
```

NAME	QUOTA	CITY	TARGET
Bill Adams	$350,000.00	Denver	$300,000.00
Sue Smith	$350,000.00	Denver	$300,000.00
Larry Fitch	$350,000.00	Denver	$300,000.00

As in all two-table queries, each row of the query results comes from a pair of rows, in this case from the SALESREPS and OFFICES tables. The search condition:

```
QUOTA > TARGET
```

selects pairs of rows where the QUOTA column from the SALESREPS row exceeds the TARGET column from the OFFICES row. Note that the pairs of SALESREPS and OFFICES rows selected are related *only* in this way; it is specifically not required that the SALESREPS row represent someone who works in the office represented by the OFFICES row. Admittedly, the example is a bit farfetched, and it illustrates why joins based on inequalities are not very common. However, they can be useful in decision-support applications and other applications that explore more complex interrelationships in the database.

SQL Considerations for Multi-Table Queries

The multi-table queries described thus far have not required any special SQL syntax or language features beyond those described for single-table queries. However, some multi-table queries cannot be expressed without the additional SQL language features described in the following sections. Specifically:

- *Qualified column names* are sometimes needed in multi-table queries to eliminate ambiguous column references.

- *All-column selections* (SELECT *) have a special meaning for multi-table queries.
- *Self-joins* can be used to create a multi-table query that relates a table to itself.
- *Table aliases* can be used in the FROM clause to simplify qualified column names and allow unambiguous column references in self-joins.

Qualified Column Names

The sample database includes several instances where two tables contain columns with the same name. The OFFICES table and the SALESREPS table, for example, both have a column named SALES. The column in the OFFICES table contains year-to-date sales for each office; the one in the SALESREPS table contains year-to-date sales for each salesperson. Normally, there is no confusion between the two columns, because the FROM clause determines which of them is appropriate in any given query, as in these examples:

Show the cities where sales exceed target.

```
SELECT CITY, SALES
  FROM OFFICES
 WHERE SALES > TARGET
```

Show all salespeople with sales over $350,000.

```
SELECT NAME, SALES
  FROM SALESREPS
 WHERE SALES > 350000.00
```

However, here is a query where the duplicate names cause a problem:

Show the name, sales, and office for each salesperson.

```
SELECT NAME, SALES, CITY
  FROM SALESREPS, OFFICES
 WHERE REP_OFFICE = OFFICE

Error: Ambiguous column name "SALES"
```

Although the English description of the query implies that you want the SALES column in the SALESREPS table, the SQL query is ambiguous. To eliminate the ambiguity, you must use a qualified column name to identify the column. Recall from Chapter 5 that a qualified column name specifies the name of a column and the table containing the column. The qualified names of the two SALES columns in the sample database are:

OFFICES.SALES and SALESREPS.SALES

A qualified column name can be used in a SELECT statement anywhere that a column name is permitted. The table specified in the qualified column name must, of course, match one of the tables specified in the FROM list. Here is a corrected version of the previous query that uses a qualified column name:

Show the name, sales, and office for each salesperson.

```
SELECT NAME, SALESREPS.SALES, CITY
   FROM SALESREPS, OFFICES
  WHERE REP_OFFICE = OFFICE

NAME              SALESREPS.SALES  CITY
--------------    ---------------  -----------
Mary Jones        $392,725.00      New York
Sam Clark         $299,912.00      New York
Bob Smith         $142,594.00      Chicago
Paul Cruz         $286,775.00      Chicago
Dan Roberts       $305,673.00      Chicago
Bill Adams        $367,911.00      Atlanta
Sue Smith         $474,050.00      Los Angeles
Larry Fitch       $361,865.00      Los Angeles
Nancy Angelli     $186,042.00      Denver
```

Using qualified column names in a multi-table query is always a good idea. The disadvantage, of course, is that they make the query text longer. When using interactive SQL, you may want to first try a query with unqualified column names and let SQL find any ambiguous columns. If SQL reports an error, you can go back and edit your query to qualify the ambiguous columns.

All-Column Selections

As discussed in Chapter 6, "SELECT *" can be used to select all columns of the table named in the FROM clause. In a multi-table query, the asterisk selects all columns of all tables in the FROM clause. The following query, for example, would produce fifteen columns of query results—the nine columns from the SALESREPS table followed by the six columns from the OFFICES table:

Tell me all about salespeople and the offices where they work.

```
SELECT *
  FROM SALESREPS, OFFICES
 WHERE REP_OFFICE = OFFICE
```

Obviously, the SELECT * form of a query becomes much less practical when there are two, three, or more tables in the FROM clause.

Many SQL dialects treat the asterisk as a special kind of wildcard column name that is expanded into a list of columns. In these dialects, the asterisk can be qualified with a table name, just like a qualified column reference. In the following query, the select item SALESREPS.* is expanded into a list containing only the columns found in the SALESREPS table:

Tell me all about salespeople and the places where they work.

```
SELECT SALESREPS.*, CITY, REGION
  FROM SALESREPS, OFFICES
 WHERE REP_OFFICE = OFFICE
```

The query would produce eleven columns of query results—Mthe nine columns of the SALESREPS table, followed by the two other columns explicitly requested from the OFFICES table. Although this type of "qualified all-columns" select item is supported in many brands of SQL-based DBMS, it is not permitted by the ANSI/ISO standard.

Self-Joins

Some multi-table queries involve a relationship that a table has with itself. For example, suppose you want to list the names of all salespeople and their managers. Each salesperson appears as a row in the SALESREPS table, and the MANAGER column contains the employee number of the salesperson's manager. It would appear that the MANAGER column should be a foreign key for the table that holds data about managers. In fact it is—it's a foreign key for the SALESREPS table itself!

If you tried to express this query like any other two-table query involving a foreign key/primary key match, it would look like this:

```
SELECT NAME, NAME
  FROM SALESREPS, SALESREPS
 WHERE MANAGER = EMPL_NUM
```

This SELECT statement is illegal because of the duplicate reference to the SALESREPS table in the FROM clause. You might also try eliminating the second reference to the SALESREPS table:

```
SELECT NAME, NAME
  FROM SALESREPS
 WHERE MANAGER = EMPL_NUM
```

This query is legal, but it won't do what you want it to do. It's a single-table query, so SQL goes through the SALESREPS table one row at a time, applying the search condition:

```
MANAGER = EMPL_NUM
```

The rows that satisfy this condition are those where the two columns have the same value—that is, rows where a salesperson is their own manager. There are no such rows, so the query would produce no results.

To understand how SQL solves this problem, imagine there were *two identical copies* of the SALESREPS table, one named EMPS, containing employees, and one named MGRS, containing managers, as shown in Figure 7-9. The MANAGER column of the EMPS table would then be a foreign key for the MGRS table, and the following query would work:

List the names of salespeople and their managers.

```
SELECT EMPS.NAME, MGRS.NAME
  FROM EMPS, MGRS
 WHERE EMPS.MANAGER = MGRS.EMPL_NUM
```

Because the columns in the two tables have identical names, all of the column references are qualified. Otherwise, this looks like an ordinary two-table query.

SQL uses exactly this "imaginary duplicate table" approach to join a table to itself. Instead of actually duplicating the contents of the table, SQL simply lets you refer to it

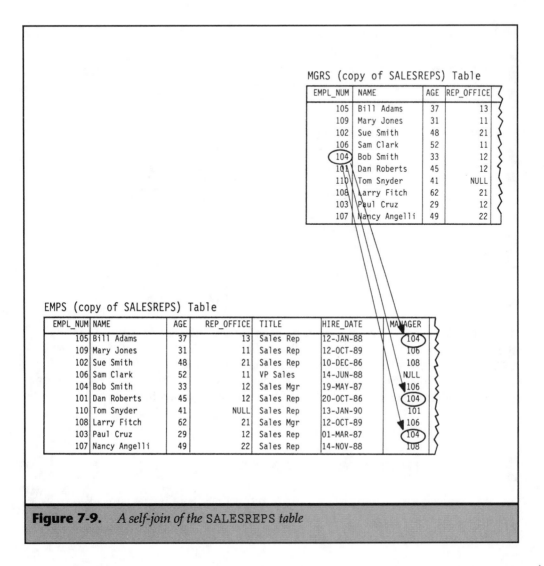

Figure 7-9. *A self-join of the* SALESREPS *table*

by a different name, called a *table alias*. Here's the same query, written using the aliases EMPS and MGRS for the SALESREPS table:

List the names of salespeople and their managers.

```
SELECT EMPS.NAME, MGRS.NAME
  FROM SALESREPS EMPS, SALESREPS MGRS
 WHERE EMPS.MANAGER = MGRS.EMPL_NUM
```

```
EMPS.NAME        MGRS.NAME
--------------   --------------
Tom Snyder       Dan Roberts
Bill Adams       Bob Smith
Dan Roberts      Bob Smith
Paul Cruz        Bob Smith
Mary Jones       Sam Clark
Bob Smith        Sam Clark
Larry Fitch      Sam Clark
Sue Smith        Larry Fitch
Nancy Angelli    Larry Fitch
```

The FROM clause assigns an alias to each "copy" of the SALESREPS table by specifying the alias name immediately after the actual table name. As the example shows, when a FROM clause contains a table alias, the alias must be used to identify the table in qualified column references. Of course it's really only necessary to use an alias for one of the two table occurrences in this query. It could just as easily have been written:

```
SELECT SALESREPS.NAME, MGRS.NAME
  FROM SALESREPS, SALESREPS MGRS
 WHERE SALESREPS.MANAGER = MGRS.EMPL_NUM
```

Here the alias MGRS is assigned to one "copy" of the table, while the table's own name is used for the other copy.

Here are some additional examples of self-joins:

List salespeople with a higher quota than their manager.

```
SELECT SALESREPS.NAME, SALESREPS.QUOTA, MGRS.QUOTA
  FROM SALESREPS, SALESREPS MGRS
 WHERE SALESREPS.MANAGER = MGRS.EMPL_NUM
   AND SALESREPS.QUOTA > MGRS.QUOTA
```

```
SALESREPS.NAME  SALESREPS.QUOTA    MGRS.QUOTA
--------------  ---------------  ------------
Bill Adams         $350,000.00  $200,000.00
Dan Roberts        $300,000.00  $200,000.00
Paul Cruz          $275,000.00  $200,000.00
Mary Jones         $300,000.00  $275,000.00
Larry Fitch        $350,000.00  $275,000.00
```

List salespeople who work in different offices than their manager, showing the name and office where each works.

```
SELECT EMPS.NAME, EMP_OFFICE.CITY, MGRS.NAME, MGR_OFFICE.CITY
  FROM SALESREPS EMPS, SALESREPS MGRS,
       OFFICES EMP_OFFICE, OFFICES MGR_OFFICE
 WHERE EMPS.REP_OFFICE = EMP_OFFICE.OFFICE
   AND MGRS.REP_OFFICE = MGR_OFFICE.OFFICE
   AND EMPS.MANAGER = MGRS.EMPL_NUM
   AND EMPS.REP_OFFICE <> MGRS.REP_OFFICE
```

```
EMPS.NAME       EMP_OFFICE.CITY MGRS.NAME       MGR_OFFICE.CITY
--------------  --------------- --------------  ---------------

Bob Smith       Chicago         Sam Clark       New York
Bill Adams      Atlanta         Bob Smith       Chicago
Larry Fitch     Los Angeles     Sam Clark       New York
Nancy Angelli   Denver          Larry Fitch     Los Angeles
```

Table Aliases

As described in the previous section, table aliases are required in queries involving self-joins. However, you can use an alias in any query. For example, if a query refers to another user's table, or if the name of a table is very long, the table name can become tedious to type as a column qualifier. This query, which references the BIRTHDAYS table owned by the user named SAM:

List names, quotas, and birthdays of salespeople.

```
SELECT SALESREPS.NAME, QUOTA, SAM.BIRTHDAYS.BIRTH_DATE
  FROM SALESREPS, BIRTHDAYS
 WHERE SALESREPS.NAME = SAM.BIRTHDAYS.NAME
```

becomes easier to read and type when the aliases S and B are used for the two tables:

List names, quotas, and birthdays of salespeople.

```
SELECT S.NAME, S.QUOTA, B.BIRTH_DATE
  FROM SALESREPS S, SAM.BIRTHDAYS B
 WHERE S.NAME = B.NAME
```

Figure 7-10 shows the form of the FROM clause for a multi-table SELECT statement, complete with table aliases. The clause has two important functions:

- The FROM clause identifies all of the tables that contribute data to the query results. Any columns referenced in the SELECT statement must come from one of the tables named in the FROM clause. (There is an exception for *outer* references contained in a subquery, as described in Chapter 9.)

- The FROM clause determines the *tag* that is used to identify the table in qualified column references within the SELECT statement. If a table alias is specified, it becomes the table tag; otherwise the table's name, exactly as it appears in the FROM clause, becomes the tag.

The only requirement for table tags in the FROM clause is that all of the table tags in a given FROM clause must be distinct from each other. The SQL2 specification optionally allows the keyword AS to appear between a table name and table alias. While this makes the FROM clause easier to read, it may not yet be supported in your specific SQL implementation.

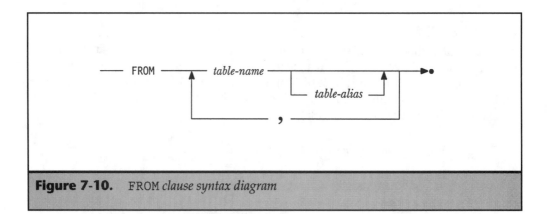

Figure 7-10. FROM *clause syntax diagram*

Multi-Table Query Performance

As the number of tables in a query grows, the amount of effort required to carry it out increases rapidly. The SQL language itself places no limit on the number of tables joined by a query. Some SQL products do limit the number of tables, with a limit of about eight tables being fairly common. The high processing cost of queries that join many tables imposes an even lower practical limit in many applications.

In on-line transaction processing (OLTP) applications, it's common for a query to involve only one or two tables. In these applications, response time is critical—the user typically enters one or two items of data and needs a response from the database within a second or two. Here are some typical OLTP queries for the sample database:

- The user enters a customer number into a form, and the DBMS retrieves the customer's credit limit, account balance, and other data (a single-table query).

- A cash register scans a product number from a package, and retrieves the product's name and price from the database (a single-table query).

- The user enters a salesperson's name, and the program lists the current orders for that salesperson (a two-table inquiry).

In decision-support applications, by contrast, it's common for a query to involve many different tables and exercise complex relationships in the database. In these applications, the query results are often used to help make expensive decisions, so a query that requires several minutes or even several hours to complete is perfectly acceptable. Here are some typical decision-support queries for the sample database:

- The user enters an office name, and the program lists the 25 largest orders taken by salespeople in that office (a three-table query).

- A report summarizes sales by product type for each salesperson, showing which salespeople are selling which products (a three-table query).

- A manager considers opening a new Seattle sales office, and runs a query analyzing the impact on orders, products, customers, and the salespeople who call on them (a four-table query).

The Structure of a Join

For simple joins, it's fairly easy to write the correct SELECT statement based on an English-language request, or to look at a SELECT statement and figure out what it does. When many tables are joined or when the search conditions become complex, however, it becomes very difficult just to look at a SELECT statement and figure out what it means. For this reason, it's useful to define more carefully what a join is and what query results are produced by a given SELECT statement.

Table Multiplication

A join is a special case of a more general combination of data from two tables, known as the *Cartesian product* (or just the *product*) of two tables. The product of two tables is another table (the *product table*), which consists of all possible pairs of rows from the two tables. The columns of the product table are all the columns of the first table, followed by all the columns of the second table. Figure 7-11 shows two small sample tables and their product.

If you specify a two-table query without a WHERE clause, SQL produces the product of the two tables as the query result. For example, this query:

Show all possible combinations of salespeople and cities.

```
SELECT NAME, CITY
   FROM SALESREPS, OFFICES
```

would produce the product of the SALESREPS and OFFICES tables, showing all possible salesperson/city pairs. There would be 50 rows of query results (5 offices * 10 salespeople = 50 combinations). Notice that the SELECT statement is exactly the same

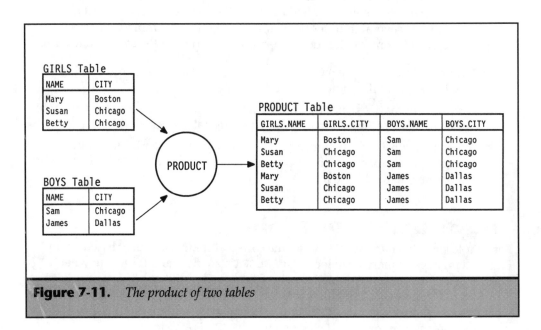

Figure 7-11. *The product of two tables*

one you would use to join the two tables, without the WHERE clause that compares the matching columns, as shown below:

Show all salespeople and the cities where they work.

```
SELECT NAME, CITY
  FROM SALESREPS, OFFICES
 WHERE REP_OFFICE = OFFICE
```

These two queries point out an important relationship between joins and products:

A join between two tables is just the product of the two tables with some of the rows removed. The removed rows are precisely those that do not meet the matching column condition for the join.

Products are important because they are part of the formal definition of how SQL processes a multi-table query, described in the next section.

Rules for Multi-Table Query Processing

Figure 7-12 restates the rules for SQL query processing originally introduced in Figure 6-14, and expands them to include multi-table queries. The rules define the meaning of any multi-table SELECT statement by specifying a procedure that always generates the correct set of query results. To see how the procedure works, consider this query:

List the company name and all orders for customer number 2103.

```
SELECT COMPANY, ORDER_NUM, AMOUNT
  FROM CUSTOMERS, ORDERS
 WHERE CUST_NUM = CUST
   AND CUST_NUM = 2103
 ORDER BY ORDER_NUM
```

COMPANY	ORDER_NUM	AMOUNT
Acme Mfg.	112963	$3,276.00
Acme Mfg.	112983	$702.00
Acme Mfg.	112987	$27,500.00
Acme Mfg.	113027	$4,104.00

To generate the query results for a SELECT statement:

1. If the statement is a UNION of SELECT statements, apply Steps 2 through 5 to each of the statements to generate their individual query results.

2. Form the product of the tables named in the FROM clause. If the FROM clause names a single table, the product is that table.

3. If there is a WHERE clause, apply its search condition to each row of the product table, retaining those rows for which the search condition is TRUE (and discarding those for which it is FALSE or NULL).

4. For each remaining row, calculate the value of each item in the select list to produce a single row of query results. For each column reference, use the value of the column in the current row.

5. If SELECT DISTINCT is specified, eliminate any duplicate rows of query results that were produced.

6. If the statement is a UNION of SELECT statements, merge the query results for the individual statements into a single table of query results. Eliminate duplicate rows unless UNION ALL is specified.

7. If there is an ORDER BY clause, sort the query results as specified.

The rows generated by this procedure comprise the query results.

Figure 7-12. *SQL query processing rules (multi-table queries)*

Following the steps in Figure 7-12:

1. The FROM clause generates all possible combinations of rows from the CUSTOMERS table (21 rows) and the ORDERS table (30 rows), producing a product table of 630 rows.

2. The WHERE clause selects only those rows of the product table where the customer numbers match (CUST_NUM = CUST) and the customer number is the one specified (CUST_NUM = 2103). Only four rows are selected; the other 626 rows are eliminated.

3. The SELECT clause extracts the three requested columns (COMPANY, ORDER_NUM, and ORD_AMOUNT) from each remaining row of the product table to generate four rows of detailed query results.

4. The ORDER BY clause sorts the four rows on the ORDER_NUM column to generate the final query results.

Obviously no SQL-based DBMS would actually carry out the query this way, but the purpose of the definition in Figure 7-12 is not to describe how the query is carried out by a DBMS. Instead, it constitutes a *definition* of "multi-table query."

Outer Joins *

The SQL join operation combines information from two tables by forming *pairs* of related rows from the two tables. The row pairs that make up the joined table are those where the matching columns in each of the two tables have the same value. If one of the rows of a table is unmatched in this process, the join can produce unexpected results, as illustrated by these queries:

List the salespeople and the offices where they work.

```
SELECT NAME, REP_OFFICE
  FROM SALESREPS

NAME             REP_OFFICE
-------------- ----------
Bill Adams               13
Mary Jones               11
Sue Smith                21
Sam Clark                11
Bob Smith                12
Dan Roberts              12
Tom Snyder             NULL
Larry Fitch              21
Paul Cruz                12
Nancy Angelli            22
```

List the salespeople and the cities where they work.

```
SELECT NAME, CITY
  FROM SALESREPS, OFFICES
 WHERE REP_OFFICE = OFFICE

NAME             CITY
-------------- -----------
Mary Jones       New York
Sam Clark        New York
Bob Smith        Chicago
```

```
Paul Cruz       Chicago
Dan Roberts     Chicago
Bill Adams      Atlanta
Sue Smith       Los Angeles
Larry Fitch     Los Angeles
Nancy Angelli   Denver
```

On the surface, you would expect these two queries to produce the same number of rows, but the first query lists ten salespeople, and the second lists only nine. Why? Because Tom Snyder is currently unassigned and has a NULL value in the REP_OFFICE column (which is the matching column for the join). This NULL value doesn't match any of the office numbers in the OFFICES table, so Tom's row in the SALESREPS table is unmatched. As a result, it "vanishes" in the join. The standard SQL join thus has the potential to lose information if the tables being joined contain unmatched rows.

Based on the English-language version of the request, you would probably expect the second query to produce results like these:

List the salespeople and the cities where they work.

```
SELECT NAME, CITY
  FROM SALESREPS, OFFICES
 WHERE REP_OFFICE *= OFFICE

NAME              CITY
--------------    ------------
Tom Snyder        NULL
Mary Jones        New York
Sam Clark         New York
Bob Smith         Chicago
Paul Cruz         Chicago
Dan Roberts       Chicago
Bill Adams        Atlanta
Sue Smith         Los Angeles
Larry Fitch       Los Angeles
Nancy Angelli     Denver
```

These query results are generated by using a different type of join operation, called an *outer join* (indicated by the "*=" notation in the WHERE clause). The outer join is an extension of the standard join described earlier in this chapter, which is sometimes called an *inner join*. The SQL1 standard specifies only the inner join; it does not include the outer join. The earlier IBM SQL products also support only the inner join. However, the outer join is a well-understood and useful part of the relational database model, and it has been implemented in many non-IBM SQL products, including SQL Server, Oracle, and SQLBase. The outer join is also the most natural way to express a certain type of query request, as shown in the remainder of this section.

To understand the outer join, it's useful to move away from the sample database and consider the two simple tables in Figure 7-13. The GIRLS table lists five girls and the cities where they live; the BOYS table lists five boys and the cities where they live. To find the girl/boy pairs who live in the same city, you could use this query, which forms the inner join of the two tables:

List the girls and boys who live in the same city.

```
SELECT *
  FROM GIRLS, BOYS
 WHERE GIRLS.CITY = BOYS.CITY

GIRLS.NAME GIRLS.CITY BOYS.NAME BOYS.CITY
---------- ---------- --------- ---------

Mary       Boston     John      Boston
Mary       Boston     Henry     Boston
Susan      Chicago    Sam       Chicago
Betty      Chicago    Sam       Chicago
```

The inner join produces four rows of query results. Notice that two of the girls (Anne and Nancy) and two of the boys (James and George) are not represented in the query results. These rows cannot be paired with any row from the other table, and so they are missing from the inner join results. Two of the unmatched rows (Anne and James) have valid values in their CITY columns, but they don't match any cities in the opposite table. The other two unmatched rows (Nancy and George) have NULL values in their CITY columns, and by the rules of SQL NULL handling, the NULL value doesn't match *any* other value (even another NULL value).

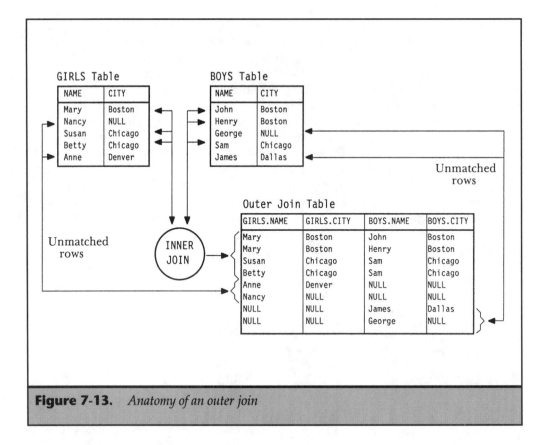

Figure 7-13. *Anatomy of an outer join*

Suppose you wanted to list the girl/boy pairs who share the same cities, and include the unmatched girls and boys in the list. The outer join of the GIRLS and BOYS tables produces exactly this result. Figure 7-14 shows the procedure for constructing the outer join, and the outer join is shown graphically in Figure 7-13. Here is the SQL statement that produces the outer join:

List girls and boys in the same city, including any unmatched girls or boys.

```
SELECT *
  FROM GIRLS, BOYS
 WHERE GIRLS.CITY *=* BOYS.CITY

GIRLS.NAME GIRLS.CITY BOYS.NAME BOYS.CITY
---------- ---------- ---------- ----------
Mary       Boston     John       Boston
Mary       Boston     Henry      Boston
```

```
Susan       Chicago     Sam       Chicago
Betty       Chicago     Sam       Chicago
Anne        Denver      NULL      NULL
Nancy       NULL        NULL      NULL
NULL        NULL        James     Dallas
NULL        NULL        George    NULL
```

The outer join of the two tables contains eight rows. Four of the rows are identical to those of the inner join between the two tables. Two other rows, for Anne and Nancy, come from the unmatched rows of the GIRLS table. These rows have been NULL-*extended* by matching them to an imaginary row of all NULLs in the BOYS table, and added to the query results. The final two rows, for James and George, come from the unmatched rows of the BOYS table. These rows have also been NULL-extended by matching them to an imaginary row of all NULLs in the GIRLS table, and added to the query results.

As this example shows, the outer join is an "information-preserving" join. Every row of the BOYS table is represented in the query results (some more than once). Similarly, every row of the GIRLS table is represented in the query results (again, some more than once).

Left and Right Outer Joins *

Technically, the outer join produced by the previous query is called the *full outer join* of the two tables. Both tables are treated symmetrically in the full outer join. There are two other well-defined outer joins that do not treat the two tables symmetrically.

---

1. Begin with the inner join of the two tables, using matching columns in the normal way.

2. For each row of the first table that is not matched by any row in the second table, add one row to the query results, using the values of the columns in the first table, and assuming a NULL value for all columns of the second table.

3. For each row of the second table that is not matched by any row in the first table, add one row to the query results, using the values of the columns in the second table, and assuming a NULL value for all columns of the first table.

4. The resulting table is the outer join of the two tables.

Figure 7-14.   *Definition of an outer join*

The *left outer join* between two tables is produced by following Step 1 and Step 2 in Figure 7-14, but omitting Step 3. The left outer join thus includes NULL-extended copies of the unmatched rows from the first (left) table, but does not include any unmatched rows from the second (right) table. Here is a left outer join between the GIRLS and BOYS tables:

List girls and boys in the same city and any unmatched girls.

```
SELECT *
  FROM GIRLS, BOYS
 WHERE GIRLS.CITY *= BOYS.CITY

GIRLS.NAME GIRLS.CITY BOYS.NAME BOYS.CITY
---------- ---------- --------- ---------
Mary       Boston     John      Boston
Mary       Boston     Henry     Boston
Susan      Chicago    Sam       Chicago
Betty      Chicago    Sam       Chicago
Anne       Denver     NULL      NULL
Nancy      NULL       NULL      NULL
```

The query produces six rows of query results, showing the matched girl/boy pairs and the unmatched girls. The unmatched boys are missing from the results.

Similarly, the *right outer join* between two tables is produced by following Step 1 and Step 3 in Figure 7-14, but omitting Step 2. The right outer join thus includes NULL-extended copies of the unmatched rows from the second (right) table, but does not include the unmatched rows of the first (left) table. Here is a right outer join between the GIRLS and BOYS tables:

List girls and boys in the same city and any unmatched boys.

```
SELECT *
  FROM GIRLS, BOYS
 WHERE GIRLS.CITY =* BOYS.CITY

GIRLS.NAME GIRLS.CITY BOYS.NAME BOYS.CITY
---------- ---------- --------- ---------
Mary       Boston     John      Boston
Mary       Boston     Henry     Boston
Susan      Chicago    Sam       Chicago
Betty      Chicago    Sam       Chicago
```

```
NULL        NULL        James       Dallas
NULL        NULL        George      NULL
```

This query also produces six rows of query results, showing the matched girl/boy pairs and the unmatched boys. This time the unmatched girls are missing from the results.

In practice, the left and right outer joins are more useful than the full outer join, especially in joins involving foreign key/primary key matching. In such a join, the foreign key column may contain NULL values, causing unmatched rows from the child table (the table containing the foreign key). An asymmetric outer join will include these unmatched child rows in the query results, without also including unmatched parent rows.

Outer Join Notation *

Because the outer join was not part of the SQL1 standard and was not implemented in early IBM SQL products, the DBMS vendors who support the outer join have used various notations in their SQL dialects. The "*=*" notation used in the earlier examples of this section is used by SQL Server. This notation indicates an outer join by appending an asterisk (*) to the comparison test in the WHERE clause that defines the join condition. To indicate the full outer join between two tables, TBL1 and TBL2, on columns COL1 and COL2, an asterisk (*) is placed before and after the standard join operator. The resulting full outer join comparison test looks like this:

```
WHERE COL1 *=* COL2
```

To indicate a left outer join, only the leading asterisk is specified, giving a comparison test like this:

```
WHERE COL1 *= COL2
```

To indicate a right outer join, only the trailing asterisk is specified, giving a comparison test like this:

```
WHERE COL1 =* COL2
```

An outer join can be used with any of the comparison operators using the same notation. For example, a left outer join using a greater than or equal (>=) comparison would produce a comparison test like this:

```
WHERE COL1 *>= COL2
```

Both Oracle and SQLBase also support the outer join operation, but use a different notation. This notation indicates the outer join in the WHERE clause by including a parenthesized plus sign following the column *whose table is to have the imaginary* NULL *row added.* The left outer join produces a search condition that looks like this:

```
WHERE COL1 = COL2 (+)
```

and the right outer join produces a search condition that looks like this:

```
WHERE COL1 (+) = COL2
```

Note that the plus sign appears on the *opposite* side of the comparison from where the asterisk appears in the SQL Server notation. Neither Oracle nor SQLBase supports a full outer join.

Although both of these outer join notations are relatively convenient, they're also somewhat deceiving. The rules for SQL query processing in Figure 7-12 begin by building the product of the two tables, and then eliminating rows that do not meet the WHERE clause search condition. But the product table doesn't include the NULL-extended rows generated by the outer join! How do they get into the query results? The answer is that the WHERE clause must be consulted when forming the product, to see whether the NULL-extended rows are to be included. In addition, a join between two tables may involve more than one pair of matching columns, and it's not clear how the notation should be used when there are two or three matching column pairs.

Other problems with the outer join notation arise when it is extended to three or more tables. Conceptually, it's easy to extend the notion of an outer join to three tables:

```
TBL1 OUTER-JOIN TBL2 OUTER-JOIN TBL3
```

But the result depends upon the order in which the outer join operations are performed. The results of:

```
(TBL1 OUTER-JOIN TBL2) OUTER-JOIN TBL3
```

will in general be different from the results of:

```
TBL1 OUTER-JOIN (TBL2 OUTER-JOIN TBL3)
```

Using either the SQL Server or Oracle/SQLBase notations, it's impossible to specify the evaluation order of the outer joins. Because of this, the results produced by the outer join of three or more tables are not very well defined.

Joins and the SQL2 Standard

Outer joins posed a problem for the writers of the SQL2 standard. Because outer joins are the only way to represent some extremely useful queries, it was important that the SQL2 standard include support for outer joins. In addition, outer joins were supported in many commercial SQL products and were becoming a more important part of the SQL language. However, the methods used to represent outer joins varied widely among the different SQL products, as shown in the preceding sections. Furthermore, the methods used to denote outer joins in commercial products all had deficiencies and had been chosen more because of their minor impact on the SQL language than because of their clarity or correctness.

Against this background, the SQL2 standard specified a brand new method for supporting outer joins, not based on any popular SQL product. The SQL2 specification puts support for outer joins in the FROM clause, with an elaborate syntax that allows the user to specify exactly how the source tables for a query are to be joined together. The extended FROM clause also supports UNION operations among tables, and allows complex combinations of joins and unions.

With these capabilities, the outer join support in the SQL2 standard has two distinct advantages. First, SQL2 standard can express even the most complex of joins. Second, existing database products can support the SQL2 extensions to SQL1 and retain support for their own proprietary outer join syntax without conflict. These advantages come at the expense of some significant added complexity for what had previously been one of the simpler parts of the SQL language.

Inner Joins in SQL2

Figure 7-15 shows a simplified form of the extended SQL2 syntax for the FROM clause. It's easiest to understand all of the options provided by considering each type of join, one by one. For example, the standard inner join of the GIRLS and BOYS tables can be expressed in SQL1 language:

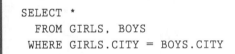

```
SELECT *
  FROM GIRLS, BOYS
 WHERE GIRLS.CITY = BOYS.CITY
```

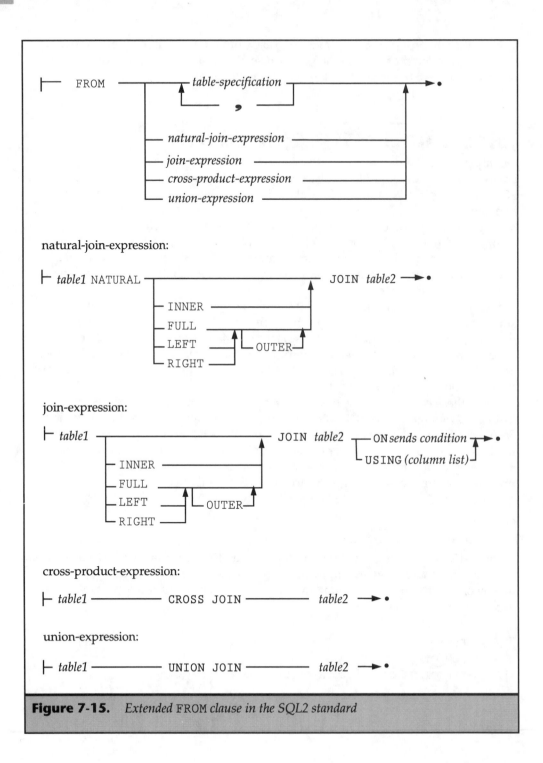

Figure 7-15.   *Extended* FROM *clause in the SQL2 standard*

This is still an acceptable statement in SQL2, but it can also be fully specified as:

```
SELECT *
   FROM GIRLS INNER JOIN BOYS ON GIRLS.CITY = BOYS.CITY
```

Note that the two tables to be joined are explicitly connected by a JOIN operation, and the search condition that describes the join is now specified in an ON clause within the FROM clause. The search condition following the keyword ON can be any search condition that specifies the criteria used to match rows of the two joined tables. For example, assume that the BOYS table and the GIRLS table were each extended by adding an AGE column. Here is a join that matches girl/boy pairs in the same city, and also requires that the boy and girl in each pair be the same age:

```
SELECT *
   FROM GIRLS INNER JOIN BOYS
      ON (GIRLS.CITY = BOYS.CITY) AND (GIRLS.AGE = BOYS.AGE)
```

In these simple two-table joins, the entire contents of the WHERE clause simply moved into the ON clause, and the ON clause doesn't add any functionality to the SQL language. However, recall from earlier in this chapter that in a outer join involving three tables or more, the order in which the joins occur affect the query results. The ON clause provides detailed control over how these multi-table joins are processed, as described later in this chapter.

The SQL2 standard permits another variation on the simple inner join query between the GIRLS and BOYS tables. Because the matching columns in the two tables have the same names and are being compared for equality (which is often the case), an alternative form of the ON clause, specifying a list of matching column names, can be used:

```
SELECT *
   FROM GIRLS INNER JOIN BOYS USING (CITY, AGE)
```

The USING clause specifies a comma-separated list of the matching column names, which must be identical in both tables. It is completely equivalent to the ON clause that specifies each matching column pair explicitly, but it's a lot more compact and therefore easier to understand. Of course, if the matching columns have different names in the BOYS table and GIRLS table, then an ON clause or a WHERE clause with an equals test must be used. The ON clause must also be used if the join does not involve equality of the matching columns. For example, if you wanted to select girl/boy pairs where the girl was required to be older than the boy, you must use an ON clause to specify the join:

```
SELECT *
  FROM GIRLS INNER JOIN BOYS
    ON (GIRLS.CITY = BOYS.CITY AND
        GIRLS.AGE > BOYS.AGE)
```

There is one final variation on this simple query that illustrates another feature of the SQL2 FROM clause. A join between two tables where the matching columns are *exactly* the columns from the two tables that have identical names is called a *natural join*, because usually this is precisely the most "natural" way to join the two tables. The query selecting girl/boy pairs who live in the same city and have the same age can be expressed as a natural join using this SQL2 query:

```
SELECT *
  FROM GIRLS NATURAL INNER JOIN BOYS
```

If the NATURAL keyword is specified, the ON and USING clauses may not be used in the join specification, because the natural join specifically defines the search condition to be used to join the tables—all of the columns with identical column names in the both tables are to be matched.

The SQL2 standard assumes that the "default" join between two tables is an inner join. You can omit keyword "INNER" from any of the preceding examples, and the resulting query remains a legal SQL2 statement with the same meaning.

Outer Joins in SQL2

The SQL2 standard provides complete support for outer joins by extending the language used for inner joins. For example, the full outer join of the GIRLS and BOYS tables (without the AGE columns) is generated by this query:

```
SELECT *
  FROM GIRLS FULL OUTER JOIN BOYS ON GIRLS.CITY = BOYS.CITY
```

As explained earlier in this chapter, the query results will contain a row for each matched girl/boy pair, as well as one row for each unmatched boy, extended with NULL values in the columns from the other, unmatched table. SQL2 allows the same variations for outer joins as for inner joins; the query could also have been written:

```
SELECT *
  FROM GIRLS NATURAL FULL OUTER BOYS
```

or

```
SELECT *
  FROM GIRLS FULL OUTER JOIN BOYS USING (CITY)
```

Just as the keyword INNER is optional in the SQL2 language, the SQL2 standard also allows you to omit the keyword OUTER. The preceding query could also have been written:

```
SELECT *
  FROM GIRLS FULL JOIN BOYS USING (CITY)
```

The DBMS can infer from the word FULL that an outer join is required.

By specifying LEFT or RIGHT instead of FULL, the SQL2 language extends quite naturally to left or right outer joins. Here is the left outer join version of the same query:

```
SELECT *
  FROM GIRLS LEFT OUTER JOIN BOYS USING (CITY)
```

As described earlier in the chapter, the query results will include matched girl/boy pairs and NULL-extended rows for each unmatched row in the GIRLS table (the "left" table join), but it does not include unmatched rows from the BOYS table. Conversely, the right outer join version of the same query, specified like this:

```
SELECT *
  FROM GIRLS RIGHT OUTER JOIN BOYS USING (CITY)
```

includes boy/girl pairs and unmatched rows in the BOYS table (the "right" table in the join), but does not include unmatched rows from the GIRLS table.

Cross Joins and Unions in SQL2

The SQL2 extended FROM clause also supports two other methods for combining data from two tables—Cartesian products (described earlier in this chapter) and unions (described in Chapter 6). Neither of these is strictly a "join" operation, but the SQL2 standard supports them using the same language clauses used to support inner and outer joins. Here is a query that generates the complete product of the GIRLS and BOYS tables:

```
SELECT *
  FROM GIRLS CROSS JOIN BOYS
```

By definition, the Cartesian product (also sometimes called the "cross product", hence the name "CROSS JOIN") contains every possible pair of rows from the two tables. It "multiplies" the two tables, turning a table of 3 girls and a table of 2 boys into a table of six (3 x 2 = 6) boy/girl pairs. There are no "matching columns" or "selection criteria" associated with the cross products, so the ON clause and the USING clause are not allowed.

If the Cartesian product of the GIRLS and BOYS tables is a "multiplication" the union of the two tables is an "addition". The union of the two tables can be specified in SQL2 as:

```
SELECT *
  FROM UNION JOIN BOYS
       GIRLS
```

The result is a five (3 + 2 = 5) row table, listing the NAME and CITY of each boy and girl.

Multi-Table Joins in SQL2

One of the major advantages of the SQL2 extended FROM clause is that it provides a uniform standard for specifying inner and outer joins, products and unions. Another, even more important, advantage is that it allows very clear specification of three-table or four-table joins, products and unions. To build up these more complex joins, any of the join expressions shown in Figure 7-15 and described in the preceding sections can be enclosed in parentheses. The resulting join expression can itself be used in another join expression, as if it were a simple table. Just as SQL allows you to combine mathematical operations (+, -, *, and /) with parentheses and build up more complex expressions, the SQL2 standard allows you to build up more complex join expressions in the same way.

To illustrate multi-table joins, assume that a new PARENTS table has been added to the GIRLS and BOYS example. The PARENTS table has three columns:

CHILD	Matches the NAME column in GIRLS or BOYS table
TYPE	Specifies "FATHER" or "MOTHER"
PNAME	First name of the parent

A row in the GIRLS or BOYS table can have two matching rows in the PARENTS table, one specifying a MOTHER and one a FATHER, or it can have only one of these rows, or it can have no matching rows if no data on the child's parents is available. The GIRLS, BOYS and PARENTS tables together provide a rich set of data for some multi-table join examples.

For example, suppose you wanted to make a list of all of the children and their parents. Here is one query that produces the list:

```
SELECT *
  FROM ((GIRLS UNION JOIN BOYS) JOIN
        PARENTS ON (PARENT.CHILD = NAME))
```

Because this is an inner join, girls or boys who do not have any matching rows in the PARENTS table will be missing from the query results. You can include (NULL-extended) rows for these children by modifying the query into left outer join:

```
SELECT *
  FROM ((GIRLS UNION JOIN BOYS) LEFT OUTER JOIN
        PARENTS ON (PARENTS.CHILD = NAME))
```

If for some reason you wanted to include unmatched girls, but not unmatched boys, you can rearrange the query into the union of two joins, one inner and one outer, to achieve the desired result:

```
SELECT *
  FROM (GIRLS LEFT JOIN PARENTS ON (CHILD = GIRLS.NAME))
       UNION
       (BOYS INNER JOIN PARENTS ON (CHILD = BOYS.NAME))
```

As another example, suppose you again want to identify boy/girl pairs in the same city, as in previous examples, but this time you want to include the name of the boy's father and the girl's mother in the query results. The potential for unmatched rows in the joins in this example means there are several possible "right" answers to the query. For example, suppose you want to include all girls and boys in the boy/girl pairing, even if the boy or girl does not have a matching row in the PARENTS table. You need to use outer joins for the (BOYS join PARENTS) and (GIRLS join PARENTS) parts of the query, but an inner join for the (BOYS join GIRLS) part of the query. This SQL2 query yields the desired results:

```
SELECT *
  FROM ((GIRLS LEFT JOIN PARENTS
                   ON ((CHILD = GIRLS.NAME) AND
                       (TYPE = "MOTHER")))
        JOIN
        ((BOYS LEFT JOIN PARENTS
                   ON ((CHILD = BOYS.NAME)) AND
                       (TYPE = "FATHER")))
        USING(CITY)
```

As the example shows, even a three-join query like this one can become quite complex with the SQL2 syntax. However, despite the complexity, the SQL2 query does specify *precisely* the query that the DBMS is to carry out. There is no ambiguity about the order in which the tables are joined, or about which joins are inner or outer joins. The ability to freely intermix UNION and JOIN operations provides flexibility in the FROM clause. Overall, the added capability is well worth the added complexity introduced by the extended SQL2 FROM clause.

Although none of the query examples included in this section had WHERE or ORDER BY clauses, they can be freely used with the extended FROM clause in SQL2. The relationship among the clauses is simple, and remains as described in Figure 7-12. The processing specified in the FROM clauses occurs first, including any joins or unions. The join criteria specified in a USING or ON clause are applied as a part of the particular join specification where they appear. When processing of the FROM class is complete, the resulting table is used to apply the selection criteria in the WHERE clause. Thus, the ON clause specifies search criteria that apply to specific joins; the WHERE clause specifies search criteria that apply to the entire table resulting from these joins.

Summary

This chapter described how SQL handles queries that combine data from two or more tables:

- In a multi-table query, the tables containing the data are named in the FROM clause.

- Each row of query results is a combination of data from a single row in each of the tables, and it is the *only* row that draws its data from that particular combination.

- The most common multi-table queries use the parent/child relationships created by primary keys and foreign keys.

- In general, joins can be built by comparing *any* pair(s) of columns from the two joined tables, using either a test for equality or any other comparison test.

- A join can be thought of as the product of two tables from which some of the rows have been removed.

- A table can be joined to itself; self-joins require the use of a table alias.

- Outer joins extend the standard (inner) join by retaining unmatched rows of the joined tables in the query results.

Chapter Eight

Summary
Queries

M any requests for information don't require the level of detail provided by the SQL queries described in the last two chapters. For example, each of the following requests asks for a single value or a small number of values that summarize the contents of the database:

- What is the total quota for all salespeople?
- What are the smallest and largest assigned quotas?
- How many salespeople have exceeded their quota?
- What is the size of the average order?
- What is the size of the average order for each sales office?
- How many salespeople are assigned to each sales office?

SQL supports these requests for summary data through column functions and the GROUP BY and HAVING clauses of the SELECT statement, which are described in this chapter.

Column Functions

SQL lets you summarize data from the database through a set of *column functions*. A SQL column function takes an entire column of data as its argument and produces a single data item that summarizes the column. For example, the AVG() column function takes a column of data and computes its average. Here is a query that uses the AVG() column function to compute the average value of two columns from the SALESREPS table:

What are the average quota and average sales of our salespeople?

```
SELECT AVG(QUOTA), AVG(SALES)
  FROM SALESREPS

   AVG(QUOTA)    AVG(SALES)
 -------------  ------------
  $300,000.00   $289,353.20
```

Figure 8-1 graphically shows how the query results are produced. The first column function in the query takes values in the QUOTA column and computes their average; the second one averages the values in the SALES column. The query produces a single row of query results summarizing the data in the SALESREPS table.

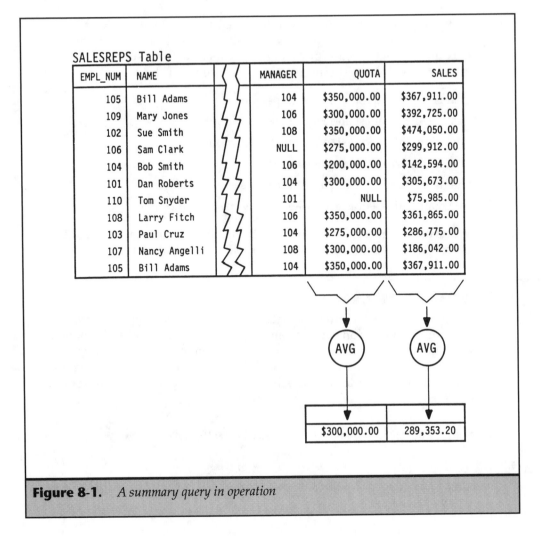

Figure 8-1. *A summary query in operation*

SQL offers six different column functions, as shown in Figure 8-2. The column functions offer different kinds of summary data:

- SUM() computes the total of a column.
- AVG() computes the average value in a column.
- MIN() finds the smallest value in a column.
- MAX() finds the largest value in a column.
- COUNT() counts the number of values in a column.
- COUNT(*) counts rows of query results.

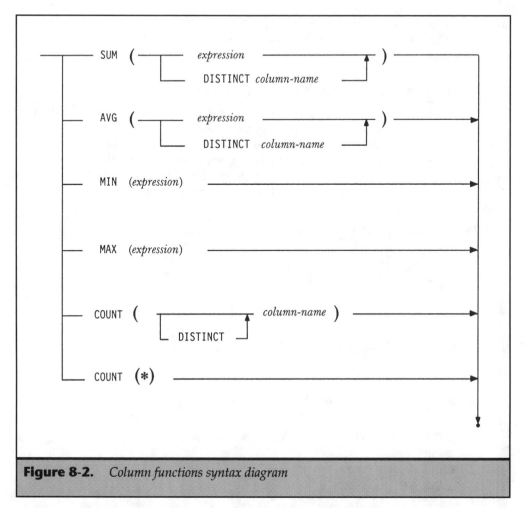

Figure 8-2. *Column functions syntax diagram*

The argument to a column function can be a simple column name, as in the previous example, or it can be a SQL expression, as shown here:

What is the average quota performance of our salespeople?

```
SELECT AVG(100 * (SALES/QUOTA))
  FROM SALESREPS

AVG(100*(SALES/QUOTA))
----------------------
              102.60
```

To process this query, SQL constructs a temporary column containing the value of the expression (100 * (SALES/QUOTA)) for each row of the SALESREPS table, and then computes the averages of the temporary column.

Computing a Column Total (SUM)

The SUM() column function computes the sum of a column of data values. The data in the column must have a numeric type (integer, decimal, floating point, or money). The result of the SUM() function has the same basic data type as the data in the column, but the result may have a higher precision. For example, if you apply the SUM() function to a column of 16-bit integers, it may produce a 32-bit integer as its result.

Here are some examples that use the SUM() column function:

What are the total quotas and sales for all salespeople?

```
SELECT SUM(QUOTA), SUM(SALES)
  FROM SALESREPS

    SUM(QUOTA)       SUM(SALES)
- - - - - - - - - - - - - -   - - - - - - - - - - - - - -
 $2,700,000.00   $2,893,532.00
```

What is the total of the orders taken by Bill Adams?

```
SELECT SUM(AMOUNT)
  FROM ORDERS, SALESREPS
 WHERE NAME = 'Bill Adams'
   AND REP = EMPL_NUM

 SUM(AMOUNT)
- - - - - - - - - - -
  $39,327.00
```

Computing a Column Average (AVG)

The AVG() column function computes the average of a column of data values. As with the SUM() function, the data in the column must have a numeric type. Because the AVG() function adds the values in the column and then divides by the number of values, its result may have a different data type than that of the values in the column. For example, if you apply the AVG() function to a column of integers, the result will be either a decimal or a floating point number, depending on the brand of DBMS you are using.

Here are some examples of the AVG() column function:

Calculate the average price of products from manufacturer ACI.

```
SELECT AVG(PRICE)
  FROM PRODUCTS
 WHERE MFR_ID = 'ACI'

AVG(PRICE)
-----------
   $804.29
```

Calculate the average size of an order placed by Acme Mfg. (customer number 2103).

```
SELECT AVG(AMOUNT)
  FROM ORDERS
 WHERE CUST = 2103

AVG(AMOUNT)
-----------
 $8,895.50
```

Finding Extreme Values (MIN and MAX)

The MIN() and MAX() column functions find the largest and smallest values in a column, respectively. The data in the column can contain numeric, string, or date/time information. The result of the MIN() or MAX() function has exactly the same data type as the data in the column.

Here are some examples that show the use of these column functions:

What are the smallest and largest assigned quotas?

```
SELECT MIN(QUOTA), MAX(QUOTA)
  FROM SALESREPS

  MIN(QUOTA)    MAX(QUOTA)
------------  ------------
$200,000.00  $350,000.00
```

What is the earliest order date in the database?

```
SELECT MIN(ORDER_DATE)
  FROM ORDERS

MIN(ORDER_DATE)
- - - - - - - - - - - - - - -
04-JAN-89
```

What is the best sales performance of any salesperson?

```
SELECT MAX(100 * (SALES/QUOTA))
  FROM SALESREPS

MAX(100*(SALES/QUOTA))
- - - - - - - - - - - - - - - - - - - - -
                 135.44
```

When the MIN() and MAX() column functions are applied to numeric data, SQL compares the numbers in algebraic order (large negative numbers are less than small negative numbers, which are less than zero, which is less than all positive numbers). Dates are compared sequentially (earlier dates are smaller than later ones). Durations are compared based on their length (shorter durations are smaller than longer ones).

When using MIN() and MAX() with string data, the comparison of two strings depends upon the character set being used. On a personal computer or minicomputer, both of which use the ASCII character set, digits come before the letters in the sorting sequence, and all of the uppercase characters come before all of the lowercase characters. On IBM mainframes, which use the EBCDIC character set, the lowercase characters precede the uppercase characters, and digits come after the letters. Here is a comparison of the ASCII and EBCDIC collating sequences of a list of strings, from smallest to largest:

ASCII	EBCDIC
1234ABC	acme mfg.
5678ABC	zeta corp.
ACME MFG.	Acme Mfg.
Acme Mfg.	ACME MFG.
ZETA CORP.	Zeta Corp.
Zeta Corp.	ZETA CORP.
acme mfg.	1234ABC
zeta corp.	5678ABC

The difference in the collating sequences means that a query with an ORDER BY clause can produce different results on two different systems.

International characters (such as Ä, ô, ç) may pose additional problems. Some brands of DBMS use special international sorting algorithms to sort these characters into their correct position for each language. Others simply sort them according to the numeric value of the code assigned to the character. To address these issues, the SQL2 standard includes elaborate support for national character sets, user-defined character sets, and alternate collating sequences. Unfortunately, these features are not yet supported in many popular DBMS products. If your application involves international text, you will want to experiment with your particular DBMS to find out how it handles these characters.

Counting Data Values (COUNT)

The COUNT() column function counts the number of data values in a column. The data in the column can be of any type. The COUNT() function always returns an integer, regardless of the data type of the column. Here are some examples of queries that use the COUNT() column function:

How many customers are there?

```
SELECT COUNT(CUST_NUM)
  FROM CUSTOMERS

COUNT(CUST_NUM)
- - - - - - - - - - - - - -
            21
```

How many salespeople are over quota?

```
SELECT COUNT(NAME)
  FROM SALESREPS
 WHERE SALES > QUOTA

COUNT(NAME)
- - - - - - - - - - -
          7
```

How many orders for more than $25,000 are on the books?

```
SELECT COUNT(AMOUNT)
  FROM ORDERS
 WHERE AMOUNT > 25000.00

COUNT(AMOUNT)
- - - - - - - - - - - -
            4
```

Note that the COUNT() function ignores the values of the data items in the column; it simply counts how many data items there are. As a result, it doesn't really matter which column you specify as the argument of the COUNT() function. The last example could just as well have been written:

```
SELECT COUNT(ORDER_NUM)
  FROM ORDERS
 WHERE AMOUNT > 25000.00

COUNT(ORDER_NUM)
- - - - - - - - - - - - - - -
            4
```

In fact, it's awkward to think of the query as "counting how many order amounts" or "counting how many order numbers"; it's much easier to think about "counting how many orders." For this reason, SQL supports a special COUNT(*) column function, which counts rows rather than data values. Here is the same query, rewritten once again to use the COUNT(*) function:

```
SELECT COUNT(*)
  FROM ORDERS
 WHERE AMOUNT > 25000.00

COUNT(*)
- - - - - - - -
       4
```

If you think of the COUNT(*) function as a "rowcount" function, it makes the query easier to read. In practice, the COUNT(*) function is almost always used instead of the COUNT() function to count rows.

Column Functions in the Select List

Simple queries with a column function in their select list are fairly easy to understand. However, when the select list includes several column functions, or when the argument to a column function is a complex expression, the query can be harder to read and understand. Figure 8-3 shows the rules for SQL query processing from Figure 7-12, expanded once more to describe how column functions are handled. As before, the rules are intended to provide a precise definition of what a query means, not a description of how the DBMS actually goes about producing the query results.

One of the best ways to think about summary queries and column functions is to imagine the query processing broken down into two steps. First, imagine how the query would work *without* the column functions, producing many rows of detailed query results. Then imagine SQL applying the column functions to the detailed query results, producing a single summary row. For example, consider the following complex query:

Find the average order amount, total order amount, average order amount as a percentage of the customer's credit limit, and average order amount as a percentage of the salesperson's quota.

```
SELECT AVG(AMOUNT), SUM(AMOUNT), (100 * AVG(AMOUNT/CREDIT_LIMIT)),
       (100 * AVG(AMOUNT/QUOTA))
  FROM ORDERS, CUSTOMERS, SALESREPS
 WHERE CUST = CUST_NUM
   AND REP = EMPL_NUM
```

AVG(AMOUNT)	SUM(AMOUNT)	(100*AVG(AMOUNT/CREDIT_LIMIT))	(100*AVG(AMOUNT/QUOTA))
$8,256.37	$247,691.00	24.45	2.51

Without the column functions it would look like this:

```
SELECT AMOUNT, AMOUNT, AMOUNT/CREDIT_LIMIT, AMOUNT/QUOTA
  FROM ORDERS, CUSTOMERS, SALESREPS
 WHERE CUST = CUST_NUM AND
   AND REP = EMPL_NUM
```

and would produce one row of detailed query results for each order. The column functions use the columns of this detailed query results table to generate a single-row table of summary query results.

To generate the query results for a SELECT statement:

1. If the statement is a UNION of SELECT statements, apply Steps 2 through 5 to each of the statements to generate their individual query results.

2. Form the product of the tables named in the FROM clause. If the FROM clause names a single table, the product is that table.

3. If there is a WHERE clause, apply its search condition to each row of the product table, retaining those rows for which the search condition is TRUE (and discarding those for which it is FALSE or NULL).

4. For each remaining row, calculate the value of each item in the select list to produce a single row of query results. For a simple column reference, use the value of the column in the current row (or row group). For a column function, use the entire set of rows as its argument.

5. If SELECT DISTINCT is specified, eliminate any duplicate rows of query results that were produced.

6. If the statement is a UNION of SELECT statements, merge the query results for the individual statements into a single table of query results. Eliminate duplicate rows unless UNION ALL is specified.

7. If there is an ORDER BY clause, sort the query results as specified.

The rows generated by this procedure comprise the query results.

Figure 8-3. *SQL query processing rules (with column functions)*

A column function can appear in the select list anywhere that a column name can appear. It can, for example, be part of an expression that adds or subtracts the values of two column functions. However, the argument of a column function cannot contain another column function, because the resulting expression doesn't make sense. This rule is sometimes summarized as "it's illegal to nest column functions."

It's also illegal to mix column functions and ordinary column names in a select list, again because the resulting query doesn't make sense. For example, consider this query:

```
SELECT NAME, SUM(SALES)
  FROM SALESREPS
```

The first select item asks SQL to generate a ten-row table of detailed query results—one row for each salesperson. The second select item asks SQL to generate a one-row column of summary query results containing the total of the SALES column. The two SELECT items contradict one another, producing an error. For this reason, either all column references in the select list must appear within the argument of a column function (producing a summary query), or the select list must not contain any column functions (producing a detailed query). Actually, the rule is slightly more complex when grouped queries and subqueries are considered. The necessary refinements are described later in this chapter.

NULL **Values and Column Functions**

The SUM(), AVG(), MIN(), MAX(), and COUNT() column functions each take a column of data values as their argument and produce a single data value as a result. What happens if one or more of the data values in the column is a NULL value? The ANSI/ISO SQL standard specifies that NULL values in the column are *ignored* by the column functions.

This query shows how the COUNT() column function ignores any NULL values in a column:

```
SELECT COUNT(*), COUNT(SALES), COUNT(QUOTA)
  FROM SALESREPS

COUNT(*) COUNT(SALES) COUNT(QUOTA)
-------- ------------ ------------
      10           10            9
```

The SALESREPS table contains ten rows, so COUNT(*) returns a count of ten. The SALES column contains ten non-NULL values, so the function COUNT(SALES) also returns a count of ten. The QUOTA column is NULL for the newest salesperson. The COUNT(QUOTA) function ignores this NULL value and returns a count of nine. Because of these anomalies, the COUNT(*) function is almost always used instead of the COUNT() function, unless you specifically want to exclude NULL values in a particular column from the total.

Ignoring NULL values has little impact on the MIN() and MAX() column functions. However, it can also cause subtle problems for the SUM() and AVG() column functions, as illustrated by this query:

```
SELECT SUM(SALES), SUM(QUOTA),
       (SUM(SALES) - SUM(QUOTA)), SUM(SALES-QUOTA)
  FROM SALESREPS

  SUM(SALES)     SUM(QUOTA)  (SUM(SALES)-SUM(QUOTA))  SUM(SALES-QUOTA)
------------- ------------- ----------------------- ---------------
$2,893,532.00 $2,700,000.00           $193,532.00      $117,547.00
```

You would expect the two expressions:

    (SUM(SALES) - SUM(QUOTA))   and   SUM(SALES-QUOTA)

in the select list to produce identical results, but the example shows that they do not. The salesperson with a NULL value in the QUOTA column is again the reason. The expression:

    SUM(SALES)

totals the sales for all ten salespeople, while the expression:

    SUM(QUOTA)

totals only the nine non-NULL quota values. The expression:

    SUM(SALES) - SUM(QUOTA)

computes the difference of these two amounts. However, the column function:

    SUM(SALES-QUOTA)

has a non-NULL argument value for only nine of the ten salespeople. In the row with a NULL quota value, the subtraction produces a NULL, which is ignored by the SUM() function. Thus, the sales for the salesperson without a quota, which are included in the previous calculation, are excluded from this calculation.

Which is the "correct" answer? Both are! The first expression calculates exactly what it says: "the sum of SALES, less the sum of QUOTA." The second expression also calculates exactly what it says: "the sum of (SALES – QUOTA)." When NULL values occur, however, the two calculations are not quite the same.

The ANSI/ISO standard specifies these precise rules for handling NULL values in column functions:

- If any of the data values in a column are NULL, they are ignored for the purpose of computing the column function's value.

- If every data item in the column is NULL, then the SUM(), AVG(), MIN(), and MAX() column functions return a NULL value; the COUNT() function returns a value of zero.

- If there are no data items in the column (that is, the column is empty), then the SUM(), AVG(), MIN(), and MAX() column functions return a NULL value; the COUNT() function returns a value of zero.
- The COUNT(*) counts rows, and does not depend on the presence or absence of NULL values in a column. If there are no rows, it returns a value of zero.

Although the standard is very clear in this area, commercial SQL products may produce results different from the standard, especially if all of the data values in a column are NULL or when a column function is applied to an empty table. Before assuming the behavior specified by the standard, you should test your particular DBMS.

Duplicate Row Elimination (DISTINCT)

Recall from Chapter 6 that you can specify the DISTINCT keyword at the beginning of the select list to eliminate duplicate rows of query results. You can also ask SQL to eliminate duplicate values from a column before applying a column function to it. To eliminate duplicate values, the keyword DISTINCT is included before the column function argument, immediately after the opening parenthesis.

Here are two queries that illustrate duplicate row elimination for column functions:

How many different titles are held by salespeople?

```
SELECT COUNT(DISTINCT TITLE)
  FROM SALESREPS

COUNT(DISTINCT TITLE)
---------------------
                    3
```

How many sales offices have salespeople who are over quota?

```
SELECT COUNT(DISTINCT REP_OFFICE)
  FROM SALESREPS
 WHERE SALES > QUOTA

COUNT(DISTINCT REP_OFFICE)
--------------------------
                         4
```

The SQL1 standard specifies that when the DISTINCT keyword is used, the argument to the column function must be a simple column name; it cannot be an expression. The standard allows the DISTINCT keyword for the SUM() and AVG() column functions. The standard does not permit use of the DISTINCT keyword with the MIN() and MAX() column functions, because it has no impact on their results, but many SQL implementations allow it anyway. The standard also *requires* the DISTINCT keyword for the COUNT() column function, but many SQL implementations permit the use of the COUNT() function without it. DISTINCT cannot be specified for the COUNT(*) function, because it doesn't deal with a column of data values at all—it simply counts rows. The SQL2 standard relaxes these restrictions, allowing DISTINCT to be applied for any of the column functions, and permitting expressions as arguments for any of the functions as well.

In addition, the DISTINCT keyword can only be specified *once* in a query. If it appears in the argument of one column function, it can't appear in any others. If it is specified before the select list, it can't appear in any column functions. The only exception is that DISTINCT may be specified a second time inside a subquery (contained within the query). Subqueries are described in Chapter 9.

Grouped Queries (GROUP BY **Clause**)

The summary queries described thus far are like the totals at the bottom of a report. They condense all of the detailed data in the report into a single, summary row of data. Just as subtotals are useful in printed reports, it's often convenient to summarize query results at a "subtotal" level. The GROUP BY clause of the SELECT statement provides this capability.

The function of the GROUP BY clause is most easily understood by example. Consider these two queries:

What is the average order size?

```
SELECT AVG(AMOUNT)
  FROM ORDERS

AVG(AMOUNT)
- - - - - - - - - - -
  $8,256.37
```

What is the average order size for each salesperson?

```
SELECT REP, AVG(AMOUNT)
  FROM ORDERS
 GROUP BY REP
```

```
REP  AVG(AMOUNT)
----  -----------
101    $8,876.00
102    $5,694.00
103    $1,350.00
105    $7,865.40
106   $16,479.00
107   $11,477.33
108    $8,376.14
109    $3,552.50
110   $11,566.00
```

The first query is a simple summary query like the previous examples in this chapter. The second query produces several summary rows—one row for each group, summarizing the orders taken by a single salesperson. Figure 8-4 shows how the second query works. Conceptually, SQL carries out the query as follows:

1. SQL divides the orders into groups of orders, with one group for each salesperson. Within each group, all of the orders have the same value in the REP column.

2. For each group, SQL computes the average value of the AMOUNT column for all of the rows in the group, and generates a single, summary row of query results. The row contains the value of the REP column for the group and the calculated average order size.

A query that includes the GROUP BY clause is called a *grouped query*, because it groups the data from its source tables and produces a single summary row for each row group. The columns named in the GROUP BY clause are called the *grouping columns* of the query, because they determine how the rows are divided into groups. Here are some additional examples of grouped queries:

What is the range of assigned quotas in each office?

```
SELECT REP_OFFICE, MIN(QUOTA), MAX(QUOTA)
  FROM SALESREPS
  GROUP BY REP_OFFICE
```

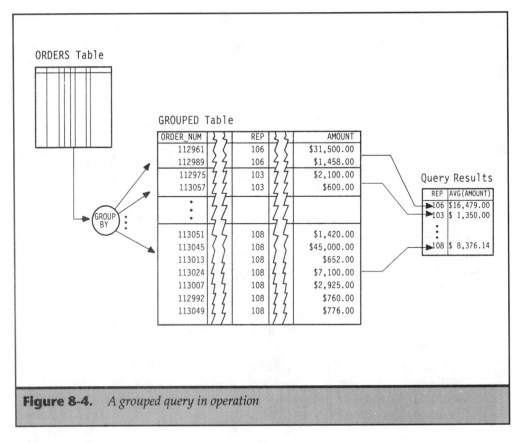

Figure 8-4. *A grouped query in operation*

```
REP_OFFICE    MIN(QUOTA)    MAX(QUOTA)
----------  ------------  ------------

      NULL          NULL          NULL
        11  $275,000.00   $300,000.00
        12  $200,000.00   $300,000.00
        13  $350,000.00   $350,000.00
        21  $350,000.00   $350,000.00
        22  $300,000.00   $300,000.00
```

How many salespeople are assigned to each office?

```
SELECT REP_OFFICE, COUNT(*)
  FROM SALESREPS
 GROUP BY REP_OFFICE
```

```
REP_OFFICE COUNT(*)
---------- --------
      NULL        1
        11        2
        12        3
        13        1
        21        2
        22        1
```

How many different customers are served by each salesperson?

```
SELECT COUNT(DISTINCT CUST_NUM), 'customers for salesrep', CUST_REP
  FROM CUSTOMERS
 GROUP BY CUST_REP

COUNT(DISTINCT CUST_NUM) CUSTOMERS FOR SALESREP CUST_REP
------------------------ ---------------------- --------
                       3 customers for salesrep      101
                       4 customers for salesrep      102
                       3 customers for salesrep      103
                       1 customers for salesrep      104
                       2 customers for salesrep      105
                       2 customers for salesrep      106
                       .
                       .
                       .
```

There is an intimate link between the SQL column functions and the GROUP BY clause. Remember that the column functions take a column of data values and produce a single result. When the GROUP BY clause is present, it tells SQL to divide the detailed query results into groups and to apply the column function separately to each group, producing a single result for each group. Figure 8-5 shows the rules for SQL query processing, expanded once again for grouped queries.

Multiple Grouping Columns

SQL can group query results based on the contents of two or more columns. For example, suppose you want to group the orders by salesperson and by customer. This query groups the data based on both criteria:

To generate the query results for a SELECT statement:

1. If the statement is a UNION of SELECT statements, apply Steps 2 through 6 to each of the statements to generate their individual query results.

2. Form the product of the tables named in the FROM clause. If the FROM clause names a single table, the product is that table.

3. If there is a WHERE clause, apply its search condition to each row of the product table, retaining those rows for which the search condition is TRUE (and discarding those for which it is FALSE or NULL).

4. If there is a GROUP BY clause, arrange the remaining rows of the product table into row groups, so that the rows in each group have identical values in all of the grouping columns.

5. For each remaining row (or row group), calculate the value of each item in the select list to produce a single row of query results. For a simple column reference, use the value of the column in the current row (or row group). For a column function, use the current row group as its argument if GROUP BY is specified; otherwise, use the entire set of rows.

6. If SELECT DISTINCT is specified, eliminate any duplicate rows of query results that were produced.

7. If the statement is a UNION of SELECT statements, merge the query results for the individual statements into a single table of query results. Eliminate duplicate rows unless UNION ALL is specified.

8. If there is an ORDER BY clause, sort the query results as specified.

The rows generated by this procedure comprise the query result.

Figure 8-5. *SQL query processing rules (with* GROUP BY*)*

Calculate the total orders for each customer of each salesperson.

```
SELECT REP, CUST, SUM(AMOUNT)
  FROM ORDERS
 GROUP BY REP, CUST

 REP   CUST   SUM(AMOUNT)
 ----  -----  ------------
 101   2102    $3,978.00
```

```
101   2108      $150.00
101   2113    $22,500.00
102   2106     $4,026.00
102   2114    $15,000.00
102   2120     $3,750.00
103   2111     $2,700.00
105   2103    $35,582.00
105   2111     $3,745.00
       .
       .
       .
```

Even with multiple grouping columns, SQL provides only a single level of grouping. The query produces a separate summary row for each salesperson/customer pair. It's impossible to create groups and subgroups with two levels of subtotals in SQL. The best you can do is sort the data so that the rows of query results appear in the appropriate order. In many SQL implementations, the GROUP BY clause will automatically have the side effect of sorting the data, but you can override this sort with an ORDER BY clause, as shown here:

Calculate the total orders for each customer of each salesperson, sorted by customer, and within each customer by salesperson.

```
SELECT CUST, REP, SUM(AMOUNT)
  FROM ORDERS
 GROUP BY CUST, REP
 ORDER BY CUST, REP

 CUST   REP   SUM(AMOUNT)
 -----  ----  ------------
 2101   106     $1,458.00
 2102   101     $3,978.00
 2103   105    $35,582.00
 2106   102     $4,026.00
 2107   110    $23,132.00
 2108   101       $150.00
 2108   109     $7,105.00
 2109   107    $31,350.00
 2111   103     $2,700.00
 2111   105     $3,745.00
         .
         .
         .
```

Note that it's also impossible to get both detailed and summary query results from a single query. To get detailed query results with subtotals, or to get multilevel subtotals, you must write an application program using programmatic SQL and compute the subtotals within the program logic. SQL Server addresses this limitation of standard SQL by adding an optional COMPUTE clause to the end of the SELECT statement. The COMPUTE clause calculates subtotals and sub-subtotals as shown in this example:

Calculate the total orders for each customer of each salesperson, sorted by salesperson, and within each salesperson by customer.

```
SELECT REP, CUST, AMOUNT
  FROM ORDERS
 ORDER BY REP, CUST
COMPUTE SUM(AMOUNT) BY REP, CUST
COMPUTE SUM(AMOUNT), AVG(AMOUNT) BY REP

REP  CUST        AMOUNT
----  -----  --------------
101   2102       $3,978.00


             sum
             --------------
                 $3,978.00

REP  CUST        AMOUNT
----  -----  --------------
101   2108         $150.00
             sum
             --------------
                   $150.00

REP  CUST        AMOUNT
----  -----  --------------
101   2113      $22,500.00
             sum
             --------------
                $22,500.00
             sum
             --------------
                $26,628.00
```

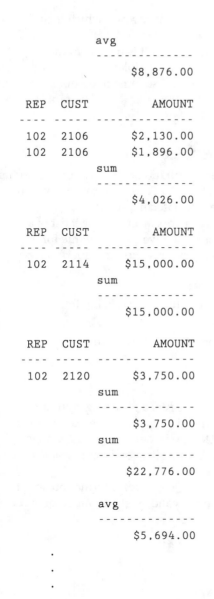

```
                    avg
                    - - - - - - - - - - - - -
                         $8,876.00

     REP   CUST            AMOUNT
     - - - - - - - - -  - - - - - - - - - - - - -
     102   2106          $2,130.00
     102   2106          $1,896.00
                    sum
                    - - - - - - - - - - - - -
                         $4,026.00

     REP   CUST            AMOUNT
     - - - - - - - - -  - - - - - - - - - - - - -
     102   2114         $15,000.00
                    sum
                    - - - - - - - - - - - - -
                        $15,000.00

     REP   CUST            AMOUNT
     - - - - - - - - -  - - - - - - - - - - - - -
     102   2120          $3,750.00
                    sum
                    - - - - - - - - - - - - -
                         $3,750.00
                    sum
                    - - - - - - - - - - - - -
                        $22,776.00

                    avg
                    - - - - - - - - - - - - -
                         $5,694.00
          .
          .
          .
```

The query produces one row of detailed query results for each row of the ORDERS table, sorted by CUST within REP. In addition, it computes the sum of the orders for each customer/salesperson pair (a low-level subtotal) and computes the sum of the orders and average order size for each salesperson (a high-level subtotal). The query results thus contain a mixture of detail rows and summary rows, which include both subtotals and sub-subtotals.

The COMPUTE clause is very nonstandard, and in fact it is unique to the Transact-SQL dialect used by SQL Server. Furthermore, it violates the basic principles of relational queries, because the results of the SELECT statement are not a table, but a strange combination of different types of rows. Nonetheless, as the example shows, it can be very useful.

Restrictions on Grouped Queries

Grouped queries are subject to some rather strict limitations. The grouping columns must be actual columns of the tables named in the FROM clause of the query. You cannot group the rows based on the value of a calculated expression.

There are also restrictions on the items that can appear in the select list of a grouped query. All of the items in the select list must have a single value for each group of rows. Basically, this means that a select item in a grouped query can be:

- a *constant,*
- a *column function,* which produces a single value summarizing the rows in the group,
- a *grouping column,* which by definition has the same value in every row of the group, or
- an *expression* involving combinations of the above.

In practice, a grouped query will always include *both* a grouping column and a column function in its select list. If no column function appears, the query can be expressed more simply using SELECT DISTINCT, without GROUP BY. Conversely, if you don't include a grouping column in the query results, you won't be able to tell which row of query results came from which group!

Another limitation of grouped queries is that SQL ignores information about primary keys and foreign keys when analyzing the validity of a grouped query. Consider this query:

Calculate the total orders for each salesperson.

```
SELECT EMPL_NUM, NAME, SUM(AMOUNT)
  FROM ORDERS, SALESREPS
 WHERE REP = EMPL_NUM
 GROUP BY EMPL_NUM

Error: "NAME" not a GROUP BY expression
```

Given the nature of the data, the query makes perfectly good sense, because grouping on the salesperson's employee number is in effect the same as grouping on the salesperson's name. More precisely, EMPL_NUM, the grouping column, is the primary key of the SALESREPS table, so the NAME column must be single-valued for each group. Nonetheless, SQL reports an error, because the NAME column is not explicitly specified as a grouping column. To correct the problem, you simply include the NAME column as a second (redundant) grouping column:

Calculate the total orders for each salesperson.

```
SELECT EMPL_NUM, NAME, SUM(AMOUNT)
  FROM ORDERS, SALESREPS
 WHERE REP = EMPL_NUM
 GROUP BY EMPL_NUM, NAME

EMPL_NUM NAME             SUM(AMOUNT)
-------- --------------- ------------
     101 Dan Roberts      $26,628.00
     102 Sue Smith        $22,776.00
     103 Paul Cruz         $2,700.00
     105 Bill Adams       $39,327.00
     106 Sam Clark        $32,958.00
     107 Nancy Angelli    $34,432.00
     108 Larry Fitch      $58,633.00
     109 Mary Jones        $7,105.00
     110 Tom Snyder       $23,132.00
```

Of course, if the salesperson's employee number is not needed in the query results, you can eliminate it entirely from the select list, giving:

Calculate the total orders for each salesperson.

```
SELECT NAME, SUM(AMOUNT)
  FROM ORDERS, SALESREPS
 WHERE REP = EMPL_NUM
 GROUP BY NAME

NAME            SUM(AMOUNT)
--------------- ------------
Bill Adams       $39,327.00
Dan Roberts      $26,628.00
```

```
Larry Fitch       $58,633.00
Mary Jones         $7,105.00
Nancy Angelli     $34,432.00
Paul Cruz          $2,700.00
Sam Clark         $32,958.00
Sue Smith         $22,776.00
Tom Snyder        $23,132.00
```

NULL **Values in Grouping Columns**

A NULL value poses a special problem when it occurs in a grouping column. If the value of the column is unknown, which group should the row be placed into? In the WHERE clause, when two different NULL values are compared, the result is NULL (not TRUE), that is, the two NULL values are *not* considered to be equal. Applying the same convention to the GROUP BY clause would force SQL to place each row with a NULL grouping column into a separate group, by itself.

In practice this rule proves too unwieldy. Instead, the ANSI/ISO SQL standard considers two NULL values to be equal for purposes of the GROUP BY clause. If two rows have NULLs in the same grouping columns and identical values in all of their non-NULL grouping columns, they are grouped together into the same row group. The small sample table in Figure 8-6 illustrates the ANSI/ISO handling of NULL values by the GROUP BY clause, as shown in this query:

```
SELECT HAIR, EYES, COUNT(*)
  FROM PEOPLE
 GROUP BY HAIR, EYES

HAIR    EYES    COUNT(*)
------  ------  --------
Brown   Blue          1
NULL    Blue          2
NULL    NULL          2
Brown   NULL          3 4
Brown   Brown         2 1
Brown   Brown         2
```

Although this behavior of NULLs in grouping columns is clearly specified in the ANSI/ISO standard, it is not implemented in all SQL dialects. It's a good idea to build a small test table and check the behavior of your DBMS brand before counting on a specific behavior.

NAME	HAIR	EYES
Cindy	Brown	Blue
Louise	NULL	Blue
Harry	NULL	Blue
Samantha	NULL	NULL
Joanne	NULL	NULL
George	Brown	NULL
Mary	Brown	NULL
Paula	Brown	NULL
Kevin	Brown	NULL
Joel	Brown	Brown
Susan	Blonde	Blue
Marie	Blonde	Blue

Figure 8-6. *The* PEOPLE *table*

Group Search Conditions (HAVING **Clause**)

Just as the WHERE clause can be used to select and reject the individual rows that participate in a query, the HAVING clause can be used to select and reject row groups. The format of the HAVING clause parallels that of the WHERE clause, consisting of the keyword HAVING followed by a search condition. The HAVING clause thus specifies a search condition for groups.

An example provides the best way to understand the role of the HAVING clause. Consider this query:

What is the average order size for each salesperson whose orders total more than $30,000?

```
SELECT REP, AVG(AMOUNT)
  FROM ORDERS
 GROUP BY REP
HAVING SUM(AMOUNT) > 30000.00
```

```
REP  AVG(AMOUNT)
----  -----------
105    $7,865.40
106   $16,479.00
107   $11,477.33
108    $8,376.14
```

Figure 8-7 shows graphically how SQL carries out the query. The GROUP_BY clause first arranges the orders into groups by salesperson. The HAVING clause then eliminates any group where the total of the orders in the group does not exceed $30,000. Finally, the SELECT clause calculates the average order size for each of the remaining groups and generates the query results.

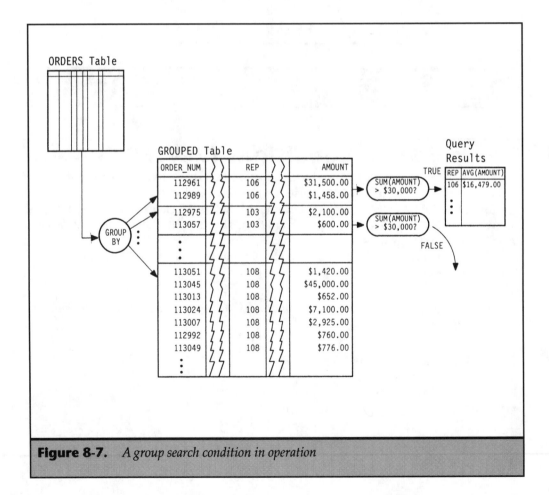

Figure 8-7. *A group search condition in operation*

The search conditions you can specify in the HAVING clause are the same ones used in the WHERE clause, as described in Chapters 6 and 9. Here is another example of the use of a group search condition:

For each office with two or more people, compute the total quota and total sales for all salespeople who work in the office.

```
SELECT CITY, SUM(QUOTA), SUM(SALESREPS.SALES)
  FROM OFFICES, SALESREPS
 WHERE OFFICE = REP_OFFICE
 GROUP BY CITY
HAVING COUNT(*) >= 2

CITY              SUM(QUOTA) SUM(SALESREPS.SALES)
------------      ---------------   --------------------
Chicago           $775,000.00            $735,042.00
Los Angeles       $700,000.00            $835,915.00
New York          $575,000.00            $692,637.00
```

Figure 8-8 shows the rules for SQL query processing, expanded once again to include group search conditions. Following the steps in the figure, SQL handles this query as follows:

1. Joins the OFFICES and SALESREPS tables to find the city where each salesperson works.

2. Groups the resulting rows by office.

3. Eliminates groups with two or fewer rows—these represent offices that don't meet the HAVING clause criterion.

4. Calculates the total quota and total sales for each group.

Here is one more example, which uses all of the SELECT statement clauses:

Show the price, quantity on hand and total quantity on order for each product where the total quantity on order is more than 75 percent of the quantity on hand.

```
SELECT DESCRIPTION, PRICE, QTY_ON_HAND, SUM(QTY)
  FROM PRODUCTS, ORDERS
 WHERE MFR = MFR_ID
   AND PRODUCT = PRODUCT_ID
 GROUP BY MFR_ID, PRODUCT_ID, DESCRIPTION, PRICE, QTY_ON_HAND
HAVING SUM(QTY) > (.75 * QTY_ON_HAND)
 ORDER BY QTY_ON_HAND DESC
```

```
DESCRIPTION           PRICE QTY_ON_HAND   SUM(QTY)
----------------    --------- -----------   ----------
Reducer             $355.00          38          32
Widget Adjuster      $25.00          37          30
Motor Mount         $243.00          15          16
Right Hinge       $4,500.00          12          15
500-lb Brace      $1,425.00           5          22
```

To process this query, SQL conceptually performs the following steps:

1. Joins the ORDERS and PRODUCTS tables to find the description, price, and quantity on hand for each product ordered.

2. Groups the resulting rows by manufacturer and product id.

3. Eliminates groups where the quantity ordered (the total of the QTY column for all orders in the group) is less than 75 percent of the quantity on hand.

4. Calculates the total quantity ordered for each group.

5. Generates one summary row of query results for each group.

6. Sorts the query results so that products with the largest quantity on hand appear first.

As described previously, DESCRIPTION, PRICE, and QTY_ON_HAND must be specified as grouping columns in this query solely because they appear in the select list. They actually contribute nothing to the grouping process, because the MFR_ID and PRODUCT_ID completely specify a single row of the PRODUCTS table, automatically making the other three columns single-valued per group.

Restrictions on Group Search Conditions

The HAVING clause is used to include or exclude row groups from the query results, so the search condition it specifies must be one that applies to the group as a whole rather than to individual rows. This means that an item appearing within the search condition in a HAVING clause can be:

- a *constant*,
- a *column function*, which produces a single value summarizing the rows in the group,
- a *grouping column*, which by definition has the same value in every row of the group, or
- an *expression* involving combinations of the above.

To generate the query results for a SELECT statement:

1. If the statement is a UNION of SELECT statements, apply Steps 2 through 7 to each of the statements to generate their individual query results.

2. Form the product of the tables named in the FROM clause. If the FROM clause names a single table, the product is that table.

3. If there is a WHERE clause, apply its search condition to each row of the product table, retaining those rows for which the search condition is TRUE (and discarding those for which it is FALSE or NULL).

4. If there is a GROUP BY clause, arrange the remaining rows of the product table into row groups, so that the rows in each group have identical values in all of the grouping columns.

5. If there is a HAVING clause, apply its search condition to each row group, retaining those groups for which the search condition is TRUE (and discarding those for which it is FALSE or NULL).

6. For each remaining row (or row group), calculate the value of each item in the select list to produce a single row of query results. For a simple column reference, use the value of the column in the current row (or row group). For a column function, use the current row group as its argument if GROUP BY is specified; otherwise, use the entire set of rows.

7. If SELECT DISTINCT is specified, eliminate any duplicate rows of query results that were produced.

8. If the statement is a UNION of SELECT statements, merge the query results for the individual statements into a single table of query results. Eliminate duplicate rows unless UNION ALL is specified.

9. If there is an ORDER BY clause, sort the query results as specified.

The rows generated by this procedure comprise the query results.

Figure 8-8.   *SQL query processing rules (with* HAVING*)*

In practice, the search condition in the HAVING clause will always include at least one column function. If it did not, the search condition could be moved to the WHERE clause and applied to individual rows. The easiest way to figure out whether a search condition belongs in the WHERE clause or in the HAVING clause is to remember how the two clauses are applied:

- The WHERE clause is applied to *individual rows,* so the expressions it contains must be computable for individual rows.

- The HAVING clause is applied to *row groups,* so the expressions it contains must be computable for a group of rows.

NULL **Values and Group Search Conditions**

Like the search condition in the WHERE clause, the HAVING clause search condition can produce one of three results:

- If the search condition is TRUE, the row group is retained, and it contributes a summary row to the query results.

- If the search condition is FALSE, the row group is discarded, and it does not contribute a summary row to the query results.

- If the search condition is NULL, the row group is discarded, and it does not contribute a summary row to the query results.

The anomalies that can occur with NULL values in the search condition are the same as those for the WHERE clause, and have been described in Chapter 6.

HAVING **Without** GROUP BY

The HAVING clause is almost always used in conjunction with the GROUP BY clause, but the syntax of the SELECT statement does not require it. If a HAVING clause appears without a GROUP BY clause, SQL considers the entire set of detailed query results to be a single group. In other words, the column functions in the HAVING clause are applied to one and only one group to determine whether the group is included or excluded from the query results, and that group consists of all the rows. The use of a HAVING clause without a corresponding GROUP BY clause is almost never seen in practice.

Summary

This chapter described summary queries, which summarize data from the database:

- Summary queries use SQL column functions to collapse a column of data values into a single value that summarizes the column.

- Column functions can compute the average, sum, minimum, and maximum values of a column, count the number of data values in a column, or count the number of rows of query results.

- A summary query without a GROUP BY clause generates a single row of query results, summarizing all the rows of a table or a joined set of tables.

- A summary query with a GROUP BY clause generates multiple rows of query results, each summarizing the rows in a particular group.

- The HAVING clause acts as a WHERE clause for groups, selecting the row groups that contribute to the summary query results.

Chapter Nine

Subqueries

The SQL subquery feature lets you use the results of one query as part of another query. The ability to use a query within a query was the original reason for the word "structured" in the name Structured Query Language. The subquery feature is less well-known than SQL's join feature, but it plays an important role in SQL for three reasons:

- A SQL statement with a subquery is often the most natural way to express a query, because it most closely parallels the English-language description of the query.

- Subqueries make it easier to write SELECT statements, because they let you "break a query down into pieces" (the query and its subqueries) and then "put the pieces together."

- There are some queries that cannot be expressed in the SQL language without using a subquery.

This chapter describes subqueries and how they are used in the WHERE and HAVING clauses of a SQL statement.

Using Subqueries

A *subquery* is a query that appears within the WHERE or HAVING clause of another SQL statement. Subqueries provide an efficient, natural way to handle query requests that are themselves expressed in terms of the results of other queries. Here is an example of such a request:

"List the offices where the sales target for the office exceeds the sum of the individual salespeople's quotas."

The request asks for a list of offices from the OFFICES table, where the value of the TARGET column meets some condition. It seems reasonable that the SELECT statement that expresses the query should look something like this:

```
SELECT CITY
  FROM OFFICES
 WHERE TARGET > ???
```

The value "? ? ?" needs to be filled in, and should be equal to "the sum of the quotas of the salespeople assigned to the office in question." How can you specify that value in the query? From Chapter 8, you know that the sum of the quotas for a specific office (say, office number 21) can be obtained with this query:

```
SELECT SUM(QUOTA)
  FROM SALESREPS
 WHERE REP_OFFICE = 21
```

But how can you put the results of this query into the earlier query in place of the question marks? It would seem reasonable to start with the first query and replace the "? ? ?" with the second query, as follows:

```
SELECT CITY
  FROM OFFICES
 WHERE TARGET > (SELECT SUM(QUOTA)
                   FROM SALESREPS
                  WHERE REP_OFFICE = OFFICE)
```

In fact, this is a correctly formed SQL query. For each office, the "inner query" (the subquery) calculates the sum of the quotas for the salespeople working in that office. The "outer query" (the *main query*) compares the office's target to the calculated total and decides whether to add the office to the main query results. Working together, the main query and the subquery express the original request and retrieve the requested data from the database.

SQL subqueries always appear as part of the WHERE clause or the HAVING clause. In the WHERE clause, they help to select the individual rows that appear in the query results. In the HAVING clause, they help to select the row groups that appear in the query results.

What Is a Subquery?

Figure 9-1 shows the form of a SQL subquery. The subquery is always enclosed in parentheses, but otherwise it has the familiar form of a SELECT statement, with a FROM clause and optional WHERE, GROUP BY, and HAVING clauses. The form of these clauses in a subquery is identical to that in a SELECT statement, and they perform their normal functions when used within a subquery. There are, however, a few differences between a subquery and an actual SELECT statement:

- A subquery must produce a single column of data as its query results. This means that a subquery always has a single select item in its SELECT clause.

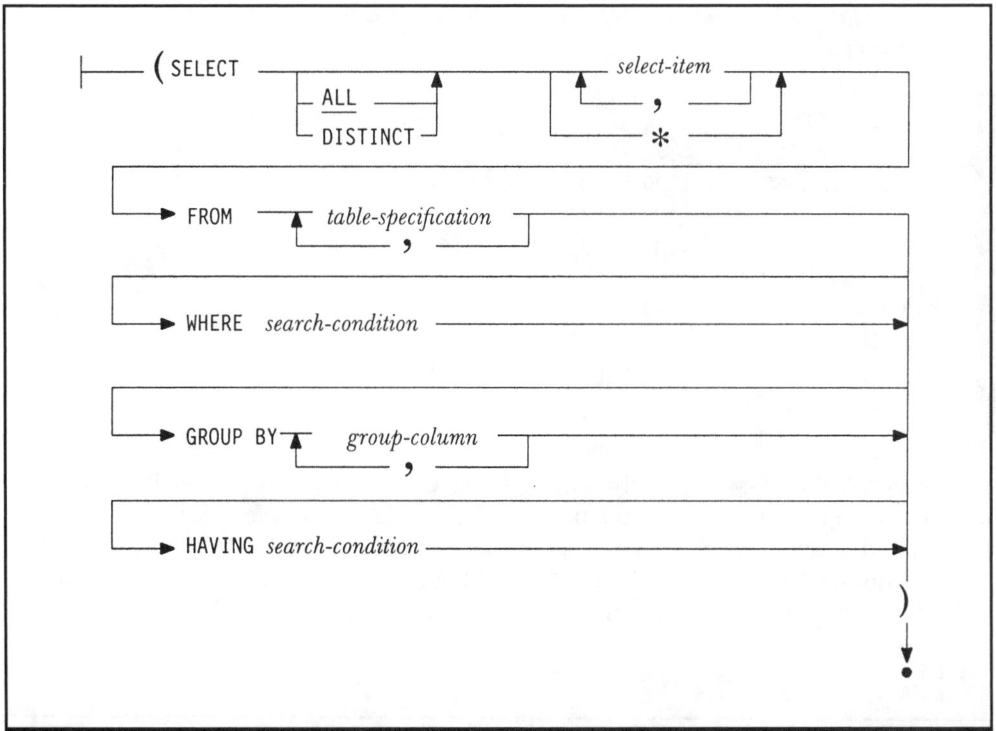

Figure 9-1. *Subquery syntax diagram*

- The ORDER BY clause cannot be specified in a subquery. The subquery results are used internally by the main query and are never visible to the user, so it makes little sense to sort them anyway.

- A subquery cannot be the UNION of several different SELECT statements; only a single SELECT is allowed.

- Column names appearing in a subquery may refer to columns of tables in the main query. These *outer references* are described in detail later in this chapter.

Subqueries in the WHERE Clause

Subqueries are most frequently used in the WHERE clause of a SQL statement. When a subquery appears in the WHERE clause, it works as part of the row selection process. Consider once again the query from the previous section:

List the offices where the sales target for the office exceeds the sum of the individual salespeople's quotas.

```
SELECT CITY
  FROM OFFICES
 WHERE TARGET > (SELECT SUM(QUOTA)
                   FROM SALESREPS
                  WHERE REP_OFFICE = OFFICE)

CITY
------------
Chicago
Los Angeles
```

Figure 9-2 shows conceptually how SQL carries out the query. The main query draws its data from the OFFICES table, and the WHERE clause selects which offices will be included in the query results. SQL goes through the rows of the OFFICES table one-by-one, applying the test stated in the WHERE clause. The WHERE clause compares the value of the TARGET column in the current row to the value produced by the

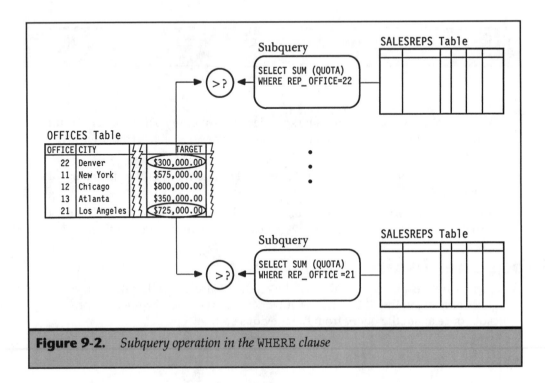

Figure 9-2. *Subquery operation in the* WHERE *clause*

subquery. To test the TARGET value, SQL carries out the subquery, finding the sum of the quotas for salespeople in the "current" office. The subquery produces a single number, and the WHERE clause compares the number to the TARGET value, selecting or rejecting the current office based on the comparison. As the figure shows, SQL carries out the subquery repeatedly, once for each row tested by the WHERE clause of the main query.

Outer References

Within the body of a subquery, it's often necessary to refer to the value of a column in the "current" row of the main query. Consider once again the query from the previous sections:

List the offices where the sales target for the office exceeds the sum of the individual salespeople's quotas.

```
SELECT CITY
  FROM OFFICES
 WHERE TARGET > (SELECT SUM(QUOTA)
                  FROM SALESREPS
                 WHERE REP_OFFICE = OFFICE)
```

The role of the subquery in this SELECT statement is to calculate the total quota for those salespeople who work in a particular office—specifically, the office currently being tested by the WHERE clause of the main query. The subquery does this by scanning the SALESREPS table. But notice that the OFFICE column in the WHERE clause of the subquery doesn't refer to a column of the SALESREPS table; it refers to a column of the OFFICES table, which is a part of the main query. As SQL moves through each row of the OFFICES table, it uses the OFFICE value from the current row when it carries out the subquery.

The OFFICE column in this subquery is an example of an *outer reference*. An outer reference is a column name that does not refer to any of the tables named in the FROM clause of the subquery in which the column name appears. Instead, the column name refers to a column of a table specified in the FROM clause of the *main* query. As the previous example shows, the value of the column in an outer reference is taken from the row currently being tested by the main query.

Subquery Search Conditions

A subquery is always part of a search condition in the WHERE or HAVING clause. Chapter 6 described the simple search conditions that can be used in these clauses. In addition, SQL offers these *subquery search conditions*:

■ *Subquery comparison test.* Compares the value of an expression to a single value produced by a subquery. This test resembles the simple comparison test.

■ *Subquery set membership test.* Checks whether the value of an expression matches one of the set of values produced by a subquery. This test resembles the simple set membership test.

■ *Existence test.* Tests whether a subquery produces any rows of query results.

■ *Quantified comparison test.* Compares the value of an expression to each of the set of values produced by a subquery.

Subquery Comparison Test (=, <>, <, <=, >, >=)

The subquery comparison test is a modified form of the simple comparison test, as shown in Figure 9-3. It compares the value of an expression to the value produced by a subquery, and returns a TRUE result if the comparison is true. You use this test to compare a value from the row being tested to a *single* value produced by a subquery, as in this example:

List the salespeople whose quotas are equal to or higher than the target of the Atlanta sales office.

```
SELECT NAME
  FROM SALESREPS
 WHERE QUOTA >= (SELECT TARGET
                   FROM OFFICES
                  WHERE CITY = 'Atlanta')


NAME
--------------
Bill Adams
Sue Smith
Larry Fitch
```

The subquery in the example retrieves the sales target of the Atlanta office. The value is then used to select the salespeople whose quotas are higher than the target.

The subquery comparison test offers the same six comparison operators (=, <>, <, <=, >, >=) available with the simple comparison test. The subquery specified in this test must produce a *single row* of query results. If the subquery produces multiple rows, the comparison does not make sense, and SQL reports an error condition. If the subquery produces no rows or produces a NULL value, the comparison test returns NULL.

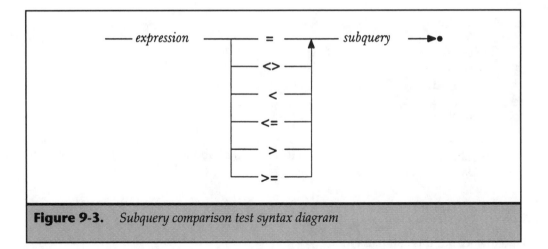

Figure 9-3. *Subquery comparison test syntax diagram*

Here are some additional examples of subquery comparison tests:

List all customers served by Bill Adams.

```
SELECT COMPANY
  FROM CUSTOMERS
 WHERE CUST_REP = (SELECT EMPL_NUM
                     FROM SALESREPS
                    WHERE NAME = 'Bill Adams')

COMPANY
------------------
Acme Mfg.
Three-Way Lines
```

List all products from manufacturer ACI where the quantity on hand is above the quantity on hand of product ACI-41004.

```
SELECT DESCRIPTION, QTY_ON_HAND
  FROM PRODUCTS
 WHERE MFR_ID = 'ACI'
   AND QTY_ON_HAND > (SELECT QTY_ON_HAND
                        FROM PRODUCTS
                       WHERE MFR_ID = 'ACI'
                         AND PRODUCT_ID = '41004')
```

```
DESCRIPTION          QTY_ON_HAND
-----------------    -----------
Size 3 Widget               207
Size 1 Widget               277
Size 2 Widget               167
```

Note that the subquery comparison test allows a subquery only on the right side of the comparison operator. This comparison:

A < (*subquery*)

is allowed, but this comparison:

(*subquery*) > A

is not permitted. This doesn't limit the power of the comparison test, because the operator in any unequal comparison can always be "turned around" so that the subquery is put on the right side of the inequality. However, it does mean that you must sometimes "turn around" the logic of an English-language request to get a form of the request that corresponds to a legal SQL statement.

Set Membership Test (IN)

The subquery set membership test (IN) is a modified form of the simple set membership test, as shown in Figure 9-4. It compares a single data value to a column

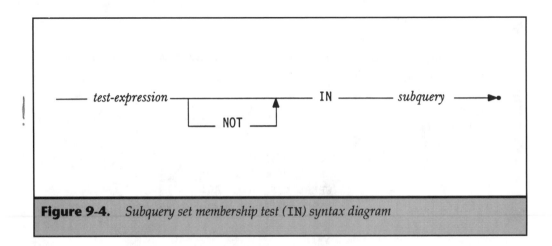

Figure 9-4. *Subquery set membership test (IN) syntax diagram*

of data values produced by a subquery and returns a TRUE result if the data value matches one of the values in the column. You use this test when you need to compare a value from the row being tested to a *set* of values produced by a subquery, as shown in these examples:

List the salespeople who work in offices that are over target.

```
SELECT NAME
  FROM SALESREPS
 WHERE REP_OFFICE IN (SELECT OFFICE
                        FROM OFFICES
                       WHERE SALES > TARGET)

NAME
--------------
Mary Jones
Sam Clark
Bill Adams
Sue Smith
Larry Fitch
```

List the salespeople who do not work in offices managed by Larry Fitch (employee 108).

```
SELECT NAME
  FROM SALESREPS
 WHERE REP_OFFICE NOT IN (SELECT OFFICE
                            FROM OFFICES
                           WHERE MGR = 108)

NAME
--------------
Bill Adams
Mary Jones
Sam Clark
Bob Smith
Dan Roberts
Paul Cruz
```

List all of the customers who have placed orders for ACI Widgets (manufacturer ACI, product numbers starting with "4100") between January and June 1990.

```
SELECT COMPANY
  FROM CUSTOMERS
 WHERE CUST_NUM IN (SELECT DISTINCT CUST
                      FROM ORDERS
                     WHERE MFR = 'ACI'
                       AND PRODUCT LIKE '4100%'
                       AND ORDER_DATE BETWEEN '01-JAN-90'
                                          AND '30-JUN-90')

COMPANY
------------------
Acme Mfg.
Ace International
Holm & Landis
JCP Inc.
```

In each of these examples, the subquery produces a column of data values, and the WHERE clause of the main query checks to see whether a value from a row of the main query matches one of the values in the column. The subquery form of the IN test thus works exactly like the simple IN test, except that the set of values is produced by a subquery instead of being explicitly listed in the statement.

Existence Test (EXISTS)

The existence test (EXISTS) checks whether a subquery produces any rows of query results, as shown in Figure 9-5. There is no simple comparison test that resembles the existence test; it is used only with subqueries.

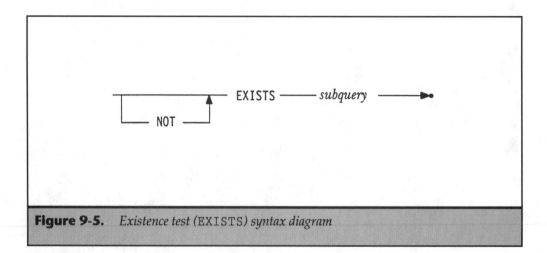

Figure 9-5. *Existence test (EXISTS) syntax diagram*

Here is an example of a request that can be expressed naturally using an existence test:

"List the products for which an order of $25,000 or more has been received."

The request could easily be rephrased as:

"List the products for which there exists at least one order in the ORDERS table (a) that is for the product in question and (b) has an amount of at least $25,000."

The SELECT statement used to retrieve the requested list of products closely resembles the rephrased request:

```
SELECT DISTINCT DESCRIPTION
  FROM PRODUCTS
 WHERE EXISTS (SELECT ORDER_NUM
                 FROM ORDERS
                WHERE PRODUCT = PRODUCT_ID
                  AND MFR = MFR_ID
                  AND AMOUNT >= 25000.00)

DESCRIPTION
------------------
500-lb Brace
Left Hinge
Right Hinge
Widget Remover
```

Conceptually, SQL processes this query by going through the PRODUCTS table and performing the subquery for each product. The subquery produces a column containing the order numbers of any orders for the "current" product that are over $25,000. If there are any such orders (that is, if the column is not empty), the EXISTS test is TRUE. If the subquery produces no rows, the EXISTS test is FALSE. The EXISTS test cannot produce a NULL value.

You can reverse the logic of the EXISTS test using the NOT EXISTS form. In this case, the test is TRUE if the subquery produces no rows, and FALSE otherwise.

Notice that the EXISTS search condition doesn't really *use* the results of the subquery at all. It merely tests to see whether the subquery produces any results. For this reason, SQL relaxes the rule that "subqueries must return a single column of data," and allows you to use the SELECT * form in the subquery of an EXISTS test. The previous subquery could thus have been written:

List the products for which an order of $25,000 or more has been received.

```
SELECT DESCRIPTION
  FROM PRODUCTS
 WHERE EXISTS (SELECT *
                 FROM ORDERS
                WHERE PRODUCT = PRODUCT_ID
                  AND MFR = MFR_ID
                  AND AMOUNT >= 25000.00)
```

In practice, the subquery in an EXISTS test is *always* written using the SELECT * notation.

Here are some additional examples of queries that use EXISTS:

List any customers assigned to Sue Smith who have not placed an order for over $3,000.

```
SELECT COMPANY
  FROM CUSTOMERS
 WHERE CUST_REP = (SELECT EMPL_NUM
                     FROM SALESREPS
                    WHERE NAME = 'Sue Smith')
   AND NOT EXISTS (SELECT *
                     FROM ORDERS
                    WHERE CUST = CUST_NUM
                      AND AMOUNT > 3000.00)

COMPANY
------------------
Carter & Sons
Fred Lewis Corp.
```

List the offices where there is a salesperson whose quota represents more than 55 percent of the office's target.

```
SELECT CITY
  FROM OFFICES
 WHERE EXISTS (SELECT *
                 FROM SALESREPS
                WHERE REP_OFFICE = OFFICE
                  AND QUOTA > (.55 * TARGET))
```

```
CITY
- - - - - - - - - - - -
Denver
Atlanta
```

Note that in each of these examples the subquery includes an outer reference to a column of the table in the main query. In practice, the subquery in an EXISTS test will always contain an outer reference that "links" the subquery to the row currently being tested by the main query.

Quantified Tests (ANY and ALL) *

The subquery version of the IN test checks whether a data value is equal to some value in a column of subquery results. SQL provides two *quantified tests*, ANY and ALL, that extend this notion to other comparison operators, such as greater than (>) and less than (<). Both of these tests compare a data value to the column of data values produced by a subquery, as shown in Figure 9-6.

THE ANY TEST * The ANY test is used in conjunction with one of the six SQL comparison operators (=, <>, <, <=, >, >=) to compare a single test value to a column of data values produced by a subquery. To perform the test, SQL uses the specified comparison operator to compare the test value to *each* data value in the column, one at

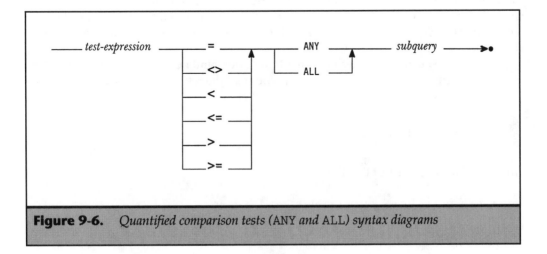

Figure 9-6. *Quantified comparison tests (ANY and ALL) syntax diagrams*

a time. If *any* of the individual comparisons yield a TRUE result, the ANY test returns a TRUE result.

Here is an example of a request that can be handled with the ANY test:

List the salespeople who have taken an order that represents more than ten percent of their quota.

```
SELECT NAME
  FROM SALESREPS
 WHERE (.1 * QUOTA) < ANY (SELECT AMOUNT
                             FROM ORDERS
                            WHERE REP = EMPL_NUM)

NAME
- - - - - - - - - - - - - -
Sam Clark
Larry Fitch
Nancy Angelli
```

Conceptually, the main query tests each row of the SALESREPS table, one-by-one. The subquery finds all of the orders taken by the "current" salesperson and returns a column containing the order amounts for those orders. The WHERE clause of the main query then computes ten percent of the current salesperson's quota and uses it as a test value, comparing it to every order amount produced by the subquery. If there is *any* order amount that exceeds the calculated test value, the "< ANY" test returns TRUE and the salesperson is included in the query results. If not, the salesperson is not included in the query results. The keyword SOME is an alternative for ANY specified by the ANSI/ISO SQL standard. Either keyword can generally be used, but some DBMS brands do not support SOME.

The ANY test can sometimes be difficult to understand because it involves an entire set of comparisons, not just one. It helps if you read the test in a slightly different way than it appears in the statement. If this ANY test appears:

```
WHERE X < ANY (SELECT Y ...)
```

instead of reading the test like this:

"where X is less than any select Y..."

try reading it like this:

"where, for *some* Y, X is less than Y"

When you use this trick, the preceding query becomes:

"Select the salespeople where, for *some* order taken by the salesperson, ten percent of the salesperson's quota is less than the order amount."

If the subquery in an ANY test produces no rows of query results, or if the query results include NULL values, the operation of the ANY test may vary from one DBMS to another. The ANSI/ISO SQL standard specifies these detailed rules describing the results of the ANY test when the test value is compared to the column of subquery results:

- If the subquery produces an empty column of query results, the ANY test returns FALSE—there is no value produced by the subquery for which the comparison test holds.

- If the comparison test is TRUE for *at least one* of the data values in the column, then the ANY search condition returns TRUE—there is indeed some value produced by the subquery for which the comparison test holds.

- If the comparison test is FALSE for *every* data value in the column, then the ANY search condition returns FALSE. In this case, you can conclusively state that there is no value produced by the subquery for which the comparison test holds.

- If the comparison test is not TRUE for any data value in the column, but it is NULL for one or more of the data values, then the ANY search condition returns NULL. In this situation, you cannot conclusively state whether there is a value produced by the subquery for which the comparison test holds; there may be or there may not be, depending on the "correct" values for the NULL (unknown) data.

The ANY comparison operator can be very tricky to use in practice, especially in conjunction with the inequality (<>) comparison operator. Here is an example that shows the problem:

"List the names and ages of all the people in the sales force who do not manage an office."

It's tempting to express this query as follows:

```
SELECT NAME, AGE
  FROM SALESREPS
  WHERE EMPL_NUM <> ANY (SELECT MGR
                           FROM OFFICES)
```

The subquery:

```
SELECT MGR
  FROM OFFICES
```

obviously produces the employee numbers of the managers, and therefore the query *seems* to be saying:

"Find each salesperson who is not the manager of any office."

But that's *not* what the query says! What it *does* say is this:

"Find each salesperson who, *for some office,* is not the manager of that office."

Of course for any given salesperson, it's possible to find *some* office where that salesperson is not the manager. The query results would include *all* the salespeople, and therefore fail to answer the question that was posed! The correct query is:

```
SELECT NAME, AGE
  FROM SALESREPS
 WHERE NOT (EMPL_NUM = ANY (SELECT MGR
                              FROM OFFICES))

NAME             AGE
--------------   ----
Mary Jones        31
Sue Smith         48
Dan Roberts       45
Tom Snyder        41
Paul Cruz         29
Nancy Angelli     49
```

You can always turn a query with an ANY test into a query with an EXISTS test by moving the comparison *inside* the search condition of the subquery. Usually this is a very good idea, because it eliminates errors like the one just described. Here is an alternative form of the query, using the EXISTS test:

```
SELECT NAME, AGE
  FROM SALESREPS
 WHERE NOT EXISTS (SELECT *
                     FROM OFFICES
                    WHERE EMPL_NUM = MGR)
```

```
NAME              AGE
--------------    ----
Mary Jones         31
Sue Smith          48
Dan Roberts        45
Tom Snyder         41
Paul Cruz          29
Nancy Angelli      49
```

THE ALL TEST * Like the ANY test, the ALL test is used in conjunction with one of the six SQL comparison operators (=, <>, <, <=, >, >=) to compare a single test value to a column of data values produced by a subquery. To perform the test, SQL uses the specified comparison operator to compare the test value to *each* data value in the column, one at a time. If *all* of the individual comparisons yield a TRUE result, the ALL test returns a TRUE result.

Here is an example of a request that can be handled with the ALL test:

List the offices and their targets where all of the salespeople have sales that exceed 50 percent of the office's target.

```
SELECT CITY, TARGET
  FROM OFFICES
 WHERE (.50 * TARGET) < ALL (SELECT SALES
                               FROM SALESREPS
                              WHERE REP_OFFICE = OFFICE)
```

```
CITY             TARGET
------------     ------------
Denver           $300,000.00
New York         $575,000.00
Atlanta          $350,000.00
```

Conceptually, the main query tests each row of the OFFICES table, one-by-one. The subquery finds all of the salespeople who work in the "current" office and returns a column containing the sales for each salesperson. The WHERE clause of the main query then computes 50 percent of the office's target and uses it as a test value, comparing it to every sales value produced by the subquery. If *all* of the sales values exceed the calculated test value, the "< ALL" test returns a TRUE and the office is included in the query results. If not, the office is not included in the query results.

Like the ANY test, the ALL test can be difficult to understand because it involves an entire set of comparisons, not just one. Again, it helps if you read the test in a slightly different way than it appears in the statement. If this ALL test appears:

```
WHERE X < ALL (SELECT Y ...)
```

instead of reading like this:

"where X is less than all select Y. . .,"

try reading the test like this:

"where, for *all* Y, X is less than Y"

When you use this trick, the preceding query becomes:

"Select the offices where, for *all* salespeople who work in the office, 50 percent of the office's target is less than the salesperson's sales."

If the subquery in an ALL test produces no rows of query results, or if the query results include NULL values, the operation of the ALL test may vary from one DBMS to another. The ANSI/ISO SQL standard specifies these detailed rules describing the results of the ALL test when the test value is compared to the column of subquery results:

- If the subquery produces an empty column of query results, the ALL test returns TRUE. The comparison test *does* hold for every value produced by the subquery; there just aren't any values.

- If the comparison test is TRUE for *every* data value in the column, then the ALL search condition returns TRUE. Again, the comparison test holds true for every value produced by the subquery.

- If the comparison test is FALSE for *any* data value in the column, then the ALL search condition returns FALSE. In this case, you can conclusively state that the comparison test does not hold true for every data value produced by the query.

- If the comparison test is not FALSE for any data value in the column, but it is NULL for one or more of the data values, then the ALL search condition returns NULL. In this situation, you cannot conclusively state whether there is a value produced by the subquery for which the comparison test does not hold true; there may be or there may not be, depending on the "correct" values for the NULL (unknown) data.

The subtle errors that can occur when the ANY test is combined with the inequality (<>) comparison operator also occur with the ALL test. As with the ANY test, the ALL test can always be converted into an equivalent EXISTS test by moving the comparison inside the subquery.

Subqueries and Joins

You may have noticed as you read through this chapter that many of the queries that were written using subqueries could also have been written as multi-table queries, or joins. This is often the case, and SQL allows you to write the query either way. This example illustrates the point:

List the names and ages of salespeople who work in offices in the Western region.

```
SELECT NAME, AGE
  FROM SALESREPS
 WHERE REP_OFFICE IN (SELECT OFFICE
                        FROM OFFICES
                       WHERE REGION = 'Western')

NAME              AGE
--------------    ----
Sue Smith          48
Larry Fitch        62
Nancy Angelli      49
```

This form of the query closely parallels the stated request. The subquery yields a list of offices in the Western region, and the main query finds the salespeople who work in one of the offices in the list. Here is an alternative form of the query, using a two-table join:

List the names and ages of salespeople who work in offices in the Western region.

```
SELECT NAME, AGE
  FROM SALESREPS, OFFICES
 WHERE REP_OFFICE = OFFICE
   AND REGION = 'Western'

NAME              AGE
--------------    ----
Sue Smith          48
Larry Fitch        62
Nancy Angelli      49
```

This form of the query joins the SALESREPS table to the OFFICES table to find the region where each salesperson works, and then eliminates those that do not work in the Western region.

Either of the two queries will find the correct salespeople, and neither one is "right" or "wrong." Many people will find the first form (with the subquery) more natural, because the English request doesn't ask for any information about offices, and because it seems a little strange to join the SALESREPS and OFFICES tables to answer the request. Of course if the request is changed to ask for some information from the OFFICES table:

"List the names and ages of the salespeople who work in offices in the Western region and the cities where they work."

the subquery form will no longer work, and the two-table query must be used. Conversely, there are many queries with subqueries that *cannot* be translated into an equivalent join. Here is a simple example:

List the names and ages of salespeople who have above-average quotas.

```
SELECT NAME, AGE
  FROM SALESREPS
 WHERE QUOTA > (SELECT AVG(QUOTA)
                  FROM SALESREPS)

NAME              AGE
-------------     ----
Bill Adams         37
Sue Smith          48
Larry Fitch        62
```

In this case, the inner query is a summary query and the outer query is not, so there is no way the two queries can be combined into a single join.

Nested Subqueries

All of the queries described thus far in this chapter have been "two-level" queries, involving a main query and a subquery. Just as you can use a subquery "inside" a main query, you can use a subquery inside another subquery. Here is an example of a request that is naturally represented as a three-level query, with a main query, a subquery, and a subsubquery:

List the customers whose salespeople are assigned to offices in the Eastern sales region.

```
SELECT COMPANY
  FROM CUSTOMERS
 WHERE CUST_REP IN (SELECT EMPL_NUM
                      FROM SALESREPS
                     WHERE REP_OFFICE IN (SELECT OFFICE
                                            FROM OFFICES
                                           WHERE REGION = 'Eastern'))

COMPANY
------------------
First Corp.
Smithson Corp.
AAA Investments
JCP Inc.
Chen Associates
QMA Assoc.
Ian & Schmidt
Acme Mfg.
     .
     .
     .
```

In this example, the innermost subquery:

```
SELECT OFFICE
  FROM OFFICES
 WHERE REGION = 'Eastern'
```

produces a column containing the office numbers of the offices in the Eastern region.
The next subquery:

```
SELECT EMPL_NUM
  FROM SALESREPS
 WHERE REP_OFFICE IN (subquery)
```

produces a column containing the employee numbers of the salespeople who work in
one of the selected offices. Finally, the outermost query:

```
SELECT COMPANY
  FROM CUSTOMERS
 WHERE CUST_REP IN (subquery)
```

finds the customers whose salespeople have one of the selected employee numbers.

The same technique used in this three-level query can be used to build queries with four or more levels. The ANSI/ISO SQL standard does not specify a maximum number of nesting levels, but in practice a query becomes much more time-consuming as the number of levels increases. The query also becomes more difficult to read, understand, and maintain when it involves more than one or two levels of subqueries. Many SQL implementations restrict the number of subquery levels to a relatively small number.

Correlated Subqueries *

In concept, SQL performs a subquery over and over again—once for each row of the main query. For many subqueries, however, the subquery produces the *same* results for every row or row group. Here is an example:

List the sales offices whose sales are below the average target.

```
SELECT CITY
  FROM OFFICES
 WHERE SALES < (SELECT AVG(TARGET)
                  FROM OFFICES)

CITY
- - - - - - - - - - - -
Denver
Atlanta
```

In this query, it would be silly to perform the subquery five times (once for each office). The average target doesn't change with each office; it's completely independent of the office currently being tested. As a result, SQL can handle the query by first performing the subquery, yielding the average target ($550,000), and then converting the main query into:

```
SELECT CITY
  FROM OFFICES
 WHERE SALES < 550000.00
```

Commercial SQL implementations use this shortcut whenever possible to reduce the amount of processing required by a subquery. However, the shortcut cannot be used if the subquery contains an outer reference, as in this example:

List all of the offices whose targets exceed the sum of the quotas of the salespeople who work in them:

```
SELECT CITY
  FROM OFFICES
 WHERE TARGET > (SELECT SUM(QUOTA)
                   FROM SALESREPS
                  WHERE REP_OFFICE = OFFICE)

CITY
------------
Chicago
Los Angeles
```

For each row of the OFFICES table to be tested by the WHERE clause of the main query, the OFFICE column (which appears in the subquery as an outer reference) has a different value. Thus SQL has no choice but to carry out this subquery five times—once for each row in the OFFICES table. A subquery containing an outer reference is called a *correlated subquery,* because its results are correlated with each individual row of the main query. For the same reason, an outer reference is sometimes called a *correlated reference.*

A subquery can contain an outer reference to a table in the FROM clause of *any query that contains the subquery,* no matter how deeply the subqueries are nested. A column name in a fourth-level subquery, for example, may refer to one of the tables named in the FROM clause of the main query, or to a table in any of the subqueries that contain the subquery in which the column name appears. Regardless of the level of nesting, an outer reference always takes on the value of the column in the "current" row of the table being tested.

Because a subquery can contain outer references, there is even more potential for ambiguous column names in a subquery than in a main query. When an unqualified column name appears within a subquery, SQL must determine whether it refers to a table in the subquery's own FROM clause, or to a FROM clause in a query containing the subquery. To minimize the possibility of confusion, SQL always interprets a column reference in a subquery *using the nearest FROM clause possible.* To illustrate this point, here is an example where the same table is used in the query and in the subquery:

List the salespeople who are over 40 and who manage a salesperson over quota.

```
SELECT NAME
  FROM SALESREPS
 WHERE AGE > 40
```

```
      AND EMPL_NUM IN (SELECT MANAGER
                         FROM SALESREPS
                        WHERE SALES > QUOTA)

 NAME
 --------------
 Sam Clark
 Larry Fitch
```

The `MANAGER, QUOTA`, and `SALES` columns in the subquery are references to the `SALESREPS` table in the subquery's own `FROM` clause; SQL does *not* interpret them as outer references, and the subquery is not a correlated subquery. As discussed earlier, SQL can perform the subquery first in this case, finding the salespeople who are over quota and generating a list of the employee numbers of their managers. SQL can then turn its attention to the main query, selecting managers whose employee numbers appear in the generated list.

If you want to use an outer reference within a subquery like the one in the previous example, you must use a table alias to force the outer reference. This request, which adds one more qualifying condition to the previous one, shows how:

List the managers who are over 40 and who manage a salesperson who is over quota and who does not work in the same sales office as the manager.

```
 SELECT NAME
   FROM SALESREPS MGRS
  WHERE AGE > 40
    AND MGRS.EMPL_NUM IN (SELECT MANAGER
                            FROM SALESREPS EMPS
                           WHERE EMPS.QUOTA > EMPS.SALES
                             AND EMPS.REP_OFFICE <> MGRS.REP_OFFICE)

 NAME
 --------------
 Sam Clark
 Larry Fitch
```

The copy of the `SALESREPS` table used in the main query now has the tag `MGRS`, and the copy in the subquery has the tag `EMPS`. The subquery contains one additional search condition, requiring that the employee's office number does not match that of the manager. The qualified column name `MGRS.OFFICE` in the subquery is an outer reference, and this subquery is a correlated subquery.

Subqueries in the HAVING **Clause ***

Although subqueries are most often found in the WHERE clause, they can also be used in the HAVING clause of a query. When a subquery appears in the HAVING clause, it works as part of the row group selection performed by the HAVING clause. Consider this query with a subquery:

List the salespeople whose average order size for products manufactured by ACI is higher than overall average order size.

```
SELECT NAME, AVG(AMOUNT)
  FROM SALESREPS, ORDERS
 WHERE EMPL_NUM = REP
   AND MFR = 'ACI'
 GROUP BY NAME
HAVING AVG(AMOUNT) > (SELECT AVG(AMOUNT)
                        FROM ORDERS)

NAME             AVG(AMOUNT)
--------------   -----------
Sue Smith         $15,000.00
Tom Snyder        $22,500.00
```

Figure 9-7 shows conceptually how this query works. The subquery calculates the "overall average order size." It is a simple subquery and contains no outer references, so SQL can calculate the average once and then use it repeatedly in the HAVING clause. The main query goes through the ORDERS table, finding all orders for ACI products, and groups them by salesperson. The HAVING clause then checks each row group to see whether the average order size in that group is bigger than the average for all orders, calculated earlier. If so, the row group is retained; if not, the row group is discarded. Finally, the SELECT clause produces one summary row for each group, showing the name of the salesperson and the average order size for each.

You can also use a correlated subquery in the HAVING clause. Because the subquery is evaluated once for each row *group*, however, all outer references in the correlated subquery must be single-valued for each row group. Effectively, this means that the outer reference must either be a reference to a grouping column of the outer query or be contained within a column function. In the latter case, the value of the column function for the row group being tested is calculated as part of the subquery processing.

If the previous request is changed slightly, the subquery in the HAVING clause becomes a correlated subquery:

List the salespeople whose average order size for products manufactured by ACI is at least as big as that salesperson's overall average order size.

```
SELECT NAME, AVG(AMOUNT)
  FROM SALESREPS, ORDERS
 WHERE EMPL_NUM = REP
   AND MFR = 'ACI'
 GROUP BY NAME, EMPL_NUM
HAVING AVG(AMOUNT) >= (SELECT AVG(AMOUNT)
                         FROM ORDERS
                        WHERE REP = EMPL_NUM)
```

```
NAME              AVG(AMOUNT)
--------------    -----------
Bill Adams         $7,865.40
Sue Smith         $15,000.00
Tom Snyder        $22,500.00
```

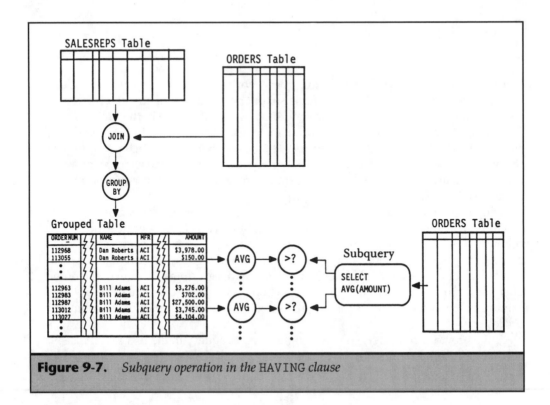

Figure 9-7. *Subquery operation in the HAVING clause*

In this new example, the subquery must produce "the overall average order size" for the salesperson whose row group is currently being tested by the HAVING clause. The subquery selects orders for that particular salesperson, using the outer reference EMPL_NUM. The outer reference is legal, because EMPL_NUM has the same value in all rows of a group produced by the main query.

Summary

This chapter described subqueries, which allow you to use the results of one query to help define another query:

- A subquery is a "query within a query." Subqueries appear within one of the subquery search conditions in the WHERE or HAVING clause.

- When a subquery appears in the WHERE clause, the results of the subquery are used to select the individual rows that contribute data to the query results.

- When a subquery appears in the HAVING clause, the results of the subquery are used to select the row groups that contribute data to the query results.

- Subqueries can be nested within other subqueries.

- The subquery form of the comparison test uses one of the simple comparison operators to compare a test value to the single value returned by a subquery.

- The subquery form of the set membership test (IN) matches a test value to the set of values returned by a subquery.

- The existence test (EXISTS) checks whether a subquery returns any values.

- The quantified tests (ANY and ALL) use one of the simple comparison operators to compare a test value to all of the values returned by a subquery, checking to see whether the comparison holds for some or all of the values.

- A subquery may include an *outer reference* to a table in any of the queries that contain it, linking the subquery to the "current" row of that query.

SQL Queries—A Final Summary

This concludes the discussion of the SQL queries and the SELECT statement that began in Chapter 6. As described in the last four chapters, the clauses of the SELECT statement provide a powerful, flexible set of capabilities for retrieving data from the database. Each clause plays a specific role in data retrieval:

- The FROM clause specifies the source tables that contribute data to the query results. Every column name in the body of the SELECT statement must unambiguously identify a column from one of these tables, or it must be an outer reference to a column from a source table of an outer query.

- The WHERE clause, if present, selects individual combinations of rows from the source tables to participate in the query results. Subqueries in the WHERE clause are evaluated for each individual row.

- The GROUP BY clause, if present, groups the individual rows selected by the WHERE clause into row groups.

- The HAVING clause, if present, selects row groups to participate in the query results. Subqueries in the HAVING clause are evaluated for each row group.

- The SELECT clause determines which data values actually appear as columns in the final query results.

- The DISTINCT keyword, if present, eliminates duplicate rows of query results.

- The UNION operator, if present, merges the query results produced by individual SELECT statements into a single set of query results.

- The ORDER BY clause, if present, sorts the final query results based on one or more columns.

Figure 9-8 shows the final version of the rules for SQL query processing, extended to include subqueries. It provides a complete definition of the query results produced by a SELECT statement.

To generate the query results for a SELECT statement:

1. If the statement is a UNION of SELECT statements, apply Steps 2 through 7 to each of the statements to generate their individual query results.

2. Form the product of the tables named in the FROM clause. If the FROM clause names a single table, the product is that table.

3. If there is a WHERE clause, apply its search condition to each row of the product table, retaining those rows for which the search condition is TRUE (and discarding those for which it is FALSE or NULL). If the WHERE clause contains a subquery, the subquery is performed for each row as it is tested.

4. If there is a GROUP BY clause, arrange the remaining rows of the product table into row groups, so that the rows in each group have identical values in all of the grouping columns.

5. If there is a HAVING clause, apply its search condition to each row group, retaining those groups for which the search condition is TRUE (and discarding those for which it is FALSE or NULL). If the HAVING clause contains a subquery, the subquery is performed for each row group as it is tested.

6. For each remaining row (or row group), calculate the value of each item in the select list to produce a single row of query results. For a simple column reference, use the value of the column in the current row (or row group). For a column function, use the current row group as its argument if GROUP BY is specified; otherwise, use the entire set of rows.

7. If SELECT DISTINCT is specified, eliminate any duplicate rows of query results that were produced.

8. If the statement is a UNION of SELECT statements, merge the query results for the individual statements into a single table of query results. Eliminate duplicate rows unless UNION ALL is specified.

9. If there is an ORDER BY clause, sort the query results as specified.

The rows generated by this procedure comprise the query results.

Figure 9-8.   *SQL query processing rules (final version)*

PART THREE

Updating Data

SQL is not only a query language, it's a complete language for retrieving and modifying data in a database. The next three chapters focus on database updates. Chapter 10 describes the SQL statements that add data to a database, remove data from a database, and modify existing database data. Chapter 11 describes how SQL maintains the integrity of stored data when the data is modified. Chapter 12 describes the SQL transaction-processing features that support concurrent database updates by many different users.

Chapter Ten

Database
Updates

S QL is a complete data manipulation language that is used not only for database queries, but also to modify and update data in the database. Compared to the complexity of the SELECT statement, which supports SQL queries, the SQL statements that modify database contents are extremely simple. However, database updates pose some challenges for a DBMS beyond those presented by database queries. The DBMS must protect the integrity of stored data during changes, ensuring that only valid data is introduced into the database, and that the database remains self-consistent, even in the event of system failures. The DBMS must also coordinate simultaneous updates by multiple users, ensuring that the users and their changes do not interfere with one another.

This chapter describes the three SQL statements that are used to modify the contents of a database:

- INSERT, which adds new rows of data to a table,
- DELETE, which removes rows of data from a table, and
- UPDATE, which modifies existing data in the database.

In Chapter 11, SQL facilities for maintaining data integrity are described. Chapter 12 covers SQL support for multi-user concurrency.

Adding Data to the Database

Typically, a new row of data is added to a relational database when a new entity represented by the row "appears in the outside world." For example, in the sample database:

- When you hire a new salesperson, a new row must be added to the SALESREPS table to store the salesperson's data.
- When a salesperson signs a new customer, a new row must be added to the CUSTOMERS table, representing the new customer.
- When a customer places an order, a new row must be added to the ORDERS table to contain the order data.

In each case, the new row is added to maintain the database as an accurate model of the real world. The smallest unit of data that can be added to a relational database is a single row. In general, a SQL-based DBMS provides three ways to add new rows of data to a database:

- A *single-row* INSERT statement adds a single new row of data to a table. It is commonly used in daily applications, for example, data entry programs.

■ A *multi-row* INSERT statement extracts rows of data from another part of the database and adds them to a table. It is commonly used in end-of-month or end-of-year processing when "old" rows of a table are moved to an inactive table.

■ A *bulk load* utility adds data to a table from a file which is outside of the database. It is commonly used to initially load the database or to incorporate data downloaded from another computer system or collected from many sites.

The Single-Row INSERT Statement

The single-row INSERT statement, shown in Figure 10-1, adds a new row to a table. The INTO clause specifies the table that receives the new row (the *target* table), and the VALUES clause specifies the data values that the new row will contain. The column list indicates which data value goes into which column of the new row.

Suppose you just hired a new salesperson, Henry Jacobsen, with the following personal data:

Name:	Henry Jacobsen
Age:	36
Employee Number:	111
Title:	Sales Manager
Office:	Atlanta (office number 13)
Hire Date:	July 25, 1990
Quota:	Not yet assigned
Year-to-Date Sales:	$0.00

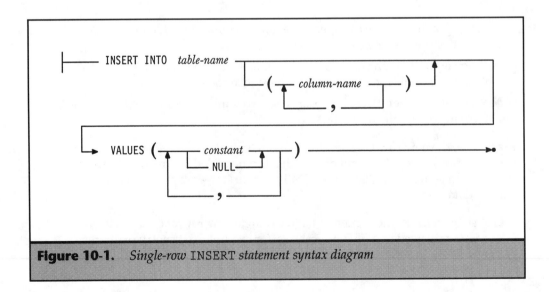

Figure 10-1. *Single-row INSERT statement syntax diagram*

Here is the INSERT statement that adds Mr. Jacobsen to the sample database:

Add Henry Jacobsen as a new salesperson.

```
INSERT INTO
  SALESREPS (NAME, AGE, EMPL_NUM, SALES, TITLE, HIRE_DATE, REP_OFFICE)
     VALUES ('Henry Jacobsen', 36, 111, 0.00, 'Sales Mgr', '25-JUL-90', 13)

1 row inserted.
```

Figure 10-2 graphically illustrates how SQL carries out this INSERT statement. Conceptually, the INSERT statement builds a single row of data that matches the column structure of the table, fills it with the data from the VALUES clause, and then adds the new row to the table. The rows of a table are unordered, so there is no notion of inserting the row "at the top" or "at the bottom" or "between two rows" of the table. After the INSERT statement, the new row is simply a part of the table. A subsequent

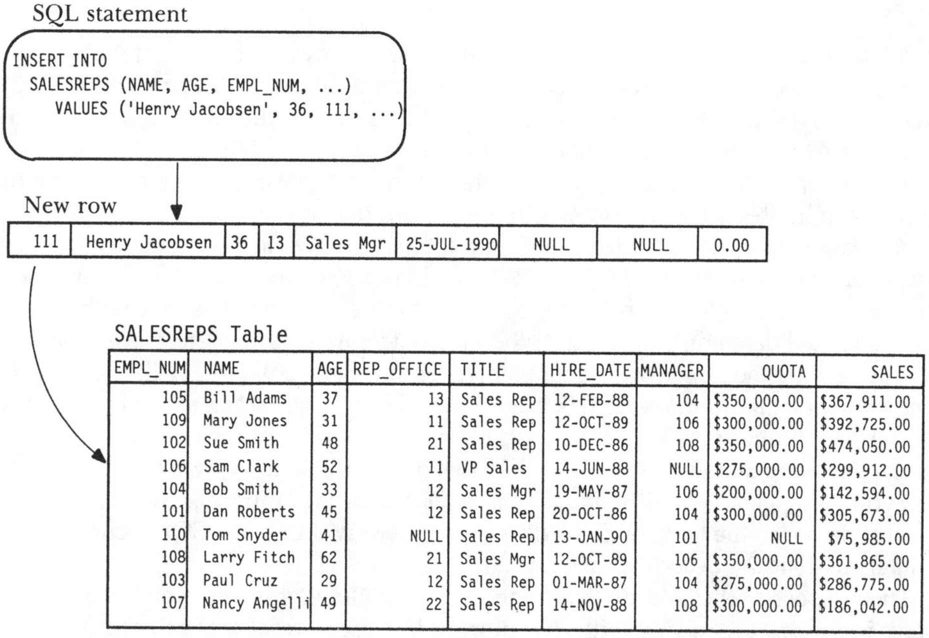

EMPL_NUM	NAME	AGE	REP_OFFICE	TITLE	HIRE_DATE	MANAGER	QUOTA	SALES
105	Bill Adams	37	13	Sales Rep	12-FEB-88	104	$350,000.00	$367,911.00
109	Mary Jones	31	11	Sales Rep	12-OCT-89	106	$300,000.00	$392,725.00
102	Sue Smith	48	21	Sales Rep	10-DEC-86	108	$350,000.00	$474,050.00
106	Sam Clark	52	11	VP Sales	14-JUN-88	NULL	$275,000.00	$299,912.00
104	Bob Smith	33	12	Sales Mgr	19-MAY-87	106	$200,000.00	$142,594.00
101	Dan Roberts	45	12	Sales Rep	20-OCT-86	104	$300,000.00	$305,673.00
110	Tom Snyder	41	NULL	Sales Rep	13-JAN-90	101	NULL	$75,985.00
108	Larry Fitch	62	21	Sales Mgr	12-OCT-89	106	$350,000.00	$361,865.00
103	Paul Cruz	29	12	Sales Rep	01-MAR-87	104	$275,000.00	$286,775.00
107	Nancy Angelli	49	22	Sales Rep	14-NOV-88	108	$300,000.00	$186,042.00

Figure 10-2. *Inserting a single row*

query against the SALESREPS table will include the new row, but it may appear anywhere among the rows of query results.

Suppose that Mr. Jacobsen now receives his first order, from InterCorp, a new customer who is assigned customer number 2126. The order is for 20 ACI-41004 Widgets, for a total price of $2,340, and has been assigned order number 113069. Here are the INSERT statements that add the new customer and the order to the database:

Insert a new customer and order for Mr. Jacobsen.

```
INSERT INTO
   CUSTOMERS (COMPANY, CUST_NUM, CREDIT_LIMIT, CUST_REP)
      VALUES ('InterCorp', 2126, 15000.00, 111)

1 row inserted.

INSERT INTO
      ORDERS (AMOUNT, MFR, PRODUCT, QTY, ORDER_DATE, ORDER_NUM, CUST, REP)
      VALUES (2340.00, 'ACI', '41004', 20, CURRENT DATE, 113069, 2126, 111)

   1 row inserted.
```

As this example shows, the INSERT statement can become lengthy if there are many columns of data, but its format is still very straightforward. The second INSERT statement uses the system constant CURRENT DATE in its VALUES clause, causing the current date to be inserted as the order date. DB2 and several other popular SQL products support this system constant. Other brands of DBMS provide other system constants or built-in functions to obtain the current date and time.

You can use the INSERT statement with interactive SQL to add rows to a table that grows very rarely, such as the OFFICES table. In practice, however, data about a new customer, order, or salesperson is almost always added to a database through a forms-oriented data entry program. When the data entry is complete, the application program inserts the new row of data using programmatic SQL. Regardless of whether interactive or programmatic SQL is used, however, the INSERT statement is the same.

The table name specified in the INSERT statement is normally an unqualified table name, specifying a table that you own. To insert data into a table owned by another user, you can specify a qualified table name. Of course you must also have permission to insert data into the table or the INSERT statement will fail. The SQL security scheme and permissions are described in Chapter 15.

The purpose of the column list in the INSERT statement is to match the data values in the VALUES clause with the columns that are to receive them. The list of values and the list of columns must both contain the same number of items, and the data type of each value must be compatible with the data type of the corresponding column, or an error will occur. The ANSI/ISO standard mandates unqualified column names in the column list, but many implementations allow qualified names. Of course there can be no ambiguity in the column names anyway, because they must all reference columns of the target table.

INSERTING NULL VALUES When SQL inserts a new row of data into a table, it automatically assigns a NULL value to any column whose name is missing from the column list in the INSERT statement. In this INSERT statement, which added Mr. Jacobsen to the SALESREPS table, the QUOTA and MANAGER columns were omitted:

```
INSERT INTO
   SALESREPS (NAME, AGE, EMPL_NUM, SALES, TITLE, HIRE_DATE, REP_OFFICE)
      VALUES ('Henry Jacobsen', 36, 111, 0.00, 'Sales Mgr', '25-JUL-90', 13)
```

As a result, the newly added row has a NULL value in the QUOTA and MANAGER columns, as shown in Figure 10-2. You can make the assignment of a NULL value more explicit by including these columns in the column list and specifying the keyword NULL in the values list. This INSERT statement has exactly the same effect as the previous one:

```
INSERT INTO
   SALESREPS (NAME, AGE, EMPL_NUM, SALES, QUOTA, TITLE,
               MANAGER, HIRE_DATE, REP_OFFICE)
      VALUES ('Henry Jacobsen', 36, 111, 0.00, NULL, 'Sales Mgr',
               NULL, '25-JUL-90', 13)
```

INSERTING ALL COLUMNS As a convenience, SQL allows you to omit the column list from the INSERT statement. When the column list is omitted, SQL automatically generates a column list consisting of all columns of the table, in left-to-right sequence. This is the same column sequence generated by SQL when you use a SELECT * query. Using this shortcut, the previous INSERT statement could be rewritten equivalently as:

```
INSERT INTO SALESREPS
      VALUES (111, 'Henry Jacobsen', 36, 13, 'Sales Mgr',
               '25-JUL-90', NULL, NULL, 0.00)
```

When you omit the column list, the NULL keyword *must* be used in the values list to explicitly assign NULL values to columns, as shown in the example. In addition, the sequence of data values must correspond *exactly* to the sequence of columns in the table.

Omitting the column list is convenient in interactive SQL, because it reduces the length of the INSERT statement you must type. For programmatic SQL, the column list should always be specified, because it makes the program easier to read and understand.

The Multi-Row `INSERT` Statement

The second form of the `INSERT` statement, shown in Figure 10-3, adds multiple rows of data to its target table. In this form of the `INSERT` statement, the data values for the new rows are not explicitly specified within the statement text. Instead, the source of new rows is a database query, specified in the statement.

Adding rows whose values come from within the database itself may seem strange at first, but it's very useful in some special situations. For example, suppose that you want to copy the order number, date, and amount of all orders placed before January 1, 1990, from the `ORDERS` table into another table, called `OLDORDERS`. The multi-row `INSERT` statement provides a compact, efficient way to copy the data:

Copy old orders into the `OLDORDERS` *table.*

```
INSERT INTO OLDORDERS (ORDER_NUM, ORDER_DATE, AMOUNT)
    SELECT ORDER_NUM, ORDER_DATE, AMOUNT
      FROM ORDERS
      WHERE ORDER_DATE < '01-JAN-90'

9 rows inserted.
```

This `INSERT` statement looks complicated, but it's really very simple. The statement identifies the table to receive the new rows (`OLDORDERS`) and the columns to receive the data, just like the single-row `INSERT` statement. The remainder of the statement is a query that retrieves data from the `ORDERS` table. Figure 10-4 graphically illustrates the operation of this `INSERT` statement. Conceptually, SQL first performs the query against the `ORDERS` table, and then inserts the query results, row by row, into the `OLDORDERS` table.

Here's another situation where you could use the multi-row `INSERT` statement. Suppose you want to analyze customer buying patterns by looking at which customers and salespeople are responsible for big orders—those over $15,000. The queries that you will be running will combine data from the `CUSTOMERS`, `SALESREPS`, and `ORDERS` tables. These three-table queries will execute fairly quickly on the small sample database, but in a real corporate database with many thousands of rows, they

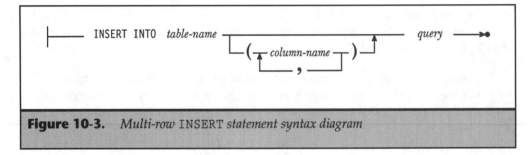

Figure 10-3. *Multi-row* INSERT *statement syntax diagram*

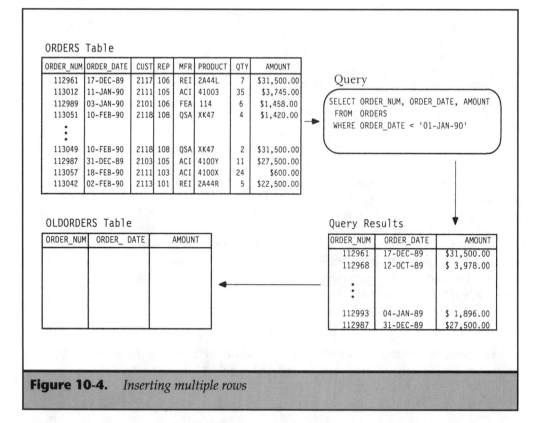

ORDERS Table

ORDER_NUM	ORDER_DATE	CUST	REP	MFR	PRODUCT	QTY	AMOUNT
112961	17-DEC-89	2117	106	REI	2A44L	7	$31,500.00
113012	11-JAN-90	2111	105	ACI	41003	35	$3,745.00
112989	03-JAN-90	2101	106	FEA	114	6	$1,458.00
113051	10-FEB-90	2118	108	QSA	XK47	4	$1,420.00
⋮							
113049	10-FEB-90	2118	108	QSA	XK47	2	$31,500.00
112987	31-DEC-89	2103	105	ACI	4100Y	11	$27,500.00
113057	18-FEB-90	2111	103	ACI	4100X	24	$600.00
113042	02-FEB-90	2113	101	REI	2A44R	5	$22,500.00

Query

```
SELECT ORDER_NUM, ORDER_DATE, AMOUNT
  FROM ORDERS
 WHERE ORDER_DATE < '01-JAN-90'
```

OLDORDERS Table

ORDER_NUM	ORDER_ DATE	AMOUNT

Query Results

ORDER_NUM	ORDER_DATE	AMOUNT
112961	17-DEC-89	$31,500.00
112968	12-OCT-89	$ 3,978.00
⋮		
112993	04-JAN-89	$ 1,896.00
112987	31-DEC-89	$27,500.00

Figure 10-4. *Inserting multiple rows*

would take a long time. Rather than running many long, three-table queries, you could create a new table named BIGORDERS to contain the required data, defined as follows:

Column	Information
AMOUNT	Order amount (from ORDERS)
COMPANY	Customer name (from CUSTOMERS)
NAME	Salesperson name (from SALESREPS)
PERF	Amount over/under quota (calculated from SALESREPS)
MFR	Manufacturer id (from ORDERS)
PRODUCT	Product id (from ORDERS)
QTY	Quantity ordered (from ORDERS)

Once you have created the BIGORDERS table, this multi-row INSERT statement can be used to populate it:

Load data into the BIGORDERS *table for analysis .*

```
INSERT INTO BIGORDERS (AMOUNT, COMPANY, NAME, PERF, PRODUCT, MFR, QTY)
    SELECT AMOUNT, COMPANY, NAME, (SALES - QUOTA), PRODUCT, MFR, QTY
      FROM ORDERS, CUSTOMERS, SALESREPS
     WHERE CUST = CUST_NUM
       AND REP = EMPL_NUM
       AND AMOUNT > 15000.00

6 rows inserted.
```

In a large database, this INSERT statement may take a while to execute, because it involves a three-table query. When the statement is complete, the data in the BIGORDERS table will duplicate information in other tables. In addition, the BIGORDERS table won't be automatically kept up to date when new orders are added to the database, so its data may quickly become outdated. Each of these factors seems like a disadvantage. However, the subsequent data analysis queries against the BIGORDERS table can be expressed very simply—they become single-table queries. Furthermore, each of those queries will run much faster than if it were a three-table join. Consequently, this is probably a good strategy for performing the analysis, especially if the three original tables are large.

The SQL1 standard specifies several logical restrictions on the query that appears within the multi-row INSERT statement:

- The query cannot contain an ORDER BY clause. It's useless to sort the query results anyway, because they're being inserted into a table which is, like all tables, unordered.

- The query results must contain the same number of columns as the column list in the INSERT statement (or the entire target table, if the column list is omitted), and the data types must be compatible, column by column.

- The query cannot be the UNION of several different SELECT statements. Only a single SELECT statement may be specified.

- The target table of the INSERT statement cannot appear in the FROM clause of the query or any subqueries that it contains. This prohibits inserting part of a table into itself.

The SQL2 standard relaxes the last two restrictions, allowing UNION and join operations and expressions in the query, and permitting "self-insertion".

Bulk Load Utilities

Data to be inserted into a database is often downloaded from another computer system or collected from other sites and stored in a sequential file. To load the data into a table, you could write a program with a loop that reads each record of the file and uses the single-row INSERT statement to add the row to the table. However, the overhead of having the DBMS repeatedly execute single-row INSERT statements may be quite high. If inserting a single row takes half of a second under a typical system load, that is probably acceptable performance for an interactive program. But that performance quickly becomes unacceptable when applied to the task of bulk loading 50,000 rows of data. In this case, loading the data would require over six hours.

For this reason, all commercial DBMS products include a bulk load feature that loads data from a file into a table at high speed. The ANSI/ISO SQL standard does not address this function, and it is usually provided as a stand-alone utility program rather than as part of the SQL language. Each vendor's utility provides a slightly different set of features, functions, and commands.

Deleting Data from the Database

Typically, a row of data is deleted from a database when the entity represented by the row "disappears from the outside world." For example, in the sample database:

- When a customer cancels an order, the corresponding row of the ORDERS table must be deleted.

- When a salesperson leaves the company, the corresponding row of the SALESREPS table must be deleted.

- When a sales office is closed, the corresponding row of the OFFICES table must be deleted. If the salespeople in the office are terminated, their rows should be deleted from the SALESREPS table as well. If they are reassigned, their REP_OFFICE columns must be updated.

In each case, the row is deleted to maintain the database as an accurate model of the real world. The smallest unit of data that can be deleted from a relational database is a single row.

The DELETE Statement

The DELETE statement, shown in Figure 10-5, removes selected rows of data from a single table. The FROM clause specifies the target table containing the rows. The WHERE clause specifies which rows of the table are to be deleted.

Suppose that Henry Jacobsen, the new salesperson hired earlier in this chapter, has just decided to leave the company. Here is the DELETE statement that removes his row from the SALESREPS table:

Remove Henry Jacobsen from the database.

```
DELETE FROM SALESREPS
 WHERE NAME = 'Henry Jacobsen'
 1 row deleted.
```

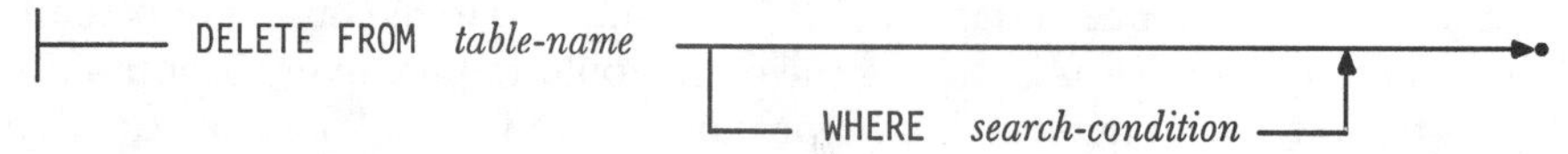

```
        ├──── DELETE FROM  table-name ──┬──────────────────────────────┬──►●
                                        └── WHERE  search-condition ──┘
```

Figure 10-5. DELETE *statement syntax diagram*

The WHERE clause in this example identifies a single row of the SALESREPS table, which SQL removes from the table. The WHERE clause should have a familiar appearance—it's exactly the same WHERE clause that you would specify in a SELECT statement to *retrieve* the same row from the table. The search conditions that can be specified in the WHERE clause of the DELETE statement are the same ones available in the WHERE clause of the SELECT statement, as described in Chapters 6 and 9.

Recall that search conditions in the WHERE clause of a SELECT statement can specify a single row or an entire set of rows, depending on the specific search condition. The same is true of the WHERE clause in a DELETE statement. Suppose, for example, that Mr. Jacobsen's customer, InterCorp (customer number 2126) has called to cancel all of their orders. Here is the delete statement that removes the orders from the ORDERS table:

Remove all orders for InterCorp (customer number 2126).

```
DELETE FROM ORDERS
  WHERE CUST = 2126

2 rows deleted.
```

In this case, the WHERE clause selects several rows of the ORDERS table, and SQL removes all of the selected rows from the table. Conceptually, SQL applies the WHERE clause to each row of the ORDERS table, deleting those where the search condition yields a TRUE result and retaining those where the search condition yields a FALSE or NULL result. Because this type of DELETE statement searches through a table for the rows to be deleted, it is sometimes called a *searched* DELETE statement. This term is used to contrast it with another form of the DELETE statement, called the *positioned* DELETE statement, which always deletes a single row. The positioned DELETE statement applies only to programmatic SQL, and is described in Chapter 17.

Here are some additional examples of searched DELETE statements:

Delete all orders placed before November 15, 1989.

```
DELETE FROM ORDERS
  WHERE ORDER_DATE < '15-NOV-89'

5 rows deleted.
```

Delete all rows for customers served by Bill Adams, Mary Jones, or Dan Roberts (employee numbers 105, 109, and 101).

```
DELETE FROM CUSTOMERS
  WHERE CUST_REP IN (105, 109, 101)

7 rows deleted.
```

Delete all salespeople hired before July 1988 who have not yet been assigned a quota.

```
DELETE FROM SALESREPS
  WHERE HIRE_DATE < '01-JUL-88'
    AND QUOTA IS NULL

0 rows deleted.
```

Deleting All Rows

The WHERE clause in a DELETE statement is optional, but it is almost always present. If the WHERE clause is omitted from a DELETE statement, *all* rows of the target table are deleted, as in this example:

Delete all orders.

```
DELETE FROM ORDERS

30 rows deleted.
```

Although this DELETE statement produces an empty table, it does not erase the ORDERS table from the database. The definition of the ORDERS table and its columns is still stored in the database. The table still exists, and new rows can still be inserted into the ORDERS table with the INSERT statement. To erase the definition of the table from the database, the DROP TABLE statement (described in Chapter 13) must be used.

Because of the potential damage from such a DELETE statement, it's important always to specify a search condition and to be careful that it actually selects the rows you want. When using interactive SQL, it's a good idea first to use the WHERE clause in a SELECT statement to display the selected rows, make sure that they are the ones you want to delete, and only then use the WHERE clause in a DELETE statement.

DELETE **with Subquery** *

DELETE statements with simple search conditions, such as those in the previous examples, select rows for deletion based solely on the contents of the rows themselves. Sometimes the selection of rows must be made based on data from other tables. For example, suppose you want to delete all orders taken by Sue Smith. Without knowing her employee number, you can't find the orders by consulting the ORDERS table alone. To find the orders, you could use a two-table query:

Find the orders taken by Sue Smith.

```
SELECT ORDER_NUM, AMOUNT
  FROM ORDERS, SALESREPS
 WHERE REP = EMPL_NUM
   AND NAME = 'Sue Smith'

ORDER_NUM      AMOUNT
---------  -----------
   112979  $15,000.00
   113065   $2,130.00
   112993   $1,896.00
   113048   $3,750.00
```

But you can't use a join in a DELETE statement. The parallel DELETE statement is illegal:

```
DELETE FROM ORDERS, SALESREPS
 WHERE REP = EMPL_NUM
   AND NAME = 'Sue Smith'

Error: More than one table specified in FROM clause
```

The way to handle the request is with one of the *subquery* search conditions. Here is a valid form of the DELETE statement that handles the request:

Delete the orders taken by Sue Smith.

```
DELETE FROM ORDERS
  WHERE REP = (SELECT EMPL_NUM
                 FROM SALESREPS
                 WHERE NAME = 'Sue Smith')

4 rows deleted.
```

The subquery finds the employee number for Sue Smith, and the WHERE clause then selects the orders with a matching value. As this example shows, subqueries can play an important role in the DELETE statement, because they let you delete rows based on information in other tables. Here are two more examples of DELETE statements that use subquery search conditions:

Delete customers served by salespeople whose sales are less than 80 percent of quota.

```
DELETE FROM CUSTOMERS
  WHERE CUST_REP IN (SELECT EMPL_NUM
                       FROM SALESREPS
                       WHERE SALES < (.8 * QUOTA))

2 rows deleted.
```

Delete any salesperson whose current orders total less than two percent of their quota.

```
DELETE FROM SALESREPS
  WHERE (.02 * QUOTA) > (SELECT SUM(AMOUNT)
                           FROM ORDERS
                           WHERE REP = EMPL_NUM)

1 row deleted.
```

Subqueries in the WHERE clause can be nested just as they can be in the WHERE clause of the SELECT statement. They can also contain outer references to the target table of the DELETE statement. In this respect, the FROM clause of the DELETE statement functions like the FROM clause of the SELECT statement. Here is an example of a deletion request that requires a subquery with an outer reference:

Delete customers who have not ordered since November 10, 1989.

```
DELETE FROM CUSTOMERS
  WHERE NOT EXISTS (SELECT *
                      FROM ORDERS
                     WHERE CUST = CUST_NUM
                       AND ORDER_DATE < '10-NOV-89')

16 rows deleted.
```

Conceptually, this DELETE statement operates by going through the CUSTOMERS table, row by row, and checking the search condition. For each customer, the subquery selects any orders placed by that customer before the cutoff date. The reference to the CUST_NUM column in the subquery is an outer reference to the customer number in the row of the CUSTOMERS table currently being checked by the DELETE statement. The subquery in this example is a correlated subquery, as described in Chapter 9.

Outer references will often be found in subqueries of a DELETE statement, because they implement the "join" between the table(s) in the subquery and the target table of the DELETE statement. The only restriction on the use of subqueries in a DELETE statement is that the target table cannot appear in the FROM clause of a subquery or any of its subqueries at any level of nesting. This prevents the subqueries from referencing the target table (some of whose rows may already have been deleted), except for outer references to the row currently being tested by the DELETE statement's search condition. The SQL2 standard eliminates this restriction by specifying that the DELETE statement should treat such a subquery as applying to the entire target table, before any rows have been deleted.

Modifying Data in the Database

Typically, the values of data items stored in a database are modified when corresponding changes occur in the outside world. For example, in the sample database:

- When a customer calls to change the quantity on an order, the QTY column in the appropriate row of the ORDERS table must be modified.
- When a manager moves from one office to another, the MGR column in the OFFICES table and the REP_OFFICE column in the SALESREPS table must be changed to reflect the new assignment.
- When sales quotas are raised by five percent in the New York sales office, the QUOTA column of the appropriate rows in the SALESREPS table must be modified.

In each case, data values in the database are updated to maintain the database as an accurate model of the real world. The smallest unit of data that can be modified in a database is a single column of a single row.

The UPDATE **Statement**

The UPDATE statement, shown in Figure 10-6, modifies the values of one or more columns in selected rows of a single table. The target table to be updated is named in the statement, and you must have the required permission to update the table as well as each of the individual columns that will be modified. The WHERE clause selects the rows of the table to be modified. The SET clause specifies which columns are to be updated and calculates the new values for them.

Here is a simple UPDATE statement that changes the credit limit and salesperson for a customer:

Raise the credit limit for Acme Manufacturing to $60,000 and reassign them to Mary Jones (employee number 109).

```
UPDATE CUSTOMERS
   SET CREDIT_LIMIT = 60000.00, CUST_REP = 109
 WHERE COMPANY = 'Acme Mfg.'

1 row updated.
```

In this example, the WHERE clause identifies a single row of the CUSTOMERS table, and the SET clause assigns new values to two of the columns in that row. The WHERE clause is exactly the same one you would use in a DELETE or SELECT statement to identify the row. In fact, the search conditions that can appear in the WHERE clause of an UPDATE statement are exactly the same as those available in the SELECT and DELETE statements.

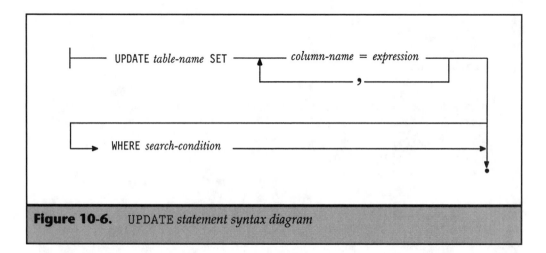

Figure 10-6. UPDATE *statement syntax diagram*

Like the DELETE statement, the UPDATE statement can update several rows at once with the proper search condition, as in this example:

Transfer all salespeople from the Chicago office (number 12) to the New York office (number 11), and lower their quotas by ten percent.

```
UPDATE SALESREPS
   SET REP_OFFICE = 11, QUOTA = .9 * QUOTA
 WHERE REP_OFFICE = 12

3 rows updated.
```

In this case, the WHERE clause selects several rows of the SALESREPS table, and the value of the REP_OFFICE and QUOTA columns are modified in all of them. Conceptually, SQL processes the UPDATE statement by going through the SALESREPS table row by row, updating those rows for which the search condition yields a TRUE result and skipping over those for which the search condition yields a FALSE or NULL result. Because it searches the table, this form of the UPDATE statement is sometimes called a *searched* UPDATE statement. This term distinguishes it from a different form of the UPDATE statement, called a *positioned* UPDATE statement, which always updates a single row. The positioned UPDATE statement applies only to programmatic SQL, and is described in Chapter 17.

Here are some additional examples of searched UPDATE statements:

Reassign all customers served by employee number 105, 106, or 107 to employee number 102.

```
UPDATE CUSTOMERS
   SET CUST_REP = 102
 WHERE CUST_REP IN (105, 106, 107)

5 rows updated.
```

Assign a quota of $100,000 to any salesperson who currently has no quota.

```
UPDATE SALESREPS
   SET QUOTA = 100000.00
 WHERE QUOTA IS NULL

1 row updated.
```

The SET clause in the UPDATE statement is a list of assignments separated by commas. Each assignment identifies a target column to be updated and specifies how to calculate the new value for the target column. Each target column should appear only once in the list; there should not be two assignments for the same target column. The ANSI/ISO specification mandates unqualified names for the target columns, but some SQL implementations allow qualified column names. There can be no ambiguity in the column names anyway, because they must refer to columns of the target table.

The expression in each assignment can be any valid SQL expression that yields a value of the appropriate data type for the target column. The expression must be computable based on the values of the row currently being updated in the target table. It may not include any column functions or subqueries.

If an expression in the assignment list references one of the columns of the target table, the value used to calculate the expression is the value of that column in the current row *before* any updates are applied. The same is true of column references that occur in the WHERE clause. For example, consider this (somewhat contrived) UPDATE statement:

```
UPDATE OFFICES
   SET QUOTA = 400000.00, SALES = QUOTA
 WHERE QUOTA < 400000.00
```

Before the update, Bill Adams had a QUOTA value of $350,000 and a SALES value of $367,911. After the update, his row has a SALES value of $350,000, *not* $400,000. The order of the assignments in the SET clause is thus immaterial; the assignments can be specified in any order.

Updating All Rows

The WHERE clause in the UPDATE statement is optional. If the WHERE clause is omitted, then *all* rows of the target table are updated, as in this example:

Raise all quotas by five percent.

```
UPDATE SALESREPS
   SET QUOTA = 1.05 * QUOTA

10 rows updated.
```

Unlike the DELETE statement, where the WHERE clause is almost never omitted, the UPDATE statement without a WHERE clause performs a useful function. It basically performs a bulk update of the entire table, as demonstrated in the preceding example.

UPDATE **with Subquery** *

As with the DELETE statement, subqueries can play an important role in the UPDATE statement because they let you select rows for update based on information contained in other tables. Here are several examples of UPDATE statements that use subqueries:

Raise by $5,000 the credit limit of any customer who has placed an order for more than $25,000.

```
UPDATE CUSTOMERS
   SET CREDIT_LIMIT = CREDIT_LIMIT + 5000.00
 WHERE CUST_NUM IN (SELECT DISTINCT CUST
                      FROM ORDERS
                      WHERE AMOUNT > 25000.00)

4 rows updated.
```

Reassign all customers served by salespeople whose sales are less than 80 percent of their quota.

```
UPDATE CUSTOMERS
   SET CUST_REP = 105
 WHERE CUST_REP IN (SELECT EMPL_NUM
                      FROM SALESREPS
                      WHERE SALES < (.8 * QUOTA))

2 rows updated.
```

Have all salespeople who serve over three customers report directly to Sam Clark (employee number 106).

```
UPDATE SALESREPS
   SET MANAGER = 106
 WHERE 3 < (SELECT COUNT(*)
              FROM CUSTOMERS
              WHERE CUST_REP = EMPL_NUM)

1 row updated.
```

As in the DELETE statement, subqueries in the WHERE clause of the UPDATE statement can be nested to any level, and can contain outer references to the target table of the UPDATE statement. The column EMPL_NUM in the subquery of the preceding example is such an outer reference; it refers to the EMPL_NUM column in the row of the SALESREPS table currently being checked by the UPDATE statement. The subquery in this example is a correlated subquery, as described in Chapter 9.

Outer references will often be found in subqueries of an UPDATE statement, because they implement the "join" between the table(s) in the subquery and the target table of the UPDATE statement. The same SQL1 restriction applies as for the DELETE statement: the target table cannot appear in the FROM clause of any subquery at any level of nesting. This prevents the subqueries from referencing the target table (some of whose rows may have already been updated). Any references to the target table in the subqueries are thus outer references to the row of the target table currently being tested by the UPDATE statement's WHERE clause. The SQL2 standard again removes this restriction, and specifies that a reference to the target table in a subquery is evaluated as if none of the target table had been updated.

Summary

This chapter described the SQL statements that are used to modify the contents of a database:

- The single-row INSERT statement adds one row of data to a table. The values for the new row are specified in the statement as constants.

- The multi-row INSERT statement adds zero or more rows to a table. The values for the new rows come from a query, specified as part of the INSERT statement.

- The DELETE statement deletes zero or more rows of data from a table. The rows to be deleted are specified by a search condition.

- The UPDATE statement modifies the values of one or more columns in zero or more rows of a table. The rows to be updated are specified by a search condition. The columns to be updated, and the expressions that calculate their new values, are specified in the UPDATE statement.

- Unlike the SELECT statement, which can operate on multiple tables, the INSERT, DELETE, and UPDATE statements work on only a single table at a time.

- The search condition used in the DELETE and UPDATE statements has the same form as the search condition for the SELECT statement.

Chapter Eleven

Data Integrity

260

T he term *data integrity* refers to the correctness and completeness of the data in a database. When the contents of a database are modified with the INSERT, DELETE, or UPDATE statements, the integrity of the stored data can be lost in many different ways. For example:

- Invalid data may be added to the database, such as an order that specifies a nonexistent product.

- Existing data may be modified to an incorrect value, such as reassigning a salesperson to a nonexistent office.

- Changes to the database may be lost due to a system error or power failure.

- Changes may be partially applied, such as adding an order for a product without adjusting the quantity available for sale.

One of the important roles of a relational DBMS is to preserve the integrity of its stored data to the greatest extent possible. This chapter describes the SQL language features that assist the DBMS in this task.

What Is Data Integrity?

To preserve the consistency and correctness of its stored data, a relational DBMS typically imposes one or more *data integrity constraints*. These constraints restrict the data values that can be inserted into the database or created by a database update. Several different types of data integrity constraints are commonly found in relational databases, including:

- *Required data.* Some columns in a database must contain a valid data value in every row; they are not allowed to contain missing or NULL values. In the sample database, every order must have an associated customer who placed the order. Therefore the CUST column in the ORDERS table is a *required column*. The DBMS can be asked to prevent NULL values in this column.

- *Validity checking.* Every column in a database has a *domain*, a set of data values that are legal for that column. The sample database uses order numbers that begin at 100001, so the domain of the ORDER_NUM column is positive integers greater than 100000. Similarly, employee numbers in the EMPL_NUM column must fall within the numeric range of 101 to 999. The DBMS can be asked to prevent other data values in these columns.

- *Entity integrity.* The primary key of a table must contain a unique value in each row, different from the values in all other rows. For example, each row of the PRODUCTS table has a unique set of values in its MFR_ID and PRODUCT_ID columns, which uniquely identifies the product represented by that row. Duplicate values are illegal, because they wouldn't allow the database to distinguish one product from another. The DBMS can be asked to enforce this unique values constraint.

■ *Referential integrity.* A foreign key in a relational database links each row in the child table containing the foreign key to the row of the parent table containing the matching primary key value. In the sample database, the value in the REP_OFFICE column of each SALESREPS row links the salesperson represented by that row to the office where he or she works. The REP_OFFICE column *must* contain a valid value from the OFFICE column of the OFFICES table, or the salesperson will be assigned to an invalid office. The DBMS can be asked to enforce this foreign key/primary key constraint.

■ *Business rules.* Updates to a database may be constrained by business rules governing the real-world transactions that are represented by the updates. For example, the company using the sample database may have a business rule that forbids accepting an order for which there is inadequate product in inventory. The DBMS can be asked to check each new row added to the ORDERS table to make sure that the value in its QTY column does not violate this business rule.

■ *Consistency.* Many real-world transactions cause multiple updates to a database. For example, accepting a customer order may involve adding a row to the ORDERS table, increasing the SALES column in the SALESREPS table for the person who took the order, and increasing the SALES column in the OFFICES table for the office where that salesperson is assigned. The INSERT and both UPDATEs must *all* take place in order for the database to remain in a consistent, correct state. The DBMS can be asked to enforce this type of consistency rule or to support applications that implement such rules.

The ANSI/ISO SQL standard specifies some of the simpler data integrity constraints. For example, the required data constraint is supported by the ANSI/ISO standard and implemented in a uniform way across almost all commercial SQL products. More complex constraints, such as business rules constraints, are not specified by the ANSI/ISO standard, and there is a wide variation in the techniques and SQL syntax used to support them. The SQL features that support the first five integrity constraints are described in this chapter. The SQL transaction mechanism, which supports the consistency constraint, is described in Chapter 12.

Required Data

The simplest data integrity constraint requires that a column contain a non-NULL value. The ANSI/ISO standard and most commercial SQL products support this constraint by allowing you to declare that a column is NOT NULL when the table containing the column is first created. The NOT NULL constraint is specified as part of the CREATE TABLE statement, described in Chapter 13.

When a column is declared NOT NULL, the DBMS enforces the constraint by ensuring the following:

■ Every INSERT statement that adds a new row or rows to the table must specify a non-NULL data value for the column. An attempt to insert a row containing a NULL value (either explicitly or implicitly) results in an error.

■ Every UPDATE statement that updates the column must assign it a non-NULL data value. Again, an attempt to update the column to a NULL value results in an error.

One disadvantage of the NOT NULL constraint is that it must usually be specified when a table is first created. Typically, you cannot go back to a previously created table and disallow NULL values for a column. Usually this disadvantage is not serious, because it's obvious when the table is first created which columns should allow NULLs and which should not.

The inability to add a NOT NULL constraint to an existing table is a result of the way most DBMS brands implement NULL values internally. Usually a DBMS reserves an extra byte in every stored row of data for each column that permits NULL values. The extra byte serves as a "null indicator" for the column and is set to some specified value to indicate a NULL value. When a column is defined as NOT NULL, the indicator byte is not present, saving disk storage space. Dynamically adding and removing NOT NULL constraints would thus require "on the fly" reconfiguration of the stored rows on the disk, which is not practical in a large database.

Validity Checking

The SQL1 standard provides limited support for restricting the legal values that can appear in a column. When a table is created, each column in the table is assigned a data type, and the DBMS ensures that only data of the specified type is introduced into the column. For example, the EMPL_NUM column in the SALESREPS table is defined as an INTEGER, and the DBMS will produce an error if an INSERT or UPDATE statement tries to store a character string or a decimal number in the column.

However, the SQL1 standard and most commercial SQL products do not provide a way to restrict a column to certain specific data values. The DBMS will happily insert a SALESREPS row with an employee number of 12345, even though employee numbers in the sample database have three digits by convention. A hire date of December 25 would also be accepted, even though the company is closed on Christmas day.

Some commercial SQL implementations provide extended features to check for legal data values. In DB2, for example, each table in the database can be assigned a corresponding *validation procedure*, a user-written program to check for valid data values. DB2 invokes the validation procedure each time a SQL statement tries to change or insert a row of the table, and gives the validation procedure the "proposed" column values for the row. The validation procedure checks the data and indicates by its return value whether the data is acceptable. The validation procedure is a conventional program (written in S/370 assembler or PL/I, for example), so it can perform whatever data value checks are required, including range checks and internal consistency checks within the row. However, the validation procedure *cannot* access the database, so it cannot be used to check for unique values or foreign key/primary key relationships.

SQL Server also provides a data validation capability by allowing you to create a *rule* that determines what data can be entered into a particular column. SQL Server checks the rule each time an INSERT or UPDATE statement is attempted for the table that contains the column. Unlike DB2's validation procedures, SQL Server rules are written in the Transact-SQL dialect that is used by SQL Server. For example, here is a Transact-SQL statement that establishes a rule for the QUOTA column in the SALESREPS table:

```
CREATE RULE QUOTA_LIMIT
    AS @VALUE BETWEEN 0.00 AND 500000.00
```

This rule prevents you from inserting or updating a quota to a negative value or to a value greater than $500,000. As shown in the example, SQL Server allows you to assign the rule a name ("QUOTA_LIMIT" in this example). Like DB2 validation procedures, however, SQL Server rules may not reference columns or other database objects.

The SQL2 standard provides extended support for validity checking through a *check constraint.* A check constraint is a search condition, like the search condition in a WHERE clause, that produces a true/false value. When a check constraint is specified for a column, the DBMS automatically checks the value of that column each time a new row is inserted or a row is updated to insure that the search condition is true. If not, the INSERT or UPDATE statement fails. A check constraint is specified as part of the CREATE TABLE statement, described in Chapter 13.

Several DBMS products provide validity checking as part of their data entry or forms packages rather than supporting it within the SQL language. For example, the data entry package may allow you to specify a range of legal values that can be entered into a field of a data entry form. Some products allow you to specify that an entered data value is to be checked against values in the database, allowing validity checks that cannot be implemented with either the DB2 or the SQL Server approach.

Entity Integrity

A table's primary key must have a unique value for each row of the table or the database will lose its integrity as a model of the outside world. For example, if two rows of the SALESREPS table both had value 106 in their EMPL_NUM column, it would be impossible to tell which row really represented the real-world entity associated with that key value—Bill Adams, who is employee number 106. For this reason the requirement that primary keys have unique values is called the *entity integrity* constraint.

Support for primary keys was rare in commercial SQL databases but is now becoming much more common. It was added to DB2 in 1988 and was added to the original ANSI/ISO SQL standard in an intermediate update, before the full SQL2 standard appeared. In both DB2 and the ANSI/ISO standard you specify the primary key as part of the CREATE TABLE statement, described in Chapter 13. The DBMS automatically checks the uniqueness of the primary key value for every INSERT and UPDATE statement. An attempt to insert a row with a duplicate primary key value or to update a row so that its primary key would be a duplicate will fail with an error message.

Other Uniqueness Constraints

It is sometimes appropriate to require a column that is not the primary key of a table to contain a unique value in every row. For example, suppose you wanted to restrict the data in the SALESREPS table so that no two salespeople could have exactly the same name in the table. You could achieve this goal by imposing a *uniqueness* constraint on the NAME column. The DBMS enforces a uniqueness constraint in the same way that it enforces the primary key constraint. Any attempt to insert or update a row in the table that violates the uniqueness constraint will fail.

The ANSI/ISO SQL standard uses the CREATE TABLE statement to specify uniqueness constraints for columns or combinations of columns. However, uniqueness constraints were implemented in DB2 long before the publication of the ANSI/ISO standard, and DB2 makes them a part of its CREATE INDEX statement. This statement is one of the SQL database administration statements that deals with physical storage of the database on the disk. Normally the SQL user doesn't have to worry about these statements at all; they are used only by the database administrator. Unfortunately, if the user wants to impose a uniqueness constraint on a DB2 table, the CREATE INDEX statement must be used. Both CREATE TABLE and CREATE INDEX are described in Chapter 13.

Many commercial SQL products followed the DB2 practice rather than the ANSI/ISO standard for uniqueness constraints. Specifically, SQL Server, Oracle, Ingres, SQLBase, and VAX SQL all use the CREATE INDEX statement to implement uniqueness constraints. Most vendors plan to support the ANSI/ISO syntax for the uniqueness constraint as they add support for SQL2 features.

Uniqueness and NULL Values

NULL values pose a problem when they occur in the primary key of a table or in a column that is specified in a uniqueness constraint. Suppose you tried to insert a row with a primary key that was NULL (or partially NULL, if the primary key is composed of more than one column). Because of the NULL value, the DBMS cannot conclusively decide whether the primary key does or does not duplicate one that is already in the table. The answer must be "maybe," depending on the "real" value of the missing (NULL) data.

For this reason, SQL requires that every column that is part of a primary key and every column named in a uniqueness constraint must be declared NOT NULL.

Referential Integrity

Chapter 4 discussed primary keys, foreign keys, and the parent/child relationships that they create between tables. Figure 11-1 shows the SALESREPS and OFFICES tables, and illustrates once again how foreign keys and primary keys work. The OFFICE column is the primary key for the OFFICES table, and it uniquely identifies each row. The REP_OFFICE column, in the SALESREPS table, is a foreign key for the OFFICES table. It identifies the office where each salesperson is assigned.

The REP_OFFICE and OFFICE columns create a parent/child relationship between the OFFICES and SALESREPS rows. Each OFFICES (parent) row has zero or more SALESREPS (child) rows with matching office numbers. Similarly, each SALESREPS (child) row has exactly one OFFICES (parent) row with a matching office number.

Suppose you tried to insert a new row into the SALESREPS table that contained an invalid office number, as in this example:

```
INSERT INTO SALESREPS (EMPL_NUM, NAME, REP_OFFICE, AGE, HIRE_DATE, SALES)
     VALUES (115, 'George Smith', 31, 37, '01-APR-90', 0.00)
```

On the surface, there's nothing wrong with this INSERT statement. In fact, many current SQL implementations will successfully add the row. The database will show that George Smith works in office number 31, even though there is no office number 31 listed in the OFFICES table. The newly inserted row clearly "breaks" the parent/child relationship between the OFFICES and SALESREPS tables. In fact, the office number in the INSERT statement is probably an error—the user may have intended office number 11, 21, or 13.

It seems clear that every legal value in the REP_OFFICE column should be forced to match some value that appears in the OFFICE column. This rule is known as a *referential integrity* constraint. It ensures the integrity of the parent/child relationships created by foreign keys and primary keys.

Referential integrity has been a key part of the relational model since it was first proposed by Codd. However, referential integrity constraints were not included in IBM's prototype System/R DBMS, nor in early releases of DB2 or SQL/DS. IBM added referential integrity support to DB2 in 1989, and referential integrity was added to the SQL1 standard after its initial release. Most DBMS vendors have now either implemented referential integrity or indicated plans to include referential integrity support in future releases of their products.

OFFICES Table

OFFICE	CITY	REGION	MGR	TARGET	SALES
22	Denver	Western	108	$300,000.00	$186,042.00
11	New York	Eastern	106	$575,000.00	$692,637.00
12	Chicago	Eastern	104	$800,000.00	$735,042.00
13	Atlanta	Eastern	NULL	$350,000.00	$367,911.00
21	Los Angeles	Western	108	$725,000.00	$835,915.00

Primary key   Reference

SALESREPS Table   Foreign key

EMPL_NUM	NAME	AGE	REP_OFFICE	TITLE
105	Bill Adams	37	13	Sales Rep
109	Mary Jones	31	11	Sales Rep
102	Sue Smith	48	21	Sales Rep
106	Sam Clark	52	11	VP Sales
104	Bob Smith	33	12	Sales Mgr
101	Dan Roberts	45	12	Sales Rep
110	Tom Snyder	41	NULL	Sales Rep
108	Larry Fitch	62	21	Sales Mgr
103	Paul Cruz	29	12	Sales Rep
107	Nancy Angelli	49	22	Sales Rep

Figure 11-1. *A foreign key/primary key reference*

Referential Integrity Problems

There are four types of database updates that can corrupt the referential integrity of the parent/child relationships in a database. Using the OFFICES and SALESREPS tables in Figure 11-1 for illustration, these four update situations are:

- *Inserting a new child row.* When a new row is inserted into the child (SALESREPS) table, its foreign key (REP_OFFICE) value *must* match one of the primary key (OFFICE) values in the parent table (OFFICES). If the foreign key value does not match any primary key, inserting the row will corrupt the database, because there will be a child without a parent (an "orphan"). Note that inserting a row in the parent table never poses a problem; it simply becomes a parent without any children.

- *Updating the foreign key in a child row.* This is a different form of the previous problem. If the foreign key (REP_OFFICE) is modified by an UPDATE statement, the new value must match a primary key (OFFICE) value in the parent (OFFICES) table. Otherwise the updated row will be an orphan.

■ *Deleting a parent row.* If a row of the parent table (OFFICES), which has one or more children (in the SALESREPS table) is deleted, the child rows will become orphans. The foreign key (REP_OFFICE) values in these rows will no longer match any primary key (OFFICE) value in the parent table. Note that deleting a row from the child table never poses a problem; the parent of this row simply has one less child after the deletion.

■ *Updating the primary key in a parent row.* This is a different form of the previous problem. If the primary key (OFFICE) of a row in the parent table (OFFICES) is modified, all of the current children of that row become orphans, because their foreign keys no longer match a primary key value.

The referential integrity features of DB2 and the ANSI/ISO SQL standard handle each of these four situations. The first problem (INSERT into the child table) is handled by checking the values of the foreign key columns before the INSERT statement is permitted. If they don't match a primary key value, the INSERT statement is rejected with an error message. In Figure 11-1 this means that before a new salesperson can be added to the SALESREPS table, the office to which the salesperson is assigned must already be in the OFFICES table. As you can see, this restriction "makes sense" in the sample database.

The second problem (UPDATE of the child table) is similarly handled by checking the updated foreign key value. If there is no matching primary key value, the UPDATE statement is rejected with an error message. In Figure 11-1 this means that before a salesperson can be reassigned to a different office, that office must already be in the OFFICES table. Again, this restriction makes sense in the sample database.

The fourth problem (UPDATE of the primary key in the parent table) is also handled by prohibition. Before the primary key can be modified, the DBMS checks to make sure there are no child rows that have matching foreign key values. If there are such child rows, the UPDATE statement is rejected with an error message. In Figure 11-1 this means that an office number cannot be changed in the OFFICES table unless there are no salespeople in the SALESREPS table currently assigned to that office. In practice, this restriction doesn't often cause problems, because primary key values are almost never modified.

The third problem (DELETE of a parent row) is more complex. For example, suppose you closed the Los Angeles office and wanted to delete the corresponding row from the OFFICES table in Figure 11-1. What should happen to the two child rows in the SALESREPS table that represent the salespeople assigned to the Los Angeles office? Depending on the situation, you might want to:

■ prevent the office from being deleted until the salespeople are reassigned,

■ automatically delete the two salespeople from the SALESREPS table as well, or

■ set the REP_OFFICE column for the two salespeople to NULL, indicating that their office assignment is unknown.

■ set the REP_OFFICE column for the two salespeople to some default value, such as the office number for the headquarters office in New York, indicating that the salespeople are automatically reassigned to that office.

The fourth problem (UPDATE of the primary key in the parent table) has similar complexity. For example, suppose for some reason you wanted to change the office number of the Los Angeles office from 21 to 23. As with the previous example, the question is what should happen to the two child rows in the SALESREPS table that represent salespeople from the Los Angeles office. Again, there are four logical possibilities:

■ prevent the office number from being changed until the salespeople are reassigned. In this case, you should first add a new row to the OFFICES table with the new office number for Los Angeles, then update the SALESREPS table, and finally delete the old OFFICES row for Los Angeles.

■ automatically update the office number for the two salespeople in the SALESREPS table, so that their rows still are linked to the Los Angeles row in the OFFICES table, via its new office number.

■ set the REP_OFFICE column for the two salespeople to NULL, indicating that their office assignment is unknown.

■ set the REP_OFFICE column for the two salespeople to some default value, such as the office number for the headquarters office in New York, indicating that the salespeople are automatically reassigned to that office.

Although some of these alternatives may seem more logical than others in this particular example, it's relatively easy to come up with examples where any one of the four possibilities is the "right" thing to do, if you want the database to accurately model the real world situation. The SQL1 standard provided only the first possibility for the examples above—it prohibited the modification of a primary key value that was "in use" and prohibited the deletion of a row containing such a primary key. DB2, however, permitted other options through its concept of *delete rules*. The SQL2 standard has expanded these delete rules into *delete and update rules* that cover both deleting of parent rows and updating of primary keys.

Delete and Update Rules *

For each parent/child relationship created by a foreign key in a DB2 database, you can specify an associated delete rule and an associated update rule. The delete rule tells the DBMS what to do when a user tries to delete a row of the parent table. One of four possible delete rules can be specified:

■ the RESTRICT delete rule prevents you from deleting a row from the parent table if the row has any children. A DELETE statement that attempts to delete such a parent row is rejected with an error message. Deletions from the parent table are thus restricted to rows without any children. Applied to Figure 11-1, this rule can be summarized as "You can't delete an office if any salespeople are assigned to it."

■ the CASCADE delete rule tells the DBMS that when a parent row is deleted, all of its child rows should *also* automatically be deleted from the child table. For Figure 11-1, this rule can be summarized as "Deleting an office automatically deletes all the salespeople assigned to that office."

■ the SET NULL delete rule tells the DBMS that when a parent row is deleted, the foreign key values in all of its child rows should automatically be set to NULL. Deletions from the parent table thus cause a "set to NULL" update on selected columns of the child table. For the tables in Figure 11-1, this rule can be summarized as "If an office is deleted, indicate that the current office assignment of its salespeople is unknown."

■ the SET DEFAULT delete rule tells the DBMS that when a parent row is deleted, the foreign key values in all of its child rows should automatically be set to the default value for that particular column. Deletions from the parent table thus cause a "set to DEFAULT" update on selected columns of the child table. For the tables in Figure 11-1, this rule can be summarized as "If an office is deleted, indicate that the current office assignment of its salespeople is the default office specified in the definition of the SALESREPS table."

Just as the delete rule tells the DBMS what to do when a user tries to delete a row of the parent table, the update rule tells the DBMS what to do when a user tries to update the value of one of the primary key columns in the parent table. Again, there are four possibilities, paralleling those available for delete rules:

■ the RESTRICT update rule prevents you from updating the primary key of a row in the parent table if that row has any children. An UPDATE statement that attempts to modify the primary key of such a parent row is rejected with an error message. Changes to primary keys in the parent table are thus restricted to rows without any children. Applied to Figure 11-1, this rule can be summarized as "You can't change an office number if salespeople are assigned to the office."

■ the CASCADE update rule tells the DBMS that when a primary key value is changed in a parent row, the corresponding foreign key value in all of its child rows should *also* automatically be changed in the child table, to match the new primary key. For Figure 11-1, this rule can be summarized as "Changing an office number automatically changes the office number for all the salespeople assigned to that office."

■ the SET NULL update rule tells the DBMS that when a primary key value in a parent row is updated, the foreign key values in all of its child rows should automatically be set to NULL. Primary key changes in the parent table thus cause a "set to NULL" update on selected columns of the child table. For the tables in Figure 11-1, this rule can be summarized as "If an office number is changed, indicate that the current office assignment of its salespeople is unknown."

■ the SET DEFAULT update rule tells the DBMS that when a primary key value in a parent row is updated, the foreign key values in all of its child rows should automatically be set to the default value for that particular column. Primary key changes in the parent table thus cause a "set to DEFAULT" update on selected columns of the child table. For the tables in Figure 11-1, this rule can be summarized as "If an office number is changed, automatically change the office assignment of its salespeople to the default office specified in the definition of the SALESREPS table."

You can specify two different rules as the delete rule and the update rule for a parent/child relationship, although in most cases, the two rules will be the same. If you do not specify a rule, the RESTRICT rule is the default, because it has the least potential for accidental destruction or modification of data. Each of the rules is appropriate in different situations. Usually, the real-world behavior modeled by the database will indicate which rule is appropriate. In the sample database, the ORDERS table contains three foreign key/primary key relationships, as shown in Figure 11-2. These three relationships link each order to (a) the product that was ordered, (b) the customer who placed the order, and (c) the salesperson who took the order. For each of these relationships, different rules seem appropriate:

■ The relationship between an order and the product that is ordered should probably use the RESTRICT rule for delete and update. It shouldn't be possible to delete product information from the database if there are still current orders for that product, or to change the product number.

■ The relationship between an order and the customer who placed it should probably use the CASCADE rule for delete and update. You probably will only delete a customer row from the database if the customer is inactive or ends their relationship with the company. In this case, when you delete the customer, any current orders for that customer should also be deleted. Similarly, changes in a customer number should automatically propagate to orders for that customer.

■ The relationship between an order and the salesperson who took it should probably use the SET NULL rule. If the salesperson leaves the company, any orders taken by that salesperson become the responsibility of an "unknown salesperson" until they are reassigned. Alternatively, the SET DEFAULT rule could be used to automatically assign these orders to the Sales Vice President. This relationship should probably use the CASCADE update rule, so that employee number changes automatically propagate to the ORDERS table.

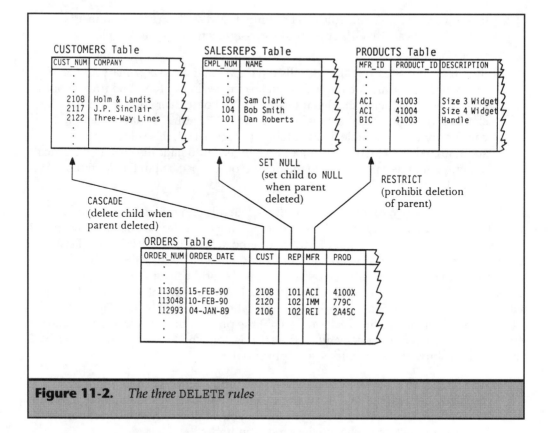

Figure 11-2.   *The three* DELETE *rules*

Cascaded Deletes and Updates *

The RESTRICT rule is a "single-level" rule—it affects only the parent table in a relationship. The CASCADE rule, on the other hand, is a "multilevel" rule, as shown in Figure 11-3.

Assume for this discussion that the OFFICES/SALESREPS and SALESREPS/ORDERS relationships shown in the figure both have CASCADE rules. What happens when you delete Los Angeles from the OFFICES table? The CASCADE rule for the OFFICES/SALESREPS relationship tells the DBMS to automatically delete all of the SALESREPS rows that refer to the Los Angeles office (office number 21) as well. But deleting the SALESREPS row for Sue Smith brings into play the CASCADE rule for the SALESREPS/ORDERS relationship. This rule tells the DBMS to automatically delete all of the ORDERS rows that refer to Sue (employee number 102). Deleting an office thus causes cascaded deletion of salespeople, which causes cascaded deletion of orders. As the example shows, CASCADE delete rules must be specified with care, because they can cause widespread automatic deletion of data if they're

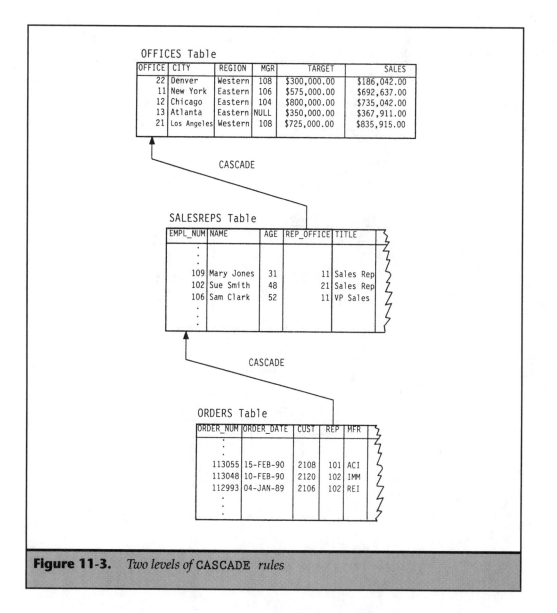

OFFICES Table

OFFICE	CITY	REGION	MGR	TARGET	SALES
22	Denver	Western	108	$300,000.00	$186,042.00
11	New York	Eastern	106	$575,000.00	$692,637.00
12	Chicago	Eastern	104	$800,000.00	$735,042.00
13	Atlanta	Eastern	NULL	$350,000.00	$367,911.00
21	Los Angeles	Western	108	$725,000.00	$835,915.00

CASCADE

SALESREPS Table

EMPL_NUM	NAME	AGE	REP_OFFICE	TITLE
.				
.				
109	Mary Jones	31	11	Sales Rep
102	Sue Smith	48	21	Sales Rep
106	Sam Clark	52	11	VP Sales
.				
.				

CASCADE

ORDERS Table

ORDER_NUM	ORDER_DATE	CUST	REP	MFR
.				
.				
113055	15-FEB-90	2108	101	ACI
113048	10-FEB-90	2120	102	IMM
112993	04-JAN-89	2106	102	REI
.				
.				

Figure 11-3. *Two levels of* CASCADE *rules*

used incorrectly. Cascaded update rules can cause similar multilevel updates if the foreign key in the child table is also its primary key. In practice, this is not very common, so cascaded updates typically have less far-reaching effects than cascaded deletes.

The SET NULL delete rule is a two-level rule; its impact stops with the child table. Figure 11-4 shows the OFFICES, SALESREPS, and ORDERS tables again, with a SET

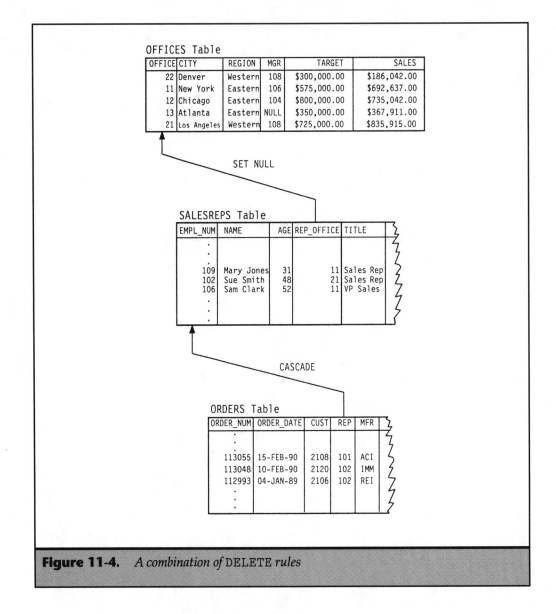

OFFICES Table

OFFICE	CITY	REGION	MGR	TARGET	SALES
22	Denver	Western	108	$300,000.00	$186,042.00
11	New York	Eastern	106	$575,000.00	$692,637.00
12	Chicago	Eastern	104	$800,000.00	$735,042.00
13	Atlanta	Eastern	NULL	$350,000.00	$367,911.00
21	Los Angeles	Western	108	$725,000.00	$835,915.00

SET NULL

SALESREPS Table

EMPL_NUM	NAME	AGE	REP_OFFICE	TITLE
.				
.				
109	Mary Jones	31	11	Sales Rep
102	Sue Smith	48	21	Sales Rep
106	Sam Clark	52	11	VP Sales
.				
.				

CASCADE

ORDERS Table

ORDER_NUM	ORDER_DATE	CUST	REP	MFR
.				
.				
113055	15-FEB-90	2108	101	ACI
113048	10-FEB-90	2120	102	IMM
112993	04-JAN-89	2106	102	REI
.				
.				

Figure 11-4. *A combination of* DELETE *rules*

NULL delete rule for the OFFICES/SALESREPS relationship. This time, when the Los Angeles office is deleted, the SET NULL delete rule tells the DBMS to set the REP_OFFICE column to NULL in the SALESREPS rows that refer to office number 21. The rows remain in the SALESREPS table, however, and the impact of the delete operation extends only to the child table.

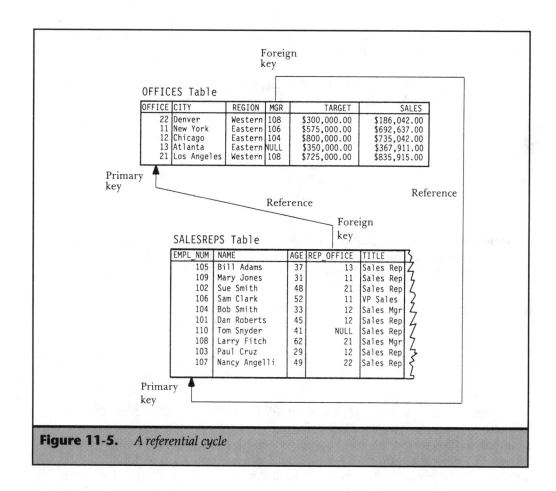

Figure 11-5. *A referential cycle*

Referential Cycles *

In the sample database, the SALESREPS table contains the REP_OFFICE column, a foreign key for the OFFICES table. The OFFICES table contains the MGR column, a foreign key for the SALESREPS table. As shown in Figure 11-5, these two relationships form a *referential cycle*. Any given row of the SALESREPS table refers to a row of the OFFICES table, which refers to a row of the SALESREPS table, and so on. This cycle includes only two tables, but it's also possible to construct cycles of three or more tables.

Regardless of the number of tables that they involve, referential cycles pose special problems for referential integrity constraints. For example, suppose that NULL values were not allowed in the primary or foreign keys of the two tables in Figure 11-5. (This is not, in fact, the way the sample database is actually defined, for reasons that will become obvious in a moment.) Consider this database update request and the INSERT statements that attempt to implement it:

You have just hired a new salesperson, Ben Adams (employee number 115), who is the manager of a new sales office in Detroit (office number 14).

```
INSERT INTO SALESREPS (EMPL_NUM, NAME, REP_OFFICE, HIRE_DATE, SALES)
    VALUES (115,'Ben Adams', 14, '01-APR-90', 0.00)

INSERT INTO OFFICES (OFFICE, CITY, REGION, MGR, TARGET, SALES)
    VALUES (14,'Detroit', 'Eastern', 115, 0.00, 0.00)
```

Unfortunately, the first INSERT statement (for Ben Adams) will fail. Why? Because the new row refers to office number 14, which is not yet in the database! Of course reversing the order of the INSERT statements doesn't help:

```
INSERT INTO OFFICES (OFFICE, CITY, REGION, MGR, TARGET, SALES)
    VALUES (14,'Detroit', 'Eastern', 115, 0.00, 0.00)

INSERT INTO SALESREPS (EMPL_NUM, NAME, REP_OFFICE, HIRE_DATE, SALES)
    VALUES (115,'Ben Adams', 14, '01-APR-90', 0.00)
```

The first INSERT statement (for Detroit this time) will still fail, because the new row refers to employee number 115 as the office manager, and Ben Adams is not yet in the database! To prevent this "insertion deadlock," at least one of the foreign keys in a referential cycle *must* permit NULL values. In the actual definition of the sample database, the MGR column does not permit NULLs, but the REP_OFFICE does. The two-row insertion can then be accomplished with two INSERTS and an UPDATE, as shown here:

```
INSERT INTO SALESREPS (EMPL_NUM, NAME, REP_OFFICE, HIRE_DATE, SALES)
    VALUES (115,'Ben Adams', NULL, '01-APR-90', 0.00)

INSERT INTO OFFICES (OFFICE, CITY, REGION, MGR, TARGET, SALES)
    VALUES (14,'Detroit', 'Eastern', 115, 0.00, 0.00)

UPDATE SALESREPS
   SET REP_OFFICE = 14
 WHERE EMPL_NUM = 115
```

As the example shows, there are times when it would be convenient if the referential integrity constraint were not checked until after a series of interrelated updates are performed. Unfortunately, this type of complex "deferred checking" is not provided by SQL.

Referential cycles also restrict the delete and update rules that can be specified for the relationships that form the cycle. Consider the three tables in the referential cycle shown in Figure 11-6. The PETS table shows three pets and the boys they like, the GIRLS table shows three girls and the pets they like, and the BOYS table shows four

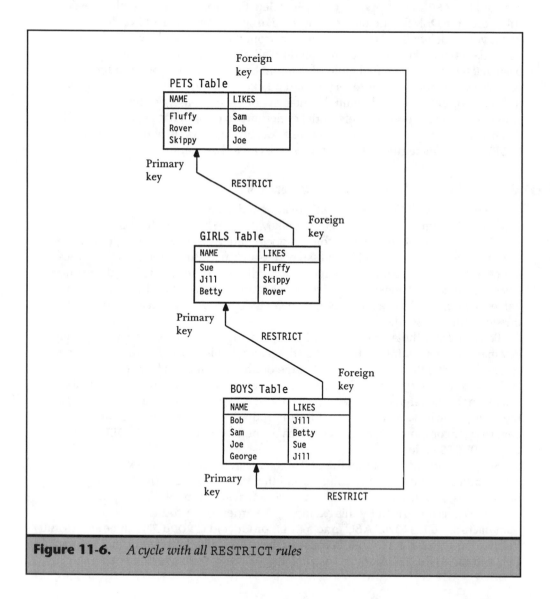

Figure 11-6. *A cycle with all RESTRICT rules*

boys and the girls they like, forming a referential cycle. All three of the relationships in the cycle specify the RESTRICT delete rule. Note that George's row is the *only* row you can delete from the three tables. Every other row is the parent in some relationship, and is therefore protected from deletion by the RESTRICT rule. Because of this anomaly, you should not specify the RESTRICT rule for all of the relationships in a referential cycle.

The CASCADE rule presents a similar problem, as shown in Figure 11-7. This figure contains exactly the same data as in Figure 11-6, but all three delete rules have been changed to CASCADE. Suppose you try to delete Bob from the BOYS table. The delete rules force the DBMS to delete Rover (who likes Bob) from the PETS table, which forces you to delete Betty (who likes Rover) from the GIRLS table, which forces you to delete Sam (who likes Betty), and so on until all of the rows in all three tables have been deleted! For these small tables this might be practical, but for a production database with thousands of rows it would quickly become impossible to keep track of the cascaded deletions and retain the integrity of the database. For this reason DB2 enforces a rule that prevents referential cycles of two or more tables where all of the delete rules are CASCADE. At least one relationship in the cycle *must* have a RESTRICT or SET NULL delete rule to break the cycle of cascaded deletions.

Foreign Keys and NULL Values *

Unlike primary keys, foreign keys in a relational database are allowed to contain NULL values. In the sample database the foreign key REP_OFFICE, in the SALESREPS table, permits NULL values. In fact, this column does contain a NULL value in Tom Snyder's row, because Tom has not yet been assigned to an office. But the NULL value poses an interesting question about the referential integrity constraint created by the primary key/foreign key relationship. Does the NULL value match one of the primary key values or doesn't it? The answer is "maybe"—it depends on the "real" value of the missing or unknown data.

Both DB2 and the ANSI/ISO SQL1 standard automatically assume that a foreign key that contains a NULL value satisfies the referential integrity constraint. In other words, they give the row "the benefit of the doubt" and allow it to be part of the child table, even though its foreign key value doesn't match any row in the parent table. Interestingly, the referential integrity constraint is assumed to be satisfied if *any part* of the foreign key has a NULL value. This can produce unexpected and unintuitive behavior for compound foreign keys, such as the one that links the ORDERS table to the PRODUCTS table.

Suppose for a moment that the ORDERS table in the sample database permitted NULL values for the PRODUCT column, and that the PRODUCTS/ORDERS relationship had a SET NULL delete rule. (This is not the actual structure of the sample database, for the reasons illustrated by this example.) An order for a product with a manufacturer id (MFR) of "ABC" and a NULL product id (PRODUCT) can be successfully inserted into the ORDERS table, because of the NULL value in the PRODUCT column. DB2 and the ANSI/ISO standard assume that the row meets the referential integrity

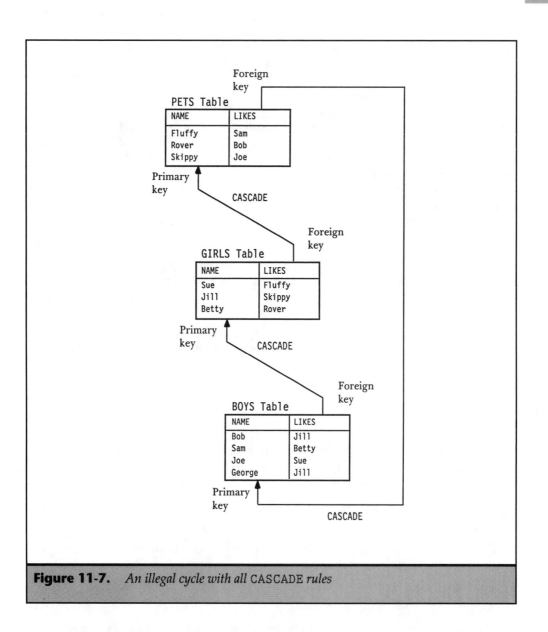

Figure 11-7. *An illegal cycle with all* CASCADE *rules*

constraint for ORDERS and PRODUCTS, even though no product in the PRODUCTS table has a manufacturer id of "ABC."

The SET NULL delete rule can produce a similar effect. Deleting a row from the PRODUCTS table will cause the foreign key value in all of its child rows in the ORDERS table to be set to NULL. Actually, only those columns of the foreign key that accept NULL values are set to NULL. If there were a single row in the PRODUCTS table for manufacturer "DEF," deleting that row would cause its child rows in the ORDERS table to have their PRODUCT column set to NULL, but their MFR column would continue to have the value "DEF." As a result, the rows would have a MFR value that did not match any row in the PRODUCTS table.

To avoid creating this situation, you should be very careful with NULL values in compound foreign keys. An application that enters or updates data in the table that contains the foreign key should usually enforce an "all NULLs or no NULLs" rule on the columns of the foreign key. Foreign keys that are partially NULL and partially non-NULL can easily create problems.

The SQL2 standard addresses this problem by giving the database administrator more control over the handling of NULL values in foreign keys for integrity constraints. The integrity constraint in the CREATE TABLE statement provides two options:

- The MATCH FULL option requires that foreign keys in a child table fully match a primary key in the parent table. With this option, no part of the foreign key can contain a NULL value, so the issue of NULL value handling in delete and update rules does not arise.

- The MATCH PARTIAL option allows NULL values in parts of a foreign key, so long as the non-NULL values match the corresponding parts of some primary key in the parent table. With this option, NULL value handling in delete and update rules proceeds as described above.

Business Rules

Many of the data integrity issues in the real world have to do with the rules and procedures of an organization. For example, the company that is modelled by the sample database might have rules like these:

- No customer is allowed to place orders that would exceed the customer's credit limit.

- The sales vice-president must be notified whenever any customer is assigned a credit limit higher than $50,000.

- Orders may only remain on the books for six months; orders older than six months must be cancelled and re-entered.

In addition, there are often "accounting rules" that must be followed to maintain the integrity of totals, counts, and other amounts stored in a database. For the sample database, these rules probably make sense:

- Whenever a new order is taken, the SALES column for the salesperson who took the order and for the office where that salesperson works should be increased by the order amount. Deleting an order or changing the order amount should also cause the SALES columns to be adjusted.

■ Whenever a new order is taken, the QTY_ON_HAND column for the product being ordered should be decreased by the quantity of products ordered. Deleting an order, changing the quantity, or changing the product ordered should also cause corresponding adjustments to the QTY_ON_HAND column.

These rules fall outside the realm of the SQL language as defined by the SQL1 standard and implemented by many SQL-based DBMS products today. The DBMS takes responsibility for storing and organizing data and ensuring its basic integrity, but enforcing the business rules is the responsibility of the application programs that access the database.

Placing the burden of enforcing business rules on the application programs that access the database has several disadvantages:

■ *Duplication of effort.* If six different programs deal with various updates to the ORDERS table, each of them must include code that enforces the rules relating to ORDERS updates.

■ *Lack of consistency.* If several programs written by different programmers handle updates to a table, they will probably enforce the rules somewhat differently.

■ *Maintenance problems.* If the business rules change, the programmers must identify every program that enforces the rules, locate the code, and modify it correctly.

■ *Complexity.* There are often many rules to remember. Even in the small sample database, a program that handles order changes must worry about enforcing credit limits, adjusting sales totals for salespeople and offices, and adjusting quantities-on-hand. A program that handles simple updates can become complex very quickly.

The requirement that application programs enforce business rules is not unique to SQL. Application programs have had that responsibility since the earliest days of COBOL programs and file systems. However, there has been a steady trend over the years to put more "understanding" of the data and more responsibility for its integrity into the database itself. In 1986 the Sybase DBMS introduced the concept of a *trigger* as a step toward including business rules in a relational database. The concept proved to be very popular, so support for triggers began to appear in many SQL DBMS products in the early 1990s.

What Is a Trigger?

The concept of a trigger is relatively straightforward. For any event that causes a change in the contents of a table, a user can specify an associated action that the DBMS should carry out. The three events that can trigger an action are attempts to INSERT, DELETE, or UPDATE rows of the table. The action triggered by an event is specified by a sequence of SQL statements.

To understand how a trigger works, let's examine a concrete example. When a new order is added to the ORDERS table, these two changes to the database should also take place:

- The SALES column for the salesperson who took the order should be increased by the amount of the order.

- The QTY_ON_HAND amount for the product being ordered should be decreased by the quantity ordered.

This Transact-SQL statement defines a SQL Server trigger, named NEWORDER, that causes these database updates to happen automatically:

```
CREATE TRIGGER NEWORDER
    ON ORDERS
   FOR INSERT
    AS UPDATE SALESREPS
          SET SALES = SALES + INSERTED.AMOUNT
         FROM SALESREPS, INSERTED
        WHERE SALESREPS.EMPL_NUM = INSERTED.REP
       UPDATE PRODUCTS
          SET QTY_ON_HAND = QTY_ON_HAND - INSERTED.QTY
         FROM PRODUCTS, INSERTED
        WHERE PRODUCTS.MFR_ID = INSERTED.MFR
          AND PRODUCTS.PRODUCT_ID = INSERTED.PRODUCT
```

The first part of the trigger definition tells SQL Server that the trigger is to be invoked whenever an INSERT statement is attempted on the ORDERS table. The remainder of the definition (after the keyword AS) defines the action of the trigger. In this case, the action is a sequence of two UPDATE statements, one for the SALESREPS table and one for the PRODUCTS table. The row being inserted is referred to using the pseudo-table name INSERTED within the UPDATE statements. As the example shows, SQL Server extends the SQL language substantially to support triggers. Other extensions not shown here include IF/THEN/ELSE tests, looping, procedure calls, and even PRINT statements that display user messages.

Triggers and Referential Integrity

Triggers provide an alternative way to implement the referential integrity constraints provided by foreign keys and primary keys. In fact, advocates of the trigger feature point out that the trigger mechanism is more flexible than the strict referential integrity provided by DB2 and the ANSI/ISO standard. For example, here is a trigger that enforces referential integrity for the OFFICES/SALESREPS relationship, and also displays a message when an attempted update fails:

```
CREATE TRIGGER REP_UPDATE
    ON SALESREPS
    FOR INSERT, UPDATE
    AS IF ((SELECT COUNT(*)
            FROM OFFICES, INSERTED
            WHERE OFFICES.OFFICE = INSERTED.REP_OFFICE) = 0)
        BEGIN
          PRINT "Invalid office number specified."
          ROLLBACK TRANSACTION
        END
```

Triggers can also be used to provide extended forms of referential integrity. For example, DB2 initially provided cascaded deletes through its CASCADE delete rule, but did not support "cascaded updates" if a primary key value is changed. This limitation need not apply to triggers, however. The following SQL Server trigger cascades any update of the OFFICE column in the OFFICES table down into the REP_OFFICE column of the SALESREPS table:

```
CREATE TRIGGER CHANGE_REP_OFFICE
    ON OFFICES
    FOR UPDATE
    AS IF UPDATE (OFFICE)
        BEGIN
           UPDATE SALESREPS
               SET SALESREPS.REP_OFFICE = INSERTED.OFFICE
             FROM SALESREPS, INSERTED, DELETED
            WHERE SALESREPS.REP_OFFICE = DELETED.OFFICE
        END
```

The references DELETED.OFFICE and INSERTED.OFFICE in the trigger refer, respectively, to the values of the OFFICE column before and after the UPDATE statement.

Trigger Advantages and Disadvantages

A complete discussion of triggers is beyond the scope of this book, but even this simple example shows the power of the trigger mechanism. The major advantage of triggers is that business rules can be stored in the database and enforced consistently with each update to the database. This can dramatically reduce the complexity of application programs that access the database. Triggers also have some disadvantages, including these two:

■ *Database complexity.* When the rules are moved into the database, setting up the database becomes a more complex task. Users who could reasonably be expected to create small, ad hoc applications with SQL will find that the programming logic of triggers makes the task much more difficult.

■ *Hidden rules.* With the rules hidden away inside the database, programs that appear to perform straightforward database updates may, in fact, generate an enormous amount of database activity. The programmer no longer has total control over what happens to the database. Instead, a program-initiated database action may cause other, hidden actions.

Triggers and the SQL Standard

Triggers were completely absent from the SQL1 standard, and despite their growing popularity in commercial SQL products, they were not explicitly included in the SQL2 standard. Instead, the SQL2 standard supports a more limited form of data validity checking through a *check constraint*. Under the SQL2 standard, a check constraint is specified as a logical expression that evaluates to either TRUE or FALSE, just like the search condition in the WHERE clause of various SQL statements. One or more check constraints can be optionally associated with each table defined in a database. The check constraints are specified in a CHECK clause in the CREATE TABLE statement.

Once the constraint is in place, the DBMS automatically evaluates the check constraints expression whenever a SQL UPDATE, INSERT or DELETE statement tries to modify the data in the table. If the expression is TRUE, the modification is allowed to continue. If the expression is not TRUE, the SQL statement fails with an error condition.

For example, suppose you wanted to enforce a business rule that the quota for any salesperson must be between $200,000 and $500,000. Under the SQL2 standard, you could augment the CREATE TABLE statement for the SALESREPS table as follows to enforce the rule:

```
CREATE TABLE SALEREPS
    (EMPL_NUM INTEGER NOT NULL,
       ...
       CHECK (QUOTA BETWEEN 200000.00 AND 500000.00),
       ...
```

The SQL2 standard permits complex search conditions in the check constraint, so check constraints can be used to enforce business rules about the relationships among data items in the database as well. For example, to enforce the business rule that the total amount of orders outstanding for a customer must not exceed the customer's credit limit, you could specify a check constraint for the ORDERS table that references the CUSTOMER table as well:

```
CREATE TABLE ORDERS
   (ORDER_NUM INTEGER NOT NULL,
      ...
      CHECK (CUSTOMER.CREDIT_LIMIT <=
                      SELECT SUM(AMOUNT)
                         FROM ORDERS
                        WHERE CUST = CUSTOMER.CUST_NUM),
   ...
```

Note that check constraints such as this one involve a query to be performed each time the ORDERS table is updated. This may require a considerable amount of effort on the part of the DBMS. However, if the application that handles order entry is enforcing the constraint, it will have to perform virtually the same query to check the customer's outstanding order balance and compare it to the credit limit. As a result, it is often more efficient to store the constraint within the database, where it can be specified and analyzed once by the DBMS when the table is created, and automatically enforced.

Future Evolution of Triggers

Triggers were one of the most widely praised and publicized features of Sybase SQL Server when it was first introduced, and they have since found their way into many commercial SQL products. Although the SQL2 standard provided an opportunity to standardize the DBMS implementation of triggers, the standards committee included check constraints instead. As the trigger and check constraint examples in the preceding sections show, check constraints can be effectively used to limit the data that can be added to a table or modified in a table. However, unlike triggers, they lack the ability to cause an independent action in the database, such as adding a row or changing a data item in another table.

The extra capability provided by triggers have led several industry experts to advocate that they be included in a future SQL3 standard. Other experts have argued that triggers are a pollution of the data management function of a database, and that the functions performed by triggers belong in fourth generation languages (4GLs) and other database tools, rather than in the DBMS itself. While the debate continues, several commercial DBMS products have now expanded the notion of triggers beyond actions within the database itself. These "extended trigger" capabilities allow modifications to data in a database to automatically cause actions such as sending mail, alerting a user or launching another program to perform a task. This makes triggers even more useful, and will add to the debate over including them in future official SQL standards. Regardless of the official stance, it appears that triggers will become a more important part of the SQL language over the next several years.

Summary

The SQL language provides a number of features that help to protect the integrity of data stored in a relational database:

■ Required columns can be specified when a table is created, and the DBMS will prevent NULL values in these columns.

■ Data validation is limited to data type checking in standard SQL, but many DBMS products offer other data validation features.

■ Entity integrity constraints ensure that the primary key uniquely identifies each entity represented in the database.

■ Referential integrity constraints ensure that relationships among entities in the database are preserved during database updates.

■ The SQL2 standard and newer implementations provide extensive referential integrity support, including delete and update rules that tell the DBMS how to handle the deletion and modification of rows that are referenced by other rows.

■ Business rules can be enforced by the DBMS through the trigger mechanism popularized by Sybase and SQL Server. Triggers allow the DBMS to take complex actions in response to events such as attempted INSERT, DELETE, or UPDATE statements. Check constraints provide a more limited way to include business rules in the definition of a database and have the DBMS enforce them.

Chapter Twelve

Transaction Processing

288

Database updates are usually triggered by real-world events, such as the receipt of a new order from a customer. In fact, receiving a new order would generate not just one, but this series of *four* updates to the sample database:

- Add the new order to the ORDERS table.
- Update the sales total for the salesperson who took the order.
- Update the sales total for the salesperson's office.
- Update the quantity-on-hand total for the ordered product.

To leave the database in a self-consistent state, all four updates must occur as a unit. If a system failure or another error creates a situation where some of the updates are processed and others are not, the integrity of the database will be lost. Similarly, if another user calculates totals or ratios part way through the sequence of updates, the calculations will be incorrect. The sequence of updates must thus be an "all-or-nothing" proposition in the database. SQL provides precisely this capability through its transaction processing features, which are described in this chapter.

What Is a Transaction?

A *transaction* is a sequence of one or more SQL statements that together form a logical unit of work. The SQL statements that form the transaction are typically closely related and perform interdependent actions. Each statement in the transaction performs some part of a task, but all of them are required to complete the task. Grouping the statements as a single transaction tells the DBMS that the entire statement sequence should be executed atomically; *all* of the statements must be completed for the database to be in a consistent state.

Here are some examples of typical transactions for the sample database, along with the SQL statement sequence that comprises each transaction:

- *Add-an-order.* To accept a customer's order, the order entry program should (a) query the PRODUCTS table to ensure that the product is in stock, (b) insert the order into the ORDERS table, (c) update the PRODUCTS table, subtracting the quantity ordered from the quantity-on-hand of the product, (d) update the SALESREPS table, adding the order amount to the total sales of the salesperson who took the order, and (e) update the OFFICES table, adding the order amount to the total sales of the office where the salesperson works.

- *Cancel-an-order.* To cancel a customer's order, the program should (a) delete the order from the ORDERS table, (b) update the PRODUCTS table, adjusting the quantity-on-hand total for the product, (c) update the SALESREPS table, subtracting the order amount from the salesperson's total sales, and (d) update the OFFICES table, subtracting the order amount from the office's total sales.

■ *Reassign-a-customer.* When a customer is reassigned from one salesperson to another, the program should (a) update the CUSTOMERS table to reflect the change, (b) update the ORDERS table to show the new salesperson for all orders placed by the customer, (c) update the SALESREPS table, reducing the quota for the salesperson losing the customer, and (d) update the SALESREPS table, raising the quota for the salesperson gaining the customer.

In each of these cases a sequence of four or five actions, each comprising a single SQL statement, is required to handle the single "logical" transaction.

The transaction concept is critical for programs that update a database, because it ensures the integrity of the database. A SQL-based DBMS makes this commitment about the statements in a transaction:

The statements in a transaction will be executed as an atomic unit of work in the database. Either *all* of the statements will be executed successfully, or *none* of the statements will be executed.

The DBMS is responsible for keeping this commitment even if the application program aborts or there is a hardware failure during the middle of the transaction, as shown in Figure 12-1. In each case, the DBMS must make sure that when failure recovery is complete, the database never reflects a "partial transaction."

COMMIT **and** ROLLBACK

SQL supports database transactions through two SQL transaction processing statements, shown in Figure 12-2:

■ The COMMIT statement signals the successful end of a transaction. It tells the DBMS that the transaction is now complete; all of the statements that comprise the transaction have been executed, and the database is self-consistent.

■ The ROLLBACK statement signals the unsuccessful end of a transaction. It tells the DBMS that the user does not want to complete the transaction; instead, the DBMS should *back out* any changes made to the database during the transaction. In effect, the DBMS restores the database to its state before the transaction began.

The COMMIT and ROLLBACK statements are executable SQL statements, just like SELECT, INSERT, and UPDATE. Here is an example of a successful update transaction that changes the quantity and amount of an order and adjusts the totals for the

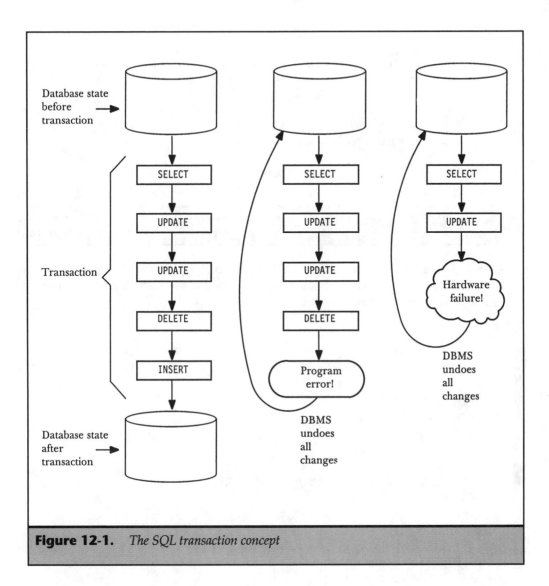

Figure 12-1. *The SQL transaction concept*

product, salesperson, and office associated with the order. A change like this would typically be handled by a forms-based "change order" program, which would use programmatic SQL to execute the statements shown:

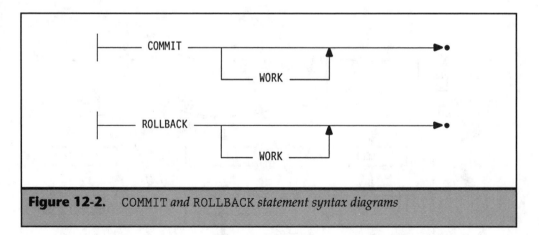

Figure 12-2. COMMIT *and* ROLLBACK *statement syntax diagrams*

Change the quantity on order number 113051 from 4 to 10, which raises its amount from $1,458 to $3,550. The order is for QSA-XK47 Reducers, and was placed with Larry Fitch (employee number 108) who works in Los Angeles (office number 21).

```
UPDATE ORDERS
   SET QTY = 10, AMOUNT = 3550.00
 WHERE ORDER_NR = 113051

UPDATE SALESREPS
   SET SALES = SALES - 1458.00 + 3550.00
 WHERE EMPL_NUM = 108

UPDATE OFFICES
   SET SALES = SALES - 1458.00 + 3550.00
 WHERE OFFICE = 21

UPDATE PRODUCTS
   SET QTY_ON_HAND = QTY_ON_HAND + 4 - 10
 WHERE MFR_ID = 'QSA'
   AND PRODUCT_ID = 'XK47'
```

. . . confirm the change one last time with the customer . . .

```
COMMIT WORK
```

Here is the same transaction, but this time assume that the user makes an error entering the product number. To correct the error, the transaction is rolled back, so that it can be reentered correctly:

Change the quantity on order number 113051 from 4 to 10, which raises its amount from $1,458 to $3,550. The order is for QAS-XK47 Reducers, and was placed with Larry Fitch (employee number 108), who works in Los Angeles (office number 21).

```
UPDATE ORDERS
   SET QTY = 10, AMOUNT = 3550.00
 WHERE ORDER_NR = 113051

UPDATE SALESREPS
   SET SALES = SALES - 1458.00 + 3550.00
 WHERE EMPL_NUM = 108

UPDATE OFFICES
   SET SALES = SALES - 1458.00 + 3550.00
 WHERE OFFICE = 21

UPDATE PRODUCTS
   SET QTY_ON_HAND = QTY_ON_HAND + 4 - 10
 WHERE MFR_ID = 'QAS'
   AND PRODUCT_ID = 'XK47'
```

. . . oops! the manufacturer is "QSA", not "QAS" . . .

```
ROLLBACK WORK
```

The ANSI/ISO Transaction Model

The ANSI/ISO SQL standard defines a SQL *transaction model* and the roles of the COMMIT and ROLLBACK statements. Most, but not all, commercial SQL products use this transaction model, which is based on DB2. The standard specifies that a SQL transaction *automatically* begins with the first SQL statement executed by a user or a program. The transaction continues through subsequent SQL statements until it ends in one of four ways:

- A COMMIT statement ends the transaction successfully, making its database changes permanent. A new transaction begins immediately after the COMMIT statement.

- A ROLLBACK statement aborts the transaction, backing out its database changes. A new transaction begins immediately after the ROLLBACK statement.

- Successful program termination (for programmatic SQL) also ends the transaction successfully, just as if a COMMIT statement had been executed. Because the program is finished, there is no new transaction to begin.

- Abnormal program termination (for programmatic SQL) also aborts the transaction, just as if a ROLLBACK statement had been executed. Because the program is finished, there is no new transaction to begin.

Figure 12-3 shows some typical transactions that illustrate these four conditions. Note that the user or program is *always* in a transaction under the ANSI/ISO transaction model. No explicit action is required to begin a transaction; it begins automatically with the first SQL statement or immediately after the preceding transaction ends.

Recall that the ANSI/ISO SQL standard specifies a *programmatic* SQL language for use in application programs. Transactions play an important role in programmatic SQL, because even a simple application program often needs to carry out a sequence of two or three SQL statements to accomplish its task. Because users can change their minds and other conditions can occur (such as being out-of-stock on a product that a customer wants to order), an application program must be able to proceed part way through a transaction and then choose to abort or continue. The COMMIT and ROLLBACK statements provide precisely this capability.

The COMMIT and ROLLBACK statements can also be used in interactive SQL, but in practice they are rarely seen in this context. Interactive SQL is generally used for

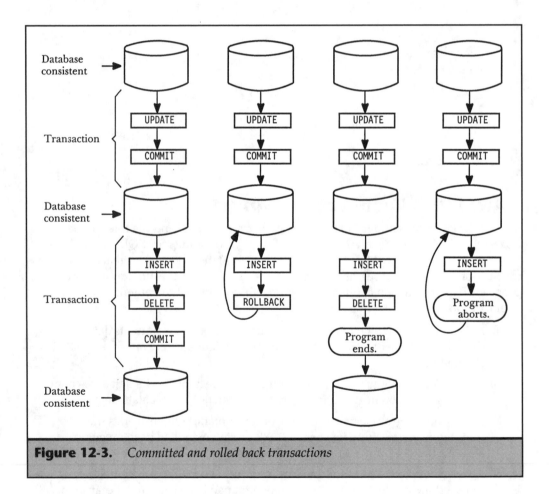

Figure 12-3. *Committed and rolled back transactions*

database queries; updates are less common, and multi-statement updates are almost never performed by typing the statements into an interactive SQL facility. As a result, transactions are typically a minor concern in interactive SQL. In fact, many interactive SQL products default to an "auto-commit" mode, where a COMMIT statement is automatically executed after each SQL statement typed by the user. This effectively makes each interactive SQL statement its own transaction.

Other Transaction Models

A few commercial SQL products depart from the ANSI/ISO and DB2 transaction model to provide additional transaction processing capability for their users. The Sybase DBMS, which is designed for on-line transaction processing applications, is one example. SQL Server, which is derived from the Sybase product, also uses the Sybase transaction model.

The Transact-SQL dialect used by Sybase includes four transaction processing statements:

- The BEGIN TRANSACTION statement signals the beginning of a transaction. Unlike the ANSI/ISO transaction model, which implicitly begins a new transaction when the previous one ends, Sybase requires an explicit statement to start a transaction.

- The COMMIT TRANSACTION statement signals the successful end of a transaction. As in the ANSI/ISO model, all changes made to the database during the transaction become permanent. However, a new transaction is not automatically started.

- The SAVE TRANSACTION statement establishes a *savepoint* in the middle of a transaction. Sybase saves the state of the database at the current point in the transaction and assigns the saved state a *savepoint name*, specified in the statement.

- The ROLLBACK TRANSACTION statement has two roles. If a savepoint is named in the ROLLBACK statement, Sybase backs out the database changes made since the savepoint, effectively rolling the transaction back to the point where the SAVE TRANSACTION statement was executed. If no savepoint is named, the ROLLBACK statement backs out all database changes made since the BEGIN TRANSACTION statement.

The Sybase savepoint mechanism is especially useful in complex transactions involving many statements, as shown in Figure 12-4. The application program in the figure periodically saves its status as the transaction progresses, establishing two named savepoints. If problems develop later during the transaction, the application program does not have to abort the entire transaction. Instead, it can roll the transaction back to *any* of its savepoints and proceed from there. All of the statements

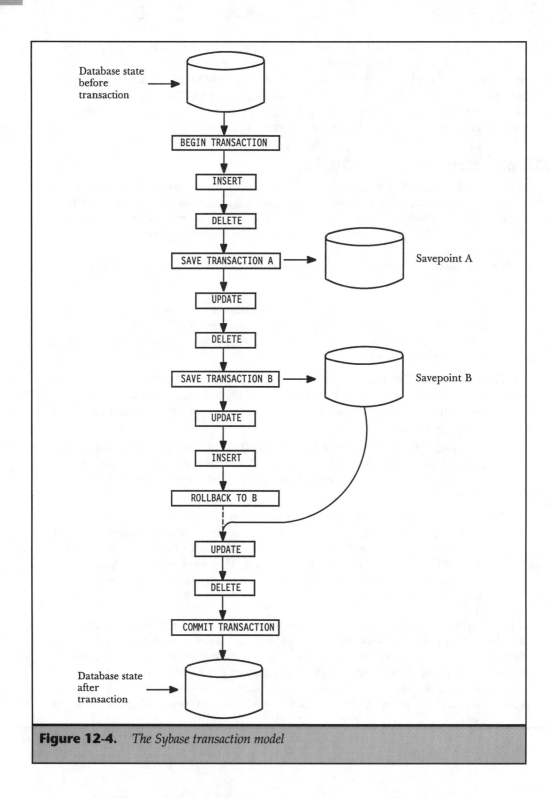

Figure 12-4. *The Sybase transaction model*

executed before the savepoint remain in effect; those executed since the savepoint are backed out by the rollback operation.

Note that the *entire transaction* is still the logical unit of work for Sybase, as it is for the ANSI/ISO model. If a system or hardware failure occurs in the middle of a transaction, for example, the entire transaction is backed out of the database. Thus, savepoints are a convenience for the application program, but not a fundamental change to the ANSI/ISO transaction model.

The explicit use of a BEGIN TRANSACTION statement is, however, a significant departure from the ANSI/ISO model. SQL statements that are executed "outside a transaction" (that is, statements that do not appear between a BEGIN/COMMIT or a BEGIN/ROLLBACK statement pair) are effectively handled in "auto-commit" mode. Each statement is committed as it is executed; there is no way to roll back the statement once it has succeeded.

Sybase specifically prohibits certain statements from occurring within a transaction, including those that alter the structure of a database (such as CREATE TABLE, ALTER TABLE, and DROP TABLE, discussed in Chapter 13), those that alter database security (GRANT and REVOKE, discussed in Chapter 15), and those that create temporary tables. These statements must be executed outside a Sybase transaction. This restriction makes the transaction model easier to implement, because it ensures that the structure of the database cannot change during a transaction. In contrast, the structure of a database can be altered significantly during an ANSI/ISO style transaction (tables can be dropped, created, and populated, for example), and the DBMS must be able to undo all the alterations if the user later decides to roll back the transaction. In practice, the Sybase prohibitions do not affect the usefulness of the DBMS. Because these prohibitions probably contribute to faster transaction performance, most users gladly make this trade-off.

Transactions: Behind the Scenes *

The "all or nothing" commitment that a DBMS makes for the statements in a transaction seems almost like magic to a new SQL user. How can the DBMS possibly back out the changes made to a database, especially if a system failure occurs during the middle of a transaction? The actual techniques used by brands of DBMS vary, but almost all of them are based on a *transaction log*, as shown in Figure 12-5.

Here is how the transaction log works, in simplified form. When a user executes a SQL statement that modifies the database, the DBMS automatically writes a record in the transaction log showing two copies of each row affected by the statement. One copy shows the row *before* the change, and the other copy shows the row *after* the change. Only after the log is written does the DBMS actually modify the row on the disk. If the user subsequently executes a COMMIT statement, the end-of-transaction is noted in the transaction log. If the user executes a ROLLBACK statement, the DBMS examines the log to find the "before" images of the rows that have been modified since the transaction began. Using these images, the DBMS restores the rows to their earlier

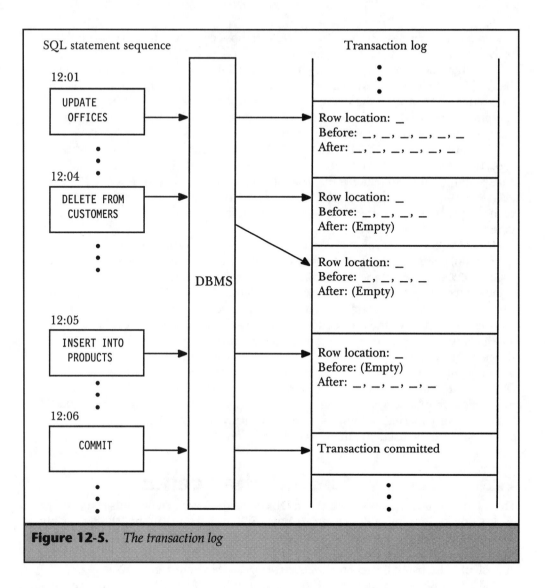

Figure 12-5. *The transaction log*

state, effectively backing out all changes to the database that were made during the transaction.

If a system failure occurs, the system operator typically recovers the database by running a special recovery utility supplied with the DBMS. The recovery utility examines the end of the transaction log, looking for transactions that were not committed before the failure. The utility rolls back each of these incomplete transactions, so that only committed transactions are reflected in the database; transactions in process at the time of the failure have been rolled back.

The use of a transaction log obviously imposes an overhead on updates to the database. Some personal computer DBMS brands allow you to disable transaction logging to increase the performance of the DBMS. While this may be acceptable for personal applications, the transaction log is essential in production databases to provide database recovery and the ROLLBACK capability. In a modern multi-user DBMS, the transaction log is usually stored on a fast disk drive, different from the one that stores the database, to minimize disk access contention.

Transactions and Multi-User Processing

When two or more users concurrently access a database, transaction processing takes on a new dimension. Now the DBMS must not only recover properly from system failures or errors, it must also ensure that the users' actions do not interfere with one another. Ideally, each user should be able to access the database as if he or she had exclusive access to it, without worrying about the actions of other users. The SQL transaction model allows a SQL-based DBMS to insulate users from one another in this way.

The best way to understand how SQL handles concurrent transactions is to look at the problems that result if transactions are not handled properly. Although they can show up in many different ways, there are four fundamental problems that can occur. The next four sections give a simple example of each problem.

The Lost Update Problem

Figure 12-6 shows a simple application where two users accept telephone orders from customers. The order entry program checks the PRODUCT file for adequate inventory before accepting the customer's order. In the figure, Joe starts entering an order for 100 ACI-41004 Widgets from his customer. At the same time, Mary starts entering her customer's order for 125 ACI-41004 Widgets. Each order entry program does a query on the PRODUCTS file, and each finds that there are 139 Widgets in stock—more than enough to cover the customer's request. Joe asks his customer to confirm the order, and his copy of the order entry program updates the PRODUCTS file to show (139 – 100) = 39 Widgets remaining for sale and inserts a new order for 100 Widgets into the ORDERS table. A few seconds later, Mary asks her customer to confirm their order. Her copy of the order entry program updates the PRODUCTS file to show (139 – 125) = 14 Widgets remaining in stock and inserts a new order for 125 Widgets into the ORDERS table.

The handling of the two orders has obviously left the database in an inconsistent state. The first of the two updates to the PRODUCTS file has been lost! Both customers' orders have been accepted, but there are not enough Widgets in inventory to satisfy both orders. Further, the database shows that there are still 14 Widgets remaining for sale! This example illustrates the "lost update" problem that can occur whenever two programs read the same data from the database, use the data as the basis for a calculation, and then try to update the data.

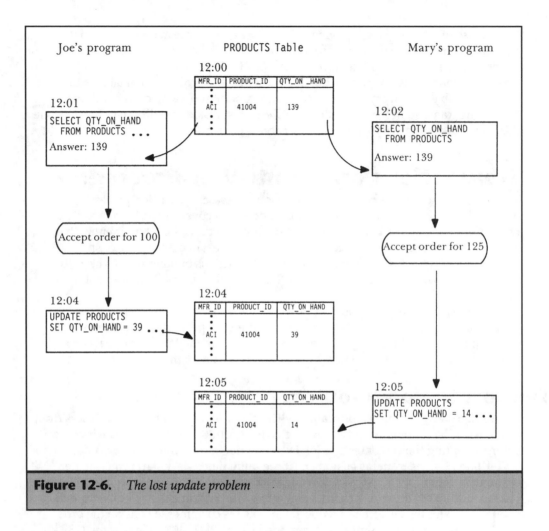

Figure 12-6. *The lost update problem*

The Uncommitted Data Problem

Figure 12-7 shows the same order processing application as Figure 12-6. Joe again begins taking an order for 100 ACI-41004 Widgets from his customer. This time, Joe's copy of the order processing program queries the PRODUCTS table, finds 139 Widgets available, and updates the PRODUCTS table to show 39 Widgets remaining after the customer's order. Then Joe begins to discuss with the customer the relative merits of the ACI-41004 and ACI-41005 Widgets. In the meantime, Mary's customer tries to order 125 ACI-41004 Widgets. Mary's copy of the order processing program queries the PRODUCTS table, finds only 39 Widgets available, and refuses the order. It also generates a notice telling the purchasing manager to buy more ACI-41004 Widgets, which are in great demand. Now Joe's customer decides that they don't want the Size

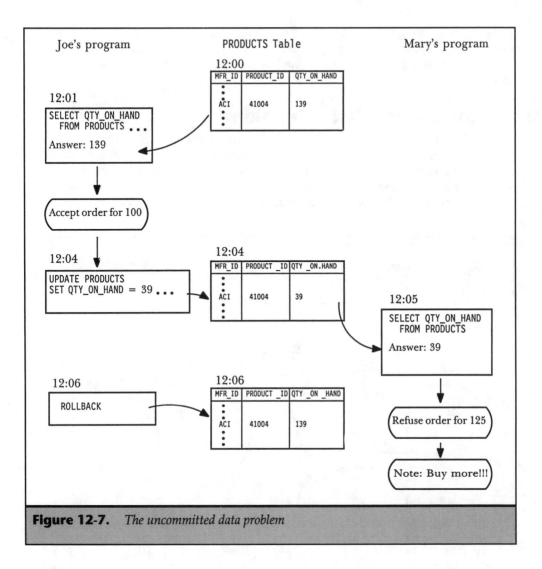

Figure 12-7. *The uncommitted data problem*

4 Widgets after all, and Joe's order entry program does a ROLLBACK to abort its transaction.

Because Mary's order processing program was allowed to see the uncommitted update of Joe's program, the order from Mary's customer was refused, and the purchasing manager will order more Widgets, even though there are still 139 of them in stock. The situation would have been even worse if Mary's customer had decided to settle for the 39 available Widgets. In this case, Mary's program would have updated the PRODUCTS table to show zero units available. But when the ROLLBACK of Joe's transaction occurred, the DBMS would have set the available inventory back to 139

Widgets, even though 39 of them are committed to Mary's customer. The problem in this example is that Mary's program has been allowed to see the uncommitted updates from Joe's program and has acted upon them, producing the erroneous results.

The Inconsistent Data Problem

Figure 12-8 shows the order processing application once more. Again, Joe begins taking an order for 100 ACI-41004 Widgets from his customer. A short time later, Mary also begins talking to her customer about the same Widgets, and her program does a single-row query to find out how many are available. This time Mary's customer inquires about the ACI-41005 Widgets as an alternative, and Mary's program does a

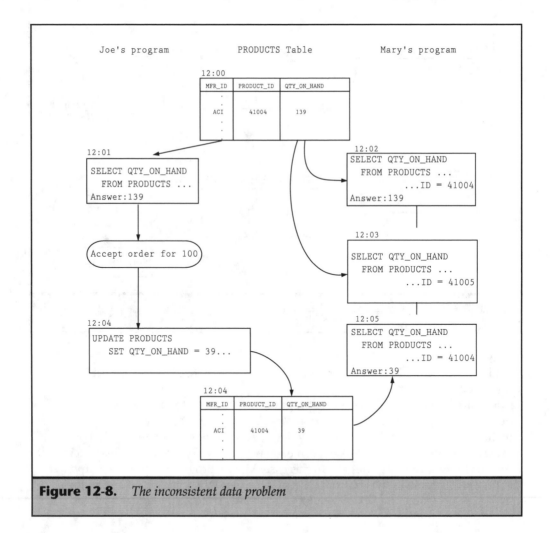

Figure 12-8. *The inconsistent data problem*

single-row query on that row. Meanwhile, Joe's customer decides to order the Widgets, so his program updates that row of the database and does a COMMIT to finalize the order in the database. After considering the ACI-41005 Widgets as an alternative, Mary's customer decides to order the ACI-41004 Widgets that Mary originally proposed. Her program does a new single-row query to get the information for the ACI-41004 Widgets again. But instead of finding the 139 Widgets that were in stock just a moment ago, the new query shown only 39 in stock.

In this example, unlike the preceding two, the status of the database has remained an accurate model of the real-world situation. There *are* only 39 ACI-41004 Widgets left, because Joe's customer has purchased 100 of them. There is no problem with Mary having seen uncommitted data from Joe's program—the order was complete, and committed to the database. However, from the point-of-view of Mary's program, the database did not remain consistent during her transaction. At the beginning of the transaction, a row contained certain data, and later in the same transaction, it contained different data, so "external events" have interfered with her consistent view of the database. This inconsistency can cause problems even if Mary's program never tries to update the database based on the results of the first query. For example, if the program is accumulating totals or calculating statistics, it cannot be sure that the statistics reflect a stable, consistent view of the data. The problem in this case is that Mary's program has been allowed to see committed updates from Joe's program that affect rows that it has already examined.

The Phantom Insert Problem

Figure 12-9 shows an order processing application once more. This time, the sales manager runs a report program that scans the ORDERS table, printing a list of the orders from customers of Bill Adams and computing their total. In the meantime, a customer calls Bill to place an additional order for $5000. The order is inserted into the database, and the transaction is committed. A short time later, the sales manager's program again scans the ORDERS table, running the very same query. This time, there is an additional order, and the total is $5000 higher than for the first query.

Like the previous example, the problem here is inconsistent data. The database remains an accurate model of the real-world situation, and its integrity is intact, but the same query executed twice during the same transaction yielded two different results. In the previous example, the query was a single-row query, and the inconsistency in the data was caused by a committed UPDATE statement. A committed DELETE statement could cause the same kind of problem. In the example of Figure 12-9, the problem is caused by a committed INSERT statement. The additional row did not participate in the first query, but it shows up as a "phantom row, out of nowhere" in the second query. Like the inconsistent data problem, the consequences of the phantom insert problem can be inconsistent and incorrect calculations.

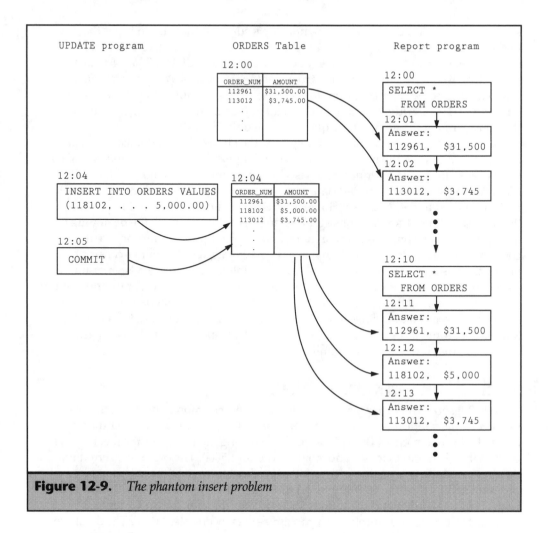

Figure 12-9. *The phantom insert problem*

Concurrent Transactions

As the three multi-user update examples show, when users share access to a database and one or more users is updating data, there is a potential for database corruption. SQL uses its transaction mechanism to eliminate this source of database corruption. In addition to the "all-or-nothing" commitment for the statements in a transaction, a SQL-based DBMS makes this commitment about transactions:

During a transaction, the user will see a completely consistent view of the database. The user will never see the uncommitted changes of other users, and even committed changes made by others will not affect data seen by the user in mid-transaction.

Transactions are thus the key to both recovery and concurrency control in a SQL database. The commitment above can be restated explicitly in terms of concurrent transaction execution:

If two transactions, A and B, are executing concurrently, the DBMS ensures that the results will be the same as they would be if *either* (a) Transaction A were executed first, followed by Transaction B, *or* (b) Transaction B were executed first, followed by Transaction A.

This concept is known as the *serializability* of transactions. Effectively, it means that each database user can access the database as if there were no other users concurrently accessing the database.

The fact that SQL insulates you from the actions of other concurrent users doesn't mean, however, that you can forget all about the other users. In fact, the situation is quite the opposite. Because other users want to concurrently update the database, you should keep your transactions as short and simple as possible, to maximize the amount of parallel processing that can occur.

Suppose, for example, that you run a program that performs a sequence of three large queries. Since the program doesn't update the database, it might seem that it doesn't need to worry about transactions. It certainly seems unnecessary to use COMMIT statements. But in fact the program should use a COMMIT statement after *each* query. Why? Recall that SQL *automatically* begins a transaction with the first SQL statement in a program. Without a COMMIT statement, the transaction continues until the program ends. Further, SQL guarantees that the data retrieved during a transaction will be self-consistent, unaffected by other users' transactions. This means that once your program retrieves a row from the database, *no other user can modify the row until your transaction ends,* because you might try to retrieve the row again later in your transaction, and the DBMS must guarantee that you will see the same data. Thus, as your program performs its three queries, it will prevent other users from updating larger and larger portions of the database.

The moral of this example is simple: you must *always* worry about transactions when writing programs for a production SQL database. Transactions should always be as short as possible. "COMMIT early and COMMIT often" is good advice when one is using programmatic SQL.

There are several possible schemes for implementing the concurrency required of SQL transactions, but all commercial SQL products use a technique based on *locking*. Locking is automatically handled by the DBMS and is invisible to you as a SQL user. You don't need to understand it to use SQL transactions. However, an understanding of locking and how it works inside the DBMS can help you use transactions more efficiently. The remainder of this chapter discusses locking in some detail.

Locking *

Major DBMS products like DB2 and SQL Server use sophisticated locking techniques to handle concurrent SQL transactions for many simultaneous users. However, the basic concepts behind locking and transactions are very simple. Figure 12-10 shows a simple locking scheme and how it handles contention between two concurrent transactions.

As Transaction A in the figure accesses the database, the DBMS automatically locks each piece of the database that the transaction retrieves or modifies. Transaction B proceeds in parallel, and the DBMS also locks the pieces of the database that it accesses. If Transaction B tries to access part of the database which has been locked by Transaction A, the DBMS blocks Transaction B, causing it to wait for the data to be unlocked. The DBMS releases the locks held by Transaction A only when it ends in a COMMIT or ROLLBACK operation. The DBMS then "unblocks" Transaction B, allowing it to proceed. Transaction B can now lock that piece of the database on its own behalf, protecting it from the effects of other transactions.

As the figure shows, the locking technique temporarily gives a transaction exclusive access to a piece of a database, preventing other transactions from modifying the locked data. Locking thus solves all three of the concurrent transaction problems. It prevents lost updates, uncommitted data, and inconsistent data from corrupting the database. However, locking introduces a new problem—it may cause a transaction to wait for a long time while the pieces of the database that it wants to access are locked by other transactions.

Locking Levels

Locking can be implemented at various levels of the database. In its crudest form, the DBMS could lock the entire database for each transaction. This locking strategy would be simple to implement, but it would allow processing of only one transaction at a time. If the transaction included any "think time" at all (such as time to discuss an order with a customer), all other access to the database would be blocked during that time, leading to unacceptably slow performance.

An improved form of locking is *table-level* locking. In this scheme, the DBMS locks only the tables accessed by a transaction. Other transactions can concurrently access other tables. This technique permits more parallel processing, but still leads to unacceptably slow performance in applications such as order entry, where many users must share access to the same table or tables.

Many DBMS products implement locking at the *page level*. In this scheme, the DBMS locks individual blocks of data from the disk ("pages") as they are accessed by a transaction. Other transactions are prevented from accessing the locked pages, but may access (and lock for themselves) other pages of data. Page sizes of 2KB, 4KB, and

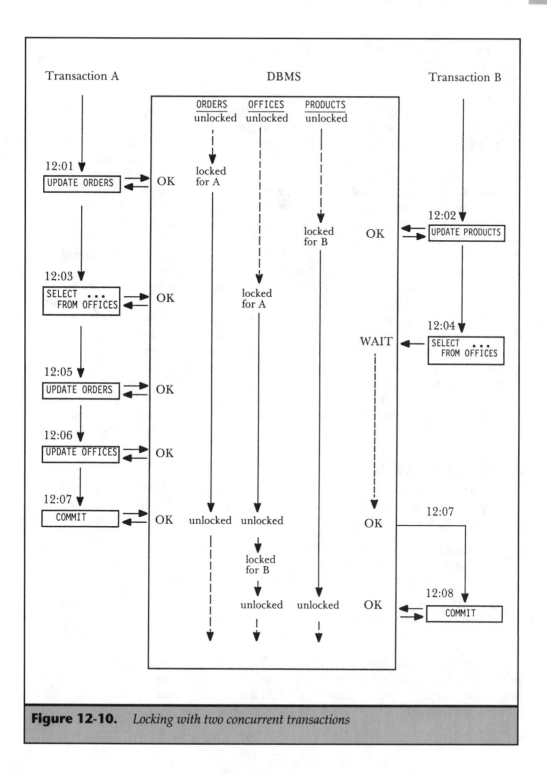

Figure 12-10. *Locking with two concurrent transactions*

16KB are commonly used. Since a large table will be spread out over hundreds or thousands of pages, two transactions trying to access two different rows of a table will usually be accessing two different pages, allowing the two transactions to proceed in parallel.

A few brands of DBMS have moved beyond page-level locking to *row-level* locks. Row-level locking allows two concurrent transactions that access two different rows of a table to proceed in parallel, even if the two rows fall in the same disk block. While this may seem a remote possibility, it can be a real problem with small tables containing small records, such as the OFFICES table in the sample database.

Row-level locking provides a high degree of parallel transaction execution. Unfortunately, keeping track of locks on variable-length pieces of the database (in other words, rows) rather than fixed-size pages is a much more complex task, so increased parallelism comes at the cost of more sophisticated locking logic and increased overhead. The DBMS vendors that stress on-line transaction processing performance are increasingly supporting row-level locking as an option.

It's theoretically possible to move beyond row-level locking to locking at the individual data item level. In theory this would provide even more parallelism than row-level locks, because it would allow concurrent access to the same row by two different transactions, provided they were accessing different sets of columns. The overhead in managing item-level locking, however, has thus far outweighed its potential advantages. No commercial SQL DBMS uses item-level locking. In fact, locking is an area of considerable research in database technology, and the locking schemes used in commercial DBMS products are much more sophisticated than the fundamental scheme described here. The most straightforward of these advanced locking schemes, using shared and exclusive locks, is described in the next section.

Shared and Exclusive Locks

To increase concurrent access to a database, most commercial DBMS products use a locking scheme with more than one type of lock. A scheme using shared and exclusive locks is quite common:

■ A *shared* lock is used by the DBMS when a transaction wants to read data from the database. Another concurrent transaction can also acquire a shared lock on the same data, allowing the other transaction to also read the data.

■ An *exclusive* lock is used by the DBMS when a transaction wants to update data in the database. When a transaction has an exclusive lock on some data, other transactions cannot acquire any type of lock (shared or exclusive) on the data.

Figure 12-11 shows the rules for this locking scheme and the permitted combinations of locks that can be held by two concurrent transactions. Note that a transaction can acquire an exclusive lock only if no other transaction currently has a shared or an exclusive lock on the data. If a transaction tries to acquire a lock not

		Transaction B		
		Unlocked	Shared lock	Exclusive lock
Transaction A	Unlocked	OK	OK	OK
	Shared lock	OK	OK	NO
	Exclusive lock	OK	NO	NO

Figure 12-11. *Rules for shared and exclusive locks*

permitted by the rules in Figure 12-11, it is blocked until other transactions unlock the data that it requires.

Figure 12-12 shows the same transactions shown in Figure 12-10, this time using shared and exclusive locks. If you compare the two figures, you can see how the new locking scheme improves concurrent access to the database. Mature and complex DBMS products, such as DB2, have more than two types of locks and use different locking techniques at different levels of the database. Despite the increased complexity, the goal of the locking scheme remains the same: to prevent unwanted interference between transactions while providing the greatest possible concurrent access to the database, all with minimal locking overhead.

Deadlocks *

Unfortunately, the use of any locking scheme to support concurrent SQL transactions leads to a problem called a *deadlock*. Figure 12-13 illustrates a deadlock situation. Program A updates the ORDERS table, thereby locking part of it. Meanwhile, Program B updates the PRODUCTS table, locking part of it. Now Program A tries to update the PRODUCTS table and Program B tries to update the ORDERS table, in each case trying to update a part of the table that has been previously locked by the other program. Without outside intervention, each program will wait forever for the other program to commit its transaction and unlock the data. The situation in the figure is a simple deadlock between two programs, but more complex situations can occur where three, four, or more programs are in a "cycle" of locks, each waiting for data that is locked by one of the other programs.

To deal with deadlocks, a DBMS typically includes logic that periodically (say, once every five seconds) checks the locks held by various transactions. When it detects a

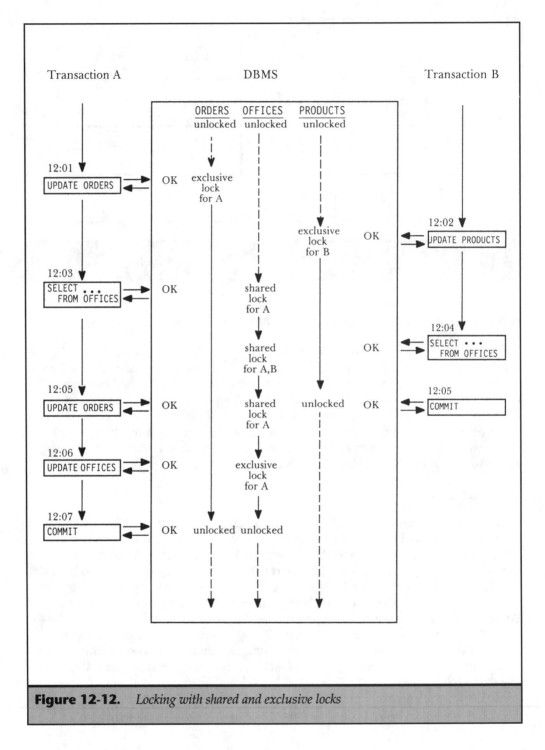

Figure 12-12. *Locking with shared and exclusive locks*

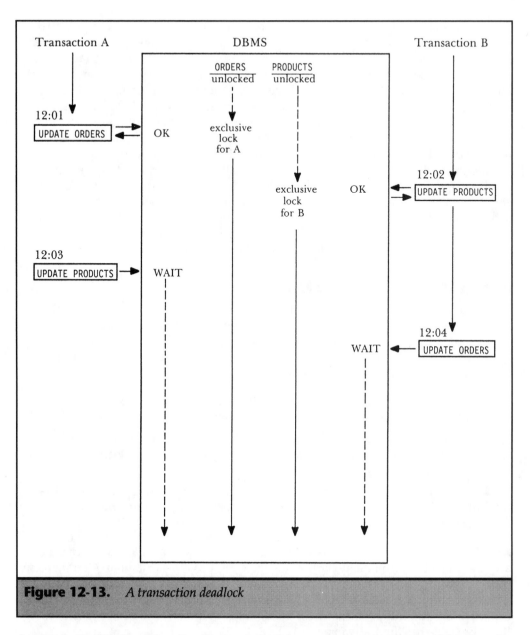

Figure 12-13. *A transaction deadlock*

deadlock, the DBMS arbitrarily chooses one of the transactions as the deadlock "loser" and rolls back the transaction. This frees the locks held by the losing transaction, allowing the deadlock "winner" to proceed. The losing program receives an error code informing it that it has lost a deadlock and that its current transaction has been rolled back.

This scheme for breaking deadlocks means that *any* SQL statement can potentially return a "deadlock loser" error code, even if there is nothing wrong with the statement per se. The transaction attempting the statement is rolled back through no fault of its own, but because of other concurrent activity in the database. This may seem unfair, but in practice it's much better than the other two alternatives—eternal deadlock or database corruption. If a deadlock loser error occurs in interactive SQL, the user can simply retype the SQL statement(s). In programmatic SQL, the application program must be prepared to handle the deadlock loser error code. Typically, the program will respond by either alerting the user or by automatically retrying the transaction.

The probability of deadlocks can be dramatically reduced by carefully planning database updates. All programs that update multiple tables during a transaction should, whenever possible, update the tables in the same sequence. This allows the locks to flow smoothly across the tables, minimizing the possibility of deadlocks. In addition, some of the advanced locking features described in later sections of this chapter can be used to further reduce the number of deadlocks that occur.

Advanced Locking Techniques *

Many commercial database products offer advanced locking facilities that go well beyond those provided by standard SQL transactions. These facilities are, by their nature, non-standard and product-specific. However, several of them, particularly those available in DB2, have been implemented in several commercial SQL products and have achieved the status of common, if not standard, features. These include:

- *Explicit locking.* A program can explicitly lock an entire table or some other part of the database if it will be repeatedly accessed by the program.

- *Isolation levels.* You can tell the DBMS that a specific program will not re-retrieve data during a transaction, allowing the DBMS to release locks before the transaction ends.

- *Locking parameters.* The database administrator can manually adjust the size of the "lockable piece" of the database and other locking parameters to tune locking performance.

EXPLICIT LOCKING *   If a transaction repeatedly accesses a table, the overhead of acquiring small locks on many parts of the table can be very substantial. A bulk update program which walks through every row of a table, for example, will lock the entire table, piece by piece, as it proceeds. For this type of transaction, the program should explicitly lock the entire table, process the updates, and then unlock the table. Locking the entire table has three advantages:

- It eliminates the overhead of row-by-row (or page-by-page) locking.

- It eliminates the possibility that another transaction will lock part of the table, forcing the bulk update transaction to wait.

■ It eliminates the possibility that another transaction will lock part of the table and deadlock the bulk update transaction, forcing it to be restarted.

Of course, locking the table has the disadvantage that all other transactions attempting to access the table must wait while the update is in process. However, because the bulk update transaction can proceed much more quickly, the overall throughput of the DBMS can be increased by explicitly locking the table.

In the IBM databases (DB2, SQL/DS, and OS/2 Extended Edition), the LOCK TABLE statement, shown in Figure 12-14, is used to explicitly lock an entire table. It offers two locking modes:

■ EXCLUSIVE mode acquires an exclusive lock on the entire table. No other transaction can access any part of the table for any purpose while the lock is held. This is the mode you would request for a bulk update transaction.

■ SHARE mode acquires a shared lock on the entire table. Other transactions can read parts of the table (that is, they can also acquire shared locks), but they cannot update any part of it. Of course if the transaction issuing the LOCK TABLE statement now updates part of the table, it will still incur the overhead of acquiring exclusive locks on the parts of the table that it updates. This is the mode you would request if you wanted a "snapshot" of a table, accurate at a particular point in time.

Oracle also supports a DB2-style LOCK TABLE statement. The same effect can be achieved in Ingres with a different statement. Several other database management systems, including SQL Server and SQLBase, do not support explicit locking at all, choosing instead to optimize their implicit locking techniques.

ISOLATION LEVELS * Under the strict definition of a SQL transaction, no action by a concurrently executing transaction is allowed to impact the data visible during the course of your transaction. If your program performs a database query during a transaction, proceeds with other work, and later performs the same database query a second time, the SQL transaction mechanism guarantees that the data returned by the two queries will be identical (unless *your* transaction acted to change the data). This ability to reliably re-retrieve a row during a transaction is the highest level of isolation that your program can have from other programs and users. The level of isolation is called the *isolation level* of your transaction.

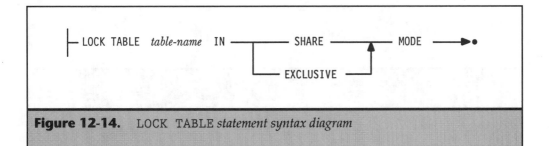

Figure 12-14. LOCK TABLE *statement syntax diagram*

This absolute isolation of your transaction from all other concurrently executing transactions is very costly in terms of database locking. As your program reads each row of query results, the DBMS must lock the row (with a shared lock) to prevent concurrent transactions from modifying the row. These locks must be held until the end of your transaction, just in case your program performs the query again. In many cases, the DBMS can significantly reduce its locking overhead if it knows in advance how a program will access a database during a transaction. To gain this efficiency, the major IBM mainframe databases added support for the concept of a user-specified *isolation level* that gives the user control over the trade-off between isolation and processing efficiency. The SQL2 specification formalized the IBM isolation level concept, and expanded it to include four isolation levels, shown in Figure 12-15. The isolation levels are linked directly to the three fundamental multi-user update problems discussed earlier in this chapter. As the level of isolation decreases (moving down the rows of the table), the DBMS insulates the user from fewer of the multi-user update problems.

The SERIALIZABLE isolation level is the highest level provided. At this level, the DBMS guarantees that the effects of concurrently executing transactions are exactly the same as if they executed in sequence. This is the default isolation level, because it is "the way SQL databases are supposed to work." If your program needs to perform the same multi-row query twice during a transaction and be guaranteed that the results will be identical regardless of other activity in the database, then it should use the SERIALIZABLE isolation level.

Multi-User Update Problem

Isolation Level	Lost Update	Uncommitted Data	Inconsistent Data	Phantom Insert
SERIALIZABLE	Prevented by DBMS	Prevented by DBMS	Prevented by DBMS	Prevented by DBMS
REPEATABLE READ	Prevented by DBMS	Prevented by DBMS	Prevented by DBMS	Can occur
READ COMMITTED	Prevented by DBMS	Prevented by DBMS	Can occur	Can occur
READ UNCOMMITTED	Prevented by DBMS	Can occur	Can occur	Can occur

Figure 12-15. *Isolation levels and multi-user updates*

The REPEATABLE READ isolation level is the second highest level. At this level, your transaction is not allowed to see either committed or uncommitted updates from other transactions, so the Lost Update, Uncommitted Data and Modified Data problems cannot occur. However, a row inserted into the database by another concurrent transaction may become visible during your transaction. As a result, a multi-row query run early in your transaction may yield different results than the same query run later in the same transaction (the Phantom Insert problem). If your program does not depend on the ability to repeat a multi-row query during a single transaction, you can safely use the REPEATABLE READ isolation level to improve DBMS performance without sacrificing data integrity. This is one of the isolation levels supported in the IBM mainframe database products.

The READ COMMITTED isolation level is the third highest level. In this mode, your transaction is not allowed to see uncommitted updates from other transactions, so the Lost Update and the Uncommitted Data problems cannot occur. However, updates that are committed by other concurrently-executing transactions may become visible during the course of your transaction. Your program could, for example, perform a single-row SELECT statement twice during the course of a transaction and find that the data in the row had been modified by another user. If your program does not depend on the ability to re-read a single row of data during a transaction, and it is not accumulating totals or doing other calculations that rely on a self-consistent set of data, it can safely use the READ COMMITTED isolation level. Note that if your program attempts to update a row that has already been updated by another user, your transaction will automatically be rolled back, to prevent the Lost Update problem from occurring.

The READ UNCOMMITTED isolation level is the lowest level specified in the SQL standard. In this mode, your transaction may be impacted by committed or uncommitted updates from other transaction, so the Uncommitted Data, Modified Data and Phantom Insert problems can occur. The DBMS still prevents the Lost Update problem. Generally, the READ UNCOMMITTED level is appropriate only for certain ad hoc query applications where the user can tolerate the fact that the query results may contain "dirty" data. If it is important that query results contain only information that has, in fact, been committed to the database, your program should not use this mode.

The SQL2 standard specifies a SET TRANSACTION statement, shown in Figure 12-16, which is used to set the isolation level of the current transaction. The SET TRANSACTION statement also allows you to specify whether the transaction is READ ONLY (i.e. it will only query the database) or READ WRITE (it may query or update the database). The DBMS uses this information, along with the isolation level, to optimize its database processing. The default isolation level is SERIALIZABLE. If READ UNCOMMITTED isolation level is specified, then READ ONLY is assumed and you may not specify a READ WRITE transaction. Otherwise, a READ WRITE transaction is the default.

The IBM mainframe databases (DB2 and SQL/DS) offer a choice of two isolation levels—REPEATABLE READ or READ COMMITTED (called *cursor stability mode* in IBM

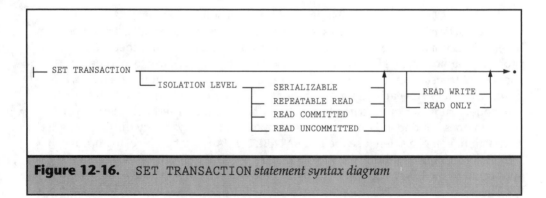

Figure 12-16. SET TRANSACTION *statement syntax diagram*

terminology). In the IBM implementations, the choice is made during the program development process, during the BIND step described in Chapter 17. Although the modes are not strictly part of the SQL language, the choice of mode strongly impacts how the application performs and how it can use retrieved data.

The Ingres DBMS offers a capability similar to the isolation modes of the IBM databases, but provides it in a different form. Using the SET LOCKMODE statement, an application program can tell Ingres what type of locking to use when handling a database query. The options are:

- *no locking*, which is similar to the IBM cursor stability mode just described,
- *shared locking*, which is similar to the IBM repeatable read mode just described, or
- *exclusive locking*, which provides exclusive access to the table during the query and offers a capability like the IBM LOCK TABLE statement.

The Ingres default is shared locking, which parallels the repeatable read default in the IBM scheme. Note, however, that the Ingres locking modes are set by an executable SQL statement. Unlike the IBM modes, which must be chosen at compile time, the Ingres modes can be chosen when the program executes, and can even be changed from one query to the next.

LOCKING PARAMETERS * A mature DBMS such as DB2, SQL/DS, Oracle, or Ingres employs much more complex locking techniques than those described here. The database administrator can improve the performance of these systems by manually setting their locking parameters. Typical parameters that can be tuned include:

- *Lock size.* Some DBMS products offer a choice of table-level, page-level, row-level, and other lock sizes. Depending on the specific application, a different size lock may be appropriate.

■ *Number of locks.*   Typically a DBMS allows each transaction to have some finite number of locks. The database administrator can often set this limit, raising it to permit more complex transactions or lowering it to encourage earlier lock escalation.

■ *Lock escalation.*   Often a DBMS will automatically "escalate" locks, replacing many small locks with a single larger lock (for example, replacing many page-level locks with a table-level lock). The database administrator may have some control over this escalation process.

■ *Lock timeout.*   Even when a transaction is not deadlocked with another transaction, it may wait a very long time for the other transaction to release its locks. Some DBMS brands implement a *timeout* feature, where a SQL statement fails with a SQL error code if it cannot obtain the locks it needs within a certain period of time. The timeout period can usually be set by the database administrator.

Summary

This chapter described the transaction mechanism provided by the SQL language:

■ A transaction is a logical unit of work in a SQL-based database. It consists of a sequence of SQL statements that are effectively executed as a single unit by the DBMS.

■ The COMMIT statement signals successful completion of a transaction, making all of its database modifications permanent.

■ The ROLLBACK statement asks the DBMS to abort a transaction, backing out all of its database modifications.

■ Transactions are the key to recovering a database after a system failure; only transactions that were committed at the time of failure remain in the recovered database.

■ Transactions are the key to concurrent access in a multi-user database. A user or program is guaranteed that its transaction will not be interfered with by other concurrent transactions.

■ Occasionally a conflict with another concurrently executing transaction may cause the DBMS to roll back a transaction through no fault of its own. An application program that uses SQL must be prepared to deal with this situation if it occurs.

PART FOUR

Database Structure

An important role of SQL is to define the structure and organization of a database. The next four chapters describe the SQL features that support this role. Chapter 13 explains how to create a database and its tables. Chapter 14 describes views, an important SQL feature that lets users see alternate organizations of database data. The SQL security features that protect stored data are described in Chapter 15. Finally, Chapter 16 discusses the system catalog, a collection of system tables that describe the structure of a database.

Chapter Thirteen

Creating a Database

320

M any SQL users don't have to worry about creating a database; they use interactive or programmatic SQL to access a database of corporate information or to access some other database that has already been created by someone else. In a typical corporate database, for example, the database administrator may give you permission to retrieve and perhaps to update the stored data. However, the administrator will not allow you to create new databases or to modify the structure of the existing tables.

As you grow more comfortable with SQL, you will probably want to start creating your own private tables to store personal data such as engineering test results or sales forecasts. If you are using a multi-user database, you may want to create tables or even entire databases that will be shared with other users. If you are using a personal computer database, you will certainly want to create your own tables and databases to support your personal applications.

This chapter describes the SQL language features that let you create databases and tables and define their structure.

The Data Definition Language

The SELECT, INSERT, DELETE, UPDATE, COMMIT, and ROLLBACK statements described in Parts Two and Three of this book are all concerned with manipulating the data in a database. These statements collectively are called the SQL *Data Manipulation Language,* or DML. The DML statements can modify the data stored in a database, but they cannot change its structure. None of these statements creates or deletes tables or columns, for example.

Changes to the structure of a database are handled by a different set of SQL statements, called the SQL *Data Definition Language,* or DDL. Using DDL statements, you can:

- define and create a new table
- remove a table that's no longer needed
- change the definition of an existing table
- define a virtual table (or view) of data
- establish security controls for a database
- build an index to make table access faster
- control the physical storage of data by the DBMS

For the most part, the DDL statements insulate you from the low-level details of how data is physically stored in the database. They manipulate abstract database objects, such as tables and columns. However, the DDL cannot avoid physical storage issues entirely, and, by necessity, the DDL statements and clauses that control physical storage vary from one DBMS to another.

The core of the Data Definition Language is based on three SQL verbs:

- CREATE, which defines and creates a database object
- DROP, which removes an existing database object
- ALTER, which changes the definition of a database object

In all major SQL-based DBMS products, these three DDL verbs can be used while the DBMS is running. The database structure is thus dynamic. The DBMS can be creating, dropping, or changing the definition of the tables in the database, for example, while it is simultaneously providing access to the database for its users. This is a major advantage of SQL and relational databases over earlier systems, where the DBMS had to be stopped before one could change the structure of the database. It means that a relational database can grow and change easily over time. Production use of a database can continue while new tables and applications are added.

Although the DDL and DML are two distinct parts of the SQL language, in most SQL-based DBMS products the split is a conceptual one only. Usually the DDL and DML statements are submitted to the DBMS in exactly the same way, and they can be freely intermixed in both interactive SQL sessions and programmatic SQL applications. If a program or user needs a table to store its temporary results, it can create the table, populate it, manipulate the data, and then delete the table. Again, this is a major advantage over earlier data models, where the structure of the database was fixed when the database was created.

Although virtually all commercial SQL products support the DDL as an integral part of the SQL language, the ANSI/ISO SQL standard does not require it. In fact, the SQL1 standard implies a strong separation between the DML and the DDL. The SQL2 standard still retains some of this separation, but it moves the SQL standard much closer to the actual usage of SQL in popular products. The differences between the ANSI/ISO standard and the DDL as implemented in popular SQL products are described later in this chapter.

Creating a Database

In a large mainframe DBMS installation, the database administrator is solely responsible for creating new databases. On smaller minicomputer DBMS installations, individual users may be allowed to create their own personal databases, but it's much more common for databases to be created centrally and then accessed by individual users. If you are using a personal computer DBMS, you are probably both the database administrator and the user, and you will have to create the database(s) that you use personally.

The SQL1 standard specifies the SQL language used to describe a database structure, but it does not specify how databases are created, and each DBMS brand takes a slightly different approach. The techniques used by some leading SQL products illustrate the differences:

- Oracle creates a database as part of the Oracle software installation process. For the most part, user tables are always placed in this single, system-wide database.

- Ingres includes a special utility program, called CREATEDB, which creates a new Ingres database. A companion program, DESTROYDB, erases an unneeded database.

- SQL Server includes a CREATE DATABASE statement as part of its data definition language. A companion DROP DATABASE statement destroys previously created databases. These statements can be used with interactive or programmatic SQL.

- OS/2 Extended Edition provides a CREATE DATABASE utility for creating databases and a DROP DATABASE utility for erasing databases. It also provides special function calls that can be used by application programs to create and drop databases.

- SQLBase uses the MS-DOS COPY command to create a new database. The user simply makes a duplicate copy of an empty database template supplied with the SQLBase software. The database can be erased later with the MS-DOS DEL command.

The SQL standard does not require a particular technique, but the structure of the standard strongly implies an executable set of DDL statements, like the SQL server approach. Major DBMS vendors have moved in this direction with their more recent releases. However, differences remain, so you must consult the manuals for your particular DBMS before you create a database. After an empty database is created, the next step is to populate it with tables, as described in the next section.

Table Definitions

The most important structure in a relational database is the table. In a multi-user database, the major tables are typically created once by the database administrator and then used day after day. As you use the database you will often find it convenient to define your own tables to store personal data or data extracted from other tables. These tables may be temporary, lasting only for a single interactive SQL session, or more permanent, lasting weeks or months. In a personal computer database, the table structure is even more fluid. Because you are both the user and the database administrator, you can create and destroy tables to suit your own needs, without worrying about other users.

Creating a Table (CREATE TABLE)

The CREATE TABLE statement, shown in Figure 13-1, defines a new table in the database and prepares it to accept data. The various clauses of the statement specify

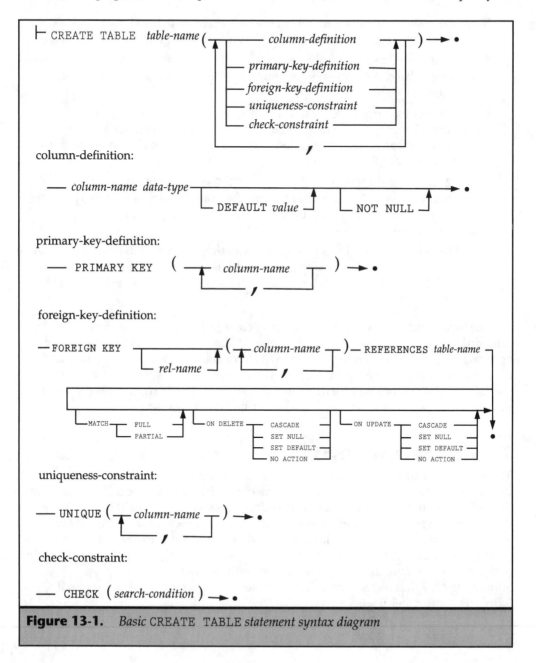

column-definition:

primary-key-definition:

foreign-key-definition:

uniqueness-constraint:

check-constraint:

Figure 13-1. *Basic CREATE TABLE statement syntax diagram*

the elements of the table definition. The syntax diagram for the statement appears complex, because there are so many parts of the definition to be specified and so many options for each element. In addition, some of the options are available in some DBMS brands or in the SQL2 standard, but not in other brands. In practice, creating a new table is relatively straightforward.

When you execute a CREATE TABLE statement, you become the owner of the newly created table, which is given the name specified in the statement. The table name must be a legal SQL name, and it must not conflict with the name of one of your existing tables. The newly created table is empty, but the DBMS prepares it to accept data added with the INSERT statement.

COLUMN DEFINITIONS   The columns of the newly created table are defined in the body of the CREATE TABLE statement. The column definitions appear in a comma-separated list enclosed in parentheses. The order of the column definitions determines the left-to-right order of the columns in the table. Each column definition specifies:

- the *column name*, which is used to refer to the column in SQL statements. Every column in the table must have a unique name, but the names may duplicate those of columns in other tables.

- the *data type* of the column, identifying the kind of data that the column stores. Data types were discussed in Chapter 5. Some data types, such as VARCHAR and DECIMAL, require additional information, such as the length or number of decimal places in the data. This additional information is enclosed in parentheses following the keyword that specifies the data type.

- whether the column contains *required data*. The NOT NULL clause prevents NULL values from appearing in the column; otherwise NULL values are allowed.

- an optional *default value* for the column. The DBMS uses this value when an INSERT statement for the table does not specify a value for the column.

The SQL2 standard allows several different parts of a column definition, which can be used to require that the column contains unique values, to specify that the column is a primary key or a foreign key, or to restrict the data values that the column may contain. These are single-column versions of capabilities provided by other clauses in the CREATE TABLE statement and are described as part of that statement in the following sections.

Here are some simple CREATE TABLE statements for the tables in the sample database:

Define the OFFICES *table and its columns.*

```
CREATE TABLE OFFICES
    (OFFICE INTEGER NOT NULL,
       CITY VARCHAR(15) NOT NULL,
     REGION VARCHAR(10) NOT NULL,
        MGR INTEGER,
     TARGET MONEY,
      SALES MONEY NOT NULL)
```

Define the ORDERS *table and its columns.*

```
CREATE TABLE ORDERS
  (ORDER NUM INTEGER NOT NULL,
   ORDER DATE DATE NOT NULL,
        CUST INTEGER NOT NULL,
         REP INTEGER,
         MFR CHAR(3) NOT NULL,
     PRODUCT CHAR(5) NOT NULL,
         QTY INTEGER NOT NULL,
      AMOUNT MONEY NOT NULL)
```

The CREATE TABLE statement varies slightly from one DBMS brand to another, because each DBMS supports its own set of data types and uses its own keywords to identify them in the column definitions. In addition, Sybase and SQL Server differ from most other DBMS brands and from the ANSI/ISO standard in their handling of NULL values. The standard specifies that a column may contain NULL values unless it is specifically declared NOT NULL. Sybase and SQL Server use the opposite convention, assuming that NULL values are not allowed unless the column is explicitly declared NULL.

DEFAULT VALUES   Both the ANSI/ISO standard and the IBM SQL products support default values for columns, but they support them in different ways. The ANSI/ISO standard allows you to specify a default value for each column. For example, here is an ANSI/ISO CREATE TABLE statement for the OFFICES table that specifies default values:

Define the OFFICES *table with default values (ANSI/ISO syntax).*

```
CREATE TABLE OFFICES
    (OFFICE INTEGER NOT NULL,
       CITY VARCHAR(15) NOT NULL,
     REGION VARCHAR(10) NOT NULL DEFAULT 'Eastern',
```

```
        MGR INTEGER DEFAULT 106,
     TARGET MONEY DEFAULT NULL,
      SALES MONEY NOT NULL DEFAULT 0.00)
```

With this table definition, only the office number and the city need to be specified when you insert a new office. The region defaults to Eastern, the office manager to Sam Clark (employee number 106), the sales to zero, and the target to NULL. Note that the target would default to NULL even without the DEFAULT NULL specification.

The IBM SQL products do not allow you to specify a different default value for each column. Instead, they provide a specific default value for each supported data type. The default value for numeric data is zero (0), the default for VARCHAR data is the empty string (""), the default for CHAR data is all blanks, and the default for date and time data is the current date and time. Here is a redefinition of the OFFICES table, using the IBM syntax for default values:

Define the OFFICES *table with default values (IBM syntax).*

```
CREATE TABLE OFFICES
    (OFFICE INTEGER NOT NULL,
       CITY VARCHAR(15) NOT NULL,
     REGION VARCHAR(10) NOT NULL WITH DEFAULT,
        MGR INTEGER WITH DEFAULT,
     TARGET MONEY,
      SALES MONEY NOT NULL WITH DEFAULT)
```

With this definition of the table, if you insert a new office and specify only the office number and city, the REGION column will be set to the empty string, the MGR and SALES columns will have zero values, and the TARGET column will be NULL.

PRIMARY AND FOREIGN KEY DEFINITIONS   In addition to defining the columns of a table, the CREATE TABLE statement identifies the table's primary key and the table's relationships to other tables in the database. The PRIMARY KEY and FOREIGN KEY clauses handle these functions. These clauses have been supported by the IBM databases (DB2, SQL/DS, and OS/2 Extended Edition) for some time and have been added to the ANSI/ISO specification. Most major SQL products have added support for them.

The PRIMARY KEY clause specifies the column or columns that form the primary key for the table. Recall from Chapter 4 that this column (or column combination) serves as a unique identifier for each row of the table. The DBMS automatically requires that the primary key value be unique in every row of the table. In addition, the column definition for every column in the primary key must specify that the column is NOT NULL.

The FOREIGN KEY clause specifies a foreign key in the table and the relationship that it creates to another (parent) table in the database. The clause specifies:

■ the column or columns that form the foreign key, all of which are columns of the table being created.

■ the table that is referenced by the foreign key. This is the parent table in the relationship; the table being defined is the child.

■ an optional name for the relationship. The name is not used in any SQL statements, but it may appear in error messages and is required if you want to be able to drop the foreign key later.

■ how the DBMS should treat a NULL value in one or more columns of the foreign key, when matching it against rows of the parent table.

■ an optional delete rule for the relationship (CASCADE, SET NULL, SET DEFAULT, or NO ACTION as described in Chapter 11), which determines the action to take when a parent row is deleted.

■ an optional update rule for the relationship as described in Chapter 11, which determines the action to take when part of the primary key in a parent row is updated.

■ an optional check constraint which restricts the data in the table so that its rows meet a specified search condition.

Here is an expanded CREATE TABLE statement for the ORDERS table, which includes a definition of its primary key and the three foreign keys that it contains:

Define the ORDERS *table with its primary and foreign keys.*

```
CREATE TABLE ORDERS
    (ORDER_NUM INTEGER NOT NULL,
    ORDER_DATE DATE NOT NULL,
          CUST INTEGER NOT NULL,
           REP INTEGER,
           MFR CHAR(3) NOT NULL,
       PRODUCT CHAR(5) NOT NULL,
           QTY INTEGER NOT NULL,
        AMOUNT MONEY NOT NULL,
    PRIMARY KEY (ORDER_NUM),
    FOREIGN KEY PLACEDBY (CUST)
     REFERENCES CUSTOMERS
      ON DELETE CASCADE,
```

```
FOREIGN KEY TAKENBY (REP)
  REFERENCES SALESREPS
    ON DELETE SET NULL,
FOREIGN KEY ISFOR (MFR, PRODUCT)
  REFERENCES PRODUCTS
    ON DELETE RESTRICT)
```

Figure 13-2 shows the three relationships created by this statement and the names it assigns to them. In general it's a good idea to assign a relationship name, because it helps to clarify the relationship created by the foreign key. For example, each order was placed by the customer whose number appears in the CUST column of the ORDERS table. The relationship created by this column has been given the name PLACEDBY.

When the DBMS processes the CREATE TABLE statement, it checks each foreign key definition against the definition of the table that it references. The DBMS makes sure that the foreign key and the primary key of the referenced table agree in the number of columns they contain and their data types. The referenced table must already be defined in the database for this checking to succeed.

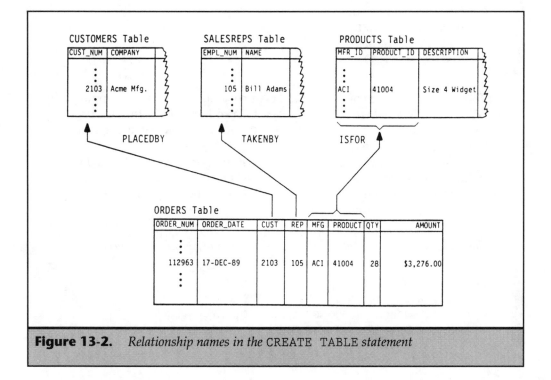

Figure 13-2. *Relationship names in the* CREATE TABLE *statement*

If two or more tables form a referential cycle (like the OFFICES and SALESREPS tables), you cannot define the foreign key for the table that you create first, because the referenced table does not yet exist. Instead, you must create the table without its foreign key definition and add the foreign key later using the ALTER TABLE statement.

UNIQUENESS CONSTRAINTS   The ANSI/ISO standard specifies that uniqueness constraints are also defined in the CREATE TABLE statement, using the UNIQUE clause shown in Figure 13-1. Here is a CREATE TABLE statement for the OFFICES table, modified to require unique CITY values:

Define the OFFICES *table with a uniqueness constraint.*

```
CREATE TABLE OFFICES
     (OFFICE INTEGER NOT NULL,
        CITY VARCHAR(15) NOT NULL,
      REGION VARCHAR(10) NOT NULL,
         MGR INTEGER,
      TARGET MONEY,
       SALES MONEY NOT NULL,
 PRIMARY KEY (OFFICE),
 FOREIGN KEY HASMGR (MGR)
   REFERENCES SALESREPS
    ON DELETE SET NULL,
       UNIQUE (CITY))
```

Unfortunately, this form of the UNIQUE clause is only slowly being supported by major SQL-based DBMS. Instead, all popular SQL products follow the DB2 practice and make uniqueness constraints a part of the CREATE INDEX statement, which is described later in this chapter.

If a primary key, foreign key, uniqueness constraint, or check constraint involves a single column, the ANSI/ISO standard permits a "shorthand" form of the definition. The primary key, foreign key, uniqueness constraint, or check constraint is simply added to the end of the column definition, as shown in this example:

Define the OFFICES *table with a uniqueness constraint (ANSI/ISO syntax).*

```
CREATE TABLE OFFICES
     (OFFICE INTEGER NOT NULL PRIMARY KEY,
        CITY VARCHAR(15) NOT NULL UNIQUE,
      REGION VARCHAR(10) NOT NULL,
```

```
        MGR INTEGER REFERENCES SALESREPS,
   TARGET MONEY,
    SALES MONEY NOT NULL)
```

Although this shorthand is part of the ANSI/ISO standard, it is not accepted by the IBM SQL products, which have pioneered primary key and foreign key support, nor by most other major commercial DBMS today.

PHYSICAL STORAGE DEFINITION * The CREATE TABLE statement typically includes one or more optional clauses that specify physical storage characteristics for a table. Generally these clauses are used only by the database administrator to optimize the performance of a production database. By their nature these clauses are very specific to a particular DBMS. Although they are of little practical interest to most SQL users, the different physical storage structures provided by various DBMS products illustrate their different intended applications and levels of sophistication.

Most of the personal computer databases provide very simple physical storage mechanisms. The dBASE IV DBMS, for example, uses an individual MS-DOS file to store each table of data. SQLBase uses a single file to store each database. In each case the use of MS-DOS files limits the size of a single table or database. They also require that the entire table or database be stored on a single physical disk volume.

Multi-user databases typically provide more sophisticated physical storage schemes to support improved database performance. For example, Ingres allows the database administrator to define multiple named *locations*, which are physical directories where database data can be stored. The locations can be spread across multiple disk volumes to take advantage of parallel disk input/output operations. You can optionally specify one or more locations for a table in the Ingres CREATE TABLE statement:

```
CREATE TABLE OFFICES (table-definition)
   WITH LOCATION = (AREA1, AREA2, AREA3)
```

By specifying multiple locations, you can spread a table's contents across several disk volumes for greater parallel access to the table.

SQL Server offers a similar approach, allowing the database administrator to specify multiple named *database files* that are used to store data. The SQL Server CREATE DATABASE statement can specify one or more database files:

```
CREATE DATABASE OPDATA
    ON DBFILE1, DBFILE2, DBFILE3
```

The SQL Server approach allows the contents of a database to be distributed across several disk volumes, but it provides less table-by-table control than the Ingres scheme.

Finally, DB2 offers a very complex scheme for managing physical storage. The entire collection of tables managed by a DB2 subsystem can be divided into two or more DB2 *databases.* Note that this use of the term "database" is confusing, because a DB2 database is an internal structure used to manage the physical storage of data, not a structure visible to the user. Each of these databases is in turn divided into DB2 *tablespaces* and *indexspaces,* logical storage entities that store tables and indexes, respectively. Tablespaces and indexspaces can be assigned in turn to a *storage group,* a physical storage entity maintained by DB2. Finally, a storage group consists of one or more volumes of direct access storage on the mainframe. Databases, tablespaces, and storage groups are managed using the CREATE DATABASE, CREATE TABLESPACE, and CREATE STOGROUP statements in the DB2 DDL. When you create a DB2 table, you can optionally assign it to a specific tablespace:

```
CREATE TABLE OFFICES (table-definition)
    IN ADMINDB.OPSPACE
```

This scheme allows precise, table-by-table control over the location of data. DB2 allows the database administrator to recover tablespaces individually after a system failure, and it allows the database administrator to start and stop access to individual databases using special database administration statements. Thus these DB2 structures work together to provide a powerful, if complex, facility for managing the physical storage of a DB2 database.

Removing a Table (DROP TABLE)

Over time the structure of a database will grow and change. New tables will be created to represent new entities, and some old tables will no longer be needed. You can remove an unneeded table from the database with the DROP TABLE statement, shown in Figure 13-3.

The table name in the statement identifies the table to be dropped. Normally you will be dropping one of your own tables and will use an unqualified table name. With

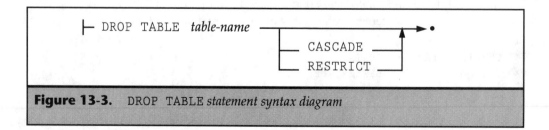

Figure 13-3. DROP TABLE *statement syntax diagram*

proper permission, you can also drop a table owned by another user by specifying a qualified table name. Here are some examples of the DROP TABLE statement:

The CUSTOMERS *table has been replaced by two new tables,* CUST_INFO *and* ACCOUNT_INFO*, and is no longer needed.*

```
DROP TABLE CUSTOMERS
```

Sam gives you permission to drop his table, named BIRTHDAYS*.*

```
DROP TABLE SAM.BIRTHDAYS
```

When the DROP TABLE statement removes a table from the database, its definition and all of its contents are lost. There is no way to recover the data, and you would have to use a new CREATE TABLE statement to recreate the table definition. Because of its serious consequences, you should use the DROP TABLE statement with care.

The SQL2 standard requires that a DROP TABLE statement include either CASCADE or RESTRICT, which specify the impact of dropping a table on other database objects (such as views, described in Chapter 14) that depend on the table. If CASCADE is specified, the DROP TABLE statement will fail if there are other database objects that reference the table. Most commercial DBMS products accept the DROP TABLE statement with no option specified.

Changing a Table Definition (ALTER TABLE)

After a table has been in use for some time, users often discover that they want to store additional information about the entities represented in the table. In the sample database, for example, you might want to:

- Add the name and phone number of a key contact person to each row of the CUSTOMERS table, as you begin to use it for contacting customers.
- Add a minimum inventory level column to the PRODUCTS table, so the database can automatically alert you when stock of a particular product is low.
- Make the REGION column in the OFFICES table a foreign key for a newly created REGIONS table, whose primary key is the region name.
- Drop the foreign key definition linking the CUST column in the ORDERS table to the CUSTOMERS table, replacing it with two foreign key definitions linking the CUST column to the newly created CUST_INFO and ACCOUNT_INFO tables.

Each of these changes, and some others, can be handled with the ALTER TABLE statement, shown in Figure 13-4. As with the DROP TABLE statement, you will normally use the ALTER TABLE statement on one of your own tables. With proper

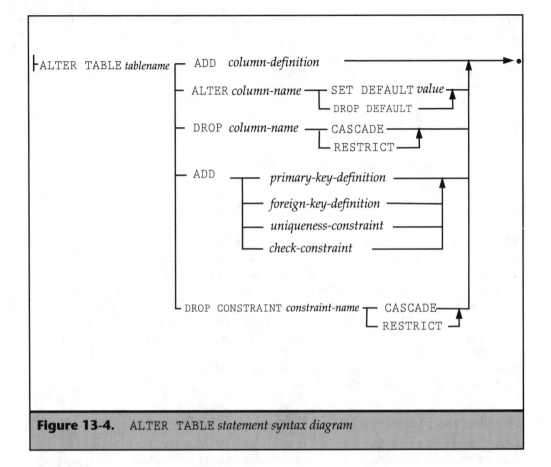

Figure 13-4. ALTER TABLE *statement syntax diagram*

permission, however, you can specify a qualified table name and alter the definition of another user's table. As shown in the figure, the ALTER TABLE statement can:

- add a column definition to a table
- change the default value for a column
- add or drop a primary key for a table
- add or drop a new foreign key for a table
- add or drop a uniqueness constraint for a table
- add or drop a check constraint for a table
- add or drop a uniqueness constraint for a table
- add or drop a check constraint for a table

The clauses in Figure 13-4 are specified in the SQL standard. Many DBMS brands lack support for some of these clauses or offer clauses unique to the DBMS, which alter other table characteristics. For example, you can use the DB2 ALTER TABLE statement to add or remove a validation procedure for the table. Each of the clauses in the ALTER TABLE statement can appear only once in the statement. You can add a column and define a foreign key in a single ALTER TABLE statement, but you must use two successive ALTER TABLE statements to add two columns.

ADDING A COLUMN   The most common use of the ALTER TABLE statement is to add a column to an existing table. The column definition clause in the ALTER TABLE statement is just like the one in the CREATE TABLE statement, and it works the same way. The new column is added to the end of the column definitions for the table, and it appears as the rightmost column in subsequent queries. The DBMS normally assumes a NULL value for a newly added column in all existing rows of the table. If the column is declared to be NOT NULL with a default value, the DBMS instead assumes the default value. Note that you cannot simply declare the new column NOT NULL, because the DBMS would assume NULL values for the column in the existing rows, immediately violating the constraint! (When you add a new column, the DBMS doesn't actually go through all of the existing rows of the table adding a NULL or default value. Instead, it detects the fact that an existing row is "too short" for the new table definition when the row is retrieved, and extends it with a NULL or default value before displaying it or passing it to your program.)

Some sample ALTER TABLE statements that add new columns are:

Add a contact name and phone number to the CUSTOMERS *table.*

```
ALTER TABLE CUSTOMERS
   ADD CONTACT_NAME VARCHAR(30)

ALTER TABLE CUSTOMERS
   ADD CONTACT_PHONE CHAR(10)
```

Add a minimum inventory level column to the PRODUCTS *table.*

```
ALTER TABLE PRODUCTS
   ADD MIN_QTY INTEGER NOT NULL WITH DEFAULT
```

In the first example, the new columns will have NULL values for existing customers. In the second example, the MIN_QTY column will have the value zero (0) for existing products, which is appropriate.

DROPPING A COLUMN   The ALTER TABLE statement cannot be used to drop an existing column, and in fact SQL does not provide a single statement method for dropping a column. Of course you can simply ignore a column that's no longer needed, keeping it in the table definition. If you really want to drop a column from a table, however, you must:

1. Unload all of the data from the table.
2. Use the DROP TABLE statement to erase the table definition.
3. Use a CREATE TABLE statement to redefine the table without the unwanted column.
4. Reload all of the data that was previously unloaded.

The bulk unloading and reloading of data in Steps 1 and 4 are typically performed with special-purpose utility programs, rather than with the SELECT or INSERT statements.

CHANGING PRIMARY AND FOREIGN KEYS   The other common use for the ALTER TABLE statement is to change or add primary key and foreign key definitions for a table. Since primary key and foreign key support is being provided in new releases of several SQL-based database systems, this form of the ALTER TABLE statement is particularly useful. It can be used to inform the DBMS about inter-table relationships that already exist in a database, but which have not been explicitly specified before.

Unlike column definitions, primary key and foreign key definitions can be added *and* dropped from a table with the ALTER TABLE statement. The clauses that add primary key and foreign key definitions are exactly the same as those in the CREATE TABLE statement, and they work the same way. The clauses that drop a primary key or foreign key are straightforward, as shown in the following examples. Note that you can only drop a foreign key if the relationship that it creates was originally assigned a name. If the relationship was unnamed, there is no way to specify it in the ALTER TABLE statement. In this case you cannot drop the foreign key unless you drop and recreate the table, using the procedure described for dropping a column.

Here is an example that adds a foreign key definition to an existing table:

Make the REGION *column in the* OFFICES *table a foreign key for the newly created* REGIONS *table, whose primary key is the region name.*

```
ALTER TABLE OFFICES
FOREIGN KEY INREGION (REGION)
 REFERENCES REGIONS
```

Here is an example of an ALTER TABLE statement that modifies a primary key. Note that the foreign key corresponding to the original primary key must be dropped, because it is no longer a foreign key for the altered table:

Change the primary key of the OFFICES *table.*

```
ALTER TABLE SALESREPS
      DROP FOREIGN KEY WORKSIN

ALTER TABLE OFFICES
      DROP PRIMARY KEY
PRIMARY KEY (CITY)
```

Constraint Definitions

The tables in a dsatabase define its basic structure, and in most early commercial SQL products the table definitions were the only specification of database structure. With the advent of primary key/foreign key support in DB2 and in the SQL2 standard, the definition of database structure was expanded to include the *relationships* among the tables in a database. More recently, through the SQL2 standard and the evolution of commercial products, the definition of database structure has expanded to include a new area—restrictions on the data that can be entered into the database. These restrictions are typically known as database *constraints*.

The previous sections described three specific types of database constraints:

- a *uniqueness constraint*, which forces the data in some column or combination of columns to be unique for every row in a table.

- a *primary key constraint*, which enforces the same uniqueness requirement, but also designates a column or combination of columns as the key for a "parent" row, constrained by a parent/child relationship to another table.

- a *foreign key constraint*, which forces the value of a column or combination of columns to match the value of a primary key in some other table.

Each of these constraints applies to a single table, is specified in the CREATE TABLE statement, and can be modified by the ALTER TABLE statement. The SQL2 standard adds support for three other kinds of data constraints, assertions and domain definitions. The standard also allows all types of constraints to be explicitly named, so that they can be manipulated by name after they have been initially defined. Finally, the standard provides explicit control over when constraints are checked, and what happens when an attempt is made to modify the database contents in a way that would violate the constraint.

Check Constraints

A *check constraint* is a database constraint that restricts the contents of a particular table. In the SQL2 standard, a check constraint is specified as a search condition, and it appears as part of the table definition. For example, you could specify a (rather artificial) check constraint for the SALESREPS table to enforce the rule "salespeople whose hire date is later than January 1, 1988 shall not be assigned quotas higher than $300,000." This SQL2-compliant table definition implements this constraint:

```
CREATE TABLE SALESREPS
   (EMPL_NUM INTEGER NOT NULL,
        NAME VARCHAR (15) NOT NULL,
           .
           .
 FOREIGN KEY WORKSIN (REP_OFFICE)
  REFERENCES OFFICES
   ON DELETE SET NULL
       CHECK ((HIRE_DATE < "01-JAN-88") OR
              (QUOTA <= 300000)))
```

The check constraint is checked every time a SQL statement attempts to update or insert data into the table.

Assertions

An *assertion* is a database constraint that restricts the contents of the database as a whole. Like a check constraint, an assertion is specified as a search condition. But unlike a check constraint, the search condition in an assertion can restrict the contents of multiple tables and the data relationships among them. For that reason, an assertion is specified as part of the overall database definition, via a SQL2 CREATE ASSERTION statement. Suppose you wanted to restrict the contents of the sample database so that the total orders for any given customer may not exceed that customer's credit limit. You can implement that restriction with the statement:

```
CREATE ASSERTION CREDLIMIT
        CHECK ((CUSTOMERS.CUST_NUM = ORDERS.CUST) AND
               (SUM (AMOUNT) <= CREDIT_LIMIT))
```

With this assertion, named "CREDITLIMIT,"as part of the database definition, the DBMS is required to check that the assertion remains true each time a SQL statement attempts to modify the CUSTOMER or ORDERS tables. The overhead in this checking may be significant, but it may be more desirable than the overload and inconsistency that might result if the checking were instead implemented within every application program that modified either of the two tables.

Domain Definitions

The contents of a particular column in a relational database table are always restricted so that the value of the column in every row of the table has the same data type. All of the city names in the CITY column of the OFFICES table, for example, are variable-length character strings of up to 15 characters. The SALES column contains all MONEY data, and the OFFICE column (containing the office number) is always an integer.

In real world situations, the data values that can appear in a particular column are actually even more constrained. For example, the OFFICE column should not *really* contain any integer. An office number of 17 or 1,246 is clearly "wrong," given the way in which the company has chosen to code its office numbers. All of the office numbers in the table are three-digit numbers with a non-zero leading digit, and presumably the company wants to continue to use this convention. In formal relational database terms, the *domain* of the OFFICE column (i.e. the set of data values it should be allowed to contain) should not be "all integers," it should be "integers between 100 and 999, inclusive."

The SQL2 standard implements the formal concept of a domain as a part of a database definition. Under SQL, a domain is a named collection of data values that effectively functions as an additional data type, for use in database definition. A domain is created with a CREATE DOMAIN statement. Once created, the domain can be referenced as if it were a data type within a table definition.

Synonyms (CREATE/DROP SYNONYM)

Production databases are often organized like the copy of the sample database shown in Figure 13-5, with all of their major tables collected together and owned by the database administrator. The database administrator gives other users permission to access the tables, using the SQL security scheme described in Chapter 15. Recall, however, that you must use qualified table names to refer to another user's tables. In practice, this means that *every* query against the major tables in Figure 13-5 must use qualified table names, which makes queries like the following one long and tedious to type:

List the name, sales, office, and office sales for everyone.

```
SELECT NAME, OP_ADMIN.SALESREPS.SALES, OFFICE, OP_ADMIN.OFFICES.SALES
  FROM OP_ADMIN.SALESREPS, OP_ADMIN.OFFICES
```

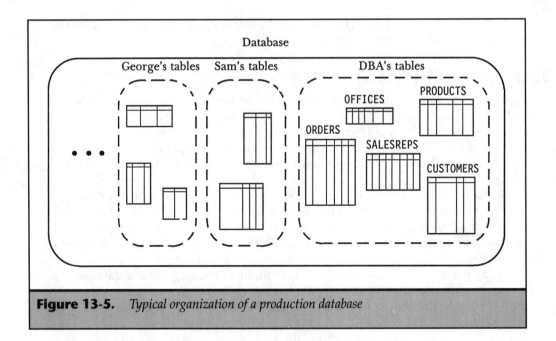

Figure 13-5.   *Typical organization of a production database*

To address this problem, the IBM SQL products provide a *synonym* capability. A synonym is a name that you define that stands for the name of some other table. You create a synonym using the CREATE SYNONYM statement. If you were the user named George in Figure 13-5, for example, here are a pair of CREATE SYNONYM statements that you might use:

Create synonyms for two tables owned by another user.

```
CREATE SYNONYM REPS
   FOR OP_ADMIN.SALESREPS

CREATE SYNONYM OFFICES
   FOR OP_ADMIN.OFFICES
```

Once you have defined a synonym, you can use it just like a table name in SQL queries. The previous query thus becomes:

```
SELECT NAME, REPS.SALES, OFFICE, OFFICES.SALES
   FROM REPS, OFFICES
```

The use of synonyms doesn't change the meaning of the query, and you must still have permission to access the other users' tables. Nonetheless, synonyms simplify the SQL statements you use and make it appear as if the tables were your own. If you decide later that you no longer want to use the synonyms, they can be removed with the DROP SYNONYM statement:

Drop the synonyms created earlier.

```
DROP SYNONYM REPS

DROP SYNONYM OFFICES
```

Synonyms are provided by the IBM databases (DB2, SQL/DS, and OS/2 Extended Edition) and Oracle, SQLBase, and Informix. They are not specified by the ANSI/ISO SQL standard.

Indexes (CREATE/DROP INDEX)

One of the physical storage structures that is provided by most SQL-based database management systems is an *index*. An index is a structure that provides rapid access to the rows of a table based on the values of one or more columns. Figure 13-6 shows the PRODUCTS table and two indexes that have been created for it. One of the indexes provides access based on the DESCRIPTION column. The other provides access based on the primary key of the table, which is a combination of the MFR_ID and PRODUCT_ID columns.

The DBMS uses the index as you might use the index of a book. The index stores data values and pointers to the rows where those data values occur. In the index the data values are arranged in ascending or descending order, so that the DBMS can quickly search the index to find a particular value. It can then follow the pointer to locate the row containing the value.

The presence or absence of an index is completely transparent to the SQL user who accesses a table. For example, consider this SELECT statement:

Find the quantity and price for Size 4 Widgets.

```
SELECT QTY_ON_HAND, PRICE
  FROM PRODUCTS
 WHERE DESCRIPTION = 'Size 4 Widget'
```

The statement doesn't say whether there is an index on the DESCRIPTION column or not, and the DBMS will carry out the query in either case.

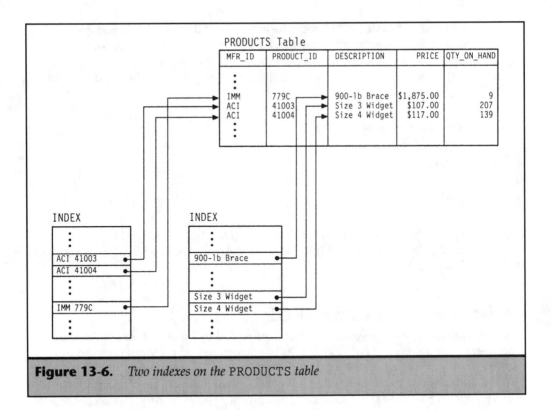

Figure 13-6. *Two indexes on the* PRODUCTS *table*

If there were no index for the DESCRIPTION column, the DBMS would be forced to process the query by sequentially scanning the PRODUCTS table, row by row, examining the DESCRIPTION column in each row. To make sure it had found all of the rows that satisfied the search condition, it would have to examine *every* row in the table. For a large table with thousands or millions of rows, the scan of the table could take minutes or hours.

With an index for the DESCRIPTION column, the DBMS can locate the requested data with much less effort. It searches the index to find the requested value ("Size 4 Widget") and then follows the pointer to find the requested row(s) of the table. The index search is very rapid because the index is sorted and because its rows are very small. Moving from the index to the row(s) is also very rapid, because the index tells the DBMS where on the disk the row(s) are located.

As this example shows, the advantage of having an index is that it greatly speeds the execution of SQL statements with search conditions that refer to the indexed column(s). One disadvantage of having an index is that it consumes additional disk space. Another disadvantage is that the index must be updated every time a row is added to the table and every time the indexed column is updated in an existing row. This imposes additional overhead on INSERT and UPDATE statements for the table.

In general it's a good idea to create an index for columns that are used frequently in search conditions. Indexing is also more appropriate when queries against a table are more frequent than inserts and updates. The DBMS *always* establishes an index for the primary key of a table, because it anticipates that access to the table will most frequently be via the primary key. In the sample database, these columns are good candidates for additional indexes:

- The COMPANY column in the CUSTOMERS table should be indexed if customer data is often retrieved by company name.

- The NAME column in the SALESREPS table should be indexed if data about salespeople is often retrieved by salesperson name.

- The REP column in the ORDERS table should be indexed if orders are frequently retrieved based on the salesperson who took them.

- The CUST column in the ORDERS table should similarly be indexed if orders are frequently retrieved based on the customer who placed them.

- The MFR and PRODUCT columns, together, in the ORDERS table should be indexed if orders are frequently retrieved based on the product ordered.

To create an index, you use the CREATE INDEX statement, shown in Figure 13-7. The statement assigns a name to the index and specifies the table for which the index is created. The statement also specifies the column(s) to be indexed and whether they should be indexed in ascending or descending order. The keyword UNIQUE is used in the DB2 version of the statement to specify that the column(s) being indexed must contain unique values. As described earlier, the ANSI/ISO standard makes the UNIQUE clause a part of the CREATE TABLE statement, but DB2 associates it with the index.

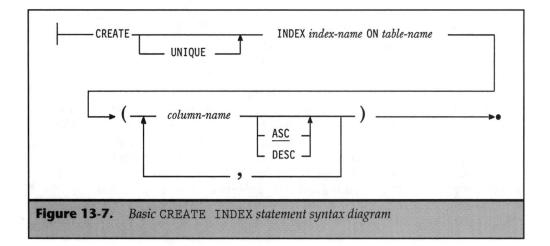

Figure 13-7. *Basic* CREATE INDEX *statement syntax diagram*

Here is an example of a CREATE INDEX statement that builds an index for the ORDERS table based on the MFR and PRODUCT columns and that requires combinations of columns to have a unique value:

Create an index for the ORDERS *table.*

```
CREATE UNIQUE INDEX ORD_PROD_IDX
    ON ORDERS (MFR, PRODUCT)
```

In addition to the clauses shown in the example, the CREATE INDEX statement almost always includes additional DBMS-specific clauses that specify the disk location for the index and for performance-tuning parameters such as the size of the index pages and the percentage of free space that the index should allow for additional rows.

If you create an index for a table and later decide that it is not needed, the DROP INDEX statement removes the index from the database. The statement removes the index created in the previous example:

Drop the index created earlier.

```
DROP INDEX ORD_PROD_IDX
```

Other Database Objects

The CREATE, DROP, and ALTER verbs form the cornerstone of the SQL Data Definition Language. Statements based on these verbs are used in all SQL implementations to manipulate tables, indexes, and views (as described in Chapter 14). Most of the popular SQL-based DBMS products also use these verbs to form additional DDL statements that create, destroy, and modify other database objects unique to that particular brand of DBMS.

In the Sybase or SQL Server DBMS, for example, a trigger is created using the CREATE TRIGGER statement. The trigger can later be removed from the database using the DROP TRIGGER statement. Except for using the standard verb names and a convention that the next word is the name of the object, these statements are all very DBMS-specific and nonstandard. Nonetheless, they give a uniform feel to the various SQL dialects. If you encounter a new SQL-based DBMS and know that it supports an object known as a BLOB, the odds are that it supports a CREATE BLOB and a DROP BLOB statement. Table 13-1 shows how some of the popular SQL products use the CREATE, DROP, and ALTER verbs in their expanded DDL.

SQL DDL Statements   **Managed Object**

Supported by most DBMS brands

SQL DDL Statements	Managed Object
CREATE/DROP/ALTER TABLE	table
CREATE/DROP/ALTER VIEW	view
CREATE/DROP/ALTER INDEX	index

Supported by DB2

CREATE/DROP DATABASE	group of tables and indexes
CREATE/DROP/ALTER STOGROUP	physical storage group
CREATE/DROP SYNONYM	table synonym
CREATE/DROP/ALTER TABLESPACE	tablespace (group of tables)

Supported by SQL/DS

CREATE/DROP PROGRAM	database access module
DROP STATEMENT	statement in database access module
ACQUIRE/DROP DBSPACE	logical storage group

Supported by Oracle

CREATE/DROP/ALTER DATABASE	database
CREATE/DROP/ALTER/ROLLBACK SEGMENT	rollback segment
CREATE/DROP/ALTER SEQUENCE	sequence of unique keys
CREATE/DROP/ALTER TABLESPACE	tablespace (group of tables)

Supported by Ingres

CREATE INTEGRITY	table integrity constraint
CREATE PERMIT	table access permission

Supported by VAX SQL

CREATE/DROP DATABASE	database

Supported by Informix

CREATE/DROP AUDIT	audit trail
CREATE/DROP DATABASE	database
CREATE/DROP SYNONYM	synonym

Supported by Sybase / SQL Server

CREATE/DROP/ALTER DATABASE	database
CREATE/DROP DEFAULT	default column value
CREATE/DROP PROCEDURE	stored procedure
CREATE/DROP RULE	column integrity rule
CREATE/DROP TRIGGER	stored trigger

Table 13-1. *DDL Statements in Popular SQL-Based Products*

Database Structure

The SQL1 standard specifies a simple structure for the contents of a database, shown in Figure 13-8. Each user of the database has a collection of tables that are owned by that user. Virtually all major DBMS products support this scheme, although some (such as Rdb/VMS and dBASE IV) do not support the concept of table ownership. In these systems all of the tables in a database are part of one large collection.

Although different brands of SQL-based database management systems provide the same structure within a single database, there is wide variation in how they organize and structure the various databases on a particular computer system. Some brands assume a single, system-wide database that stores all of the data on that system. Other DBMS brands support multiple databases on a single computer, with each database identified by name. Still other DBMS brands support multiple databases within the context of the computer's directory system.

These variations don't change the way you use SQL to access the data within a database. However, they do affect the way you organize your data—for example do you mix order processing and accounting data in one database or do you divide it into two databases? They also affect the way you initially gain access to the database—for example, if there are multiple databases, you need to tell the DBMS which one you want to use. To illustrate how various DBMS brands deal with these issues, suppose the sample database were expanded to support a payroll and an accounting application, in addition to the order processing tasks it now supports.

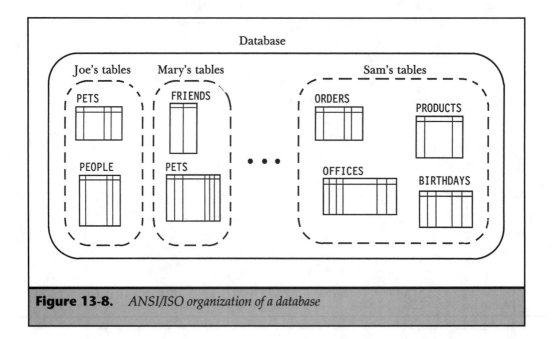

Figure 13-8. *ANSI/ISO organization of a database*

Single-Database Architecture

Figure 13-9 shows a single-database architecture where the DBMS supports one system-wide database. DB2 and Oracle both use this approach. Order processing, accounting, and payroll data are all stored in tables within the database. The major tables for each application are gathered together and owned by a single user, who is probably the person in charge of that application on this computer.

An advantage of this architecture is that the tables in the various applications can easily reference one another. The TIMECARDS table of the payroll application, for example, can contain a foreign key that references the OFFICES table, and the applications can use that relationship to calculate commissions. With proper permission, users can run queries that combine data from the various applications.

A disadvantage of this architecture is that the database will grow huge over time as more and more applications are added to it. A DB2 or Oracle database with several hundred tables is not uncommon. The problems of managing a database of that size—performing backups, recovering data, analyzing performance, and so on—usually require a full-time database administrator.

In the single-database architecture, gaining access to the database is very simple—there's only one database, so no choices need to be made. For example, the programmatic SQL statement that connects you to an Oracle database is CONNECT, and users speak in terms of "connecting to Oracle," rather than connecting to a specific database.

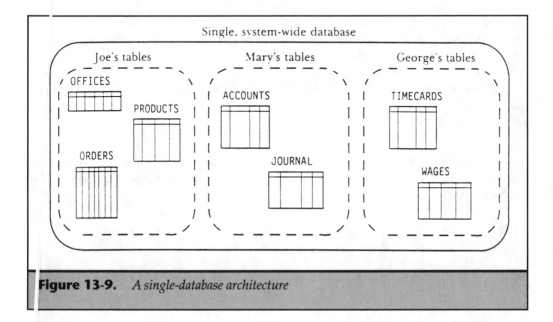

Figure 13-9. *A single-database architecture*

In fact Oracle and DB2 installations frequently do run two separate databases, one for production work and one for testing. Fundamentally, however, all production data is collected into a single database.

Multi-Database Architecture

Figure 13-10 shows a multi-database architecture where each database is assigned a unique name. Ingres, Sybase, and SQL Server all use this scheme. As shown in the figure, each of the databases in this architecture is usually dedicated to a particular application. When you add a new application, you will probably create a new database.

The main advantage of the multi-database architecture over the single-database architecture is that it divides the data management tasks into smaller, more manageable pieces. Each person responsible for an application can now be the database administrator of their own database, with less worry about overall coordination. When it's time to add a new application, it can be developed in its own database, without disturbing the existing databases. It's also more likely that users and programmers can remember the overall structure of their own databases.

The main disadvantage of the multi-database architecture is that the individual databases may become "islands" of information, unconnected to one another. Typically a table in one database cannot contain a foreign key reference to a table in a different database. Often the DBMS does not support queries across database boundaries, making it impossible to relate data from two applications. If cross-database queries are supported, they may impose substantial overhead or require the purchase of additional distributed DBMS software from the DBMS vendor.

If a DBMS uses a multi-database architecture and supports queries across databases, it must extend the SQL table and column naming conventions. A qualified table name must specify not only the owner of the table, but also which database contains the table. Typically the DBMS extends the "dot notation" for table names by prefixing the database name to the owner name, separated by a period (.). For example, in a Sybase or SQL Server database, this table reference:

```
OP.JOE.OFFICES
```

refers to the OFFICES table owned by the user JOE in the order processing database named OP, and the following query joins the SALESREPS table in the payroll database with that OFFICES table:

```
SELECT OP.JOE.OFFICES.CITY, PAYROLL.GEORGE.SALESREPS.NAME
  FROM OP.JOE.OFFICES, PAYROLL.GEORGE.SALESREPS
 WHERE OP.JOE.OFFICES.MGR = PAYROLL.GEORGE.SALESREPS.EMPL_NUM
```

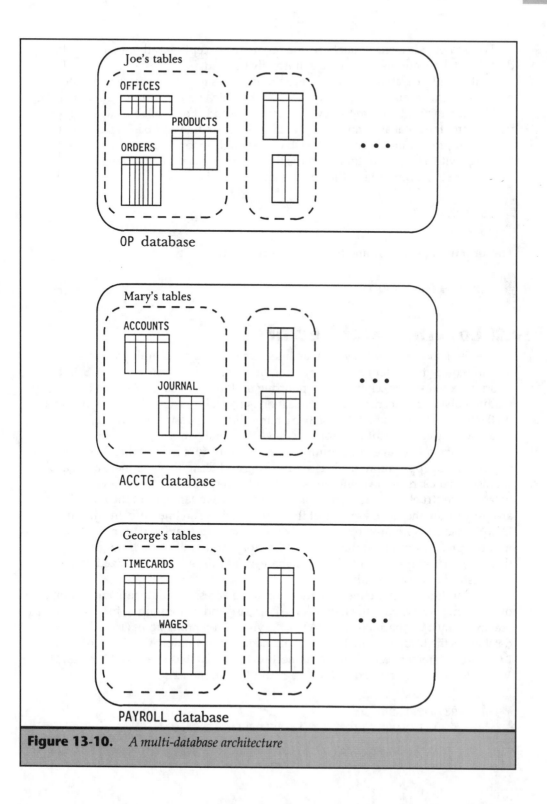

Figure 13-10.   *A multi-database architecture*

Fortunately, such cross-database queries are the exception rather than the rule, and default database and user names can normally be used.

With a multi-database architecture, gaining access to a database becomes slightly more complex, because you must tell the DBMS which database you want to use. The DBMS's interactive SQL program will often display a list of available databases or ask you to enter the database name along with your user name and password to gain access. For programmatic access, the DBMS generally extends the embedded SQL language with a statement that connects the program to a particular database. The Ingres form for connecting to the database named OP is:

```
CONNECT 'OP'
```

The form used by Sybase and SQL Server is:

```
USE DATABASE 'OP'
```

Multi-Location Architecture

Figure 13-11 shows a multi-location architecture that supports multiple databases and uses the computer system's directory structure to organize them. Rdb/VMS and Informix both use this scheme for supporting multiple databases. As with the multi-database architecture, each application is typically assigned to its own database. As the figure shows, each database has a name, but it's possible for two different databases in two different directories to have the same name.

The major advantage of the multi-location architecture is flexibility. It is especially appropriate in applications such as engineering and design, where there are many sophisticated users of the computer system, who may all want to use several databases to structure their own information. The disadvantages of the multi-location architecture are the same as those of the multi-database architecture. In addition, the DBMS typically doesn't know about all of the databases that have been created, which may be spread throughout the system's directory structure. There is no "master database" that keeps track of all the databases, and this makes centralized database administration very difficult.

The multi-location architecture makes gaining access to a database more complex once again, because both the name of the database and its location in the directory hierarchy must be specified. The VAX SQL syntax for gaining access to an Rdb/VMS database is the DECLARE DATABASE statement. For example, this DECLARE DATABASE statement establishes a connection to the database named OP in the VAX/VMS directory named SYS$ROOT:[DEVELOPMENT.TEST]:

```
DECLARE DATABASE
        FILENAME 'SYS$ROOT:[DEVELOPMENT.TEST]OP'
```

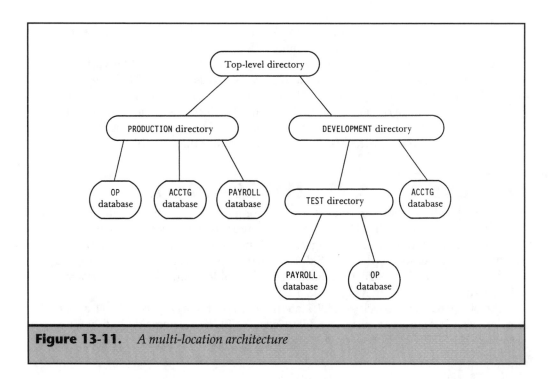

Figure 13-11. *A multi-location architecture*

If the database is in the user's current directory (which is often the case), the statement simplifies to:

```
DECLARE DATABASE
        FILENAME 'OP'
```

Some of the DBMS brands that use this scheme allow you to have access to several databases concurrently, even if they don't support queries across database boundaries. Again, the most common technique used to distinguish among the multiple databases is with a "superqualified" table name. Since two databases in two different directories can have the same name, it's also necessary to introduce a *database alias* to eliminate ambiguity. These VAX SQL statements open two different Rdb/VMS databases that happen to have the same name:

```
DECLARE DATABASE OP1
        FILENAME 'SYS$ROOT:[PRODUCTION\]OP'
DECLARE DATABASE OP2
        FILENAME "SYS$ROOT:[DEVELOPMENT.TEST]OP
```

The statements assign the aliases OP1 and OP2 to the two databases, and these aliases are used to qualify table names in subsequent VAX SQL statements.

As this discussion shows, there is tremendous variety in the way that various DBMS brands organize their databases and provide access to them. This area of SQL is one of the most nonstandard, and yet it is often the first one that a user encounters when trying to access a database for the first time. The inconsistencies also make it impossible to move programs developed for one DBMS to another transparently, although the conversion process is usually tedious rather than complex.

DDL and the ANSI/ISO Standard

The ANSI/ISO SQL1 standard makes a very strong distinction between the SQL Data Manipulation Language and Data Definition Language, defining them as two separate, relatively unrelated languages. The standard does not require that the DDL statements be accepted by the DBMS during its normal operation. In fact, the standard permits a static database structure like that used by older hierarchical and network DBMS products, as shown in Figure 13-12.

The SQL1 standard specifies DDL statements as part of a *database schema*, a map of the database that shows its structure. Here is an ANSI/ISO schema definition for a user (called an *authorization-id* in the standard) named Joe:

```
CREATE SCHEMA AUTHORIZATION JOE
  CREATE TABLE PEOPLE
         (NAME VARCHAR(30),
          AGE INTEGER)
  CREATE TABLE PLACES
         (CITY VARCHAR(30),
          STATE VARCHAR(30))
         GRANT ALL PRIVILEGES
             ON PEOPLE
             TO PUBLIC
         GRANT SELECT
             ON PLACES
             TO MARY
```

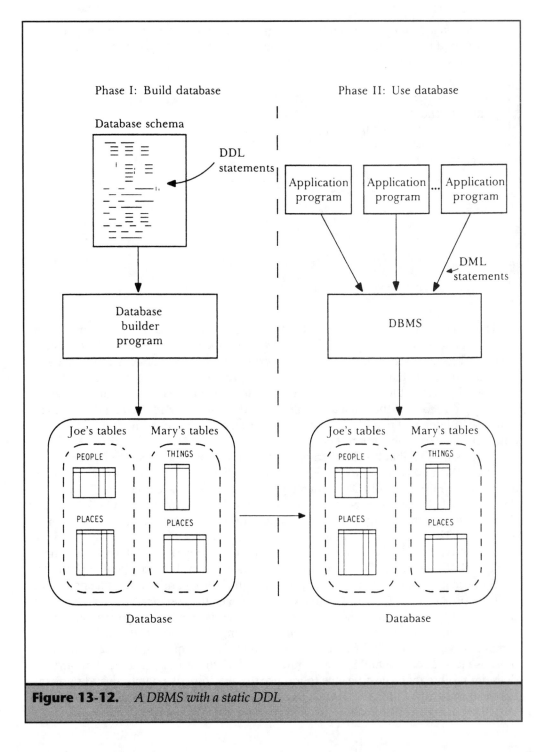

Phase I: Build database   Phase II: Use database

Database schema

DDL statements

Application program   Application program ... Application program

DML statements

Database builder program

DBMS

Joe's tables   Mary's tables

PEOPLE   THINGS

PLACES   PLACES

Database

Joe's tables   Mary's tables

PEOPLE   THINGS

PLACES   PLACES

Database

Figure 13-12. *A DBMS with a static DDL*

The schema defines the two tables and gives certain other users permission to access them. If there is another user of the database, named Mary, her tables are defined by a separate schema:

```
CREATE SCHEMA AUTHORIZATION MARY
  CREATE TABLE THINGS
   (THING_NAME VARCHAR(30),
    THING_COUNT INTEGER))
  CREATE TABLE PLACES
          (CITY VARCHAR(30),
           STATE VARCHAR(30))
          GRANT SELECT, INSERT
              ON THINGS
              TO JOE
          GRANT INSERT, UPDATE
              ON PLACES
              TO PUBLIC
```

These two schemas can be submitted to a database builder utility program, which builds a database with the specified structure. Once the database is created, its tables, users, and security scheme are frozen and permanent. DML statements can then be used to add data to the database or retrieve data from it, but the structure cannot be changed. To change the structure (for instance, to drop a table or add a column), you must stop all access to the database, unload the data, submit a revised schema to the database builder, and reload the data. While the structure is being modified, the database is not available for access.

Despite the fact that the SQL1 standard permits a static database structure with a separate DML and DDL, no major SQL-based DBMS uses this approach. Instead, they all provide a fully dynamic DDL and allow free intermixing of data definition and data manipulation statements. The IBM databases (DB2, SQL/DS, and OS/2 Extended Edition) all have this architecture, as do Oracle, Informix, SQLBase, Ingres, SQL Server, and others. The SQL products that do not offer a dynamic DDL are typically those that have "layered" the SQL language on top of an older, nonrelational database structure. The dBASE IV version of SQL is the most prominent example of this type of product.

Because it does not require a dynamic DDL, the SQL1 standard did not specify the DROP TABLE or ALTER TABLE statements. However, these statements have been in the IBM SQL products since their earliest releases, and other SQL implementations have used them as part of their Data Definition Language. The DROP and ALTER statements were added to the SQL2 standard, effectively requiring a SQL2-compliant database to support dynamic table definition and modification. The SQL standard does not require that a user be able to modify the structure of a database and perform data manipulation within the context of a single transaction. Thus, a conforming DBMS product can still effectively isolate changes to the structure of a database

(CREATE/ALTER/DROP) from changes to database contents
(UPDATE/INSERT/DELETE). However, a user or a program must be able to perform
both data definition and data manipulation operations "on the fly."

Summary

This chapter described the SQL Data Definition Language features that define and
change the structure of a database:

- The CREATE TABLE statement creates a table and defines its columns, primary
  key, and foreign keys.

- The DROP TABLE statement removes a previously created table from the
  database.

- The ALTER TABLE statement can be used to add a column to an existing table
  and to change primary key and foreign key definitions.

- The CREATE INDEX and DROP INDEX statements define indexes, which speed
  database queries but add overhead to database updates.

- Most DBMS brands support other CREATE, DROP, and ALTER statements used
  with DBMS-specific objects.

- Various DBMS brands use very different approaches to organizing the one or
  more databases that they manage, and these differences affect the way you
  design your databases and gain access to them.

Chapter Fourteen

Views

The tables of a database define the structure and organization of its data. However, SQL also lets you look at the stored data in other ways by defining alternative views of the data. A *view* is a SQL query that is permanently stored in the database and assigned a name. The results of the stored query are "visible" through the view, and SQL lets you access these query results as if they were, in fact, a "real" table in the database.

Views are an important part of SQL, for several reasons:

■ Views let you tailor the appearance of a database so that different users see it from different perspectives.

■ Views let you restrict access to data, allowing different users to see only certain rows or certain columns of a table.

■ Views simplify database access by presenting the structure of the stored data in the way that is most natural for each user.

This chapter describes how to create views and how to use views to simplify processing and enhance the security of a database.

What Is a View?

A *view* is a "virtual table" in the database whose contents are defined by a query, as shown in Figure 14-1. To the database user, the view appears just like a real table, with a set of named columns and rows of data. But unlike a real table, a view does not exist in the database as a stored set of data values. Instead, the rows and columns of data visible through the view are the query results produced by the query that defines the view. SQL creates the illusion of the view by giving the view a name like a table name and storing the definition of the view in the database.

The view shown in Figure 14-1 is typical. It has been given the name REPDATA and is defined by this two-table query:

```
SELECT NAME, CITY, REGION, QUOTA, SALESREPS.SALES
  FROM SALESREPS, OFFICES
 WHERE REP_OFFICE = OFFICE
```

The data in the view comes from the SALESREPS and OFFICES tables. These tables are called the *source tables* for the view, because they are the source of the data that is visible through the view. This view contains one row of information for each salesperson, extended with the name of the city and region where the salesperson works. As shown in the figure, the view appears as a table, and its contents look just like the query results that you would obtain if you actually ran the query.

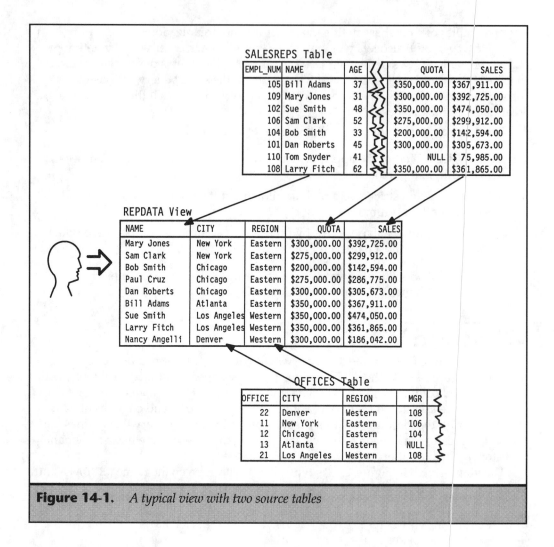

Figure 14-1. *A typical view with two source tables*

Once a view is defined, you can use it in a SELECT statement, just like a real table, as in this query:

List the salespeople who are over quota, showing the name, city, and region for each salesperson.

```
SELECT NAME, CITY, REGION
  FROM REPDATA
 WHERE SALES > QUOTA

NAME             CITY           REGION
---------------  -------------  --------
Mary Jones       New York       Eastern
Sam Clark        New York       Eastern
Dan Roberts      Chicago        Eastern
Paul Cruz        Chicago        Eastern
Bill Adams       Atlanta        Eastern
Sue Smith        Los Angeles    Western
Larry Fitch      Los Angeles    Western
```

The name of the view, REPDATA, appears in the FROM clause just like a table name, and the columns of the view are referenced in the SELECT statement just like the columns of a real table. For some views you can also use the INSERT, DELETE, and UPDATE statements to modify the data visible through the view, as if it were a real table. Thus, for all practical purposes, the view can be used in SQL statements as if it *were* a real table.

How the DBMS Handles Views

When the DBMS encounters a reference to a view in a SQL statement, it finds the definition of the view stored in the database. Then the DBMS translates the request that references the view into an *equivalent* request against the source tables of the view and carries out the equivalent request. In this way the DBMS maintains the illusion of the view while maintaining the integrity of the source tables.

For simple views, the DBMS may construct each row of the view "on the fly," drawing the data for the row from the source table(s). For more complex views, the DBMS must actually *materialize* the view; that is, the DBMS must actually carry out the query that defines the view and store its results in a temporary table. The DBMS fills your requests for view access from this temporary table and discards the table when it is no longer needed. Regardless of how the DBMS actually handles a particular view, the result is the same for the user—the view can be referenced in SQL statements exactly as if it were a real table in the database.

Advantages of Views

Views provide a variety of benefits and can be useful in many different types of databases. In a personal computer database, views are usually a convenience, defined to simplify database requests. In a production database installation, views play a central role in defining the structure of the database for its users and enforcing its security. Views provide these major benefits:

- *Security.* Each user can be given permission to access the database only through a small set of views that contain the specific data the user is authorized to see, thus restricting the user's access to stored data.

- *Query simplicity.* A view can draw data from several different tables and present it as a single table, turning multi-table queries into single-table queries against the view.

- *Structural simplicity.* Views can give a user a "personalized" view of the database structure, presenting the database as a set of virtual tables that make sense for that user.

- *Insulation from change.* A view can present a consistent, unchanged image of the structure of the database, even if the underlying source tables are split, restructured, or renamed.

- *Data integrity.* If data is accessed and entered through a view, the DBMS can automatically check the data to ensure that it meets specified integrity constraints.

Disadvantages of Views

While views provide substantial advantages, there are also two major disadvantages to using a view instead of a real table:

- *Performance.* Views create the *appearance* of a table, but the DBMS must still translate queries against the view into queries against the underlying source tables. If the view is defined by a complex, multi-table query, then even a simple query against the view becomes a complicated join, and it may take a long time to complete.

- *Update restrictions.* When a user tries to update rows of a view, the DBMS must translate the request into an update on rows of the underlying source tables. This is possible for simple views, but more complex views cannot be updated; they are "read-only."

These disadvantages mean that you cannot indiscriminately define views and use them instead of the source tables. Instead, you must in each case consider the advantages provided by using a view and weigh them against the disadvantages.

Creating a View (CREATE VIEW)

The CREATE VIEW statement, shown in Figure 14-2, is used to create a view. The statement assigns a name to the view and specifies the query that defines the view. To create the view successfully, you must have permission to access all of the tables referenced in the query.

The CREATE VIEW statement can optionally assign a name to each column in the newly created view. If a list of column names is specified, it must have the same number of items as the number of columns produced by the query. Note that only the column names are specified; the data type, length, and other characteristics of each column are derived from the definition of the columns in the source tables. If the list of column names is omitted from the CREATE VIEW statement, each column in the view takes the name of the corresponding column in the query. The list of column names must be specified if the query includes calculated columns or if it produces two columns with identical names.

Although all views are created in the same way, in practice different types of views are typically used for different purposes. The next few sections examine these types of views and give examples of the CREATE VIEW statement.

Horizontal Views

A common use of views is to restrict a user's access to only selected rows of a table. For example, in the sample database, you may want to let a sales manager see only the SALESREPS rows for salespeople in the manager's own region. To accomplish this, you can define two views, as follows:

Create a view showing Eastern region salespeople.

```
CREATE VIEW EASTREPS AS
    SELECT *
      FROM SALESREPS
     WHERE REP_OFFICE IN (11, 12, 13)
```

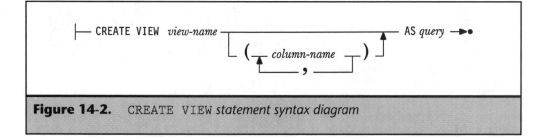

Figure 14-2. CREATE VIEW *statement syntax diagram*

Create a view showing Western region salespeople.

```
CREATE VIEW WESTREPS AS
    SELECT *
      FROM SALESREPS
      WHERE REP_OFFICE IN (21, 22)
```

Now you can give each sales manager permission to access either the EASTREPS or the WESTREPS view, denying them permission to access the other view and the SALESREPS table itself. This effectively gives the sales manager a customized view of the SALESREPS table, showing only salespeople in the appropriate region.

A view like EASTREPS or WESTREPS is often called a *horizontal view*. As shown in Figure 14-3, a horizontal view "slices" the source table horizontally to create the view. All of the columns of the source table participate in the view, but only some of its rows are visible through the view. Horizontal views are appropriate when the source table contains data that relates to various organizations or users. They provide a "private table" for each user, composed only of the rows needed by that user.

Here are some more examples of horizontal views:

Define a view containing only Eastern region offices.

```
CREATE VIEW EASTOFFICES AS
    SELECT *
      FROM OFFICES
      WHERE REGION = 'Eastern'
```

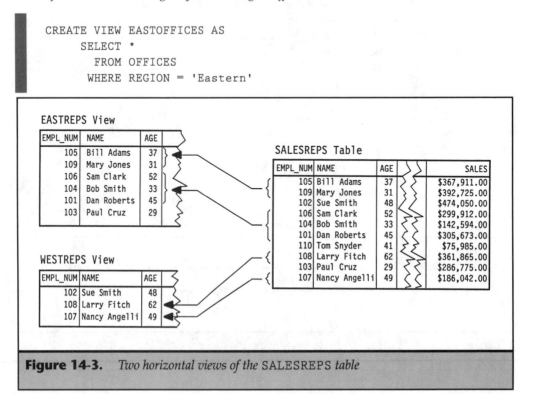

Figure 14-3. *Two horizontal views of the* SALESREPS *table*

Define a view for Sue Smith (employee number 102) containing only orders placed by customers assigned to her.

```
CREATE VIEW SUEORDERS AS
    SELECT *
      FROM ORDERS
     WHERE CUST IN (SELECT CUST_NUM
                      FROM CUSTOMERS
                     WHERE CUST_REP = 102)
```

Define a view showing only those customers who have more than $30,000 worth of orders currently on the books.

```
CREATE VIEW BIGCUSTOMERS AS
    SELECT *
      FROM CUSTOMERS
     WHERE 30000.00 < (SELECT SUM(AMOUNT)
                         FROM ORDERS
                        WHERE CUST = CUST_NUM)
```

In each of these examples, the view is derived from a single source table. The view is defined by a SELECT * query and therefore has exactly the same columns as the source table. The WHERE clause determines which rows of the source table are visible in the view.

Vertical Views

Another common use of views is to restrict a user's access to only certain columns of a table. For example, in the sample database, the order processing department may need access to the employee number, name, and office assignment of each salesperson, because this information may be needed to process an order correctly. However, there is no need for the order processing staff to see the salesperson's year-to-date sales or quota. This selective view of the SALESREPS table can be constructed with the following view:

Create a view showing selected salesperson information.

```
CREATE VIEW REPINFO AS
    SELECT EMPL_NUM, NAME, REP_OFFICE
      FROM SALESREPS
```

By giving the order processing staff access to this view and denying access to the SALESREPS table itself, access to sensitive sales and quota data is effectively restricted.

A view like the REPINFO view is often called a *vertical view.* As shown in Figure 14-4, a vertical view "slices" the source table vertically to create the view. Vertical views are commonly found where the data stored in a table is used by various users or groups of users. They provide a "private table" for each user, composed only of the columns needed by that user.

Here are some more examples of vertical views:

Define a view of the OFFICES *table for the order processing staff that includes the office's city, office number, and region.*

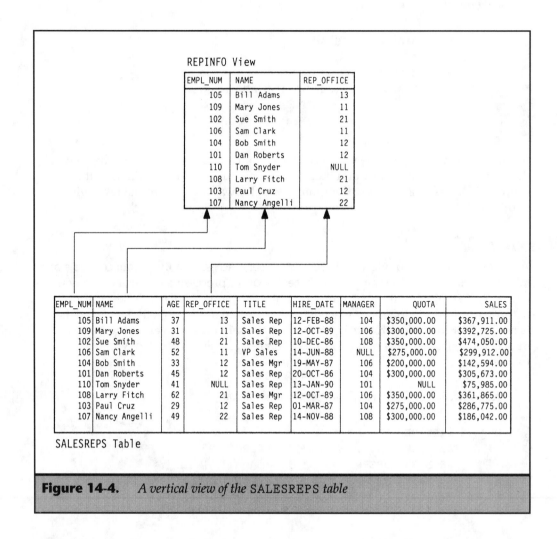

Figure 14-4. *A vertical view of the* SALESREPS *table*

```
CREATE VIEW OFFICEINFO AS
    SELECT OFFICE, CITY, REGION
        FROM OFFICES
```

Define a view of the CUSTOMERS *table that includes only customer names and their assignment to salespeople.*

```
CREATE VIEW CUSTINFO AS
    SELECT COMPANY, CUST_REP
        FROM CUSTOMERS
```

In each of these examples, the view is derived from a single source table. The select list in the view definition determines which columns of the source table are visible in the view. Because these are vertical views, every row of the source table is represented in the view, and the view definition does not include a WHERE clause.

Row/Column Subset Views

When you define a view, SQL does not restrict you to purely horizontal or vertical slices of a table. In fact, the SQL language does not include the notion of horizontal and vertical views. These concepts merely help you to visualize how the view presents the information from the source table. It's quite common to define a view that slices a source table in *both* the horizontal and vertical dimensions, as in this example:

Define a view that contains the customer number, company name, and credit limit of all customers assigned to Bill Adams (employee number 105).

```
CREATE VIEW BILLCUST AS
    SELECT CUST_NUM, COMPANY, CREDIT_LIMIT
        FROM CUSTOMERS
        WHERE CUST_REP = 105
```

The data visible through this view is a row/column subset of the CUSTOMERS table. Only the columns explicitly named in the select list of the view and the rows that meet the search condition are visible through the view.

Grouped Views

The query specified in a view definition may include a GROUP BY clause. This type of view is called a *grouped view,* because the data visible through the view is the result of a grouped query. Grouped views perform the same function as grouped queries; they group related rows of data and produce one row of query results for each group, summarizing the data in that group. A grouped view makes these grouped query results into a virtual table, allowing you to perform further queries on them.

Here is an example of a grouped view:

Define a view that contains summary order data for each salesperson.

```
CREATE VIEW ORD_BY_REP (WHO, HOW_MANY, TOTAL, LOW, HIGH, AVERAGE) AS
    SELECT REP, COUNT(*), SUM(AMOUNT), MIN(AMOUNT), MAX(AMOUNT), AVG(AMOUNT)
      FROM ORDERS
      GROUP BY REP
```

As this example shows, the definition of a grouped view will always include a column name list. The list assigns names to the columns in the grouped view which are derived from column functions, such as SUM() and MIN(). It may also specify a modified name for a grouping column. In this example, the REP column of the ORDERS table becomes the WHO column in the ORD_BY_REP view.

Once this grouped view is defined, it can be used to simplify queries. For example, this query generates a simple report that summarizes the orders for each salesperson:

Show the name, number of orders, total order amount, and average order size for each salesperson.

```
SELECT NAME, HOW_MANY, TOTAL, AVERAGE
  FROM SALESREPS, ORD_BY_REP
 WHERE WHO = EMPL_NUM
 ORDER BY TOTAL DESC
```

NAME	HOW_MANY	TOTAL	AVERAGE
Larry Fitch	7	$58,633.00	$8,376.14
Bill Adams	5	$39,327.00	$7,865.40
Nancy Angelli	3	$34,432.00	$11,477.33
Sam Clark	2	$32,958.00	$16,479.00
Dan Roberts	3	$26,628.00	$8,876.00
Tom Snyder	2	$23,132.00	$11,566.00
Sue Smith	4	$22,776.00	$5,694.00
Mary Jones	2	$7,105.00	$3,552.50
Paul Cruz	2	$2,700.00	$1,350.00

Unlike a horizontal or vertical view, the rows in a grouped view do not have a one-to-one correspondence with the rows in the source table. A grouped view is not just a filter on its source table that screens out certain rows and columns. It is a summary of the source tables, and therefore a substantial amount of DBMS processing is required to maintain the illusion of a virtual table for grouped views.

Grouped views can be used in queries just like other, simpler views. A grouped view cannot be updated, however. The reason should be obvious from the example. What would it mean to "update the average order size for salesrep number 105?" Because each row in the grouped view corresponds to a *group* of rows from the source table, and because the columns in the grouped view generally contain calculated data, there is no way to translate the update request into an update against the rows of the source table. Grouped views thus function as "read-only" views, which can participate in queries, but not in updates.

Grouped views are also subject to the SQL restrictions on nested column functions. Recall from Chapter 8 that nested column functions, such as:

```
MIN(MIN(A))
```

are not legal in SQL expressions. Although the grouped view "hides" the column functions in its select list from the user, the DBMS still knows about them and enforces the restriction. Consider this example:

For each sales office, show the range of average order sizes for all salespeople who work in the office.

```
SELECT REP_OFFICE, MIN(AVERAGE), MAX(AVERAGE)
  FROM SALESREPS, ORD_BY_REP
 WHERE EMPL_NUM = WHO
 GROUP BY REP_OFFICE

Error: Nested column function reference
```

This query produces an error, even though it appears perfectly reasonable. It's a two-table query that groups the rows of the ORD_BY_REP view based on the office to which the salesperson is assigned. But the column functions MIN() and MAX() in the select list cause a problem. The argument to these column functions, the AVERAGE column, is itself the result of a column function. The "actual" query being requested from SQL is:

```
SELECT REP_OFFICE, MIN(AVG(AMOUNT)), MAX(AVG(AMOUNT))
  FROM SALESREPS, ORDERS
 WHERE EMPL_NUM = REP
 GROUP BY REP
 GROUP BY REP_OFFICE
```

This query is illegal because of the double GROUP BY and the nested column functions. Unfortunately, as this example shows, a perfectly reasonable grouped SELECT statement may, in fact, cause an error if one of its source tables turns out to be a grouped view. There's no way to anticipate this situation; you must just understand the cause of the error when SQL reports it to you.

Joined Views

One of the most frequent reasons for using views is to simplify multi-table queries. By specifying a two-table or three-table query in the view definition, you can create a *joined view* that draws its data from two or three different tables and presents the query results as a single virtual table. Once the view is defined, you can often use a simple, single-table query against the view for requests that would otherwise each require a two-table or three-table join.

For example, suppose that Sam Clark, the vice president of sales, often runs queries against the ORDERS table in the sample database. However, Sam doesn't like to work with customer and employee numbers. Instead, he'd like to be able to use a version of the ORDERS table that has names instead of numbers. Here is a view that meets Sam's needs:

Create a view of the ORDERS *table with names instead of numbers.*

```
CREATE VIEW ORDER_INFO (ORDER_NUM, COMPANY, REP_NAME, AMOUNT) AS
    SELECT ORDER_NUM, COMPANY, NAME, AMOUNT
      FROM ORDERS, CUSTOMERS, SALESREPS
     WHERE CUST = CUST_NUM
       AND REP = EMPL_NUM
```

This view is defined by a three-table join. As with a grouped view, the processing required to create the illusion of a virtual table for this view is considerable. Each row of the view is derived from a *combination* of one row from the ORDERS table, one row from the CUSTOMERS table, and one row from the SALESREPS table.

Although it has a relatively complex definition, this view can provide some real benefits. Here is a query against the view that generates a report of orders, grouped by salesperson:

Show the total current orders for each company for each salesperson.

```
SELECT REP_NAME, COMPANY, SUM(AMOUNT)
  FROM ORDER_INFO
 GROUP BY REP_NAME, COMPANY
```

REP_NAME	COMPANY	SUM(AMOUNT)
Bill Adams	Acme Mfg.	$35,582.00
Bill Adams	JCP Inc.	$3,745.00
Dan Roberts	First Corp.	$3,978.00
Dan Roberts	Holm & Landis	$150.00
Dan Roberts	Ian & Schmidt	$22,500.00
Larry Fitch	Midwest Systems	$3,608.00
Larry Fitch	Orion Corp.	$7,100.00
Larry Fitch	Zetacorp	$47,925.00

Note that this query is a single-table SELECT statement, which is considerably simpler than the equivalent three-table SELECT statement for the source tables:

```
SELECT NAME, COMPANY, SUM(AMOUNT)
  FROM SALESREPS, ORDERS, CUSTOMERS
 WHERE REP = EMPL_NUM
   AND CUST = CUST_NUM
 GROUP BY NAME, COMPANY
```

Similarly, it's easy to generate a report of the largest orders, showing who placed them and who received them, with this query against the view:

Show the largest current orders, sorted by amount.

```
SELECT COMPANY, AMOUNT, REP_NAME
  FROM ORDER_INFO
 WHERE AMOUNT > 20000.00
 ORDER BY AMOUNT DESC
```

```
COMPANY                 AMOUNT REP_NAME
------------------   ----------- ----------------
Zetacorp             $45,000.00 Larry Fitch
J.P. Sinclair        $31,500.00 Sam Clark
Chen Associates      $31,350.00 Nancy Angelli
Acme Mfg.            $27,500.00 Bill Adams
Ace International    $22,500.00 Tom Snyder
Ian & Schmidt        $22,500.00 Dan Roberts
```

The view makes it much easier to see what's going on in the query than if it were expressed as the equivalent three-table join. Of course the DBMS must work just as hard to generate the query results for the single-table query against the view as it would to generate the query results for the equivalent three-table query. In fact, the DBMS must perform slightly more work to handle the query against the view. However, for the human user of the database it's much easier to write and understand the single-table query that references the view.

Updating a View

What does it mean to insert a row of data into a view, delete a row from a view, or update a row of a view? For some views these operations can obviously be translated into equivalent operations against the source table(s) of the view. For example, consider once again the EASTREPS view, defined earlier in this chapter:

Create a view showing Eastern region salespeople.

```
CREATE VIEW EASTREPS AS
    SELECT *
      FROM SALESREPS
     WHERE REP_OFFICE IN (11, 12, 13)
```

This is a straightforward horizontal view, derived from a single source table. As shown in Figure 14-5, it makes sense to talk about inserting a row into this view; it means the new row should be inserted into the underlying SALESREPS table from which the view is derived. It also makes sense to delete a row from the EASTREPS view; this would delete the corresponding row from the SALESREPS table. Finally, updating a row of the EASTREPS view makes sense; this would update the corresponding row of the SALESREPS table. In each case the action can be carried out against the corresponding row of the source table, preserving the integrity of both the source table and the view.

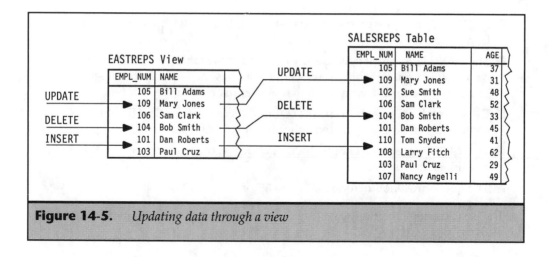

Figure 14-5. *Updating data through a view*

However, consider the ORDS_BY_REP grouped view, also defined earlier in this chapter:

Define a view that contains summary order data for each salesperson.

```
CREATE VIEW ORD_BY_REP (WHO, HOW_MANY, TOTAL, LOW, HIGH, AVERAGE) AS
     SELECT REP, COUNT(*), SUM(AMOUNT), MIN(AMOUNT),
            MAX(AMOUNT), AVG(AMOUNT)
       FROM ORDERS
      GROUP BY REP
```

There is no one-to-one correspondence between the rows of this view and the rows of the underlying ORDERS table, so it makes no sense to talk about inserting, deleting, or updating rows of this view. The ORD_BY_REP view is not updatable; it is a read-only view.

The EASTREPS view and the ORD_BY_REP view are two extreme examples in terms of the complexity of their definitions. There are views more complex than EASTREPS where it still makes sense to update the view, and there are views less complex than ORD_BY_REP where updates do not make sense. In fact, which views can be updated and which cannot has been an important relational database research problem over the years.

View Updates and the ANSI/ISO Standard

The ANSI/ISO SQL1 standard specifies the views that must be updatable in a database that claims conformance to the standard. Under the standard, a view can be updated if the query that defines the view meets all of these restrictions:

- `DISTINCT` must not be specified; that is, duplicate rows must *not* be eliminated from the query results.
- The `FROM` clause must specify only one updatable table; that is, the view must have a single source table for which the user has the required privileges. If the source table is itself a view, then that view must meet these criteria.
- Each select item must be a simple column reference; the select list cannot contain expressions, calculated columns, or column functions.
- The `WHERE` clause must not include a subquery; only simple row-by-row search conditions may appear.
- The query must not include a `GROUP BY` or a `HAVING` clause.

The basic concept behind the restrictions is easier to remember than the rules themselves:

For a view to be updatable, the DBMS must be able to trace any row of the view back to its source row in the source table. Similarly, the DBMS must be able to trace each individual column to be updated back to its source column in the source table.

If the view meets this test, then it's possible to define meaningful `INSERT`, `DELETE` and `UPDATE` operations for the view in terms of the source table(s).

View Updates in Commercial SQL Products

The SQL1 standard rules on view updates are very restrictive. There are many views that can be theoretically updated that do not satisfy all of the restrictions. In addition, there are views that can support some of the update operations but not others, and there are views that can support updates on certain columns but not others. Most commercial SQL implementations have view update rules that are considerably more permissive than the SQL1 standard. For example, consider this view:

Create a view showing the sales, quota, and the difference between the two for each salesperson.

```
CREATE VIEW SALESPERF (EMPL_NUM, SALES, QUOTA, DIFF) AS
    SELECT EMPL_NUM, SALES, QUOTA, (SALES - QUOTA)
        FROM SALESREPS
```

The SQL1 standard disallows all updates to this view, because its fourth column is a calculated column. However, note that each row in the view can be traced back to a single row in the source table (`SALESREPS`). For this reason DB2 (and several other commercial SQL implementations) will allow `DELETE` operations against this view.

Further, DB2 allows UPDATE operations on the EMPL_NUM, SALES, and QUOTA columns, because they are directly derived from the source table. Only the DIFF column cannot be updated. DB2 does not allow the INSERT statement for the view, because inserting a value for the DIFF column would be meaningless.

The specific rules that determine whether a view can be updated or not vary from one brand of DBMS to another, and they are usually fairly detailed. Some views, such as those based on grouped queries, cannot be updated by any DBMS, because the update operations simply do not make sense. Other views may be updatable in one brand of DBMS, partially updatable in another brand, and not updatable in a third brand. The SQL2 standard recognized this and includes a broader definition of updatable views along with considerable latitude for variation among DBMS brands. The best way to find out about updatability of views in your particular DBMS is to consult the user's guide or experiment with different types of views.

Checking View Updates (CHECK OPTION)

If a view is defined by a query that includes a WHERE clause, only rows that meet the search condition are visible in the view. Other rows may be present in the source table(s) from which the view is derived, but they are not visible through the view. For example, the EASTREPS view described earlier in this chapter contains only those rows of the SALESREPS table with specific values in the REP_OFFICE column:

Create a view showing Eastern region salespeople.

```
CREATE VIEW EASTREPS AS
    SELECT *
      FROM SALESREPS
     WHERE REP_OFFICE IN (11, 12, 13)
```

This is an updatable view according to the ANSI/ISO standard and for most commercial SQL implementations. You can add a new salesperson with this INSERT statement:

```
INSERT INTO EASTREPS (EMPL_NUM, NAME, REP_OFFICE, AGE, SALES)
    VALUES (113, 'Jake Kimball', 11, 43, 0.00)
```

The DBMS will add the new row to the underlying SALESREPS table, and the row will be visible through the EASTREPS view. But consider what happens when you add a new salesperson with this INSERT statement:

```
INSERT INTO EASTREPS (EMPL_NUM, NAME, REP_OFFICE, AGE, SALES)
    VALUES (114, 'Fred Roberts', 21, 47, 0.00)
```

This is a perfectly legal SQL statement, and the DBMS will insert it into the SALESREPS table. However, the newly inserted row doesn't meet the search condition for the view. Its REP_OFFICE value (21) specifies the Los Angeles office, which is in the Western region. As a result, if you run this query immediately after the INSERT statement:

```
SELECT EMPL_NUM, NAME, REP_OFFICE
  FROM EASTREPS

EMPL_NUM NAME             REP_OFFICE
-------- -------------- ----------
     105 Bill Adams             13
     109 Mary Jones             11
     106 Sam Clark              11
     104 Bob Smith              12
     101 Dan Roberts            12
     103 Paul Cruz              12
```

the newly added row doesn't show up in the view. The same thing happens if you change the office assignment for one of the salespeople currently in the view. This UPDATE statement:

```
UPDATE EASTREPS
   SET REP_OFFICE = 21
 WHERE EMPL_NUM = 104
```

modifies one of the columns for Bob Smith's row and immediately causes it to disappear from the view. Of course both of the "vanishing" rows show up in a query against the underlying table:

```
SELECT EMPL_NUM, NAME, REP_OFFICE
  FROM SALESREPS

EMPL_NUM NAME             REP_OFFICE
-------- -------------- ----------
     105 Bill Adams             13
     109 Mary Jones             11
     102 Sue Smith              21
     106 Sam Clark              11
     104 Bob Smith              21
     101 Dan Roberts            12
```

```
110 Tom Snyder          NULL
108 Larry Fitch           21
103 Paul Cruz             12
107 Nancy Angelli         22
114 Fred Roberts          21
```

The fact that the rows vanish from the view as a result of an INSERT or UPDATE statement is disconcerting, at best. You probably want the DBMS to detect and prevent this type of INSERT or UPDATE from taking place through the view. SQL allows you to specify this kind of integrity checking for views by creating the view with a *check option*. The check option is specified in the CREATE VIEW statement, as shown in this redefinition of the EASTREPS view:

```
CREATE VIEW EASTREPS AS
     SELECT *
       FROM SALESREPS
      WHERE REP_OFFICE IN (11, 12, 13)
 WITH CHECK OPTION
```

When the check option is requested for a view, SQL *automatically* checks each INSERT and each UPDATE operation for the view to make sure that the resulting row(s) meet the search criteria in the view definition. If an inserted or modified row would not meet the condition, the INSERT or UPDATE statement fails and the operation is not carried out.

The check option adds overhead to the INSERT and UPDATE operations, but it helps to ensure the integrity of the database. When you create an updatable view as part of a security scheme, you should always specify the check option. It prevents modifications made through the view from affecting data that isn't accessible to the user in the first place.

Dropping a View (DROP VIEW)

Recall that the SQL1 standard treated the SQL Data Definition Language (DDL) as a static specification of the structure of a database, including its tables and views. For this reason, the SQL1 standard did not provide the ability to drop a view when it was no longer needed. However, all major DBMS brands provide this capability. Because views behave like tables, and a view cannot have the same name as a table, many DBMS brands use the DROP TABLE statement to drop views as well. Other SQL implementations provide a separate DROP VIEW statement.

The SQL2 standard formalized support for dropping views through a DROP VIEW statement. It also provides for detailed control over what happens when a user attempts to drop a view when the definition of another view depends on it. For example, suppose two views on the SALESREPS table have been created by these two CREATE VIEW statements:

```
CREATE VIEW EASTREPS AS
     SELECT *
       FROM SALESREPS
      WHERE REP_OFFICE IN (11, 12, 13)

CREATE VIEW NYREPS AS
     SELECT *
       FROM EASTREPS
      WHERE REP_OFFICE = 11
```

For purposes of illustration, the NYREPS view is defined in terms of the EASTREPS view, although it could just as easily have been defined in terms of the underlying table. Under the SQL2 standard, the following DROP VIEW statement will remove *both* of the views from the database:

```
DROP VIEW EASTREPS CASCADE
```

The CASCADE option tells the DBMS to delete not only the named view, but also any views that depend on its definition. In contrast this DROP VIEW statement:

```
DROP VIEW EASTREPS RESTRICT
```

will fail with an error, because the RESTRICT option tells the DBMS to remove the view only if no other views depend on it. This provides an added precaution against unintentional side-effects of a DROP VIEW statement. The SQL2 standard requires that either RESTRICT or CASCADE be specified, but many commercial SQL products support a version of the DROP VIEW statement without an explicitly-specified option.

Summary

Views allow you to redefine the structure of a database, giving each user a personalized view of the database structure and contents:

- A view is a virtual table defined by a query. The view appears to contain rows and columns of data, just like a "real" table, but the data visible through the view is, in fact, the results of the query.

- A view can be a simple row/column subset of a single table, it can summarize a table (a grouped view), or it can draw its data from two or more tables (a joined view).

- A view can be referenced like a real table in a SELECT, INSERT, DELETE, or UPDATE statement. However, more complex views cannot be updated; they are read-only views.

- Views are commonly used to simplify the apparent structure of a database, to simplify queries, and to protect certain rows and/or columns from unauthorized access.

Chapter Fifteen

SQL Security

W hen you entrust your data to a database management system, the security of the stored data is a major concern. Security is especially important in a SQL-based DBMS, because interactive SQL makes database access very easy. The security requirements of a typical production database are many and varied:

■ The data in any given table should be accessible to some users, but access by other users should be prevented.

■ Some users should be allowed to update data in a particular table; others should only be allowed to retrieve data.

■ For some tables, access should be restricted on a column-by-column basis.

■ Some users should be denied interactive SQL access to a table, but should be allowed to use applications programs that update the table.

The SQL security scheme, described in this chapter, provides these types of protection for data in a relational database.

SQL Security Concepts

Implementing a security scheme and enforcing security restrictions are the responsibility of the DBMS software. The SQL language defines an overall framework for database security, and SQL statements are used to specify security restrictions. The SQL security scheme is based on three central concepts:

■ *Users* are the actors in the database. Each time the DBMS retrieves, inserts, deletes, or updates data, it does so on behalf of some user. The DBMS will permit or prohibit the action depending on which user is making the request.

■ *Database objects* are the items to which SQL security protection can be applied. Security is usually applied to tables and views, but other objects such as forms, application programs, and entire databases can also be protected. Most users will have permission to use certain database objects, but will be prohibited from using others.

■ *Privileges* are the actions that a user is permitted to carry out for a given database object. A user may have permission to SELECT and INSERT rows in a certain table, for example, but may lack permission to DELETE or UPDATE rows of the table. A different user may have a different set of privileges.

Figure 15-1 shows how these security concepts might be used in a security scheme for the sample database.

To establish a security scheme for a database, you use the SQL GRANT statement to specify which users have which privileges on which database objects. For example, here is a GRANT statement that lets Sam Clark retrieve and insert data in the OFFICES table of the sample database:

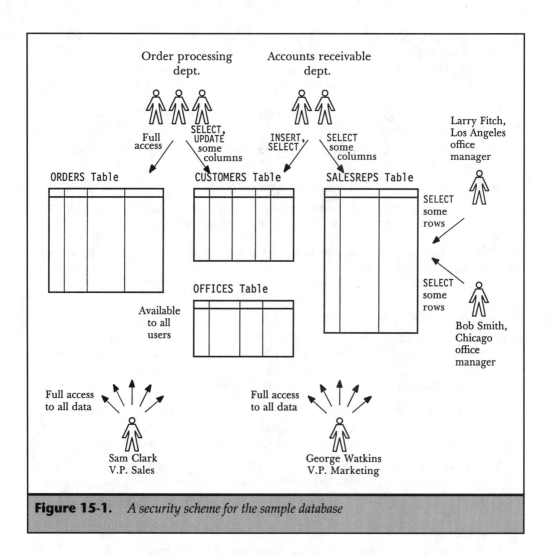

Figure 15-1. *A security scheme for the sample database*

Let Sam Clark retrieve and insert data in the OFFICES *table.*

```
GRANT SELECT, INSERT
   ON OFFICES
   TO SAM
```

The GRANT statement specifies a combination of a user-id (SAM), an object (the OFFICES table), and privileges (SELECT and INSERT). Once granted, the privileges can be rescinded later with this REVOKE statement:

Take away the privileges granted earlier to Sam Clark.

```
REVOKE SELECT, INSERT
    ON OFFICES
  FROM SAM
```

The GRANT and REVOKE statements are described in detail later in this chapter.

User-Ids

Each user of a SQL-based database is assigned a *user-id,* a short name that identifies the user to the DBMS software. The user-id is at the heart of SQL security. Every SQL statement executed by the DBMS is carried out on behalf of a specific user-id. The user-id determines whether the statement will be permitted or prohibited by the DBMS. In a production database, user-ids are assigned by the database administrator. In a personal computer database, there may be only a single user-id, identifying the user who created and who owns the database.

The SQL1 standard permits user-ids of up to 18 characters and requires them to be valid SQL names, but many commercial DBMS brands have different restrictions. In DB2 and SQL/DS, for example, user-ids may have no more than eight characters. In Sybase and SQL Server, user-ids may have up to 30 characters. If portability is a concern, it's best to limit user-ids to eight or fewer characters. Figure 15-2 shows various users who need access to the sample database and typical user-ids assigned to them. Note that all of the users in the order processing department can be assigned the same user-id, because they are to have identical privileges in the database.

The ANSI/ISO SQL standard uses the term *authorization-id* instead of user-id, and you will occasionally find this term used in other SQL documentation. Technically, "authorization-id" is a more accurate term, because the role of the id is to determine authorization or privileges in the database. There are situations, as in Figure 15-2, where it makes sense to assign the same user-id to different users. In other situations, a single person may use two or three different user-ids. In a production database, authorization-ids may be associated with programs and groups of programs, rather than with human users. In each of these situations, "authorization-id" is a more precise and less confusing term than "user-id". However, the most common practice is to assign a different user-id to each person, and most SQL-based DBMS use the term "user-id" in their documentation.

USER AUTHENTICATION   The SQL1 standard specifies that user-ids provide database security, but it says nothing about the mechanism for associating a user-id with a SQL statement. For example, when you type SQL statements into an interactive SQL utility, how does the DBMS determine what user-id is associated with the statements? Most commercial SQL implementations establish a user-id for each database *session.* In interactive SQL, the session begins when you start the interactive

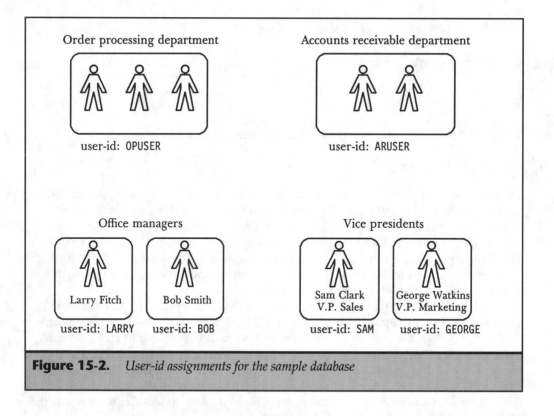

Figure 15-2. *User-id assignments for the sample database*

SQL program, and it lasts until you exit the program. In an application program using programmatic SQL, the session begins when the application program connects to the DBMS, and it ends when the application program terminates. All of the SQL statements used during the session are associated with the user-id specified for the session.

Usually you must supply both a user-id and an associated password at the beginning of a session. The DBMS checks the password to verify that you are, in fact, authorized to use the user-id that you supply. Although user-ids and passwords are common across most SQL products, the specific techniques used to specify the user-id and password vary from one product to another.

Some DBMS brands implement their own user-id/password security. For example, when you use Oracle's interactive SQL program, called SQLPLUS, you specify a user name and associated password in the command that starts the program, like this:

```
SQLPLUS SCOTT/TIGER
```

The Sybase interactive SQL program, called ISQL, also accepts a user name and password, using this command format:

```
ISQL /USER=SCOTT /PASSWORD=TIGER
```

In each case, the DBMS validates the user-id (SCOTT) and the password (TIGER) before beginning the interactive SQL session.

Many other DBMS brands, including Ingres and Informix, use the user names of the host computer's operating system as database user-ids. For example, when you log in to a VAX/VMS computer system, you must supply a valid VMS user name and password to gain access. To start the Ingres interactive SQL utility, you simply give the command:

```
ISQL SALESDB
```

where SALESDB is the name of the Ingres database you want to use. Ingres automatically obtains your VMS user name and makes it your Ingres user-id for the session. Thus you don't have to specify a separate database user-id and password. DB2's interactive SQL, running under MVS/TSO, uses a similar technique. Your TSO login name automatically becomes your DB2 user-id for the interactive SQL session.

SQL security also applies to programmatic access to a database, so the DBMS must determine and authenticate the user-id for every application program that tries to access the database. Again, the techniques and rules for establishing the user-id vary from one brand of DBMS to another. They are described in Chapter 17, which covers programmatic SQL.

USER GROUPS   In a large production database, there are often groups of users with similar needs. In the sample database, for example, the three people in the order processing department form a natural user group, and the two people in the accounts receivable department form another natural group. Within each group, all of the users have identical needs for data access and should have identical privileges.

Under the ANSI/ISO SQL security scheme, you can handle groups of users with similar needs in one of two ways:

- You can assign the same user-id to every person in the group, as shown in Figure 15-2. This scheme simplifies security administration, because it allows you to specify data access privileges once for the single user-id. However, under this scheme the people sharing the user-id cannot be distinguished from one another in system operator displays and DBMS reports.

- You can assign a different user-id to every person in the group. This scheme lets you differentiate between the users in reports produced by the DBMS, and it lets you establish different privileges for the individual users later. However, you must specify privileges for each user individually, making security administration tedious and error-prone.

The scheme you choose will depend upon the trade-offs in your particular database and application.

Sybase and SQL Server offer a third alternative for dealing with groups of similar users. They support group-ids, which identify groups of related user-ids. Privileges can be granted both to individual user-ids and to group-ids, and a user may carry out a database action if it is permitted by either the user-id or group-id privileges. Group-ids thus simplify the administration of privileges given to groups of users. However, they are nonstandard and are unique to SQL Server and Sybase.

DB2 also supports groups of users, but takes a different approach. The DB2 database administrator can configure DB2 so that when you first connect to DB2 and supply your user-id (known as your *primary authorization-id*), DB2 automatically looks up a set of additional user-ids (known as *secondary authorization-ids*) that you may use. When DB2 later checks your privileges, it checks the privileges for all of your authorization-ids, primary and secondary. The DB2 database administrator normally sets up the secondary authorization-ids so that they are the same as the user group names used by RACF, the IBM mainframe security facility. Thus the DB2 approach effectively provides group-ids, but does so without adding to the user-id mechanism.

Security Objects

SQL security protections apply to specific *objects* contained in a database. The SQL1 standard specifies two types of security objects—tables and views. Thus each table and view can be individually protected. Access to a table or view can be permitted for certain user-ids and prohibited for other user-ids. The SQL2 standard expands security protections to include other objects, including domains and user-defined character sets.

Most commercial SQL products support additional security objects. In a SQL Server database, for example, a stored procedure is an important database object. The SQL security scheme determines which users can create and drop stored procedures, and which users are allowed to execute them. In IBM's DB2, the physical tablespaces where tables are stored are treated as security objects. The database administrator can give some user-ids permission to create new tables in a particular tablespace and deny that permission to other user-ids. Other SQL implementations support other security objects.

Privileges

The set of actions that a user can carry out against a database object are called the *privileges* for the object. The SQL1 standard specifies four privileges for tables and views:

■ The SELECT privilege allows you to retrieve data from a table or view. With this privilege, you can specify the table or view in the FROM clause of a SELECT statement or subquery.

- The INSERT privilege allows you to insert new rows into a table or view. With this privilege, you can specify the table or view in the INTO clause of an INSERT statement.

- The DELETE privilege allows you to delete rows of data from a table or view. With this privilege, you can specify the table or view in the FROM clause of a DELETE statement.

- The UPDATE privilege allows you to modify rows of data in a table or view. With this privilege, you can specify the table or view as the target table in an UPDATE statement. The UPDATE privilege can be restricted to specific columns of the table or view, allowing updates to these columns, but disallowing updates to any other columns.

These four privileges are supported by virtually all commercial SQL products.

OWNERSHIP PRIVILEGES   When you create a table with the CREATE TABLE statement, you become its owner and receive full privileges for the table (SELECT, INSERT, DELETE, UPDATE, and any other privileges supported by the DBMS). Other users initially have no privileges on the newly created table. If they are to be given access to the table, you must explicitly grant privileges to them, using the GRANT statement.

When you create a view with the CREATE VIEW statement, you become the owner of the view, but you do not necessarily receive full privileges on it. In order to create the view successfully you must already have the SELECT privilege on each of the source tables for the view; therefore the DBMS gives you the SELECT privilege for the view automatically. For each of the other privileges (INSERT, DELETE, and UPDATE), the DBMS gives you the privilege on the view only if you hold that same privilege on *every* source table for the view.

OTHER PRIVILEGES   Many commercial DBMS products offer additional table and view privileges beyond the SELECT, INSERT, DELETE, and UPDATE privileges specified in the SQL1 standard. For example, the IBM mainframe databases (DB2 and SQL/DS) and Oracle support an ALTER and an INDEX privilege for tables. A user with the ALTER privilege on a particular table can use the ALTER TABLE statement to modify the definition of the table; a user with the INDEX privilege can create an index for the table with the CREATE INDEX statement. In DBMS brands that do not support the ALTER and INDEX privileges, only the owner may use the ALTER TABLE and CREATE INDEX statements.

Another example of additional table and view privileges is the extended SELECT privilege offered by Sybase and SQL Server. Like the ANSI/ISO UPDATE privilege, this SELECT privilege can be specified for individual columns of a table or view. Thus one user may be allowed to retrieve certain columns of a table while another user is restricted to other columns.

Additional privileges are frequently supported for DBMS security objects other than tables and views. For example, Sybase and SQL Server support an EXECUTE privilege for stored procedures, which determines whether a user is allowed to execute a stored procedure. DB2 supports a USE privilege for tablespaces, which determines whether a user can create tables in a specific tablespace.

The SQL2 standard expanded the SQL1 table and view privileges in several ways. It allows the INSERT privilege for specific columns, like the UPDATE privilege. It adds a REFERENCES privilege to foreign key support and a USAGE privilege for other database objects. These privileges, and commercial DBMS extended privileges, are administered using variations on the GRANT and REVOKE statements.

Views and SQL Security

In addition to the restrictions on table access provided by the SQL privileges, views also play a key role in SQL security. By carefully defining a view and giving a user permission to access the view but not its source tables, you can effectively restrict the user's access to only selected columns and rows. Views thus offer a way to exercise very precise control over what data is made visible to which users.

For example, suppose you wanted to enforce this security rule in the sample database:

"Accounts receivable personnel should be able to retrieve employee numbers, names, and office numbers from the SALESREPS table, but data about sales and quotas should not be available to them."

You can implement this security rule by defining a view as follows:

```
CREATE VIEW REPINFO AS
    SELECT EMPL_NUM, NAME, REP_OFFICE
        FROM SALESREPS
```

and giving the SELECT privilege for the view to the ARUSER user-id, as shown in Figure 15-3. This example uses a vertical view to restrict access to specific columns. Horizontal views are also effective for enforcing security rules such as this one:

"The sales managers in each region should have full access to SALESREPS data for the salespeople assigned to that region."

As shown in Figure 15-4, you can define two views, EASTVIEWS and WESTVIEWS, containing SALESREPS data for each of the two regions, and then grant each office manager access to the appropriate view.

Of course views can be much more complex than the simple row and column subsets of a single table shown in these examples. By defining a view with a grouped query, you can give a user access to summary data, but not to the detailed rows in the

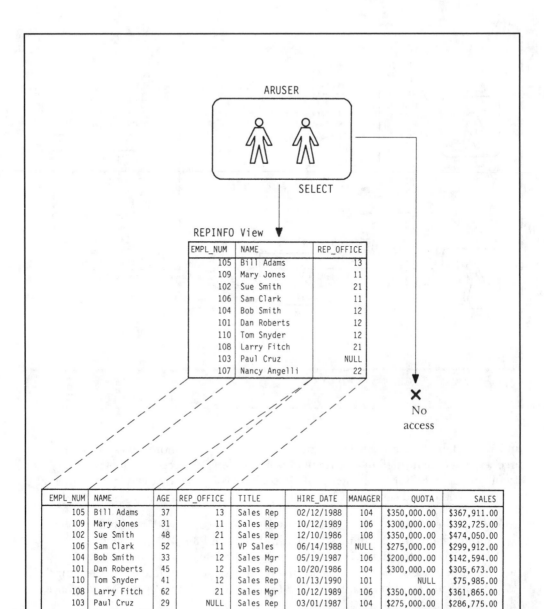

Figure 15-3. *Using a view to restrict column access*

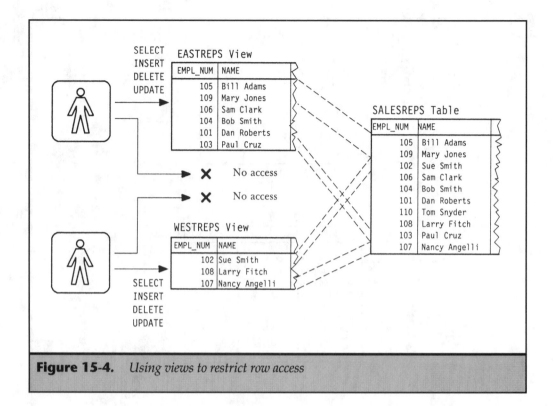

Figure 15-4. *Using views to restrict row access*

underlying table. A view can also combine data from two or more tables, providing precisely the data needed by a particular user and denying access to all other data. The usefulness of views for implementing SQL security is limited by the two fundamental restrictions described earlier in Chapter 14:

■ *Update restrictions.* The SELECT privilege can be used with read-only views to limit data retrieval, but the INSERT, DELETE, and UPDATE privileges are meaningless for these views. If a user must update the data visible in a read-only view, the user must be given permission to update the underlying tables, and must use INSERT, DELETE, and UPDATE statements that reference those tables.

■ *Performance.* Because the DBMS translates every access to a view into a corresponding access to its source tables, views can add significant overhead to database operations. Views cannot be used indiscriminately to restrict database access without causing overall database performance to suffer.

Granting Privileges (GRANT)

The basic GRANT statement, shown in Figure 15-5, is used to grant security privileges on database objects to specific users. Normally the GRANT statement is used by the owner of a table or view to give other users access to the data. As shown in the figure, the GRANT statement includes a specific list of the privileges to be granted, the name of the table to which the privileges apply, and the user-id to which the privileges are granted.

The GRANT statement shown in the syntax diagram conforms to the ANSI/ISO SQL standard. Many DBMS brands follow the DB2 GRANT statement syntax, which is more flexible. The DB2 syntax allows you to specify a list of user-ids and a list of tables, making it simpler to grant many privileges at once. Here are some examples of simple GRANT statements for the sample database:

Give order processing users full access to the ORDERS *table.*

```
GRANT SELECT, INSERT, DELETE, UPDATE
   ON ORDERS
   TO OPUSER
```

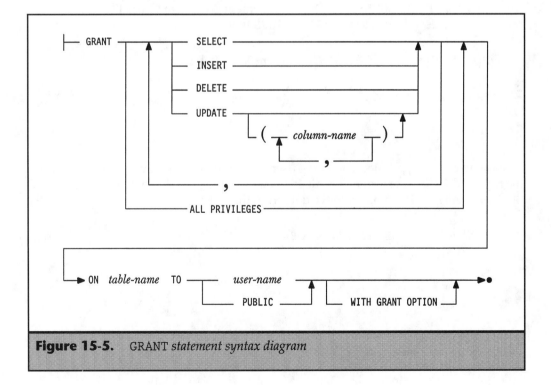

Figure 15-5. GRANT *statement syntax diagram*

Let accounts receivable users retrieve customer data and add new customers to the CUSTOMERS *table, but give order processing users read-only access.*

```
GRANT SELECT, INSERT
    ON CUSTOMERS
    TO ARUSER

GRANT SELECT
    ON CUSTOMERS
    TO OPUSER
```

Allow Sam Clark to insert or delete an office.

```
GRANT INSERT, DELETE
    ON OFFICES
    TO SAM
```

For convenience, the GRANT statement provides two shortcuts that you can use when granting many privileges or when granting them to many users. Instead of specifically listing all of the privileges available for a particular object, you can use the keywords ALL PRIVILEGES. This GRANT statement gives Sam Clark, the vice president of sales, full access to the SALESREPS table:

Give all privileges on the SALESREPS *table to Sam Clark.*

```
GRANT ALL PRIVILEGES
    ON SALESREPS
    TO SAM
```

Instead of giving privileges to every user of the database one-by-one, you can use the keyword PUBLIC to grant a privilege to every authorized database user. This GRANT statement lets anyone retrieve data from the OFFICES table:

Give all users SELECT *access to the* OFFICES *table.*

```
GRANT SELECT
    ON OFFICES
    TO PUBLIC
```

Note that this GRANT statement grants access to all present and future authorized users, not just to the user-ids currently known to the DBMS. This eliminates the need for you to explicitly grant privileges to new users as they are authorized.

Column Privileges

The SQL1 standard allows you to grant the UPDATE privilege for individual columns of a table or view, and the SQL2 standard allows a column list for INSERT and REFERENCES privileges as well. The columns are listed after the UPDATE, INSERT, or REFERENCES keyword and enclosed in parentheses. Here is a GRANT statement that allows the order processing department to update only the company name and assigned salesperson columns of the CUSTOMERS table:

Let order processing users change company names and salesperson assignments.

```
GRANT UPDATE (COMPANY, CUST_REP)
   ON CUSTOMERS
   TO OPUSER
```

If the column list is omitted, the privilege applies to all columns of the table or view, as in this example:

Let accounts receivable users change any customer information.

```
GRANT UPDATE
   ON CUSTOMERS
   TO ARUSER
```

The ANSI/ISO standard does not permit a column list for the SELECT privilege; it requires that the SELECT privilege apply to all of the columns of a table or view. In practice, this isn't a serious restriction. To grant access to specific columns you first define a view on the table that includes only those columns, and then grant the SELECT privilege for the view only, as described earlier in this chapter. However, views defined solely for security purposes can clog the structure of an otherwise simple database. For this reason some DBMS brands allow a column list for the SELECT privilege. For example, the following GRANT statement is legal for the Sybase, SQL Server, and Informix DBMS brands:

Give accounts receivable users read-only access to the employee number, name, and sales office columns of the SALESREPS table.

```
GRANT SELECT (EMPL_NUM, NAME, REP_OFFICE)
   ON SALESREPS
   TO ARUSER
```

This GRANT statement eliminates the need for the REPINFO view defined in Figure 15-3, and in practice it can eliminate the need for many views in a production database. However, the use of a column list for the SELECT privilege is unique to certain SQL dialects, and it is not permitted by the ANSI/ISO standard or by the IBM SQL products.

Passing Privileges (GRANT OPTION)

When you create a database object and become its owner, you are the only person who can grant privileges to use the object. When you grant privileges to other users, they are allowed to use the object, but they cannot pass those privileges on to other users. In this way the owner of an object maintains very tight control both over who has permission to use the object, and over what forms of access are allowed.

Occasionally you may want to allow other users to grant privileges on an object that you own. For example, consider again the EASTREPS and WESTREPS views in the sample database. Sam Clark, the vice president of sales, created these views and owns them. He can give the Los Angeles office manager, Larry Fitch, permission to use the WESTREPS view with this GRANT statement:

```
GRANT SELECT
   ON WESTREPS
   TO LARRY
```

What happens if Larry wants to give Sue Smith (user-id SUE) permission to access the WESTREPS data because she is doing some sales forecasting for the Los Angeles office? With the preceding GRANT statement, he cannot give her the required privilege. Only Sam Clark can grant the privilege, because he owns the view.

If Sam wants to give Larry discretion over who may use the WESTREPS view, he can use this variation of the previous GRANT statement:

```
GRANT SELECT
   ON WESTREPS
   TO LARRY
 WITH GRANT OPTION
```

Because of the WITH GRANT OPTION clause, this GRANT statement conveys, along with the specified privileges, the right to grant those privileges to other users.

Larry can now issue this GRANT statement:

```
GRANT SELECT
   ON WESTREPS
   TO SUE
```

which allows Sue Smith to retrieve data from the WESTREPS view. Figure 15-6 graphically illustrates the flow of privileges, first from Sam to Larry, and then from Larry to Sue. Because the GRANT statement issued by Larry did not include the WITH GRANT OPTION clause, the chain of permissions ends with Sue; she can retrieve the WESTREPS data, but cannot grant access to another user. However, if Larry's grant of privileges to Sue had included the grant option, the chain could continue to another level, allowing Sue to grant access to other users.

Alternatively, Larry might construct a view for Sue including only the salespeople in the Los Angeles office and give her access to that view:

```
CREATE VIEW LAREPS AS
     SELECT *
       FROM WESTREPS
      WHERE OFFICE = 21

GRANT ALL PRIVILEGES
   ON LAREPS
   TO SUE
```

Larry will be the owner of the LAREPS view, but he does not own the WESTREPS view from which this new view is derived. To maintain effective security, the DBMS requires that Larry not only have SELECT privilege on WESTREPS, but also requires that he have the grant option for that privilege before allowing him to grant the SELECT privilege on LAREPS to Sue.

Once a user has been granted certain privileges with the grant option, that user may grant those privileges *and the grant option* to other users. Those other users can, in turn, continue to grant both the privileges and the grant option. For this reason you should use great care when giving other users the grant option. Note that the grant option applies only to the specific privileges named in the GRANT statement. If you want to grant certain privileges with the grant option and to grant other privileges without it, you must use two separate GRANT statements, as in this example:

Let Larry Fitch retrieve, insert, update, and delete data from the WESTREPS *table, and let him grant retrieval permission to other users.*

```
GRANT SELECT
   ON WESTREPS
```

```
      TO LARRY
  WITH GRANT OPTION

GRANT INSERT, DELETE, UPDATE
   ON WESTREPS
   TO LARRY
```

Revoking Privileges (REVOKE)

In most SQL-based databases, the privileges that you have granted with the GRANT statement can be taken away with the REVOKE statement, shown in Figure 15-7. The REVOKE statement has a structure that closely parallels the GRANT statement, specifying a specific set of privileges to be taken away, for a specific database object, from one or more user-ids.

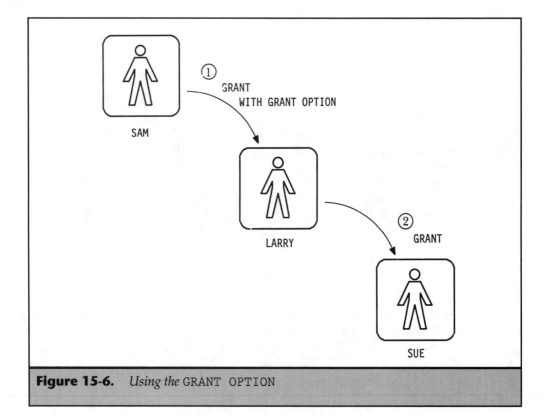

Figure 15-6. *Using the* GRANT OPTION

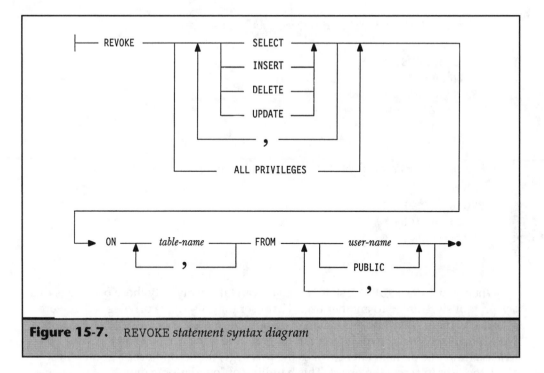

Figure 15-7. REVOKE *statement syntax diagram*

A REVOKE statement may take away all or some of the privileges that you previously granted to a user-id. For example, consider this statement sequence:

Grant and then revoke some SALESREPS *table privileges.*

```
GRANT SELECT, INSERT, UPDATE
    ON SALESREPS
    TO ARUSER, OPUSER

REVOKE INSERT, UPDATE
    ON SALESREPS
  FROM OPUSER
```

The INSERT and UPDATE privileges on the SALESREPS table are first given to the two users and then revoked from one of them. However, the SELECT privilege remains for both user-ids. Here are some other examples of the REVOKE statement:

Take away all privileges granted earlier on the OFFICES *table.*

```
REVOKE ALL PRIVILEGES
    ON OFFICES
  FROM ARUSER
```

Take away UPDATE *and* DELETE *privileges for two user-ids.*

```
REVOKE UPDATE, DELETE
   ON OFFICES
 FROM ARUSER, OPUSER
```

Take away all privileges on the OFFICES *that were formerly granted to all users.*

```
REVOKE ALL PRIVILEGES
   ON OFFICES
 FROM PUBLIC
```

When you issue a REVOKE statement, you can take away only those privileges that *you* previously granted to another user. That user may also have privileges that were granted by other users; those privileges are not affected by your REVOKE statement. Note specifically that if two different users grant the same privilege on the same object to a user and one of them later revokes the privilege, the second user's grant will still allow the user to access the object. This handling of "overlapping grants" of privileges is illustrated in the following example sequence.

Suppose that Sam Clark, the sales vice president, gives Larry Fitch SELECT privileges for the SALESREPS table, and SELECT and UPDATE privileges for the ORDERS table, using the following statements:

```
GRANT SELECT
   ON SALESREPS
   TO LARRY

GRANT SELECT, UPDATE
   ON ORDERS
   TO LARRY
```

A few days later George Watkins, the marketing vice president, gives Larry the SELECT and DELETE privileges for the ORDERS table, and the SELECT privilege for the CUSTOMERS table, using these statements:

```
GRANT SELECT, DELETE
    ON ORDERS
    TO LARRY

GRANT SELECT
    ON CUSTOMERS
    TO LARRY
```

Note that Larry has received privileges on the ORDERS table from two different sources. In fact, the SELECT privilege on the ORDERS table has been granted by both sources. A few days later, Sam revokes the privileges he previously granted to Larry for the ORDERS table:

```
REVOKE SELECT, UPDATE
    ON ORDERS
    FROM LARRY
```

After the DBMS processes the REVOKE statement, Larry still retains the SELECT privilege on the SALESREPS table, the SELECT and DELETE privileges on the ORDERS table, and the SELECT privilege on the CUSTOMERS table, but he has lost the UPDATE privilege on the ORDERS table.

REVOKE **and the Grant Option**

When you grant privileges with the grant option and later revoke these privileges, most DBMS brands will *automatically* revoke all privileges derived from the original grant. Consider again the chain of privileges in Figure 15-6, from Sam Clark, the sales vice president, to Larry Fitch, the Los Angeles office manager, and then to Sue Smith. If Sam now revokes Larry's privileges for the WESTREPS view, Sue's privilege is automatically revoked as well.

The situation gets more complicated if two or more users have granted privileges and one of them later revokes the privileges. Consider Figure 15-8, a slight variation on the last example. Here Larry receives the SELECT privilege with the grant option from *both* Sam (the sales vice president) *and* George (the marketing vice president), and then grants privileges to Sue. This time when Sam revokes Larry's privileges, the grant of privileges from George remains. Furthermore, Sue's privileges also remain, because they can be derived from George's grant.

However, consider another variation on the chain of privileges, with the events slightly rearranged, as shown in Figure 15-9. Here Larry receives the privilege with the grant option from Sam, grants the privilege to Sue, and *then* receives the grant, with the grant option, from George. This time when Sam revokes Larry's privileges, the results are slightly different, and they may vary from one DBMS to another. As in Figure 15-8, Larry retains the SELECT privilege on the WESTREPS view, because the

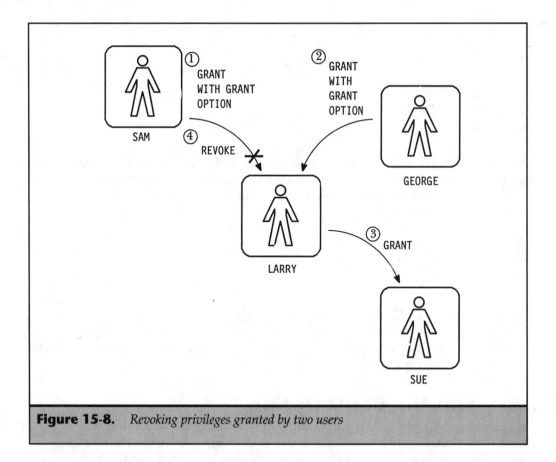

Figure 15-8. *Revoking privileges granted by two users*

grant from George is still intact. But in a DB2 or SQL/DS database, Sue will automatically lose her SELECT privilege on the table. Why? Because the grant from Larry to Sue was clearly derived from the grant from Sam to Larry, which has just been revoked. It could not have been derived from George's grant to Larry, because that grant had not yet taken place when the grant from Larry to Sue was made.

In a different brand of DBMS, Sue's privileges might remain intact, because the grant from George to Larry remains intact. Thus the time sequence of GRANT and REVOKE statements, rather than just the privileges themselves, can determine how far the effects of a REVOKE statement will cascade. Granting and revoking privileges with the grant option must be handled very carefully, to ensure that the results are those you intend.

REVOKE **and the ANSI/ISO Standard**

The SQL1 standard specifies the GRANT statement as part of the SQL Data Definition Language (DDL). Recall from Chapter 13 that the SQL1 standard treats the DDL as a

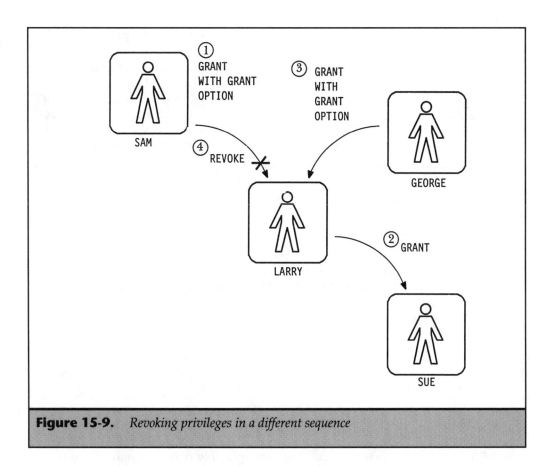

Figure 15-9. *Revoking privileges in a different sequence*

separate, static definition of a database, and does not require that the DBMS permit dynamic changes to database structure. This approach applies to database security as well. Under the SQL1 standard, accessibility to tables and views in the database is determined by a series of GRANT statements included in the database schema. There is no mechanism for changing the security scheme once the database structure is defined. The REVOKE statement is therefore absent from the SQL1 standard, just as the DROP TABLE statement is missing from the standard.

Despite its absence from the SQL1 standard, the REVOKE statement has been provided by virtually all commercial SQL-based DBMS products since their earliest versions. As with the DROP and ALTER statements, the DB2 dialect of SQL has effectively set the standard for the REVOKE statement. The SQL2 standard includes a specification for the REVOKE statement, based on the DB2 statement with some extensions. One of the extensions gives the user more explicit control over how privileges are revoked when the privileges have, in turn, been granted to others. The other provides a way to revoke the grant option without revoking the privileges themselves.

To specify how the DBMS should handle the revoking of privileges that have been in turn granted to others, the SQL2 standard requires that a CASCADE or RESTRICT option be specified in a REVOKE statement. (A similar requirement applies to many of the DROP statements in the SQL2 standard, as described in Chapter 13.) Suppose that SELECT and UPDATE privileges have previously been granted to Larry on the ORDERS table, with the grant option, and that Larry has further granted these options to Bill. Then this REVOKE statement:

```
REVOKE SELECT, UPDATE
    ON ORDERS
  FROM LARRY CASCADE
```

revokes not only Larry's privileges, but Bill's as well. The effect of the REVOKE statement thus "cascades" to all other users whose privileges have flowed from the original GRANT.

Now, assume the same circumstances and this REVOKE statement:

```
REVOKE SELECT, UPDATE
    ON ORDERS
  FROM LARRY RESTRICT
```

In this case, the REVOKE will fail. The RESTRICT option tells the DBMS not to execute the statement if it will affect any other privileges in the database. The resulting error calls the user's attention to the fact that there are (possibly unintentional) side-effects of the REVOKE statement, and allows the user to reconsider the action. If the user wants to go ahead and revoke the privileges, the CASCADE option can be specified.

The SQL2 version of the REVOKE statement also gives a user more explicit, separate control over privileges and the grant option for those privileges. Suppose again that Larry has been granted privileges on the ORDERS table, with the grant option for those privileges. The usual REVOKE statement for those privileges:

```
REVOKE SELECT, UPDATE
    ON ORDERS
  FROM LARRY
```

takes away both the privileges and the ability to grant those privileges to others. The SQL2 standard permits this version of the REVOKE statement:

```
REVOKE GRANT OPTION FOR SELECT, UPDATE
    ON ORDERS
  FROM LARRY CASCADE
```

If the statement is successful, Larry will lose the ability to grant these privileges to other users, but he will not lose the privileges themselves. As before, the SQL2 standard requires the CASCADE or the RESTRICT option to specify how the DBMS should handle the statement if Larry has, in turn, granted the grant option to other users.

Summary

The SQL language is used to specify the security restrictions for a SQL-based database:

- The SQL security scheme is built around privileges (permitted actions) that can be granted on specific database objects (such as tables and views) to specific user-ids (users or groups of users).

- Views also play a key role in SQL security, because they can be used to restrict access to specific rows or specific columns of a table.

- The GRANT statement is used to grant privileges; privileges that you grant to a user with the grant option can in turn be granted by that user to others.

- The REVOKE statement is used to revoke privileges previously granted with the GRANT statement.

Chapter Sixteen

The System Catalog

SQL

DB2

ODBC

Oracle

Sybase

402

A database management system must keep track of a great deal of information about the structure of a database in order to perform its data management functions. In a relational database, this information is typically stored in the *system catalog,* a collection of system tables that the DBMS maintains for its own use. The information in the system catalog describes the tables, views, columns, privileges, and other structural features of the database.

Although the DBMS maintains the system catalog primarily for its own internal purposes, the system tables are usually accessible to database users as well through standard SQL queries. A relational database is thus self-describing; using queries against the system tables, you can ask the database to describe its own structure. General-purpose database "front-ends," such as query tools and report writers, use this self-describing feature to generate lists of tables and columns for user selection, simplifying database access.

This chapter describes the system catalogs provided by several popular SQL-based DBMS products, and the information that the catalogs contain.

What Is the System Catalog?

The system catalog is a collection of special tables in a database that are owned, created, and maintained by the DBMS itself. These *system tables* contain data that describes the structure of the database. The tables in the system catalog are automatically created when the database is created. Usually they are gathered together under a special "system user-id" with a name like SYSTEM, SYSIBM, MASTER, or DBA.

The DBMS constantly refers to the data in the system catalog while processing SQL statements. For example, to process a two-table SELECT statement, the DBMS must:

- verify that the two named tables actually exist
- ensure that the user has permission to access them
- check whether the columns referenced in the query exist
- resolve any unqualified column names to one of the tables
- determine the data type of each column

By storing structural information in system tables, the DBMS can use its own access methods and logic to rapidly and efficiently retrieve the information it needs to perform these tasks.

If the system tables were only used internally to the DBMS, they would be of little interest to database users. However, the DBMS generally makes the system tables available for user access as well. User queries against the system catalogs are almost always permitted by personal computer and minicomputer databases. These queries are also supported by mainframe DBMS products, but the database administrator may restrict system catalog access to provide an additional measure of database security. By

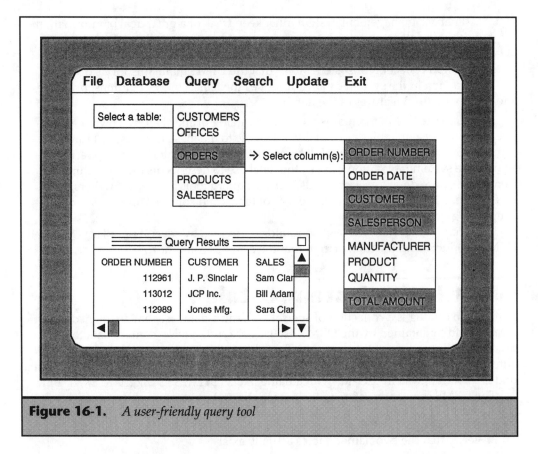

Figure 16-1. *A user-friendly query tool*

querying the system catalogs, you can discover information about the structure of a database, even if you have never used it before.

User access to the system catalog is read-only. The DBMS prevents users from directly updating or modifying the system tables, because such modifications would destroy the integrity of the database. Instead, the DBMS itself takes care of inserting, deleting, and updating rows of the system tables as it modifies the structure of a database. DDL statements such as CREATE, ALTER, DROP, GRANT, and REVOKE produce changes in the system tables as a by-product of their actions.

The Catalog and Query Tools

One of the most important benefits of the system catalog is that it makes possible user-friendly query tools, as shown in Figure 16-1. The objective of such a tool is to let users simply and transparently access the database without learning the SQL language. Typically, the tool leads the user through a series of steps like this one:

1. The user gives a name and password for database access.

2. The query tool displays a list of available tables.

3. The user chooses a table, causing the query tool to display a list of the columns it contains.

4. The user chooses columns of interest, perhaps by clicking on their names as they appear on a PC screen.

5. The user chooses columns from other tables or restricts the data to be retrieved with a search condition.

6. The query tool retrieves the requested data and displays it on the user's screen.

A general-purpose query tool like the one in Figure 16-1 must be able to dynamically learn about the tables and columns of a database. The tool uses system catalog queries for this purpose.

The Catalog and the ANSI/ISO Standard

The ANSI/ISO SQL1 standard did not specify the structure and contents of the system catalog. In fact, the standard does not require a system catalog at all. However, all of the major SQL-based DBMS products provide a system catalog in one form or another. The structure of the catalog and the tables it contains vary considerably from one brand of DBMS to another.

Because of the growing importance of general-purpose database tools that must access the system catalog, the SQL2 standard includes a specification of a set of views that provide standardized access to information typically found in the system catalog. A DBMS that conforms to the SQL2 standard must support these views, which are collectively called the INFORMATION_SCHEMA. Because this schema is more complex than the actual system catalogs used by commercial DBMS products, and is only slowly being supported, it is described in a separate section near the end of this chapter.

Catalog Contents

Each table in the system catalog contains information about a single kind of structural element in the database. Although the details vary, almost all commercial SQL products include system tables that describe each of these five entities:

- *Tables.* The catalog describes each table in the database, identifying its table name, its owner, the number of columns it contains, its size, and so on.

- *Columns.* The catalog describes each column in the database, giving the column's name, the table to which it belongs, its data type, its size, whether NULLs are allowed, and so on.

- *Users.* The catalog describes each authorized database user, including the user's name, an encrypted form of the user's password, and other data.

■ *Views.* The catalog describes each view defined in the database, including its name, the name of its owner, the query that defines the view, and so on.

■ *Privileges.* The catalog describes each set of privileges granted in the database, including the names of the grantor and grantee, the privileges granted, the object on which the privileges have been granted, and so on.

DBMS	Tables	Columns	Users	Views	Privileges
DB2	SYSTABLES SYSFOREIGNKEYS SYSRELS	SYSCOLUMNS	SYSUSERAUTH	SYSVIEWS SYSVIEWDEP SYSVTREE SYSVLTREE	SYSDBAUTH SYSCOLAUTH SYSPLANAUTH SYSRESAUTH SYSTABAUTH
SQL/DS	SYSCATALOG	SYSCOLUMNS	SYSUSERAUTH SYSUSERLIST	SYSVIEWS	SYSCOLAUTH SYSPROGAUTH SYSTABAUTH
Oracle	CATALOG TAB	COL COLUMNS SYSCOLUMNS	SYSUSERAUTH SYSUSERLIST	SYSVIEWS VIEWS	SYSCOLAUTH SYSTABAUTH
Ingres	IITABLES IIPHYSICAL_TABLES IIINGRES_TABLES IIINTEGRITIES IIMULTI_LOCATIONS	IICOLUMNS IISTATS		IIVIEWS	IIPERMITS
Rdb/VMS	RDB$RELATIONS	RDB$FIELDS RDB$FIELD_VERSIONS RDB$RELATION_FIELDS		RDB$VIEW_RELATIONS	
OS/2 EE	SYSTABLES	SYSCOLUMNS		SYSVIEWS SYSVIEWDEP	
SQL Server	SYSOBJECTS SYSKEYS	SYSCOLUMNS	SYSUSERS SYSLOGINS SYSALTERNATES	SYSDEPENDS SYSCOMMENTS	SYSPROTECTS
SQLBase	SYSTABLES	SYSCOLUMNS	SYSUSERAUTH	SYSVIEWS	SYSCOLAUTH SYSTABAUTH

Table 16-1. *Selected System Tables in Popular SQL-Based Products*

Table 16-1 shows the names of the system tables that provide this information in each of the major SQL-based DBMS products. The remainder of this chapter describes some typical system tables in more detail and gives examples of system catalog access.

Table Information

Each of the major SQL products has a system table that keeps track of the tables in the database. In DB2, this system table is called SYSTABLES. It contains one row for each table or view defined in the database. Table 16-2 shows the columns of the OS/2 SYSTABLES table.

You can use queries like the following examples to find out information about the tables in an OS/2 database. Similar queries, using different table and column names, can be used to obtain the same information from other DBMS brands.

List the names and owners of all tables in the database.

```
SELECT CREATOR, NAME
  FROM SYSIBM.SYSTABLES
  WHERE TYPE = 'T'
```

Column Name	Data Type	Information
NAME	VARCHAR(18)	Name of the table or view
CREATOR	CHAR(18)	Owner of table or view
TYPE	CHAR(1)	'T' for table; 'V' for view
CTIME	TIMESTAMP	Date/time of table creation
REMARKS	VARCHAR(254)	Up to 254 characters of comments
PACKED_DESC	LONG VARCHAR	Internal form of table description
VIEW_DESC	LONG VARCHAR	Internal form of view definition
COLCOUNT	SMALLINT	Number of columns in the table
FID	SMALLINT	Internal file id of file containing data
TID	SMALLINT	Internal table id of the table
CARD	INTEGER	Cardinality (number of rows)
NPAGES	INTEGER	Number of storage pages used
FPAGES	INTEGER	Number of total storage pages
OVERFLOW	INTEGER	Number of overflow records

Table 16-2. *The SYSTABLES Table (OS/2)*

List the names of all tables and views in the database.

```
SELECT NAME
  FROM SYSIBM.SYSTABLES
```

List the names and creation times of my tables only.

```
SELECT NAME, CTIME
  FROM SYSIBM.SYSTABLES
 WHERE TYPE = 'T'
   AND CREATOR = USER
```

The DB2 version of the SYSTABLES system table is very similar to the OS/2 version, but there are some subtle differences that arise from feature differences between the two products. In OS/2 Extended Edition, the user who creates a table automatically becomes its owner. The CREATOR column in the OS/2 SYSTABLES table thus identifies *both* the owner and the creator of a table. In DB2, a user can create a table and give ownership of it to another user. For this reason the DB2 catalog includes both a CREATOR column, specifying the owner of a table, and a CREATED_BY column, specifying the user who actually created the table. Similarly, the FID (file id) column of the OS/2 catalog, which identifies the OS/2 file containing the data for a table, is replaced in the DB2 catalog by a column that specifies the tablespace (a DB2 physical storage entity) where the table is stored.

In a SQL/DS database, the system table SYSCATALOG performs the same function as the OS/2 and DB2 SYSTABLES table. The SYSCATALOG table also contains one row for each table or view in the database. The table tracks the name (TNAME), creator (CREATOR), number of columns (NCOLS), and so on, for each table or view.

The SQL Server equivalent of the OS/2 SYSTABLES table is a system table named SYSOBJECTS, described in Table 16-3. The SYSOBJECTS table stores information about SQL Server tables and views, and other SQL Server objects such as stored procedures, rules, and triggers. Note also how the SYSOBJECTS table uses an internal id number instead of a name to identify the table owner.

It's interesting to note that even the IBM SQL products, which have been under strong pressure to offer uniform, standard features, have different definitions of the same system table. The differences between the IBM tables and the SQL Server catalog are even more pronounced. These catalog differences, even among DBMS products produced by the same manufacturer, arise from differences in DBMS features, from differences in the underlying hardware and operating system, and from historical choices.

Column Information

All of the major SQL products have a system table that keeps track of the columns in the database. The IBM SQL products all call this system table SYSCOLUMNS. There is

Column Name	Data Type	Information
name	SYSNAME	Name of the object
id	INT	Internal object id number
uid	SMALLINT	User-id of object owner
type	CHAR(2)	Object type code *
refdate	DATETIME	Reserved for future use
crdate	DATETIME	Date/time object was created
expdate	DATETIME	Reserved for future use
deltrig	INT	Procedure id of DELETE trigger
instrig	INT	Procedure id of INSERT trigger
updtrig	INT	Procedure id of UPDATE trigger
seltrig	INT	Reserved for future use

* S = system table, U = user table, V = view, L = log, P = stored procedure, R = rule, D = default, TR = trigger

Table 16-3. *Selected Columns of the* SYSOBJECTS *Table (SQL Server)*

one row in the SYSCOLUMNS table for each column in each table or view in the database. Table 16-4 shows the definition of the SYSCOLUMNS system table in OS/2 Extended Edition.

Most of the information in the SYSCOLUMNS table stores the definition of a column—its name, its data type, its length, whether it can take NULL values, and so on. In addition, the SYSCOLUMNS table includes information about the distribution of data values found in each column. This statistical information helps the DBMS decide how to carry out a query in the optimal way.

You can use queries like those in the following examples to find out about the columns in an OS/2 Extended Edition database. Similar queries, using different table and column names, can be used to obtain the same information for other DBMS brands.

List the names and data types of the columns in my OFFICES *table.*

```
SELECT NAME, COLTYPE
  FROM SYSIBM.SYSCOLUMNS
 WHERE TBNAME = 'OFFICES'
   AND TBCREATOR = USER
```

Column Name	Data Type	Information
NAME	VARCHAR(18)	Name of the column
TBNAME	VARCHAR(18)	Name of table or view containing the column
TBCREATOR	CHAR(8)	Owner of table or view
REMARKS	VARCHAR(254)	Up to 254 characters of comments
COLTYPE	CHAR(8)	The column's data type (e.g. "INTEGER")
NULLS	CHAR(1)	'Y' if NULLs allowed; 'N' if not
CODEPAGE	SMALLINT	IBM character set (for text data)
DBCSCODEPG	SMALLINT	Used internally by DBMS
LENGTH	SMALLINT	Length of the column
SCALE	SMALLINT	Scale of the column (for decimal columns)
COLNO	SMALLINT	Position of the column within the table
COLCARD	INTEGER	Number of distinct values in the column
HIGH2KEY	VARCHAR(16)	Second highest data value in the column
LOW2KEY	VARCHAR(16)	Second lowest data value in the column
AVGCOLLEN	INTEGER	Average length of the column

Table 16-4. *The SYSCOLUMNS Table (OS/2)*

Find all columns in the database with a DATE data type.

```
SELECT TBCREATOR, TBNAME, NAME
  FROM SYSIBM.SYSCOLUMNS
 WHERE COLTYPE = 'DATE'
```

List the owner, view name, column name, data type, and length for all text columns longer than ten characters defined in views.

```
SELECT TBCREATOR, TBNAME, SYSIBM.SYSCOLUMNS.NAME, COLTYPE, LENGTH
  FROM SYSIBM.SYSCOLUMNS, SYSIBM.SYSTABLES
 WHERE TBCREATOR = CREATOR
   AND TBNAME = SYSIBM.SYSTABLES.NAME
```

```
AND (COLTYPE = 'VARCHAR' OR COLTYPE = 'CHAR')
AND LENGTH > 10
AND TYPE = 'V'
```

There is considerable variation in the way that the column definition is provided by the system catalogs of various DBMS brands. For comparison, Table 16-5 shows the definition of the SQL Server SYSCOLUMNS table. Some of the differences between the OS/2 and SQL Server tables are simply matters of style:

- The names of the columns in the two tables are completely different, even when they contain similar data.

- The OS/2 Extended Edition catalog uses a combination of the owner name and table name to identify the table containing a given column; the SQL Server catalog uses an internal table id number, which is a foreign key to its SYSOBJECTS table.

- The OS/2 Extended Edition catalog specifies data types in text form (for example, VARCHAR); the SQL Server catalog uses integer data type codes.

Column Name	Data Type	Information
id	INT	Internal id of table containing the column
number	SMALLINT	Zero for column definitions
colid	TINYINT	Internal column id number
status	TINYINT	NULLs allowed?
type	TINYINT	Data type code for the column
length	TINYINT	Length of the column
offset	TINYINT	Physical column offset from beginning of row
usertype	SMALLINT	Data type code for user-defined data type
cdefault	INT	Id of stored procedure for default value
domain	INT	Id of stored procedure for column's rule
name	SYSNAME	Column name
printfmt	VARCHAR(255)	Display format for column

Table 16-5. *The* SYSCOLUMNS *Table (SQL Server)*

Other differences reflect the different capabilities provided by the two DBMS brands:

- OS/2 Extended Edition allows you to specify up to 254 characters of remarks about each column; SQL Server does not provide this feature.

- SQL Server lets you specify a rule that defines the valid data for a column; OS/2 Extended Edition does not provide this feature.

- OS/2 Extended Edition uses a standard default value for each data type (0 for integers, for example); SQL Server requires you to write a stored procedure that generates a default value, and stores the id number of the stored procedure in the SYSCOLUMNS table.

View Information

The definitions of the views in a database are stored in the system catalog. The OS/2 Extended Edition catalog contains two system tables that keep track of views. The SYSVIEWS table, described in Table 16-6, contains the SQL text definition of each view. If the definition exceeds 3900 characters, it is stored in multiple rows, with sequence numbers 1, 2, 3, and so on.

The SYSVIEWDEP table, described in Table 16-7, describes how each view depends on other tables or views. There is one row in the table for each dependency, so a view with three source tables will be represented by three rows.

Using these two tables, you can see the definitions of the views in the database and quickly determine which tables in the database serve as the source tables for a view.

Column Name	Data Type	Information
NAME	VARCHAR(18)	Name of the view
CREATOR	CHAR(8)	Owner of view
SEQNO	SMALLINT	Sequence number of this row (1, 2, etc.)
CHECK	CHAR(1)	'Y' if view has check option; 'N' if not
TEXT	VARCHAR(3900)	Up to 3900 characters of view definition

Table 16-6. *The SYSVIEWS Table (OS/2)*

Column Name	Data Type	Information
BNAME	VARCHAR(18)	Name of table or view on which view depends
BCREATOR	CHAR(8)	Owner of table or view specified in BNAME
BTYPE	CHAR(1)	'T' if BNAME names a table; 'V' if a view
DNAME	VARCHAR(18)	Name of dependent view
DCREATOR	CHAR(8)	Owner of dependent view

Table 16-7. *The SYSVIEWDEP Table (OS/2)*

The easiest way to find out the names of the views themselves is to query the SYSTABLES catalog, which includes both views and base tables:

List the views defined in the database.

```
SELECT NAME, CREATOR
  FROM SYSTABLES
 WHERE TYPE = 'V'
```

Remarks and Labels

The IBM SQL products allow you to associate up to 254 characters of *remarks* with each table, view, and column defined in the database. The remarks allow you to store a brief description of the table or data item in the system catalog. In addition to the remarks, you can specify a *label* of up to 30 characters for each table, view, and column. The label is used as the default heading in database reports and output.

The remarks and labels are stored in the SYSTABLES and SYSCOLUMNS system tables of the system catalog. Unlike the other elements of table and column definitions, the remarks and labels are not specified by the CREATE TABLE statement. Instead, the COMMENT and LABEL statements, shown in Figure 16-2, are used to specify the remarks and labels in the system catalog.

Here are some examples of the COMMENT and LABEL statements:

Define remarks and a label for the OFFICES table.

```
COMMENT ON TABLE OFFICES
    IS 'This table stores data about our sales offices'

LABEL ON TABLE OFFICES
   IS 'Sales Offices'
```

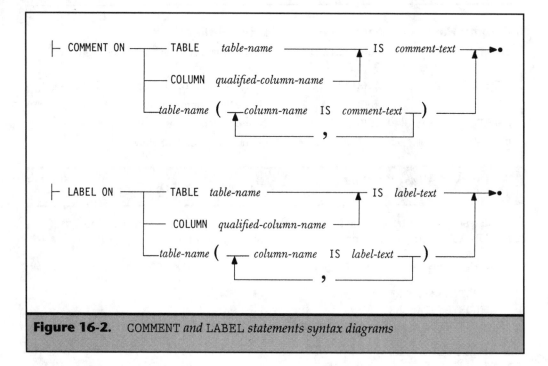

Figure 16-2.   COMMENT *and* LABEL *statements syntax diagrams*

Associate some remarks with the TARGET *and* SALES *columns of the* OFFICES *table.*

```
COMMENT ON OFFICES
(TARGET IS 'This is the annual sales target for the office',
  SALES IS 'This is the year-to-date sales for the office')
```

Define a label for the TARGET *column.*

```
LABEL ON COLUMN OFFICES.TARGET
  IS 'Sales Target'
```

Relationship Information

With the introduction of referential integrity in DB2 Version 2, the DB2 catalog was expanded to describe primary keys, foreign keys, and the parent/child relationships that they create. The description is spread over four tables in the system catalog named SYSTABLES, SYSCOLUMNS, SYSFOREIGNKEYS, and SYSRELS, the first two of which were described in previous sections.

Column Name	Data Type	Information
CREATOR	CHAR(8)	Owner of child table in the relationship
TBNAME	VARCHAR(18)	Name of child table
RELNAME	CHAR(8)	Name of relationship
REFTBNAME	VARCHAR(18)	Name of parent table in the relationship
REFTBCREATOR	CHAR(8)	Owner of parent table
COLCOUNT	SMALLINT	Number of columns in the foreign key
DELETERULE	CHAR(1)	'C', 'R', 'N' for CASCADE, RESTRICT, SET NULL
TIMESTAMP	TIMESTAMP	Date/time when relationship defined

Table 16-8. *Selected Columns of the* SYSRELS *Table (DB2)*

Every parent/child relationship between two tables in the database is represented by a single row in the SYSRELS system table, described in Table 16-8. The row identifies the names of the parent and child tables, the name of the relationship, and the delete rule for the relationship. You can query it to find out about the relationships in the database:

List all of the parent/child relationships among my tables, showing the name of the relationship, the name of the parent table, the name of the child table, and the delete rule for each one.

```
SELECT RELNAME, REFTBNAME, TBNAME, DELETERULE
  FROM SYSIBM.SYSRELS
 WHERE CREATOR = USER
```

List all of the tables related to the SALESREPS *table as either a parent or a child.*

```
SELECT REFTBNAME
  FROM SYSIBM.SYSRELS
 WHERE CREATOR = USER
   AND TBNAME = 'SALESREPS'
 UNION
SELECT TBNAME
```

```
   FROM SYSIBM.SYSRELS
  WHERE REFTBCREATOR = USER
    AND REFTBNAME = 'SALESREPS'
```

Each foreign key that creates a relationship is described in one or more rows of the SYSFOREIGNKEYS system table, shown in Table 16-9. There is one row in this system table for each column in each foreign key defined in the database. A sequence number defines the order of the columns in a compound foreign key. You can use this system table to find out the names of the columns that link a table to its parent, using a query like this one:

List the columns that link ORDERS *to* PRODUCTS *in the relationship named* ISFOR.

```
SELECT COLNAME, COLSEQ
  FROM SYSIBM.SYSFOREIGNKEYS
 WHERE CREATOR = USER
   AND RELNAME = 'ISFOR'
 ORDER BY COLSEQ
```

The primary key of a table is described in the SYSTABLES and SYSCOLUMNS system tables, shown previously in Tables 16-2 and 16-4. If a table has a primary key, the KEYCOLUMNS column in its row of the SYSTABLES system table is nonzero and tells how many columns comprise the primary key (1 for a simple key; 2 or more for a

Column Name	Data Type	Information
CREATOR	CHAR(8)	Owner of tabel containing the foreign key
TBNAME	VARCHAR(18)	Name of tabel containing the foreign key
RELNAME	CHAR(8)	Name of relationship created by foreign key
COLNAME	VARCHAR(18)	Name of a column in the foreign key
COLNO	SMALLINT	Position of column in its table (1, 2, etc.)
COLSEQ	SMALLINT	Position of column in foreign key (1, 2, etc.)

Table 16-9. *Selected Columns of the* SYSFOREIGNKEYS *Table (DB2)*

composite key). In the SYSCOLUMNS system table, the rows for the columns that comprise the primary key have a nonzero value in their KEYSEQ column. The value in this column indicates the position (1, 2, and so on) of the primary key column within the primary key.

You can query the SYSCOLUMNS table to find a table's primary key:

List the columns that form the primary key of the PRODUCTS *table.*

```
SELECT NAME, KEYSEQ, COLTYPE, REMARKS
  FROM SYSIBM.SYSCOLUMNS
 WHERE TBCREATOR = USER
   AND KEYSEQ > 0
   AND TBNAME = 'PRODUCTS'
 ORDER BY KEYSEQ
```

User Information

The system catalog generally contains a table that identifies the users who are authorized to access the database. The DBMS may use this system table to validate the user name and password when a user first attempts to connect to the database. The table may also store other data about the user.

SQL Server stores user information in its SYSUSERS system table, shown in Table 16-10. Each row of this table describes a single user or user group in the SQL Server security scheme. The DB2 system catalog takes a slightly different approach. It includes a SYSUSERAUTH system table, shown in Table 16-11, which stores basic user information and information about the user's privileges in the database. The rows in SYSUSERAUTH describe both "real" users and application programs that access the database.

Column Name	Data Type	Information
suid	SMALLINT	Internal server user-id number
uid	SMALLINT	Internal user-id number in this database
gid	SMALLINT	Internal user group id number in database
name	SYSNAME	User or group name

Table 16-10. *Selected Columns of the* SYSUSERS *Table (SQL Server)*

Column Name	Data Type	Information
GRANTOR	CHAR(8)	The user who granted the privileges
GRANTEE	CHAR(8)	User or application given the privileges
TIMESTAMP	CHAR(12)	Date/time when privileges granted
DATEGRANTED	CHAR(6)	Date when privileges granted
TIMEGRANTED	CHAR(8)	Time when privileges granted
GRANTEETYPE	CHAR(1)	'' for user; 'P' for application program
CREATEDBAUTH	CHAR(1)	User can create new databases?
SYSADMAUTH	CHAR(1)	User has system administrator authority?
SYSOPRAUTH	CHAR(1)	User has system operator authority?

Table 16-11. *Selected Columns of the* SYSUSERAUTH *Table (DB2)*

Here are two equivalent queries that list the authorized users for SQL Server and DB2:

List all the user-ids known to SQL Server.

```
SELECT NAME
  FROM SYSUSERS
 WHERE UID <> GID
```

List all the user-ids known to DB2.

```
SELECT DISTINCT GRANTEE
  FROM SYSIBM.SYSUSERAUTH
 WHERE GRANTEETYPE = ' '
```

Privileges Information

In addition to storing database structure information, the system catalog generally stores the information required by the DBMS to enforce database security. As described in Chapter 15, various DBMS products offer different variations on the basic SQL privileges scheme. These variations are reflected in the structure of the system catalogs for the various DBMS brands.

DB2 has one of the most comprehensive schemes for user privileges, extending down to the individual columns of a table. Table 16-12 shows the DB2 system catalogs that store information about privileges and briefly describes the role of each one.

System Table	Role
SYSTABAUTH	Implements the basic privileges scheme by telling which users have permission to access which tables, for which operations (SELECT, INSERT, DELETE, UPDATE, ALTER, and INDEX)
SYSCOLAUTH	Implements column-level update privileges by telling which users have permission to update which columns of which tables
SYSDBAUTH	Determines which users have permission to create tables and run various DB2 utility programs (for instance, to bulk load data)
SYSPLANAUTH	Determines which users have permission to execute which application programs that access the database
SYSRESAUTH	Determines which users have permission to create tables and allocate space in various tablespaces, storage groups, and so on
SYSUSERAUTH	Determines which users have system administration, system operator, system maintenance, and other privileges

Table 16-12. *DB2 Tables that Implement Permissions*

The authorization scheme used by SQL Server is more fundamental and streamlined than that of DB2. It treats databases, tables, stored procedures, triggers, and other entities uniformly as objects to which privileges apply. This streamlined structure is reflected in the system table, SYSPROTECTS, shown in Table 16-13, which implements the entire privileges scheme for SQL Server. Each row in the table represents a single GRANT or REVOKE statement that has been issued.

Column Name	Data Type	Information
id	INT	Internal id of protected object
uid	SMALLINT	Internal id of user or group with privilege
action	TINYINT	Numerical privilege code (e.g., SELECT =193)
protecttype	TINYINT	Numerical code for grant or revoke
columns	VARBINARY(32)	Bit map for column-level update privileges

Table 16-13. *The SYSPROTECTS Table (SQL Server)*

The SQL2 Information Schema

The SQL2 standard does not directly specify a system catalog that must be supported by DBMS implementations. In practice, given the widely differing features supported by different DBMS brands and the large differences in the system catalogs that were already being used by commercial SQL products when the SQL2 standard was adopted, it would have been impossible to reach an agreement on a standard catalog definition. Instead, the writers of the SQL2 standard defined an "idealized" system catalog that a DBMS vendor might design if they were building a DBMS to support the SQL2 standard "from scratch". The tables in this idealized system catalog (called the *definition schema* in the standard) are summarized in Table 16-14.

System Table	Contents
USERS	One row for each user ("authorization-id") in the catalog cluster
SCHEMATA	One row for each schema in the catalog cluster
DATA_TYPE_DESCRIPTOR	One row for each domain or column defined with a data type
DOMAINS	One row for each domain
DOMAIN_CONSTRAINTS	One row for each domain constraint
TABLES	One row for each table or view
VIEWS	One row for each or view
COLUMNS	One row for each column in each table or view definition
VIEW_TABLE_USAGE	One row for each table referenced in each view definition (if a view is defined by a query on multiple tables, there will be a row for each table)
VIEW_COLUMN_USAGE	One row for each column referenced by a view
TABLE_CONSTRAINTS	One row for each table constraint specified in a table definition
KEY_COLUMN_USAGE	One row for each column specified in each primary key, each foreign key and each uniqueness constraint (if multiple columns are specified in a key definition or uniqueness constraint, there will be multiple rows representing that constraint)
REFERENTIAL_CONSTRAINTS	One row for each foreign key definition specified in a table definition

Table 16-14.   *Idealized System Catalog Used by the SQL2 Standard*

System Table	Contents
CHECK_CONSTRAINTS	One row for each check-constraint specified in a table definition
CHECK_TABLE_USAGE	One row for each table referenced in each check constraint, domain constraint, or assertion
CHECK_COLUMN_USAGE	One row for each column referenced in each check constraint, domain constraint, or assertion
ASSERTIONS	One row for each assertion defined
TABLE_PRIVILEGES	One row for each privilege granted on each table
COLUMN_PRIVILEGES	One row for each privilege granted on each column
USAGE_PRIVILEGES	One row for each privilege granted on each domain, character set, etc.
CHARACTER_SETS	One row for each character set defined
COLLATIONS	One row for each collation defined
TRANSLATIONS	One row for each translation defined
SQL_LANGUAGES	One row for each language (e.g. COBOL, C, etc.) supported by this DBMS brand

Table 16-14. *Idealized System Catalog Used by the SQL2 Standard* (continued)

The SQL2 standard does not require a DBMS to actually support the system catalog tables in Table 16-14, or any system catalog at all. Instead, it defines a series of views on these catalog tables which identify database objects that are accessible to the current user. (These "catalog views" are called an *information schema* in the standard.) Any DBMS that claims to conform to the SQL2 standard must support these views. This effectively gives a user a standardized way to find out about the objects in the database that are available to him or her by issuing standard SQL queries against the catalog views.

In practice, commercial DBMS products support the standard catalog views by defining corresponding views on the tables in their own system catalogs. In most cases, the information in the DBMS's own system catalogs is similar enough to that required by the standard that the definition of the standard catalog views is relatively straightforward.

The catalog views required by the SQL2 standard are summarized in Table 16-15, along with a brief description of the information contained in each view. The standard also defines three domains which are used by the catalog views and are also available to users. These domains are summarized in Table 16-16. Here are some sample queries

System Catalog View	Contents
INFORMATION_SCHEMA_ CATALOG_NAME	A single row, specifying the name of the database for each user ("catalog in the language of the SQL2 standard) described by this information_schema
SCHEMATA	One row for each schema in the database that is owned by the current user, specifying the schema name, default character set, etc.
DOMAINS	One row for each domain accessible by the current user, specifying the name of the domain, the underlying data type, character set, maximum length, scale, precision, etc.
DOMAIN_CONSTRAINTS	One row for each domain constraint, specifying the name of the constraint and its deferrability characteristics
TABLES	One row for each table or view accessible to the current user, specifying its name and type (table or view)
VIEWS	One row for each view accessible to the current user, specifying its name, check option, and updatability
COLUMNS	One row for each column accessible to the current user, specifying its name, the table or view that contains it, its data type, precision, scale, character set, etc.
TABLE_PRIVILEGES	One row for each privilege on a table granted to or granted by the current user, specifying the table, the type of privilege, the grantor and grantee, and whether the privilege is grantable by the current user
COLUMN_PRIVILEGES	One row for each privilege on column granted to or granted by the current user, specifying the table and column, the type of privilege, the grantor and grantee, and whether the privilege is grantable by the current user
USAGE_PRIVILEGES	One row for each usage privilege granted to or by the current user
TABLE_CONSTRAINTS	One row for each table constraint (primary key, foreign key, uniqueness constraint or check constraint) specified on a table owned by the current user, specifying the name of the constraint, the table, the type of constraint, and its deferrability

Table 16-15. *Catalog Views Mandated by the SQL2 Standard*

System Catalog View	Contents
REFERENTIAL_CONSTRAINTS	One row for each referential constraint (foreign key definition) for a table owned by the current user, specifying the names of the constraint and the child and parent tables
CHECK_CONSTRAINTS	One row for each check-constraint for a table owned by the current user
KEY_COLUMN_USAGE	One row for each column specified in each primary key, each foreign key and each uniqueness constraint in a table owned by the current user, specifying the column and table names, and the position of the column in the key
ASSERTIONS	One row for each assertion owned by current user, specifying its name and its deferrability
CHARACTER_SETS	One row for each character set definition accessible to the current user
COLLATIONS	One row for each collation definition accessible to the current user
TRANSLATIONS	One row for each translation definition accessible to the current user
VIEW_TABLE_USAGE	One row for each table referenced in each view definition owned by the current user, specifying the name of the table
VIEW_COLUMN_USAGE	One row for each column referenced by a view owned by the current user, specifying its name and the table containing it
CONSTRAINT_TABLE_USAGE	One row for each table referenced in each check constraint, uniqueness constraint, foreign key definition and assertion owned by the current user
CONSTRAINT_COLUMN_USAGE	One row for each column referenced in each check constraint, uniqueness constraint, foreign key definition and assertion owned by the current user
SQL_LANGUAGES	One row for each language (e.g. COBOL, C, etc.) supported by this DBMS brand, specifying its level of conformance to the SQL2 standard, the type of SQL supported, etc.

Table 16-15. *Catalog Views Mandated by the SQL2 Standard* (continued)

System Domain	Values
SQL_IDENTIFIER	The domain of all variable-length character strings that are legal SQL identifiers under the SQL2 standard. A value drawn from this domain is a legal table name, column name, etc.
CHARACTER_DATA	The domain of all variable-length character strings with a length between zero and the maximum length supported by this DBMS. A value drawn from this domain is a legal character string.
CARDINAL_NUMBER	The domain of all non-negative numbers, from zero up to the maximum number represented by an INTEGER for this DBMS. A value drawn from this domain is zero or a legal positive number.

Table 16-16.   *Domains Defined by the SQL2 Standard*

that can be used to extract information about database structure from the SQL2-defined system catalog views:

List the names of all tables and views owned by the current user.

```
SELECT TABLE_NAME
  FROM TABLES
```

List the name, position, and data type of all columns in all views.

```
SELECT TABLE_NAME, C.COLUMN_NAME, ORDINAL_POSITION, DATA_TYPE
  FROM COLUMNS
 WHERE (COLUMNS.TABLE_NAME IN (SELECT TABLE_NAME FROM VIEWS))
```

Determine how many columns are in the table named OFFICES.

```
SELECT COUNT(*)
  FROM COLUMNS
 WHERE (TABLE_NAME = 'OFFICES')
```

Other Information

The system catalog is a reflection of the capabilities and features of the DBMS that uses it. Because of the many SQL extensions and additional features offered by popular DBMS products, their system catalogs always contain several tables unique to the DBMS. Here are just a few examples:

- DB2 and Oracle support synonyms (alternate names for tables). Synonym definitions are stored in a system table named SYSSYNONYMS.

- SQL Server supports multiple named databases. It has a system table called SYSDATABASES that identifies the databases managed by a single server.

- Ingres supports tables that are distributed across several disk volumes. Its IIMULTI_LOCATIONS system table keeps track of the locations of multivolume tables.

Summary

The system catalog is a collection of system tables that describe the structure of a relational database:

- The DBMS maintains the data in the system tables, updating it as the structure of the database changes.

- A user can query the system tables to find out information about tables, columns, and privileges in the database.

- Front-end query tools use the system tables to help users navigate their way through the database in a user-friendly way.

- The names and organization of the system tables differ widely from one brand of DBMS to another; even the IBM SQL products have differences in their system catalogs.

PART FIVE

Programming with SQL

In addition to its role as an interactive data access language, SQL supports database access by application programs. The next three chapters describe the special SQL features and techniques that apply to programmatic SQL. Chapter 17 describes embedded SQL, the programmatic SQL technique used by most SQL products. Dynamic SQL, an advanced form of embedded SQL that is used to build general-purpose database tools, is described in Chapter 18. Chapter 19 describes an alternative to embedded SQL —the function call interface provided by several popular DBMS products.

Chapter Seventeen

Embedded SQL

428

S QL is a *dual-mode language.* It is both an interactive database language used for ad hoc queries and updates, and a programmatic database language used by application programs for database access. For the most part, the SQL language is identical in both modes. The dual-mode nature of SQL has several advantages:

■ It is relatively easy for programmers to learn how to write programs that access the database.

■ Capabilities available through the interactive query language are also automatically available to application programs.

■ The SQL statements to be used in a program can be tried out first using interactive SQL and then coded into the program.

■ Programs can work with tables of data and query results instead of navigating their way through the database.

This chapter summarizes the types of programmatic SQL offered by the leading SQL-based products and then describes the programmatic SQL used by the IBM SQL products, called *embedded SQL.*

Programmatic SQL Techniques

SQL is a language, and it can be used programmatically, but it would be incorrect to call SQL a programming language. SQL lacks even the most primitive features of "real" programming languages. It has no provision for declaring variables, no GOTO statement, no IF statement for testing conditions, no FOR, DO, or WHILE statement to construct loops, no block structure, and so on. SQL is a database *sublanguage* that handles special-purpose database management tasks. To write a program that accesses a database, you must start with a conventional programming language, such as COBOL, PL/I, FORTRAN, Pascal, or C, and then "add SQL to the program."

The ANSI/ISO SQL1 standard was concerned exclusively with this programmatic use of SQL. The standard did not even include the interactive SELECT statement described in Chapters 6 through 9. It only specifies the programmatic SELECT statement described later in this chapter.

Commercial SQL database vendors offer two basic techniques for using SQL within an application program:

■ *Embedded SQL.* In this approach, SQL statements are embedded directly into the program's source code, intermixed with the other programming language statements. Special embedded SQL statements are used to retrieve data into the program. A special SQL precompiler accepts the combined source code and, along with other programming tools, converts it into an executable program.

■ *Application program interface.* In this approach, the program communicates with the DBMS through a set of function calls called an *application program interface,* or API. The program passes SQL statements to the DBMS through the API calls and uses API calls to retrieve query results. This approach does not require a special precompiler.

The IBM SQL products use an embedded SQL approach, and this approach has been adopted by most commercial SQL products. The ANSI/ISO standard originally specified a separate "module language" for programmatic SQL, but in 1989 the standard was extended to include a definition of embedded SQL for the Ada, C, COBOL, FORTRAN, Pascal, and PL/I programming languages. However, SQL Server and the Sybase DBMS from which it is derived both use the API approach exclusively, as does the Gupta Technologies SQLBase product. Microsoft's ODBC is another leading example of the API approach, based on the draft SQL API standard from the SQL Access Group. Table 17-1 summarizes the programmatic interfaces offered by the leading SQL-based DBMS products.

The basic techniques of embedded SQL, called *static* SQL, are described in this chapter. Some advanced features of embedded SQL, called *dynamic* SQL, are discussed in Chapter 18. The SQL API provided by Sybase and SQL Server is discussed in Chapter 19.

DBMS	API	Embedded Language Support
DB2	No*	APL, Assembler, BASIC, COBOL, FORTRAN, PL/I
SQL/DS	No	APL, Assembler, BASIC, COBOL, FORTRAN, PL/I, Prolog
Oracle	Yes	Ada, C, COBOL, FORTRAN, Pascal, PL/I
Ingres	No	Ada, BASIC, C, COBOL, FORTRAN, Pascal, PL/I
Sybase	Yes	none
Informix	No	Ada, C, COBOL
OS/2 EE	No	C
SQLBase	Yes	none
ODBC	Yes	none

*Function interface not available for application programming; however, the DB2 Call Attach Facility provides a function interface for systems programmers.

Table 17-1. *Programmatic SQL Interfaces for Popular SQL Products*

DBMS Statement Processing

To understand any of the programmatic SQL techniques, it helps to understand a little bit more about how the DBMS processes SQL statements. To process a SQL statement, the DBMS goes through a series of five steps, shown in Figure 17-1:

1. The DBMS begins by *parsing* the SQL statement. It breaks the statement up into individual words, makes sure that the statement has a valid verb and legal clauses, and so on. Syntax errors and misspellings can be detected in this step.

2. The DBMS *validates* the statement. It checks the statement against the system catalog. Do all the tables named in the statement exist in the database? Do all of the columns exist and are the column names unambiguous? Does the user have the required privileges to execute the statement? Semantic errors are detected in this step.

3. The DBMS *optimizes* the statement. It explores various ways to carry out the statement. Can an index be used to speed a search? Should the DBMS first apply a search condition to Table A and then join it to Table B, or should it begin with the join and use the search condition afterward? Can a sequential search through a table be avoided or reduced to a subset of the table? After exploring alternatives, the DBMS chooses one of them.

4. The DBMS then generates an *application plan* for the statement. The application plan is a binary representation of the steps that are required to carry out the statement; it is the DBMS equivalent of "executable code."

5. Finally, the DBMS carries out the statement by executing the application plan.

Note that the steps in Figure 17-1 vary in the amount of database access they require and the amount of CPU time they take. Parsing a SQL statement does not require access to the database, and typically can be done very quickly. Optimization, on the other hand, is a very CPU-intensive process and requires access to the database's system catalog. For a complex, multi-table query, the optimizer may explore more than a dozen different ways of carrying out the query. However, the cost in computer processing time of doing the query the "wrong" way is usually so high compared to the cost of doing it the "right" way (or at least a "better" way) that the time spent in optimization is more than gained back in increased query execution speed.

When you type a SQL statement to interactive SQL, the DBMS goes through all five steps while you wait for its response. The DBMS has little choice in the matter—it doesn't know what statement you are going to type until you type it, and so none of the processing can be done ahead of time. In programmatic SQL, however, the situation is quite different. Some of the early steps can be done at *compile-time*, when the programmer is developing the program. This leaves only the later steps to be done at *run-time*, when the program is executed by a user. When you use programmatic SQL, all DBMS products try to move as much processing as possible to compile-time, because once the final version of the program is developed, it may be executed

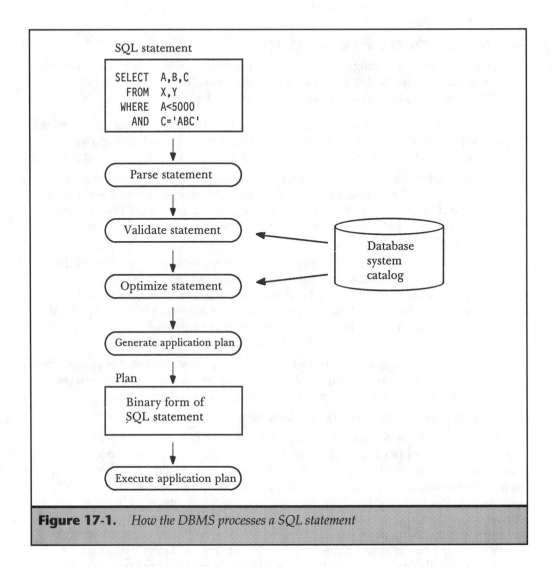

Figure 17-1. *How the DBMS processes a SQL statement*

thousands of times by users in a production application. In particular, the goal is to move optimization to compile-time if at all possible.

Embedded SQL Concepts

The central idea of embedded SQL is to blend SQL language statements directly into a program written in a "host" programming language, such as C, Pascal, COBOL, FORTRAN, PL/I, or Assembler. Embedded SQL uses the following techniques to embed the SQL statements:

■ SQL statements are intermixed with statements of the host language in the source program. This "embedded SQL source program" is submitted to a SQL *precompiler,* which processes the SQL statements.

■ Variables of the host programming language can be referenced in the embedded SQL statements, allowing values calculated by the program to be used by the SQL statements.

■ Program language variables also are used by the embedded SQL statements to receive the results of SQL queries, allowing the program to use and process the retrieved values.

■ Special program variables are used to assign NULL values to database columns and to support the retrieval of NULL values from the database.

■ Several new SQL statements that are unique to embedded SQL are added to the interactive SQL language, to provide for row-by-row processing of query results.

Figure 17-2 shows a simple embedded SQL program, written in C. The program illustrates many, but not all, of the embedded SQL techniques. The program prompts the user for an office number, retrieves the city, region, sales, and target for the office, and displays them on the screen.

Don't worry if the program appears strange, or if you can't understand all of the statements that it contains before reading the rest of this chapter. One of the disadvantages of the embedded SQL approach is that the source code for a program becomes an impure "blend" of two different languages, making the program hard to understand without training in both SQL and the programming language. Another disadvantage is that embedded SQL uses SQL language constructs not used in interactive SQL, such as the WHENEVER statement and the INTO clause of the SELECT statement—both used in this program.

Developing an Embedded SQL Program

An embedded SQL program contains a mix of SQL and programming language statements, so it can't be submitted directly to a compiler for the programming language. Instead, it moves through a multi-step development process, shown in Figure 17-3. The steps in the figure are actually those used by the IBM databases (DB2, SQL/DS, and OS/2 Extended Edition), but all products that support embedded SQL use a similar process:

1. The embedded SQL source program is submitted to the SQL *precompiler,* a programming tool. The precompiler scans the program, finds the embedded SQL statements, and processes them. A different precompiler is required for each programming language supported by the DBMS. Commercial SQL products typically offer precompilers for one or more languages, including C, Pascal, COBOL, FORTRAN, Ada, PL/I, RPG, and various assembly languages.

```
main()
{
    exec sql include sqlca;
    exec sql begin declare section;
        int   officenum;                /* office number (from user) */
        char  cityname[16];             /* retrieved city name */
        char  regionname[11];           /* retrieved region name */
        float targetval;                /* retrieved target and sales */
        float salesval;                 /* retrieved target and sales */
    exec sql end declare section;

    /* Set up error processing */
    exec sql whenever sqlerror goto query_error;
    exec sql whenever not found goto bad_number;

    /* Prompt the user for the employee number */
    printf("Enter office number: ");
    scanf("%d", &officenum);

    /* Execute the SQL query */
    exec sql select city, region, target, sales
             from offices
             where office = :officenum
             into :cityname, :regionname, :targetval, :salesval;

    /* Display the results */
    printf("City:   %s\n", cityname);
    printf("Region: %s\n", regionname);
    printf("Target: %f\n", targetval);
    printf("Sales:  %f\n", salesval);
    exit();

query_error:
    printf("SQL error: %ld\n", sqlca.sqlcode);
    exit();

bad_number:
    printf("Invalid office number.\n");
    exit();
}
```

Figure 17-2. *A typical embedded SQL program*

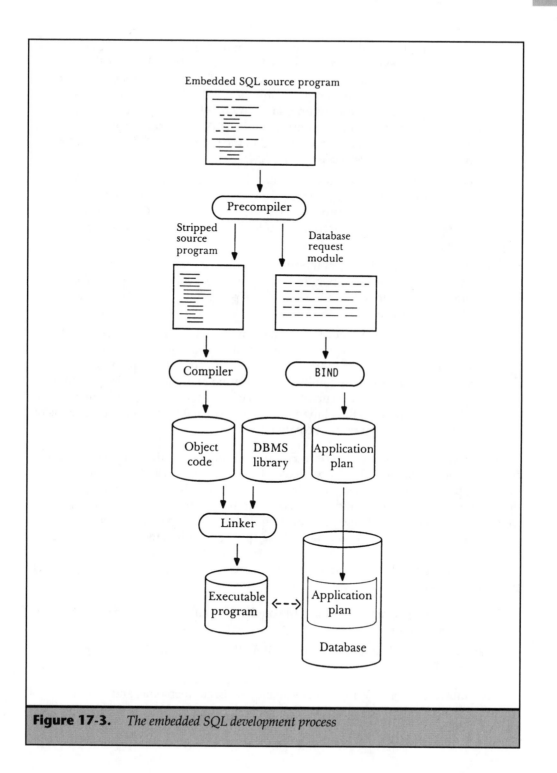

Figure 17-3. *The embedded SQL development process*

2. The precompiler produces two files as its output. The first file is the source program, stripped of its embedded SQL statements. In their place, the precompiler substitutes calls to the "private" DBMS routines that provide the run-time link between the program and the DBMS. Typically, the names and calling sequences of these routines are known only to the precompiler and the DBMS; they are not a public interface to the DBMS. The second file is a copy of all the embedded SQL statements used in the program. This file is sometimes called a *database request module,* or DBRM.

3. The source file output from the precompiler is submitted to the standard compiler for the host programming language (such as a C or COBOL compiler). The compiler processes the source code and produces object code as its output. Note that this step has nothing in particular to do with the DBMS or with SQL.

4. The *linker* accepts the object modules generated by the compiler, links them with various library routines, and produces an executable program. The library routines linked into the executable program include the "private" DBMS routines described in Step 2.

5. The database request module generated by the precompiler is submitted to a special BIND program. This program examines the SQL statements, parses, validates, and optimizes them, and produces an application plan for each statement. The result is a combined application plan for the entire program, representing a DBMS-executable version of its embedded SQL statements. The BIND program stores the plan in the database, usually assigning it the name of the application program that created it.

The program development steps in Figure 17-3 correlate with the DBMS statement processing steps in Figure 17-1. In particular, the precompiler usually handles statement parsing (the first step), and the BIND utility handles verification, optimization, and plan generation (the second, third, and fourth steps). Thus the first four steps of Figure 17-1 all take place at compile-time when you use embedded SQL. Only the fifth step, the actual execution of the application plan, remains to be done at run-time.

The embedded SQL development process turns the original embedded SQL source program into two executable parts:

- an *executable program,* stored in a file on the computer in the same format as any executable program

- an *executable application plan,* stored within the database in the format expected by the DBMS

The embedded SQL development cycle may seem cumbersome, and it is more awkward than developing a standard C or COBOL program. In most cases, all of the steps in Figure 17-3 are automated by a single command procedure, so the individual steps are made invisible to the application programmer. The process does have several major advantages from a DBMS point of view:

- The blending of SQL and programming language statements in the embedded SQL source program is an effective way to merge the two languages. The host programming language provides flow of control, variables, block structure, and input/output functions; SQL handles database access and does not have to provide these other constructs.

- The use of a precompiler means that the compute-intensive work of parsing and optimization can take place *during the development cycle.* The resulting executable program is very efficient in its use of CPU resources.

- The database request module produced by the precompiler provides portability of applications. An application program can be written and tested on one system, and then its executable program and DBRM can be moved to another system. After the BIND program on the new system creates the application plan and installs it in the database, the application program can use it without being recompiled itself.

- The program's actual run-time interface to the private DBMS routines is completely hidden from the application programmer. The programmer works with embedded SQL at the source code level and does not have to worry about other, more complex interfaces.

Running an Embedded SQL Program

Recall from Figure 17-3 that the embedded SQL development process produces two executable components, the executable program itself and the program's application plan, stored in the database. When you run an embedded SQL program, these two components are brought together to do the work of the application:

1. When you ask the computer system to run the program, the computer loads the executable program in the usual way and begins to execute its instructions.

2. One of the first calls generated by the precompiler is a call to a DBMS routine that finds and loads the application plan for the program.

3. For each embedded SQL statement, the program calls a private DBMS routine, requesting execution of the corresponding statement in the application plan. The DBMS finds the statement, executes that part of the plan, and then returns control to the program.

4. Execution continues in this way, with the executable program and the DBMS cooperating to carry out the task defined by the original embedded SQL source program.

RUN-TIME SECURITY   When you use interactive SQL, the DBMS enforces its security based on the user-id you supply to the interactive SQL program. You can type any SQL statement you want, but the privileges granted to your user-id determine whether the DBMS will or will not execute the statement you type. When you run a program that uses embedded SQL, there are *two* user-ids to consider:

- the user-id of the person who *developed* the program, or more specifically, the person who ran the BIND program to create the application plan
- the user-id of the person who is now *executing* the program and the corresponding application plan

It may seem strange to consider the user-id of the person who ran the BIND program, but in fact DB2 and several other commercial SQL products use both user-ids in their security scheme. To see how the security scheme works, suppose that user JOE runs the ORDMAINT order maintenance program, which updates the ORDERS, SALES, and OFFICES tables. The application plan for the ORDMAINT program was originally bound by user-id OPADMIN, which belongs to the order processing administrator.

In the DB2 scheme, each application plan is a database object, protected by DB2 security. To execute a plan, JOE must have the EXECUTE privilege for it. If he does not, execution fails immediately. As the ORDMAINT program executes, its embedded INSERT, UPDATE, and DELETE statements update the database. The privileges of the OPADMIN user determine whether the plan will be allowed to perform these updates. Note that the plan may update the tables even if JOE does not have the required privileges. However, the updates that can be performed are *only* those that have been explicitly coded into the embedded SQL statements of the program. Thus DB2 provides very fine control over database security. The privileges of users to access tables can be very limited, without diminishing their ability to use "canned" programs.

Not all DBMS products provide security protection for application plans. For those that do not, the privileges of the user executing an embedded SQL program determine the privileges of the program's application plan. Under this scheme, the user must have privileges to perform all of the actions performed by the plan, or the program will fail. If the user is not to have these same permissions in an interactive SQL environment, access to the interactive SQL program itself must be restricted, which is a disadvantage of this approach.

AUTOMATIC REBINDING   Note that an application plan is optimized for the database structure as it exists at the time the plan is placed in the database by the BIND program. If the structure changes later (for example, if an index is dropped or a column is deleted from a table), any application plan that references the changed structures may become invalid. To handle this situation, the DBMS stores, with the application plan, a copy of the original SQL statements that produced it. The DBMS also keeps track of all the database objects upon which each application plan depends. If any of these objects are modified by a DDL statement, the DBMS automatically marks the plan as "invalid". The next time the program tries to use the plan, the DBMS detects the situation and *automatically rebinds* the statements to produce a new bind image. This automatic rebinding is completely transparent to the application program, except that a SQL statement may take much longer to execute when its plan is rebound than when the plan is simply executed.

Although the DBMS automatically rebinds a plan when one of the structures upon which it depends is changed, the DBMS cannot automatically detect changes in the database that may make a better plan possible. For example, if the plan uses a sequential scan of a table because no appropriate index existed when it was bound, it's possible that a subsequent CREATE INDEX statement will create an appropriate index. To take advantage of the new structure, you must explicitly run the BIND program to rebind the plan.

Simple Embedded SQL Statements

The simplest SQL statements to embed in a program are those that are self-contained and do not produce any query results. For example, consider this interactive SQL statement:

Delete all salespeople with sales under $150,000.

```
DELETE FROM SALESREPS
 WHERE SALES < 150000.00
```

Figures 17-4, 17-5, and 17-6 show three programs that perform the same task as this interactive SQL statement, using embedded SQL. The program in Figure 17-4 is written in C, the program in Figure 17-5 is written in COBOL, and the program in Figure 17-6 is written in FORTRAN. Although the programs are extremely simple, they illustrate the most basic features of embedded SQL:

- The embedded SQL statements appear in the midst of host programming language statements. It usually doesn't matter whether the SQL statement is written in uppercase or lowercase; the most common practice is to follow the style of the host language.

- Every embedded SQL statement begins with an *introducer* that flags it as a SQL statement. The IBM SQL products use the introducer EXEC SQL for most host languages, and the ANSI/ISO standard has been updated to specify it as well. Some embedded SQL products still use other introducers.

- If an embedded SQL statement extends over multiple lines, the host language strategy for statement continuation is used. For COBOL, PL/I, and C programs, no special continuation character is required. For FORTRAN programs, the second and subsequent lines of the statement must have a continuation character in column 6.

```
                main()
                {
                    exec sql include sqlca;
                    exec sql declare salesreps table
                                    (empl_num integer not null,
                                         name varchar(15) not null,
                                          age integer,
                                   rep_office integer,
                                        title varchar(10),
                                    hire_date date not null,
                                      manager integer,
                                        quota money,
                                        sales money not null);

                    /* Display a message for the user */
                    printf("Deleting salesreps with low quota.\n");

                    /* Execute the SQL statement */
                    exec sql delete from salesreps
                             where sales < 150000.00;

                    /* Display another message */
                    printf("Finished deleting.\n");
                    exit();
                }
```

Figure 17-4.   *An embedded SQL program written in C*

■ Every embedded SQL statement ends with a *terminator* that signals the end of
   the SQL statement. The terminator varies with the style of the host language. In
   COBOL, the terminator is the string "END-EXEC.", which ends in a period like
   other COBOL statements. For PL/I and C, the terminator is a semicolon (;),
   which also is the statement termination character in those languages. In
   FORTRAN, the embedded SQL statement ends when no more continuation
   lines are indicated.

The embedding technique shown in the three figures works for any SQL statement
that (a) does not depend on the values of host language variables for its execution and
(b) does not retrieve data from the database. For example, the C program in Figure
17-7 creates a new REGIONS table and inserts two rows into it, using exactly the same
embedded SQL features as the program in Figure 17-4. For consistency, all of the
remaining program examples in the book will use the C programming language,
except when a particular host language feature is being illustrated.

```
      IDENTIFICATION DIVISION.
      PROGRAM-ID.  SAMPLE.
      ENVIRONMENT DIVISION.
      DATA DIVISION.
      FILE SECTION.
      WORKING-STORAGE SECTION.
            EXEC SQL INCLUDE SQLCA.
            EXEC SQL DECLARE SALESREPS TABLE
                            (EMPL_NUM INTEGER NOT NULL,
                                NAME VARCHAR(15) NOT NULL,
                                 AGE INTEGER,
                          REP_OFFICE INTEGER,
                               TITLE VARCHAR(10),
                           HIRE_DATE DATE NOT NULL,
                             MANAGER INTEGER,
                               QUOTA MONEY,
                               SALES MONEY NOT NULL)
            END-EXEC.
      PROCEDURE DIVISION.
      *
      *     DISPLAY A MESSAGE FOR THE USER
            DISPLAY "Deleting salesreps with low quota.".
      *
      *     EXECUTE THE SQL STATEMENT
            EXEC SQL DELETE FROM SALESREPS
                     WHERE QUOTA < 150000
            END-EXEC.
      *
      *     DISPLAY ANOTHER MESSAGE
            DISPLAY "Finished deleting.".
```

Figure 17-5. *An embedded SQL program written in COBOL*

Declaring Tables

The DECLARE TABLE statement, shown in Figure 17-8, declares a table that will be referenced by one or more embedded SQL statements in your program. This is an optional statement that aids the precompiler in its task of parsing and validating the embedded SQL statements. By using the DECLARE TABLE statement, your program explicitly specifies its assumptions about the columns in the table and their data types and sizes. The precompiler checks the table and column references in your program to make sure they conform to your table declaration.

```
              PROGRAM SAMPLE
      100 FORMAT(' ',A35)
          EXEC SQL INCLUDE SQLCA
          EXEC SQL DECLARE SALESREPS TABLE
          C                (EMPL_NUM INTEGER NOT NULL,
          C                    NAME VARCHAR(15) NOT NULL,
          C                     AGE INTEGER,
          C              REP_OFFICE INTEGER,
          C                   TITLE VARCHAR(10),
          C               HIRE_DATE DATE NOT NULL,
          C                 MANAGER INTEGER,
          C                   QUOTA MONEY,
          C                   SALES MONEY NOT NULL)
      *
      *     DISPLAY A MESSAGE FOR THE USER
            WRITE (6,100) 'Deleting salesreps with low quota.'
      *
      *     EXECUTE THE SQL STATEMENT
            EXEC SQL DELETE FROM REPS
          C           WHERE QUOTA < 150000
      *
      *     DISPLAY ANOTHER MESSAGE
            WRITE (6,100) 'Finished deleting.'
            RETURN
            END
```

Figure 17-6. *An embedded SQL program written in FORTRAN*

The programs in Figures 17-4, 17-5, and 17-6 all use the DECLARE TABLE statement. It's important to note that the statement appears purely for documentation purposes and for the use of the precompiler. It is not an executable statement, and you do not need to explicitly declare tables before referring to them in embedded DML or DDL statements. However, using the DECLARE TABLE statement does make your program more self-documenting and simpler to maintain. The IBM SQL products all support the DECLARE TABLE statement, but most other SQL products do not yet support it, and their precompilers will generate an error message if you use it.

Error Handling

When you type an interactive SQL statement that causes an error, the interactive SQL program displays an error message, aborts the statement, and prompts you to type a new statement. In embedded SQL, error handling becomes the responsibility of the

```
main()
{
   exec sql include sqlca;

   /* Create a new REGIONS table */
   exec sql create table regions
                (name char(15),
              hq_city char(15),
              manager integer,
               target money,
                sales money,
           primary key name,
           foreign key manager
            references salesreps);
   printf("Table created.\n");

   /* Insert two rows; one for each region */
   exec sql insert into regions
              values ('Eastern', 'New York', 106, 0.00, 0.00);
   exec sql insert into regions
              values ('Western', 'Los Angeles', 108, 0.00, 0.00);
   printf("Table populated.\n");

   exit();
}
```

Figure 17-7. *Using embedded SQL to create a table*

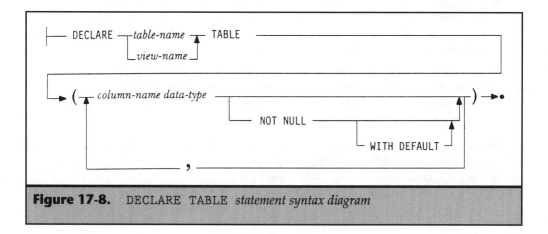

Figure 17-8. DECLARE TABLE *statement syntax diagram*

application program. Actually, embedded SQL statements can produce two distinct types of errors:

- *Compile-time errors.* Misplaced commas, misspelled SQL keywords, and similar errors in embedded SQL statements are detected by the SQL precompiler and reported to the programmer. The programmer can fix the errors and recompile the application program.

- *Run-time errors.* References to nonexistent columns or lack of permission to update a table can be detected only at run-time. Errors like these must be detected and handled by the application program.

The DBMS reports run-time errors to the application program through a *SQL Communications Area,* or SQLCA. The SQLCA is a data structure that contains error variables and status indicators. By examining the SQLCA, the application program can determine the success or failure of its embedded SQL statements and act accordingly.

Notice in Figures 17-4, 17-5, 17-6, and 17-7 that the first embedded SQL statement in the program is INCLUDE SQLCA. This statement tells the SQL precompiler to include a SQL Communications Area in this program. The specific contents of the SQLCA vary slightly from one brand of DBMS to another, but the SQLCA always provides the same type of information. Figure 17-9 shows the definition of the SQLCA used by the IBM databases (DB2, SQL/DS, and OS/2 Extended Edition). The most important part of the SQLCA, the SQLCODE variable, is supported by all embedded SQL products, and is specified by the ANSI/ISO standard.

THE SQLCODE VARIABLE   As it executes each embedded SQL statement, the DBMS sets the value of the variable SQLCODE in the SQLCA to indicate the completion status of the statement:

- A SQLCODE of zero indicates successful completion of the statement, without any errors or warnings.

- A negative SQLCODE value indicates a serious error that prevented the statement from executing correctly. For example, an attempt to update a read-only view would produce a negative SQLCODE value. A separate negative value is assigned to each run-time error that can occur.

- A positive SQLCODE value indicates a warning condition. For example, truncation or rounding of a data item retrieved by the program would produce a warning. A separate positive value is assigned to each run-time warning that can occur.

Because every executable embedded SQL statement can potentially generate an error, a well written program will check the SQLCODE value after *every* executable embedded SQL statement. Figure 17-10 shows a C program excerpt that checks the SQLCODE value. Figure 17-11 shows a similar excerpt from a COBOL program.

```
struct sqlca {
   unsigned char sqlcaid[8];          /* the string "SQLCA    " */
   long          sqlcabc;             /* length of SQLCA, in bytes */
   long          sqlcode;             /* SQL status code */
   short         sqlerrml;            /* length of sqlerrmc array data */
   unsigned char sqlerrmc[70];        /* name(s) of object(s) causing error */
   unsigned char sqlerrp[8];          /* diagnostic information */
   long          sqlerrd[6];          /* various counts and error codes */
   unsigned char sqlwarn[8];          /* warning flag array */
   unsigned char sqlext[8];           /* extension to sqlwarn array */
}

#define SQLCODE  sqlca.sqlcode        /* SQL status code */

/* A 'W' in any of the SQLWARN fields signals a warning condition;
   otherwise these fields each contain a blank */

#define SQLWARN0 sqlca.sqlwarn[0]     /* master warning flag */
#define SQLWARN1 sqlca.sqlwarn[1]     /* string truncated */
#define SQLWARN2 sqlca.sqlwarn[2]     /* NULLs eliminated from column function */
#define SQLWARN3 sqlca.sqlwarn[3]     /* too few/too many host variables */
#define SQLWARN4 sqlca.sqlwarn[4]     /* prepared UPDATE/DELETE without WHERE */
#define SQLWARN5 sqlca.sqlwarn[5]     /* SQL/DS vs DB2 incompatibility */
#define SQLWARN6 sqlca.sqlwarn[6]     /* invalid date in arithmetic expr */
#define SQLWARN7 sqlca.sqlwarn[7]     /* reserved */
```

Figure 17-9.   *The SQL Communications Area* (SQLCA) *for IBM databases*

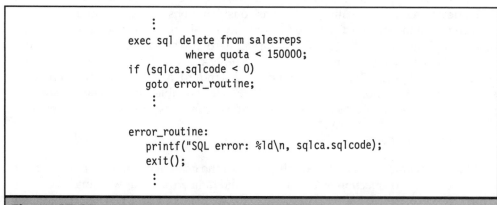

```
            ⋮
         exec sql delete from salesreps
                 where quota < 150000;
         if (sqlca.sqlcode < 0)
            goto error_routine;
            ⋮

         error_routine:
            printf("SQL error: %ld\n, sqlca.sqlcode);
            exit();
            ⋮
```

Figure 17-10.   *A C program excerpt with* SQLCODE *error checking*

```
                  ⋮
         01  PRINT-MESSAGE.
               02  FILLER    PIC X(11) VALUE 'SQL error: '.
               02  PRINT-CODE PIC SZ(9).
               ⋮
                   EXEC SQL DELETE FROM SALESREPS
                           WHERE QUOTA < 150000
                   END-EXEC.
                   IF SQLCODE NOT = ZERO GOTO ERROR-ROUTINE.
               ⋮
         ERROR-ROUTINE.
                   MOVE SQLCODE TO PRINT-CODE.
                   DISPLAY PRINT-MESSAGE.
               ⋮
```

Figure 17-11.   *A COBOL program excerpt with* SQLCODE *error checking*

THE SQLSTATE **VARIABLE**   By the time the SQL2 standard was being written, virtually all commercial SQL products were using the SQLCODE variable to report error conditions in an embedded SQL program. However, there was no standardization of the error numbers used by the different products to report the same or similar error conditions. Further, because of the significant differences among SQL implementations permitted by the SQL1 standard, there were considerable differences in the errors that could occur from one implementation to another.

Instead of tackling the impossible task of getting all of the DBMS vendors to agree to change their SQLCODE values to some standard, the writers of the SQL2 standard took a different approach. They included the SQLCODE error value, but identified it as a "depricated feature", meaning that it was considered obsolete and would be removed from the standard at some future time. To take its place, they introduced a new error variable, called SQLSTATE. The standard also specifies, in detail, the error conditions that can be reported through the SQLSTATE variable, and the error code assigned to each error. To conform to the SQL2 standard, a SQL product must report errors using *both* the SQLCODE and SQLSTATE error variables. In this way, existing programs that use SQLCODE will still function, but new programs can be written to use the standardized SQLSTATE error codes.

The SQLSTATE variable consists of two parts:

- a two-character *error class* which identifies the general classification of the error (such as a "connection error" or an "invalid data error" or a "warning")

- a three-character *error subclass* which identifies a specific type of error within a general error class. For example, within the "invalid data" class, the error subclass might identify a "divide by zero" error or an "invalid numeric value" error or "invalid datetime data"

Errors specified in the SQL2 standard have an error class code that begins with a digit from zero to four (inclusive) or a letter between "A" and "H" (inclusive). For example, data errors are indicated by error class "22". A transaction rollback is indicated by error class "40". A violation of an integrity constraint (such as a foreign key definition) is indicated by error class "23".

The standard specifically reserves error class codes that begin with digits from five to nine (inclusive) and letters between "I" and "Z" (inclusive) as implementation-specific errors which are not standardized. While this allows differences among DBMS brands to continue, all of the most common errors caused by SQL statements are included in the standardized error class codes. As commercial DBMS implementations move to support the SQLSTATE variable, one of the most troublesome incompatibilities between different SQL products will slowly but surely be eliminated.

THE WHENEVER **STATEMENT**   It quickly becomes tedious for a programmer to write programs that explicitly check the SQLCODE value after each embedded SQL statement. To simplify error handling, embedded SQL supports the WHENEVER statement, shown in Figure 17-12. The WHENEVER statement is a directive to the SQL precompiler, not an executable statement. It tells the precompiler to *automatically* generate error-handling code following every executable embedded SQL statement and specifies what the generated code should do.

You can use the WHENEVER statement to tell the precompiler how to handle three different exception conditions:

- WHENEVER SQLERROR tells the precompiler to generate code to handle errors (negative SQLCODEs).

- WHENEVER SQLWARNING tells the precompiler to generate code to handle warnings (positive SQLCODEs).

- WHENEVER NOT FOUND tells the precompiler to generate code that handles a particular warning—the warning generated by the DBMS when your program tries to retrieve query results when there are no more remaining. This use of the

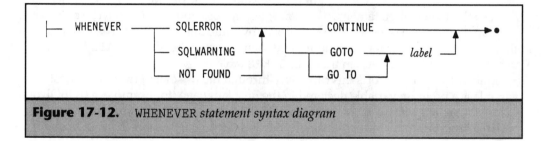

Figure 17-12.   WHENEVER *statement syntax diagram*

WHENEVER statement is specific to the singleton SELECT and the FETCH statements, and is described later in this chapter.

Note that the SQL2 standard does not specify the SQLWARNING form of the WHENEVER statement, but most commercial SQL products support it.

For any of these three conditions, you can tell the precompiler to generate code that takes one of two actions:

■ WHENEVER/GOTO tells the precompiler to generate a branch to the specified *label*, which must be a statement label or statement number in the program.

■ WHENEVER/CONTINUE tells the precompiler to let the program's flow of control proceed to the next host language statement.

The WHENEVER statement is a directive to the precompiler, and its effect can be superseded by another WHENEVER statement appearing later in the program text. Figure 17-13 shows a program excerpt with three WHENEVER statements and four executable SQL statements. In this program, an error in either of the two DELETE statements results in a branch to error1 because of the first WHENEVER statement. An error in the embedded UPDATE statement flows directly into the following statements of the program. An error in the embedded INSERT statement results in a branch to error2. As this example shows, the main use of the WHENEVER/CONTINUE form of the statement is to cancel the effect of a previous WHENEVER statement.

The WHENEVER statement makes embedded SQL error handling much simpler, and it is more common for an application program to use it than to check SQLCODE directly. Remember, however, that after a WHENEVER/GOTO statement appears, the precompiler will generate a test and a branch to the specified label for *every* embedded SQL statement that follows it. You must arrange your program so that the specified label is a valid target for branching from these embedded SQL statements, or use another WHENEVER statement to specify a different destination or cancel the effects of the WHENEVER/GOTO.

Using Host Variables

The embedded SQL programs in the previous figures don't provide any real interaction between the programming statements and the embedded SQL statements. In most applications, you will want to use the value of one or more program variables in the embedded SQL statements. For example, suppose you wanted to write a program to adjust all sales quotas up or down by some dollar amount. The program should prompt the user for the amount and then use an embedded UPDATE statement to change the QUOTA column in the SALESREPS table.

Embedded SQL supports this capability through the use of *host variables*. A host variable is a program variable declared in the host language (for example, a COBOL or C variable) that is referenced in an embedded SQL statement. To identify the host variable, the variable name is prefixed by a colon (:) when it appears in an embedded

```
                  ⋮
         exec sql whenever sqlerror goto error1;

         exec sql delete from salesreps
                  where quota < 150000;

         exec sql delete from customers
                  where credit_limit < 20000;

         exec sql whenever sqlerror continue;

         exec sql update salesreps
                  set quota = quota * 1.05;

         exec sql whenever sqlerror goto error2;

         exec sql insert into salesreps (empl_num, name, quota)
                  values (116, 'Jan Hamilton', 100000.00);
                  ⋮

error1:
    printf("SQL DELETE error: %ld\n", sqlca.sqlcode);
    exit();

error2:
    printf("SQL INSERT error: %ld\n", sqlca.sqlcode);
    exit();
                  ⋮
```

Figure 17-13. *Using the* WHENEVER *statement*

SQL statement. The colon allows the precompiler to distinguish easily between host variables and database objects (such as tables or columns) which may have the same name.

Figure 17-14 shows a C program that implements the quota adjustment application using a host variable. The program prompts the user for the adjustment amount and stores the entered value in the variable named `amount`. This host variable is referenced in the embedded UPDATE statement. Conceptually, when the UPDATE statement is executed, the value of the `amount` variable is obtained, and that value is substituted for the host variable in the SQL statement. For example, if you enter the

```
    main()
    {
       exec sql include sqlca;
       exec sql begin declare section;
          float amount;                    /* amount (from user) */
       exec sql end declare section;

       /* Prompt the user for the amount of quota increase/decrease */
       printf("Raise/lower quotas by how much: ");
       scanf("%f", &amount);

       /* Update the QUOTA column in the SALESREPS table */
       exec sql update salesreps
                   set quota = quota + :amount;

       /* Check results of statement execution */
       if (sqlqa.sqlcode != 0)
          printf("Error during update.\n");
       else
          printf("Update successful.\n");

       exit();
    }
```

Figure 17-14. *Using host variables*

amount 500 in response to the prompt, the DBMS effectively executes this UPDATE
statement:

```
exec sql update salesreps
          set quota = quota + 500;
```

A host variable can appear in an embedded SQL statement wherever a constant
can appear. In particular, a host variable can be used in an assignment expression:

```
exec sql update salesreps
          set quota = quota + :amount;
```

A host variable can appear in a search condition:

```
exec sql delete from salesreps
         where quota < :amount;
```

A host variable can also be used in the VALUES clause of an insert statement:

```
exec sql insert into salesreps (empl_num, name, quota)
         values (116, 'Bill Roberts', :amount);
```

In each case, note that the host variable is part of the program's *input* to the DBMS; it forms part of the SQL statement submitted to the DBMS for execution. Later in this chapter, you will see how host variables are also used to receive *output* from the DBMS; they receive query results returned from the DBMS to the program.

Note that a host variable *cannot* be used instead of a SQL identifier. This attempted use of the host variable colname is illegal:

```
char *colname = "quota";

exec sql insert into salesreps (empl_num, name, :colname)
         values (116, 'Bill Roberts', 0.00);
```

DECLARING HOST VARIABLES   When you use a host variable in an embedded SQL statement, you must declare the variable using the normal method for declaring variables in the host programming language. For example, in Figure 17-14, the host variable amount is declared using the normal C language syntax (float amount;). When the precompiler processes the source code for the program, it notes the name of each variable it encounters, along with its data type and size. The precompiler uses this information to generate correct code later when it encounters a use of the variable as a host variable in a SQL statement.

The two embedded SQL statements BEGIN DECLARE SECTION and END DECLARE SECTION bracket the host variable declarations, as shown in Figure 17-14. These two statements are unique to embedded SQL, and they are not executable. They are directives to the precompiler, telling it when it must "pay attention" to variable declarations and when it can ignore them.

In a simple embedded SQL program, it may be possible to gather all of the host variable declarations together in one "declare section." Usually, however, the host variables must be declared at various points within the program, especially in block-structured languages such as C, Pascal, and PL/I. In this case each declaration of host variables must be bracketed with a BEGIN DECLARE SECTION/END DECLARE SECTION statement pair.

The BEGIN DECLARE SECTION and END DECLARE SECTION statements are relatively new to the embedded SQL language. They are specified in the ANSI/ISO SQL standard, and DB2 requires them in embedded SQL for C, which was introduced in DB2 Version 2. However, DB2 and many other DBMS brands did not historically require declare sections, and some SQL precompilers do not yet support the BEGIN DECLARE SECTION and END DECLARE SECTION statements. In this case the precompiler scans and processes all variable declarations in the host program.

When you use a host variable, the precompiler may limit your flexibility in declaring the variable in the host programming language. For example, consider the following C language source code:

```
#define BIGBUFSIZE    256
      .
      .
      .
exec sql begin declare section;
    char bigbuffer[BIGBUFSIZE+1];
exec sql end declare section;
```

This is a valid C declaration of the variable bigbuffer. However, if you try to use bigbuffer as a host variable in an embedded SQL statement like this:

```
exec sql update salesreps
           set quota = 300000
         where name = :bigbuffer;
```

many precompilers will generate an error message, complaining about an illegal declaration of bigbuffer. The problem is that many precompilers don't recognize symbolic constants like BIGBUFSIZE. This is just one example of the special considerations that apply when using embedded SQL and a precompiler. Fortunately, the precompilers offered by the major DBMS vendors are being improved steadily, and the number of special case problems like this one is decreasing.

HOST VARIABLES AND DATA TYPES   The data types supported by a SQL-based DBMS and the data types supported by a programming language such as C or FORTRAN are often quite different. These differences impact host variables, because they play a dual role. On the one hand, a host variable is a program variable, declared using the data types of the programming language and manipulated by programming language statements. On the other hand, a host variable is used in embedded SQL statements to contain database data.

Consider the four embedded UPDATE statements in Figure 17-15. In the first UPDATE statement, the MANAGER column has an INTEGER data type, so hostvar1 should be declared as a C integer variable. In the second statement, the NAME column has a VARCHAR data type, so hostvar2 should contain string data. The program should declare hostvar2 as an array of C character data, and most DBMS products

```
                                 ⋮
                    exec sql begin declare section;
                        int   hostvar1  = 106;
                        char  *hostvar2 = "Joe Smith";
                        float hostvar3  = 150000.00;
                        char  *hostvar4 = "01-JUN-1990";
                    exec sql end declare section;

                    exec sql update salesreps
                                set manager = :hostvar1
                            where empl_num = 102;

                    exec sql update salesreps
                                set name = :hostvar2
                            where empl_num = 102;

                    exec sql update salesreps
                                set quota = :hostvar3
                            where empl_num = 102;

                    exec sql update salesreps
                                set hire_date = :hostvar4
                            where empl_num = 102;
                                 ⋮
```

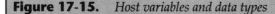

Figure 17-15. *Host variables and data types*

will expect the data in the array to be terminated by a null character (0). In the third
UPDATE statement, the QUOTA column has a MONEY data type. There is no
corresponding data type in C, and C does not support a packed decimal data type. For
most DBMS brands, you can declare hostvar3 as a C floating point variable, and the
DBMS will automatically translate the floating-point value into the DBMS MONEY
format. Finally, in the fourth UPDATE statement, the HIRE_DATE column has a DATE
data type in the database. For most DBMS brands, you should declare hostvar4 as
an array of C character data, and fill the array with a text form of the date acceptable
to the DBMS. As Figure 17-15 shows, the data types of host variables must be chosen
carefully to match their intended usage in embedded SQL statements. Table 17-2
shows the most frequently used SQL data types and the corresponding data types in
various programming languages. Note, however, that in many cases there is not a
one-to-one correspondence between data types. In addition, each brand of DBMS has
its own data type idiosyncrasies and its own rules for data type conversion when
using host variables. Before counting on a specific data conversion behavior, consult

SQL Type	C Type	COBOL Type	FORTRAN Type	PL/I Type
SMALLINT	short	PIC S9 (4) COMP	INTEGER*2	FIXED BIN(15)
INTEGER	int	PIC S9 (9) COMP	INTEGER*4	FIXED BIN(31)
FLOAT	float	COMP-1	REAL*4	BIN FLOAT(21)
DOUBLE	double	COMP-2	REAL*8	BIN FLOAT(53)
DECIMAL(*p,s*)	double[1]	PIC S9 (*p-s*) V9(*s*) COMP-3	REAL*8[1]	FIXED DEC(*p,s*)
MONEY(*p,s*)	double[1]	PIC S9 (*p-s*) V9(*s*) COMP-3	REAL*8[1]	FIXED DEC(*p,s*)
CHAR(*n*)	char x[*n+1*][2]	PIC X (*n*)	CHARACTER**n*	CHAR(*n*)

VARCHAR(*n*)	struct { [3]
	  short len;
	  char x[*n+1*] }
	}
		01 X
		  02 LEN PIC S9 (4) COMP
		  02 DATA PIC X(*n*)
			CHARACTER**n*[4]	CHAR(*n*) VAR

DATE	char x[12][5]	PIC X(11)[5]	CHARACTER*11[5]	CHAR(11)[5]
TIME	char x[9][5]	PIC X(8)[5]	CHARACTER*8[5]	CHAR(8)[5]
TIMESTAMP	char x[28][5]	PIC X(27)[5]	CHARACTER*27[5]	CHAR(27)[5]

Notes:

[1] Host language does not support packed decimal data; conversion to or from floating-point data may cause truncation or round off errors.

[2] The DBMS may or may not return a C string with a null-terminator character.

[3] Some DBMS brands (including DB2, OS/2 EE, and Oracle) use this VARCHAR structure; other brands (including Informix and Ingres) support normal null-terminated C strings.

[4] Host language does not support variable-length strings; all string data is treated as fixed-length, blank-padded strings.

[5] Assumes date/time data types converted to character strings in "dd-mmm-yyyy", "hh:mm:ss", and "dd-mmm-yyyy hh:mm:ss:fffff" formats. Some DBMS brands return date/time data in a binary representation.

Table 17-2. *Data Types in SQL and Host Languages*

the documentation for your particular DBMS brand and carefully read the description for the particular programming language you are using.

HOST VARIABLES AND NULL **VALUES**   Most programming languages do not provide SQL-style support for unknown or missing values. A C, COBOL, or FORTRAN variable, for example, always has a value. There is no concept of the value being NULL or missing. This causes a problem when you want to store NULL values in the database or retrieve NULL values from the database using programmatic SQL. Embedded SQL solves this problem by allowing each host variable to have a companion *host indicator variable.* In an embedded SQL statement, the host variable and the indicator variable *together* specify a single SQL-style value, as follows:

- An indicator value of zero means that the host variable contains a valid value and that this value is to be used.

- A negative indicator value means that the host variable should be assumed to have a NULL value; the actual value of the host variable is irrelevant and should be disregarded.

- A positive indicator value means that the host variable contains a valid value, which may have been rounded off or truncated. This situation only occurs when data is retrieved from the database, and is described later in this chapter.

When you specify a host variable in an embedded SQL statement, you can follow it immediately with the name of the corresponding indicator variable. Both variable names are preceded by a colon. Here is an embedded UPDATE statement that uses the host variable amount with the companion indicator variable amount_ind:

```
exec sql update salesreps
        set quota = :amount :amount_ind, sales = :amount2
        where quota < 20000.00;
```

If amount_ind has a nonnegative value when the UPDATE statement is executed, the DBMS treats the statement as if it read:

```
exec sql update salesreps
        set quota = :amount, sales = :amount2
        where quota < 20000.00;
```

If amount_ind has a negative value when the UPDATE statement is executed, the DBMS treats the statement as if it read:

```
exec sql update salesreps
        set quota = NULL, sales = :amount2
        where quota < 20000.00;
```

A host variable/indicator variable pair can appear in the assignment clause of an embedded UPDATE statement (as shown here), or in the values clause of an embedded INSERT statement. You cannot use an indicator variable in a search condition, so this embedded SQL statement is illegal:

```
exec sql delete from salesreps
        where quota = :amount :amount_ind;
```

This prohibition exists for the same reason that the NULL keyword is not allowed in the search condition — it makes no sense to test whether QUOTA and NULL are equal, because the answer will always be NULL (unknown). Instead of using the indicator variable, you must use an explicit IS NULL test. This pair of embedded SQL statements accomplishes the intended task of the preceding illegal statement:

```
if (amount_ind < 0)  {
   exec sql delete from salesreps
           where quota is null;
}
else {
   exec sql delete from salesreps
           where quota = :amount;
}
```

Indicator variables are especially useful when you are retrieving data from the database into your program and the retrieved data values may be NULL. This use of indicator variables is described later in this chapter.

Data Retrieval in Embedded SQL

Using the embedded SQL features described thus far, you can embed any interactive SQL statement *except* the SELECT statement in an application program. Retrieving data with an embedded SQL program requires some special extensions to the SELECT statement. The reason for these extensions is that there is a fundamental mismatch between the SQL language and programming languages such as C and COBOL: a SQL query produces an entire *table* of query results, but most programming languages can only manipulate individual data items or individual records (rows) of data.

Embedded SQL must build a "bridge" between the table-level logic of the SQL
`SELECT` statement and the row-by-row processing of C, COBOL, and other host
programming languages. For this reason, embedded SQL divides SQL queries into
two groups:

- *Single-row queries,* where you expect the query results to contain a single row of
  data. Looking up a customer's credit limit or retrieving the sales and quota for a
  particular salesperson are examples of this type of query.

- *Multi-row queries,* where you expect that the query results may contain zero,
  one, or many rows of data. Listing the orders with amounts over $20,000 or
  retrieving the names of all salespeople who are over quota are examples of this
  type of query.

Interactive SQL does not distinguish between these two types of queries; the same
interactive `SELECT` statement handles them both. In embedded SQL, however, the
two types of queries are handled very differently. Single-row queries are simpler to
handle, and are discussed in the next section. Multi-row queries are discussed later in
this chapter.

Single-Row Queries

Many useful SQL queries return a single row of query results. Single-row queries are
especially common in transaction processing programs, where a user enters a
customer number or an order number and the program retrieves relevant data about
the customer or order. In embedded SQL, single-row queries are handled by the
singleton `SELECT` statement, shown in Figure 17-16. The singleton `SELECT` statement
has a syntax much like that of the interactive `SELECT` statement. It has a `SELECT`
clause, a `FROM` clause, and an optional `WHERE` clause. Because the singleton `SELECT`
statement returns a single row of data, there is no need for a `GROUP  BY`, `HAVING`, or
`ORDER  BY` clause. The `INTO` clause specifies the host variables which are to receive
the data retrieved by the statement.

Figure 17-17 shows a simple program with a singleton `SELECT` statement. The
program prompts the user for an employee number, and then retrieves the name,
quota, and sales of the corresponding salesperson. The DBMS places the three
retrieved data items into the host variables `repname`, `repquota`, and `repsales`,
respectively.

Recall that the host variables used in the `INSERT`, `DELETE`, and `UPDATE`
statements in the previous examples were input host variables. By contrast, the host
variables specified in the `INTO` clause of the singleton `SELECT` statement are *output*
host variables. Each host variable named in the `INTO` clause receives a single column
from the row of query results. The select list items and the corresponding host
variables are paired in sequence, as they appear in their respective clauses, and the
number of query results columns must be the same as the number of host variables. In

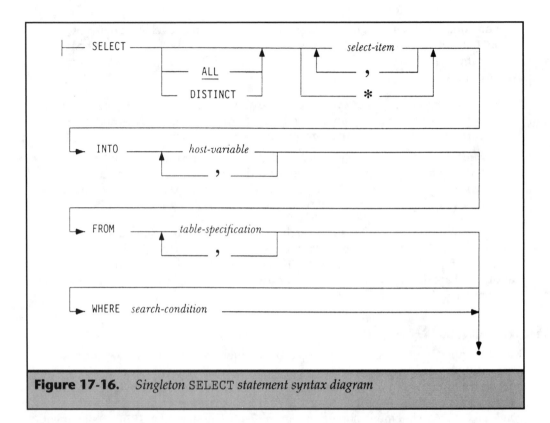

Figure 17-16. *Singleton* SELECT *statement syntax diagram*

addition, the data type of each host variable must be compatible with the data type of the corresponding column of query results.

As discussed earlier, most DBMS brands will automatically handle "reasonable" conversions between DBMS data types and the data types supported by the programming language. For example, most DBMS products will convert MONEY data retrieved from the database into packed decimal (COMP-3) data before storing it in a COBOL variable, or into floating-point data before storing it in a C variable. The precompiler uses its knowledge of the host variable's data type to handle the conversion correctly.

Variable-length text data must also be converted before being stored in a host variable. Typically, a DBMS converts VARCHAR data into a null-terminated string for C programs and into a variable-length string (with a leading character count) for Pascal programs. For COBOL and FORTRAN programs, the host variable must generally be declared as a data structure with an integer "count" field and a character array. The DBMS returns the actual characters of data in the character array, and it returns the length of the data in the count field of the data structure.

If a DBMS supports date/time data or other data types, other conversions are necessary. Some DBMS products return their internal date/time representations into an integer host variable. Others convert the date/time data to text format and return it into a string host variable. Table 17-2 summarized the data type conversions typically provided by DBMS products, but you must consult the embedded SQL documentation for your particular DBMS brand for specific information.

THE NOT FOUND **CONDITION**   Like all embedded SQL statements, the singleton SELECT statement sets the value of SQLCODE to indicate its completion status:

- If a *single row* of query results is successfully retrieved, SQLCODE is set to zero; the host variables named in the INTO clause contain the retrieved values.
- If the query produced an *error,* SQLCODE is set to a negative value; the host variables do not contain retrieved values.
- If the query produced *no rows* of query results, a special NOT FOUND warning value is returned in SQLCODE.
- If the query produced *more than one row* of query results, it is treated as an error, and a negative SQLCODE is returned.

The SQL1 standard specifies the NOT FOUND warning condition, but it does not specify a particular value to be returned. DB2 uses the value +100, and most other SQL products follow this convention, including the other IBM SQL products, Ingres, and SQLBase. This value is also specified in the SQL2 standard, but as noted previously, SQL2 strongly encourages the use of the new SQLSTATE error variable instead of the older SQLCODE values.

RETRIEVING NULL **VALUES**   If the data to be retrieved from a database may contain NULL values, the singleton SELECT statement must provide a way for the DBMS to communicate the NULL values to the application program. To handle NULL values, embedded SQL uses indicator variables in the INTO clause, just as they are used in the VALUES clause of the INSERT statement and the SET clause of the UPDATE statement.

When you specify a host variable in the INTO clause, you can follow it immediately with the name of a companion host indicator variable. Figure 17-18 shows a revised version of the program in Figure 17-17 that uses the indicator variable repquota_ind with the host variable repquota. Because the NAME and SALES columns are declared NOT NULL in the definition of the SALESREPS table, they cannot produce NULL output values, and no indicator variable is needed for those columns.

After the SELECT statement has been executed, the value of the indicator variable tells the program how to interpret the returned data:

■ An indicator value of zero means the host variable has been assigned a retrieved value by the DBMS. The application program can use the value of the host variable in its processing.

■ A negative indicator value means the retrieved value was NULL. The value of the host variable is irrelevant and should not be used by the application program.

■ A positive indicator value indicates a warning condition of some kind, such as a rounding error or string truncation.

```
main()
{
    exec sql begin declare section;
        int    repnum;                /* employee number (from user) */
        char   repname[16];           /* retrieved salesperson name */
        float  repquota;              /* retrieved quota */
        float  repsales;              /* retrieved sales */
    exec sql end declare section;

    /* Prompt the user for the employee number */
    printf("Enter salesrep number: ");
    scanf("%d", &repnum);

    /* Execute the SQL query */
    exec sql select name, quota, sales
            from salesreps
          where empl_num = :repnum
            into :repname, :repquota, :repsales;

    /* Display the retrieved data */
    if (sqlca.sqlcode == 0) {
        printf("Name:  %s\n", repname);
        printf("Quota: %f\n", repquota);
        printf("Sales: %f\n", repsales);
    }
    else if (sqlca.sqlcode == 100)
        printf("No salesperson with that employee number.\n");
    else
        printf("SQL error: %ld\n", sqlca.sqlcode);

    exit();
}
```

Figure 17-17.   *Using the singleton* SELECT *statement*

Because you cannot tell in advance when a NULL value will be retrieved, you should *always* specify an indicator variable in the INTO clause for any column of query results that may contain a NULL value. If the SELECT statement produces a column containing a NULL value and you have not specified an indicator variable for the column, the DBMS will treat the statement as an error and return a negative SQLCODE. Thus indicator variables *must* be used to retrieve rows containing NULL data successfully.

Although the major use of indicator variables is for handling NULL values, the DBMS also uses indicator variables to signal warning conditions. For example, if an arithmetic overflow or division by zero makes one of the query results columns invalid, DB2 returns a warning SQLCODE of +802 and sets the indicator variable for the affected column to –2. The application program can respond to the SQLCODE and examine the indicator variables to determine which column contains invalid data.

DB2 also uses indicator variables to signal string truncation. If the query results contain a column of character data that is too large for the corresponding host variable, DB2 copies the first part of the character string into the host variable and sets the corresponding indicator variable to the full length of the string. The application program can examine the indicator variable and may want to retry the SELECT statement with a different host variable that can hold a larger string.

These additional uses of indicator variables are fairly common in commercial SQL products, but the specific warning code values vary from one product to another. They are not specified by the ANSI/ISO SQL standard.

RETRIEVAL USING DATA STRUCTURES   Some programming languages support *data structures*, which are named collections of variables. For these languages, a SQL precompiler may allow you to treat the entire data structure as a single, composite host variable in the INTO clause. Instead of specifying a separate host variable as the destination for each column of query results, you can specify a data structure as the destination for the entire row. Figure 17-19 shows the program from Figure 17-18, rewritten to use a C data structure.

When the precompiler encounters a data structure reference in the INTO clause, it replaces the structure reference with a list of the individual variables in the structure, in the order they are declared within the structure. Thus the number of items in the structure and their data types must correspond to the columns of query results. The use of data structures in the INTO clause is, in effect, a "shortcut." It does not fundamentally change the way the INTO clause works.

The use of data structures as host variables is not supported by all DBMS brands today. However, it has been added to DB2 and will probably be adopted by other DBMS products over time. The use of data structures is also restricted to certain programming languages. DB2 supports C and PL/I structures, but does not support COBOL or assembly language structures, for example.

INPUT AND OUTPUT HOST VARIABLES   Host variables provide two-way communication between the program and the DBMS. In the program shown in Figure

```
main()
{
   exec sql include sqlca;
   exec sql begin declare section;
      int   repnum;                 /* employee number (from user) */
      char  repname[16];            /* retrieved salesperson name */
      float repquota;               /* retrieved quota */
      float repsales;               /* retrieved sales */
      short repquota_ind;           /* null quota indicator */
   exec sql end declare section;

   /* Prompt the user for the employee number */
   printf("Enter salesrep number: ");
   scanf("%d", &repnum);

   /* Execute the SQL query */
   exec sql select name, quota, sales
            from salesreps
            where empl_num = :repnum
            into :repname, :repquota :repquota_ind, :repsales;

   /* Display the retrieved data */
   if (sqlca.sqlcode == 0) {
      printf("Name:  %s\n", repname);
      if (repquota_ind < 0)
         printf("Quota is NULL\n");
      else
         printf("Quota: %f\n", repquota);
      printf("Sales: %f\n", repsales);
   }
   else if (sqlca.sqlcode == 100)
      printf("No salesperson with that employee number.\n");
   else
      printf("SQL error: %ld\n", sqlca.sqlcode);

   exit();
}
```

Figure 17-18. *Using singleton* SELECT *with indicator variables*

```
main()
{
   exec sql include sqlca;
   exec sql begin declare section;
      int repnum;                  /* employee number (from user) */
      struct {
         char  name[16];           /* retrieved salesperson name */
         float quota;              /* retrieved quota */
         float sales;              /* retrieved sales */
      } repinfo;
      short rep_ind[3];            /* null indicator array */
   exec sql end declare section;

   /* Prompt the user for the employee number */
   printf("Enter salesrep number: ");
   scanf("%d", &repnum);

   /* Execute the SQL query */
   exec sql select name, quota, sales
            from salesreps
            where empl_num = :repnum
            into :repinfo :rep_ind;

   /* Display the retrieved data */
   if (sqlca.sqlcode == 0) {
      printf("Name:  %s\n",repinfo.name);
      if (rep_ind[1] < 0)
         printf("Quota is NULL\n");
      else
         printf("Quota: %f\n", repinfo.quota);
      printf("Sales: %f\n", repinfo.sales);
   }
   else if (sqlca.sqlcode == 100)
      printf("No salesperson with that employee number.\n");
   else
      printf("SQL error: %ld\n", sqlca.sqlcode);

   exit();
}
```

Figure 17-19. *Using a data structure as a host variable*

17-18, the host variables `repnum` and `repname` illustrate the two different roles played by host variables:

- The `repnum` host variable is an *input* host variable, used to pass data from the program to the DBMS. The program assigns a value to the variable before executing the embedded statement, and that value becomes part of the `SELECT` statement to be executed by the DBMS. The DBMS does nothing to alter the value of the variable.

- The `repname` host variable is an *output* host variable, used to pass data back from the DBMS to the program. The DBMS assigns a value to this variable as it executes the embedded `SELECT` statement. After the statement has been executed, the program can use the resulting value.

Input and output host variables are declared the same way and are specified using the same colon notation within an embedded SQL statement. However, it's often useful to think in terms of input and output host variables when you're actually coding an embedded SQL program. Input host variables can be used in any SQL statement where a constant can appear. Output host variables are used only with the singleton `SELECT` statement and with the `FETCH` statement, described later in this chapter.

Multi-Row Queries

When a query produces an entire table of query results, embedded SQL must provide a way for the application program to process the query results one row at a time. Embedded SQL supports this capability by defining a new SQL concept, called a *cursor,* and adding several statements to the interactive SQL language. Here is an overview of embedded SQL technique for multi-row query processing and the new statements it requires:

1. The `DECLARE CURSOR` statement specifies the query to be performed and associates a *cursor* name with the query.

2. The `OPEN` statement asks the DBMS to start executing the query and generating query results. It positions the cursor before the first row of query results.

3. The `FETCH` statement advances the cursor to the first row of query results and retrieves its data into host variables for use by the application program. Subsequent `FETCH` statements move through the query results row by row, advancing the cursor to the next row of query results and retrieving its data into the host variables.

4. The `CLOSE` statement ends access to the query results and breaks the association between the cursor and the query results.

Figure 17-20 shows a program that uses embedded SQL to perform a simple multi-row query. The numbered callouts in the figure correspond to the numbers in the steps above. The program retrieves and displays, in alphabetical order, the name,

```
main()
{
    exec sql include sqlca;
    exec sql begin declare section;
        char  repname[16];              /* retrieved salesperson name */
        float repquota;                 /* retrieved quota */
        float repsales;                 /* retrieved sales */
        short repquota_ind;             /* null quota indicator */
    exec sql end declare section;

    /* Declare the cursor for the query */
    exec sql declare repcurs cursor for        ◄───────────────── ①
            select name, quota, sales
                from salesreps
                where sales > quota
                order by name;

    /* Set up error processing */
    whenever sqlerror goto error;
    whenever not found goto done;

    /* Open the cursor to start the query */
    exec sql open repcurs;             ◄─────────────────────── ②

    /* Loop through each row of query results */
    for ( ; ; ) {

        /* Fetch the next row of query results */
        exec sql fetch repcurs         ◄───────────────────── ③
                into :repname, :repquota :repquota_ind, :repsales;

        /* Display the retrieved data */
        printf("Name: %s\n", repname);
        if (repquota_ind < 0)
            printf("Quota is NULL\n");
        else
            printf("Quota: %f\n", repquota);
        printf("Sales: %f\n", repsales);
    }

error:
    printf("SQL error: %ld\n", sqlca.sqlcode);
    exit();

done:
    /* Query complete; close the cursor */
    exec sql close repcurs;            ◄───────────────────── ④
    exit();
}
```

Figure 17-20. *Multi-row query processing*

quota, and year-to-date sales of each salesperson whose sales exceed quota. The interactive SQL query that prints this information is:

```
SELECT NAME, QUOTA, SALES
  FROM SALESREPS
 WHERE SALES > QUOTA
 ORDER BY NAME
```

Notice that this query appears, word for word, in the embedded DECLARE CURSOR statement in Figure 17-20. The statement also associates the cursor name repcurs with the query. This cursor name is used later in the OPEN CURSOR statement to start the query and position the cursor before the first row of query results.

The FETCH statement inside the for loop fetches the next row of query results each time the loop is executed. The INTO clause of the FETCH statement works just like the INTO clause of the singleton SELECT statement. It specifies the host variables that are to receive the fetched data items—one host variable for each column of query results. As in previous examples, a host indicator variable (repquota_ind) is used when a fetched data item may contain NULL values.

When there are no more rows of query results to be fetched, the DBMS returns the NOT FOUND warning in response to the FETCH statement. This is exactly the same warning code that is returned when the singleton SELECT statement does not retrieve a row of data. In this program, the WHENEVER NOT FOUND statement causes the precompiler to generate code that checks the SQLCODE value after the FETCH statement. This generated code branches to the label done when the NOT FOUND condition arises, and to the label error if an error occurs. At the end of the program, the CLOSE statement ends the query and terminates the program's access to the query results.

CURSORS   As the program in Figure 17-20 illustrates, an embedded SQL cursor behaves much like a filename or "file handle" in a programming language such as C or COBOL. Just as a program opens a file to access the file's contents, it opens a cursor to gain access to the query results. Similarly, the program closes a file to end its access and closes a cursor to end access to the query results. Finally, just as a file handle keeps track of the program's current position within an open file, a cursor keeps track of the program's current position within the query results. These parallels between file input/output and SQL cursors make the cursor concept relatively easy for application programmers to understand.

Despite the parallels between files and cursors, there are also some differences. Opening a SQL cursor usually involves much more overhead than opening a file, because opening the cursor actually causes the DBMS to begin carrying out the associated query. In addition, SQL cursors support only forward, sequential motion through the query results, like sequential file processing. In most current SQL implementations, there is no cursor analog to the random access provided to the individual records of a file.

Cursors provide a great deal of flexibility for processing queries in an embedded SQL program. By declaring and opening multiple cursors, the program can process several sets of query results in parallel. For example, the program might retrieve some rows of query results, display them on the screen for its user, and then respond to a user's request for more detailed data by launching a second query. The following sections describe in detail the four embedded SQL statements that define and manipulate cursors.

THE DECLARE CURSOR **STATEMENT**   The DECLARE CURSOR statement, shown in Figure 17-21, defines a query to be performed. The statement also associates a cursor name with the query. The cursor name must be a valid SQL identifier. It is used to identify the query and its results in other embedded SQL statements. The cursor name is specifically *not* a host language variable; it is declared by the DECLARE CURSOR statement, not in a host language declaration.

The SELECT statement in the DECLARE CURSOR statement defines the query associated with the cursor. The select statement can be any valid interactive SQL SELECT statement, as described in Chapters 6 through 9. In particular, the SELECT statement must include a FROM clause and may optionally include WHERE, GROUP BY, HAVING, and ORDER BY clauses. The SELECT statement may also include the UNION operator, as described in Chapter 6. Thus an embedded SQL query can use any of the query capabilities that are available in the interactive SQL language.

The query specified in the DECLARE CURSOR statement may also include input host variables. These host variables perform exactly the same function as in the embedded INSERT, DELETE, UPDATE, and singleton SELECT statements. An input host variable can appear within the query anywhere that a constant can appear. Note that output host variables *cannot* appear in the query. Unlike the singleton SELECT statement, the SELECT statement within the DECLARE CURSOR statement has no INTO clause and does not retrieve any data. The INTO clause appears as part of the FETCH statement, described later in this chapter.

As its name implies, the DECLARE CURSOR statement is a declaration of the cursor. In most SQL implementations, including the IBM SQL products, this statement is a directive for the SQL precompiler; it is not an executable statement, and the precompiler does not produce any code for it. Like all declarations, the DECLARE CURSOR statement must physically appear in the program before any statements that reference the cursor that it declares. Most SQL implementations treat the cursor name

├──   DECLARE *cursor-name* CURSOR FOR *select-statement* ──────▶●

Figure 17-21.   DECLARE CURSOR *statement syntax diagram*

as a global name that can be referenced inside any procedures, functions, or subroutines that appear after the DECLARE CURSOR statement.

It's worth noting that not all SQL implementations treat the DECLARE CURSOR statement strictly as a declarative statement, and this can lead to subtle problems. Some SQL precompilers actually generate code for the DECLARE CURSOR statement (either host language declarations, or calls to the DBMS, or both), giving it some of the qualities of an executable statement. For these precompilers, the DECLARE CURSOR statement must not only physically precede the OPEN, FETCH, and CLOSE statements that reference its cursor, it must sometimes precede these statements in the flow of execution or be placed in the same block as the other statements.

In general you can avoid problems with the DECLARE CURSOR statement by following these guidelines:

■ Place the DECLARE CURSOR statement right before the OPEN statement for the cursor. This placement ensures the correct physical statement sequence, it puts the DECLARE CURSOR and the OPEN statements in the same block, and it ensures that the flow of control passes through the DECLARE CURSOR statement, if necessary. It also helps to document just what query is being requested by the OPEN statement.

■ Make sure that the FETCH and CLOSE statements for the cursor follow the OPEN statement physically as well as in the flow of control.

THE OPEN STATEMENT   The OPEN statement, shown in Figure 17-22, conceptually "opens" the table of query results for access by the application program. In practice, the OPEN statement actually causes the DBMS to process the query, or at least to begin processing it. The OPEN statement thus causes the DBMS to perform the same work as an interactive SELECT statement, stopping just short of the point where it produces the first row of query results.

The single parameter of the OPEN statement is the name of the cursor to be opened. This cursor must have been previously declared by a DECLARE CURSOR statement. If the query associated with the cursor contains an error, the OPEN statement will produce a negative SQLCODE value. Most query processing errors, such as a reference to an unknown table, an ambiguous column name, or an attempt to retrieve data from

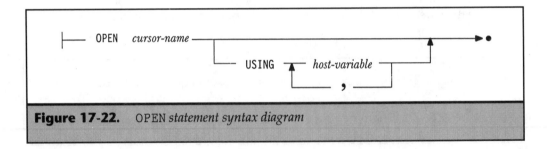

Figure 17-22.   OPEN *statement syntax diagram*

a table without the proper permission, will be reported as a result of the OPEN statement. In practice, very few errors occur during the subsequent FETCH statements.

Once opened, a cursor remains in the open state until it is closed with the CLOSE statement. The DBMS also closes all open cursors automatically at the end of a transaction (that is, when the DBMS executes a COMMIT or ROLLBACK statement). After the cursor has been closed, it can be reopened by executing the OPEN statement a second time. Note that the DBMS restarts the query "from scratch" each time it executes the OPEN statement.

THE FETCH **STATEMENT**   The FETCH statement, shown in Figure 17-23, retrieves the *next* row of query results for use by the application program. The cursor named in the FETCH statement specifies which row of query results is to be fetched. It must identify a cursor previously opened by the OPEN statement.

The FETCH statement fetches the row of data items into a list of host variables, which are specified in the INTO clause of the statement. An indicator variable can be associated with each host variable to handle retrieval of NULL data. The behavior of the indicator variable and the values that it can assume are identical to those described for the singleton SELECT statement earlier in this chapter. The number of host variables in the list must be the same as the number of columns in the query results, and the data types of the host variables must be compatible, column by column, with the columns of query results.

As shown in Figure 17-24, the FETCH statement moves the cursor through the query results, row by row, according to these rules:

- The OPEN statement positions the cursor *before* the first row of query results. In this state, the cursor has no current row.

- The FETCH statement advances the cursor to the *next* available row of query results, if there is one. This row becomes the current row of the cursor.

- If a FETCH statement advances the cursor past the last row of query results, the FETCH statement returns a NOT FOUND warning. In this state, the cursor again has no current row.

- The CLOSE statement ends access to the query results and places the cursor in a closed state.

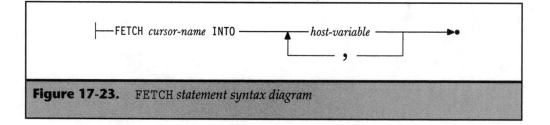

Figure 17-23.   FETCH *statement syntax diagram*

If there are no rows of query results, the OPEN statement still positions the cursor *before* the (empty) query results and returns successfully. The program cannot detect that the OPEN statement has produced an empty set of query results. However, the very first FETCH statement produces the NOT FOUND warning and positions the cursor after the end of the (empty) query results.

THE CLOSE STATEMENT The CLOSE statement, shown in Figure 17-25, conceptually "closes" the table of query results created by the OPEN statement, ending access by the application program. Its single parameter is the name of the cursor associated with the query results, which must be a cursor previously opened by an OPEN statement. The CLOSE statement can be executed at any time after the cursor has been opened. In particular, it is not necessary to FETCH all rows of query results before closing the cursor, although this will usually be the case. All cursors are automatically closed at the end of a transaction. Once a cursor is closed, its query results are no longer available to the application program.

SCROLL CURSORS The SQL1 standard specifies that a cursor can only move forward through the query results. The IBM SQL products and most commercial SQL products support this form of cursor. If the program wants to re-retrieve a row once the cursor has moved past it, the program must CLOSE the cursor and re-OPEN it (causing the DBMS to perform the query again), and then FETCH through the rows until the desired row is reached.

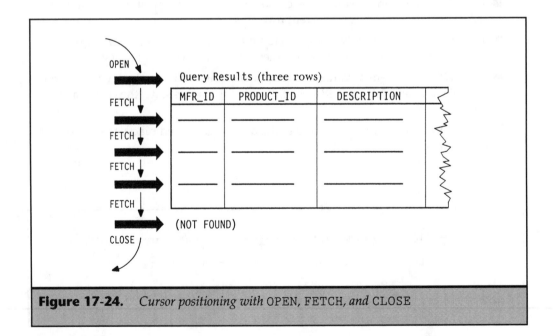

Figure 17-24.   *Cursor positioning with OPEN, FETCH, and CLOSE*

In the early 1990s a few commercial SQL products extended the cursor concept with the concept of a *scroll cursor*. Unlike standard cursors, a scroll cursor provides random access to the rows of query results. The program specifies which row it wants to retrieve through an extension of the FETCH statement, shown in Figure 17-26:

- FETCH FIRST retrieves the first row of query results.
- FETCH LAST retrieves the last row of query results.
- FETCH PRIOR retrieves the row of query results that immediately precedes the current row of the cursor.
- FETCH NEXT retrieves the row of query results that immediately follows the current row of the cursor. This is the default behavior if no motion is specified and corresponds to the standard cursor motion.
- FETCH ABSOLUTE retrieves a specific row by its row number.
- FETCH RELATIVE moves the cursor forward or backward a specific number of rows relative to its current position.

Scroll cursors can be especially useful in programs that allow a user to browse database contents. In response to the user's request to move forward or backward through the data a row or a screenful at a time, the program can simply fetch the required rows of the query results. However, scroll cursors are also a great deal harder for the DBMS to implement than a normal, unidirectional cursor. To support a scroll cursor, the DBMS must keep track of the previous query results that it provided for a program, and the order in which it supplied those rows of results. The DBMS must also insure that no other concurrently executing transaction modifies any data that has become visible to a program through a scroll cursor, because the program can use the extended FETCH statement to re-retrieve the row, even after the cursor has moved past the row.

If you use a scroll cursor, you should be aware that certain FETCH statements on a scroll cursor may have a very high overhead for some DBMS brands. If the DBMS brand normally carries out a query step-by-step as your program FETCH-es its way down through the query results, your program may wait a much longer time than normal if you request a FETCH NEXT operation when the cursor is positioned at the first row of query results. It's best to understand the performance characteristics of your particular DBMS brand before writing programs that depend on scroll cursor functionality for production applications.

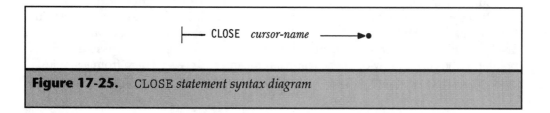

Figure 17-25. CLOSE *statement syntax diagram*

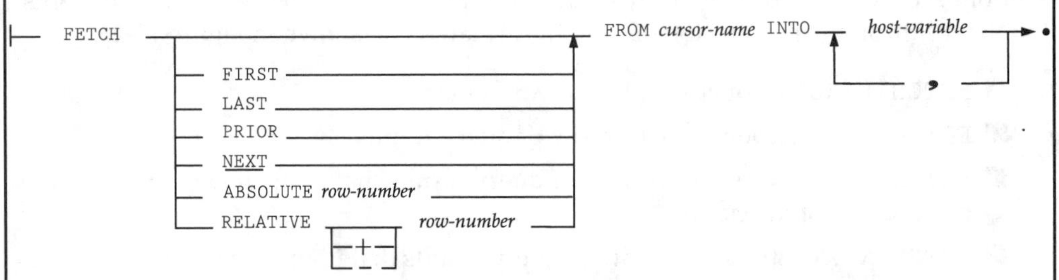

Figure 17-26. *Extended* FETCH *statement for scroll cursors*

Because of the usefulness of scroll cursors, and because a few DBMS vendors had begun to ship scroll cursor implementations that were slightly different from one another, the SQL2 standard included support for scroll cursors. The syntax shown in Figure 17-26 is from the SQL2 standard. The standard also specifies that if any motion other than FETCH NEXT (the default) is used on a cursor, its DECLARE CURSOR statement must explicitly identify it as a scroll cursor. Using the SQL2 syntax, the cursor declaration in Figure 17-20 would appear as:

```
exec sql declare repcurs scroll cursor for
        select name, quota, sales
          from salesreps
         where sales > quota
         order by name;
```

Cursor-Based Deletes and Updates

Application programs often use cursors to allow the user to browse through a table of data row by row. For example, the user may ask to see all of the orders placed by a particular customer. The program declares a cursor for a query of the ORDERS table and displays each order on the screen, possibly in a computer-generated form, waiting for a signal from the user to advance to the next row. Browsing continues in this fashion until the user reaches the end of the query results. The cursor serves as a pointer to the current row of query results. If the query draws its data from a single table, and it is not a summary query, as in this example, the cursor implicitly points to a row of a database table, because each row of query results is drawn from a single row of the table.

While browsing the data, the user may spot data that should be changed. For example, the order quantity in one of the orders may be incorrect, or the customer may want to delete one of the orders. In this situation, the user wants to update or delete "this" order. The row is not identified by the usual SQL search condition; rather, the program uses the cursor as a pointer to indicate which particular row is to be updated or deleted.

Embedded SQL supports this capability through special versions of the DELETE and UPDATE statements, called the *positioned* DELETE and *positioned* UPDATE statements, respectively.

The positioned DELETE statement, shown in Figure 17-27, deletes a single row from a table. The deleted row is the current row of a cursor that references the table. To process the statement, the DBMS locates the row of the base table that corresponds to the current row of the cursor, and deletes that row from the base table. After the row is deleted, the cursor has no current row. Instead, the cursor is effectively positioned in the "empty space" left by the deleted row, waiting to be advanced to the next row by a subsequent FETCH statement.

The positioned UPDATE statement, shown in Figure 17-28, updates a single row of a table. The updated row is the current row of a cursor that references the table. To process the statement, the DBMS locates the row of the base table that corresponds to the current row of the cursor, and updates that row as specified in the SET clause. After the row is updated, it remains the current row of the cursor. Figure 17-29 shows an order browsing program that uses the positioned UPDATE and DELETE statements:

1. The program first prompts the user for a customer number and then queries the ORDERS table to locate all of the orders placed by that customer.

2. As it retrieves each row of query results, it displays the order information on the screen and asks the user what to do next.

3. If the user types an "N", the program does not modify the current order, but moves directly to the next order.

4. If the user types a "D", the program deletes the current order using a positioned DELETE statement.

5. If the user types a "U", the program prompts the user for a new quantity and amount, and then updates these two columns of the current order using a positioned UPDATE statement.

6. If the user types an "X", the program halts the query and terminates.

```
├──── DELETE FROM  table-name  WHERE CURRENT OF  cursor-name  ──────▶●
```

Figure 17-27. *Positioned* DELETE *statement syntax diagram*

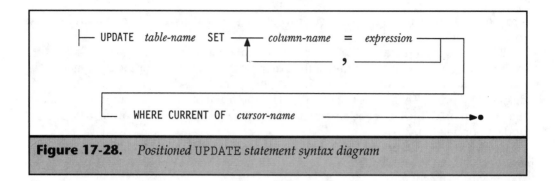

Figure 17-28. *Positioned* UPDATE *statement syntax diagram*

Although it is primitive compared to a real application program, the example in Figure 17-29 shows all of the logic and embedded SQL statements required to implement a browsing application with cursor-based database updates.

The SQL1 standard specifies that the positioned DELETE and UPDATE statements can be used only with cursors that meet these very strict criteria:

■ The query associated with the cursor must draw its data from a single source table; that is, there must be only one table named in the FROM clause of the query specified in the DECLARE CURSOR statement.

■ The query cannot specify an ORDER BY clause; the cursor must not identify a sorted set of query results.

■ The query cannot specify the DISTINCT keyword.

■ The query must not include a GROUP BY or a HAVING clause.

■ The user must have the UPDATE or DELETE privilege (as appropriate) on the base table.

The IBM databases (DB2, SQL/DS) extended the SQL1 restrictions a step further. They require that the cursor be explicitly declared as an updatable cursor in the DECLARE CURSOR statement. The extended IBM form of the DECLARE CURSOR statement is shown in Figure 17-30. In addition to declaring an updatable cursor, the FOR UPDATE clause can optionally specify particular columns that may be updated through the cursor. If the column list is specified in the cursor declarations, positioned UPDATE statements for the cursor may update only those columns.

In practice, all commercial SQL implementations that support positioned DELETE and UPDATE statements follow the IBM SQL approach. It is a great advantage for the DBMS to know, in advance, whether a cursor will be used for updates or whether its data will be read-only, because read-only processing is simpler. The FOR UPDATE clause provides this advance notice and can be considered a *de facto* standard part of the embedded SQL language.

```
main()
{
    exec sql include sqlca;
    exec sql begin declare section;
        int    custnum;                 /* customer number entered by user */
        int    ordnum;                  /* retrieved order number */
        char   orddate[12];             /* retrieved order date */
        char   ordmfr[4];               /* retrieved manufacturer-id */
        char   ordproduct[6];           /* retrieved product-id */
        int    ordqty;                  /* retrieved order quantity */
        float  ordamount;               /* retrieved order amount */
    exec sql end declare section;
    char inbuf[101]                     /* character entered by user */

    /* Declare the cursor for the query */
    exec sql declare ordcurs cursor for
            select order_num, ord_date, mfr, product, qty, amount
              from orders
             where cust = cust_num
             order by order_num
               for update of qty, amount;

    /* Prompt the user for a customer number */
    printf("Enter customer number: ");
    scanf("%d", &custnum);

    /* Set up error processing */
    whenever sqlerror goto error;
    whenever not found goto done;

    /* Open the cursor to start the query */
    exec sql open ordcurs;

    /* Loop through each row of query results */
    for ( ; ; ) {

        /* Fetch the next row of query results */
        exec sql fetch ordcurs
                into :ordnum, :orddate, :ordmfr, :ordproduct,
                     :ordqty, :ordamount;

        /* Display the retrieved data */
        printf("Order Number: %d\n", ordnum);
        printf("Order Date:   %s\n", orddate);
        printf("Manufacturer: %s\n", ordmfr);
```

①

②

Figure 17-29. *Using the positioned* DELETE *and* UPDATE *statements*

```
            printf("Product:      %s\n", ordproduct);
            printf("Quantity:     %d\n", ordqty);      ◄─────────────② 
            printf("Total Amount: %f\n", ordamount);

            /* Prompt user for action on this order */
            printf("Enter action (Next/Delete/Update/eXit): "); ◄
            gets(inbuf);

            switch (inbuf[0]) {

            case 'N':
              /* Continue on to next order */  ◄─────────────────③
              break;

            case 'D':
              /* Delete the current order */
              exec sql delete from orders   ◄─────────────────────④
                      where current of ordcurs;
              break;

            case 'U':
              /* Update the current order */
              printf("Enter new quantity: ");
              scanf("%d", &ordqty);
              printf("Enter new amount: ");
              scanf("%f", &ordamount);
              exec sql update orders      ◄────────────────────────⑤
                      set qty = :ordqty, amount = :ordamount
                      where current of ordcurs;
              break;

            case 'X':
              /* Stop retrieving orders and exit */  ◄──────────────⑥
              goto done;

          }
        }

done:
   exec sql close ordcurs;
   exec sql commit;
   exit();

error:
   printf("SQL error: %ld\n", sqlca.sqlcode);
   exit();
}
```

Figure 17-29.   *Using the positioned* DELETE *and* UPDATE *statements* (continued)

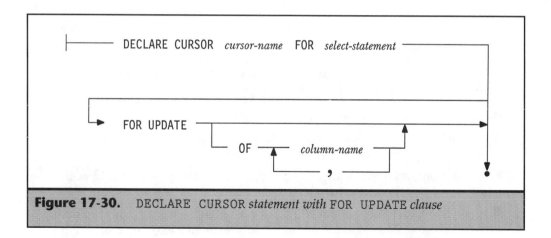

Figure 17-30. DECLARE CURSOR *statement with* FOR UPDATE *clause*

Because of its widespread use, the SQL2 standard included the IBM-style FOR UPDATE clause as an option in its DECLARE CURSOR statement. However, unlike the IBM products, the SQL2 standard automatically assumes that a cursor is opened for update unless it is a scroll cursor or it is explicitly declared FOR READ ONLY. The FOR READ ONLY specification in the SQL2 DECLARE CURSOR statement appears in exactly the same position as the FOR UPDATE clause, and explicitly tells the DBMS that the program will not attempt a positioned DELETE or UPDATE operation using the cursor. Because it can have a significant effect on database overhead and performance, it is a good idea to understand the specific assumptions that your particular DBMS brand makes about the updatability of cursors and the clauses or statements that can be used to override them.

Cursors and Transaction Processing

The way that your program handles its cursors can have a major impact on database performance. Recall from Chapter 12 that the SQL transaction model guarantees the consistency of data during a transaction. In cursor terms, this means that your program can declare a cursor, open it, fetch the query results, close it, reopen it, and fetch the query results again—and be guaranteed that the query results will be identical both times. The program can also fetch the same row through two different cursors and be guaranteed that the results will be identical. In fact, the data is guaranteed to remain consistent until your program issues a COMMIT or ROLLBACK to end the transaction. Because the consistency is not guaranteed across transactions, both the COMMIT and ROLLBACK statements automatically close all open cursors.

Behind the scenes, the DBMS provides this consistency guarantee by locking all of the rows of query results, preventing other users from modifying them. If the query produces many rows of data, a major portion of a table may be locked by the cursor. Furthermore, if your program waits for user input after fetching each row (for example, to let the user verify data displayed on the screen), parts of the database may be locked for a very long time. In an extreme case, the user might leave for lunch in mid-transaction, locking out other users for an hour or more!

To minimize the amount of locking required, you should follow these guidelines when writing interactive query programs:

- Keep transactions as short as possible.

- Issue a COMMIT statement immediately after every query and as soon as possible after your program has completed an update.

- Avoid programs that require a great deal of user interaction or that browse through many rows of data.

- If you know that the program will not try to re-fetch a row of data after the cursor has moved past it, use one of the less restrictive isolation modes described in Chapter 12. This allows the DBMS to unlock a row as soon as the next FETCH statement is issued.

- Avoid the use of scroll cursors unless you have taken other actions to eliminate or minimize the extra database locking they will cause.

- Explicitly specify a READ ONLY cursor, if possible.

Summary

In addition to its role as an interactive database language, SQL is used for programmatic access to relational databases:

- The most common technique for programmatic use of SQL is embedded SQL, where SQL statements are embedded into the application program, intermixed with the statements of a host programming language such as C or COBOL.

- Embedded SQL statements are processed by a special SQL precompiler. They begin with a special introducer (usually EXEC SQL) and end with a terminator, which varies from one host language to another.

- Variables from the application program, called host variables, can be used in embedded SQL statements wherever a constant can appear. These input host variables tailor the embedded SQL statement to the particular situation.

- Host variables are also used to receive the results of database queries. The values of these output host variables can then be processed by the application program.

- Queries that produce a single row of data are handled with the singleton SELECT statement of embedded SQL, which specifies both the query and the host variables to receive the retrieved data.

■ Queries that produce multiple rows of query results are handled with cursors in embedded SQL. The DECLARE CURSOR statement defines the query, the OPEN statement begins query processing, the FETCH statement retrieves successive rows of query results, and the CLOSE statement ends query processing.

■ The positioned UPDATE and DELETE statements can be used to update or delete the row currently selected by a cursor.

Chapter Eighteen

Dynamic SQL *

480

T he embedded SQL programming features described in the preceding chapter are collectively known as *static SQL*. Static SQL is adequate for writing all of the programs typically required in a data processing application. For example, in the order processing application of the sample database, you can use static SQL to write programs that handle order entry, order updates, order inquiries, customer inquiries, customer file maintenance, and programs that produce all types of reports. In every one of these programs, the pattern of database access is decided by the programmer and "hard-coded" into the program as a series of embedded SQL statements.

There is an important class of applications, however, where the pattern of database access cannot be determined in advance. A graphic query tool or a report writer, for example, must be able to decide at run-time what SQL statements it will use to access the database. A personal computer spreadsheet that supports host database access must also be able to send a query to the host DBMS for execution "on the fly." These programs and other general-purpose database front-ends cannot be written using static SQL techniques. They require an advanced form of embedded SQL, called *dynamic SQL*, described in this chapter.

Limitations of Static SQL

As the name "static SQL" implies, a program built using the embedded SQL features described in Chapter 17 (host variables, cursors, and the DECLARE CURSOR, OPEN, FETCH, and CLOSE statements) has a predetermined, fixed pattern of database access. For each embedded SQL statement in the program, the tables and columns referenced by that statement are determined in advance by the programmer and hard-coded into the embedded SQL statement. Input host variables provide some flexibility in static SQL, but they don't fundamentally alter its static nature. Recall that a host variable can appear anywhere a constant is allowed in a SQL statement. You can use a host variable to alter a search condition:

```
exec sql select name, quota, sales
         from salesreps
         where quota > :cutoff_amount;
```

You can also use a host variable to change the data inserted or updated in a database:

```
exec sql update salesreps
         set quota = quota + :increase
         where quota >:cutoff_amount;
```

However, you cannot use a host variable in place of a table name or a column reference. The attempted use of the host variables which_table and which_column in these statements is illegal:

```
exec sql update :which_table
          set :which_column = 0;

exec sql declare cursor cursor7 for
        select *
          from :which_table;
```

Even if you could use a host variable in this way (and you cannot), another problem would immediately arise. The number of columns produced by the query in the second statement would vary, depending on which table was specified by the host variable. For the OFFICES table, the query results would have six columns; for the SALESREPS table, they would have nine columns. Furthermore, the data types of the columns will be different for the two tables. But to write a FETCH statement for the query, you must know in advance how many columns of query results there will be and their data types, because you must specify a host variable to receive each column:

```
exec sql fetch cursor7
        into :var1, :var2, :var3;
```

As this discussion illustrates, if a program must be able to determine at run-time which SQL statements it will use, or which tables and columns it will reference, static SQL is inadequate for the task. Dynamic SQL overcomes these limitations.

Dynamic SQL has been supported by the IBM SQL products since their introduction, and it is supported by Oracle, Ingres, VAX SQL, Informix, and many other DBMS brands. However, dynamic SQL was not specified by the ANSI/ISO SQL1 standard; the standard defined only static SQL. The absence of dynamic SQL from the SQL1 standard was ironic, given the popular notion that the standard allowed you to build front-end database tools that are portable across many different DBMS brands. In fact, such front-end tools must be built using dynamic SQL.

In the absence of an ANSI/ISO standard, DB2 set the *de facto* standard for dynamic SQL. The other IBM databases (SQL/DS and OS/2 Extended Edition) are nearly identical to DB2 in their dynamic SQL support, and most other SQL products also followed the DB2 standard. In 1992, the SQL standard added "official" support for dynamic SQL, mostly following the path set by IBM.

Dynamic SQL Concepts

The central concept of dynamic SQL is simple: don't hard-code an embedded SQL statement into the program's source code. Instead, let the program build the text of a SQL statement in one of its data areas at run-time, and then pass the statement text to the DBMS for execution "on the fly." Although the details get quite complex, all of dynamic SQL is built on this simple concept, and it's a good idea to keep it in mind.

To understand dynamic SQL and how it compares with static SQL, it's useful to consider once again the process the DBMS goes through to execute a SQL statement, originally shown in Figure 17-1 and repeated here in Figure 18-1. Recall from Chapter 17 that a static SQL statement goes through the first four steps of the process at compile-time. The BIND utility stores the application plan for the statement in the database as part of the program development process. When the static SQL statement is executed at run-time, the DBMS simply executes the stored application plan.

In dynamic SQL, the situation is quite different. The SQL statement to be executed isn't known until run-time, so the DBMS cannot prepare for the statement in advance. When the program is actually executed, the DBMS receives the text of the statement to be dynamically executed (called the *statement string*), and goes through all five of the steps shown in Figure 18-1 at run-time.

As you might expect, dynamic SQL is less efficient than static SQL. For this reason, static SQL is used whenever possible, and most application programmers never need to learn about dynamic SQL. However, dynamic SQL is growing in importance as database access moves to a client/server, front-end/back-end architecture. Database access is beginning to appear in personal computer applications such as spreadsheets, word processors, and graphics programs, and front-end data access tools are one of the most active areas of database development. All of these applications require the features of dynamic SQL.

Dynamic Statement Execution (EXECUTE IMMEDIATE)

The simplest form of dynamic SQL is provided by the EXECUTE IMMEDIATE statement, shown in Figure 18-2. This statement passes the text of a dynamic SQL statement to the DBMS and asks the DBMS to execute the dynamic statement immediately. To use this statement, your program goes through the following steps:

1. The program constructs a SQL statement as a string of text in one of its data areas (usually called a *buffer*). The statement can be almost any SQL statement that does not retrieve data.

2. The program passes the SQL statement to the DBMS with the EXECUTE IMMEDIATE statement.

3. The DBMS executes the statement and sets SQLCODE to indicate the completion status, exactly as if the statement had been hard-coded using static SQL.

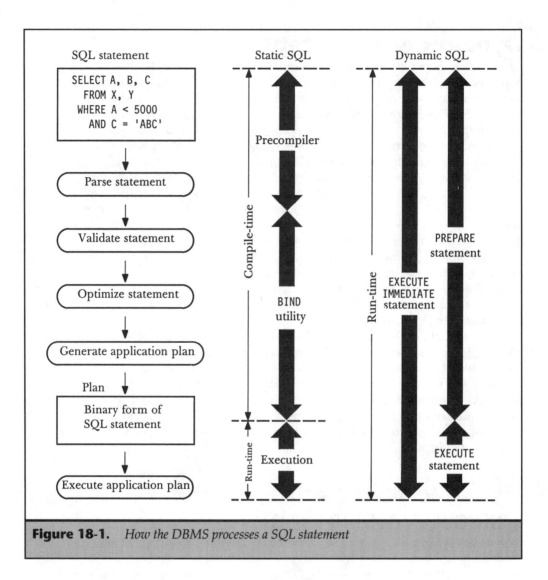

Figure 18-1. *How the DBMS processes a SQL statement*

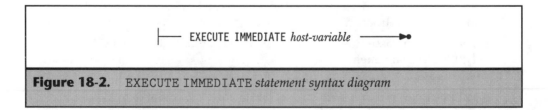

Figure 18-2. EXECUTE IMMEDIATE *statement syntax diagram*

Figure 18-3 shows a simple C program that follows these steps. The program prompts the user for a table name and a SQL search condition, and builds the text of a DELETE statement based upon the user's responses. The program uses the EXECUTE IMMEDIATE statement to execute the DELETE statement. This program cannot use a static SQL embedded DELETE statement, because neither the table name nor the

```
main()
{
  /* This program deletes rows from a user-specified table
     according to a user-specified search condition.
  */

  exec sql include sqlca;
  exec sql begin declare section;
    char stmtbuf[301];              /* SQL text to be executed */
  exec sql end declare section;

  char tblname[101];               /* table name entered by user */
  char search_cond[101];           /* search condition entered by user */

  /* Start building the DELETE statement in stmtbuf */
  strcpy(stmtbuf,"delete from ");

  /* Prompt user for table name; add it to the DELETE statement text */
  printf("Enter table name:      ");
  gets(tblname);
  strcat(stmtbuf, tblname);

  /* Prompt user for search condition; add it to the text */
  printf("Enter search condition: ");
  gets(search_cond);
  if (strlen(search_cond) > 0) {
     strcat(stmtbuf, " where ");
     strcat(stmtbuf, search_cond);
  }

  /* Now ask the DBMS to execute the statement */
  exec sql execute immediate :stmtbuf;
  if (sqlca.sqlcode < 0)
     printf("SQL error: %ld\n", sqlca.sqlcode);
  else
     printf("Delete from %s successful.\n", tblname);

  exit();
}
```

Figure 18-3. *Using the EXECUTE IMMEDIATE statement*

search condition are known until the user enters them at run-time. It must use dynamic SQL. If you run the program in Figure 18-3 with these inputs:

```
Enter table name:        staff
Enter search condition: quota < 20000
Delete from staff successful.
```

the program passes this statement text to the DBMS:

```
delete from staff
 where quota < 20000
```

If you run the program with these inputs:

```
Enter table name:        orders
Enter search condition: cust = 2105
Delete from orders successful
```

the program passes this statement text to the DBMS:

```
delete from orders
 where cust = 2105
```

The EXECUTE IMMEDIATE statement thus gives the program great flexibility in the type of DELETE statement that it executes.

The EXECUTE IMMEDIATE statement uses exactly one host variable—the variable containing the entire SQL statement string. The statement string itself cannot include host variable references, but there's no need for them. Instead of using a static SQL statement with a host variable like this:

```
exec sql delete from orders
         where cust = :cust_num;
```

a dynamic SQL program achieves the same effect by building the *entire* statement in a buffer and executing it:

```
sprintf(buffer, "delete from orders where cust = %d", cust_num)
exec sql execute immediate :buffer;
```

The EXECUTE IMMEDIATE statement is the simplest form of dynamic SQL, but it is very versatile. You can use it to dynamically execute most DML statements, including INSERT, DELETE, UPDATE, COMMIT, and ROLLBACK. You can also use EXECUTE IMMEDIATE to dynamically execute most DDL statements, including the CREATE, DROP, GRANT, and REVOKE statements.

The EXECUTE IMMEDIATE statement does have one significant limitation, however. You cannot use it to dynamically execute a SELECT statement, because it does not provide a mechanism to process the query results. Just as static SQL requires cursors and special-purpose statements (DECLARE CURSOR, OPEN, FETCH, and CLOSE) for programmatic queries, dynamic SQL uses cursors and some new special-purpose statements to handle dynamic queries. The dynamic SQL features that support dynamic queries are discussed later in this chapter.

Two-Step Dynamic Execution

The EXECUTE IMMEDIATE statement provides one-step support for dynamic statement execution. As described previously, the DBMS goes through all five steps of Figure 18-1 for the dynamically executed statement. The overhead of this process can be significant if your program executes many dynamic statements, and it's wasteful if the statements to be executed are very similar.

To address this situation, dynamic SQL offers an alternative, two-step method for executing SQL statements dynamically. Here is an overview of the two-step technique:

1. The program constructs a SQL statement string in a buffer, just as it does for the EXECUTE IMMEDIATE statement. A question mark (?) can be substituted for a constant anywhere in the statement text to indicate that a value for the constant will be supplied later. The question mark is called a *parameter marker*.

2. The PREPARE statement asks the DBMS to parse, validate, and optimize the statement and to generate an application plan for it. The DBMS sets SQLCODE to indicate any errors found in the statement and retains the application plan for later execution. Note that the DBMS does *not* execute the plan in response to the PREPARE statement.

3. When the program wants to execute the previously prepared statement, it uses the EXECUTE statement and passes a value for each parameter marker to the DBMS. The DBMS substitutes the parameter values, executes the previously generated application plan, and sets SQLCODE to indicate its completion status.

4. The program can use the EXECUTE statement repeatedly, supplying different parameter values each time the dynamic statement is executed.

Figure 18-4 shows a C program that uses these steps. The program is a general-purpose table update program. It prompts the user for a table name and two column names, and constructs an UPDATE statement for the table that looks like this:

```
update table-name
  set second-column-name = ?
where first-column-name = ?
```

The user's input thus determines the table to be updated, the column to be updated, and the search condition to be used. The search comparison value and the updated data value are specified as parameters, to be supplied later when the UPDATE statement is actually executed.

After building the UPDATE statement text in its buffer, the program asks the DBMS to compile it with the PREPARE statement. The program then enters a loop, prompting the user to enter pairs of parameter values to perform a sequence of table updates. This user dialog shows how you could use the program in Figure 18-4 to update the quotas for selected salespeople:

```
Enter name of table to be updated:    staff
Enter name of column to be searched:  empl_num
Enter name of column to be updated:   quota

Enter search value for empl_num: 106
Enter new value for quota: 150000.00
Another (y/n)? y

Enter search value for empl_num: 102
Enter new value for quota: 225000.00
Another (y/n)? y

Enter search value for empl_num: 107
Enter new value for quota: 215000.00
Another (y/n)? n

Updates complete.
```

This program is an excellent example of a situation where two-step dynamic execution is appropriate. The DBMS compiles the dynamic UPDATE statement only once, but executes it three times, once for each set of parameter values entered by the user. If the program had been written using EXECUTE IMMEDIATE instead, the dynamic UPDATE statement would have been compiled three times and executed three times. Thus the two-step dynamic execution of PREPARE and EXECUTE helps to eliminate some of the performance disadvantage of dynamic SQL.

```
main()
{
   /* This is a general-purpose update program.  It can be used
      for any update where a numeric column is to be updated in
      all rows where a second numeric column has a specified
      value.  For example, you can use it to update quotas for
      selected salespeople or to update credit limits for
      selected customers.
   */

   exec sql include sqlca;
   exec sql begin declare section;
      char  stmtbuf[301];          /* SQL text to be executed */
      float search_value;          /* parameter value for searching */
      float new_value;             /* parameter value for update */
   exec sql end declare section;

   char tblname[31];               /* table to be updated */
   char searchcol[31];             /* name of search column */
   char updatecol[31];             /* name of update column */
   char yes_no[31];                /* yes/no response from user */

   /* Prompt user for tablename and column name */
   printf("Enter name of table to be updated:   ");
   gets(tblname);
   printf("Enter name of column to be searched: ");
   gets(searchcol);
   printf("Enter name of column to be updated:  ");
   gets(updatecol);

   /* Build SQL statement in buffer; ask DBMS to compile it */
   sprintf(stmtbuf, "update %s set %s = ? where %s = ?",    ◄─────────────① 
                    tblname, searchcol, updatecol);
   exec sql prepare mystmt from :stmtbuf;    ◄─────────────②
   if (sqlca.sqlcode) {
      printf("PREPARE error: %ld\n", sqlca.sqlcode);
      exit();
   }

   /* Loop prompting user for parameters and performing updates */
   for ( ; ; ) {
      printf("\nEnter search value for %s: ", searchcol);
      scanf("%f", &search_value);
      printf("Enter new value for %s: ", updatecol);
      scanf("%f", &new_value);
```

Figure 18-4. *Using the* PREPARE *and* EXECUTE *statements*

```
        /* Ask the DBMS to execute the UPDATE statement */
        execute mystmt using :search_value, :new_value;          ③
        if (sqlca.sqlcode) {
           printf("EXECUTE error: %ld\n", sqlca.sqlcode);
           exit();
        }

        /* Ask user if there is another update */
        printf("Another (y/n)? ");                               ④
        gets(yes_no);
        if (yes_no[0] == 'n')
           break;
     }

     printf("\nUpdates complete.\n");

     exit();
}
```

Figure 18-4. *Using the* PREPARE *and* EXECUTE *statements* (continued)

The PREPARE **Statement**

The PREPARE statement, shown in Figure 18-5, is unique to dynamic SQL. It accepts a host variable containing a SQL statement string and passes the statement to the DBMS. The DBMS compiles the statement text and prepares it for execution by generating an application plan. The DBMS sets the SQLCODE variable to indicate any errors detected in the statement text. As described previously, the statement string can contain a parameter marker, indicated by a question mark, anywhere that a constant can appear. The parameter marker signals the DBMS that a value for the parameter will be supplied later, when the statement is actually executed.

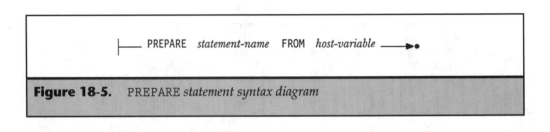

PREPARE *statement-name* FROM *host-variable* ━━▶•

Figure 18-5. PREPARE *statement syntax diagram*

As a result of the PREPARE statement, the DBMS assigns the specified *statement name* to the prepared statement. The statement name is a SQL identifier, like a cursor name. You specify the statement name in subsequent EXECUTE statements when you want to execute the statement. The DBMS retains the prepared statement and associated statement name until the end of the current transaction (that is, until the next COMMIT or ROLLBACK statement). If you want to execute the same dynamic statement later during another transaction, you must prepare it again.

The PREPARE statement can be used to prepare almost any executable DML or DDL statement, including the SELECT statement. SQL statements that are precompiler directives (such as the WHENEVER or DECLARE CURSOR statements) cannot be prepared, of course, because they are not executable.

The EXECUTE **Statement**

The EXECUTE statement, shown in Figure 18-6, is unique to dynamic SQL. It asks the DBMS to execute a statement previously prepared with the PREPARE statement. You can execute any statement that can be prepared, with one exception. Like the EXECUTE IMMEDIATE statement, the EXECUTE statement cannot be used to execute a SELECT statement, because it lacks a mechanism for handling query results.

If the dynamic statement to be executed contains one or more parameter markers, the EXECUTE statement must provide a value for each of the parameters. The values can be provided in two different ways, described in the next two sections.

EXECUTE **WITH HOST VARIABLES**   The easiest way to pass parameter values to the EXECUTE statement is by specifying a list of host variables in the USING clause. The EXECUTE statement substitutes the values of the host variables, in sequence, for the parameter markers in the prepared statement text. The host variables thus serve as input host variables for the dynamically executed statement. This technique was used in the program shown in Figure 18-4.

The number of host variables in the USING clause must match the number of parameter markers in the dynamic statement, and the data type of each host variable must be compatible with the data type required for the corresponding parameter. Each

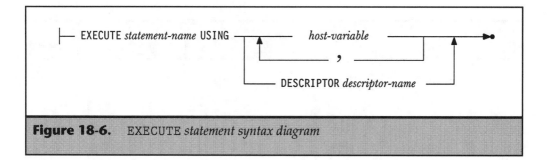

Figure 18-6.   EXECUTE *statement syntax diagram*

host variable in the list may also have a companion host indicator variable. If the indicator variable contains a negative value when the EXECUTE statement is processed, the corresponding parameter marker is assigned the NULL value.

EXECUTE **WITH** SQLDA   The second way to pass parameters to the EXECUTE statement is with a special dynamic SQL data structure called a *SQL Data Area*, or SQLDA. You must use a SQLDA to pass parameters when you don't know the number of parameters to be passed and their data types at the time that you write the program. For example, suppose you wanted to modify the general-purpose update program in Figure 18-4 so that the user could select more than one column to be updated. You could easily modify the program to generate an UPDATE statement with a variable number of assignments, but the list of host variables in the EXECUTE statement poses a problem; it must be replaced with a variable-length list. The SQLDA provides a way to specify such a variable-length parameter list.

Figure 18-7 shows the layout of the SQLDA used by the IBM databases (DB2, SQL/DS, and OS/2 Extended Edition). Most other DBMS products also use the IBM

```
struct sqlda {
   unsigned char sqldaid[8];
   long          sqldabc;
   short         sqln;
   short         sqld;
   struct sqlvar {
      short          sqltype;
      short          sqllen;
      unsigned char *sqldata;
      short         *sqlind;
      struct sqlname {
         short          length;
         unsigned char data[30];
      } sqlname;
   } sqlvar[1];
} ;
```

Figure 18-7.   *The SQL Data Area* (SQLDA) *for IBM databases*

SQLDA format or one very similar to it. The SQLDA is a variable-size data structure with two distinct parts:

■ The *fixed part* is located at the beginning of the SQLDA. Its fields identify the data structure as a SQLDA and specify the size of this particular SQLDA.

■ The *variable part* is an array of one or more SQLVAR data structures. When you use a SQLDA to pass parameters to an EXECUTE statement, there must be one SQLVAR structure for each parameter.

The fields in the SQLVAR structure describe the data being passed to the EXECUTE statement as a parameter value:

■ The SQLTYPE field contains an integer *data type code* that specifies the data type of the parameter being passed. For example, the DB2 data type code is 500 for a two-byte integer, 496 for a four-byte integer, and 448 for a variable-length character string.

■ The SQLLEN field specifies the *length* of the data being passed. It will contain a 2 for a two-byte integer and a 4 for a four-byte integer. When you pass a character string as a parameter, SQLLEN contains the number of characters in the string.

■ The SQLDATA field is a pointer to the *data area* within your program that contains the parameter value. The DBMS uses this pointer to find the data value as it executes the dynamic SQL statement. The SQLTYPE and SQLLEN fields tell the DBMS what type of data is being pointed to, and its length.

■ The SQLIND field is a pointer to a two-byte integer that is used as an *indicator variable* for the parameter. The DBMS checks the indicator variable to determine whether you are passing a NULL value. If you are not using an indicator variable for a particular parameter, the SQLIND field must be set to zero.

The other fields in the SQLVAR and SQLDA structures are not used to pass parameter values to the EXECUTE statement. They are used when you use a SQLDA to retrieve data from the database, as described later in this chapter.

Figure 18-8 shows a dynamic SQL program that uses a SQLDA to specify input parameters. The program updates the SALESREPS table, but it allows the user to select which columns are to be updated at the beginning of the program. Then it enters a loop, prompting the user for an employee number, and then prompting for a new value for each column to be updated. If the user types an asterisk (*) in response to the "new value" prompt, the program assigns the corresponding column a NULL value.

```
main()
{
    /* This program updates user-specified columns of the
       SALESREPS table.  It first asks the user to select the
       columns to be updated, and then prompts repeatedly for the
       employee number of a salesperson and new values for the
       selected columns.
    */

    #define COLCNT 6                  /* six columns in SALESREPS table */

    exec sql include sqlca;
    exec sql include sqlda;
    exec sql begin declare section;
        char stmtbuf[2001];           /* SQL text to be executed */
    exec sql end declare section;

    char *malloc()
    struct {
        char   prompt[31];            /* prompt for this column */
        char   name[31];              /* name for this column */
        short typecode;               /* its data type code */
        short buflen;                 /* length of its buffer */
        char   selected;              /* "selected" flag (y/n) */
    } columns[] = { "Name",      "NAME",        449, 16, 'n',
                    "Office",    "REP_OFFICE",  497, 4,  'n',
                    "Manager",   "MANAGER",     497, 4,  'n',
                    "Hire Date", "HIRE_DATE",   449, 12, 'n',
                    "Quota",     "QUOTA",       481, 8,  'n',
                    "Sales",     "SALES",       481, 8,  'n' } ;

    struct sqlda  *parmda;            /* SQLDA for parameter values */
    struct sqlvar *parmvar;           /* SQLVAR for current parm value */
    int           parmcnt;            /* running parameter count */
    int           empl_num;           /* employee number entered by user */
    int           i;                  /* index for columns[] array */
    int           j;                  /* index for sqlvar array in sqlda */
    char          inbuf[101];         /* input entered by user */

    /* Prompt the user to select the columns to be updated */
    printf("*** Salesperson Update Program ***\n\n");
    parmcnt = 1;
    for (i = 0; i < COLCNT; i++) {

        /* Ask about this column */
        printf("Update %s column (y/n)? ");
        gets(inbuf);
```

Figure 18-8.   *Using* EXECUTE *with a* SQLDA

```
    if (inbuf[0] == 'y') {
       columns[i].selected = 'y';
       parmcnt += 1;
    }
}

/* Allocate a SQLDA structure to pass parameter values */
parmda = malloc(16 + (44 * parmcnt));                    ◀──────────────①
strcpy(parmda -> sqldaid, "SQLDA    ");
parmda -> sqldabc = (16 + (44 * parmcnt));
parmda -> sqln = parmcnt;

/* Start building the UPDATE statement in statement buffer */
strcpy(stmtbuf, "update orders set ");

/* Loop through columns, processing the selected ones */
for (i = 0; j = 0; i++; i < COLCNT) {                    ◀──────────────②

    /* Skip over non-selected columns */
    if (columns[i].selected == 'n')
       continue;

    /* Add an assignment to the dynamic UPDATE statement */
    if (parmcnt > 0)  strcat(stmtbuf, ", ");
    strcat(stmtbuf, columns[i].name);
    strcat(stmtbuf, " = ?");

    /* Allocate space for data and indicator variable, and */
    /* fill in the SQLVAR with information for this column */
    parmvar = parmda -> sqlvar + j;
    parmvar -> sqltype = columns[i].typecode;            ◀──────────────③
    parmvar -> sqllen  = columns[i].buflen;              ◀──────────────④
    parmvar -> sqldata = malloc(columns[i].buflen);      ◀────────────⑤
    parmvar -> sqlind  = malloc(2);   ◀───────────────────────────────⑥
    strcpy(parmvar -> sqlname.data, columns[i].prompt);
    j += 1;
}

/* Fill in last SQLVAR for parameter in the WHERE clause */
strcat(stmtbuf, " where empl_num = ?");
parmvar = parmda + parmcnt;
parmvar -> sqltype = 496;
parmvar -> sqllen  = 4;
parmvar -> sqldata = &empl_num;
parmvar -> sqlind  = 0;
parmda -> sqld = parmcnt;                                ◀──────────────⑦
```

Figure 18-8. *Using EXECUTE with a SQLDA (continued)*

```
/* Ask the DBMS to compile the complete dynamic UPDATE statement */
exec sql prepare updatestmt from :stmtbuf;
if (sqlca.sqlcode < 0) {
   printf("PREPARE error: %ld\n", sqlca.sqlcode);
   exit();
}

/* Now loop, prompting for parameters and doing UPDATEs */
for ( ; ; ) {

   /* Prompt user for order number of order to be updated */
   printf("\nEnter Salesperson's Employee Number: ");
   scanf("%ld", &empl_num);
   if (empl_num == 0) break;

   /* Get new values for the updated columns */
   for (j = 0; j < (parmcnt-1); j++) {
      parmvar = parmda + j;
      printf("Enter new value for %s: ", parmvar -> sqlname.data);
      gets(inbuf);
      if (inbuf[0] == '*') {
         /* If user enters '*', set column to a NULL value */
         *(parmvar -> sqlind) = -1;
         continue;
      }
      else {
         /* Otherwise, set indicator for non-NULL value */
         *(parmvar -> sqlind) = 0;

         switch(parmvar -> sqltype) {

         case 481:
            /* Convert entered data to 8-byte floating point */
            sscanf(inbuf, "%lf", parmvar -> sqldata);
            break;

         case 449:
            /* Pass entered data as variable-length string */
            stccpy(parmvar -> sqldata, inbuf, strlen(inbuf));
            parmvar -> sqllen = strlen(inbuf);
            break;

         case 501:
            /* Convert entered data to 4-byte integer */
            sscanf(inbuf, "%ld", parmvar -> sqldata);
            break;
         }
      }
   }
}
```

⑧

Figure 18-8. *Using* EXECUTE *with a* SQLDA (continued)

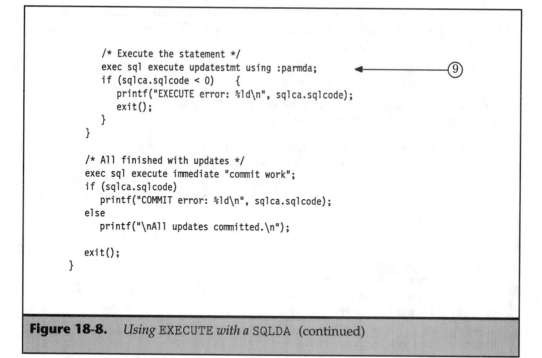

```
      /* Execute the statement */
      exec sql execute updatestmt using :parmda;                        ⑨
      if (sqlca.sqlcode < 0)     {
         printf("EXECUTE error: %ld\n", sqlca.sqlcode);
         exit();
      }
   }

   /* All finished with updates */
   exec sql execute immediate "commit work";
   if (sqlca.sqlcode)
      printf("COMMIT error: %ld\n", sqlca.sqlcode);
   else
      printf("\nAll updates committed.\n");

   exit();
}
```

Figure 18-8.   *Using* EXECUTE *with a* SQLDA   (continued)

Because the user can select different columns each time the program is run, this program must use a SQLDA to pass the parameter values to the EXECUTE statement. The program illustrates the general technique for using a SQLDA, indicated by callouts in Figure 18-8:

1. The program allocates a SQLDA large enough to hold a SQLVAR structure for each parameter to be passed. It sets the SQLN field to indicate how many SQLVARs can be accommodated.

2. For each parameter to be passed, the program fills in one of the SQLVAR structures with information describing the parameter.

3. The program determines the data type of a parameter and places the correct data type code in the SQLTYPE field.

4. The program determines the length of the parameter and places it in the SQLLEN field.

5. The program allocates memory to hold the parameter value and puts the address of the allocated memory in the SQLDATA field.

6. The program allocates memory to hold an indicator variable for the parameter and puts the address of the indicator variable in the SQLIND field.

7. Now, the program sets the SQLD field in the SQLDA header to indicate how many parameters are being passed. This tells the DBMS how many SQLVAR structures within the SQLDA contain valid data.

8. The program prompts the user for data values and places them into the data areas allocated in Steps 5 and 6.

9. The program uses an EXECUTE statement with the USING DESCRIPTOR clause to pass parameter values via the SQLDA.

Note that this particular program copies the "prompt string" for each parameter value into the SQLNAME structure. The program does this solely for its own convenience; the DBMS ignores the SQLNAME structure when you use the SQLDA to pass parameters. Here is a sample user dialog with the program in Figure 18-8:

```
*** Salesperson Update Program ***

Update Name column (y/n)? y
Update Office column (y/n)? y
Update Manager column (y/n)? n
Update Hire Date column (y/n)? n
Update Quota column (y/n)? y
Update Sales column (y/n)? n

Enter Salesperson's Employee Number: 106
Enter new value for Name: Sue Jackson
Enter new value for Office: 22
Enter new value for Quota: 175000.00

Enter Salesperson's Employee Number: 104
Enter new value for Name: Joe Smith
Enter new value for Office: *
Enter new value for Quota: 275000.00

Enter Salesperson's Employee Number: 0

All updates committed.
```

Based on the user's response to the initial questions, the program generates this dynamic UPDATE statement and prepares it:

```
update salesreps
   set name = ?, office = ?, quota = ?
 where empl_num = ?
```

The statement specifies four parameters, and the program allocates a SQLDA big enough to handle four SQLVAR structures. When the user supplies the first set of parameter values, the dynamic UPDATE statement becomes:

```
update salesreps
   set name = 'Sue Jackson', office = 22, quota = 175000.00
 where empl_num = 106
```

and with the second set of parameter values, it becomes:

```
update salesreps
   set name = 'Joe Smith', office = NULL, quota = 275000.00
 where empl_num = 104
```

This program is somewhat complex, but it's simple compared to a real general-purpose database update utility. It also illustrates all of the dynamic SQL features required to dynamically execute statements with a variable number of parameters.

The DECLARE STATEMENT Statement

The DECLARE STATEMENT statement, shown in Figure 18-9, is unique to dynamic SQL. It declares one or more statement names that will be used in your program. This statement is an optional directive to the SQL precompiler and is used purely for documentation purposes. You do not need to explicitly declare statement names before using them. However, using the DECLARE STATEMENT statement does make your program more self-documenting and easier to maintain. If you use the DECLARE STATEMENT statement, it should appear in your program before any DECLARE CURSOR or PREPARE statements that reference the statement name(s) that it declares. Figure 18-10 shows a program excerpt that illustrates its use.

The IBM SQL products all support the DECLARE STATEMENT statement, but most other SQL products do not yet support it, and their precompilers will generate an error message if you use it.

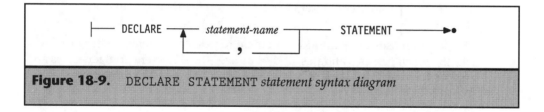

Figure 18-9. DECLARE STATEMENT *statement syntax diagram*

```
         ⋮
    exec sql declare statement updtstmt, delstmt;
         ⋮
    /* Prepare a dynamic UPDATE statement */
    exec sql prepare updtstmt from :stmtbuf;
         ⋮
    /* Prepare a dynamic DELETE statement */
    exec sql prepare delstmt from :stmtbuf;
         ⋮
    /* Execute one of the two statements */
    if (choice = 1)
       exec sql execute updtstmt using :var1, :var2;
    else
       exec sql execute delstmt;
         ⋮
```

Figure 18-10.   *Using the* DECLARE STATEMENT *statement*

Dynamic Queries

The EXECUTE IMMEDIATE, PREPARE, and EXECUTE statements as described thus far support dynamic execution of most SQL statements. However, they can't support dynamic queries, because they lack a mechanism for retrieving the query results. To support dynamic queries, SQL *combines* the dynamic SQL features of the PREPARE and EXECUTE statements with extensions to the static SQL query processing statements, and adds a new statement. Here is an overview of how a program performs a dynamic query:

1. A dynamic version of the DECLARE CURSOR statement declares a cursor for the query. Unlike the static DECLARE CURSOR statement, which includes a hard-coded SELECT statement, the dynamic form of the DECLARE CURSOR statement specifies the statement name that will be associated with the dynamic SELECT statement.

2. The program constructs a valid SELECT statement in a buffer, just as it would construct a dynamic UPDATE or DELETE statement. The SELECT statement may contain parameter markers like those used in other dynamic SQL statements.

3. The program uses the PREPARE statement to pass the statement string to the DBMS, which parses, validates, and optimizes the statement and generates an application plan. This is identical to the PREPARE processing used for other dynamic SQL statements.

4. The program uses the DESCRIBE statement to request a description of the query results that will be produced by the query. The DBMS returns a column-by-column description of the query results in a SQL Data Area (SQLDA) supplied by the program, telling the program how many columns of query results there are, and the name, data type, and length of each column. The DESCRIBE statement is used exclusively for dynamic queries.

5. The program uses the column descriptions in the SQLDA to allocate a block of memory to receive each column of query results. The program may also allocate space for an indicator variable for the column. The program places the address of the data area and the address of the indicator variable into the SQLDA to tell the DBMS where to return the query results.

6. A dynamic version of the OPEN statement asks the DBMS to start executing the query and passes values for the parameters specified in the dynamic SELECT statement. The OPEN statement positions the cursor before the first row of query results.

7. A dynamic version of the FETCH statement advances the cursor to the first row of query results and retrieves the data into the program's data areas and indicator variables. Unlike the static FETCH statement, which specifies a list of host variables to receive the data, the dynamic FETCH statement uses the SQLDA to tell the DBMS where to return the data. Subsequent FETCH statements move through the query results row by row, advancing the cursor to the next row of query results and retrieving its data into the program's data areas.

8. The CLOSE statement ends access to the query results and breaks the association between the cursor and the query results. This CLOSE statement is identical to the static SQL CLOSE statement; no extensions are required for dynamic queries.

The programming required to perform a dynamic query is more extensive than the programming for any other embedded SQL statement. However, the programming is typically more tedious than complex. Figure 18-11 shows a small query program that uses dynamic SQL to retrieve and display selected columns from a user-specified table. The callouts in the figure identify the eight steps in the preceding list.

The program in the figure begins by prompting the user for the table name and then queries the system catalog to discover the names of the columns in that table. It asks the user to select the column(s) to be retrieved and constructs a dynamic SELECT statement based on the user's responses. The step-by-step construction of a select list in this example is very typical of database front-end programs that generate dynamic SQL. In real applications, the generated select list might include expressions or aggregate functions, and there might be additional program logic to generate GROUP BY, HAVING, and ORDER BY clauses. Notice that the generated SELECT statement is identical to the interactive SELECT statement that you would use to perform the requested query.

```
main()
{
   /* This is a simple general-purpose query program.  It prompts
      the user for a table name, and then asks the user which
      columns of the table are to be included in the query.
      After the user's selections are complete, the program runs
      the requested query and displays the results.
   */

   exec sql include sqlca;
   exec sql include sqlda;
   exec sql begin declare section;
      char stmtbuf[2001];          /* SQL text to be executed */
      char querytbl[32];           /* user-specified table */
      char querycol[32];           /* user-specified column */
   exec sql end declare section;

   /* Cursor for system catalog query that retrieves column names */
   exec sql declare tblcurs cursor for
           select colname from system.syscolumns
             where tblname = :querytbl and owner = user;

   exec sql declare qrycurs cursor for querystmt;  ◄──────────────① 

   /* Data structures for the program */
   int          colcount = 0;      /* number of columns chosen */
   struct sqlda *qry_da;           /* allocated SQLDA for query */
   struct sqlvar *qry_var;         /* SQLVAR for current column */
   int          i;                 /* index for SQLVAR array in SQLDA */
   char         inbuf[101];        /* input entered by user */

   /* Prompt the user for which table to query */
   printf("*** Mini-Query Program ***\n\n");
   printf("Enter name of table for query: ");
   gets(querytbl);

   /* Start the SELECT statement in the buffer */
   strcpy(stmtbuf, "select ");  ◄──────────────────────────────② 

   /* Set up error processing */
   exec sql whenever sqlerror goto handle_error;
   exec sql whenever not found goto no_more_columns;

   /* Query the system catalog to get column names for the table */
   exec sql open tblcurs;
   for ( ; ; ) {

      /* Get name of next column and prompt the user */
      exec sql fetch tblcurs into :querycol;
      printf("Include column %s (y/n)? ", querycol);
```

Figure 18-11. *Data retrieval with dynamic SQL*

```
      gets(inbuf);
      if (inbuf[0] == 'y') {
        /* User wants the column; add it to the select list */
        if (colcount++ > 0)
           strcat(stmtbuf, ", ");
        strcat(stmtbuf, querycol);  ◄─────────────────────────── ②
      }
    }

no_more_columns:
  exec sql close tblcurs;

  /* Finish the SELECT statement with a FROM clause */
  strcat(stmtbuf, "from ");
  strcat(stmtbuf, querytbl);

  /* Allocate SQLDA for the dynamic query */
  qry_da = (SQLDA *) malloc(sizeof(SQLDA) + colcount * sizeof(SQLVAR));
  qry_da -> sqln = colcount;

  /* Prepare the query and ask the DBMS to describe it */
  exec sql prepare querystmt from :stmtbuf;  ◄─────────────── ③
  exec sql describe querystmt into qry_da;   ◄─────────────── ④

  /* Loop through SQLVARs, allocating memory for each column */
  for (i = 0; i < colcount; i++) {
     qry_var = qry_da -> sqlvar + i;
     qry_var -> sqldat = malloc(qry_var -> sqllen);  ◄──────── ⑤
     qry_var -> sqlind = malloc(sizeof(short));
  }

  /* SQLDA is all set; do the query and retrieve the results! */
  exec sql open qrycurs;  ◄──────────────────────────────── ⑥
  exec sql whenever not found goto no_more_data;
  for ( ; ; ) {

     /* Fetch the row of data into our buffers */
     exec sql fetch sqlcurs using descriptor qry_da;  ◄────── ⑦
     printf("\n");

     /* Loop, printing data for each column of the row */
     for (i = 0; i < colcount; i++) {

        /* Find the SQLVAR for this column; print column label */
        qry_var = qry_da -> sqlvar + i;
        printf(" Column # %d (%s): ", i+1, qry_var -> sqlname);

        /* Check indicator variable for NULL indication */
```

Figure 18-11. *Data retrieval with dynamic SQL* (continued)

```
                    if (*(qry_var -> sqlind)) != 0) {
                        puts("is NULL!\n");
                        continue;
                    }

                    /* Actual data returned; handle each type separately */
                    switch (qry_var -> sqltype) {

                    case 448:
                    case 449:
                        /* VARCHAR data -- just display it */
                        puts(qry_var -> sqldata);
                        break;

                    case 496:
                    case 497:
                        /* Four-byte integer data -- convert & display it */
                        printf("%ld", *((int *) (qry_var -> sqldata)));
                        break;

                    case 500:
                    case 501:
                        /* Two-byte integer data -- convert & display it */
                        printf("%d", *((short *) (qry_var -> sqldata)));
                        break;

                    case 480:
                    case 481:
                        /* Floating-point data -- convert & display it */
                        printf("%lf", *((double *) (qry_var -> sqldat)));
                        break;
                    }
                }
            }

    no_more_data:
        printf("\nEnd of data.\n");

        /* Clean up allocated storage */
        for (i = 0; i < colcount; i++) {
            qry_var = qry_da -> sqlvar + i;
            free(qry_var -> sqldata);
            free(qry_var -> sqlind);
        }
        free(qry_da);
        close qrycurs;  ◄──────────────────────────────────────⑧

        exit();
    }
```

Figure 18-11. *Data retrieval with dynamic SQL* (continued)

The handling of the PREPARE and DESCRIBE statements and the method of allocating storage for the retrieved data in this program are also typical of dynamic query programs. Note how the program uses the column descriptions placed in the SQLVAR array to allocate a data storage block of the proper size for each column. This program also allocates space for an indicator variable for each column. The program places the address of the data block and indicator variable back into the SQLVAR structure.

The OPEN, FETCH, and CLOSE statements play the same role for dynamic queries as they do for static queries, as illustrated by this program. Note that the FETCH statement specifies the SQLDA instead of a list of host variables. Because the program has previously filled in the SQLDATA and SQLIND fields of the SQLVAR array, the DBMS knows where to place each retrieved column of data.

As this example shows, much of the programming required for a dynamic query is concerned with setting up the SQLDA and allocating storage for the SQLDA and the retrieved data. The program must also sort out the various types of data that can be returned by the query and handle each one correctly, taking into account the possibility that the returned data will be NULL. These characteristics of the sample program are typical of production applications that use dynamic queries. Despite the complexity, the programming is not too difficult in C, Pascal, or PL/I. Languages such as COBOL and FORTRAN, which lack the ability to dynamically allocate storage and work with variable-length data structures, cannot be used for dynamic query processing.

The following sections discuss the DESCRIBE statement and the dynamic versions of the DECLARE CURSOR, OPEN, and FETCH statements.

The DESCRIBE **Statement**

The DESCRIBE statement, shown in Figure 18-12, is unique to dynamic queries. It is used to request a description of a dynamic query from the DBMS. The DESCRIBE statement is used after the dynamic query has been compiled with the PREPARE statement, but before it is executed with the OPEN statement. The query to be described is identified by its statement name. The DBMS returns the query description in a SQLDA supplied by the program.

The SQLDA is a variable-length structure with an array of one or more SQLVAR structures, as described earlier in this chapter and shown in Figure 18-7. Before passing the SQLDA to the DESCRIBE statement, your program must fill in the SQLN

|— DESCRIBE *statement-name* INTO *descriptor-name* ——————▶●

Figure 18-12. DESCRIBE *statement syntax diagram*

field in the SQLDA header, telling the DBMS how large the SQLVAR array is in this particular SQLDA. As the first step of its DESCRIBE processing, the DBMS fills in the SQLD field in the SQLDA header with the number of columns of query results. If the size of the SQLVAR array (as specified by the SQLN field) is too small to hold all of the column descriptions, the DBMS does not fill in the remainder of the SQLDA. Otherwise, the DBMS fills in one SQLVAR structure for each column of query results, in left-to-right order. The fields of each SQLVAR describe the corresponding column:

■ The SQLNAME structure specifies the name of the column (with the name in the DATA field and the length of the name in the LENGTH field). If the column is derived from an expression, the SQLNAME field is not used.

■ The SQLTYPE field specifies an integer data type code for the column. The data type codes used by different brands of DBMS vary. For the IBM SQL products, the data type code indicates both the data type and whether NULL values are allowed, as shown in Table 18-1.

■ The SQLLEN field specifies the length of the column. For variable-length data types (such as VARCHAR), the reported length is the maximum length of the data; the length of the columns in individual rows of query results will not exceed this length. For DB2 (and many other SQL products), the length returned for a DECIMAL data type specifies both the size of the decimal number (in the upper byte) and the scale of the number (in the lower byte).

Data Type	NULL **Allowed**	NOT NULL
CHAR	452	453
VARCHAR	448	449
LONG VARCHAR	456	457
SMALLINT	500	501
INTEGER	496	497
FLOAT	480	481
DECIMAL	484	485
DATE	384	385
TIME	388	389
TIMESTAMP	392	393
GRAPHIC	468	469
VARGRAPHIC	464	465

Table 18-1. SQLDA *Data Type Codes for DB2*

■ The SQLDATA and SQLIND fields are not filled in by the DBMS. Your application program fills in these fields with the addresses of the data buffer and indicator variable for the column before using the SQLDA later in a FETCH statement.

A complication of using the DESCRIBE statement is that your program may not know in advance how many columns of query results there will be, and therefore it may not know how large a SQLDA must be allocated to receive the description. One of three strategies is typically used to ensure that the SQLDA has enough space for the returned descriptions.

■ If the program has generated the select list of the query, it can keep a running count of the select items as it generates them. In this case, the program can allocate a SQLDA with exactly the right number of SQLVAR structures to receive the column descriptions. This approach was used in the program shown in Figure 18-11.

■ If it is inconvenient for the program to count the number of select list items, it can initially DESCRIBE the dynamic query into a minimal SQLDA with a one-element SQLVAR array. When the DESCRIBE statement returns, the SQLD value tells the program how large the SQLDA must be. It can then allocate a SQLDA of the correct size and re-execute the DESCRIBE statement, specifying the new SQLDA. There is no limit to the number of times that a prepared statement can be described.

■ Alternatively, the program can allocate a SQLDA with a SQLVAR array large enough to accommodate a typical query. A DESCRIBE statement using this SQLDA will succeed most of the time. If the SQLDA turns out to be too small for the query, the SQLD value tells the program how large the SQLDA must be, and it can allocate a larger one and DESCRIBE the statement again into that SQLDA.

The DESCRIBE statement is normally used for dynamic queries, but you can ask the DBMS to DESCRIBE any previously prepared statement. This feature is useful, for example, if a program needs to process an unknown SQL statement typed by a user. The program can PREPARE and DESCRIBE the statement and examine the SQLD field in the SQLDA. If the SQLD field is zero, the statement text was not a query, and the EXECUTE statement can be used to execute it. If the SQLD field is positive, the statement text was a query, and the OPEN/FETCH/CLOSE statement sequence must be used to execute it.

The DECLARE CURSOR Statement

The dynamic DECLARE CURSOR statement, shown in Figure 18-13, is a variation of the static DECLARE CURSOR statement. Recall from Chapter 17 that the static DECLARE CURSOR statement literally specifies a query by including the SELECT statement as one of its clauses. By contrast, the dynamic DECLARE CURSOR statement specifies the

```
        ┌─── DECLARE  cursor-name  CURSOR FOR  statement-name ───►●
```

Figure 18-13. *Dynamic* DECLARE CURSOR *statement syntax diagram*

query indirectly, by specifying the statement name associated with the query by the PREPARE statement.

Like the static DECLARE CURSOR statement, the dynamic DECLARE CURSOR statement is a directive to the SQL precompiler rather than an executable statement. It must appear before any other references to the cursor that it declares. The cursor name declared by this statement is used in subsequent OPEN, FETCH, and CLOSE statements to process the results of the dynamic query.

The Dynamic OPEN Statement

The dynamic OPEN statement, shown in Figure 18-14, is a variation of the static OPEN statement. It causes the DBMS to begin executing a query and positions the associated cursor just before the first row of query results. When the OPEN statement completes successfully, the cursor is in an open state and is ready to be used in a FETCH statement.

The role of the OPEN statement for dynamic queries parallels the role of the EXECUTE statement for other dynamic SQL statements. Both the EXECUTE and the OPEN statements cause the DBMS to execute a statement previously compiled by the PREPARE statement. If the dynamic query text includes one or more parameter markers, then the OPEN statement, like the EXECUTE statement, must supply values for these parameters. The USING clause is used to specify parameter values, and it has an identical format in both the EXECUTE and OPEN statements.

If the number of parameters that will appear in a dynamic query is known in advance, the program can pass the parameter values to the DBMS through a list of

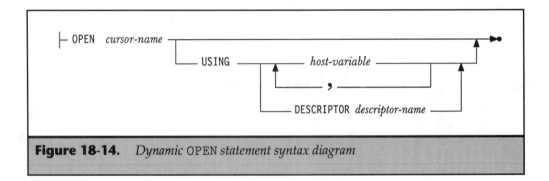

Figure 18-14. *Dynamic* OPEN *statement syntax diagram*

host variables in the USING clause of the OPEN statement. As in the EXECUTE statement, the number of host variables must match the number of parameters, the data type of each host variable must be compatible with the type required by the corresponding parameter, and an indicator variable can be specified for each host variable, if necessary. Figure 18-15 shows a program excerpt where the dynamic query has three parameters whose values are specified by host variables.

If the number of parameters is not known until run-time, the program must pass the parameter values using a SQLDA structure. This technique for passing parameter values was described for the EXECUTE statement earlier in this chapter. The same technique is used for the OPEN statement. Figure 18-16 shows a program excerpt like the one in Figure 18-15, except that it uses a SQLDA to pass parameters.

Note carefully that the SQLDA used in the OPEN statement has *absolutely nothing* to do with the SQLDA used in the DESCRIBE and FETCH statements:

- The SQLDA in the OPEN statement is used to pass parameter values *to* the DBMS for dynamic query execution. The elements of its SQLVAR array correspond to the *parameter markers* in the dynamic statement text.

- The SQLDA in the DESCRIBE and FETCH statements receives descriptions of the query results columns *from* the DBMS and tells the DBMS where to place the retrieved query results. The elements of its SQLVAR array correspond to the *columns of query results* produced by the dynamic query.

```
       ⋮
   /* Program has previously generated and prepared a SELECT statement like this one:

        SELECT A, B, C ... FROM SALESREPS
        WHERE SALES BETWEEN ? AND ?

     with two parameters to be specified
   */

   /* Prompt the user for low & high values and do the query */
   printf("Enter low end of sales range: ");
   scanf("%f", &low_end);
   printf("Enter high end of sales range: ");
   scanf("%f", &high_end);

   /* Open the cursor to start the query, passing parameters */
   exec sql open qrycursor using :low_end, :high_end;
       ⋮
```

Figure 18-15. OPEN *statement with host variable parameter passing*

The Dynamic FETCH Statement

The dynamic FETCH statement, shown in Figure 18-17, is a variation of the static FETCH statement. It advances the cursor to the next available row of query results and retrieves the values of its columns into the program's data areas. Recall from Chapter 17 that the static FETCH statement includes an INTO clause with a list of host variables that receive the retrieved column values. In the dynamic FETCH statement, the list of host variables is replaced by a SQLDA.

```
          ⋮
      /* Program has previously generated and prepared a SELECT
         statement like this one:

             SELECT A, B, C ... FROM SALESREPS
             WHERE EMPL_NUM IN (?, ?, ... ?)

         with a variable number of parameters to be specified.  The
         number of parameters for this execution is stored in the
         variable parmcnt.
      */

      char    *malloc()
      SQLDA  *parmda;
      SQLVAR *parmvar;
      long    parm_value[101];

      /* Allocate a SQLDA to pass parameter values */
      parmda = (SQLDA *) malloc(sizeof(SQLDA) + parmcnt * sizeof(SQLVAR));
      parmda -> sqln = parmcnt;

      /* Prompt the user for parameter values */
      for (i = 0; i < parmcnt; i++) {
         printf("Enter employee number: ");
         scanf("%ld", &(parm_value[i]));
         parmvar = parmda -> sqlvar + i;
         parmvar -> sqltype = 496;
         parmvar -> sqllen  = 4;
         parmvar -> sqldata = &(parm_value[i]);
         parmvar -> sqlind  = 0;
      }

      /* Open the cursor to start the query, passing parameters */
      exec sql open qrycursor using descriptor :parmda;
          ⋮
```

Figure 18-16.   OPEN *statement with* SQLDA *parameter passing*

Before using the dynamic FETCH statement, it is the application program's responsibility to provide data areas to receive the retrieved data and indicator variable for each column. The application program must also fill in the SQLDATA, SQLIND, and SQLLEN fields in the SQLVAR structure for each column, as follows:

- The SQLDATA field must point to the data area for the retrieved data.

- The SQLLEN field must specify the length of the data area pointed to by the SQLDATA field. This value must be correctly specified to make sure the DBMS does not copy retrieved data beyond the end of the data area.

- The SQLIND field must point to an indicator variable for the column (a two-byte integer). If no indicator variable is used for a particular column, the SQLIND field for the corresponding SQLVAR structure should be set to zero.

Normally, the application program allocates a SQLDA, uses the DESCRIBE statement to get a description of the query results, allocates storage for each column of query results, and sets the SQLDATA and SQLIND values, all before opening the cursor. This same SQLDA is then passed to the FETCH statement. However, there is no requirement that the same SQLDA be used, or that the SQLDA specify the same data areas for each FETCH statement. It is perfectly acceptable for the application program to change the SQLDATA and SQLIND pointers between FETCH statements, retrieving two successive rows into different locations.

The Dynamic CLOSE Statement

The dynamic form of the CLOSE statement is identical in syntax and function to the static CLOSE statement shown in Figure 17-25. In both cases, the CLOSE statement ends access to the query results. When a program closes a cursor for a dynamic query, the program normally should also deallocate the resources associated with the dynamic query, including:

- the SQLDA allocated for the dynamic query and used in the DESCRIBE and FETCH statements

- a possible second SQLDA, used to pass parameter values to the OPEN statement

- the data areas allocated to receive each column of query results retrieved by a FETCH statement

- the data areas allocated as indicator variables for the columns of query results

```
├── FETCH  cursor-name USING DESCRIPTOR descriptor-name ──▶●
```

Figure 18-17.   *Dynamic* FETCH *statement syntax diagram*

It may not be necessary to deallocate these data areas if the program will terminate immediately after the CLOSE statement.

Dynamic SQL Dialects

Like the other parts of the SQL language, dynamic SQL varies from one brand of DBMS to another. In fact, the differences in dynamic SQL support are more serious than for static SQL, because dynamic SQL exposes more of the "nuts and bolts" of the underlying DBMS —data types, data formats, and so on. These differences make it impossible to write a general-purpose database front-end that is portable across different DBMS brands. Instead, database front-end programs must include a "translation layer" for each brand of DBMS that they support to accommodate the differences.

A detailed description of the dynamic SQL features supported by all of the major DBMS brands is beyond the scope of this book. However, it is instructive to examine the dynamic SQL support provided by SQL/DS and by Oracle as examples of the kinds of differences and extensions to dynamic SQL that you may find in your particular DBMS.

Dynamic SQL in SQL/DS

SQL/DS supports all of the dynamic features supported by DB2 and described in the preceding sections of this chapter. In addition, SQL/DS supports a feature called *extended dynamic SQL*. With extended dynamic SQL, you can write a program that prepares a statement string and permanently stores the compiled statement in the database. The compiled statement can then be executed very efficiently, either by the same program or by a different program, without having to be prepared again. Thus extended dynamic SQL provides some of the performance advantages of static SQL in a dynamic SQL context.

The prepared statements in a SQL/DS database are stored in an *access module*, which is a named collection of compiled statements. SQL/DS users may have their own sets of access modules, protected by SQL/DS privileges. To create an empty access module, you use the SQL/DS CREATE PROGRAM statement, specifying a name of up to eight characters:

```
CREATE PROGRAM OPSTMTS
```

You can later remove the access module from the database with the DROP PROGRAM statement:

```
DROP PROGRAM OPSTMTS
```

Note that although the statements are called CREATE PROGRAM and DROP PROGRAM, they actually operate on access modules. Often, however, the set of compiled statements stored in an access module are, in fact, the set of statements used by a single program.

Once an access module has been created, a program can store compiled statements in it and execute those compiled statements. Special extended versions of the dynamic SQL PREPARE, DROP, DESCRIBE, EXECUTE, DECLARE CURSOR, OPEN, FETCH, and CLOSE statements, shown in Figure 18-18, are used for this purpose. These statements are supported by the SQL/DS precompiler for use in host programs written in IBM S/370 assembly language.

To compile a SQL statement string and store the compiled statement in an access module, your program must use the extended PREPARE statement. SQL/DS assigns the compiled statement a unique *statement-id* (a 32-bit number) and returns the statement-id into a host variable in your program. This statement-id is used by all of the other extended dynamic SQL statements to identify the compiled statement. An

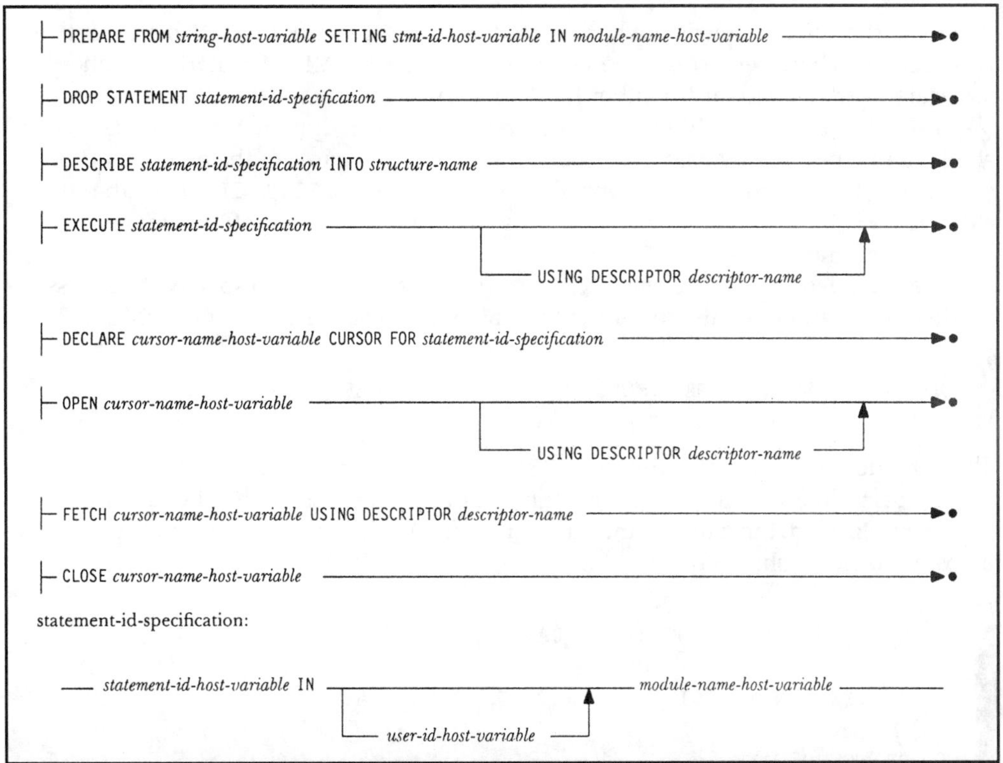

Figure 18-18. *Extended dynamic SQL statements in SQL/DS*

individual statement can be removed from the access module with the DROP STATEMENT statement.

To execute a stored statement, your program uses an extended EXECUTE statement like this one:

```
EXECUTE :STMT_ID IN :MODULE_NAME USING DESCRIPTOR :PARM_DA
```

The program passes the name of the access module and the statement-id for the statement to be executed in a pair of host variables (:MODULENAME and :STMT_ID). It also passes any parameters for the dynamic statement through a SQLDA (:PARM_DA), as described earlier in this chapter. Like the "standard" EXECUTE statement, the extended dynamic EXECUTE statement cannot be used to execute queries.

To execute a stored query, your program uses an extended DECLARE CURSOR statement like this one to associate a cursor name with the query:

```
DECLARE :CURS_NAME CURSOR FOR :STMT_ID IN :MODULE_NAME
```

Note that the cursor name is not hard-coded into the DECLARE CURSOR statement, but is passed as a character string in a host variable (:CURS_NAME). Similarly, the query associated with the cursor is neither hard-coded into the DECLARE CURSOR statement (as in static SQL) nor specified by a statement name (as in dynamic SQL). Instead, the statement is specified by using host variables to pass the name of the access module (:MODULE_NAME) and the statement-id for the statement (:STMT_ID). Thus the extended DECLARE CURSOR statement provides a dynamic association between a cursor name and a query.

The extended DESCRIBE statement also uses host variables to specify the access module name and the statement-id of the statement to be described into a SQLDA:

```
DESCRIBE :STMT_ID IN :MODULE_NAME INTO :QUERY_DA
```

The extended OPEN, FETCH, and CLOSE statements are similar to their dynamic SQL counterparts. In each case, however, the name of the cursor is not hard-coded into the statement. Instead, the name of the cursor to be opened, fetched, or closed is passed in a host variable, as shown here:

```
OPEN :CURS_NAME USING :PARM_DA

FETCH :CURS_NAME USING DESCRIPTOR :QUERY_DA

CLOSE :CURS_NAME
```

This allows a single set of OPEN, FETCH, and CLOSE statements to be used with different queries at different times, increasing the flexibility of a program that uses extended dynamic SQL.

Extended dynamic SQL provides significantly more flexibility than dynamic SQL, and it can be used to gain performance advantages over dynamic SQL as well. Currently it is a feature of SQL/DS only. It is not supported by the other IBM SQL products, and IBM's plans for such support in the future are not clear.

Dynamic SQL in Oracle *

The Oracle DBMS preceded DB2 into the market and based its dynamic SQL support upon IBM's System/R prototype. For this reason, the Oracle support for dynamic SQL differs somewhat from the IBM SQL standard. Although Oracle and DB2 are broadly compatible, Oracle differs from DB2 in its use of parameter markers, its use of the SQLDA, the format of its SQLDA, and its support for data type conversion. The Oracle differences from DB2 are similar to those you may encounter in other DBMS brands. For that reason it is instructive to briefly examine Oracle's dynamic SQL support and its points of difference from DB2.

NAMED PARAMETERS   Recall that DB2 does not allow host variable references in a dynamically prepared statement. Instead, parameters in the statement are identified by question marks (parameter markers), and values for the parameters are specified in the EXECUTE or OPEN statement. Oracle allows you to specify parameters in a dynamically prepared statement using the syntax for host variables. For example, this sequence of embedded SQL statements is legal for Oracle:

```
exec sql begin declare section;
   char   stmtbuf[1001];
   int    employee_number;
exec sql end declare section;
     .
     .
     .
strcpy(stmtbuf, "delete from salesreps where empl_num = :rep_number;");
exec sql prepare delstmt from :stmtbuf;
exec sql execute delstmt using :employee_number;
```

Although rep_number appears to be a host variable in the dynamic DELETE statement, it is in fact a *named parameter*. As shown in the example, the named parameter behaves exactly like the parameter markers in DB2. A value for the parameter is supplied from a "real" host variable in the EXECUTE statement. Named parameters are a real convenience when you use dynamic statements with a variable number of parameters.

THE DESCRIBE **STATEMENT**   The Oracle DESCRIBE statement is used, like the DB2 DESCRIBE statement, to describe the query results of a dynamic query. Like DB2, Oracle returns the descriptions in a SQLDA. The Oracle DESCRIBE statement can also be used to request a description of the named parameters in a dynamically prepared statement. Oracle also returns these parameter descriptions in a SQLDA.

This Oracle DESCRIBE statement requests a description of the columns of query results from a previously prepared dynamic query:

```
exec sql describe select list for qrystmt into qry_sqlda;
```

It corresponds to the DB2 statement:

```
exec sql describe qrystmt into qry_sqlda;
```

This Oracle DESCRIBE statement requests a description of the named parameters in a previously prepared dynamic statement. The statement might be a query or some other SQL statement:

```
exec sql describe bind list for thestmt into the_sqlda;
```

This Oracle statement has no DB2 equivalent. Following this DESCRIBE statement, your program would typically examine the information in the SQLDA, fill in the pointers in the SQLDA to point to the parameter values the program wants to supply, and then execute the statement using the SQLDA form of the OPEN or EXECUTE statement:

```
exec sql execute thestmt using descriptor the_sqlda;

exec sql open qrycursor using descriptor the_sqlda;
```

The information returned by both forms of the Oracle DESCRIBE statement is the same, and is described in the next section.

THE ORACLE SQLDA   The Oracle SQLDA performs the same functions as the DB2 SQLDA, but its format, shown in Figure 18-19, differs substantially from that of DB2. The two important fields in the DB2 SQLDA header both have counterparts in the Oracle SQLDA:

■ The N field in the Oracle SQLDA specifies the size of the arrays used to hold column definitions. It corresponds to the SQLN field in the DB2 SQLDA.

■ The F field in the Oracle SQLDA indicates how many columns are currently described in the arrays of the SQLDA. It corresponds to the SQLD field in the DB2 SQLDA.

Instead of DB2's single array of SQLVAR structures that contain column descriptions, the Oracle SQLDA contains pointers to a series of arrays, each of which describes one aspect of a column:

■ The T field points to an array of integers that specify the data type for each query results column or named parameter. The integers in this array correspond to the SQLTYPE field in each DB2 SQLVAR structure.

■ The V field points to an array of pointers that specify the buffer for each column of query results or each passed parameter value. The pointers in this array correspond to the SQLDATA field in each DB2 SQLVAR structure.

■ The L field points to an array of integers that specify the length of each buffer pointed to by the V array. The integers in this array correspond to the SQLLEN field in each DB2 SQLVAR structure.

■ The I field points to an array of data pointers that specify the indicator variable for each query results column or named parameter. The pointers in this array correspond to the SQLIND field in each DB2 SQLVAR structure.

■ The S field points to an array of string pointers that specify the buffers where Oracle is to return the name of each query results column or named parameter. The buffers pointed to by this array correspond to the SQLNAME structure in each DB2 SQLVAR structure.

```
struct sqlda {
    int     N;  /* number of entries in the SQLDA arrays */
    char  **V;  /* pointer to array of pointers to data areas */
    int    *L;  /* pointer to array of buffer lengths */
    short  *T;  /* pointer to array of data type codes */
    short **I;  /* pointer to array of pointers to indicator variables */
    int     F;  /* number of active entries in the SQLDA arrays */
    char  **S;  /* pointer to array of pointers to column/parameter names */
    short  *M;  /* pointer to array of name buffer lengths */
    short  *C;  /* pointer to array of current lengths of names */
    char  **X;  /* pointer to array of pointers to indicator parameter names */
    short  *Y;  /* pointer to array of indicator name buffer lengths */
    short  *Z;  /* pointer to array of current lengths of indicator names */
} ;

typedef struct sqlda sqlda;
```

Figure 18-19. *The Oracle* SQLDA

- The M field points to an array of integers that specify the size of each buffer pointed to by the S array. For DB2, the SQLNAME structure has a fixed-length buffer, so there is no equivalent to the M field.

- The C field points to an array of integers that specify the actual lengths of the names pointed to by the S array. When Oracle returns the column or parameter names, it sets the integers in this array to indicate their actual lengths. For DB2, the SQLNAME structure has a fixed-length buffer, so there is no equivalent to the C field.

- The X field points to an array of string pointers that specify the buffers where Oracle is to return the name of each named indicator parameter. These buffers are used only by the Oracle DESCRIBE BLIND LIST statement; they have no DB2 equivalent.

- The Y field points to an array of integers that specify the size of each buffer pointed to by the X array. There is no DB2 equivalent.

- The Z field points to an array of integers that specify the actual lengths of the indicator parameter names pointed to by the X array. When Oracle returns the indicator parameter names, it sets the integers in this array to indicate their actual lengths. There is no DB2 equivalent.

DATA TYPE CONVERSIONS   The data type formats that DB2 uses to receive parameter values and return query results are those supported by the IBM S/370 architecture mainframes that run DB2. Because it was designed as a portable DBMS, Oracle uses its own internal data type formats. Oracle automatically converts between its internal data formats and those of the computer system on which it is running when it receives parameter values from your program and when it returns query results to your program.

Your program can use the Oracle SQLDA to control the data type conversion performed by Oracle. For example, suppose that your program uses the DESCRIBE statement to describe the results of a dynamic query and discovers (from the data type code in the SQLDA) that the first column contains numeric data. Your program can request conversion of the numeric data by changing the data type code in the SQLDA before it fetches the data. If the program places the data type code for a character string into the SQLDA, for example, Oracle will convert the first column of query results and return it to your program as a string of digits.

The data type conversion feature of the Oracle SQLDA provides excellent portability, both across different computer systems and across different programming languages. A similar feature is supported by several other DBMS brands, but not by the IBM SQL products.

Dynamic SQL and the SQL2 Standard

The SQL1 standard did not address dynamic SQL, so the *de facto* standard for dynamic SQL, as described in the preceding sections, was set by IBM's implementation in DB2. The SQL2 standard explicitly included a standard for dynamic SQL, specified in a separate chapter of the standard which is nearly 50 pages long. In the simplest areas of dynamic SQL, the new SQL2 standard follows the dynamic SQL currently used by commercial DBMS products very closely. But in other areas, including even the most basic dynamic SQL queries, the new standard introduces incompatibilities with existing DBMS products which will require rewriting of applications.

In practice, support for SQL2-style dynamic SQL is appearing slowly in commercial DBMS products, and most dynamic SQL programming still requires the use of the "old," DB2-style dynamic SQL. Even when a new version of a DBMS product supports the new SQL2 statements, the DBMS vendor always provides a precompiler option that accepts the "old" dynamic SQL structure used by the particular DBMS. Often, this is the default option for the precompiler, because with thousands and thousands of SQL programs already in existence, the DBMS vendor has an absolute requirement that new DBMS versions do not "break" old programs. Thus, the migration to portions of SQL2 that represent incompatibilities with current practice will be a slow and evolutionary one.

The SQL2 statements that implement dynamic SQL are shown in Figure 18-20. The statements for basic dynamic SQL (i.e. dynamic SQL that does not involve database queries) follow the DB2 structure and language closely. Specifically:

■ SQL2 specifies an EXECUTE IMMEDIATE statement, for immediate execution of a SQL statement passed in the character buffer. The form of the EXECUTE IMMEDIATE statement precisely follows the DB2 style. For example, the EXECUTE IMMEDIATE statement in Figure 18-3 conforms to the SQL2 standard.

■ SQL2 specifies a PREPARE statement that passes a SQL statement to the DBMS and causes the DBMS to analyze the statement, optimize it, and build an application plan for it. The form of the PREPARE statement follows the DB2 style. For example, the PREPARE statement in Figure 18-4 (called out as item 2) conforms to the SQL2 standard.

■ SQL2 specifies an EXECUTE statement that causes a previously-prepared statement to be executed. Like the DB2 version, the SQL2 EXECUTE statement optionally accepts host variables that pass the specific values to be used when executing the SQL statement. The EXECUTE statement in Figure 18-4 (called out as item 2) conforms to the SQL2 standard.

These similarities mean that basic dynamic SQL programs using EXECUTE IMMEDIATE and PREPARE/EXECUTE with host variables will conform to the SQL2 standard.

The new standard also specifies a useful companion to the PREPARE statement that "unprepares" a previously-compiled dynamic SQL statement. The DEALLOCATE

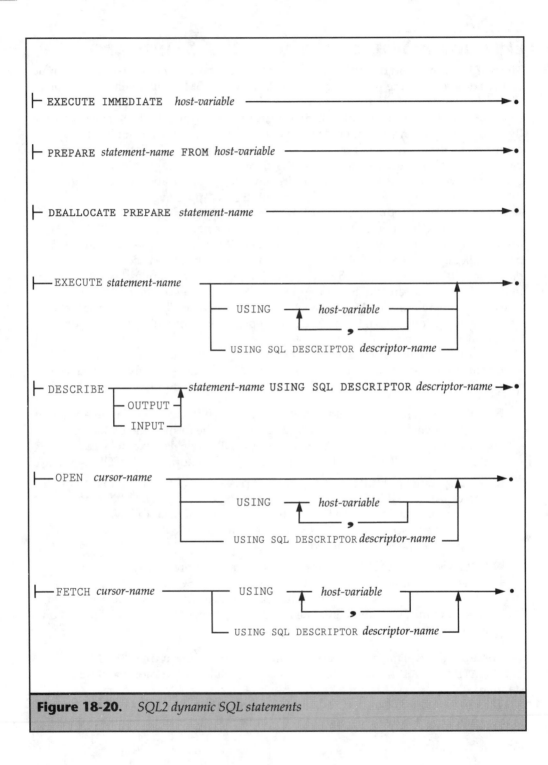

Figure 18-20.   *SQL2 dynamic SQL statements*

PREPARE statement provides this capability. When the DBMS processes this statement, it can free up the resources associated with the compiled statement, which will usually include some internal representation of the application plan for the statement. The statement named in the DEALLOCATE PREPARE must match the name specified in a previously-executed PREPARE statement. Note that in the absence of a capability like that provided by DEALLOCATE PREPARE, the DBMS has no way of knowing whether a previously-prepared statement will be executed again or not, and so must retain all of the information associated with the statement. The DEALLOCATE PREPARE is thus a useful, but not essential, addition to dynamic SQL. It does not introduce any incompatibilities for existing dynamic SQL programs.

SQL2 and the SQLDA

The SQL2 standard includes major changes to the support provided by the DB2 SQL Data Area (SQLDA). Recall from the previous description in this chapter that a SQL Data Area (SQLDA) provides two important functions:

■ a flexible way to pass parameters to be used in the execution of a dynamic SQL statement (passing data from the host program *to* the DBMS)

■ *the* way that the query results are returned to the program in the execution of a dynamic SQL query (passing data from the DBMS back to the host program)

The SQLDA handles these functions with flexibility, but it has some serious disadvantages. It is a very low-level data structure, which tends to be very specific to a particular programming language. For example, the variable-length structure of a DB2-style SQLDA makes it very difficult to represent in the FORTRAN language. The SQLDA structure also implicitly makes assumptions about the memory of the computer system on which the dynamic SQL program is running, how data items in a structure are aligned on such a system, etc. For the writers if the SQL2 standard, these low-level dependencies were unacceptable barriers to portability. Therefore, they replaced the DB2 SQLDA structure with a set of statements for manipulating a dynamic SQL *descriptor*.

The structure of a SQL2 descriptor is shown in Figure 18-21. Conceptually, the SQL2 descriptor is parallel to, and plays exactly the same role as the DB2-style SQLDA shown in Figure 18-7. The fixed part of the SQL2 descriptor specifies a count of the number of items in the variable part of the descriptor. Each item in the variable part contains information about a single parameter being passed, such as its data type, its length, an indicator telling whether or not a NULL value is being passed, etc. But unlike the DB2 SQLDA, the SQL2 descriptor is not an actual data structure within the host program. Instead it is a collection of data items "owned" by the DBMS software. The host program manipulates SQL2 descriptors — creating them, destroying them, placing data items into them, extracting data from them— via a new set of dynamic SQL statements specially designed for that purpose. Figure 18-22 summarizes these SQL2 descriptor management statements.

Fixed part	
COUNT	number of items described

Variable part—one occurrence per item (parameter or query results column):

TYPE	data type of item
LENGTH	length of item
OCTET_LENGTH	length of item (in 8-bit octets)
RETURNED_LENGTH	length of returned data item
RETURNED_OCTET_LENGTH	length of returned data (in 8-bit octets)
PRECISION	precision of data item
SCALE	scale of data item
DATETIME_INTERVAL_CODE	type of date/time interval data
DATETIME_INTERVAL_PRECISION	precision of date/time interval data
NULLABLE	can item be NULL?
INDICATOR	is data item NULL? (indicator value)
DATA	data item itself
NAME	name of data item
UNNAMED	is data item unnamed?

Figure 18-21. *SQL2 descriptor structure*

To understand how the SQL2 descriptor management statements work, it's instructive to re-examine the dynamic SQL update program in Figure 18-8. This program illustrates the use of a DB2-style SQLDA in an EXECUTE statement. The flow of the program remains identical if a SQL2 descriptor is used instead, but the specifics change quite a lot.

Before using the descriptor, the program must create it, using the statement:

```
ALLOCATE DESCRIPTOR parmdesc WITH MAX :parmcnt;
```

This statement replaces the allocation of storage for the parmda data structure at callout 1 in Figure 18-8. The descriptor (named "parmdesc") will perform the same functions as the parmda. Note that the program in Figure 18-8 had to calculate how much storage would be required for the parmda structure before allocating it. With the SQL2 descriptor, that calculation is eliminated and the host program simply tells the DBMS how many items the variable part of the descriptor must be able to hold.

The next step in the program is to set up the descriptor so that it describes the parameters to be passed—their data types, lengths, and so on. The loop callout 2 of the

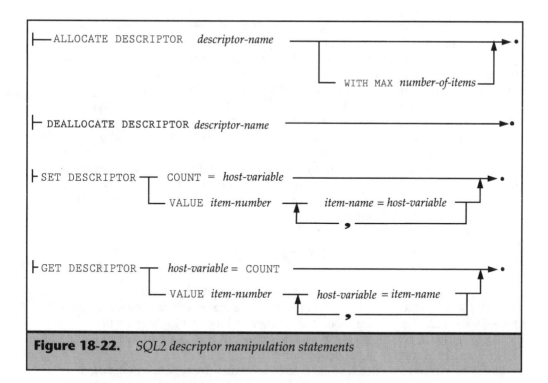

Figure 18-22. *SQL2 descriptor manipulation statements*

program remains intact, but again the details of how the descriptor is initialized differ from those for the SQLDA. At callout 3 and callout 4, the data type and length for the parameter are specified with a form of the SET DESCRIPTOR statement, with this code excerpt:

```
typecode = columns [i] .typecode;
length = columns [j].buflen;
SET DESCRIPTOR parmdesc VALUE (:i + 1) TYPE = :typecode
SET DESCRIPTOR parmdesc VALUE (:i + 1) LENGTH = :length;
```

The differences from Figure 18-8 are instructive. Because the descriptor is maintained by the DBMS, the data type and length must be passed to the DBMS, through the SET DESCRIPTOR statement, using host variables. In this particular example, the simple variables typecode and length are used. Additionally, the data type codes in Figure 18-8 were specific to DB2. The fact that each DBMS vendor used different codes to represent different SQL data types was a major source of portability problems in dynamic SQL. The SQL2 standard specifies integer data type codes for all of the data types specified in the standard, eliminating this issue. So, in addition to the other changes, the data type codes in the columns structure of Figure 18-8 would need to be modified to use these SQL2 standard data type codes.

The statements at callouts 5 and 6 in Figure 18-8 were used to "bind" the SQLDA structure to the program buffers used to contain the parameter data and the corresponding indicator variable. Effectively, they put pointers to these program buffers into the SQLDA for the use of DBMS. With SQL2 descriptors, this type of "binding" is not possible. Instead, the data value and indicator value are specifically passed as host variables, later in the program. Thus, the statements at callouts 5 and 6 would be eliminated in the conversion to SQL2.

The statement at callout 7 in Figure 18-8 sets the SQLDA to indicate how many parameter values are actually being passed to the DBMS. The SQL2 descriptor must similarly be set to indicate the number of passed parameters. This is done with a form of the SET DESCRIPTOR statement:

```
SET DESCRIPTOR parmdesc COUNT = :parmcnt;
```

The flow of the program in Figure 18-8 can now continue unmodified. The PREPARE statement compiles the dynamic UPDATE statement, and its form does not change for SQL2. The program then enters the for loop, prompting the user for parameters. Her again, the concepts are the same, but the details of manipulating the SQLDA structure and the SQL2 descriptor differ.

If the user indicates a NULL value is to be assigned (by typing an asterisk in response to the prompt), the program in Figure 18- 8 sets the parameter indicator buffer appropriately with the statement:

```
*(parmvar -> sqlind) = -1;
```

and if the value is not NULL, the program again sets the indicator buffer with the statement:

```
*(parmvar -> sqlind) = 0;
```

For the SQL2 descriptor, these statements would again be converted to a pair of SET DESCRIPTOR statements:

```
SET DESCRIPTOR parmdesc VALUE (:j + 1) INDICATOR = -1;
SET DESCRIPTOR parmdesc VALUE (:j + 1) INDICATOR = 0;
```

Note again the use of the loop control variable to specify which item in the descriptor is being set, and the direct passing of data (in this case, constants) rather than the use of pointers to buffers in the SQLDA structure.

Finally the program in Figure 18-8 passes the actual parameter value typed by the user to the DBMS, via the SQLDA. The statements at callout 8 accomplish this for data of different types, by first converting the typed characters into binary representations of the data and placing the binary data into the data buffers pointed to by the SQLDA. Again, the conversion to SQL2 involves replacing these pointers and direct SQLDA manipulation with a SET DESCRIPTOR statement. For example, theses statements pass the data and its length for a variable-length character string:

```
length = strlen(inbuf);
SET DESCRIPTOR parmdesc VALUE (:j + 1) DATA = :inbuf;
SET DESCRIPTOR parmdesc VALUE (:j + 1) LENGTH = :length;
```

For data items that do not require a length specification, passing the data is even easier, since only the DATA form of the SET DESCRIPTOR statement is required. It's also useful to note that SQL2 specifies implicit data type conversions between host variables (such as inbuf) and SQL data types. Following the SQL standard, it would be necessary for the program in Figure 18-8 to perform all of the data type conversion in the sscanf() functions. Instead, the data could be passed to the DBMS as character data, for automatic conversion and error detection.

With the SQLDA finally set up as required, the program in Figure 18-8 executes the dynamic UPDATE statement with the passed parameters at callout 9, using an EXECUTE statement that specifies a SQLDA. The conversion of this statement to a SQL2 descriptor is straightforward; it becomes

```
EXECUTE updatestmt USING SQL DESCRIPTOR parmdesc;
```

The keywords in the EXECUTE statement change slightly, and the name of the descriptor is specified instead of the name of the SQLDA.

Finally, the program in Figure 18-8 should be modified like this to tell the DBMS to deallocate the SQL2 descriptor. The statement that does this is:

```
DEALLOCATE DESCRIPTOR parmdesc;
```

In a simple program like this one, the DEALLOCATE is not very necessary, but in a more complex real-world program with multiple descriptors, it's a very good idea to deallocate them when the program no longer requires them.

SQL2 and Dynamic SQL Queries

In the dynamic SQL statements of the preceding sections, the SQL2 descriptor, like the SQLDA it replaces, is used to pass parameter information from the host program to the DBMS, for use in dynamic statement execution. The SQL2 standard also uses the

SQL descriptor in dynamic query statements where, like the SQLDA it replaces, it controls the passing of query result from the DBMS back to the host program. Figure 18-11 lists a DB2-style dynamic SQL query program. It's useful to examine how the program in Figure 18-11 would change to conform to the SQL2 standard. Again the flow of the program remains identical under SQL2, but the specifics change quite a lot.

The declaration of the cursor for the dynamic query, in callout 1 of Figure 18-11, remains unchanged under SQL2. The construction of the dynamic SELECT statement in callout 2 is also unchanged, as is the PREPARE statement of callout 3. The changes to the program begin at callout 4, where the program uses the DESCRIBE statement to obtain a description of the query results, which is returned in a SQLDA named qry_da. For SQL2, this DESCRIBE statement must be modified to refer to a SQL2 descriptor, which must have been previously allocated. Assuming the descriptor is named qrydesc, the statements would be:

```
ALLOCATE DESCRIPTOR qrydesc WITH MAX :colcount;
DESCRIBE querystmt USING SQL DESCRIPTOR qrydesc;
```

The SQL2 form of the DESCRIBE statement has a parallel effect on the one it replaces. Descriptions of the query result columns are returned, column by column, into the SQL2 descriptor, instead of into the SQLDA. Because the descriptor is a DBMS structure, rather than an actual data structure in the program, the host program must retrieve the information from the descriptor, piece by piece, as required. The GET DESCRIPTOR statement performs this function, just as the SET DESCRIPTOR function performs the opposite function of putting information into the SQL2 descriptor. In the program of Figure 18-11, the statements at callout 5, which obtains the length of a particular column of query results from a SQLDA, would be replaced with this statement:

```
GET DESCRIPTOR qrydesc VALUE (:i + 1) :length = LENGTH;
qry_var -> sqldat = malloc(length);
```

The statements at callout 5 that allocate buffers for indicator variables are not needed with the SQL2 descriptor. Instead, the descriptor can be queried for each column of query results, as it is being processed, as seen later in the program example.

In this particular example, the number of columns in the query results are calculated by the program as it builds the query. The program could also obtain the number of columns from the SQL2 descriptor with this form of the GET DESCRIPTOR statement:

```
GET DESCRIPTOR qrydesc :colcount = COUNT;
```

Having obtained the description of the query results, the program performs the query by opening the cursor at callout 6. The simple form of the OPEN statement, without any input parameters, conforms to the SQL2 standard. If the dynamic query specified parameters, they could be passed to the DBMS either as a series of host variables or via a SQL2 descriptor. The SQL2 OPEN statement using host variables is identical to the DB2 style, shown in Figure 18-15. The SQL2 OPEN statement using a descriptor is parallel to the SQL2 EXECUTE statement using a descriptor, and differs from the DB2 style. For example, the OPEN statement of Figure 18-16:

```
OPEN qrycursor USING DESCRIPTOR :parmda;
```

is changed for SQL2 into this OPEN statement:

```
Open qrycursor USING SQL DESCRIPTOR parmdesc;
```

The technique for passing input parameters to the OPEN statement via the SQL2 descriptor is exactly the same as that described earlier for the EXECUTE statement.

Like the Oracle implementation of dynamic SQL, the SQL2 standard provides a way for the host program to obtain a description of the parameters in a dynamic query as well as a description of the query results. For the program fragment in Figure 18-16, this DESCRIBE statement:

```
DESCRIBE INPUT querystmt USING SQL DESCRIPTOR parmdesc;
```

will return, in the SQL2 descriptor named parmdesc, a description of each of the parameters that appears in the dynamic query. The number of parameters can be obtained with the GET DESCRIPTOR statement, retrieving the COUNT item from the descriptor. As with the Oracle implementation, the SQL2 standard can have two descriptors associated with a dynamic query. The input descriptor, obtained with the DESCRIBE INPUT statement, contains descriptions of the parameters. The output descriptor contains descriptions of the query results columns. The standard allows you to explicitly ask for the output description:

```
DESCRIBE OUTPUT querystmt USING SQL DESCRIPTOR qrydesc;
```

but the DESCRIBE OUTPUT form of the statement is the default, and the most common practice is to omit the keyword "OUTPUT".

Returning to the dynamic query example of Figure 18-11, the cursor has been opened at callout 7, and it's time to fetch rows of query results at callout 8. Again, the SQL2 form of the FETCH statement is slightly modified to use the SQL2-style descriptor:

```
FETCH sqlcurs USING SQL DESCRIPTOR qrydesc;
```

Because the SQL2 descriptor is a DBMS structure and not a program data structure, the SQL2 dynamic FETCH statement does not actually retrieve any data into program variables like the DB2-style dynamic FETCH statement. Instead, it advances the cursor to the next row of query results and, conceptually, places those results into the SQL2 descriptor, where they are not available for retrieval by the program. The program retrieves the results from the descriptor using the GET DESCRIPTOR statement. For example, to retrieve a column of query results containing character data and determine its length, the program might use the statement:

```
GET DESCRIPTOR qrydesc VALUE (:i + 1) :buffer = DATA
GET DESCRIPTOR qrydesc VALUE (:i + 1)
                    :length = RETURNED_LENGTH;
```

To determine whether the value in the column was NULL, the program can use the statement:

```
GET DESCRIPTOR qrydesc VALUE (:i + 1) :indbuf = INDICATOR;
```

and similarly to determine the data type of the column, the program can use the statement:

```
GET DESCRIPTOR qrydesc VALUE (:i + 1) :type = TYPE;
```

As you can see, the details of row-by-row query processing within the for loop of the program will differ dramatically from those in Figure 18-11. Instead of manipulating data retrieved into program locations via pointers in the SQLDA structure, the program must obtain the columns of query results, item by item, by fetching them from the SQL2 descriptor. While this is more cumbersome than the DB2 style, and will result in many more lines of code, it is a much more portable and machine-independent approach.

Having processed all rows of query results, the program closes the cursor at callout 8. The CLOSE statement remains unchanged under SQL2. Following the closing of the cursor, it would be good practice to deallocate the SQL2 descriptor(s), which would have been allocated at the very beginning of the program.

The changes required to the dynamic SQL programs in Figures 18-8, 18-11, and 18-16 to make them conform to the SQL2 standard illustrate, in detail, the new features specified by the standard and the degree to which they differ from common dynamic SQL usage today. In summary, the changes from DB2-style dynamic SQL are:

- The SQLDA structure is replaced with a named SQL2 descriptor.

- The ALLOCATE DESCRIPTOR and DEALLOCATE DESCRIPTOR statement are used to create and destroy descriptors, replacing allocation and deallocation of host program SQLDA data structures.

- Instead of directly manipulating elements of the SQLDA, the program specifies parameter values and information through the SET DESCRIPTOR statement.

- Instead of directly manipulating elements of the SQLDA, the program obtains information about query results and obtains the query result data itself through the GET DESCRIPTOR statement.

- The DESCRIBE statement is used both to obtain descriptions of query results (DESCRIBE OUTPUT) and to obtain descriptions of parameters (DESCRIBE INPUT).

- The EXECUTE, OPEN, and FETCH statements are slightly modified to specify the SQL2 descriptor by name instead of the SQLDA.

Summary

This chapter described dynamic SQL, an advanced form of embedded SQL. Dynamic SQL is rarely needed to write simple data processing applications, but it is crucial for building general-purpose database front-ends. Static SQL and dynamic SQL present a classic trade-off between efficiency and flexibility, which can be summarized as follows:

- *Simplicity.* Static SQL is relatively simple; even its most complex feature, cursors, can be easily understood in terms of familiar file input/output concepts. Dynamic SQL is complex, requiring dynamic statement generation, variable-length data structures, and memory allocation.

- *Performance.* Static SQL is compiled into an application plan at compile-time; dynamic SQL must be compiled at run-time. As a result, static SQL performance is generally much better than that of dynamic SQL.

- *Flexibility.* Dynamic SQL allows a program to decide at run-time what specific SQL statements it will execute. Static SQL requires that all SQL statements be coded in advance, when the program is written, limiting the flexibility of the program.

Dynamic SQL uses a set of extended embedded SQL statements to support its dynamic features:

- The EXECUTE IMMEDIATE statement passes the text of a dynamic SQL statement to the DBMS, which executes it immediately.

- The PREPARE statement passes the text of a dynamic SQL statement to the DBMS, which compiles it into an application plan but does not execute it. The dynamic statement may include parameter markers whose values are specified when the statement is executed.

- The EXECUTE statement asks the DBMS to execute a dynamic statement previously compiled by a PREPARE statement. It also supplies parameter values for the statement that is to be executed.

- The DESCRIBE statement returns a description of a previously prepared dynamic statement into a SQLDA. If the dynamic statement is a query, the description includes a description of each column of query results.

- The DECLARE CURSOR statement for a dynamic query specifies the query by the statement name assigned to it when it was compiled by the PREPARE statement.

- The OPEN statement for a dynamic query passes parameter values for the dynamic SELECT statement and requests query execution.

- The FETCH statement for a dynamic query fetches a row of query results into program data areas specified by a SQLDA structure.

- The CLOSE statement for a dynamic query ends access to the query results.

Chapter Nineteen

SQL APIs

532

S everal SQL-based DBMS products take an approach to programmatic SQL that is very different from the embedded SQL approach taken by IBM and the ANSI/ISO standard. Instead of trying to blend SQL with another programming language, these products provide a library of function calls as an application programming interface (API) for the DBMS. To pass SQL statements to the DBMS, an application program calls functions in the API, and it calls other functions to retrieve query results and status information from the DBMS.

For many programmers, a SQL API is a very straightforward way to use SQL. Most programmers have some experience in using function libraries for other purposes, such as string manipulation, mathematical functions, file input/output, and screen forms management. The SQL API thus becomes "just another library" for the programmer to learn.

This chapter describes the general concepts used in a SQL API interface and then describes three of the most important APIs — those provided by SQL Server, Oracle, and SQLBase.

API Concepts

When a DBMS supports a function call interface, an application program communicates with the DBMS exclusively through a set of calls that are collectively known as an *application program interface*, or API. The basic operation of a typical DBMS API is illustrated in Figure 19-1:

- The program begins its database access with one or more API calls that connect the program to the DBMS, and often to a specific database.

- To send a SQL statement to the DBMS, the program builds the statement as a text string in a buffer, and then makes an API call to pass the buffer contents to the DBMS.

- The program makes API calls to check the status of its DBMS request and to handle errors.

- If the request is a query, the program uses API calls to retrieve the query results into the program's buffers. Typically, the calls return data a row at a time or a column at a time.

- The program ends its database access with an API call that disconnects it from the DBMS.

A SQL API is often used when the application program and the database are on two different systems in a client/server architecture, as shown in Figure 19-2. In this configuration, the code for the API functions is located on the client system, where the application program executes. The DBMS software is located on the server system, where the database resides. Calls from the application program to the API take place locally within the client system, but communication between the API and the DBMS

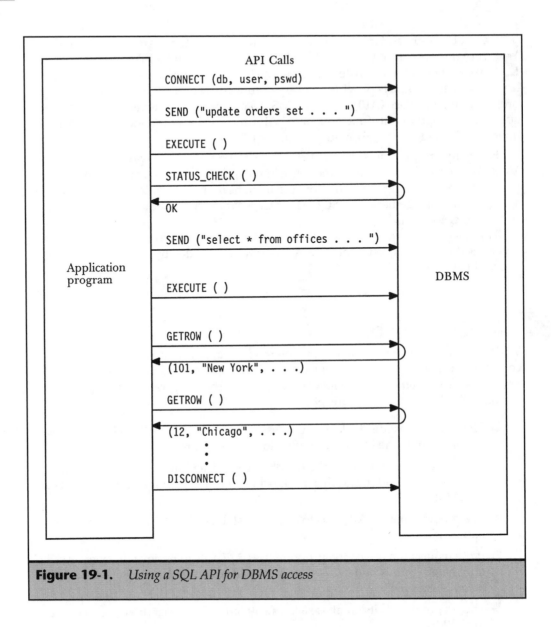

API Calls

CONNECT (db, user, pswd)

SEND ("update orders set . . . ")

EXECUTE ( )

STATUS_CHECK ( )

OK

SEND ("select * from offices . . . ")

Application
program

EXECUTE ( )

DBMS

GETROW ( )

(101, "New York", . . .)

GETROW ( )

(12, "Chicago", . . .)

DISCONNECT ( )

Figure 19-1. *Using a SQL API for DBMS access*

takes place over a network. As explained later in this chapter, a SQL API offers
particular advantages for a client/server architecture, because it can minimize the
amount of network traffic between the API and the DBMS.

The APIs offered by various DBMS products differ substantially from one another.
Unlike the embedded SQL interface, where DB2 provided an early standard and
where there is now an official ANSI/ISO standard, there is not yet an official standard

SQL API. Nonetheless, all of the SQL APIs available in commercial SQL products are based on the fundamental concepts illustrated in Figures 19-1 and 19-2, as is the SQL API standard proposed by the SQL Access Group.

The SQL Server API

One of the most important DBMS products that offers an API is SQL Server. The SQL Server API is important because it is the *only* interface offered by SQL Server, and it provided the model for much of Microsoft's ODBC API. SQL Server and its API are also an excellent example of a DBMS designed from the ground up around a client/server architecture.

The SQL Server API, which is called the *database library* or *dblib*, consists of about 100 functions available to an application program. The API is very comprehensive, but a typical program uses only about a dozen of the function calls, which are summarized in Table 19-1. The other calls provide advanced features, alternative methods of interacting with the DBMS, or single-call versions of features that otherwise would require multiple calls.

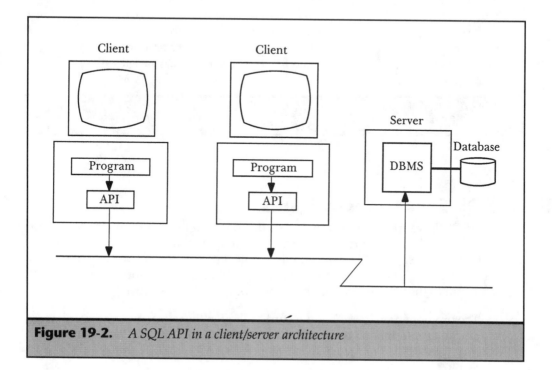

Figure 19-2. *A SQL API in a client/server architecture*

Function	Description
Database Connection/Disconnection	
dblogin()	Provides a data structure for login information
dbopen()	Opens a connection to SQL Server
dbuse()	Establishes the default database
dbexit()	Closes a connection to SQL Server
Basic Statement Processing	
dbcmd()	Passes SQL statement text to dblib
dbsqlexec()	Requests execution of a statement batch
dbresults()	Obtains results of next SQL statement in a batch
dbcancel()	Cancels the remainder of a statement batch
Error Handling	
dbmsghandle()	Establishes a user-written message handler procedure
dberrhandle()	Establishes a user-written error handler procedure
Query Results Processing	
dbbind()	Binds a query results column to a program variable
dbnextrow()	Fetches the next row of query results
dbnumcols()	Obtains the number of columns of query results
dbcolname()	Obtains the name of a query results column
dbcoltype()	Obtains the data type of a query results column
dbcollen()	Obtains the maximum length of a query results column
dbdata()	Obtains a pointer to a retrieved data value
dbdatlen()	Obtains the actual length of a retrieved data value
dbcanquery()	Cancels a query before all rows are fetched

Table 19-1. *Basic dblib API Functions*

Basic SQL Server Techniques

A simple SQL Server program that updates a database can use a very small set of dblib calls to do its work. The program in Figure 19-3 implements a simple quota update application for the SALESREPS table in the sample database. It is identical to the program in Figure 17-14, but uses the SQL Server API instead of embedded SQL. The figure illustrates the basic interaction between a program and SQL Server:

1. The program prepares a "login record," filling in the user name, password, and any other information required to connect to the DBMS.

2. The program calls `dbopen()` to establish a connection to the DBMS. A connection must exist before the program can send SQL statements to SQL Server.

3. The program builds a SQL statement in a buffer and calls `dbcmd()` to pass the SQL text to dblib. Successive calls to `dbcmd()` add to the previously passed text; there is no requirement that a complete SQL statement be sent in a single `dbcmd()` call.

4. The program calls `dbsqlexec()`, instructing SQL Server to execute the statement previously passed with `dbcmd()`.

5. The program calls `dbresults()` to determine the success or failure of the statement.

6. The program calls `dbexit()` to close down the connection to SQL Server.

It's instructive to compare the programs in Figure 19-3 and Figure 17-14 to see the differences between the embedded SQL and the dblib approach:

- The embedded SQL program either implicitly connects to the only available database (as in DB2), or it includes an embedded SQL statement for connection (such as the Oracle CONNECT statement, the Informix DATABASE statement, or the VAX SQL DECLARE DATABASE statement). The dblib program connects to a particular SQL Server with the `dbopen()` call.

- The actual SQL UPDATE statement processed by the DBMS is identical in both programs. With embedded SQL, the statement is part of the program's source code. With dblib, the statement is passed to the API as a sequence of one or more character strings. In fact, the dblib approach more closely resembles the dynamic SQL EXECUTE IMMEDIATE statement than static SQL.

- In the embedded SQL program, host variables provide the link between the SQL statements and the values of program variables. With dblib, the program passes variable values to the DBMS in the same way that it passes program text—as part of a SQL statement string.

- With embedded SQL, errors are returned in the SQLCODE field of the SQLCA structure. With dblib, the `dbresults()` call retrieves the status of each SQL statement.

Overall, the embedded SQL program in Figure 17-14 is shorter and probably easier to read. However, the program is neither purely C nor purely SQL, and a programmer must be trained in the use of embedded SQL to understand it. The use of host variables means that the interactive and embedded forms of the SQL statement are different. Additionally, the embedded SQL program must be processed both by the SQL precompiler and by the C compiler, lengthening the compilation cycle. In contrast, the SQL Server program is a "plain vanilla" C program, directly acceptable to the C compiler, and does not require special coding techniques.

```
main()
{
    LOGINREC  *loginrec;              /* data structure for login information */
    DBPROCESS *dbproc;                /* data structure for connection */
    char      amount_str[31];         /* amount entered by user (as a string) */
    int       status;                 /* dblib call return status */

    /* Get a login structure and set user name & password */
    loginrec = dblogin();                                              ◄──────── ①
    DBSETLUSER(loginrec, "scott");    ◄────────
    DBSETLPWD (loginrec, "tiger");    ◄────────

    /* Connect to SQL Server */
    dbproc = dbopen(loginrec, "");    ◄──────────────────────────────────────── ②

    /* Prompt the user for the amount of quota increase/decrease */
    printf("Raise/lower quotas by how much: ");
    gets(amount_str);

    /* Pass SQL statement to dblib */
    dbcmd(dbproc, "update salesreps set quota = quota + ");
    dbcmd(dbproc, amount_str);        ◄──────────                       ③

    /* Ask SQL Server to execute the statement */
    dbsqlexec(dbproc);                ◄──────────────────────────────── ④

    /* Get results of statement execution */
    status = dbresults(dbproc);       ◄──────────────────────────────── ⑤
    if (status != SUCCEED)
       printf("Error during update.\n");
    else
       printf("Update successful.\n");

    /* Break connection to SQL Server */
    dbexit(dbproc);                   ◄──────────────────────────────── ⑥
    exit();
}
```

Figure 19-3. *A simple SQL Server program*

STATEMENT BATCHES The program in Figure 19-3 sends a single SQL statement to SQL Server and checks its status. If an application program must execute several SQL statements, it can repeat the dbcmd() / dbsqlexec() / dbresults() cycle for each statement. Alternatively, the program can send several statements as a single *statement batch* to be executed by SQL Server.

Figure 19-4 shows a program that uses a batch of three SQL statements. As in Figure 19-3, the program calls dbcmd() to pass SQL text to dblib. The API simply

```
    main()
    {
        LOGINREC  *loginrec;            /* data structure for login information */
        DBPROCESS *dbproc;              /* data structure for connection */
            .
            .
            .
        /* Delete salespeople with low sales */
        dbcmd(dbproc, "delete from salesreps where sales < 100000.00 ");

        /* Increase quota for salespeople with moderate sales */
        dbcmd(dbproc, "update salesreps set quota = quota + 10000.00 ")
        dbcmd(dbproc, "where sales <= 150000.00 ");

        /* Increase quota for salespeople with high sales */
        dbcmd(dbproc, "update salesreps set quota = quota + 20000.00 ");
        dbcmd(dbproc, "where sales > 150000.00 ");

        /* Ask SQL Server to execute the statement batch */
        dbsqlexec(dbproc);

        /* Check results of each of the three statements */
        if (dbresults(dbproc) != SUCCEED) goto do_error;
        if (dbresults(dbproc) != SUCCEED) goto do_error;
        if (dbresults(dbproc) != SUCCEED) goto do_error;
            .
            .
            .
    }
```

Figure 19-4. *Using a SQL Server statement batch*

concatenates the text from each call. Note that it's the program's responsibility to include any required spaces or punctuation in the passed text. SQL Server does not begin executing the statements until the program calls dbsqlexec(). In this example, three statements have been sent to SQL Server, so the program calls dbresults() three times in succession. Each call to dbresults() "advances" the API to the results of the next statement in the batch and tells the program whether the statement succeeded or failed.

In the program shown in Figure 19-4, the programmer knows in advance that there are three statements in the batch, and can code three corresponding calls to dbresults(). If the number of statements in the batch is not known in advance, the program can call dbresults() repeatedly until it receives the error code NO_MORE_RESULTS. The program excerpt in Figure 19-5 illustrates this technique.

```
            ⋮

    /* Execute statements previously generated with dbcmd() calls */
    dbsqlexec(dbproc);

    /* Loop checking results of each statement in the batch */
    while (status = dbresults(dbproc) != NO_MORE_RESULTS) {
        if (status == FAIL)
            goto handle_error;
        else
            printf("Statement succeeded.\n");
    }

    /* Done with loop; batch completed successfully */
    printf("Batch complete.\n");
    exit();
            ⋮
```

Figure 19-5. *Processing the results of a SQL Server statement batch*

ERROR HANDLING The value returned by the dbresults() function tells the program whether the corresponding statement in the statement batch succeeded or failed. To get more detailed information about a failure, your program must provide its own *message-handling function.* The dblib software automatically calls the message-handling function when SQL Server encounters an error while executing SQL statements. Note that dblib calls the message-handling function during its processing of the dbsqlexec() or dbresults() function calls, before it returns to your program. This allows the message-handling function to do its own error processing.

Figure 19-6 shows an excerpt from a SQL Server program which includes a message-handling function called msg_rtn(). When the program begins, it activates the message-handling function by calling msghandle(). Suppose that an error occurs later, while SQL Server is processing the DELETE statement. When the program calls dbsqlexec() or dbresults() and dblib receives the error message from SQL Server, it "up-calls" the msg_rtn() routine in the program, passing it five parameters:

- dbproc, the connection on which the error occurred
- msgno, the SQL Server error number identifying the error
- msgstate, providing information about the error context
- severity, a number indicating the seriousness of the error
- msgtext, an error message corresponding to msgno

```
          ⋮
    /* External variables to hold error information */
    int  errcode;                        /* saved error code */
    char errmsg[256];                    /* saved error message */

    /* Define our own message-handling function */
    int msg_rtn(dbproc, msgno, msgstate, severity, msgtext)
    DBPROCESS  *dbproc;
    DBINT      msgno;
    int        msgstate;
    int        severity;
    char       *msgtext;
    extern int  errcode;
    extern char *errmsg;
    {
        /* Print out the error number and message */
        printf("*** Error: %d  Message: %s\n", msgno, msgtext);

        /* Save the error information for the application program */
        errcode = msgno;
        strcpy(errmsg, msgtext);

        /* Return to dblib to complete the API call */
        return(0);
    }

    main()
    {
        DBPROCESS *dbproc;                 /* data structure for connection */
          ⋮
        /* Install our own error handling function */
        dberrhandle(msg_rtn)
          ⋮
        /* Execute a DELETE statement */
        dbcmd(dbproc, "delete from salesreps where quota < 100000.00");
        dbsqlexec(dbproc);
        dbresults(dbproc);
          ⋮
```

Figure 19-6. *Error handling in a SQL Server program*

The `msg_rtn()` function in this program handles the message by printing it and saving the error number in a program variable for use later in the program. When the message-handling function returns to dblib (which called it), dblib completes its own processing and then returns to the program with a `FAIL` status. The program can detect this return value and perform further error processing, if appropriate.

The program excerpt in the figure actually presents a simplified view of SQL Server error handling. In addition to SQL statement errors detected by SQL Server, errors can also occur within the dblib API itself. For example, if the network connection to the SQL Server is lost, a dblib call may timeout waiting for a response from SQL Server, resulting in an error. The API handles these errors by up-calling a separate *error-handling function*, which operates much like the message-handling function described here.

A comparison of Figure 19-6 with Figures 17-10 and 17-13 illustrates the differences in error-handling techniques between dblib and embedded SQL:

- In embedded SQL, the SQLCA structure is used to signal errors and warnings to the program. SQL Server communicates errors and warnings by up-calling special functions within the application program and returning a failure status for the API function that encountered the error.

- In embedded SQL, error processing is synchronous. The embedded SQL statement fails, control returns to the program, and the SQLCODE value is tested. SQL Server error processing is asynchronous. When an API call fails, SQL Server calls the application program's error-handling or message-handling function *during* the API call. It returns to the application program with an error status later.

- Embedded SQL has only a single type of error and a single mechanism for reporting it. The SQL Server scheme has two types of errors, and two parallel mechanisms.

In summary, error handling in embedded SQL is simple and straightforward, but there are a limited number of responses that the application program can take when an error occurs. A SQL Server program has more flexibility in handling errors. However, the "up-call" scheme used by dblib is more sophisticated, and while it is familiar to systems programmers, it may be unfamiliar to application programmers.

SQL Server Queries

The SQL Server technique for handling programmatic queries is very similar to its technique for handling other SQL statements. To perform a query, a program sends a SELECT statement to SQL Server and uses dblib to retrieve the query results row by row. The program in Figure 19-7 illustrates the SQL Server query processing technique:

1. The program uses the dbcmd() and dbsqlexec() calls to pass a SELECT statement to SQL Server and request its execution.

2. When the program calls dbresults() for the SELECT statement, dblib returns the completion status for the query and also makes the query results available for processing.

```
main()
{
   LOGINREC  *loginrec;           /* data structure for login information */
   DBPROCESS *dbproc;             /* data structure for connection */
   char      repname[16];         /* retrieved city for the office */
   short     repquota;            /* retrieved employee number of mgr */
   float     repsales;            /* retrieved sales for office */

   /* Open a connection to SQL Server */
   loginrec = dblogin();
   DBSETLUSER(loginrec, "scott");
   DBSETLPWD (loginrec, "tiger");
   dbproc = dbopen(loginrec, "");

   /* Pass query to dblib and ask SQL Server to execute it */
   dbcmd(dbproc, "select name, quota, sales from salesreps ");
   dbcmd(dbproc, "where sales > quota order by name ");          ①
   dbsqlexec(dbproc);

   /* Get to first statement in the batch */
   dbresults(dbproc);                                            ②

   /* Bind each column to a variable in this program */
   dbbind(dbproc, 1, NTBSTRINGBIND, 16, &repname);
   dbbind(dbproc, 2, FLT4BIND,       0, &repquota);              ③
   dbbind(dbproc, 3, FLT4BIND,       0, &repsales);

   /* Loop retrieving rows of query results */
   while (status = dbnextrow(dbproc) == SUCCEED) {               ④

      /* Print data for this salesperson */
      printf("Name:  %s\n",   repname);
      printf("Quota: %f\n\n", repquota);
      printf("Sales: %f\n",   repsales);
   }

   /* Check for errors and close the connection */
   if (status == FAIL) {                                         ⑤
      printf("SQL error.\n");
   dbexit(dbproc);
   exit();
}
```

Figure 19-7.   *Retrieving SQL Server query results*

3. The program calls `dbbind()` once for each column of query results, telling dblib where it should return the data for that particular column. The arguments to `dbbind()` indicate the column number, the buffer to receive its data, the size of the buffer, and the expected data type.

4. The program loops, calling `dbnextrow()` repeatedly to obtain the rows of query results. The API places the returned data into the data areas indicated in the previous `dbbind()` calls.

5. When no more rows of query results are available, the `dbnextrow()` call returns the value `NO_MORE_ROWS`. If there were more statements in the statement batch following the `SELECT` statement, the program could call `dbresults()` to advance to the next statement.

Two of the dblib calls in Figure 19-7, `dbbind()` and `dbnextrow()`, support processing of the SQL Server query results. The `dbbind()` call sets up a one-to-one correspondence between each column of query results and the program variable that is to receive the retrieved data. This process is called *binding* the column. In the figure, the first column (`NAME`) is bound to a 16-byte character array and will be returned as a null-terminated string. The second and third columns, `QUOTA` and `SALES`, are both bound to floating-point numbers. It is the programmer's responsibility to make sure that the data type of each column of query results is compatible with the data type of the program variable to which it is bound.

Once again, it is useful to compare the SQL Server query processing in Figure 19-7 with the embedded SQL queries in Figure 17-17 and Figure 17-20:

■ Embedded SQL has two different query processing techniques—one for single-row queries (singleton `SELECT`) and one for multi-row queries (cursors). SQL Server uses a single technique, regardless of the number of rows of query results.

■ To specify the query, embedded SQL replaces the interactive `SELECT` statement with the singleton `SELECT` statement or the `DECLARE CURSOR` statement. With SQL Server, the `SELECT` statement sent by the program is *identical* to the interactive `SELECT` statement for the query.

■ With embedded SQL, the host variables that receive the query results are named in the `INTO` clause of the singleton `SELECT` or the `FETCH` statement. With SQL Server, the variables to receive query results are specified in the `dbbind()` calls.

■ With embedded SQL, row-by-row access to query results is provided by special-purpose embedded SQL statements (`OPEN`, `FETCH`, and `CLOSE`). With SQL Server, access to query results is through dblib function calls (`dbresults()` and `dbnextrow()`), which keep the SQL language itself more streamlined.

Because of its relative simplicity and its similarity to the interactive SQL interface, many programmers find the SQL Server interface easier to use for query processing than the embedded SQL interface.

RETRIEVING NULL VALUES   The dbnextrow() and dbbind() calls shown in Figure 19-7 provide a simple way to retrieve query results, but they do not support NULL values. When a row retrieved by dbnextrow() includes a column with a NULL value, SQL Server replaces the NULL with a *null substitution value.* By default, SQL Server uses zero as a substitution value for numeric data types, a string of blanks for fixed-length strings, and an empty string for variable-length strings. The applications program can change the default value for any data type by calling the API function dbsetnull().

In the program shown in Figure 19-7, if one of the offices had a NULL value in its QUOTA column, the dbnextrow() call for that office would retrieve a zero into the quota_value variable. Note that the program cannot tell from the retrieved data whether the QUOTA column for the row really has a zero value, or whether it is NULL. In some applications the use of substitution values is acceptable, but in others it is important to be able to detect NULL values. These latter applications must use an alternative scheme for retrieving query results, described in the next section.

RETRIEVAL USING POINTERS   With the standard SQL Server data retrieval technique, the dbnextrow() call copies the data value for each column into one of your program's variables. If there are many rows of query results or many long columns of text data, copying the data into your program's data areas can create a significant overhead. In addition, the dbnextrow() call lacks a mechanism for returning NULL values to your program.

To solve these two problems, dblib offers an alternate method of retrieving query results. Figure 19-8 shows the program excerpt from Figure 19-7, rewritten to use this alternate method:

1. The program sends the query to SQL Server and uses dbresults() to access the results, as it does for any SQL statement. However, the program does *not* call dbbind() to bind the columns of query results to program variables.

2. The program calls dbnextrow() to advance, row by row, through the query results.

3. For each column of each row, the program calls dbdata() to obtain a *pointer* to the data value for the column. The pointer points to a location within dblib's internal buffers.

4. If a column contains variable-length data, such as a VARCHAR data item, the program calls dbdatlen() to find out the length of the data item.

5. If a column has a NULL value, the dbdata() function returns a null pointer (0) and dbdatlen() returns 0 as the length of the item. These return values give the program a way to detect and respond to NULL values in the query results.

The program in Figure 19-8 is more cumbersome than the one in Figure 19-7. In general, it's easier to use the dbbind() function than the dbdata() approach, unless your program needs to handle NULL values or will be handling a large volume of query results.

RANDOM ROW RETRIEVAL   A program normally processes SQL Server query results by moving through them sequentially using the dbnextrow() call. For browsing applications, dblib also provides limited random access to the rows of query results. Your program must explicitly enable random row access by turning on a dblib option. The dbgetrow() call can then be used to retrieve a row by its row number.

To support random row retrieval, dblib stores the rows of query results in an internal buffer. If the query results fit entirely within the dblib buffer, dbgetrow() supports random retrieval of any row. If the query results exceed the size of the buffer, only the initial rows of query results are stored. The program can randomly retrieve these rows, but a dbnextrow() call that attempts to retrieve a row past the end of the buffer returns the special BUF_FULL error condition. The program must then discard some of the saved rows from the buffer, using the dbclrbuf() call, to make room for the new row. Once the rows are discarded, they cannot be re-retrieved with the dbgetrow() function. Thus dblib supports random retrieval of query results within a limited "window," dictated by the size of the row buffer, as shown in Figure 19-9. Your program can specify the size of the dblib row buffer by calling the dblib routine dbsetopt().

The random access provided by dbgetrow() is similar to the scroll cursors supported by several DBMS products and specified by the SQL2 standard. In both cases, random retrieval by row number is supported. However, a scroll cursor is a true pointer into the entire set of query results; it can range from the first to the last row, even if the query results contain thousands of rows. By contrast, the dbgetrow() function provides random access only within a limited window. This is adequate for limited browsing applications, but cannot easily be extended to large queries.

Stored Procedures

One of the most important and heavily promoted features of SQL Server is its support for *stored procedures.* A stored procedure is a sequence of Transact-SQL statements that is assigned a name, compiled, and stored in a SQL Server database. Once the stored procedure has been defined in the database, an application program can call it by name, using the dblib interface.

Figures 19-10 and 19-11 offer a simple example of how stored procedures work. Figure 19-10 is a procedure definition, written in SQL Server's Transact-SQL dialect. The procedure, named get_custinfo(), accepts a customer number as its argument and executes two queries. The argument of the procedure, cust_num, is a variable in the Transact-SQL language that can be used within the stored procedure in other Transact-SQL statements. In this example, the variable is used within the WHERE

```
main()
{
   LOGINREC  *loginrec;              /* data structure for login information */
   DBPROCESS *dbproc;                /* data structure for connection */
   char      *namep;                 /* pointer to NAME column data */
   int       citylen;                /* length of NAME column data */
   float     *quotap;                /* pointer to QUOTA column data */
   float     *salesp;                /* pointer to SALES column data */

   /* Open a connection to SQL Server */
   loginrec = dblogin();
   DBSETLUSER(loginrec, "scott");
   DBSETLPWD (loginrec, "tiger");
   dbproc = dbopen(loginrec, "");

   /* Pass query to dblib and ask SQL Server to execute it */
   dbcmd(dbproc, "select name, quota, sales from salesreps ");
   dbcmd(dbproc, "where sales > quota order by name ");
   dbsqlexec(dbproc);

   /* Get to first statement in the batch */            ————————————①
   dbresults(dbproc);

   /* Retrieve the single row of query results */
   while (status = dbnextrow(dbproc) == SUCCEED) {————————————②

      /* Get the address of each data item in this row */
      namep   = dbdata(dbproc, 1);  ◄
      quotap  = dbdata(dbproc, 2);  ◄—————————————③
      salesp  = dbdata(dbproc, 3);  ◄
      namelen = dbdatlen(dbproc, 1); ◄————————————④

      /* Copy NAME value into our own buffer & null-terminate it */
      strncpy(namebuf, namep, namelen);
      *(namebuf + namelen) = (char) 0;

      /* Print data for this salesperson */
      printf("Name:  %s\n", namebuf);
      if (quotap == 0)  ◄—————————————————⑤
         printf("Quota is NULL.\n");
      else
         printf("Quota: %f\n", *quotap);
      printf("Sales: %f\n", *salesp);
   }

   /* Check for successful completion */
   if (status == FAIL)
      printf("SQL error.\n");
   dbexit(dbproc);
   exit();
}
```

Figure 19-8.   *Retrieval using the SQL Server* dbdata() *function*

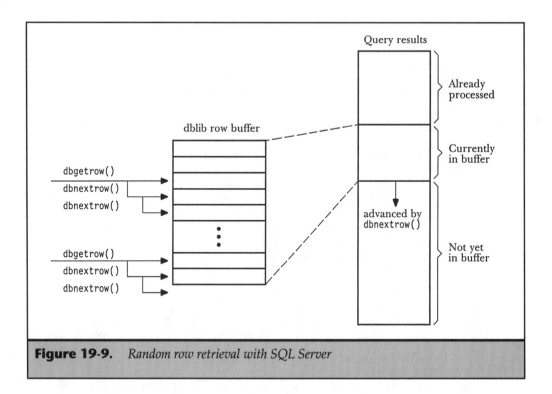

Figure 19-9. *Random row retrieval with SQL Server*

clauses of the two SELECT statements. When SQL Server executes the CREATE PROCEDURE statement, it compiles the procedure and stores it in the database.

Figure 19-11 shows an excerpt from a customer inquiry application. It prompts the user for a customer number and then calls the stored procedure in Figure 19-10 to

```
create procedure get_custinfo ( @cust_num integer) as

    /* Retrieve the customer's company name and credit limit */
    select company, credit_limit
      from customers
     where cust_num = @cust_num

    /* Retrieve info about each order placed by the customer */
    select order_num, amount
      from orders
     where cust = @cust_num
```

Figure 19-10. *A SQL Server stored procedure*

```
main()
{
    LOGINREC  *loginrec;          /* data structure for login information */
    DBPROCESS *dbproc;            /* data structure for connection */
    char      number[11];         /* customer number entered by user */
    char      company[31];        /* retrieved company name */
    float     limit;              /* retrieved credit limit */
    long      order_num;          /* retrieved order number */
    float     amount;             /* retrieved order amount */
        .
        .
    /* Prompt user to enter a customer number */
    printf("Enter customer number: ");
    gets(number);

    /* Ask SQL Server to execute the stored procedure */
    dbcmd(dbproc, "execute get_custinfo ");
    dbcmd(dbproc, number);
    dbsqlexec(dbproc);

    /* Retrieve results of the first query and display them */
    dbresults(dbproc);
    dbbind(dbproc, 1, NTBSTRINGBIND, 31, &company);
    dbbind(dbproc, 2, FLT4BIND,       0, &credit);
    status = dbnextrow(dbproc);
    if (status != SUCCEED) {
        printf("No such customer.\n");
        exit();
    }
    printf("Customer: %s  Credit Limit: %f\n", company, limit);

    /* Process second query, printing order information */
    dbresults(dbproc);
    dbbind(dbproc, 1, INTBIND,  0, &order_num);
    dbbind(dbproc, 2, FLT4BIND, 0, &amount);
    while (status = dbnextrow(dbproc) == SUCCEED) {
        /* Print data for this salesperson */
        printf("Order number: %ld  Amount: %f\n", order_num, amount);
    }

        .
        .
        .
```

Figure 19-11.   *Using a SQL Server stored procedure*

retrieve the customer's name and credit limit from the CUSTOMERS table and to retrieve all of the current orders placed by that customer from the ORDERS table. Notice that the program calls dbresults() twice to process the results of the two queries in the stored procedure.

The example in Figure 19-10 barely scratches the surface of the SQL Server stored procedure capability. The Transact-SQL language provides a complete set of procedural extensions to SQL, including condition testing (IF/THEN/ELSE), iteration (FOR and WHILE loops with BREAK and CONTINUE), branching (GOTO), procedure calls (EXECUTE), statement blocks (BEGIN/END), and both local and global variables. Using these features, you can create very complex stored procedures.

STORED PROCEDURES AND DBMS PERFORMANCE   SQL Server and the Sybase DBMS from which it is derived are both positioned as high-performance database management systems for OLTP applications. Stored procedures are a critical part of this performance claim. To understand why, it's useful to consider how SQL Server processes a SQL statement, as shown in Figure 19-12. The five steps in the figure are the same as those introduced in Chapter 17 and shown in Figure 17-1. Figure 18-1 showed how the five steps applied to static embedded SQL and dynamic embedded SQL, and Figure 19-12 shows how they apply to SQL Server.

A comparison of Figure 18-1 and Figure 19-12 shows that dblib is basically a *dynamic* interface to SQL Server. Each statement that a program sends to SQL Server goes through all five steps (parsing, validation, optimization, compilation, and finally execution) at *run-time*. But recall from Chapter 18 that one of the disadvantages of dynamic SQL is its relatively poor performance compared to static SQL. Doesn't SQL Server's use of a dynamic interface contradict its performance claims?

The answer is no, for two reasons. First, the typical transactions in an OLTP program (make a reservation, change an order, add a customer, and so on) use INSERT, DELETE, UPDATE, and SELECT statements that access a single row of data based on the row's primary key. It's relatively easy to optimize this type of SQL statement. Thus the overhead of run-time optimization and compilation is relatively low for the simple, high-usage OLTP programs that need the highest performance.

Second, and more important, SQL Server's stored procedures provide a way to parse, validate, optimize, and compile an entire *sequence* of SQL statements in advance. To get the best possible performance from a program, the programmer takes the SQL statements to be executed, defines a procedure containing them, and stores the compiled procedure in the database. At run-time, the program simply asks SQL Server to execute the stored procedure. Thus stored procedures give SQL Server both the flexibility of a dynamic SQL interface and the performance benefits of precompiled statements found in static SQL.

STORED PROCEDURES AND NETWORK PERFORMANCE   Stored procedures also play a key role in improving the network performance of the client/server architecture pioneered by Sybase and SQL Server. In this architecture, the application program and the SQL API reside on a *client* system (typically a personal computer) while the DBMS resides on a different *server* system, connected to the client systems by a local area network. To get good performance from the client/server architecture, the traffic over the network must be minimized, and stored procedures help to achieve this goal.

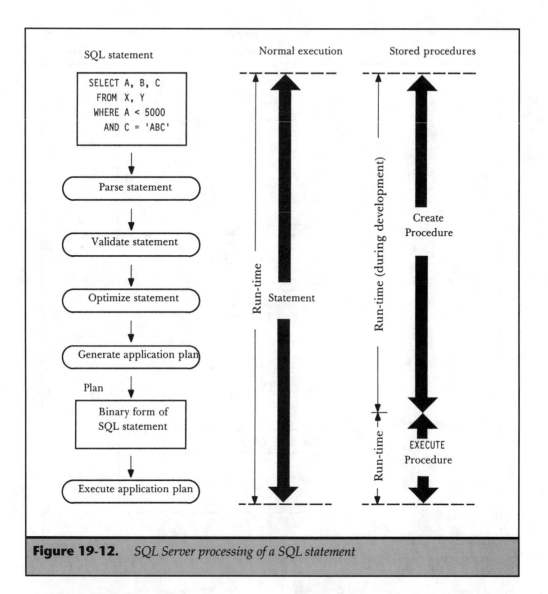

SQL statement

```
SELECT A, B, C
  FROM X, Y
 WHERE A < 5000
   AND C = 'ABC'
```

Normal execution

Stored procedures

↓

Parse statement

↓

Validate statement

↓

Optimize statement

↓

Generate application plan

Plan

Binary form of
SQL statement

↓

Execute application plan

Run-time

Statement

Run-time (during development)

Create
Procedure

Run-time

EXECUTE
Procedure

Figure 19-12.   *SQL Server processing of a SQL statement*

Figures 19-13 and 19-14 compare two client/server implementations—one using an embedded SQL interface and the other using the SQL Server API and a stored procedure. In both figures, the applications program performs an update and a simple query that generates a dozen rows of query results. Notice the difference in network traffic between the two schemes.

With the embedded SQL approach in Figure 19-13, every SQL statement must be sent across the network from client to server for processing. The DBMS must send back the results of each statement to the client system, so that the SQLCODE value can

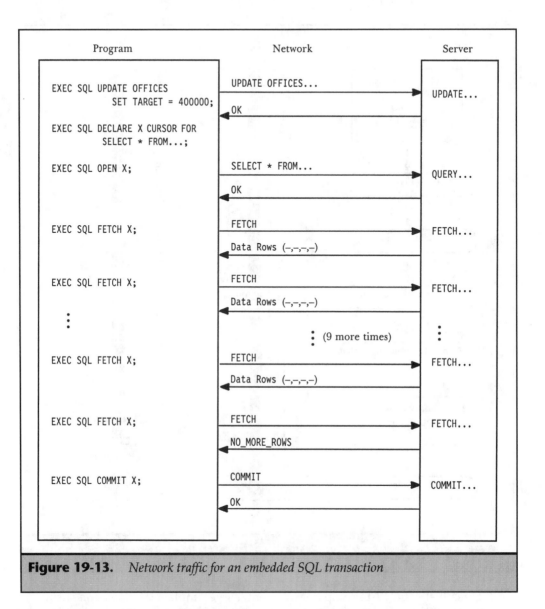

Figure 19-13. *Network traffic for an embedded SQL transaction*

be correctly set in the application program. Because the row-by-row processing of query results is handled by a SQL statement, each retrieved row also generates one complete round-trip across the network.

With the SQL Server approach in Figure 19-14, a single SQL statement invoking the stored procedure is sent across the network from client to server. The DBMS executes the stored procedure, generating a stream of status messages and query results that it sends back across the network to the client system. In this case the query results are

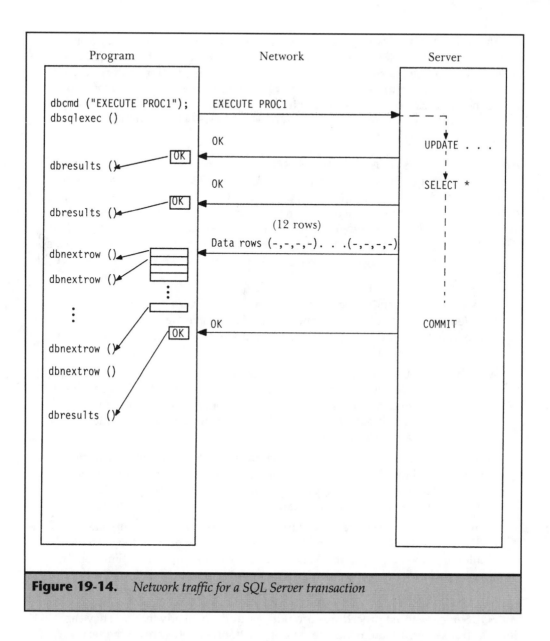

Figure 19-14. *Network traffic for a SQL Server transaction*

relatively small, and the DBMS sends them all back to the client system, where dblib stores them in buffers. The `dbnextrow()` calls from the program to dblib are then satisfied from the data in the buffers. Instead of the multiple round-trips required by the embedded SQL scheme, the SQL Server scheme generates one round-trip across the network.

The difference between the two architectures is not always so dramatic as in Figures 19-13 and 19-14. It may be impossible to incorporate all of a program's SQL statements into a single stored procedure, for example. In addition, if the query results have more than a few rows, the SQL Server DBMS must feed the query results back across the network to dblib in smaller pieces, generating more network traffic. Nonetheless, the advantages of the SQL Server architecture in a network environment are clearly shown by the two figures.

ADVANTAGES OF STORED PROCEDURES   SQL Server's stored procedures are similar in concept to the application plans stored in a DB2 database (described in Chapter 17) and to the access modules stored in a SQL/DS database (described in Chapter 18). Each of these structures stores the compiled form of one or more SQL statements. In fact, there is a logical progression from static SQL to dynamic SQL to SQL/DS's extended dynamic SQL to SQL Server's stored procedures. With each step in the progression, the compiled object stored in the database becomes more shareable and more capable:

- In static SQL, each embedded SQL statement generates its own compiled statement. The compiled statement is used exclusively at the single point in the program where the embedded statement appears. It cannot be shared by other programs, because they have no way of identifying the compiled statement.

- In dynamic SQL, each prepared SQL statement is identified by a statement name. The statement name allows other parts of the program to reuse the compiled statement during the same transaction. However, the compiled statement still cannot be shared by other programs, because the statement name is specific to a particular program.

- In extended dynamic SQL, each prepared SQL/DS statement is identified by a statement-id number. The statement-id is visible outside the confines of the database or of an individual program, allowing several programs to take advantage of a single compiled statement or a set of compiled statements.

- In SQL Server, each stored procedure is identified by a procedure name. Like the SQL/DS statement-id, the procedure name is visible outside the database, allowing several programs to take advantage of the procedure. Further, the compiled procedure may consist of an entire sequence of SQL statements, minimizing the number of requests the program must make to the DBMS.

SQL Server's stored procedures provide one additional advantage. They can include Transact-SQL statements that interact with other software on the server outside of the DBMS itself. For example, a stored procedure can send a mail message to another user or launch the execution of a user-written program on the server system. With this capability, a SQL Server DBMS can move beyond the role of a database server and take on a broader set of responsibilities as an applications server.

Positioned Updates

In an embedded SQL program, a cursor provides a direct, intimate link between the program and the DBMS query processing. The program communicates with the DBMS row by row as it uses the FETCH statement to retrieve query results. If the query is a simple, single-table query, the DBMS can maintain a direct correspondence between the current row of query results and the corresponding row within the database. Using this correspondence, the program can use the positioned update statements (UPDATE/WHERE CURRENT OF and DELETE/WHERE CURRENT OF) to modify or delete the current row of query results.

SQL Server query processing uses a much more detached, asynchronous connection between the program and the DBMS. In response to a statement batch containing one or more SELECT statements, SQL Server sends the query results back to the dblib software, which manages them. Row-by-row retrieval is handled by the dblib API calls, not by SQL language statements. As a result, SQL Server cannot support positioned updates, because the DBMS itself has no notion of a "current" row. The Transact-SQL dialect supports only the searched UPDATE and DELETE statements.

The lack of positioned update can be a real disadvantage in applications that let the user browse a set of query results and occasionally update the record currently being viewed. To minimize this disadvantage, the dblib API includes a special set of *browse mode* functions, summarized in Table 19-2. Using these functions, a program can create its own positioned update capability with this technique:

1. The table(s) to be queried and updated must have a unique index defined, and must include a TIMESTAMP column. The unique index ensures that each individual row of the table(s) can be located with a search condition; the TIMESTAMP column provides a way of determining how recently the contents of a particular row have been changed.

2. The program must open two connections to SQL Server—one to process the query and the other to handle updates to individual rows of query results.

3. The program sends a SELECT statement to SQL Server on the first connection, adding the keywords FOR BROWSE to the end of the statement. These keywords cause SQL Server to return additional information to dblib when it sends back the query results.

4. The program retrieves each row of query results normally, using the dbnextrow() call.

5. If the user wants to update the current row of query results, it generates a searched UPDATE statement. The UPDATE statement must specify the name of the table and column(s) to be updated and the new values for each column. If the programmer doesn't know the table and column names (for example, if the program calls a stored procedure to perform the query), the program can determine the names by calling the dbtabsource(), dbtabname(), dbcolsource(), and other browse mode functions.

Function	Description
dbtabcount()	Tells the number of source tables for the current query
dbtabname()	Tells the name of one of the source tables
dbtabbrowse()	Tells whether a particular table can be updated
dbcolbrowse()	Tells whether a particular column can be updated
dbtabsource()	Tells the name of the table that produced the specified column of query results
dbcolsource()	Tells the name of the column that produced the specified column of query results
dbqual()	Produces a WHERE clause that will select the row of query results currently being processed

Table 19-2. *Browse Mode dblib Functions*

6. The program calls the special dblib function dbqual() to generate an appropriate WHERE clause for the UPDATE statement. The WHERE clause specifies a match on the unique index (to ensure that the correct row is updated) and a match on the TIMESTAMP value (to ensure that no other user has updated the row since it was retrieved by the query).

7. The program sends the UPDATE statement to SQL Server on the second connection and calls dbresults() to be sure that it succeeded. If another user has modified the row or deleted it since the original query, the UPDATE statement will fail, because of its WHERE clause.

8. The program repeats Steps 4 through 7 for each row of query results.

This is the *only* way that positioned updates can be safely processed with SQL Server. The technique basically performs the update by "brute force" — pushing back on the application program responsibilities that are assumed by embedded SQL:

■ The application program must generate an UPDATE statement with a search condition that uniquely identifies the current row of query results, instead of being able to specify WHERE CURRENT OF.

■ The application must use timestamps to synchronize updates, instead of being able to rely on the SQL transaction mechanism, because two separate connections to the database, with two separate transaction contexts, are required.

Browsed updates are used relatively rarely in OLTP applications, because they tend to decrease database performance, so the browse mode functions are not normally needed by application programmers. That's fortunate, because positioned updates are an area where the SQL Server interface is much more complex than embedded SQL.

Dynamic Queries

In all of the program examples thus far in this chapter, the queries to be performed were known in advance. The columns of query results could be bound to program variables by explicit dbbind() calls hard-coded in the program. Most programs that use SQL Server can be written using this technique. (This static column binding corresponds to the fixed list of host variables used in the static SQL FETCH statement, described in Chapter 17.)

If the query to be carried out by a program is not known at the time the program is written, the program cannot include hard-coded dbbind() calls. Instead, the program must ask dblib for a description of each column of query results, using special API functions. The program can then bind the columns "on the fly" to data areas that it allocates at run-time. (This dynamic column binding corresponds to the use of the dynamic SQL DESCRIBE statement and SQLDA, described in Chapter 18.)

Figure 19-15 shows an interactive query program that illustrates the dblib technique for handling dynamic queries. The program accepts a table name entered by the user and then prompts the user to choose which columns are to be retrieved from the table. As the user selects the columns, the program constructs a SELECT statement and then uses these steps to execute the SELECT statement and display the data from the selected columns:

1. The program passes the generated SELECT statement to SQL Server using the dbcmd() call, requests its execution with the dbsqlexec() call, and calls dbresults() to advance the API to the query results, as it does for all queries.

2. The program calls dbnumcols() to find out how many columns of query results were produced by the SELECT statement.

3. For *each* column, the program calls dbcolname() to find out the name of the column, calls dbcoltype() to find out its data type, and calls dbcollen() to find out its maximum length.

4. The program allocates a buffer to receive each column of query results and calls dbbind() to bind each column to its buffer.

5. When all columns have been bound, the program calls dbnextrow() repeatedly to retrieve each row of query results.

```
main()
{
    /* This is a simple general-purpose query program.  It prompts
       the user for a table name, and then asks the user which
       columns of the table are to.be included in the query.  After
       the user's selections are complete, the program runs the
       requested query and displays the results.
    */

    LOGINREC   *loginrec;              /* data structure for login information */
    DBPROCESS  *dbproc;                /* data structure for connection */
    char       stmtbuf[2001];          /* SQL text to be executed */
    char       querytbl[32];           /* user-specified table */
    char       querycol[32];           /* user-specified column */
    int        status;                 /* dblib return status */
    int        first_col = 0;          /* is this the first column chosen? */
    int        colcount;               /* number of columns of query results */
    int        i;                      /* index for columns */
    char       inbuf[101];             /* input entered by user */
    char       *item_name[100];        /* array to track column names */
    char       *item_data[100];        /* array to track column buffers */
    int        item_type[100];         /* array to track column data types */
    char       *address;               /* address of buffer for current column */
    int        length;                 /* length of buffer for current column */

    /* Open a connection to SQL Server */
    loginrec = dblogin();
    DBSETLUSER(loginrec, "scott");
    DBSETLPWD (loginrec, "tiger");
    dbproc = dbopen(loginrec, "");

    /* Prompt the user for which table to query */
    printf("*** Mini-Query Program ***\n");
    printf("Enter name of table for query: ");
    gets(querytbl);

    /* Start the SELECT statement in the buffer */
    strcpy(stmtbuf, "select ");

    /* Query the SQL Server system catalog to get column names */
    dbcmd(dbproc, "select name from syscolumns ");
    dbcmd(dbproc, "where id = (select id from sysobjects ");
    dbcmd(dbproc, "where type = 'U' and name = ");
    dbcmd(dbproc, querytbl);
    dbcmd(dbproc, ")");
    dbsqlexec(dbproc);
```

Figure 19-15. *Using SQL Server for a dynamic query*

```
      /* Process the results of the query */
      dbresults(dbproc);
      dbbind(dbproc, querycol);
      while (status = dbnextrow(dbproc) == SUCCEED) {
         printf("Include column %s (y/n)? ", querycol);
         gets(inbuf);
         if (inbuf[0] == 'y') {
            /* User wants the column; add it to the select list */
            if (first_col++ > 0)  strcat(stmtbuf, ", ");
            strcat(stmtbuf, querycol);
         }
      }

      /* Finish the SELECT statement with a FROM clause */
      strcat(stmtbuf, "from ");
      strcat(stmtbuf, querytbl);

      /* Execute the query and advance to the query results */
      dbcmd(dbproc, stmtbuf);       ◄─────────────────────────①
      dbsqlexec(dbproc);            ◄───
      dbresults(dbproc);            ◄───

      /* Ask dblib to describe each column, allocate memory & bind it */
      colcount = dbnumcols(dbproc); ◄─────────────────────────②
      for (i = 0; i < colcount; i++) {
         item_name[i] = dbcolname(dbproc, i);  ◄──
         type = dbcoltype(dbproc, i);          ◄──────────────③
         switch(type) {

         case SQLCHAR:
         case SQLTEXT:
         case SQLDATETIME:
            length = dbcollen(dbproc, i) + 1;
            item_data[i] = address = malloc(length);    ◄──
            item_type[i] = NTBSTRINGBIND;
            dbbind(dbproc, i, NTBSTRINGBIND, length, address); ◄──④
            break;

         case SQLINT1:
         case SQLINT2:
         case SQLINT4:
            item_data[i] = address = malloc(sizeof(long));
            item_type[i] = INTBIND;
            dbbind(dbproc, i, INTBIND, sizeof(long), address);
            break;
```

Figure 19-15. *Using SQL Server for a dynamic query* (continued)

```
      case SQLFLT8:
      case SQLMONEY:
         item_data[i] = address = malloc(sizeof(double));
         item_type[i] = FLT8BIND;
         dbbind(dbproc, i, FLT8BIND, sizeof(double), address);
         break;
      }
   }

   /* Fetch and display the rows of query results */
   while (status = dbnextrow(dbproc) == SUCCEED) {          ◄————————⑤

      /* Loop, printing data for each column of the row */
      printf("\n");
      for (i = 0; i < colcount; i++) {

         /* Find the SQLVAR for this column; print column label */
         printf("Column # %d (%s): ", i+1, item_name[i]);

         /* Handle each data type separately */
         switch(item_type[i]) {

         case NTBSTRINGBIND:
            /* Text data -- just display it */
            puts(item_data[i]);
            break;

         case INTBIND:
            /* Four-byte integer data -- convert & display it */
            printf("%ld", *((int *) (item_data[i])));
            break;

         case FLT8BIND:
            /* Floating-point data -- convert & display it */
            printf("%lf", *((double *) (item_data[i])));
            break;
         }
      }
   }

   printf("\nEnd of data.\n");

   /* Clean up allocated storage */
   for (i = 0; i < colcount; i++) {
      free(item_data[i]);
   }
   dbexit (dbproc);
   exit();
}
```

Figure 19-15. *Using SQL Server for a dynamic query* (continued)

The SQL Server program in Figure 19-15 performs exactly the same function as the dynamic embedded SQL program in Figure 18-11. It's instructive to compare the two programs and the techniques they use:

- For both embedded SQL and dblib, the program builds a SELECT statement in its buffers and submits it to the DBMS for processing. With dynamic SQL, the special PREPARE statement handles this task; with the SQL Server API, the standard dbcmd() and dbsqlexec() functions are used.

- For both interfaces, the program must request a description of the columns of query results from the DBMS. With dynamic SQL, the special DESCRIBE statement handles this task, and the description is returned in a SQLDA data structure. With dblib, the description is obtained by calling API functions. Note that the program in Figure 19-15 maintains its *own* arrays to keep track of the column information.

- For both interfaces, the program must allocate buffers to receive the query results and must bind individual columns to those buffer locations. With dynamic SQL, the program binds columns by placing the buffer addresses into the SQLVAR structures in the SQLDA. With SQL Server, the program uses the dbbind() function to bind the columns.

- For both interfaces, the query results are returned into the program's buffers, row by row. With dynamic SQL, the program retrieves a row of query results using a special version of the FETCH statement that specifies the SQLDA. With SQL Server, the program calls dbnextrow() to retrieve a row.

Overall, the strategy used to handle dynamic queries is very similar for both interfaces. The dynamic SQL technique uses special statements and data structures that are unique to dynamic SQL; they are quite different from the techniques used for static SQL queries. In contrast, the SQL Server techniques for dynamic queries are basically the same as those used for all other queries. The only added features are the dblib functions that return information about the columns of query results. This makes the SQL Server approach easier to understand for the less experienced SQL programmer.

Other Function Call Interfaces

Although the SQL Server API has received much attention because of SQL Server's pioneering features, several other important DBMS products also provide a callable interface. The callable interface to Oracle is much smaller and more streamlined than the SQL Server API, and it closely parallels the Oracle embedded SQL interface in its capabilities. The SQLBase API also parallels embedded SQL, but like the SQL Server API, it provides features that go well beyond those provided by embedded SQL. These two APIs offer an excellent perspective on the different ways that SQL can be supported through a call interface. Their most interesting features are described in the next two sections.

The Oracle Call API

The primary programmatic interface to Oracle is the embedded SQL interface. However, Oracle also provides an alternative API interface, known as the *Oracle Call Interface*. The API includes about twenty calls as summarized in Table 19-3.

Function	Description
Database Connection/Disconnection	
olon()	Logs on to an Oracle database
oopen()	Opens a cursor (connection) for SQL statement processing
oclose()	Closes an open cursor (connection)
ologof()	Logs off from an Oracle database
Basic Statement Processing	
osql3()	Prepares (compiles) a SQL statement string
oexec()	Executes a previously compiled statement
oexn()	Executes with an array of bind variables
obreak()	Aborts the current Oracle call interface function
oermsg()	Obtains error message text
Statement Parameters	
obndrv()	Binds a parameter to a program variable (by name)
obndrn()	Binds a parameter to a program variable (by number)
Transaction Processing	
ocom()	Commits the current transaction
orol()	Rolls back the current transaction
ocon()	Turns on auto-commit mode
ocof()	Turns off auto-commit mode
Query Results Processing	
odsc()	Obtains a description of a query results column
oname()	Obtains the name of a query results column
odefin()	Binds a query results column to a program variable
ofetch()	Fetches the next row of query results
ofen()	Fetches multiple rows of query results into an array
ocan()	Cancels a query before all rows are fetched

Table 19-3.   *Oracle Call Interface Functions*

The Oracle call interface uses the term "cursor" to refer to a connection to the Oracle database. A program uses the `olon()` call to logon to the Oracle database, but it must use the `oopen()` call to open a cursor through which SQL statements can be executed. By issuing multiple `oopen()` calls, the applications program can establish multiple cursors (connections) and execute statements in parallel. For example, a program might be retrieving query results on one of its connections and use a different connection to issue `UPDATE` statements.

The most remarkable feature of the Oracle Call Interface is that it very closely parallels the embedded dynamic SQL interface. Figure 19-16 shows excerpts from two programs that access an Oracle database, one using embedded SQL and one using the call interface. Note that there is a one-to-one correspondence between the embedded SQL `CONNECT`, `PREPARE`, `EXECUTE`, `COMMIT`, and `ROLLBACK` statements and the equivalent calls. In the case of the `EXECUTE` statement, the host variables that supply parameter values are listed in the embedded `EXECUTE` statement and specified by `obndrv()` calls in the call interface. Note also that the embedded `UPDATE` statement in the figure has no direct counterpart in the call interface; it must be prepared and executed with calls to `osql3()` and `oexec()`.

The dynamic query processing features of the two Oracle interfaces are also very parallel:

- The embedded `DESCRIBE` statement becomes a series of calls to `oname()` and `odsc()` to retrieve the column names and data type information for query results. Each call returns data for a single column.

- Instead of having the program set `SQLDA` fields to bind query results columns to host variables, to bind columns the call interface uses calls to `odefin()`.

- The embedded `FETCH` statement becomes a call to `ofetch()` instead.

- The embedded `CLOSE` statement becomes a call to `ocan()`, which ends access to query results.

One unique and useful feature of the Oracle call interface is its ability to interrupt a long-running query. In embedded SQL and most SQL call interfaces, a program passes control to the DBMS when it issues an embedded `OPEN` statement or an "execute" call to start a query. The program does not regain control until the query processing is complete. Thus there is no mechanism for the program to interrupt the query. The Oracle call interface provides an `obreak()` function that can be called asynchronously, while the Oracle DBMS has control, to interrupt Oracle processing. Thus, if the program can regain control during a query (typically by setting a timer and receiving an interrupt when the time expires), the program can call `obreak()` to asynchronously terminate the query.

```
Embedded SQL Interface              Oracle Call Interface

EXEC SQL BEGIN DECLARE SECTION
char  text1[255];  /* stmt text */    char  text1[255];   /* stmt text */
char  text2[255];  /* stmt text */    char  text2[255];   /* stmt text */
int   parm1;       /* parameter */    int   parm1;        /* parameter */
float parm2;       /* parameter */    float parm2;        /* parameter */
char  city[31];    /* retrieved */    char  city[31];     /* retrieved */
float sales;       /* retrieved */    float sales;        /* retrieved */
EXEC SQL END DECLARE SECTION          LDA   *lda;         /* logon area */
                                      CDA   *crs;         /* cursor area */


EXEC SQL CONNECT USING SCOTT/TIGER;   olon(lda, "SCOTT/TIGER",. . .);


EXEC SQL UPDATE OFFICES               oopen(crs, lda, . . .);
         SET QUOTA = 0;               osql3(crs, "UPDATE OFFICES SET QUOTA = 0");
                                      oexec(crs);


EXEC SQL ROLLBACK WORK;               orol(lda);


EXEC SQL PREPARE stmt2 USING :text2;  osql3(crs, text2);


EXEC SQL EXECUTE stmt2                obndrn(crs, 1, &parm1, sizeof(int));
         USING :parm1, :parm2;        obndrn(crs, 2, &parm2, sizeof(float));
                                      oexec(crs);


EXEC SQL COMMIT WORK;                 ocom(lda);

EXEC SQL DECLARE C1 CURSOR FOR        osql3(crs, "SELECT CITY, SALES FROM OFFICES");
         SELECT CITY, SALES           odefin(crs, 1, city, 30, 5);
            FROM OFFICES;             odefin(crs, 2, &sales, sizeof(float), 4);
EXEC SQL OPEN C1;                     oexec(crs);

EXEC SQL FETCH C1                     ofetch(crs);
         INTO :city, :sales;


EXEC SQL CLOSE C1;                    ocan(crs);


EXEC SQL COMMIT WORK RELEASE;         oclose(crs);
                                      ologof(lda);
```

Figure 19-16. *Comparing Oracle's programmatic SQL interfaces*

The SQLBase API

The SQLBase DBMS offers an API as its sole programmatic SQL interface. The SQLBase API includes about 75 calls. The most frequently used calls are summarized in Table 19-4.

Function	Description
Database Connection/Disconnection	
sqlcon()	Connects to a SQLBase database by name
sqldis()	Disconnects from a SQLBase database
Basic Statement Execution	
sqlcom()	Compiles a SQL statement
sqlexe()	Executes a previously compiled statement
sqlcex()	Compiles and executes a statement in one step
sqlcty()	Obtains statement type of the statement just compiled
sqlerr()	Obtains error message text
sqlepo()	Obtains offset of error within statement text
Transaction Processing	
sqlcmt()	Commits a transaction
sqlrbk()	Rolls back a transaction
Statement Parameters	
sqlnbv()	Obtains the number of parameters in a statement
sqlbnn()	Binds a parameter to a program variable (by number)
sqlbnd()	Binds a parameter to a program variable (by name)
Query Results Processing	
sqlnsi()	Obtains the number of columns of query results
sqldes()	Obtains a description of a query results column
sqlssb()	Binds query results column to a program variable
sqlfqn()	Obtains the fully qualified name of a query results column
sqlefb()	Enables backwards fetching
sqlfet()	Fetches the next row of query results
sqlfbk()	Fetches the previous row of query results
sqlgfi()	Obtains information about a column in the current row

Table 19-4. *Basic SQLBase API Functions*

The SQLBase API blends some of the features of the Oracle and SQL Server APIs. Like the Oracle API, the core functions in the SQLBase API very closely parallel the statements of embedded SQL. For example:

■ The embedded FETCH statement becomes the sqlfet() call.

■ The embedded PREPARE statement becomes the sqlcom() ("compile") call.

■ The embedded EXECUTE statement becomes the sqlexe() call.

■ The embedded EXECUTE IMMEDIATE statement becomes the sqlcex() ("compile and execute") call.

■ The embedded COMMIT and ROLLBACK statements become the sqlcmt() and sqlrbk() calls.

■ The embedded DESCRIBE statement becomes a series of calls to the sqldes() function, which provides a description of an individual column of query results.

Figure 19-17 shows some program excerpts that compare the SQLBase API to the embedded SQL interface. The embedded SQL excerpts are the same ones shown in Figure 19-16, and a comparison of the figures reveals the strong parallels between the calls to the Oracle API and the corresponding calls to the SQLBase API.

Like the SQL Server API, the SQLBase API supports features and functions that go well beyond those provided in standard embedded SQL. Those features include:

■ *Scroll cursors.* A program can move both forward and backward through query results using a SQLBase cursor. The sqlefb() call enables bidirectional fetching, sqlfet() moves forward one row, and sqlfbk() moves backward one row.

■ *Named parameters.* Like Oracle, SQLBase allows parameters in statements to be assigned names, using a notation like that used by embedded SQL for host variables. The parameters can then be bound to program variables either by name (with sqlbnd()) or positionally by number (with sqlbnn()).

■ *Named statements.* Like SQL/DS, SQLBase allows you to compile a SQL statement and save its compiled form in the database for later use by one or more programs. The compiled SQL statement is given a name by the sqlsto() call and is recalled for use with the sqlres() call. The sqldst() call drops a compiled statement from the database.

■ *Result sets.* After performing a query, your program can tell SQLBase to establish the query results as a *result set*. Subsequent queries will draw their data *only* from the rows in the result set, not from the full tables in the database. In this way your program can run a sequence of queries, each of which further narrows the set of query results obtained by the previous query, to gradually focus in on the data that it needs. Table 19-5 shows the SQLBase API calls that support result set processing.

■ *Long data.* SQLBase can store very large data objects, such as documents and scanned images, as columns of a database. Special API calls, shown in Table 19-6, provide access to this "long data," allowing your program to retrieve and update the data piece by piece. For example, your program can retrieve a row that contains a 50-page document as one of its columns and retrieve the document a page at a time, allowing it to process the entire document while allocating enough memory to contain only a single page.

```
Embedded SQL Interface              SQLBase API

EXEC SQL BEGIN DECLARE SECTION
char  text1[255];  /* stmt text */   char    text1[255];  /* stmt text */
char  text2[255];  /* stmt text */   char    text2[255];  /* stmt text */
int   parm1;       /* parameter */   int     parm1;       /* parameter */
float parm2;       /* parameter */   float   parm2;       /* parameter */
char  city[31];    /* retrieved */   char    city[31];    /* retrieved */
float sales;       /* retrieved */   float   sales;       /* retrieved */
EXEC SQL END DECLARE SECTION         SQLTCUR crs;         /* stmt cursor */

EXEC SQL CONNECT USING SCOTT/TIGER;  sqlcon(&crs, "salesdb", 4, ...);

EXEC SQL UPDATE OFFICES              sqlcex(crs, "UPDATE OFFICES SET QUOTA = 0", 0);
          SET QUOTA = 0;

EXEC SQL ROLLBACK WORK;              sqlrbk(crs);

EXEC SQL PREPARE stmt2 USING :text2; sqlcom(crs, text2, 0);

EXEC SQL EXECUTE stmt2               sqlbnn(crs, 1, &parm1, sizeof(int), SQLPSIN);
          USING :parm1, :parm2;      sqlbnn(crs, 2, &parm2, sizeof(float), SQLPFLT);
                                     sqlexe(crs);

EXEC SQL COMMIT WORK RELEASE;        sqlcmt(crs);


EXEC SQL DECLARE C1 CURSOR FOR       sqlcom(crs, "SELECT CITY, SALES FROM OFFICES, 0);
          SELECT CITY, SALES         sqlssb(crs, 1, SQLPSTR, city, 30, ...);
            FROM OFFICES;            sqlssb(crs, 2, SQLPFLT, &sales, sizeof(float), ...);
EXEC SQL OPEN C1;                    sqlexe(crs);

EXEC SQL FETCH C1                    sqlfet(crs);
          INTO :city, :sales;

EXEC SQL CLOSE C1;                   sqlcan(crs);

EXEC SQL COMMIT WORK RELEASE;        sqldis(crs);
```

Figure 19-17. *Comparing embedded SQL and the SQLBase API*

Function	Description
sqlsrs()	Starts result set mode
sqlurs()	Ends result set mode, restoring normal query operation
sqlcrs()	Closes the result set, optionally saving it by name
sqlrrs()	Reopens a previously saved result set
sqldrs()	Drops a previously saved result set
sqlprs()	Positions to a specific row in a result set

Table 19-5. *SQLBase API Result Set Functions*

Function	Description
sqlgls()	Obtains the total size of a long data column in the current row of query results
sqlbld()	Establishes access to a long data column (by column name) for subsequent reading/writing
sqlbln()	Establishes access to a long data column (by column number) for subsequent reading/writing
sqlrlo()	Reads the next segment of a long data column into a program variable for a specified length
sqllsk()	Seeks to a specified byte position within a long data column; subsequent sqlrlo() calls read from this point
sqlwlo()	Adds data from a program variable to the end of a long data column
sqlelo()	Ends access to a long data column that was begun by a sqlbld() or sqlbln() call

Table 19-6. *SQLBase API Long Data Functions*

Function	Description
sqlcpy()	Copies bulk data within the database
sqlins()	Installs or creates a new database
sqldin()	De-installs a database
sqldir()	Lists available databases for this server
sqlgnr()	Obtains the number of rows in a table
sqlsta()	Retrieves database statistics
sqlsys()	Retrieves system statistics
sqltio()	Sets the lock timeout
sqlbkp()	Initiates network database backup
sqlrdc()	Reads "chunk" of database data for backup
sqlebk()	Ends network database backup
sqlres()	Initiates network database restore
sqlwdc()	Writes "chunk" of database data for restore
sqlers()	Ends network database restore

Table 19-7.   *SQLBase API Utility Functions*

■ *Utility functions.* Several calls in the SQLBase API support utility functions such as database backup and gathering of database statistics. These calls, which make the utility functions easily accessible to user-written programs, are listed in Table 19-7.

Summary

Several SQL-based DBMS products provide a callable API for programmatic database access:

■ Sybase, SQL Server, and SQLBase are examples of DBMS products that provide *only* a callable interface. Oracle is an example of a DBMS product that provides a callable API in addition to its embedded SQL interface.

■ A callable interface puts query processing, parameter passing, statement compilation, statement execution, and similar tasks into the call interface, keeping the programmatic SQL language identical to interactive SQL. With embedded SQL, these tasks are handled by special SQL statements (OPEN,

FETCH, CLOSE, DESCRIBE, PREPARE, EXECUTE, and so on) that are unique to programmatic SQL.

■ A callable interface can provide more efficient communication between the application program and the DBMS, and can be used to minimize the network traffic when the application program is on a different system than the database itself.

■ The callable APIs of the different DBMS brands all offer the same basic features, but they vary dramatically in the extended features that they offer and in the details of the calls and data structures that they use.

PART SIX

Future Directions

SQL has become an important computer industry standard, and its future evolution will have a significant impact on many parts of the industry. Chapter 20 describes the development of distributed databases, one of the most important areas of SQL research and development that is now finding its way into mainstream SQL products. Chapter 21 discusses the key trends in SQL's continuing evolution and the impact they may have through the 1990s and into the next decade.

Chapter Twenty

Distributed Database Management

One of the major computing trends over the last ten years has been the move from large centralized computers to distributed networks of computer systems. With the advent of minicomputers, data processing tasks such as inventory control and order processing moved from corporate mainframes to smaller departmental systems. The explosive increase in the popularity of the personal computer in the 1980s brought computer power directly onto the desktops of millions of people.

As computers and computer networks have spread through organizations, computer data no longer resides on a single system under the control of a single DBMS. Instead, data is spread across many different systems, each with its own database manager. Often the various computer systems and database management systems come from different manufacturers.

These trends have led to a strong focus in the computer industry and in the data management community on the problems of distributed database management. This chapter discusses the challenges of managing distributed data and the products that leading DBMS vendors have begun to offer to meet those challenges.

The Challenge of Distributed Data Management

Figure 20-1 shows a portion of a computer network that you might find in a manufacturing company, a financial services firm, or a distribution company. Data is stored on a variety of computer systems in the network:

- *Mainframes.* The company's core data processing applications, such as accounting and payroll, run on an IBM mainframe. Developed over the last 20 years, these applications store their data in IMS databases, and the company is using DB2 for a new mainframe application to be completed later this year.

- *Minicomputers.* The company's engineering organization uses a VAX minicomputer and Ingres for engineering support and time-sharing applications. Engineering test results are stored in the Ingres database. The company also uses Oracle databases on minicomputers located in its six distribution centers to manage inventory and to process orders.

- *LAN servers.* Several of the company's departments have been pioneers in the use of PC local area networks (LANs) to share printers and files. Recently the personnel department automated its personnel system using SQL Server and Windows NT. In the financial planning department, a planning application is being built by the data processing staff, which believes that DB2/2 running on OS/2 should be the DBMS of choice.

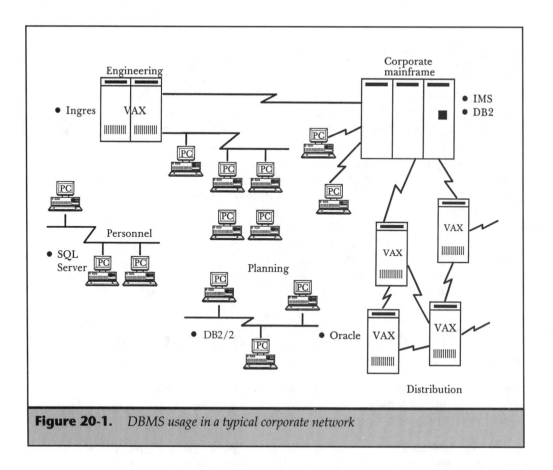

Figure 20-1. *DBMS usage in a typical corporate network*

■ *Personal computers.* Many of the company's employees use personal computers. They maintain personal databases using dBASE, Paradox, and even Lotus 1-2-3 spreadsheets. In a few cases the databases are shared with other users, using LAN versions of these products.

With data spread over many different systems, it's easy to imagine requests that span more than one database:

■ An engineer needs to combine lab test results (on a VAX) with production forecasts (on the mainframe) to choose among three alternative technologies.

■ A financial planner needs to link financial forecasts (in a DB2/2 database) to historical financial data (on the mainframe).

■ A product manager needs to know how much inventory of a particular product is in each distribution center (data stored on six VAXes) to plan product obsolescence.

■ Current pricing data needs to be downloaded from the mainframe to the distribution center VAXes daily.

■ Orders need to be uploaded from the VAXes to the mainframe daily so that the manufacturing plan can be adjusted.

■ Managers throughout the company want to query the various shared databases using the PC on their desktop.

As these examples suggest, access to distributed data is useful and will become critical as the trend toward distributed computing continues. All of the leading DBMS vendors are committed to delivering distributed database management, and some of them already offer limited distributed database capabilities. Industry pundits and others have written extensively about the features that should be provided by a distributed DBMS, and there is general agreement on these "ideal" characteristics:

■ *Location transparency.*   The user shouldn't have to worry about where the data is physically located. The DBMS should present all data as if it were local and be responsible for maintaining that illusion.

■ *Heterogeneous systems.*   The DBMS should support data stored on different systems, with different architectures and performance levels, including PCs, workstations, LAN servers, minicomputers, and mainframes.

■ *Network transparency.*   Except for differences in performance, the DBMS should work the same way over different networks, from high-speed LANs to low-speed telephone links.

■ *Distributed queries.*   The user should be able to join data from any of the tables in the (distributed) database, even if the tables are located on different physical systems.

■ *Distributed updates.*   The user should be able to update data in any table for which the user has the necessary privileges, whether that table is on the local system or on a remote system.

■ *Distributed transactions.*   The DBMS must support transactions (using COMMIT and ROLLBACK) across system boundaries, maintaining the integrity of the (distributed) database even in the face of network failures and failures of individual systems.

■ *Security.*   The DBMS must provide a security scheme adequate to protect the entire (distributed) database from unauthorized forms of access.

■ *Universal access.*   The DBMS should provide universal, uniform access to all of the organization's data.

No current distributed DBMS product even comes close to meeting this ideal. In fact, there are formidable obstacles that make it difficult to provide even simple forms of distributed database management. These obstacles include:

- *Performance.* In a centralized database, the path from the DBMS to the data has an access speed of a few milliseconds and a data transfer rate of several million characters per second. Even on a fast local area network, access speeds lengthen to tenths of a second and transfer rates fall to 100,000 characters per second or less. On a 9600 baud modem link, data access may take seconds or minutes, and 500 characters per second may be the maximum throughput. This vast difference in speeds can dramatically slow the performance of remote data access.

- *Integrity.* Distributed transactions require active cooperation by two or more independent copies of the DBMS software running on different computer systems if the transactions are to remain "all or nothing" propositions. Special "two-phase commit" transaction protocols must be used.

- *Static SQL.* A static embedded SQL statement is compiled and stored in the database as an application plan. When a query combines data from two or more databases, where should its application plan be stored? Must there be two or more cooperating plans? If there is a change in the structure of one database, how do the application plans in the other databases get notified?

- *Optimization.* When data is accessed across a network, the normal rules for SQL optimization don't apply. For example, it may be more efficient to sequentially scan an entire local table than to use an index search on a remote table. The optimization software must know about the network(s) and their speeds. Generally speaking, optimization becomes both more critical and more difficult.

- *Data compatibility.* Different computer systems support different data types, and even when two systems offer the same data type they often use different formats. For example, a VAX and a Macintosh store 16-bit integers differently. IBM mainframes store EBCDIC character codes while minicomputers and PCs use ASCII. A distributed DBMS must mask these differences.

- *System catalogs.* As a DBMS carries out its tasks, it makes very frequent access to its system catalogs. Where should the catalog be kept in a distributed database? If it is centralized on one system, remote access to it will be slow, bogging down the DBMS. If it is distributed across many different systems, changes must be propagated around the network and synchronized.

- *Mixed-vendor environment.* It's highly unlikely that all the data in an organization will be managed by a single brand of DBMS, so distributed database access will cross DBMS brand boundaries. This requires active cooperation between DBMS products from highly competitive vendors — an unlikely prospect.

- *Distributed deadlocks.* When transactions on two different systems each try to access locked data on the other system, a deadlock can occur in the distributed database, even though the deadlock is not visible on either of the two systems. The DBMS must provide global deadlock detection for a distributed database.

■ *Recovery.* If one of the systems running a distributed DBMS fails, the operator of that system must be able to run its recovery procedures independent of the other systems in the network, and the recovered state of the database must be consistent with that of the other systems.

Because of these obstacles, all of the leading DBMS vendors have taken a step-by-step approach to distributed data management. At first the DBMS may allow a user on one system to query a database located on one other system. In subsequent releases the distributed DBMS capabilities may grow, moving closer to the goal of providing universal, transparent data access.

Stages of Distributed Data Access

In 1989 IBM announced its blueprint for the step-by-step implementation of distributed data access in its SQL products. IBM was not the first vendor to offer distributed data access, and it is not the vendor with the most advanced distributed DBMS capability today. However, IBM's four stages, shown in Table 20-1, provide an excellent framework for understanding the distributed data management capabilities of IBM and other vendors. Of course the capabilities of IBM's DBMS products fall neatly into the stages described in the table.

The four stages of the IBM model deal with a simple definition of the distributed data access problem: a user of one computer system needs to access data stored on one or more other computer systems. The sophistication of the distributed access increases

Stage	Description
1. Remote request	Each SQL statement accesses a single remote database; each statement is a transaction.
2. Remote transaction	Each SQL statement accesses a single remote database; multi-statement transactions are supported for a single database.
3. Distributed transaction	Each SQL statement accesses a single remote database; multi-statement transactions are supported across multiple databases.
4. Distributed request	SQL statement may access multiple databases; multi-statement transactions are supported across multiple databases.

Table 20-1. *IBM's Four Stages of Distributed Database Access*

at each stage. Thus the capabilities provided by a given DBMS can be described in terms of which stage it has reached. In addition, within each stage a distinction can be made between read-only access (with the SELECT statement) and update access (with the INSERT, DELETE, and UPDATE statements). A DBMS product will often provide read-only capability for a given stage before full update capability is provided.

Remote Requests

The first stage of distributed data access, as defined by IBM, is a *remote request*, shown in Figure 20-2. In this stage, the PC user may issue a SQL statement that queries or updates data in a single remote database. Each individual SQL statement operates as its own transaction, similar to the "auto-commit" mode provided by many interactive SQL programs. The user can issue a sequence of SQL statements for various databases, but the DBMS doesn't support multi-statement transactions.

Remote requests are very useful when a PC user needs to query corporate data. Usually the required data will be located within a single database, such as a database of order processing or manufacturing data. Using a remote request, the PC program can retrieve the remote data for processing by a PC spreadsheet, graphics program, or desktop publishing package.

The remote request capability is not powerful enough for most transaction processing applications. For example, consider a PC-based order entry application that accesses a corporate database. To process a new order, the PC program must check inventory levels, add the order to the database, decrease the inventory totals, and

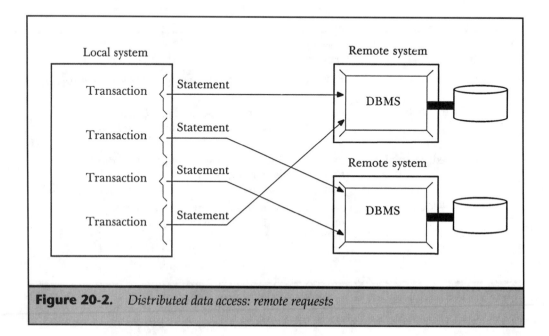

Figure 20-2.   *Distributed data access: remote requests*

adjust customer and sales totals, involving perhaps half a dozen different SQL statements. As explained in Chapter 11, database integrity can be corrupted if these statements do not execute as a single transaction. However, the remote request stage does not support multi-statement transactions, so it cannot support this application.

Remote request capability does not require a DBMS on the requesting system, and several vendors provide products that use this configuration. In the IBM product family, Host Data Base View (HDBV) provides a user interface on the IBM PC for querying a DB2 database on a mainframe, and Extended Connectivity Facility (ECF) allows a PC program to query a DB2 or SQL/DS database. Ingres offers its product, Ingres/PCLink, which provides a Lotus-style user interface for querying an Ingres database. Both Informix and Oracle offer add-in products for Lotus 1-2-3 that provide access to remote databases from within a spreadsheet.

Remote Transactions

The second stage of distributed data access, as defined by IBM, is a *remote transaction* (called a "remote unit of work" by IBM), shown in Figure 20-3. Remote transactions extend the remote request stage to include multi-statement transaction support. The PC user can issue a series of SQL statements that query or update data in a remote database and then commit or roll back the entire series of statements as a single transaction. The DBMS guarantees that the entire transaction will succeed or fail as a unit, as it does for transactions on a local database. However, all of the SQL statements that comprise the transaction must reference a single remote database.

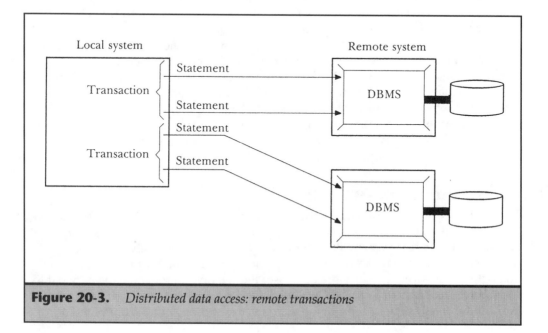

Figure 20-3. *Distributed data access: remote transactions*

Remote transactions open the door for distributed transaction processing applications. For example, in the order processing example described in the previous section, the PC program can now perform a sequence of queries, updates, and inserts in the inventory database to process a new order. The program ends the statement sequence with a COMMIT or ROLLBACK for the transaction.

Remote transaction capability typically requires a DBMS (or at least transaction processing logic) on the PC as well as the system where the database is located. The transaction logic of the DBMS must be extended across the network to ensure that the local and remote systems always have the same opinion about whether a transaction has been committed. However, the actual responsibility for maintaining database integrity remains with the remote DBMS.

Several DBMS vendors and several independent companies offer products with distributed transaction support. Digital Equipment Corporation's SQL Services product offers programmatic access to Rdb/VMS databases from a remote VAX, PC, Macintosh, or RISC-based workstation. Apple Computer's Data Access Language (DAL) allows a Macintosh application program to access a variety of host databases, including Oracle, Ingres, Sybase, Rdb/VMS, Informix, DB2, and SQL/DS, on Digital VAX and IBM mainframe systems. SQL Server's client/server architecture is based on a remote transaction capability, with the user located on a personal computer and the database located across a LAN on a server system. Microsoft's ODBC capability also provides remote transaction support.

Remote transaction capability is also often provided by database gateways that link one vendor's DBMS to other DBMS brands. For example, Oracle's SQL*Net products include gateways from Oracle to DB2 and to SQL/DS. Ingres provides similar gateways to DB2 and other brands of DBMS. Sybase has announced Open Server, an applications programming interface for SQL Server that allows independent software vendors to develop gateways from SQL Server to other DBMS brands.

Some gateway products go beyond the bounds of remote transactions, allowing a user to join, in a single query, tables from a local database with tables from a remote database managed by a different brand of DBMS. However, these gateways do not (and cannot) provide the underlying transaction logic required to support the higher stages of distributed access as defined by IBM. The gateway can ensure the integrity of the local and remote databases individually, but it cannot guarantee that a transaction will not be committed in one and rolled back in the other.

Distributed Transactions

The third stage of distributed data access, as defined by IBM, is a *distributed transaction* (a "distributed unit of work" in IBM parlance), shown in Figure 20-4. At this stage, each individual SQL statement still queries or updates a single database on a single remote computer system. However, the sequence of SQL statements within a transaction may access two or more databases located on different systems. When the transaction is committed or rolled back, the DBMS guarantees that all parts of the transaction, on all of the systems involved in the transaction, will be committed or

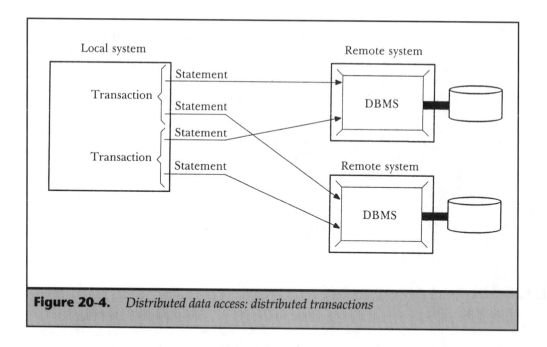

Figure 20-4. *Distributed data access: distributed transactions*

rolled back. The DBMS specifically guarantees that there will not be a "partial transaction," where the transaction is committed on one system and rolled back on another.

Distributed transactions support the development of very sophisticated transaction processing applications. For example, in the corporate network of Figure 20-1, a PC order processing application can query the inventory databases on two or three different VAX systems to check the inventory of a scarce product and then update the databases to commit inventory from multiple locations to a customer's order. The DBMS ensures that other concurrent orders will not interfere with the remote access of the first transaction.

Distributed transactions are much more difficult to provide than the first two stages of distributed data access. It's impossible to provide distributed transactions without the active cooperation of the individual DBMS systems involved in the transaction. A special transaction protocol, called the *two-phase commit* protocol, is generally used to enforce this cooperation. The details of this protocol are described later in this chapter.

Because distributed transactions are a major step, most DBMS vendors have decided to support them in stages. Both Ingres (with Ingres/Star) and Oracle (with SQL*Net) have taken this approach, announcing distributed read-only transactions for current or soon-to-be-available releases of their software, and announcing plans to support distributed read/write transactions in the future. IBM announced limited distributed transaction support in DB2 Version 2 Release 2, shipped in 1989. The DB2 support provides distributed read-only transactions across multiple mainframes running DB2. It also supports distributed updates, but restricts updates to a single system per transaction. Effectively, this means that DB2 provides distributed transactions for queries, but only remote transactions for updates. The distributed transaction support is provided only for DB2-to-DB2 connections, not across different IBM SQL products.

Sybase and SQL Server also provide distributed transactions, but they place the burden of the distributed transaction on the application program. The program must explicitly connect to two SQL Servers and must send the appropriate SQL statements over each connection. When it is time to commit or roll back a transaction, the standard COMMIT and ROLLBACK statements are not used. Instead, the program uses a special set of two-phase commit calls in the SQL Server API to synchronize the commits of the two SQL Server copies. Although the scheme provides full support for distributed transactions (including distributed updates), it has been criticized for its lack of transparency.

Distributed Requests

The final stage of distributed data access in the IBM model is a distributed request, shown in Figure 20-5. At this stage, a single SQL statement may reference tables from two or more databases located on different computer systems. The DBMS is responsible for automatically carrying out the statement across the network. A sequence of distributed request statements can be grouped together as a transaction.

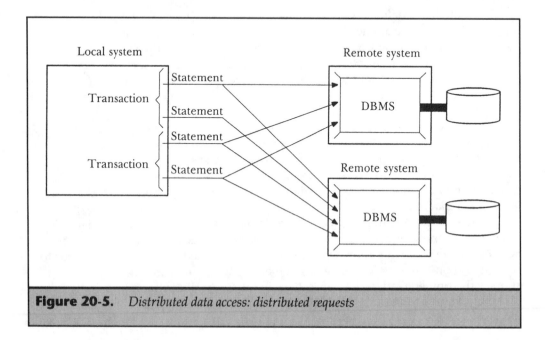

Figure 20-5. *Distributed data access: distributed requests*

As in the previous distributed transaction stage, the DBMS must guarantee the integrity of the distributed transaction on all systems that are involved.

The distributed request stage doesn't make any new demands on the DBMS transaction processing logic, because the DBMS already had to support transactions across system boundaries at the previous distributed transaction stage. However, distributed requests pose major new challenges for the DBMS optimization logic. The optimizer must now consider network speed when it evaluates alternate methods for carrying out a SQL statement. If the local DBMS must repeatedly access part of a remote table (for example, when making a join), it may be faster to copy part of the table across the network in one large bulk transfer rather than repeatedly retrieving individual rows across the network.

The optimizer must also decide which copy of the DBMS should handle statement execution. If most of the tables are on a remote system, it may be a good idea for the remote DBMS on that system to execute the statement. However, that may be a bad choice if the remote system is heavily loaded. Thus the optimizer's task is both more complex and much more important in a distributed request.

Ultimately, the goal of the distributed request stage is to make the entire distributed database look like one large database to the user. Ideally, the user would have full access to any table in the distributed database and could use SQL transactions without knowing anything about the physical location of the data. Unfortunately, this "ideal" scenario would quickly prove impractical in real networks. In a network of any size, the number of tables in the distributed database would quickly become very large, and users would find it impossible to find data of interest. The user-ids of every database in the organization would have to be coordinated to make sure that a given user-id uniquely identified a user in *all* databases. Database administration would also be very difficult.

In practice, therefore, distributed requests must be implemented selectively. Database administrators must decide which remote tables are to be made visible to local users and which will remain hidden. The cooperating DBMS copies must translate user-ids from one system to another, allowing each database to be administered autonomously while providing security for remote data access. Distributed requests that would consume too many DBMS or network resources must be detected and prohibited before they impact overall DBMS performance.

Because of their complexity, distributed requests are not fully supported by any commercial SQL-based DBMS today, and it will be some time before even a majority of their features are available. The Oracle and Ingres distributed database products provide limited distributed request capability today. With both systems, a table in a remote database can appear as if it were a local table, and the user can execute multi-table queries that combine data from local and remote tables. However, the full transaction support required by the IBM definition of a distributed request is not provided, and multi-table access is restricted to database queries only.

Distributed Tables

The IBM-defined stages of distributed data access treat a database table as an indivisible unit. They assume that a table is located on a single system, in a single database, under the control of a single copy of the DBMS. Some of the research on distributed databases has relaxed this restriction, allowing an individual table to be distributed across two or more systems. Commercial DBMS products do not yet provide distributed tables, but several of the DBMS vendors have publicly stated that they will provide the capability in the future.

At first, the idea of splitting a table across multiple computer systems may seem silly or academic. However, there are certain types of applications where it makes a great deal of sense to split a table. Two different types of table split—horizontal and vertical—are appropriate in different situations.

Horizontal Table Splits

One way to distribute a table across a network is to divide the table horizontally, placing different rows of the table on different systems. Figure 20-6 shows a simple example where a horizontal table split is useful. In this application, a company

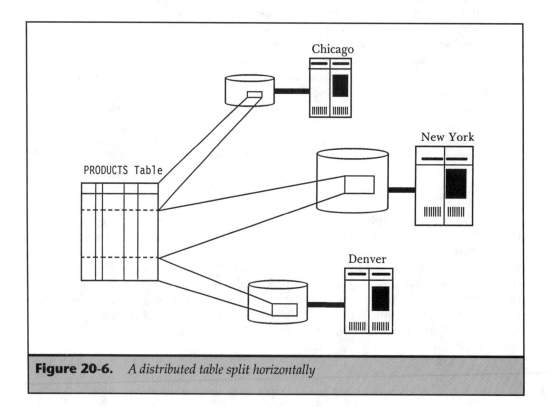

Figure 20-6.   *A distributed table split horizontally*

operates three distribution centers, each with its own computer system and DBMS to manage an inventory database. Most of the activity in each distribution center involves locally stored data, but the company has a policy of satisfying a customer's order from *any* distribution center if the local center is out of stock on a particular product.

To implement this policy, the PRODUCTS table is split horizontally into three parts and expanded to include a LOCATION column that tells where the inventory is located. The rows of the table that describe inventory in each distribution center are stored locally and managed by that center's DBMS. However, for order processing purposes, the PRODUCTS table is one large table, which may be queried and updated as a unit.

Horizontally split tables require major changes in the DBMS and its optimization logic. Consider these three queries against the PRODUCTS table, which are executed on the system located in New York:

Find all items built by ACI in the New York distribution center.

```
SELECT *
  FROM PRODUCTS
 WHERE LOCATION = 'New York'
   AND MFR_ID = 'ACI'
```

Find all items built by ACI in the Chicago distribution center.

```
SELECT *
  FROM PRODUCTS
 WHERE LOCATION = 'Chicago'
   AND MFR_ID = 'ACI'
```

Find all items manufactured by ACI.

```
SELECT *
  FROM PRODUCTS
 WHERE MFR_ID = 'ACI'
```

The three queries appear to be very similar. However, the first one can be handled locally, the second requires a remote request, and the third one requires a distributed request that spans all three systems. The DBMS must handle the three queries very differently.

Database updates also require special handling by the DBMS. For example, when the DBMS processes an INSERT statement like this one:

```
INSERT INTO PRODUCTS (MFR_ID, PRODUCT_ID, LOCATION, ...)
    VALUES ('ACI', '41004', 'New York', ...)
```

it must decide on which system it should store the new row. Further, an update to the row like this one:

```
UPDATE PRODUCTS
   SET LOCATION = 'Chicago'
 WHERE MFR = 'ACI'
   AND PRODUCT = '41004'
```

should actually cause the DBMS to delete a row on one system and insert it on another. As these statements show, the DBMS must have detailed knowledge of the split table and its contents to handle SQL requests efficiently.

Vertical Table Splits

Another way to distribute a table across a network is to divide the table vertically, placing different columns of the table on different systems. Figure 20-7 shows a simple example of a vertical table split. The SALESREPS table has been expanded to include new columns of personnel information (phone number, marital status, and so on) and is now being used by both the order processing department and the personnel department, each of which has its own computer system and DBMS. Most of the activity in each department focuses on one or two columns of the table, but there are many queries and reports that use both personnel-related and order-related columns.

To store the salesperson data, the SALESREPS table is split vertically into two parts. The columns of the table that store personnel data (NAME, AGE, HIRE_DATE, PHONE, MARRIED) are stored on the personnel system and managed by its DBMS. The other columns (EMPL_NUM, QUOTA, SALES, REP_OFFICE) are stored on the order processing system and managed by its DBMS. However, the SALESREPS table is treated as one large table, which may be queried and updated as a unit.

Note that these two queries against the SALESREPS table appear very similar, yet one will involve local access, and the other remote:

Find the names of all salespeople over 30 years old.

```
SELECT NAME, AGE
  FROM SALESREPS
 WHERE AGE > 30
```

Show the quota performance of all salespeople in Chicago.

```
SELECT EMPL_NUM, SALES, QUOTA
  FROM SALESREPS
 WHERE REP_OFFICE = 12
```

The following query requires that the DBMS collect parts of each row from the two different systems:

Show the quota performance of all salespeople in Chicago.

```
SELECT NAME, SALES, QUOTA
  FROM SALESREPS
 WHERE REP_OFFICE = 12
```

With a vertical table split, the DBMS does not have to worry about the contents of the rows to determine where data is located. However, it has the equally difficult problem of maintaining a one-to-one relationship between the partial rows located on two or more different systems. Further, vertically split tables may require major changes in the DBMS locking logic. If a program needs to lock a row, the DBMS must now lock parts of the row on more than one system. Should the DBMS lock all parts of

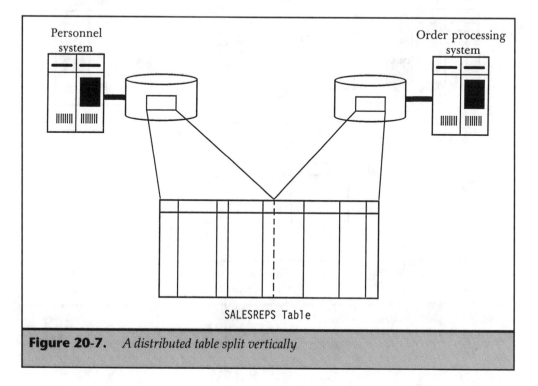

Figure 20-7. *A distributed table split vertically*

the row, or only the parts actually being updated? Depending on the decision, the DBMS may need to implement item-level locking.

Mirrored Tables

The design of a distributed database should ideally follow an *80/20 rule:* 80 percent (or more) of database access requests should be satisfied locally, with only 20 percent (or fewer) requiring remote access. If one or two of the tables in a distributed database are heavily used by many users on different systems, however, it can be difficult to achieve this 80/20 balance. No matter where these tables are located, access to them by users on other systems will generate network traffic and delays.

One solution to this problem is the use of a *mirrored table,* where duplicate copies of a table are stored on several systems, as shown in Figure 20-8. When a user runs a query that references the table, the local copy of the table can be used, reducing network traffic and speeding database throughput. However, updates to the mirrored table must be synchronized so that all copies of the table are updated at the same time, to prevent users on different systems from seeing inconsistent versions of the table. For this reason, mirrored tables are practical only for tables that have heavy read access but are infrequently updated. In the sample database, the CUSTOMERS table

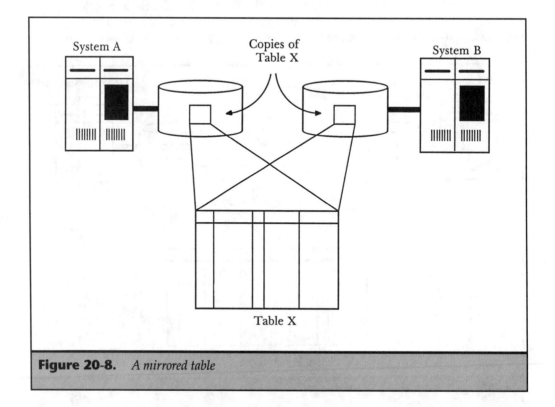

Figure 20-8. *A mirrored table*

might be a good candidate for mirroring, but the ORDERS table would not be a good candidate.

Replicated Tables

The overhead associated with keeping mirrored tables in perfect synchronization can be substantial, and in many applications it is not absolutely essential that all copies of a mirrored table be *exactly* in synchronization with one another. For example, consider the order processing in the sample database, and assume that order processing is distributed across five different computer systems that are geographically distributed around the world, through a distributed database. Incoming orders are checked against the PRODUCTS table to be certain that there is enough inventory on hand to fill the order.

Suppose the company's policy is that the order processing clerk must be able to absolutely guarantee a customer that products can be shipped within 24 hours of the time an order is accepted. In this case, the PRODUCTS table must contain absolutely up-to-the-minute data, reflecting the inventory impact of orders taken just seconds earlier. There are only two possible designs for the database in this case. There could be a single, central copy of the PRODUCTS table, shared by all users at all five order processing sites. Alternatively, there could be a fully mirrored copy of the PRODUCTS table at each of the five sites. The fully mirrored solution is probably impractical, because the frequent updates to the PRODUCTS table as each order is taken will cause excessive network traffic to keep the five copies of the table in perfect synchronization.

But suppose the company believes it can still maintain adequate customer satisfaction with a policy that is slightly less strict—for example, that it promises to notify any customer within 24 hours if their order cannot be filled immediately and give the customer an opportunity to cancel the order. In this case, a replicated PRODUCTS table becomes an excellent solution. Overnight, updates to the PRODUCTS table can be downloaded to the replicated copy at each of the five sites. During the day, orders are verified against the *local copy* of the PRODUCTS table, but only the local PRODUCTS table is updated. This prevents the company from taking an order for which there was not adequate stock on hand at the beginning of the day, but it does not prevent orders taken at two or three different sites from exceeding the available stock. The next night, when data communications costs are lower than they are during the day, the orders from each site are transmitted to a central site, which processes them against a central copy of the PRODUCTS table. Orders that cannot be filled from inventory are flagged, and a report of them is generated. When processing is complete, the updated PRODUCTS table, along with the "problem orders report" is transmitted back to each of the five sites to prepare for the next day's processing.

As this situation shows, replicated tables involve a compromise to the ideal of a transparent, distributed database. That compromise is almost always reflected in a compromise in the quality of the data processing that the database can support, as in this example. However, those compromises are often the most practical way to solve real-world business problems, given the costs and complexity of data communications and distributed databases today. Over the last several years, the new distributed database features being announced and developed for commercial SQL products have shifted from pure, ideal distributed database features to more practical approaches, such as replicated tables. Support for replicated tables includes the ability to maintain a single definition of the table, to automatically propagate changes to the definition to all copies of the table, to automatically track updates to the different copies of the table and handle synchronization in a semi-automatic batch process, etc. Over the next few years, it's likely that all popular commercial DBMS products will offer both distributed and replicated approaches to distributing data. As always, careful decision design will be required to choose the best approach for each specific application and collection data.

The Two-Phase Commit Protocol *

A distributed DBMS must preserve the "all or nothing" quality of a SQL transaction if it is to provide distributed transactions. The user of the distributed DBMS expects that a committed transaction will be committed on all of the systems where data resides, and that a rolled back transaction will be rolled back on all of the systems as well. Further, failures in a network connection or in one of the systems should cause the DBMS to abort a transaction and roll it back, rather than leaving the transaction in a partially committed state.

All commercial DBMS systems that support or plan to support distributed transactions use a technique called *two-phase commit* to provide that support. You don't have to understand the two-phase commit scheme to use distributed transactions. In fact, the whole point of the scheme is to support distributed transactions without your knowing it. However, understanding the mechanics of a two-phase commit can help you plan efficient database access.

To understand why a special two-phase commit protocol is needed, consider the database in Figure 20-9. The user, located on System A, has updated a table on System B and a table on System C, and now wants to commit the transaction. Suppose that the DBMS software on System A tried to commit the transaction by simply sending a COMMIT message to System B and System C, and then waiting for their affirmative replies. This strategy works so long as Systems B and C can both successfully commit their part of the transaction. But what happens if a problem such as a disk failure or a deadlock condition prevents System C from committing as requested? System B will commit its part of the transaction and send back an acknowledgment, System C will roll back its part of the transaction because of the error and send back an error message, and the user ends up with a partially committed, partially rolled back transaction. Note that System A can't "change its mind" at this point and ask System B to roll back the transaction. The transaction on System B has been committed, and other users may already have modified the data on System B based on the changes made by the transaction.

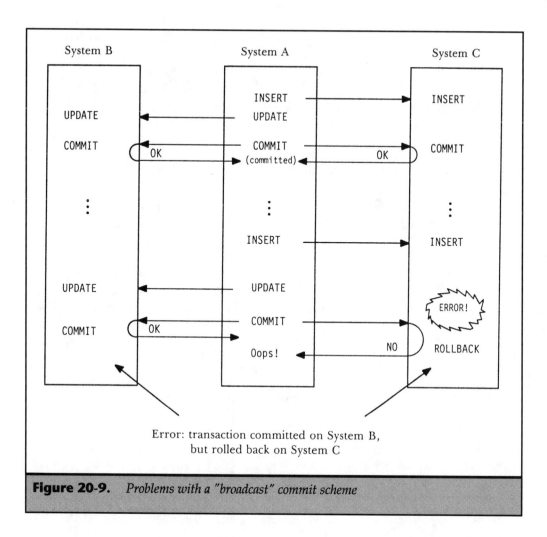

Error: transaction committed on System B,
but rolled back on System C

Figure 20-9. *Problems with a "broadcast" commit scheme*

The two-phase commit protocol eliminates the problems of the simple strategy shown in Figure 20-9. Figure 20-10 illustrates the steps involved in a two-phase commit:

1. The program on System A issues a COMMIT for the current (distributed) transaction, which has updated tables on System B and System C. System A will act as the *coordinator* of the commit process, coordinating the activities of the DBMS software on Systems B and C.

2. System A sends a GET READY message to both System B and System C, and notes the message in its own transaction log.

3. When the DBMS on System B or C receives the GET READY message, it must prepare *either* to commit or to roll back the current transaction. If the DBMS can get into this "ready to commit" state, it replies YES to System A and notes that fact in its local transaction log; if it cannot get into this state, it replies NO.

4. System A waits for replies to its GET READY message. If all of the replies are YES, System A sends a COMMIT message to both System B and System C, and notes the decision in its transaction log. If any of the replies is NO, or if all of the replies are not received within some timeout period, System A sends a ROLLBACK message to both other systems and notes that decision in its transaction log.

5. When the DBMS on System B or C receives the COMMIT or ROLLBACK message, it *must* do as it is told. The DBMS gave up the ability to decide the transaction's fate autonomously when it replied YES to the GET READY message in Step 3. The DBMS commits or rolls back its part of the transaction as requested, writes the COMMIT or ROLLBACK message in its transaction log, and returns an OK message to System A.

6. When System A has received all the OK messages, it knows the transaction has been committed or rolled back and returns the appropriate SQLCODE value to the program.

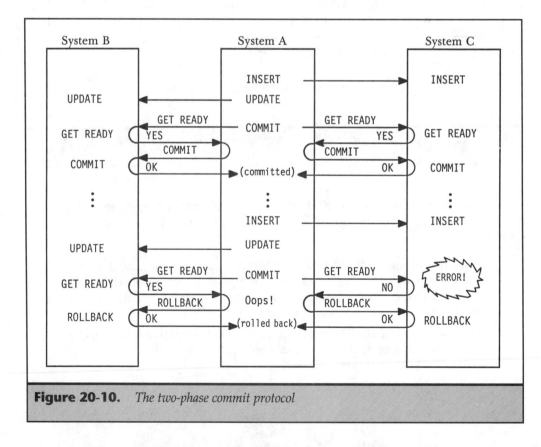

Figure 20-10. *The two-phase commit protocol*

This protocol protects the distributed transaction against any single failure in System B, System C, or the communications network. These two examples illustrate how the protocol permits recovery from failures:

- Suppose a failure occurs on System C before it sends a YES message in Step 3. System A will not receive a YES reply and will broadcast a ROLLBACK message, causing System B to roll back the transaction. The recovery program on System C will not find the YES message or a COMMIT message in the local transaction log, and it will roll back the transaction on System C as part of the recovery process. All parts of the transaction will have been rolled back at this point.

- Suppose a failure occurs on System C after it sends a YES message in Step 3. System A will decide whether to commit or roll back the distributed transaction based on the reply from System B. The recovery program on System C will find the YES message in the local transaction log, but will not find a COMMIT or ROLLBACK message to mark the end of the transaction. The recovery program then asks the coordinator (System A) what the final disposition of the transaction was and acts accordingly. Note that System A must maintain a record of its decision to commit or roll back the transaction until it receives the final OK from all of the participants, so that it can respond to the recovery program in case of failure.

The two-phase commit protocol guarantees the integrity of distributed transactions, but it generates a great deal of network traffic. If there are n systems involved in the transaction, the coordinator must send and receive a total of $(4 * n)$ messages to successfully commit the transaction. Note that these messages are *in addition* to the messages that actually carry the SQL statements and query results among the systems. However, there's no way to avoid the message traffic if a distributed transaction is to provide database integrity in the face of system failures.

Because of their heavy network overhead, distributed transactions can have a serious negative effect on database performance. For this reason, distributed databases must be carefully designed so that frequently accessed (or at least frequently updated) data is on a local system or on a single remote system. If possible, transactions that update two or more remote systems should be a relatively rare occurrence.

Summary

This chapter described the distributed data management capabilities offered by various DBMS products and the trade-offs involved in providing access to remote data:

- A distributed database is typically implemented by a network of computer systems, each running its own copy of the DBMS software and operating autonomously for local data access. The copies of the DBMS cooperate to provide remote data access when required.

- The "ideal" distributed database is one in which the user doesn't know and doesn't care that the data is distributed; to the user, all of the relevant data appears as if it were on the local system.

- Because this ideal distributed DBMS is very difficult (and perhaps impossible) to provide, commercial DBMS products are providing distributed database capability in phases.

- IBM has defined four stages of remote data access: remote requests, remote transactions, distributed transactions, and distributed requests, with each stage providing broader capability than the previous one. The IBM definitions are very rigorous, and none of IBM's DBMS products has fully achieved the third stage.

- Other DBMS vendors, such as Oracle and Ingres, have provided remote access to multiple databases within a single statement, but have either limited the update capabilities of the statement or have not provided full transaction support for distributed transactions.

- The capability of distributing individual tables across multiple systems in a network can be useful in certain applications, but this capability is still in the research stage for most DBMS vendors.

- Distributed databases present serious implementation challenges for a DBMS vendor, especially in the areas of optimization, locking, and transaction management. In these areas, the DBMS must be aware of the various systems and networks, and it must use special techniques such as two-phase commits to support remote data access.

Chapter Twenty-one

The Future of
SQL

596

SQL is one of the most important technologies driving and shaping the computer market today. From its first commercial implementation a little more than a decade ago, SQL has grown to become *the* standard database language. With the backing of IBM, the blessing of standards bodies, and the enthusiastic support of DBMS vendors, the evidence clearly shows the importance of SQL:

- IBM's flagship databases, on systems from mainframe processors to personal computers, are all based on SQL.

- Every major independent DBMS vendor and most computer hardware manufacturers either offer or plan to offer SQL-based products.

- SQL-based databases are beginning to dominate in virtually every market segment, from personal computers to OLTP systems, and especially in the "downsizing" of applications onto PC local area networks.

- SQL-based access to databases is emerging as a key feature of popular PC software products, such as spreadsheets and PC databases.

This chapter describes the current trends in the database market and the impact that they will have both on SQL and on the computer market of the 1990s.

Database Market Trends

As the 1990s began, the size of the market for database management products crossed the three billion dollar mark, and forecasters predicted continued healthy growth throughout the decade. At the same time, the neat divisions that had characterized the database market of the 1980s were rapidly fading. DBMS products could no longer be clearly categorized as "PC databases," "minicomputer databases," "OLTP databases," "mainframe databases," and so on, each participating in its own market segment. Instead, standardization on SQL and the relational database model created a new, more unified database market.

These changes in the market have produced dramatic changes in the fortunes and marketing strategies of DBMS vendors. To be successful, a DBMS vendor must provide SQL support and then provide additional value-added on top of SQL. Established DBMS vendors whose products are not based on SQL are scrambling to provide SQL support and hold on to their installed base of systems. The experiences of Ashton-Tate in the PC market and Cullinet in the mainframe market show how this phenomenon has cut across all segments of the database market. Meanwhile, DBMS vendors who already have SQL-based products are taking advantage of the opportunity, attacking both established vendors and each other.

The battle lines are particularly well drawn in two segments of the computer market. In the transaction processing segment, the major hardware vendors (such as IBM, Digital, and Tandem) have all introduced OLTP systems based on relational databases (DB2, Rdb/VMS, and NonStop SQL, respectively), competing with independent DBMS vendors (such as Oracle, Ingres, and Sybase) who tout transaction processing versions of their products. In the personal computer segment, the advent of OS/2, and more recently Windows NT, has produced a clash between the hardware giant (IBM, with OS/2), the personal computer software giant (Microsoft, with SQL Server), and the largest independent DBMS vendor (Oracle, Informix, Sybase, Gupta, et al.) for dominance of the desktop and PC LAN segment.

As the experience of these two market segments shows, the rise of SQL has produced a dramatic reorientation of the database market, which is still in progress. Competition based on market segment is giving way to competition based on other factors, including:

- DBMS features and SQL extensions
- Transaction processing performance
- Portability across multiple hardware platforms
- DBMS vendor reputation
- Distribution channels
- Support and service

With the changing competitive landscape, it seems very likely that some of the leading DBMS vendors at the beginning of the decade will no longer be leaders at the end of the decade.

Hardware Performance Trends

One of the most important contributors to the rise of SQL during the 1980s was a dramatic increase in the performance of relational databases. Part of this performance increase was due to advances in database technology and query optimization. However, most of the DBMS performance improvement came from gains in the raw processing power of the underlying computer systems. For example, with the introduction of DB2 Version 2, IBM claimed performance of 270 transactions per second (tps), up 120 percent from 123 tps for the previous release of DB2. However, a closer examination of the benchmark results showed that the performance of the DB2 software itself improved only 51 percent, from 123 tps to 186 tps. The remaining 69 percent of the performance increase was due to the more powerful mainframe on which the tests of the new DB2 software had been conducted.

The performance improvements in mainframe systems were paralleled in the minicomputer market, where the VAX 11/780 was replaced by VAXes with ten or twenty times its power, and in the personal computer market, where the Intel 8086 gave way to the 80286, 80386, 80486, and Pentium processors. These hardware advances overcame the higher overhead of the relational data model and gave it performance comparable to the nonrelational databases of a decade ago.

The improvements in computer hardware price/performance should continue unabated through the 1990s, providing continuing performance improvements for relational DBMS products.

Microprocessors based on the Reduced Instruction Set Computing (RUC) architecture will bring performance formerly found only on $50,000 workstations at popular PC prices. The Power PC processors, jointly developed by Apple, IBM and Motorola, are leading this trend. In response, Intel is moving aggressively to push the price/performance of its X86 architecture forward. Some of the most dramatic advances are coming from multiprocessor systems, where two, four, eight, or more processors operate in parallel, sharing the processing workload. A multiprocessor architecture is especially appropriate for OLTP applications, where the workload consists of many small, parallel database transactions. Traditional OLTP vendors, such as Tandem, have always used a multiprocessor architecture, but multiprocessor systems are now becoming part of the data processing mainstream. The largest mainframe systems already use a multiprocessor design, and multiprocessor systems have an important part of the VAX minicomputer product line and UNIX-based servers. These developments will drive down the cost of multiprocessor systems, further improving the price/performance of relational database systems.

Multiprocessor architectures pose a special dilemma for DBMS vendors who bypass the operating system in an attempt to improve database performance. The Sybase DBMS, for example, operates as a single process and takes responsibility for its own task management, event handling, and input/output—functions that are usually handled by an operating system such as UNIX or VMS. While this improves performance on a single-processor system, it prevents the operating system from automatically spreading the Sybase workload across multiple processors. To reap the advantages of a multiprocessor system, the Sybase DBMS software must be rewritten, duplicating the logic that is already in the operating system. By contrast, DBMS products that do not bypass the operating system can automatically benefit from the multi processor environment. Oracle and Ingres both use this argument to defend their own architectures, and they point to benchmark results on multiprocessor systems as proof of their claim.

Several companies are combining high-performance microprocessors, fast disk drives, and multiprocessor architectures to build dedicated systems that are optimized as database servers. These vendors argue that they can deliver much better database performance with a specially designed database engine than with a general-purpose computer system. In some cases, their systems include application-specific integrated circuits (ASICs) that implement some of the DBMS logic in hardware for maximum speed.

Dedicated database systems from companies such as Teradata and Sharebase (formerly Britton-Lee) have found some acceptance in applications that involve complex queries against very large databases. However, they have not become an important part of the mainstream database market and most of these vendors have met with limited success or have been acquired by larger, general-purpose computer companies. History shows that other application-specific systems (such as word processors) have had a very difficult time keeping up with the pace of technical advancement and the economies of scale in the general-purpose computer market. Dedicated database systems will have to overcome these formidable obstacles if they are to play more than a niche role.

The Benchmark Wars

Relational databases and SQL have become part of the data processing mainstream, and they are being used to implement serious data processing applications. As a result, users are paying more attention to the performance of SQL products to ensure that their chosen DBMS won't "run out of gas" as their applications expand. This user concern, coupled with the DBMS vendors' interest in the lucrative transaction processing market, has produced "benchmark wars" among DBMS vendors. Virtually all of the DBMS vendors have joined the fray, each touting benchmarks that show the superior performance of its products while trying to discredit the benchmarks of the other vendors.

Unfortunately, most of the benchmarks and the resulting data are designed to support vendor marketing claims rather than to enlighten users about DBMS performance in real applications. Most of the benchmarks are vendor-proprietary, but two vendor-independent benchmarks have emerged. The Debit/Credit benchmark simulates simple accounting transactions. The TP1 benchmark, first defined by Tandem in 1985, measures a mix of typical OLTP transactions.

In a series of 1989 benchmark results, a multiprocessor Tandem minicomputer specialized for OLTP applications performed at 40 to 50 tps on a TP1 benchmark. Oracle's TP1 performance on midrange VAX systems ranged from 30 to 40 tps. Sybase performance on midrange VAX systems was also in the 30 to 40 tps range. SQL Server running on a Compaq 386/33 PC performed at 8 to 12 tps, slightly better than the 5 to 10 tps performance of Sybase on a MicroVAX II, a low-end VAX minicomputer. This last result gave some early credibility to the claim that PC local area networks had become a viable alternative to minicomputers for data processing applications.

All indications point to a continuing escalation of the benchmark wars over the next few years. Computer systems with multiple processors, tightly coupled servers, improvements in database caching techniques, and other trends will continue to push the performance claims of the DBMS vendors higher. For example, Oracle has already claimed performance of up to a thousand transactions per second on an NCUBE, a massive parallel system that links up to 8192 processors in parallel.

In an attempt to bring more stability and meaning to the benchmark data, several vendors and database consultants have banded together to produce a standard relational database benchmark that would allow meaningful comparisons among various DBMS products. This group, called the Transaction Processing Council, has defined a series of "official" benchmarks, known as "TPC-A", "TPC-B" and "TPC-C". The Council has also assumed a role as a clearinghouse for publishing the results of benchmarks run on various brands of DBMS and computer systems, and more recently for validating benchmark claims made by database and computer system vendors. The results of TPC benchmarks are expressed in transactions per second (tps), but it's common to hear the results referred to simply by the benchmark name (e.g."Informix on a 2-processor Compaq server with SCO UNIX delivered 120 TPC-Bs"). Interestingly, the TPC benchmarks specify an increasing size of the database used for the benchmark as the claimed number of transactions per second goes up. A TPC benchmark result of 30 tps may reflect a test run on a database of 100 megabytes of data, for example, while a result of 100 tps on the same benchmark may reflect a test on a 4 gigabyte database. This provision of the TPC benchmarks is designed to add more realism to the benchmark results, since the size of database and computer system that a user would require to support an application with demands in the 30 tps range is typically much smaller than the scale required to support an application with 100 tps demands.

In addition to raw performance, the TPC benchmarks also measure database price/performance. The "price" used in the calculation is specified by the council as the five-year ownership cost of the database solution, including the purchase price of the computer system, the purchase price of the database software, five years maintenance and support costs, etc. The price/performance measure is expressed in "dollar-per-TPC" (e.g. "Oracle on an NCUBE machine broke through the $500-per-TPC-B barrier"). While higher numbers are better for transactions-per-seconds results; lower numbers are better for price/performance measure.

When the TPC-A benchmark first appeared, it sparked a new round in the benchmark wars, with competing advertisements and database "run-offs" at industry trade shows. Unfortunately, the TPC-A benchmark was relatively simple, and it was relatively easy for the DBMS vendors to artificially improve their results by tuning their DBMS software for the benchmark transactions. The TPC-B benchmark reduced this tendency by specifying a more complex transaction workload, but over time it too has become subject to heavy database tuning. The most recent benchmark, TPC-C, is growing in popularity and is widely viewed as more representative of real commercial database workload than either of its predecessors. If history is any indication, the DBMS vendors will discover how to tune for this new benchmark over the next few years, its validity will decrease as a result, and a TPC-D benchmark will emerge to continue the cycle.

Despite vendor claims about OLTP performance, there are lingering doubts about the suitability of SQL for high-volume transaction processing applications. The best advice for prospective buyers of a SQL-based DBMS is to be skeptical of vendor benchmark claims and to ask questions about how the benchmark was performed, on what kind of hardware, and by whom. For real information about how a DBMS will perform in your application, the best data can be obtained by prototyping the application and benchmarking it on your own data. A discussion with another user who has implemented an application similar to yours using the proposed DBMS can also provide useful information.

Bundled DBMS Products

With the unveiling of its SAA strategy, IBM showed that it considers a relational database to be a strategic product that is logically an extension of a computer's operating system. The IBM product offerings support this point of view. DB2 operates as a subsystem of the MVS operating system on IBM mainframes, and the OS/400 operating system for the AS/400 midrange systems includes an integrated relational DBMS. With OS/2, IBM made the point even more explicit by combining a relational DBMS with key communications functions and calling the result OS/2 Extended Edition. More recently, IBM has brought its own technology to OS/2, through its DB2/2 products.

Other computer system vendors, independently and in response to IBM, have also concluded that relational databases are a strategic technology, and they now offer vendor-proprietary DBMS products for their systems:

- Digital Equipment Corporation has poured millions of dollars into the development of Rdb/VMS and VAX SQL, its relational DBMS products for the VAX/VMS family of systems.

- Hewlett-Packard has invested heavily in Allbase, a hybrid DBMS that supports HPSQL, a relational interface, and also provides backward compatibility with Image, a popular HP DBMS based on the network data model.

- Tandem has developed NonStop SQL, a relational DBMS that supports disk mirroring and other special features for its fault-tolerant family of OLTP systems.

- Data General offers DG/SQL, an implementation of SQL for its MV family of minicomputer systems.

In the early 1990s, Digital took the most aggressive stance of these computer vendors by bundling the Rdb/VMS run-time modules with every copy of the VAX/VMS operating system. This move drew sharp criticism from the independent DBMS vendors, who charged that Digital was using its clout as a hardware vendor to gain unfair competitive advantage for what they claim is a mediocre product. In fact, the independent DBMS vendors continued to prosper and grow on the VAX platform despite Digital's decision to bundle Rdb/VMS.

Digital's bundling move and IBM's packaging of SQL across its product line indicate the new importance that computer vendors are attaching to relational database technology and SQL. In the future, these vendors may further enhance the performance of their proprietary SQL products by building database support directly into their hardware and operating systems. In response, the independent DBMS vendors will continue to offer innovative new features, portability across multiple hardware platforms, and independence from any particular computer vendor. With the emergence of UNIX, Netware and Windows NT as vendor-independent server operating system platforms, it appears that the independent DBMS vendors are poised to win this battle. As the 1990s unfold, hardware vendors — and especially those offering standards-based LAN servers — appear to be moving toward cooperative rather than competitive relationships with the DBMS vendor community.

SQL Standards

The adoption of an official ANSI/ISO SQL standard was one of the major factors that secured SQL's place as the standard relational database language in the 1980s. Compliance with the ANSI/ISO standard has become a checkoff item for evaluating DBMS products, so each DBMS vendor claims that its product is "compatible with" or "based on" the ANSI/ISO standard. Through the late 1980s and early 1990s, all of the popular DBMS products evolved to conform to the parts of the standard that represented common usage. Other parts, such as the module language, were effectively ignored. This produced slow convergence around a core SQL language in popular DBMS products.

As discussed in Chapter 3, the SQL1 standard was relatively weak, with many omissions and areas that are left as implementation choices. For several years, the standards committee worked on an expanded SQL2 standard that remedies these weaknesses and significantly extends the SQL language. Unlike the first SQL standard, which specified features that were already available in most SQL products, the SQL2 standard is an attempt to lead rather than follow the market. It specifies features and functions that are not yet widely implemented in today's DBMS products, such as scroll cursors, standardized system catalogs, much broader use of subqueries, and a new error message scheme. With the publication of the SQL2 standard, DBMS vendors have begun a new process of slowly evolving their products to support it. Most vendors are targeting full SQL2 compliance as part of their strategy for the mid-to-late 1990s.

In addition to the ANSI/ISO SQL standard, IBM's SQL products will continue to be a powerful influence on SQL in the 1990s. As the developer of SQL and the largest DBMS software vendor in the world, IBM's SQL decisions have always had a major impact on other vendors of SQL products. When the IBM and ANSI SQL dialects have differed in the past, most independent DBMS vendors have chosen to follow the IBM standard. Although the movement to open systems and vendor independence has reduced IBM's clout, it is likely that independent DBMS vendors will continue to closely watch and follow IBM's products.

While the ANSI/ISO and IBM standards focus on the SQL language itself, other groups have been working to standardize the application programming interface to SQL. The ISO Remote Data Access (RDA) standard falls into this category; it is an attempt to standardize database access across a network. The RDA work progressed very slowly, and was handicapped by its strong tie to the OSI protocols. In 1989 a group of database vendors, calling themselves the SQL Access Group, joined together to develop their own standard for remote database access. With Microsoft's strong encouragement, this effort led to publication of a standard SQL API from SQL Access

Group. Microsoft's ODBC product, based on that API, has been a strong public relations success for Microsoft. Its long-term impact, and the role of SQL APIs in future "official" standards, remains an open question.

In summary, the various SQL standards will continue to grow and evolve through the 1990s. The existence of several different standards, together with the introduction of new extensions and proprietary features from the DBMS vendors, ensures that there will not be a single, portable version of SQL in the near future. Instead, the SQL standards will continue to be treated as guidelines and goals rather than ironclad rules. An ever-expanding "core SQL" will become more and more standard, while important new SQL features continue to generate differences among SQL implementations.

SQL Language Extensions

SQL is just over ten years old as a commercial product, and it is still actively growing and changing in its adolescence. DBMS vendors are investing heavily in SQL extensions and new features, including:

- *Procedural statements.* The addition of traditional programming language statements (IF/THEN/ELSE, GOTO, FOR, and WHILE loops, and so on) to SQL allows users to "glue together" SQL DML and DDL statements into complete SQL scripts. This capability is especially useful in a client/server architecture, because the server can execute an entire SQL script without statement-by-statement interaction with the requesting program, minimizing network traffic.

- *Stored procedures.* Stored procedures allow a sequence of SQL statements to be precompiled, named, and stored in the database for later execution. They combine the flexibility of dynamic SQL (the application program can decide which procedure to execute at run-time) with the performance of static SQL (the procedure code is precompiled, and the DBMS simply executes it at run-time).

- *Triggers.* Triggers allow a DBMS to automatically execute a SQL statement or statement sequence in response to an external event, such as an attempt to update, insert, or delete data in a table. With triggers, the DBMS can take a more active role in enforcing database integrity and business rules.

- *Rules.* Several DBMS vendors have begun to incorporate rules and other features borrowed from knowledge-based systems into their relational databases. Rules allow a database to encompass the "rules of thumb" and normal operating procedures of an organization, storing not only raw data but also knowledge about how an organization operates.

- *Scroll cursors.* Scroll cursors support the development of database browsing programs that allow a user to move freely forward and backward through a set of query results. This type of user interface can be very valuable in decision support and database query applications.

The most active work on extending the SQL language is being done by the independent DBMS vendors, such as Sybase, Oracle, Ingres, and Informix. Sybase already supports procedural statements, stored procedures, and triggers in its Transact-SQL dialect. Ingres Version 6.3 added support for stored procedures and rules. Oracle supported procedural statements in the transaction processing option of Oracle Version 6, and added referential integrity and stored procedure support to Oracle Version 7. Informix currently supports scroll cursors and offers Informix-4GL, a fourth generation language that combines SQL and procedural language statements.

In this area the 1990s are likely to continue the history of the 1980s, as each vendor introduces new SQL features that it hopes will provide a compelling reason for customers to purchase its DBMS products. The result is a continuous game of technical leapfrog, with each vendor forging ahead in certain areas while playing catch-up with its competitors in other areas. In the process, those features that the market deems important (procedural statements and stored procedures are the current favorites) will find their way into all of the products from leading independent DBMS vendors.

Complex Data Types

SQL was originally conceived and designed to handle typical data processing data such as integers, floating point and decimal numbers, and short character strings. As relational databases have become more popular, however, users want them to store and organize other types of data, such as scanned images, computer-aided-design drawings, spreadsheets, entire documents, and so on. Complex data types such as these are often referred to as *binary large objects*, or "blobs".

With the SQL language and DBMS technology of the 1980s, the only way to manage blobs was to store them in files, separate from the database. The database itself stored descriptive information about the object (such as a document's author, title, date, and keywords) and the name of the file where the object was stored. The application program could then use SQL to search the database, but was forced to use conventional file input/output to process the blob itself. However, pressure has mounted to extend SQL and support blobs directly within the database.

At first it may seem straightforward to support a blob directly as a SQL data type, stored in a column of a relational table. However, blobs raise several serious issues for SQL and the relational model:

■ *Nonatomic data.* The relational model assumes that each column in each row contains a single, atomic data item, but blobs often have parts and subparts and sub-subparts. This structure cannot be represented without violating the relational model.

■ *Random retrieval.* If a blob contains a substructure, the application program may want to retrieve individual parts of the blob (for example, sections of a document or layers of a circuit board layout) without retrieving all of the blob. SQL doesn't provide any mechanism for selecting and retrieving parts of a data item.

■ *Memory limitations.* With conventional SQL, an application program fetches an entire row of data into its buffers for processing. However, a large blob can easily exceed the available main memory of a personal computer. To process such blobs, a program *must* be able to store and retrieve them piece by piece, just as it processes data files.

■ *Searching.* If a blob column contains text data, a user may want to select rows based on a full-text search of the contents of the blob. Other searches may be appropriate for other types of blobs. These nonstandard searches require extensions to the SQL language.

Despite these obstacles, support for blobs has become a hot issue, especially for DBMS products that run on personal computers and workstations that manipulate complex data objects. The major DBMS vendors have all announced support for blobs in new versions of their DBMS products, and other DBMS vendors can be expected to follow. However, the development of techniques to store, retrieve, search, and process blobs is in its infancy and will continue to be an active area of SQL development and change well into the 1990s. The demand for blobs that can handle very large data items will also expand as users move to store, retrieve and manipulate multimedia objects in SQL databases.

Client/Server Applications

The exploding popularity and aggressive pricing of personal computers has produced a major change in the way that organizations are implementing new data processing applications. Increasingly, application designers no longer assume a central minicomputer or mainframe communicating with dozens of users seated at "dumb" computer terminals. Instead, applications are migrating to personal computers, where they can take advantage of the PC's graphical user interface. The database that supports the application is stored on a database server, linked to the personal computers by a local area network. PC local area networks with OS/2-based, UNIX-based, Netware-based and Windows NT-based database servers thus pose a serious competitive threat to minicomputers for new data processing applications. These products became the fastest growing part of the SQL database market in the early 1990s.

This client/server approach to application design is accelerating the acceptance of relational databases, with the SQL language forming the interface between the personal computer and the database server. Some computer industry analysts, noting this phenomenon, have concluded that SQL database servers have become a commodity, and that the standardization of SQL will allow a SQL-based application to access data stored in any SQL-based database. Such pronouncements are at best premature, and probably off the mark. Performance and extended features are still major selling points for SQL-based DBMS servers, and major differences in SQL dialects make interchangeable front-end applications impossible to achieve with today's products.

SQL Access from PC Applications

The growing use of personal computers in corporate networks has generated intense interest in providing access to corporate databases from within desktop applications. PC users want to be able to use off-the-shelf PC-based tools to analyze and graph corporate data and incorporate it into their spreadsheets and word processing documents. DBMS vendors, PC software vendors, and personal computer vendors have all announced strategies and tools for providing this remote data access:

- Oracle, Ingres, and Sybase each offer an application programming interface on one or more PC platforms (MS-DOS, MS-Windows, OS/2, and Macintosh), providing access both to PC versions of their DBMS and, via their networking capabilities, to their DBMS products running on multi-user systems. Each of these DBMS vendors is actively lobbying PC software vendors to support its interface.

- Lotus Development Corporation announced its own data access interface, called Datalens, which is incorporated into Lotus 1-2-3 and other Lotus products. Datalens allows a spreadsheet user to select, insert, and delete data from SQL-based databases for which Datalens drivers have been developed. Datalens drivers have been announced or demonstrated for Oracle, Novell's Netware SQL, Gupta's SQLBase, and dBASE IV. While Lotus continues to support Datalens, it has also announced support for Microsoft's rival ODBC API, raising the possibility of reduced commitment to Datalens in the future.

- Several PC application vendors have positioned their products as portable front-ends for access to SQL-based databases. PC databases and spreadsheets, especially, have been demonstrated as front-ends to multiple back-end servers, including SQL Server, DB2, and Oracle Server. In each case, a separate database adapter generates the SQL dialect required by each supported server.

- Apple Computer offers Data Access Language (DAL), a standard SQL-based connectivity language that links Macintosh applications to minicomputer and mainframe databases, including Oracle, Ingres, Sybase, Informix, Rdb/VMS, DB2, and SQL/DS. DAL masks the differences between these databases, allowing a Macintosh application to make standard DAL requests for remote data access, regardless of the brand of DBMS being accessed.

■ Microsoft's ODBC product is a major entrant in this field, with drivers for many leading SQL databases either available or promised, and the mantle of "standard" conferred by SQL Access Group.

Despite a flurry of product announcements in the early 1990s, PC access to corporate data is still a relatively new phenomenon, and vendor strategies for providing that access are still evolving. In particular, the question of ODBC's role and whether it can become a widely used technology remains open. The enthusiastic response to the early products from both PC users and data processing professionals indicates the importance of this phenomenon and should further expand the set of PC applications that support remote data access over the next few years.

Database Tools

The growing popularity of SQL-based DBMS products has produced a strong secondary market for database tools. These tools support the development, administration, and use of SQL-based databases, and include:

■ application development tools, such as 4GLs, forms packages, and computer-aided software engineering (CASE) packages

■ data access tools, such as graphical query interfaces, database browsing programs, and report writers

■ database administration tools, including backup and recovery utilities and database performance monitors

■ graphical user interface tools that support popular PC and workstation environments such as MS-Windows, OS/2, Open Look, and Motif

Several DBMS vendors see the database tools market as a substantial business opportunity, either in addition to or in place of their core DBMS business. Ingres, for example, has signed an OEM agreement with Digital Equipment Corporation, under which Digital sells Ingres database tools for use with its Rdb/VMS DBMS. Unify Corporation, an early vendor of UNIX-based databases, has turned its focus on its Accell development environment and now offers it for use with other vendor's SQL-based databases.

In the PC arena, Gupta Technologies' SQL Windows provides a graphical user interface under MS-Windows, supporting Gupta's SQLBase and other SQL-based PC databases. Lotus Development Corporation, which began development of its own SQL database engine, has abandoned that strategy and repositioned its products as front-end tools for use with SQL Server and other SQL database engines. Several startup software companies in the database tools arena have also seen rapid success and acceptance of their products. PowerSoft's PowerBuilder product emerged as an early favorite tool for building database front-ends for PCs running Microsoft Windows. Other companies, such as Transaction Technologies and Forte Software, specialized in tools for transaction processing applications. In many cases, these startup companies were founded by former executives of the leading relational database vendors, who saw database tools as the "next big opportunity" in the database market. Over the next few years, database tools specifically and object-oriented development tools in general will emerge as a major application category in their own right, and the most popular database tools will provide support for a range of popular SQL-based database engines.

Distributed Databases

As discussed in Chapter 20, distributed database management is one of the most active areas of DBMS development today, and the steadily increasing support for distributed data will be one of the most important developments of the 1990s. DBMS vendors will unveil distributed database support in stages, and announcements driven by competitive pressures will typically precede actual product availability by six months or more. For example, Oracle disclosed plans for two-phase commit protocols and location transparency in Oracle Version 7 in 1989, a full year before its anticipated availability. It will take until the late 1990s or beyond until the ability to transparently update remote databases with full database integrity is a routine feature of SQL-based products.

Most DBMS vendors are primarily focused on providing distributed database capability among their own DBMS products, with secondary emphasis on gateways to other DBMS environments. Oracle, Ingres, and Rdb/VMS each provide gateways to the major IBM mainframe databases. Sybase also provides a DB2 gateway, and goes a step further with its Open Server specification, which allows third parties to build gateways to other DBMS environments. Without any standards for distributed databases or the underlying protocols, gateways will continue to play a secondary role in the DBMS market. Distributed networks that mix different DBMS brands cannot provide the same kind of transparency and transaction integrity offered by a single-vendor network without such standards.

As in many other areas, IBM's actions could produce a dramatic change in distributed databases. To date, the protocols that IBM uses for internal communications among its distributed DBMS products are closed and proprietary to IBM. If IBM were to publish and standardize these protocols, however, independent DBMS vendors would rush to support them as a way of providing distributed access to DB2 and SQL/DS. The DBMS vendors could also use these IBM protocols as a "vendor-neutral" method of communicating among their DBMS systems, effectively providing a standard for implementing a heterogeneous distributed database. Whether IBM will take such a dramatic step, or whether it will see a competitive advantage in having a closed, vendor-proprietary distributed DBMS, remains to be seen.

Object-Oriented Databases

Much of the academic research in the database area over the past several years has been concentrated on new, "post-relational" data models. Just as the relational model provided clear-cut advantages over the earlier hierarchical and network models, the goal of this research is to develop new data models that will overcome some of the disadvantages of the relational model. Today, most research on new data models is focused on so-called "object-oriented" databases. Enthusiastic supporters of object-oriented databases claim that they are the next generation of database systems and predict that they will mount a serious challenge to relational databases by the turn of the century.

Unlike the relational data model, where Codd's 1970 paper provided a clear, mathematical definition of a relational database, there is no agreement on what an object-oriented database is. When researchers use the term, they are generally describing a database that uses the same organizing principles as object-oriented programming. Those principles include:

- *Objects.* In an object-oriented database, everything is an object and is manipulated as an object. The tabular, row/column organization of a relational database is replaced by the notion of collections of objects. Generally, a collection of objects is itself an object and can be manipulated in the same way that other objects are manipulated.

- *Classes.* Object-oriented databases replace the relational notion of atomic data types with a hierarchical notion of classes and subclasses. For example, VEHICLES might be a class of object, and individual members ("instances") of that class would include a car, a bicycle, a train, or a boat. The VEHICLES class might include subclasses called CARS and BOATS, representing a more specialized form of vehicle. Similarly, the CARS class might include a subclass called CONVERTIBLES, and so on.

- *Inheritance.* Objects inherit characteristics from their class and from all of the higher-level classes to which they belong. For example, one of the characteristics of a vehicle might be "number of passengers." All members of the CARS, BOATS, and CONVERTIBLES classes also have this attribute, because they are subclasses of VEHICLES. The CARS class might also have the attribute "number of doors," and the CONVERTIBLES class would inherit this attribute. However, the BOATS class would not inherit the attribute.

- *Messages and methods.* Objects communicate with one another by sending and receiving *messages.* When it receives a message, an object responds by executing a *method,* a program stored within the object that determines how it processes the message. Thus an object includes a set of behaviors described by its methods. Usually an object shares many of the same methods with other objects in its class.

These principles and techniques make object-oriented databases well-suited to applications involving complex data types, such as computer-aided-design or compound documents that combine text, graphics, and spreadsheets. The database provides a natural way to represent the hierarchies that occur in complex data. For example, an entire document can be represented as a single object, composed of smaller objects (sections), composed of still smaller objects (paragraphs, graphs, and so on). The class hierarchy allows the database to track the "type" of each object in the document (paragraphs, charts, illustrations, titles, footnotes, and so on). Finally, the message mechanism offers natural support for a graphical user interface. The application program can send a "draw yourself" message to each part of the document, asking it to draw itself on the screen. If the user changes the shape of the window displaying the document, the application program can respond by sending a "resize yourself" message to each document part, and so on. Each object in the document bears responsibility for its own display, so new objects can easily be added to the document architecture.

There are several commercial object-oriented databases currently on the market, but they have had only limited sales success to date. However, object-oriented databases have already stirred up a storm of controversy in the database community. Proponents claim that object-oriented databases will eventually replace the relational data model. Critics claim that object-oriented databases are simply a rehash of the hierarchical databases of the 1960s, with new terminology and a new twist on old concepts. Relational database vendors claim that most, if not all, of the benefits of object-oriented databases can be achieved by adding blob support to a relational database.

Object-oriented databases will likely play an increasing role in specialized market segments, such as engineering design, compound document processing, and graphical user interfaces. However, it is unlikely that they will have a major impact on mainstream data processing applications over the next few years. With the support of an official standard, the market clout of IBM, and the backing of several major independent DBMS vendors, the SQL bandwagon is simply too powerful to be derailed by a handful of object-oriented DBMS vendors any time in the near future. Moreover, the SQL vendors have demonstrated their ability to move quickly to accommodate new features when they become serious issues for customer purchase decisions. But of all the trends in the database market, the development of object-oriented databases is the only one that threatens the continued dominance of SQL as the decade unfolds.

Appendix A

The Sample Database

612

Most of the examples in this book are based on the sample database described in this appendix. The sample database contains data that supports a simple order processing application for a small distribution company. It consists of five tables:

- CUSTOMERS, which contains one row for each of the company's customers.
- SALESREPS, which contains one row for each of the company's ten salespeople.
- OFFICES, which contains one row for each of the company's five sales offices where the salespeople work.
- PRODUCTS, which contains one row for each type of product that is available for sale.
- ORDERS, which contains one row for each order placed by a customer. For simplicity, each order is assumed to be for a single product.

Figure A-1 graphically shows the five tables, the columns that they contain, and the parent/child relationships among them. The primary key of each table is shaded.

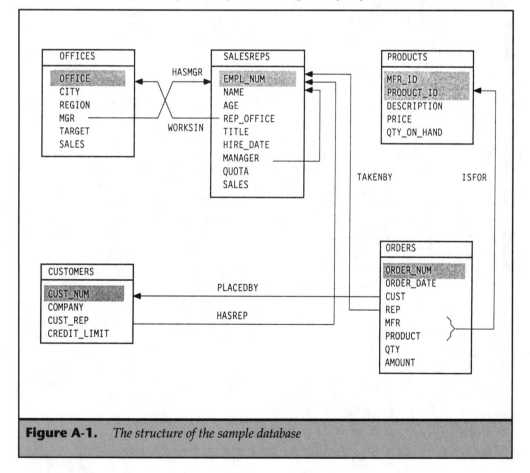

Figure A-1. *The structure of the sample database*

The five tables in the sample database can be created using the CREATE TABLE statements shown here:

```
CREATE TABLE CUSTOMERS
    (CUST_NUM INTEGER NOT NULL,
      COMPANY VARCHAR(20) NOT NULL,
     CUST_REP INTEGER,
 CREDIT_LIMIT MONEY,
  PRIMARY KEY (CUST_NUM),
  FOREIGN KEY HASREP (CUST_REP)
   REFERENCES SALESREPS
    ON DELETE SET NULL)

CREATE TABLE SALESREPS
    (EMPL_NUM INTEGER NOT NULL,
         NAME VARCHAR(15) NOT NULL,
          AGE INTEGER,
   REP_OFFICE INTEGER,
        TITLE VARCHAR(10),
    HIRE_DATE DATE NOT NULL,
      MANAGER INTEGER,
        QUOTA MONEY,
        SALES MONEY NOT NULL,
  PRIMARY KEY (EMPL_NUM),
  FOREIGN KEY (MANAGER)
   REFERENCES SALESREPS
    ON DELETE SET NULL,
  FOREIGN KEY WORKSIN (REP_OFFICE)
   REFERENCES OFFICES
    ON DELETE SET NULL)

CREATE TABLE OFFICES
    (OFFICE INTEGER NOT NULL,
       CITY VARCHAR(15) NOT NULL,
     REGION VARCHAR(10) NOT NULL,
        MGR INTEGER,
     TARGET MONEY,
```

```
        SALES MONEY NOT NULL,
  PRIMARY KEY (OFFICE),
  FOREIGN KEY HASMGR (MGR)
   REFERENCES SALESREPS
    ON DELETE SET NULL)

CREATE TABLE ORDERS
  (ORDER_NUM INTEGER NOT NULL,
  ORDER_DATE DATE NOT NULL,
        CUST INTEGER NOT NULL,
         REP INTEGER,
         MFR CHAR(3) NOT NULL,
     PRODUCT CHAR(5) NOT NULL,
         QTY INTEGER NOT NULL,
      AMOUNT MONEY NOT NULL,
  PRIMARY KEY (ORDER_NUM),
  FOREIGN KEY PLACEDBY (CUST)
   REFERENCES CUSTOMERS
    ON DELETE CASCADE,
  FOREIGN KEY TAKENBY (REP)
   REFERENCES SALESREPS
    ON DELETE SET NULL,
  FOREIGN KEY ISFOR (MFR, PRODUCT)
   REFERENCES PRODUCTS
    ON DELETE RESTRICT)
CREATE TABLE PRODUCTS
      (MFR_ID CHAR(3) NOT NULL,
   PRODUCT_ID CHAR(5) NOT NULL,
  DESCRIPTION VARCHAR(20) NOT NULL,
        PRICE MONEY NOT NULL,
  QTY_ON_HAND INTEGER NOT NULL,
  PRIMARY KEY (MFR_ID, PRODUCT_ID))
```

Figures A-2 through A-6 show the contents of each of the five tables in the sample database. The query results in examples throughout the book are based on the data shown in these figures.

CUST_NUM	COMPANY	CUST_REP	CREDIT_LIMIT
2111	JCP Inc.	103	$50,000.00
2102	First Corp.	101	$65,000.00
2103	Acme Mfg.	105	$50,000.00
2123	Carter & Sons	102	$40,000.00
2107	Ace International	110	$35,000.00
2115	Smithson Corp.	101	$20,000.00
2101	Jones Mfg.	106	$65,000.00
2112	Zetacorp	108	$50,000.00
2121	QMA Assoc.	103	$45,000.00
2114	Orion Corp.	102	$20,000.00
2124	Peter Brothers	107	$40,000.00
2108	Holm & Landis	109	$55,000.00
2117	J.P. Sinclair	106	$35,000.00
2122	Three-Way Lines	105	$30,000.00
2120	Rico Enterprises	102	$50,000.00
2106	Fred Lewis Corp.	102	$65,000.00
2119	Solomon Inc.	109	$25,000.00
2118	Midwest Systems	108	$60,000.00
2113	Ian & Schmidt	104	$20,000.00
2109	Chen Associates	103	$25,000.00
2105	AAA Investments	101	$45,000.00

Figure A-2. *The* CUSTOMERS *table*

EMPL_NUM	NAME	AGE	REP_OFFICE	TITLE	HIRE_DATE	MANAGER	QUOTA	SALES
105	Bill Adams	37	13	Sales Rep	12-FEB-88	104	$350,000.00	$367,911.00
109	Mary Jones	31	11	Sales Rep	12-OCT-89	106	$300,000.00	$392,725.00
102	Sue Smith	48	21	Sales Rep	10-DEC-86	108	$350,000.00	$474,050.00
106	Sam Clark	52	11	VP Sales	14-JUN-88	NULL	$275,000.00	$299,912.00
104	Bob Smith	33	12	Sales Mgr	19-MAY-87	106	$200,000.00	$142,594.00
101	Dan Roberts	45	12	Sales Rep	20-OCT-86	104	$300,000.00	$305,673.00
110	Tom Snyder	41	NULL	Sales Rep	13-JAN-90	101	NULL	$75,985.00
108	Larry Fitch	62	21	Sales Mgr	12-OCT-89	106	$350,000.00	$361,865.00
103	Paul Cruz	29	12	Sales Rep	01-MAR-87	104	$275,000.00	$286,775.00
107	Nancy Angelli	49	22	Sales Rep	14-NOV-88	108	$300,000.00	$186,042.00

Figure A-3. *The* SALESREPS *table*

OFFICE	CITY	REGION	MGR	TARGET	SALES
22	Denver	Western	108	$300,000.00	$186,042.00
11	New York	Eastern	106	$575,000.00	$692,637.00
12	Chicago	Eastern	104	$800,000.00	$735,042.00
13	Atlanta	Eastern	105	$350,000.00	$367,911.00
21	Los Angeles	Western	108	$725,000.00	$835,915.00

Figure A-4. *The* OFFICES *table*

ORDER_NUM	ORDER_DATE	CUST	REP	MFR	PRODUCT	QTY	AMOUNT
112961	17-DEC-89	2117	106	REI	2A44L	7	$31,500.00
113012	11-JAN-90	2111	105	ACI	41003	35	$3,745.00
112989	03-JAN-90	2101	106	FEA	114	6	$1,458.00
113051	10-FEB-90	2118	108	QSA	K47	4	$1,420.00
112968	12-OCT-89	2102	101	ACI	41004	34	$3,978.00
113036	30-JAN-90	2107	110	ACI	4100Z	9	$22,500.00
113045	02-FEB-90	2112	108	REI	2A44R	10	$45,000.00
112963	17-DEC-89	2103	105	ACI	41004	28	$3,276.00
113013	14-JAN-90	2118	108	BIC	41003	1	$652.00
113058	23-FEB-90	2108	109	FEA	112	10	$1,480.00
112997	08-JAN-90	2124	107	BIC	41003	1	$652.00
112983	27-DEC-89	2103	105	ACI	41004	6	$702.00
113024	20-JAN-90	2114	108	QSA	XK47	20	$7,100.00
113062	24-FEB-90	2124	107	FEA	114	10	$2,430.00
112979	12-OCT-89	2114	102	ACI	4100Z	6	$15,000.00
113027	22-JAN-90	2103	105	ACI	41002	54	$4,104.00
113007	08-JAN-90	2112	108	IMM	773C	3	$2,925.00
113069	02-MAR-90	2109	107	IMM	775C	22	$31,350.00
113034	29-JAN-90	2107	110	REI	2A45C	8	$632.00
112992	04-NOV-89	2118	108	ACI	41002	10	$760.00
112975	12-OCT-89	2111	103	REI	2A44G	6	$2,100.00
113055	15-FEB-90	2108	101	ACI	4100X	6	$150.00
113048	10-FEB-90	2120	102	IMM	779C	2	$3,750.00
112993	04-JAN-89	2106	102	REI	2A45C	24	$1,896.00
113065	27-FEB-90	2106	102	QSA	XK47	6	$2,130.00
113003	25-JAN-90	2108	109	IMM	779C	3	$5,625.00
113049	10-FEB-90	2118	108	QSA	XK47	2	$776.00
112987	31-DEC-89	2103	105	ACI	4100Y	11	$27,500.00
113057	18-FEB-90	2111	103	ACI	4100X	24	$600.00
113042	02-FEB-90	2113	101	REI	2A44R	5	$22,500.00

Figure A-5. *The* ORDERS *table*

MFR_ID	PRODUCT_ID	DESCRIPTION	PRICE	QTY_ON_HAND
REI	2A45C	Ratchet Link	$79.00	210
ACI	4100Y	Widget Remover	$2,750.00	25
QSA	XK47	Reducer	$355.00	38
BIC	41672	Plate	$180.00	0
IMM	779C	900-lb Brace	$1,875.00	9
ACI	41003	Size 3 Widget	$107.00	207
ACI	41004	Size 4 Widget	$117.00	139
BIC	41003	Handle	$652.00	3
IMM	887P	Brace Pin	$250.00	24
QSA	XK48	Reducer	$134.00	203
REI	2A44L	Left Hinge	$4,500.00	12
FEA	112	Housing	$148.00	115
IMM	887H	Brace Holder	$54.00	223
BIC	41089	Retainer	$225.00	78
ACI	41001	Size 1 Widget	$55.00	277
IMM	775C	500-lb Brace	$1,425.00	5
ACI	4100Z	Widget Installer	$2,500.00	28
QSA	XK48A	Reducer	$177.00	37
ACI	41002	Size 2 Widget	$76.00	167
REI	2A44R	Right Hinge	$4,500.00	12
IMM	773C	300-lb Brace	$975.00	28
ACI	4100X	Widget Adjuster	$25.00	37
FEA	114	Motor Mount	$243.00	15
IMM	887X	Brace Retainer	$475.00	32
REI	2A44G	Hinge Pin	$350.00	14

Figure A-6. *The* PRODUCTS *table*

Appendix B

DBMS Vendor Profiles

620

The vendors profiled in this appendix are leaders in their respective market segments in terms of either technology or market share, and collectively they are responsible for the vast majority of SQL-related revenues. The vendors and their products are:

- ASK Group (Ingres)
- Borland International (dBASE IV, Interbase)
- Digital Equipment (Rdb/VMS, VAX SQL)
- Gupta Technologies (SQLBase, SQLWindows)
- Hewlett-Packard (HPSQL)
- IBM (DB2, SQL/DS, SQL/400, OS/2 Extended Edition)
- Informix Software (Informix-SQL)
- Microsoft (SQL Server)
- Oracle (Oracle)
- Sybase (Sybase SQL Server)
- Tandem (NonStop SQL)
- Unify (Unify, Accell)

ASK Group

Ingres Corporation, now a division of the ASK Group, had its origins in the Ingres relational database prototype built at the University of California at Berkeley. During the early and middle 1980s, the Ingres DBMS and its QUEL database language were a major rival to SQL, and there was a particularly strong competitive rivalry between Ingres and Oracle in the midrange DBMS market. When SQL emerged as the standard database language, the company converted Ingres into a SQL-based DBMS. The product thus enjoys some of the advantages of being a more recent SQL implementation, along with the benefits of more than a decade of relational database experience.

Ingres was first implemented on Digital minicomputers, and a substantial part of the company's sales still come from DEC hardware platforms. Ingres has also been ported to several dozen different UNIX-based systems, and Ingres products for PCs run on DOS-based and Windows-based personal computers. Using Ingres/Star, an Ingres installation on one system can remotely access Ingres databases on another system where Ingres is installed.

With its academic origins, Ingres has always had a reputation as a technology leader in the DBMS market. For example, its distributed database offerings have typically been available earlier, and with more comprehensive features, than those of its competitors. In the PC arena, the company squeezed its implementation of Ingres for PCs into a standard 640K MS-DOS system, unlike the extended memory systems required by some of its competitors. Most analysts agree that the company's marketing and sales efforts have been weaker than its technology. The company sells its products directly, and through OEM relationships with computer system manufacturers.

In 1993, a major expansion of the Ingres family, under the name "ASK OpenINGRES", was announced. The new capabilities once again advanced Ingres, leadership in core DBMS technology. The OpenINGRES/Replicator provides replicated data support in a distributed database environment. Open/INGRES/DTP offers distributed transaction processing support, integrated with the most popular transaction processing monitors, CICS, Tuxedo and Encina. Ingres database gateways, previously offered for DB2, IMS, Rdb and VAX RMS files, were expanded to include CICS/VSAM datasets, where a great deal of transaction data on IBM mainframes is stored. APIs for Windows and Macintosh clients, extended support for binary large objects, and a spatial object library for manipulating graphical objects were also added. Finally, the new release of Ingres takes several major strides toward SQL2 compatibility.

The ASK Group, of which Ingres is now a part, has development and marketing activity focused on three complementary software areas:

- Core database technology, represented by the Ingres DBMS and associated products.

- Database tools, an area where the company is moving to decouple its "front-end" graphical development tools from the Ingres DBMS and offer them as a cross-database toolset.

- Manufacturing applications software, where ASK's MANMAN product, the leading manufacturing management application, has been evolved over the last several years to be more closely integrated into the Ingres DBMS environment.

With this product line, the company can be a full-line software vendor to manufacturing companies, and a vendor of key software technology to other industry segments.

Borland International

Borland is a leading supplier of personal computer software, and has become a major player in the PC database market through acquisitions. Founded in 1983, Borland distinguished itself early as a leading supplier of PC programming language products that offered exceptional productivity for programmers. In 1987, the company expanded into a new product area with an innovative spreadsheet, Quattro Pro, which featured compatibility with Lotus 1-2-3, the market leader, coupled with advanced new features and aggressive pricing. The company offers three database products—Paradox, dBASE and Interbase—each of which was originally developed by another company that was subsequently acquired by Borland.

The dBASE products, originally developed by Ashton-Tate, are the volume leaders in the PC database category. Over four million copies of dBASE software have been shipped to date, and dBASE consistently held a 70 percent or greater share of the PC DBMS market during the 1980s. Both dBASE II and dBASE III were basically flat file managers with a limited ability to join data across multiple files. Even though these databases were limited, the dBASE programming language was used to develop a wide range of business applications on PCs and has become a de facto standard.

By the late 1980s, minicomputer DBMS vendors had ported their products to personal computers and began to exert competitive pressure on the aging dBASE product line. In addition, competitors in the personal computer market offered more advanced products. Ashton-Tate responded with dBASE IV, which was designed to provide backward compatibility with earlier versions of dBASE, while providing the more advanced features that users were demanding. In addition, dBASE IV featured SQL support "grafted onto" the dBASE language. Finally, dBASE IV was to provide a front-end for SQL Server, the OS/2 version of the Sybase DBMS.

Unfortunately, the initial release of dBASE IV had some serious bugs, and Ashton-Tate's engineers discovered that all of the objectives for dBASE IV could not be achieved within the 640KB memory limitation of MS-DOS. The product was revised and was reintroduced in two versions. The stand alone dBASE IV product ran on a standard IBM PC and supported both dBASE and SQL statements that access a local database. The network dBASE IV product required an MS-DOS memory extender. It supported the same language statements as the stand-alone version, and it provided access to SQL Server databases across an OS/2 local area network.

Ashton-Tate and Microsoft originally shared marketing responsibility for the SQL Server DBMS in the OS/2 market. Ashton-Tate initially had exclusive retail distribution rights for the product and was responsible for selling it in volume through computer stores along with its other database products. With the very slow initial sales of OS/2, however, the product was less than spectacularly successful, and Microsoft sought out other retail distribution channels for the product.

The false start with dBASE IV and the SQL Server-OS/2 alliance with Microsoft was very costly for Ashton-Tate. It still had a large installed base, but was faced with increasingly serious competition from companies like Foxbase, which offered a dBASE-compatible product, and no serious entry in the full-fledged relational DBMS market. These factors, and their financial consequences, led to the acquisition of Ashton-Tate by Borland.

Borland has extended and improved the dBASE product, including the announcement of dBASE 2.0 for DOS in 1993. The new dBASE version offered performance improvements of up to 10 times over previous versions. It also featured a dBASE compiler, one of the major features of the competing dBASE "clones" which had been missing from Borland's own product suite. The compiler allows a developer to build a dBASE application and then compile into executable form, permitting higher-speed execution and eliminating the possibility that the end user will tamper with the dBASE application itself. These new capabilities make dBASE again competitive within its own domain of "desktop databases" in the DOS market.

Borland's strategies for the Windows market, and for the mainstream relational market, revolve around its other two products.

Paradox was one of the earliest PC databases to offer a graphical interface and easy, direct, end user manipulation of data. It offered the ability to view data in a variety of different ways, including the traditional forms-based view, as well as a spreadsheet-style, row/column view. The product's features made it very attractive as a data analysis tool, using data imported from production databases. Today, Paradox competes with Microsoft Access and other products in the same category in the Windows-based PC market.

Interbase is a capable relational database that runs on UNIX-based computer systems. With the acquisition of Interbase, Borland viewed its database product family as consisting of dBASE and Paradox as "desktop" databases and front-ends for the "industrial strength" back-end provided by Interbase. Interbase has been steadily enhanced to include leading-edge features, such as automatic two-phase commit for distributed transactions, triggers and event alerters, support for binary large objects and multi-dimensional arrays, appropriate for financial and scientific database applications. Current implementations of Interbase run on the most popular UNIX-based systems, on SCO UNIX for PC servers, and on Netware. While Interbase has offered good database technology, it has been hampered by Borland's PC-centric marketing, distribution and support culture. Competitors such as Oracle and Sybase have sizeable direct sales forces and support/consulting businesses backing their push into corporate accounts, a radically different approach than Borland's indirect, computer store and PC software distribution model. Borland argues that its distribution model is better suited to the future of LAN-based database management, with lower DBMS price points, but to date, the direct sales approach has proved to be the winner.

Digital Equipment Corporation

Digital Equipment Corporation, the largest minicomputer vendor in the world, is also a major player in the minicomputer database market. Digital's family of systems ranges in price and performance from personal workstations costing under $10,000 to the mainframe-class systems costing several million dollars. Digital also offers Intel-based PCs and PC servers. The Digital product line supports two major operating systems. VMS, the company's historical flagship operating system, is proprietary to Digital. Digital also offers UNIX-based operating systems that have become a much more important part of its strategy over the last few years.

Digital's flagship relational DBMS is Rdb/VMS, which runs solely under the VAX/VMS operating system. Internally the Rdb/VMS database engine supports the Digital Standard Relational Interface (DSRI), a low-level binary interface. Above the DSRI level, Rdb provides two language-based interfaces—VAX SQL, which supports embedded SQL and interactive SQL access, and RDO, which supports a proprietary Digital database language. The RDO language has effectively been phased out in favor of VAX SQL. The Rdb/VMS DBMS itself provides only a basic set of database tools for system administration. To boost its offering, Digital licensed the Ingres tools from Ingres Corporation and modified them to support Rdb/VMS. Digital has also licensed the Ingres DBMS itself and offered it as the Digital-supported RDBMS under the Ultrix UNIX-based operating system.

In 1989 Digital bundled the Rdb/VMS run-time system with the VMS operating system, making it a fundamental part of the VMS operating software. Digital also indicated its intention to build other layered VMS products on top of the Rdb/VMS foundation. Remote access to Rdb/VMS data is provided by VAX SQL Services, a SQL-based API that uses DECnet networking protocols. SQL Services access is available from VMS and Ultrix-based workstations, from MS-DOS-based personal computers, and from Macintosh systems.

In the early 1990s, Digital entered a major transition, moving virtually its entire product line from the proprietary 32-bit VAX architecture that had fueled the company's growth through the 1980s to a new, 64-bit, RISC architecture named Alpha. Industry analysts agreed that Alpha was a stunning technical achievement, offering the highest processor speeds available in a commercial RISC processor and the performance to go with them. However, the transition to Alpha has been a difficult one, because the new processor architecture is relatively expensive, and it represents an incompatible jump from the VAX line. Along with the transition in processor architectures, Digital has undergone a major shift in its attitude towards UNIX. While UNIX-based VAX systems were an important revenue source, Digital's attention and loyalties were primarily to its own VMS operating system. On Alpha, the implementation of UNIX (based on the OSF/1 UNIX technology from the Open Software Foundation) is on an equal, or slightly more prominent footing, with VMS, especially on Alpha-based workstations. Along with this emerging emphasis on UNIX and open systems has come renewed importance of products from independent DBMS vendors, and a relative reduction in the importance of Rdb in Digital's strategy.

Gupta Technologies, Inc.

Gupta Technologies is one of the smaller relational DBMS vendors, but has an impressive list of technical "firsts" to its credit. The company was founded by a former manager of Oracle Corporation's microcomputer division. The Gupta product line includes a relational DBMS and database development tools, all aimed at PCs and PC local area networks.

SQLBase, the company's SQL-based DBMS engine, runs on MS-DOS-, OS/2-, and Windows-based personal computers. SQLBase runs either on a stand-alone PC or on a local area network of PCs. In the latter configuration, the SQLBase server was the first and only major SQL-based server to run on an MS-DOS-based PC. The server supports client PCs running on a NETBIOS-based local area network. SQLBase also provides a family of gateways linking Gupta's PC products to DB2, Oracle, SQL Server, Informix, Ingres, and others. Gupta also lead the recent move to offer database servers for Netware, with an NLM implementation of SQLBase. Novell is an investor in the company. Other unique features of SQLBase include support for long data types ("blobs"), updatable scroll cursors, programmatic control over cursor isolation levels, and result sets, which allow the results of one query to be used as the data source for subsequent queries. The programmatic interface to SQLBase is through a callable API.

In addition to its database engine, Gupta offers SQLWindows, a collection of development tools that provide a graphical user interface for database processing. SQLWindows runs under Microsoft Windows and supports the development of "point-and-click" style database applications. SQLWindows works with Gupta's own SQLBase DBMS and also with other SQL-based back-ends, including DB2, SQL Server, and Oracle Server. A version of SQLWindows that runs under OS/2 was announced in 1992. As one of the early DBMS development tools for Microsoft Windows, SQLWindows has enjoyed a great deal of success in the last few years. Gupta Technologies became a public company in 1993 on the strength of that success.

Hewlett-Packard Company

Hewlett-Packard is a major vendor of minicomputer systems, and database management has always played an important role in HP's product line. In the 1970s the company pioneered database management on minicomputers with its Image/1000 DBMS, which ran on HP 1000 minicomputers in engineering and technical applications, and its Image/3000 DBMS, which ran on HP 3000 minicomputers in commercial applications. The Image DBMS was based on the network data model.

In the mid-1980s HP converted its entire minicomputer product line to a 32-bit RISC architecture and offered two new operating systems for the new product line. The first, MPE/XL, provided backward compatibility with the HP 3000 series. The second, HP/UX, was an HP implementation of UNIX and represented HP's commitment to the UNIX bandwagon.

With the help of technology purchased from an outside DBMS software vendor, HP has implemented a DBMS, called Allbase, under both MPE/XL and HP/UX. HP offers two alternative interfaces to the Allbase database engine. An Image interface provides backward compatibility for existing applications and presents a network data model view of Allbase data. HPSQL provides a relational interface for new applications and offers an embedded SQL and interactive SQL interface to Allbase data. This dual approach to database access is unique, and it represents a significant technical achievement.

HP's emerging role as the largest or second-largest UNIX workstation vendor has made its systems a major target for the independent DBMS vendors. Ingres, Informix, Oracle and Sybase all offer HP implementations. As a result, HP's proprietary DBMS technology has become less important in the overall mix of DBMS activity on HP systems.

IBM Corporation

IBM is the largest database vendor in the world, with the majority of its database revenues coming from two older, nonrelational, mainframe database products—IMS, a hierarchical DBMS, and DL/1 (Data Language/1), a hierarchical database access method. However, the fastest growing part of IBM's database business is in SQL-based relational databases, and SQL is the standard database interface for all future IBM databases.

IBM has a SQL-based product offering for each of its five major systems families:

- *DB2* is IBM's flagship relational DBMS product. It is a large, complex software product that runs on IBM mainframe systems under the MVS operating system. In its more recent releases, the performance of DB2 has improved dramatically, and IBM now markets it as an OLTP solution. However, DB2 is a substantial drain on mainframe resources and requires a sizable mainframe system to support it.

- *SQL/DS* is IBM's database management system for information center applications. It runs under the VM/CMS operating system on IBM mainframes. A fairly direct descendant of IBM's System/R relational database prototype, SQL/DS has pioneered some innovative relational database features, including extended dynamic SQL. However, from an IBM marketing perspective, it stands in the shadow of DB2.

- *SQL/400* is IBM's SQL implementation for the AS/400 series of systems. The successor to the IBM System/38, the AS/400 has a built-in relational database system with hardware support as part of its operating system. SQL/400 runs as an additional layer, providing SQL support to the underlying DBMS software. To date, most AS/400s have been sold as upgrades to IBM System/38 and System/36 systems, and the SQL interface has not been critical to these customers. As the AS/400 begins to play its own independent role as a mid-range alternative to VAXes and other minicomputers, SQL support will become more critical.

- *DB2/6000* is IBM's implementation of DB2 for its RS/6000 family of UNIX-based workstations and servers. Over the last five years, the RISC-based RS/6000 family has been one of the fastest-growing parts of IBM's business, vaulting it to a number three position in the UNIX workstation market behind Sun Microsystems and Hewlett-Packard. In 1991, IBM announced a broad-ranging alliance with Apple Computer and Motorola, which included a jointly-developed family of RISC microprocessors, called PowerPC, that significantly expand the RS/6000 line. With the support of IBM and Motorola, industry analysts believe PowerPC will emerge as a rival to Intel's dominance of the microprocessor market, and a major force in client/server computing. DB2/6000 occupies a key role as IBM's own database implementation for the PowerPC.

- *DB2/2* is IBM's implementation of DB2 for its PS/2 family of Intel-based personal computers and LAN servers, running under IBM's OS/2 operating system. It is a replacement for IBM's earlier OS/2 Extended Edition product, offering more compatibility with mainframe DB2. DB2/2 plays an important role in traditional IBM large corporate accounts who have standardized on OS/2 as part of a "buy IBM" strategy. However, the serious challenge to OS/2 posed by Microsoft Windows, and in particular by Windows NT, means that DB2/2 may not enjoy the broad PC LAN server market acceptance of SQL Server, Oracle and other cross-platform DBMS products.

IBM's stated goal is to evolve its SQL products toward a common standard to provide application portability. In the current implementations, however, significant differences between the products still remain. IBM has also announced its plans to provide distributed database access across its SQL-based products and has revealed a four-step blueprint for providing that access. Detailed timetables for distributed access within each product and between products have not been announced.

The major competitive advantage of the IBM products is, of course, the fact that they come from IBM. Each of the products is a solid, basic SQL implementation, and each product is being steadily enhanced over time. In a few cases (such as referential integrity support), IBM has set the pace for SQL innovation, but generally IBM has been the steady standard setter, leaving the independent DBMS vendors to innovate in new areas of DBMS technology.

Informix Software, Inc.

Informix Software is a leading vendor of UNIX-based relational DBMS systems. The company's first relational DBMS, Informix, was implemented on UNIX-based microcomputer systems in the early 1980s, and was known for its efficiency and compactness compared to the VAX/VMS-based DBMS systems that were introduced about the same time. In 1985 Informix was rewritten as a SQL-based DBMS and introduced as Informix-SQL. Informix-SQL has since been ported to several dozen different UNIX-based systems, ranging from UNIX-based PCs to Amdahl mainframes running UNIX. Informix has also been ported to personal computers under MS-DOS and more recently to Windows, Netware and Windows NT. But the majority of the company's sales remain in the UNIX market.

In addition to the Informix DBMS engine itself, the company offers Informix-4GL, a SQL-based fourth generation language that supports the development of forms-based interactive applications. Complementary development tools support development of forms, menus, Hypercard stacks, and complete user applications. The programmatic interface to Informix-SQL is via embedded SQL, and a variety of host programming languages are supported. The company offers two tiers of DBMS products. The Informix/Online family is a powerful DBMS targeted for OLTP applications. Informix-SE is a compatible, "lightweight" version of the DMBS for lighter-duty applications; it requires little overhead and administration.

In addition to its database engines and development tools, Informix also offers a pair of database access tools. Informix-Wingz is a versatile spreadsheet with extensive database access and "front-ending" capability. Introduced in the early 1990s, its database integration features were widely praised, but it suffered from lack of compatibility with the leading spreadsheets, 1-2-3 and Excel. It continues to play a role in the company's product line, but its pioneering work in spreadsheet/database integration will likely be eclipsed by Microsoft's heavy ODBC evangelism. A complementary product, Informix/ViewPoint is a graphical SQL query tool for end-user access to data.

Informix has tended to concentrate on the lower-priced, higher-volume portion of the UNIX market, and has been very successful in that segment. While its revenues are only one quarter of those of rival Oracle, its unit shipments are equal to or slightly greater than Oracle's. Informix has a heavier concentration of indirect distribution through value-added resellers than most of its DBMS vendor competitors, a position that could serve it well as the center of gravity in the DBMS market shifts from minicomputers and UNIX-based systems to PC-based client/server LANs.

Microsoft Corporation

Microsoft is the largest vendor of personal computer software in the world, with annual revenues in the billions of dollars. As the developer of MS-DOS and various versions of Microsoft Windows, the company is by far the leading supplier of personal computer systems software. It is also a major supplier of PC applications software, with a full line of products that includes spreadsheets, word processors, graphics packages, project management programs, and computer languages (C, Pascal, BASIC, Assembler). Microsoft is also the largest supplier of applications software for Apple Computer's Macintosh personal computer.

Until 1987, Microsoft's product lineup did not include a database management system. With the announcement of OS/2 Extended Edition in 1987, IBM effectively extended its definition of a personal computer operating system to include an integrated DBMS and data communications. In 1988, Microsoft responded with SQL Server, a version of the Sybase DBMS ported to OS/2. Although Microsoft later abandoned OS/2 in favor of its own Windows NT operating system, SQL Server has remained its flagship DBMS, now delivered as a Windows client and an NT-based database server. Other DBMS vendors complain about the "unfair" advantage Microsoft has in controlling both SQL Server and NT technology, but given Microsoft's market clout, they have little choice but to support NT with their DBMS products as well.

Expanding from its early experience with SQL Server, Microsoft has moved aggressively to establish itself as a major computer database vendor, both through product development and through acquisition. In early 1990s, Microsoft acquired Foxbase Corporation, developer of the Foxbase DBMS. Foxbase had established itself as a successful "clone" of dBASE, the most popular and widely used PC database product. Through the acquisition, Microsoft moved to challenge Borland International, which had acquired the rights to dBASE shortly before.

While the Foxbase acquisition was focused more on the installed base and the relatively mature market for character-based, "flat file" PC databases, Microsoft's internal development focused on the new, growing market for graphical, "lightweight relational" PC databases. After several false starts and abandoned development prototypes, the resulting products, Microsoft Access, was introduced. Microsoft Access is both a standalone database product, and, through its support for ODBC, a "front-end" for SQL-based, production databases.

The fourth component of Microsoft's database strategy is ODBC, a SQL-based API for database access. ODBC is Microsoft's attempt to set the standard for PC database access, just as Microsoft has set the standard for PC operating systems and is attempting to set standards for PC-based electronic mail and other technologies. Database vendors and front-end vendors have all indicated support for ODBC, and Microsoft has been aggressively implementing ODBC support in its own application products, adding competitive pressure for other vendors to do the same.

As a whole, Microsoft's efforts with SQL Server, Foxbase, Microsoft Access and ODBC constitute a formidable focus on database products, from a company with heavy clout in the personal computer industry. However, Microsoft's move from the mass-market techniques of the desktop PC business to the heavyweight sales, service and support required of a serious DBMS vendor has not evolved nearly as quickly as its product strategy. The degree of Microsoft's success and impact on the DBMS market by the turn of the century will depend at least as much on these market and channel investment as on product strategy.

Oracle Corporation

Oracle Corporation was the first DBMS vendor to offer a commercial SQL product, preceding IBM's own announcement by almost two years. During the 1980s, Oracle grew to become the largest independent DBMS vendor. Today it is a major DBMS competitor, selling its products through an aggressive direct sales force and through reseller arrangements with manufacturers of midrange computers and UNIX-based systems.

The Oracle DBMS was originally implemented on Digital minicomputers, but sales of Oracle on the VAX have been eclipsed by UNIX-based systems, which currently generate the majority of Oracle's revenues. One of the major advantages of Oracle is its portability. Oracle is currently implemented on nearly 100 different types of computer systems, giving it the broadest availability of any DBMS product. Oracle implementations are available for MS-DOS, Windows, OS/2, and the Macintosh in the personal computer market, for Sun, HP, IBM, MIPS, and many other UNIX-based systems, for a very large variety of minicomputer systems, and for IBM mainframes. Using Oracle's SQL*Net networking software, many of these Oracle implementations can participate in a distributed network of Oracle systems, providing remote access from one system to another. The company is implementing a plan to provide full distributed DBMS capabilities in stages.

The Oracle DBMS was originally based on IBM's System/R prototype, and has remained generally compatible with IBM's SQL-based products. In recent years, Oracle has been aggressively marketing the OLTP performance of its DBMS, using benchmark results from multiprocessor systems to substantiate its claim as the OLTP performance leader. More recently, the company's Oracle7 products have been positioned as "cooperative-server" databases going beyond client/server into distributed data management.

Oracle Corporation has combined good technology with an aggressive sales force and high-profile marketing campaigns. The company is attempting to exploit these advantages as it tries to extend its dominance into the personal computer arena with its database products and especially with a new family of database development tools called Cooperative Development Environment (CDE). Oracle expects CDE to be a major source of future growth. In other attempts to enhance its competitive position, Oracle has expanded into the systems integration, manufacturing software, and financial software markets. These products and services are based on the Oracle DBMS, but tap revenue opportunities that lie outside the DBMS market. The Oracle applications products also contribute to the maintenance, support, and consulting revenues that now account for over 40 percent of the company's sales. Thus Oracle is positioning itself not just as a DBMS vendor, but as a major independent software vendor across a broad spectrum of systems. The company is also using the profits from its DBMS business to fund investments in multimedia and information services as it seeks to play a major role in the creation of an "information superhighway".

Sybase, Inc.

Sybase was a mid-1980s DBMS startup company, funded by tens of millions of dollars in venture capital. The company's founding team and many of its early employees were alumni of other DBMS vendors, and for most of them, Sybase represented the second or third relational DBMS that they had built. Sybase positioned its product as "the relational DBMS for on-line applications" and stressed the technical and architectural features that distinguished it from other SQL-based DBMS products. These features included:

- A client/server architecture, with client software running on Sun and VAX workstations and IBM PCs and the server running on VAX/VMS or Sun systems

- A multi-threaded server that handled its own task management and input/output, for maximum efficiency

- A programmatic API, instead of the embedded SQL interface used by most other DBMS vendors

- Stored procedures, triggers, and a Transact-SQL dialect that extended SQL into a complete server programming language

Aggressive marketing and a first-class roster of venture capital backers gained Sybase the attention of industry analysts, but it was a subsequent OEM deal with Microsoft and Ashton-Tate that positioned the company as an up-and-coming DBMS vendor. Renamed SQL Server, the Sybase DBMS was ported to OS/2, and marketed by Microsoft to computer systems vendors (along with OS/2), and by Ashton-Tate through retail computer channels. Although sales from the alliance never met the early expectations, the publicity propelled Sybase into the DBMS market as a serious player. Today SQL Server continues to be Microsoft's strategic DBMS for Windows NT, its flagship server operating system, and Sybase is a large and successful DBMS vendor, with a second-place standing in revenue share.

The innovations in the Sybase product made it the most technically "flashy" DBMS in the late 1980s, and the company's late start gave it a technical competitive edge. By 1990, these innovations had provoked a competitive response from the other leading independent DBMS vendors, many of whom had announced plans for their own support of client/server architectures, procedural SQL dialects, stored procedures, triggers, and so on. Sybase has focused on staying "a step ahead" of these competitive developments. Sybase Systems 10 includes highly sophisticated support for replicated, distributed data, gateways for mainframe integration, open APIs that integrate database processing with e-mail and custom-written applications, and support for very large databases.

Sybase product development has tended to concentrate on the core features of the DBMS itself, with relatively less attention to the associated tools and utilities. The product line includes SQL Workbench, an application development and testing environment with a graphical user interface, but lacks the extensive set of forms packages, report writers, graphics packages, and other tools offered by some other DBMS vendors. Sybase has used its high stock market valuation to add more of these capabilities by selectively acquiring smaller companies over the last several years. It has also launched a small, but growing, consulting services business through acquisition.

Tandem Computers, Inc.

Tandem is the leading vendor of fault-tolerant computer systems. Many Tandem systems are sold to financial services and transportation companies for use in on-line transaction processing applications. Tandem's systems run the proprietary TXP operating system, and fault-tolerant applications are generally written in the proprietary Tandem Application Language (TAL). However, database management is provided by a SQL-based relational DBMS called NonStop SQL. Tandem has also added a family of UNIX-based OLTP systems, and works with the major independent DBMS vendors to provide data management on these systems.

Because of Tandem's OLTP emphasis, NonStop SQL has pioneered several special techniques, such as disk mirroring. NonStop SQL also takes advantage of the Tandem

multiprocessor architecture and provides distributed database capabilities. The
programmatic interface to NonStop SQL is through embedded SQL.

Unify Corporation

Unify Corporation is a supplier of UNIX-based relational DBMS products and
database tools. In the mid-1980s Unify, Informix, Ingres, and Oracle were the four
major UNIX-based DBMS competitors, with Oracle and Ingres battling for dominance
as the "high-end" DBMS while Informix and Unify competed at the low end of the
market. The Unify DBMS was based on the network data model, with a SQL veneer
for relational access. The embedded pointers and other features of the network data
model gave Unify excellent performance, but the lack of a true relational foundation
restricted the level of SQL support it could provide.

The Unify DBMS has been a declining part of the company's product line as
Unify's emphasis over the last few years has shifted to database tools. The company's
Accell application development environment is an advanced fourth-generation
language designed to speed the development of interactive, forms-oriented data
processing applications. Initially available only for use with the Unify DBMS, Accell
was expanded to support a range of SQL-based DBMS back-ends. It is an excellent
example of a new class of "portable" database application development tools that have
been adapted to work with a variety of SQL engines.

Appendix C

Company and Product List

634

This appendix contains a list of companies and products in the DBMS marketplace, most of which are mentioned in this book. The majority of the products listed are SQL-based database management systems or database tools. The companies appear in alphabetical order. Key products for each company appear in italics.

Acius
20883 Stevens Creek Boulevard
Cupertino, CA 95014
408-252-4444
4th DIMENSION

Apple Computer, Inc.
20525 Mariani Avenue
Cupertino, CA 95014
408-996-1010
DAL, HyperCard

ASK Group
Ingres Division
1080 Marina Village Parkway
Alameda, CA 94501
800-446-4737
INGRES

Borland International, Inc.
1800 Green Hills Road
Scotts Valley, CA 95066
408-438-8400
Paradox, dBASE IV, Interbase

Cincom Systems, Inc.
2300 Montan Avenue
Cincinnati, OH 45211
513-662-2300
Supra, TOTAL

Cognos, Inc.
67 S. Bedford Street, Suite 200 West
Burlington, MA 01803-5164
617-229-6600
PowerHouse, PowerHouse StarBase

CompuServe Data Technologies
1000 Massachusetts Avenue
Cambridge, MA 02138
617-661-9440
System 1032

Computer Associates International, Inc.
One Computer Associates Plaza
Islandia, NY 11788-7000
516-DIAL-CAI
CA-Universe, CA-Datacom/DB, Enterprise:DB

Computer Corporation of America
4 Cambridge Center
Cambridge, MA 02142
617-492-8860
Model 204

Data General Corporation
3400 Computer Drive
Westboro, MA 01580
508-898-5090
DG/SQL

DataEase International, Inc.
7 Cambridge Drive
Trumbull, CT 06611
203-374-8000
DataEase

Digital Equipment Corporation
146 Main Street
Maynard, MA 01754
508-493-5111
Rdb/VMS, VAX SQL

Empress Software, Inc.
6401 Golden Triangle Drive, Suite 220
Greenbelt, MD 20770
301-220-1919
Empress

Gupta Technologies, Inc.
1060 Marsh Road
Menlo Park, CA 94025
415-321-9500
SQLBase, SQLWindows

Hewlett-Packard Company
3000 Hanover Street
Palo Alto, CA 94304
415-857-1501
Allbase, HPSQL

IBM Corporation
Old Orchard Road
Armonk, NY 10504
914-765-1900
DB2, SQL/DS, SQL/400, DB2/2, DB2/6000

Information Builders, Inc.
1250 Broadway
New York, NY 10001
212-736-4433
Focus

Informix Software, Inc.
4100 Bohannon Drive
Menlo Park, CA 94025
415-926-6300
Informix

Microsoft Corporation
One Microsoft Way
Redmond, WA 98052
206-882-8080
SQL Server

Novell, Inc.
5918 W. Courtyard Drive
Austin, TX 78730
512-346-8380
NetWare SQL, XQL

Oracle Corporation
20 Davis Drive
Belmont, CA 94002
415-598-8000
Oracle

Progress Software Corporation
5 Oak Park
Bedford, MA 01730
617-275-4500
PROGRESS

Revelation Technologies, Inc.
181 Harbor Drive
Stanford, CT 06902
203-973-1000
Advanced Revelation

Software AG
11190 Sunrise Valley Drive
Reston, VA 22091
703-860-5050
Adabas

Sybase, Inc.
6475 Christie Avenue
Emeryville, CA 94608
415-596-3500
Sybase SQL Server

Tandem Computers, Inc.
19191 Vallco Parkway
Cupertino, CA 95014
408-725-6000
NonStop SQL

Unify Corporation
3870 Rosin Court
Sacramento, CA 32256
916-920-9092
UNIFY, ACCELL

XDB Systems, Inc.
14700 Sweitzer Lane
Laurel, MD 20707
301-377-6800
XDB-SQL, XDB-Server

Appendix D

ANSI/ISO SQL Syntax

The ANSI/ISO SQL1 standard specifies the syntax of the SQL language using a formal BNF notation. Unfortunately, the standard is difficult to read and to understand for several reasons. First, the standard specifies the language bottom-up rather than top-down, making it difficult to get the "big picture" of a SQL statement. Second, the standard uses unfamiliar terms (such as *table-expression* and *predicate*). Finally, the BNF in the standard is many layers deep, providing a very precise specification, but masking the relatively simple structure of the SQL language.

This appendix presents a complete, simplified BNF for ANSI/ISO standard SQL1 as it is commonly used. Specifically:

- The data definition statements are treated as stand-alone statements, rather than as part of a schema definition.

- The module language is omitted, because it is replaced in all current SQL implementations by embedded SQL or a SQL API.

- Components of the language are called by their common names, rather than by the technical names used in the standard.

The BNF in this appendix uses these conventions:

- SQL keywords appear in all UPPERCASE letters.

- Syntax elements are specified in *italics*.

- The notation *element-list* indicates an *element* or a list of *elements* separated by commas.

- Vertical bars (|) indicate a choice between two or more alternative syntax elements.

- Square brackets ([]) indicate an optional syntax element.

- Braces ({}) indicate a choice among required syntax elements.

Data Definition Statements

These statements define the structure and security of a database.

```
CREATE  TABLE table ( table-def-item-list )

CREATE VIEW view [ ( column-list ) ]
   AS query-spec
  [ WITH CHECK OPTION ]

GRANT { ALL [ PRIVILEGES ] | privilege-list }
   ON table
   TO { PUBLIC | user-list }
  [ WITH GRANT OPTION ]
```

Basic Data Manipulation Statements

These statements retrieve data from a database or modify the data in the database.

```
SELECT [ ALL | DISTINCT ] { select-item-list | * }
    INTO host-variable-list
    FROM table-ref-list
    [ WHERE search-condition ]

INSERT INTO table [ ( column-list ) ]
    VALUES { ( insert-item-list ) | query-spec }

DELETE FROM table [ WHERE search-condition ]

UPDATE table SET assignment-list [ WHERE search-condition ]
```

Transaction Processing Statements

These statements signal the end of a SQL transaction.

```
COMMIT WORK

ROLLBACK WORK
```

Cursor-Based Statements

These programmatic SQL statements support data retrieval and positioned update of data.

```
DECLARE cursor CURSOR FOR query-expr [ ORDER BY sort-item list ]

OPEN cursor

CLOSE cursor

FETCH cursor INTO host-variable-list

DELETE FROM table WHERE CURRENT OF cursor

UPDATE table SET assignment-list WHERE CURRENT OF cursor
```

Query Expressions

These expressions appear in SQL statements to specify the data that is to be affected by the statement.

query-expr:	*query-item* | *query-expr* UNION [ALL] *query-item*
query-item:	*query-spec* | (*query-expr*)
query-spec:	SELECT [ALL | DISTINCT] { *select-item-list* | * }
	FROM *table-ref-list*
	[WHERE *search-condition*]
	[GROUP BY *column-ref-list*]
	[HAVING *search-condition*]
subquery:	(SELECT [ALL | DISTINCT] { *select-item* | * }
	FROM *table-ref-list*
	[WHERE *search-condition*]
	[GROUP BY *column-ref-list*]
	[HAVING *search-condition*])

Search Conditions

These expressions select rows from the database for processing.

search-condition:	*Search-item* | *search-item* { AND | OR } *search-item*
search-item:	[NOT] { *search-test* | (*search-condition*) }
search-test:	*comparison-test* | *between-test* | *like-test* | *null-test* |
	set-test | *quantified-test* | *existence-test*
comparison-test:	*expr* { = | <> | < | <= | > | >= } { *expr* | *subquery* }
between-test:	*expr* [NOT] BETWEEN *expr* AND *expr*
like-test:	*column-ref* [NOT] LIKE *value* [ESCAPE *value*]
null-test:	*column-ref* IS [NOT] NULL
set-test:	*expr* [NOT] IN { *value-list* | *subquery* }
quantified-test:	*expr* { = | <> | < | <= | > | >= }
	[ALL | ANY | SOME] *subquery*
existence-test:	EXISTS *subquery*

Expressions

These expressions are used in SQL select lists and search conditions.

expr:	*expr-item* | *expr-item* { + | - | * | / } *expr-item*
expr-item:	[+ | -] [*value* | *column-ref* | *function* | (*expr*)]
value:	*literal* | USER | *host-variable*
host-variable:	*variable* [[INDICATOR] *variable*]
function:	COUNT(*) | *distinct-fcn* | *all-fcn*

distinct-function:	{ AVG | MAX | MIN | SUM | COUNT } (DISTINCT *column-ref*)
all-function:	{ AVG | MAX | MIN | SUM | COUNT } ([ALL] *expr*)

Statement Elements

These elements appear in various SQL statements.

assignment:	*column* = { *expr* | NULL }
sort-item:	{ *column-ref* | *integer* } [ASC | DESC]
insert-item:	{ *value* | NULL }
select-item:	*expr*
table-ref:	*table* [*table-alias*]
column-ref:	[{ *table* | *alias* } .] *column*
table-def-item:	*column-def* | UNIQUE (*column-list*) |
	PRIMARY KEY (*column-list*) |
	FOREIGN KEY (*column-list*)
	REFERENCES *table* [(*column-list*)]
column-def:	*column data-type*
	[DEFAULT { *literal* | USER | NULL }]
column-constraint:	[*column-constraint*]
	NOT NULL [UNIQUE | PRIMARY KEY] |
	CHECK (*search-condition*) |
	REFERENCES *table* [(*column-list*)]
privilege:	SELECT | INSERT | DELETE | UPDATE [(*column-list*)]

Simple Elements

These elements are the basic names and constants that appear in SQL statements.

table:	a table name
column:	a column name
user:	a database user name
variable:	a host language variable name
literal:	a number or a string literal enclosed in quotes
integer:	an integer number
data-type:	a SQL data type
alias:	a SQL identifier
cursor:	a SQL identifier

Index

* (asterisk)
    as multiplication operator, 78
    in outer join notation, 165
    versus percent sign (%), 111
    in queries, 95-96, 148-149
| (bar symbol), in SQL syntax notation, 641
{ } (braces), in SQL syntax notation, 641
[ ] (brackets), in SQL syntax notation, 641
| | (concatenation operator), 79
: (colon), in host variable names, 447-448
= (equal to)
    in quantified comparison tests,
      221-227
    in simple comparison tests, 101-104
    in subquery comparison tests,
      213-216
> (greater than)
    in quantified comparison tests,
      221-227

in simple comparison tests, 101-104
in subquery comparison tests,
   213-216
>= (greater than or equal to)
    in quantified comparison tests,
      221-227
    in simple comparison tests, 101-104
    in subquery comparison tests,
      213-216
< (less than)
    in quantified comparison tests,
      221-227
    in simple comparison tests, 101-104
    in subquery comparison tests,
      213-216
<= (less than or equal to)
    in quantified comparison tests,
      221-227
    in simple comparison tests, 101-104

E

F

R

LAN TIMES Free Subscription Form

○ **Yes,** I want to receive (continue to receive) LAN TIMES free of charge.　　　　○ No.

I am　○ a new subscriber　○ renewing my subscription　○ changing my address

Signature required _____ Date _____

Name_____

Title _____ Telephone _____

Company _____

Address _____

City _____

State/County _____ Zip/Postal Code _____

Free in the United States to qualified subscribers only

International Prices (Airmail Delivery)

Canada: $65　Elsewhere: $150

○ Payment enclosed　○ Bill me later

Charge my: ○ Visa　○ Mastercard　○ Amer. Exp

Card number _____

Exp. Date _____

All questions must be completed to qualify for a subscription to LAN TIMES. Publisher reserves the right to serve only those individuals who meet publication criteria.

1. Which of the following best describe your organization?

(Check only one)
- ○ A. Agriculture/Mining/Construction/Oil/Petrochemical/Environmental
- ○ B. Manufacturer (non-computer)
- ○ C. Government/Military/Public Adm.
- ○ D. Education
- ○ E. Research/Development
- ○ F. Engineering/Architecture
- ○ G. Finance/Banking/Accounting/Insurance/Real Estate
- ○ H. Health/Medical/Legal
- ○ I. VAR/VAD Systems House
- ○ J. Manufacturer Computer Hardware/Software
- ○ K. Aerospace
- ○ L. Retailer/Distributor/Wholesaler (non-computer)
- ○ M. Computer Retailer/Distributor/Sales
- ○ N. Transportation
- ○ O. Media/Marketing/Advertising/Publishing/Broadcasting
- ○ P. Utilities/Telecommunications/VAN
- ○ Q. Entertainment/Recreation/Hospitality/Non-profit/Trade Association
- ○ R. Consultant
- ○ S. Systems Integrator
- ○ T. Computer/LAN Leasing/Training
- ○ U. Information/Data Services
- ○ V. Computer/Communications Services: Outsourcing/3rd Party
- ○ W. All Other Business Services
- ○ X. Other _____

2. Which best describes your title? (Check only one)
- ○ A. Network/LAN Manager
- ○ B. MIS/DP/IS Manager
- ○ C. Owner/President/CEO/Partner
- ○ D. Data Communications Manager
- ○ E. Engineer/CNE/Technician
- ○ F. Consultant/Analyst
- ○ G. Micro Manager/Specialist/Coordinator
- ○ H. Vice President
- ○ I. All other Dept. Heads, Directors and Managers
- ○ J. Educator
- ○ K. Programmer/Systems Analyst
- ○ L. Professional
- ○ M. Other_____

3. Which of the following best describes your job function?

(Check only one)
- ○ A. Network/LAN Management
- ○ B. MIS/DP/IS Management
- ○ C. Systems Engineering/Integration
- ○ D. Administration/Management
- ○ E. Technical Services
- ○ F. Consulting
- ○ G. Research/Development
- ○ H. Sales/Marketing
- ○ I. Accounting/Finance
- ○ J. Education/Training

- ○ K. Office Automation
- ○ L. Manufacturing/Operations/Production
- ○ M. Personnel
- ○ N. Technology Assessment
- ○ O. Other _____

4. How many employees work in your entire ORGANIZATION?

(Check only one)
- ○ A. Under 25
- ○ B. 25-100
- ○ C. 101-500
- ○ D. 501-1,000
- ○ E. 1,001-5,000
- ○ F. 5,001-9,999
- ○ G. 10,000 and over

5. Which of the following are you or your clients currently using, or planning to purchase in the next 12 months? (1–Own; 2–Plan to purchase in next 12 months) (Check all that apply)

Topologies	1	2
A. Ethernet	○	○
B. Token Ring	○	○
C. Arcnet	○	○
D. LocalTalk	○	○
E. FDDI	○	○
F. Starlan	○	○
G. Other	○	○

Network Operating System	1	2
A. Novell Netware	○	○
B. Novell Netware Lite	○	○
C. Banyan VINES	○	○
D. Digital Pathworks	○	○
E. IBM LAN Server	○	○
F. Microsoft LAN Manager	○	○
G. Microsoft Windows for Workgroups	○	○
H. Artisoft LANtastic	○	○
I. Sitka TOPS	○	○
J. 10NET	○	○
K. AppleTalk	○	○

Client/Workstation Operating Sys.	1	2
A. DOS	○	○
B. DR-DOS	○	○
C. Windows	○	○
D. Windows NT	○	○
E. UNIX	○	○
F. UnixWare	○	○
G. OS/2	○	○
H. Mac System 6	○	○
I. Mac System 7	○	○

Protocols/Standards	1	2
A. IPX	○	○
B. TCP/IP	○	○
C. X.25	○	○
D. XNS	○	○
E. OSI	○	○
F. SAA/SNA	○	○
G. NFS	○	○
H. MHS	○	○

6. Is your Organization/Clients network... (Check all that apply)
- ○ A. International
- ○ B. National
- ○ C. Regional
- ○ D. Metropolitan
- ○ E. Local
- ○ F. Other _____

7. What hardware does your department/client base own/plan to purchase. (Check all that apply)

	Owns	Plan to purchase in next 12 months
A. Bridges	○	○
B. Diskless Workstations	○	○
C. Cabling System	○	○
D. Printers	○	○
E. Disk Drive	○	○
F. Optical Storage	○	○
G. Tape Backup System	○	○
H. Optical Storage	○	○
I. Application Servers	○	○
J. Communication Servers	○	○
K. Fax Servers	○	○
L. Mainframe	○	○
M. Network Adapter Cards	○	○
N. Wireless Adapters/Bridges	○	○
O. Power Conditioners/UPSs	○	○
P. Hubs/Concentrators	○	○
Q. Minicomputers	○	○
R. Modems	○	○
S. 386-based computers	○	○
T. 486-based computers	○	○
U. Pentium-based computers	○	○
V. Macintosh computers	○	○
W. RISC-based workstations	○	○
X. Routers	○	○
Y. Multimedia Cards	○	○
Z. Network Test/Diagnostic Equipment	○	○
1. Notebooks/Laptops	○	○
2. DSU/CSU	○	○
99. None of the Above	○	○

8. What network software/applications do you/your clients own/plan to purchase in the next 12 months? (Check all that apply)
- ○ A. Network Management
- ○ B. Software Metering
- ○ C. Network Inventory
- ○ D. Virus Protection
- ○ E. Menuing
- ○ F. E-mail
- ○ G. Word Processing
- ○ H. Spreadsheet
- ○ I. Database
- ○ J. Accounting
- ○ K. Document Management
- ○ L. Graphics
- ○ M. Communications
- ○ N. Application Development Tools
- ○ O. Desktop Publishing
- ○ P. Integrated Business Applications
- ○ Q. Multimedia
- ○ R. Document Imaging
- ○ S. Groupware
- ○ Z. None of the above

9. What is the annual revenue of your entire organization or budget if non-profit (Check only one)
- ○ A. Under $10 million
- ○ B. $10-$50 million
- ○ C. $50-$100 million
- ○ D. $100-$500 million
- ○ E. $500 million-$1 billion
- ○ F. Over $1 billion

10. How much does your organization (if reseller, your largest client's company) plan to spend on computer products in the next 12 months? (Check only one)
- ○ A. Under $25,000
- ○ B. $25,000-$99,999
- ○ C. $100,000-$499,999
- ○ D. $500,000-$999,999
- ○ E. $1 billion

11. Where do you purchase computer products? (Check all that apply)
- ○ A. Manufacturer
- ○ B. Distributor
- ○ C. Reseller
- ○ D. VAR
- ○ E. System Integrator
- ○ F. Consultant
- ○ G. Other _____

12. In which ways are you involved in acquiring computer products and services? (Check all that apply)
- ○ A. Determine the need
- ○ B. Define product specifications/features
- ○ C. Select brand
- ○ D. Evaluate the supplier
- ○ E. Select vendor/source
- ○ F. Approve the acquisition
- ○ G. None of the above

ICS1639

---

fold here

LAN TIMES

McGraw–Hill, INC.

P.O. Box 652

Hightstown NJ 08520-0652